DIARIES
1915-1918

'Portrait of a Lady in Black' by *Augustus John*

Lady Cynthia Asquith

DIARIES

1915-1918

With a foreword by
L. P. HARTLEY

HUTCHINSON OF LONDON

HUTCHINSON & CO (*Publishers*) LTD
178–202 Great Portland Street, London W1

London Melbourne Sydney
Auckland Bombay Toronto
Johannesburg New York

First published 1968

*This book has been set in Fournier, printed in Great Britain
on Antique Wove paper by Anchor Press, and
bound by Wm. Brendon, both of Tiptree, Essex*

09 8464 0

ILLUSTRATIONS

LINE DRAWINGS

ACKNOWLEDGMENTS

Permission to quote from personal letters has kindly been given by the beneficiaries of the estate of the Rt. Hon. Harold Baker; the Most Hon. the Marquess of Dufferin and Ava (for those of Lord Basil Blackwood); the Hon. Mrs Aubrey Herbert; Mrs Augustus John; Mr Michael MacCarthy; and William Heinemann Ltd for those of D. H. Lawrence; Lady Violet Benson gave much appreciated co-operation and Mr Lionel Tertis supplied most helpful information on the musical week-end at Chirk.

ACKNOWLEDGMENTS

FOREWORD

by

L. P. HARTLEY

It isn't easy to write about Lady Cynthia Asquith, who in her lifetime, as her diaries show, wrote so revealingly about herself. She was a complex personality, and the aspect of her that dazzled and enchanted was only one of many. To meet, she seemed all fire and air; her restless darting mind outstripped her tongue, nimble as her tongue was. She could think deeply, but she spoke lightly, and any attempt to make a *catalogue raisonné* of her qualities she would have greeted with a gust of ironic laughter. Laughter, above all laughter at herself, was outwardly an essential expression of her spirit, though not always of her face. Her face often showed that she had had more than her share of sorrows, but she made light of them; she might have said, in the words of her friend, the late Lady Salisbury, 'You must learn to laugh at nothing, for often there's nothing to laugh at.' She didn't make light of her friends' troubles, however; she lightened them by the infectious courage of her outlook.

Perhaps her favourite form of conversation with those whom she knew well was an inspired synthesis of what they would first find laughable in her, and she in them. What a tonic it was to be teased by her! In conversation she was like a butterfly that would never quite settle; before the net closed, she was off. One remembers little things: the sometimes startling abruptness of her speech and manner (especially on the telephone), her sudden plunging movements, with their strange coltish grace, and the disconcerting questions she would fire at one. 'How many eggs can you eat at one go, Mr Hartley? Do you prefer a hot bath or a cold?' were the first she put to me.

One cannot think of her apart from her physical presence and the beauty, sunshiny at one moment, shadows the next, that was as various and unpredictable as her talk. But I won't say more of the physical and mental graces that were the vesture of her spirit and that are, for each of her friends, a treasured possession, not to be disturbed by any attempt of mine to paint the lily. You could truly say of her, in the words of Shakespeare, whose plays she knew almost by heart, that a star danced when she was born and went on dancing till she died.

But underlying these gossamer qualities that so delighted the eye and ear, the mercurial emanations of her temperament, was a stable

Foreword

bedrock of character and a strong practical sense that made her, among many other things, the most reliable and dependable of friends. To them she gave herself, and her time, unstintingly. No journey was too long for her to take, if at the end of it she could help someone; no engagement too trifling or inconvenient to keep; no responsibility too heavy to shoulder. And this conscientiousness in private and public matters (for she adorned many spheres besides the one she was born to) she carried into her work as a writer. Modest about her own literary gifts, though always ready to encourage other people's, she was a most scrupulous craftsman, and no less so when she was writing for herself, in her letters, and in her diaries, than when she wrote *Married to Tolstoy*, the last of her books that she prepared for the press. She revised and revised, and into all her writing she put the faith and hope that burned in her and the charity that informed all her judgments. Except towards reckless motorists, she was the least censorious of human beings. She could take sides, often a side one didn't expect her to, but she always kept her sense of humour and of justice intact, with no lessening of sympathy for either of the protagonists.

It was her special gift to be ironically detached from herself and yet vitally concerned with other people. She saw herself in a mirror, often as a figure of fun. Perhaps we saw her in a mirror too, for in spite of her directness she had a mysterious, a moonlit, leprechaun quality that was not quite of this world. She was not called Cynthia for nothing, and she had at least as much in common with the regent of the night as with us ordinary mortals. And so, even though she has left us, she shines for us still.

L. P. HARTLEY

INTRODUCTION

Wife to Herbert, second son of Prime Minister Asquith, Lady Cynthia was one of the most fascinatingly beautiful women of her time— painted for love by McEvoy, Sargent, and Augustus John—and her lively wit and sensitivity of intelligence made her the treasured confidante of such diverse characters as D. H. Lawrence and Sir James Barrie, but when she died in 1960 she left a new generation to discover yet another of her gifts—as a rarely talented diarist.

While she lived she mentioned to few the existence of her sequence of diaries, begun in 1915 when Duff Cooper, later Lord Norwich, presented her with the first blank, handsomely bound volume. At the outset she declared: 'I would never write as though I were really convinced no other eye would ever see what I wrote', but she was a born diarist, having inherited the gift and a certain charming inconsequence in narration from her mother. Rapidly she dropped into an ever more intimate, unselfconscious record, with only a rare 'space' indication when she could not trust herself to complete an entry fully.

At the end of her life she had ample opportunity to destroy them had she wished, but instead passed on the volumes to her children, not forbidding and rather hoping that one day publication might be possible. She wrote with the bewildering fullness of a still-leisured age— and very, very frankly, so that even now many excisions have been made for reasons other than length, before it was possible to publish this selection covering the period of the First World War.

The value and fascination of her record are threefold. Familiar figures cross her pages, often in 'undress', and a pulsing cross-section of the society of her time is shown. In the political world her marriage had brought a family link with Asquith and his irrepressible Margot; Balfour she had known since childhood as a close friend of her mother; Churchill was a fellow dinner guest; and Harold 'Bluetooth' Baker— the *éminence grise* of the period—was her frequent companion. In literature, besides Lawrence (who wrote many of his best letters to her) and Barrie (whose secretary she was for twenty years), she gives interesting glimpses of Yeats, Siegfried Sassoon, Augustine Birrell, Robert Nichols, 'AE', T. S. Eliot, and Rupert Brooke. She made friends with the artists who painted her, and Augustus John, Sargent, McEvoy and Tonks are reproduced to the life. She loved the theatre, recorded her impression of H. B. Irving as Hamlet, chatted with Desmond Mac-Carthy, visited with Mrs Patrick Campbell and her daughter, and

Introduction

dipped into the world of music—her description of Suggia playing being a splendid word picture.

Secondly, the diary is also the story of the end of an era, symbolised perhaps in the curious anachronism of the Viceregal court in Dublin she describes with such delicious malice. She transports us to a world totally different from our own: 'One can hardly believe', she writes on reading Richardson's *Pamela*, 'our habits and values will ever seem as incredibly quaint to our descendants as those of our ancestors do to us'. Already, a mere fifty years later, they do. It is only through such a record as this that we can in some measure step back, the transition aided by illustration from her scrapbooks. 'As a hoarder,' she once said, 'I do outvie the most assiduous squirrel,' and it is a fault for which to be grateful.

And, finally, it is the unconscious analysis of a family and a woman's identity—developing, maturing, changing, and almost completely breaking under the pressure of the most disastrous events that any generation had ever known.

Lady Cynthia was the third child of the family of seven children born to Lord Elcho, later the eleventh Earl of Wemyss, and the time-lag between those who came before and those who came after made her sometimes feel herself an only child. Her seniors were two brothers, Ego—a nickname reflecting his inability as a child to pronounce Hugo, not his personality—and Guy. Another brother, Colin, died as a child, and she had one younger brother, Yvo, nine years her junior. Her sisters were Mary, eight years younger, and the baby Irene, nicknamed Bibs, who was fifteen years younger.

Her upbringing at the family seat of Stanway House, near Cheltenham in Gloucestershire, had the odd mixture of the spartan and the splendid which belonged to the English aristocracy. Writing in 1950 of her childish puzzlement over the state of the family fortunes, she made the point with characteristic candour: 'Since we lived in a large house, amply staffed and almost continually full of visitors, there must, according to present-day standards, have been a considerable amount of money, yet I cannot remember a time when finance was not an ever-present worry to my parents. There was always talk of the necessity for "retrenchment"—sometimes even, desecrating thought, of the letting of Stanway, and in most ways we were brought up most unluxuriously.'

Educated at home in the time-honoured tradition of the upper-class English girl, she married in 1910 Herbert Asquith, second son of the Prime Minister, who had followed in his father's early footsteps by beginning his career as a barrister. From the financial viewpoint it was an unworldy match, the wealth of the Asquith family being more widely assumed than actual. It was certainly not altogether a popular one with her own people, for it came in the midst of Asquith's battle to break the power of the House of Lords. Yet, oddly enough, her grandfather, the tenth earl, who was an extremist member of the right wing and had dubbed Asquith the 'Robber Chief', was probably the least incensed. By the outbreak of the First World War, however, such considerations had fallen into the background. During 1914 her husband, familiarly referred to in the diary as Beb, had enlisted in the Royal Field Artillery, and Lady Cynthia and her two baby sons had adopted an existence of 'cuckooing'.

This was the expressive term she coined for the flitting from temporary roof to temporary roof forced on her by lack of a permanent home—she had not, as the saying went, 'married a country house'. It is true there was a town house, in Sussex Place, but she was not wealthy enough to maintain such an establishment on her own, and it was let, with all the complications such amateur ventures usually entail. Her new way of life was only possible in that age of large, multiple residences in town and at the seaside or in the country, and of armies of servants to run them. Friends and relatives gave her frequent and varied harbour. Her mother's large, grimy corner-house in Cadogan Square tended to be limited in its usefulness. It was occupied only during three months in summer—May to the end of July—and its disadvantages were humorously summarised by Lady Cynthia: 'Built of inflamed red brick in the period of most elaborate ugliness, "Sixty-two", though I grew fond enough of it to be sad when it had to be sold, was I think a singularly depressing abode. Five storeys high, with a basement, the surface it presented to wretched maids to try—their failure was signal—to keep clean, was dauntingly large; yet the accommodation the house provided was inadequate, for it abounded in those waste spaces by house-agents grandiloquently called "entresols".'

Her best-loved resting-place, however, was Stanway. Her feeling for this house, the 'mansion' of the village of the same name which perches on a foothill of the North Cotswolds, was intense. Once the summer residence of the Abbots of Tewkesbury, it fell into the hands of the Tracy family at the dissolution of the monasteries, and before she was five Lady Cynthia had learned the story of the curse laid on the usurpers by the dispossessed clerics. The tale has been disputed as a legend, but the records seem to show that with some exceptions the curse has been remarkably effective. Undoubtedly it would have been uttered with the greater venom because the monks would have known

Introduction

that in the twelfth century an earlier member of the family, William Tracy, had been one of the four knights who left Thomas Becket weltering in his own blood on the altar-steps of Canterbury Cathedral. On the anniversary of his crime he was said to ride once again in search of a priest to shrive his soul, the clatter of his horse's hooves still audible to living ears. Such was the ill-starred inheritance that Susan Tracy, heiress of the family in the eighteenth century, brought with her when she married the eldest son of the fifth Earl of Wemyss. Susan's husband died young—the curse had transferred.

Lady Cynthia had been born at Clouds, the Wiltshire home of her mother's family, but it was to Stanway[1] that her heart belonged:

'The house is built of time-tinged golden Cotswold stone. Approached through the arch of the beautiful Inigo Jones gatehouse, the west front of the house with its four wide sixteenth-century gables, numerous mullioned windows, and one huge oriel, closely overlooks the village church and the huddled graves of the rude forefathers. The southern wing faces a lawn skirted by a wood of yew trees that makes a dark background in the spring for the brief, shimmering waxen glory of a large magnolia tree. Queened over by the great tulip tree, the eastern lawns stretch out until the ground rises in a sudden steep bank up to the long wide grass terrace that was once a pond and is still called the canal. From the "canal", you climb up, up, up, until you reach the queer stone building called the pyramid (the "Pretty Maid", I misunderstood its name to be) that has given its name to the entire hill.'

Inside it might have disappointed today's visitor of stately homes. The original panelling had been removed, the portraits were by artists as undistinguished as their subjects among the Tracy ancestors, and the furniture—much of it cumbrous Jacobean with William Morris upholstery—included no museum-pieces. All this could not be redeemed by the reputedly Tudor ceiling and gilt Queen Anne mirrors in the drawing room, but there was still the great 'oriel' window of the hall 'with hundreds of latticed panes, so mellowed by time that whenever the sun shines through their amber and green glass, the effect is of a vast honeycomb and indeed at all times and in all weathers of stored sunshine'. However, the family did not pine for grandeur, but 'loved the restful shabbiness and gentle dilapidation', and when the local decorator was called in occasionally it was 'to renovate, but never to innovate'. In winter comfort was limited to the immediate area of a fire, and piercing draughts penetrated the latticed panes and whistled through the endless intercommunicating doors, of which one bedroom boasted five. Unwary guests tended also to suffer from the paper

1. See additional notes in the index.

xiv

thinness of the walls which made any curtain-lecture clearly audible to the occupants of adjoining rooms.

Relics of feudalism still lingered about the establishment. The venerable coachman, Prew, automatically flourished his whip and cried 'Make way for her ladyship!' when he drove into the local inn yard, the only sign of changing times being the acute embarrassment he caused Lady Cynthia's mother. The vicar was still invited to the great house as he would have been in the days of Jane Austen and Trollope, although such a character as the Rev. H. B. Allen, usually referred to in the diary as 'Priest', would have been too great an eccentric for their pages. Living to a very advanced age, he was a monument to the preservative powers of whisky and a firm believer in free love, and continued in a chronic state of insolvency because of the kindness of heart which led him to maintain a retinue of sick horses and donkeys.

The diary opens in the midst of a family gathering at Stanway. A little under a year before, the tenth Earl of Wemyss had died, a zestful ninety-six, and his spirit was among them still as a cherished memory. To the historians he would be a member of the Cave of Adullam—the group of Liberals who had seceded from their party to oppose the democratic extension of the franchise in the Reform Bill of 1866. To his family he was the romantic who sketched the sunset from his home at Gosford House in East Lothian almost every night of his life and who, as a robustly lovesick widower on the way to ninety, had pursued Annie Tennant, wife of Margot Asquith's brother Frank Tennant. Equally, and contemporaneously, in his affections was Grace, whom he had ardently and tempestuously wooed and married as his second wife in 1900, and family legend has it that he often slept with a sword in the bed between himself and his wife—indeed a Viking gone to his Valhalla.

Now the presiding genius of the house was the new Countess of Wemyss. Her family links were in themselves a commentary on the vagaries of the English aristocracy. Her brother was George Wyndham, the many-talented Private Secretary to Balfour when Irish Secretary, and himself Chief Secretary for Ireland from 1900 until his economic development and local government schemes led to Unionist suspicions which forced his resignation in 1905. Their father was the Hon. Percy Scawen Wyndham, Conservative M.P. for West Cumberland for a quarter of a century, and himself the third and eldest surviving son of the first Baron Leconfield. The latter had been the natural son of the third Earl of Egremont, who is remembered for his naturalisation of Turner at Petworth, and as the probable father of the Whig premier Lord Melbourne.

Introduction

In 1883—when she was twenty-two—Mary Wyndham had married Hugo Charteris, Viscount Elcho, but he had not been alone in his admiration of her. Possessed of fine rather than classical features, she had a beauty which depended for much of its charm on expression, fascination of manner, a sympathetic eye, and a mind which combined a vivacious intelligence, ultimate reserves of wisdom, and an ability to compartmentalise her life by a quick-closing screen of vagueness. Thirteen years after her marriage she still had the enduring affection for Balfour to write: 'If only you had married me in 1881!', yet her union with Hugo Wemyss was in reality the best choice possible, widely though their interests diverged. His taste in company was altogether more earthy than her own: whereas she turned to the soulful-eyed Balfour, he relaxed in company with Lady Angela Forbes, whose language would reputedly have made a trooper blush, and had no patience with his wife's famed juxtapositions of ill-assorted guests. The idiosyncrasies and interplays of character which emerged in their house parties were a kind of experimental chemistry that dismayed him, and he literally fled from what Lady Cynthia would call 'frumps, freaks, and funnies'.

Yet, the son of the man of whom Matthew Arnold said: 'To my mind, indeed, the mere cock of his lordship's hat is one of the finest and most aristocratic things we have', was a striking character in his own right. His talents industriously applied might have sped him far —Balfour himself wrote to Lady Elcho in 1892: 'Hugo has just made one of the most amusing speeches I have ever heard in the House'— but, as Lady Cynthia commented, 'He is indolent.' Able instantly to summon an intimidating storm of wrath, he seldom bothered to sustain it, and he possessed that fatal barrier to high endeavour . . . a sense of humour. It is pleasant to think of him in the typical moment of his passionate recruiting speech of 1914, in which he coined the famous family catch-phrase 'the calm of Toddington'—referring to the nearest village to Stanway, and home of the 'simple yokels' listening to his words. Eloquently he appealed to these Cotswold labourers for more austerity to help the war effort, dwelling especially on the need to cut down on such luxuries as smoking, and at the height of his peroration —marked by an emphatic gesture—a cascade of huge cigars tumbled from his waistcoat pocket. Perhaps he was caught out, more probably he appreciated the instant roar of laughter more than anybody . . . and had known how to provoke it.

By 1915 the Countess of Wemyss—her husband had succeeded to the title in the previous year—was in her early fifties, then a much more advanced age than it appears to us today. Her once brilliant beauty lingered only in the re-read letters of her admirers, but her charm remained. Her health, however, was indifferent, and the diaries open with her reappearance after three weeks' of self-imposed imprisonment at Stanway, undertaken as a rest cure under the care of Halliwell, the local doctor. The plan had amused her family, and in her privately printed book *A Family Record* she later included the jesting comments of her youngest son Yvo in a letter to his sister Mary:

'How is your languid self and how is Stanway, and how pray is that strange recluse, or unspeakable monster, whom none may look on, closeted and communing with her spirit, dwelling on the heights until she emerge a full Mahatma? I suppose in the silence of the night the house echoes to the sound of beds, wardrobes and all manner of furniture being trundled round the room, and again to the rustlings of many sheet and blanket "manias". She will awake after a month and find Mockett[1] waiting with a sheaf of telegrams to the effect that her three sons are at the Front, her eldest daughter doing time for card-sharping, her second eloped with a young cavalry officer, her youngest truant from school and God knows where. But she will have forgotten them, so what matter? With renewed zest she will wheel the grand piano round in the drawing room and wander off over the hills with a pack of wild and aggravated chows, till Stanway falls in ruins about her. What a curious sight Halliwell must be, entering the forbidden room like the Steward of Glamis?'

Yvo wrote from Queenboro, where he was already serving with the King's Royal Rifles, but around her on that April day on which we are about to move into their lives were her daughter Lady Cynthia, her second son Guy, and his wife Frances—a niece of Margot Asquith. At the time of this return visit to her childhood home, Lady Cynthia was in her late twenties and at the height of her beauty—a delicately strange, elusive, evanescent quality of face which was unique and baffled the artists who tried again and again to capture it. To beauty she added wit, intelligence, and a literary bent which stayed with her all her life and enabled her in 1958 to astonish a television audience with her ability to survive the most searching of quizzes on the novels of Jane Austen. Like her mother, she had married a man of very different temperament, but had chosen equally well from the point of view of an enduring marriage. Beb Asquith was a man of some gifts as a poet and writer, as well as in his originally chosen career in law, but even in literature he did not agree with his wife on the cardinal point of the merits of 'beloved Dickens'. She had conquered shyness and shone in the social world, he—largely perhaps because he cared so

1. The butler.

much less for its pleasures—was still often diffident, and when absorbed in poetic composition became remote, leaving everyone (in her graphic phrase) as if hammering on layers of thick felt. Beb, too, had a sense of humour and when his father 'did not address one word of inquiry to him' on his return from the Front in 1918 after five months in the line, realised the depth of unexpressed feeling, and merely allowed himself to comment that H. H. Asquith 'had at times an excessive belief in the powers of the unspoken word'.

In the spring of 1915 the war, despite the terrible battles of the previous year which had reduced the initial German strategy to dead-lock, was still something removed, not yet stripped of excitement, and only gradually were people being converted to Kitchener's original conclusion that the war would be a long one. Lady Cynthia had herself been out with her sister-in-law (later Lady Asquith of Yarnbury) to visit the hospitals in France, but the impact of that conducted tour had been slight—'the war was still not much more than academic to me'.

In January Kitchener wrote to French—commander of the British army on the Western Front from the beginning of the war until the end of 1915—that, since the German lines in France could not be broken, they 'could be held by an investing force whilst operations proceed elsewhere'. This included the Near East, where at the end of 1914 Egypt had been declared a British protectorate, and where some of the troops were now being massed for the attack on the Dardanelles. Ego, Lady Cynthia's eldest brother, was already in Egypt, as were his friends and brother officers George Vernon and Tom Strickland. His wife, Letty, daughter of the eighth Duke of Rutland and sister of Lady Diana Manners (later the wife of Duff Cooper), was about to join him there, and was taking with her Lady Cynthia's younger sister Mary.

The dark shadows that were eventually to move on Stanway were as yet only potential, and above stairs in the nursery three small children played. For Anne Charteris, daughter of Lady Cynthia's brother Guy, tragedy was to come with another war when her husband Lord O'Neill was killed in action in 1944—she was later to become the wife of Lord Rothermere, and subsequently of Ian Fleming, creator of James Bond. The others were Lady Cynthia's own two boys, four-year-old John and Michael, still a baby-in-arms. John, preco-ciously talented in some ways, as in his gift for music, was causing his mother great anxiety. Autism was then a condition undiagnosed, and against the plunges into frivolity that Lady Cynthia so often seems to take may be set the ever-nagging worry of her cherished eldest son, whom in the course of the present diary she had gradually to accept as never to be normal. The endless quest from specialist to specialist; the confidence—always to be undermined—that the latest governess held the key to tutoring him into ordinary life; the agony of being with or away from him, all these are things which every mother similarly placed will recognise with understanding.

But on the April day when the diary opens the sun was shining . . . .

Asquith Family Tree

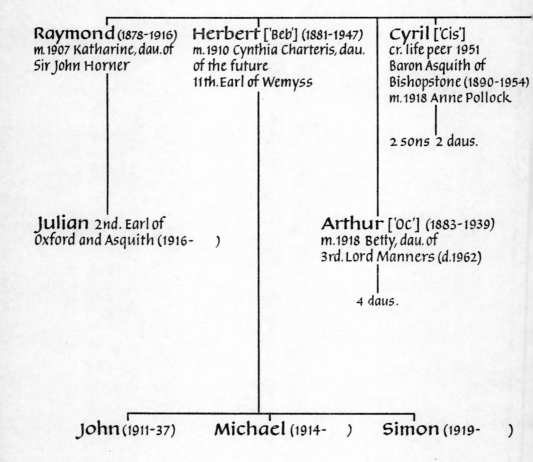

Raymond (1878-1916)
m. 1907 Katharine, dau. of
Sir John Horner

Herbert ['Beb'] (1881-1947)
m. 1910 Cynthia Charteris, dau.
of the future
11th. Earl of Wemyss

Cyril ['Cis']
cr. life peer 1951
Baron Asquith of
Bishopstone (1890-1954)
m. 1918 Anne Pollock

2 sons 2 daus.

Julian 2nd. Earl of
Oxford and Asquith (1916-   )

Arthur ['Oc'] (1883-1939)
m. 1918 Betty, dau. of
3rd. Lord Manners (d. 1962)

4 daus.

John (1911-37)   **Michael** (1914-   )   **Simon** (1919-   )

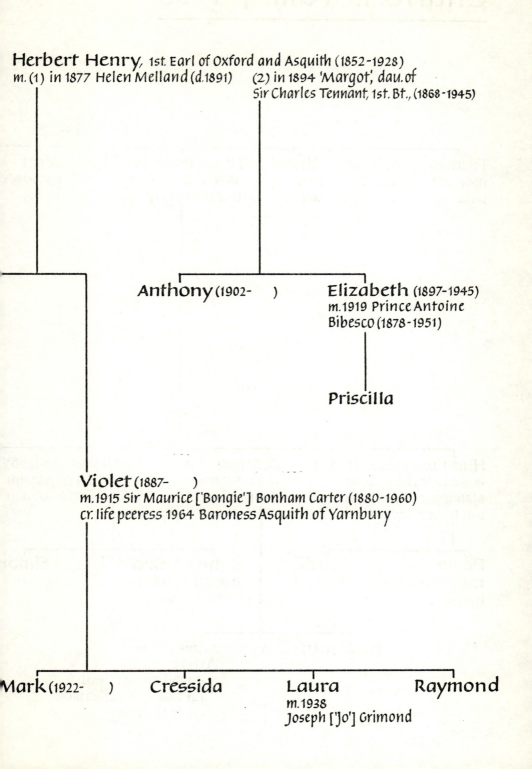

Herbert Henry, 1st. Earl of Oxford and Asquith (1852-1928)
m. (1) in 1877 Helen Melland (d.1891)   (2) in 1894 'Margot', dau.of
                                          Sir Charles Tennant, 1st. Bt., (1868-1945)

Anthony (1902-   )   **Elizabeth** (1897-1945)
                           m.1919 Prince Antoine
                           Bibesco (1878-1951)

Priscilla

Violet (1887-   )
m.1915 Sir Maurice ['Bongie'] Bonham Carter (1880-1960)
cr. life peeress 1964 Baroness Asquith of Yarnbury

Mark (1922-   )   **Cressida**   **Laura**   **Raymond**
                                        m.1938
                                        Joseph ['Jo'] Grimond

Charteris Family Tree

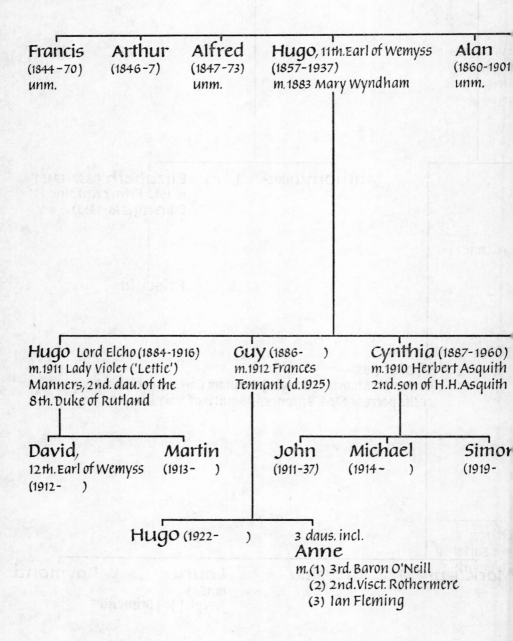

Francis	Arthur	Alfred	Hugo, 11th. Earl of Wemyss	Alan
(1844–70)	(1846–7)	(1847–73)	(1857–1937)	(1860–1901)
unm.		unm.	m. 1883 Mary Wyndham	unm.

Hugo Lord Elcho (1884-1916)
m. 1911 Lady Violet ('Lettie')
Manners, 2nd. dau. of the
8th. Duke of Rutland

Guy (1886–)
m. 1912 Frances
Tennant (d. 1925)

Cynthia (1887-1960)
m. 1910 Herbert Asquith
2nd. son of H.H. Asquith

David,
12th. Earl of Wemyss
(1912–)

Martin
(1913–)

John
(1911-37)

Michael
(1914–)

Simon
(1919–

Hugo (1922–)

3 daus. incl.
Anne
m. (1) 3rd. Baron O'Neill
(2) 2nd. Visct. Rothermere
(3) Ian Fleming

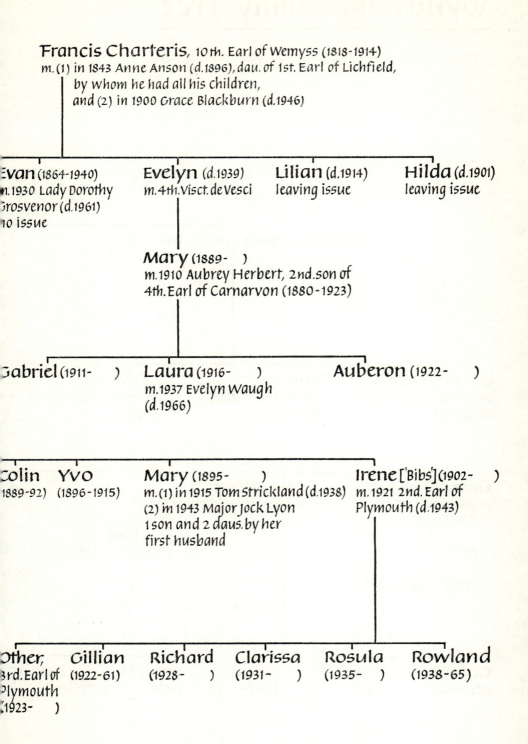

Francis Charteris, 10th. Earl of Wemyss (1818-1914)
m. (1) in 1843 Anne Anson (d.1896), dau. of 1st. Earl of Lichfield,
by whom he had all his children,
and (2) in 1900 Grace Blackburn (d.1946)

Evan (1864-1940)
m.1930 Lady Dorothy
Grosvenor (d.1961)
no issue

Evelyn (d.1939)
m. 4th. Visct. de Vesci

Lilian (d.1914)
leaving issue

Hilda (d.1901)
leaving issue

Mary (1889-   )
m.1910 Aubrey Herbert, 2nd. son of
4th. Earl of Carnarvon (1880-1923)

Gabriel (1911-   )

Laura (1916-   )
m.1937 Evelyn Waugh
(d.1966)

Auberon (1922-   )

Colin
(1889-92)

Yvo
(1896-1915)

Mary (1895-   )
m. (1) in 1915 Tom Strickland (d.1938)
(2) in 1943 Major Jock Lyon
1 son and 2 daus. by her
first husband

Irene ['Bibs'] (1902-   )
m.1921 2nd. Earl of
Plymouth (d.1943)

Other,
3rd. Earl of
Plymouth
(1923-   )

Gillian
(1922-61)

Richard
(1928-   )

Clarissa
(1931-   )

Rosula
(1935-   )

Rowland
(1938-65)

Wyndham Family Tree

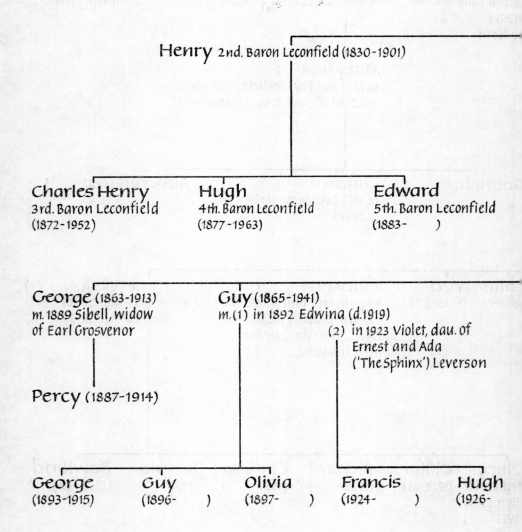

Henry 2nd. Baron Leconfield (1830-1901)

Charles Henry
3rd. Baron Leconfield
(1872-1952)

Hugh
4th. Baron Leconfield
(1877-1963)

Edward
5th. Baron Leconfield
(1883-   )

George (1863-1913)
m. 1889 Sibell, widow
of Earl Grosvenor

Guy (1865-1941)
m.(1) in 1892 Edwina (d.1919)
  (2) in 1923 Violet, dau. of
      Ernest and Ada
      ('The Sphinx') Leverson

Percy (1887-1914)

George
(1893-1915)

Guy
(1896-   )

Olivia
(1897-   )

Francis
(1924-   )

Hugh
(1926-

George Wyndham, 1st. Baron Leconfield
(the natural son of the 3rd. Earl of Egremont,
who was also the father of Lord Melbourne,
the Prime Minister) (1787-1869)
m. 1815 Mary (d.1863) only dau. of the
Rev. William Blunt of Crabbett, Sussex

Percy Scawen (1835-1911)
m. Madeline (d.1920) 6th. dau. of
Gen. Sir Guy Campbell, 1st. Bt.

Mary (1864-1937)
1883 Lord Elcho, later
th. Earl of Wemyss
mother of Cynthia Asquith,
ee Charteris family tree)

Madeline (d.1941)
leaving issue

Pamela (d.1928)
m.(1) in 1895 1st. Baron Glenconner
(d.1920) by whom she had 3 sons
and 1 dau.
(2) in 1922 1st. Visct. Grey
of Fallodon (1862-1933)

1915

I wonder if all diaries are as unrepresentative of their writers as this is of me.

LADY CYNTHIA ASQUITH

Thursday, 15th April

I have always thought it would be unwholesome for me to attempt to write a diary. I'm sure it will make me think my life drab and strain after sensation to make copy for my autobiography. I shall become morbidly self-conscious and a valetudinarian about my career, so I shall try not to be un-introspective, and confine myself to events and diagnoses of other people. In any case I am entirely devoid of the gift of sincerity, and could never write as though I were really convinced no other eye would ever see what I wrote. I am incurably self-conscious. This impromptu resolution sprung from an absurd compact I made with Duff Cooper that we would both begin a diary at the same moment, and bind each other over to keep it up. He has given me this lovely book—but instead of inspiring, it paralyses me and makes me feel my life will not be nearly sufficiently purple.

Frances and I, Guy and Mamma are here at Stanway alone—Mamma convalescing from her rest cure and Guy from a slight operation. The pyramid is starred with daffodils, but the spring is reluctant and tantalising. Letty and Mary came down for one night yesterday. They follow Ego, George and Strickland to Egypt on Saturday and are wildly excited. Letty is so emaciated that, seen from certain angles, she really has no face at all. She was in her music-hall vein and also being dazzlingly capable about the details of their journey. They were both full of passport, inoculation, money-bag thrills, and I must say I do envy them a good deal. I'm sure to be having enthralling adventures of one's own is the only distraction which can help to prevent one being either permanently raw or numb from this war. Mary is looking very beautiful and her passport photograph is exactly like a spy in a melodrama. I felt very tired and ugly.

Biographical information, with cross-references under Christian and nicknames, and also vocabulary definitions and identifications of places, is included in the annotated index. Later first references, when the index entry may be of interest, are marked by an asterisk.

1915

Thursday, 15th April

Mary and Letty went away early leaving us all feeling rather 'flat'. This reminds me of Letty's Restoration joke when poor Frances[1] said she was feeling flat: 'You don't look it, darling'—she is going to have a baby in July.

We all suffered from spring lassitude and Frances wisely dormoused most of the day. We sat out a little in the morning and she read me French's latest despatch containing sadly definite censure of poor Rawlinson. Had Anne and John in the drawing room. Instead of hearing them, I practised the piano, which is my obsession for the moment. I am beginning to read pieces for nine-year-olds. Nurse massaged me at seven. Guy, Bibs, and I dined together. We told Bibs that she was an adopted Barnardo foundling—she took it calmly. Bibs slept in my bed.

Friday, 16th April

Lovely spring day. Wrote letters and practised piano after breakfast. Frances, Bibs and I sat out and read the day's instalment of *Richard Chatterton V.C.* and some *Barrack Room Ballads* aloud. Guy was up and about and birdsnesting with Priest. Bibs lay on my bed while I rested after lunch, and we had rather an amusing talk. She is a delightful companion with a great deal of humour and sensitiveness, and astoundingly articulate. The children came down after tea. John played the piano with wonderful technique and temperament.

Guy, Frances, Mamma and I had rather a pleasant evening together. Frances was very funny in her sweet, simple arch way about Grandpapa and his octogenarian courtship of her mother. Apparently he was the most wonderfully Elizabethanly romantic of lovers. He used to send her a breakfast arranged on a tray (grapes and white violets) with his own hands every morning over from Gosford to North Berwick, and once when he was importunate in Italy and Annie fled secretly from one town to another, he took a special train, and when she alighted at her destination to her flattered consternation she found him bowing on the platform. And all the while he was getting entangled into matrimony with Grace. He was a wonderful old stag.

Poor Bibs was inoculated in preparation for a visit to the Front. She was very nervous about the operation and the needle had only just been inserted when a telegram from Angela arrived saying she wouldn't take the responsibility of having her. So probably it will be abandoned and she will have the thorn without the rose—rather bad luck.

1. Frances Charteris: see index for all names and nicknames on this page.

4

Went up to London alone by 8.14 train. It's a maddening, dilatory, philandering train. I finished *Pamela* which I had been reading at Southsea. The last volume is a tedious anticlimax, but otherwise I enjoyed it immensely. One can hardly believe our habits and values will ever seem as incredibly quaint to our descendants as those of our ancestors, thus portrayed, do to us. The language is too delicious; the men are 'sad rakes', the women 'of virtuous and amiable dispositions', and the degree of what was known as 'sensibility' too extraordinary. On every page some benefactor's hand is seized and bathed with tears of gratitude, and the combination of demonstrative, schwärmerei-ish emotions and the greatest formality of manner. They always cried and swooned when conversing with their husbands, but never neglected to call them 'Sir' or 'Mr B.' It is extremely long and trivially told, but amazingly readable. Pamela's morality is tawdry and commercially expedient to the last degree, but she is redeemed from platitudinous priggishness by a certain sprightliness and one is made sensible of her charm of appearance.

I got up to London just before twelve and had a hellish morning in pursuit of my summer tweed from Harrods. I went to Selfridges first, took back a hat which made a trench in my forehead and found a pretty black-and-white one instead. Sharp skirmish with Harrods on telephone about my skirt. Had hair waved at Emile. Went to Harrods— found it closed and skirt just despatched to fictitious address in Conduit Street. Lunched in neighbouring A.B.C. shop off two poached eggs and rusks and butter. Returned to Harrods and finally ran down skirt.

I caught the four-something train to Reigate at Charing Cross and met Evan.[1] He dug me out of my third class and we got into an extraordinary carriage with only one seat in it. I hadn't seen him since he returned from being intelligence officer to the Flying Corps. He has been out for about three months and has come back for the Parliamentary Bar. We had a delightful journey. He is learning German and had a stiff grammar. I helped him. We talked the language of the 'Huns' nearly all the time, and I thought we should be arrested on suspicion.

We arrived at Reigate Priory soon after five and had tea with Lady Essex, Kitty Somerset, and Ava Astor. Conversation mainly war gossip. Ava exquisitely dressed and looking very *larmoyante*. She is very beautiful in a decorative, Sèvres-china way, but it is an appliqué, unventilated face and she doesn't look out of it and one cannot look into it. I don't feel her in the least responsible for her beauty, but it is very perfect of its kind. I believe she is an extremely nice woman, but I'm sure she is hopelessly unwhimsical, and I think it was a very good

1. Evan Charteris: see index—also for other house-party guests.

thing Basil[1] didn't marry her. I think one might get to want to untidy her face.

Beb arrived and told me they really think they are going to the front on Thursday. It is very difficult to believe that history will interfere in one's private life to such an extent. Beb going to the front seems too melodramatic to be true. It is a thing I cannot at all imagine in anticipation until it has happened. I don't know what I shall feel like. He is excited and very keen. They have had definite orders, but of course they may be revoked.

Dinner 8.30. Kitty, Lord and Lady Essex, my father, Evan, Mrs Astor, Islingtons and Joan Poynder, General Cowans, Gwendeline Churchill, Kitty's son Bobby, Beb and self were the party. I sat between the General and Jack Islington. The General is very affable and easy. Before the war one would have thought him quite stupid, but now one knows he is Quartermaster-General and is supposed to be performing his difficult function with brilliant success. I got on quite well with him. He inveighed against Winston a good deal—very anti-Naval Division, etc. He was amusingly disapproving about Mary and Letty's camp-following, and said there was a very good chance of their being sent straight back directly they arrive. He seems practically positive that the Yeomanry will remain in Egypt. I liked him, though he isn't impressive. He loves India, where he has spent twenty years, and is homesick for it. He says his present work is terrifically severe.

After dinner there was one bridge table and I played low poker with Lady Essex, Beb, Evan, and the General. We had a joker, but the hands were very low on the whole. I won £1.18s, Beb lost £2. Talked to Adele Essex a little in her room before going to bed. We discussed war work and how we could do 'our bit'. Very, very tired when I went to bed.

Sunday, 18th April

When I got out of bed I found my neck and chest were covered with a rash. A little man exactly like Dr Dose in Happy Families came to see me and, to my horror and amusement, said he thought it must be German measles (Hun pox)—all Evan's fault for making me talk German. It was a comic bathos to have German measles just now, but I gnashed my teeth in rage. It seemed too cruel if I shouldn't be able to be with Beb at Portsmouth for these last few days, and it was uncomfortable to feel such a nuisance to Kitty, etc. I can't count how many people I kissed on Friday! Beb went off about 10.30.

1. Lord Basil Blackwood: see index.

Monday, 19th April

Woke up in tears with conviction that I was caught in a trap and that Beb would go to the front this week. It seems very hard; we had intended to have John down at Portsmouth. The rash has spread to my arms and face, so I am certain to be condemned. Papa came up and said he thought I had much better come up to Cadogan Square, and that he would send an ambulance down to fetch me. The doctor said an ordinary motor, if it was fumigated afterwards, would do quite well, so ambulance was stopped. Polly[1] and I started at about 2.30. Such a lovely day . . . the swaying, debonair daffodils made me feel mutinous. I saw Papa when I got up and went straight to bed in Mary's room, in my eyes so unaccountably shrunk since it used to seem so large as our night nursery. Ego, Guy, and I used to sleep in it, and now it seems so confined.

Dr Parkinson came at about 5.30 and could scarcely find any traces of rash, and would hardly believe I could have measles. I twitted him with the very brown brandies Margot Asquith now swills at his prescription. I asked Papa for some books and began Maupassant's *Une Vie*. Wrote to Eliza Wedgwood to ask her to find small Shakespeares to form part of Beb's active service trousseau.

Tuesday, 20th April

Slept fairly well. Rash really quite gone. I finished *Une Vie* and thought it very depressing and not sufficiently nourishing to be worth while. Went over some of my repertory of by-heart poems. I did a little knitting, but the intoxication of that sport has quite, quite left me. Papa said goodbye to me in the evening as he was going off early in the morning to the Buffet at Boulogne. Yvo, who was up from his soldiering, came and talked to me through the door.

Wednesday, 21st April

Huge budget of letters came up for me at breakfast. Such a typical one from Aubrey Herbert* in Egypt, one from Patrick Shaw-Stewart in the Dardanelles reading like a page of Homer, Beb wrote from Lee-on-Solent where he was collecting ammunition, etc. The doctor came unexpectedly and bouleversed my whole present and future by saying quite definitely that I hadn't had measles but a colitic rash. I could get up and go away tomorrow. I immediately wired Beb.

1. Maid, Polly Cliffe: see index also for other names on this page.

Thursday, 22nd April

Telegram arrived from Beb saying he would be billeted at the Mermaid Tavern at Rye. Found there was a twelve o'clock train—full of Canadian soldiers who kept re-bawling the following words:

> One—two—three. Who are we?
> We are the boys of the C.O.C.
> Are we here?
> I should say we've been here a hellish while . . .
> Are we downhearted? No.
> Are we dry? YES!

Two got into my carriage and I made great friends with them. One was a rather attractive-looking youth, a little like Yvo, with an insolent, humorous expression. The other was older and looked rather sad and sensitive. He seemed pained by his companions. One very rough diamond—if a diamond at all—came to the door and tried to coax them into a carriage full of rowdies, but they refused and there was rather a row about it.

They kept quarrelling about Canada versus England, the elder of the two being English-bred. They indulged in every kind of futile argument—the relative merit of English and Canadian trains, sweet-peas, food, etc., etc.—and I gradually got roped into the conversation. They were very funny with me. Their tone and manner to one so subtly, but greatly different from an English Tommy's. They both drew out photographs and white heather with a rather truculent sentimentality. The youth was very homesick, and I fear regretted his impulsive enlistment. He said Salisbury Plain had been too ghastly, and had given him two months in hospital with rheumatism. He made me laugh by dramatically exclaiming, after catching sight of my label, 'I say, look who's travelling in our midst like!' We shook hands warmly when I got out, and I felt the 'Soldier I wish you well' of Housman's poem in a gush.

I found the Mermaid Tavern at Rye was the most perfect specimen of 'Ye Olde Inn' I have ever seen. I think Beb is very lucky in his companions. Captain Ammon is in command of Beb's battery (C. battery). Good-looking and very young. He is a regular, but was just going to retire before the war. He is supposed to be a very good Staff College man. With him was a huge, burly, jolly man called Arkwright, of great football fame. He was captain of the English eleven for two years. They had brought the half-battery which was going out all the way from Lee-on-Solent by road that day. Beb arrived about 8.15 with inches of dust on him. One could have written with one's finger on his face. He is the only subaltern going out, which involves a lot of work—he seems to have a great deal of fagging to do. The great joke is calling him Carson.*

Beb and I dined at a little table by ourselves. I could not realise the reality of the situation and grasp that I had really come to see Beb off to the front, the setting of that lovely old inn full of soldiers and everything was so extraordinarily theatrical. It is difficult to recognise one's own identity these days; the whole of life has become such a melodrama that one always feels in a dream.

Friday, 23rd April

We were called at 5.30 as they had to chaperone the guns along the road to Dover very early. Captain Ammon offered to motor me there, and I accepted with alacrity. We started about 7.30 in the Battery Commander's beautiful car. It was a lovely drive through that curious flat country full of delicious lambs—I have never seen so many—a divine morning. We passed all the huge lorries of the battery just as they were starting. Magnificent-looking men and very grim, business-like-looking guns—quite disguised, one couldn't tell their outsides from the other lorries containing ammunition, etc. Beb was in a little motor winding up the procession, looking very official with maps and paraphernalia. They had a difficult job getting the guns up that perpendicular hill just outside Folkestone.

Talked a lot to Ammon. He was interesting, but not cheering, about the war. He estimates duration at quite three years, and thinks the Germans may still get to Calais. We went to the Lord Warden Hotel —full of officers. At last they know definitely that they are to go to-night. The order was to start at seven, and they have been very busy embarking the guns, etc., all day. My heart was torn by poor little Walter's tragedy.[1] He had thought they were not going till Sunday and his 'girl' had been coming to see him on the Saturday. Now he was in despair and desperately telephoning and telegraphing to try and get her down in time, but she never came and the poor little fellow looked so sad. He came up to where Beb and I were sitting, looking very rueful, and wistfully said, 'There's no one to see me off.'

Beb was busy most of the afternoon. I sat stupefiedly in the lounge. At about four o'clock I went down to the pier-head in his little motor. His driver is almost the best-looking man I have ever seen. Very spruce and dapper; in technique still very much more like a chauffeur

1. One of the young officers.

than a Tommy. *Princess Victoria* was the name of their transport: she looked inadequately small to carry those huge lorries. There was a great bustle, the deck creeping with muscular Lascars and huge motor cars being swung on board. The guns were all on. Beb, very well disguised as a soldier, gave orders to brilliantly efficient-looking N.C.O.s. The men were all swarming about, looking rather excited and important. We motored back and had tea, and he went soon afterwards as they were ordered to embark the men at six. I waited till about 6.30 and then I walked down to the pier accompanied by Captain Ammon, who told me he wasn't going till Sunday after all.

Beb came off and said goodbye, and then I waited there in the cold until they actually glided away. I never thought I could have done such a thing, but I felt strangely and mercifully numb, curiously narcotised and unimaginative. Luckily there was no band, nothing to dramatise the situation. They just slunk stealthily, surreptitiously, away with their grim iron freight. No cheers, no waving, and but few jokes—just one or two 'Are we downhearted? No's'. I was the only woman seer-off, and I could not convince myself of the reality and momentousness of the occasion. I couldn't believe it was really Beb who was going, or myself who was watching him go.

Captain Ammon walked me home and we had dinner together. He was so nice. Aileen Meade* telephoned me from her hotel at Folkestone, asking me to come there at once as she and her husband were remaining there over Sunday. I was too utterly tired to feel much, but it was rather forlorn alone in the hotel, so I agreed, and she sent a motor and maid to pack up my clothes for me. I got there about ten. She was very darling and put me to bed.

Saturday, 24th April

This is the most extraordinary hotel, full of the most fascinating frumps, freaks, and funnies—nearly all terribly smart and glitteringly *décolleté*. Aileen and I feel like governesses. Charlie is undergoing a military course here for a fortnight. He is very bored by military routine, poor darling, I'm afraid. He and Aileen are deliciously, really rather infectiously, happy together and quite delightful to be with. We enjoyed the human species at luncheon enormously. It was a lovely day, and Aileen and I both went out in bathchairs—a delicious occupation. We pretended to be hopelessly ill. She is one of the people I enjoy myself most with and very often feel an almost startling affinity with, though I suppose we should strike a third person as very different.

Sunday, 25th April

Stayed in bed this morning. Aileen came and talked to me. I find her rather intoxicating—she has that blessed gift of making one feel in good form as well as being, I think, very amusing herself. A superlatively good conductor. Of course, we have an enormous amount of nursery conversation—she is frighteningly devoted to Charlie. I went up to their bedroom, and Aileen and I both put on his khaki. Being so freakishly flat I really look surprisingly like a subaltern.

After dinner we all sat in my room and indulged in one of those delicious sort of Peter Ibbetson conversations about Abbeyleix.* I love quite effortless reminiscences, just reminding one another of concrete things. It brought back that happy atmosphere so vividly and made me homesick for my childhood. Aileen gave me a really intoxicating dewdrop* from Charlie. When they were engaged, he had once rather chilled her by saying, 'Nearly all women are bores—Cynthia is the only really witty one I know'!

Monday, 26th April

Aileen decided to come up to London for the day with me. I feel a peculiar appetite for buying clothes just now. So far from not wanting them in wartime, I think they are the one thing to distract one, and I long for lovely ones. Went to Miss North's where I tried on resurrected Paisley coat, réchauffé black evening dress, made fashionable, tully and sticky-out. The clothes have undergone enormous change since the war and have become practically early Victorian with real full skirts. I thought war would produce reactions to womanliness.

Caught 4.45 Paddington and came down to Stanway with Polly. Found children flourishing and only Mamma, Guy, Frances, and Bibs here—Guy with water-on-knee from fall off Yvo's motor bicycle, which has given him extension of leave. Went to Mamma's sitting room. Guy read some *Egoist* aloud, and 'so to bed'.

Tuesday, 27th April

The news seems fairly serious.[1] I am very bad at interpreting the

1. In the Battle of Neuve Chapelle, 10–13th March, first of the siege warfare battles, the British had used a short intensive bombardment to open a gap in the German defences, but had not properly exploited the initial surprise. Then, three days before the first Gallipoli landing, the Germans created a four-mile gap on 22nd April by their first use of chlorine gas in the west in the Second Battle of Ypres. This was one of the war's great crises, but this time the Germans failed fully to exploit the advantage.

papers, but they seem to admit that the Germans did make an advance of three miles on Friday, and considering the fuss we made over our appallingly expensive advance of one mile at Neuve Chapelle, it does seem as if they had had a considerable success. Superstition forbids me to breathe it, but I feel the most unaccountable, almost apathetic, want of terror about Beb. An extraordinary sense of security laps me round, only interrupted by moments of sudden sharp nerves. I have been far more anxious when he has been out shooting or has come home late at home. I can't understand it, and wonder if it can in any way be telepathic, or is it merely a merciful paralysis of my imagination.

Mamma is depressed about getting old, poor darling. Some people age when they are getting old in years, and that muffles and brings resignation, but she is, of course, one of the perennially young, and then I suppose it must be tragic.

Guy read *Egoist* aloud in Mamma's sitting room. So very sorry to hear Rupert Brooke has died in Dardanelles of poisoning or sunstroke. I have only met him once or twice, never got to know him, but always looked forward to doing so some day, and it does stab one to think of his beautiful young poet's face with the cornfield head. He had the most lovely *regard* I have ever seen I think. Poor Eddie[1] will be broken-hearted—I think he was his favourite protégé. I am told he was absolutely convinced he would be killed in this war and he wrote lovely poems bidding farewell to things he loved—the 'touch of fur' was one which I thought original. It is rather sad that it should have been an illness.

Wednesday, 28th April

The first letter arrived from Beb by the first post. He has plunged straight into the shell theatre and had a very busy day extricating mudsunk lorries, etc. It was as lovely a day as I have ever seen—enchanted sunlight and daffodils. I wore my new mysterious check skirt.

News indefinite, but apparently somewhat better. Read the debate on the prisoners' question. It is too dreadful to think of poor Bunt[2] in solitary confinement. Sat out with Mamma in Tigsy* Hut. She seems better today. Eliza Wedgwood* came to tea in very high spirits. I gave her a hat with which she was delighted, and it really did suit her extraordinarily well. She looks like Brünnhilde in it. I gave her some clothes for the Belgians, too, and she went off highly delighted with her loot. We read Beb's letter to her.

1. Edward Marsh: see index.
2. G. G. Goschen, son of Sir Edward Goschen.

Thursday, 29th April

Another absolutely enchanted day. Sat out in the morning—read papers. News seems somewhat better. Advance appears to be checked. French cruisers torpedoed and all lives lost.[1] A great deal in papers about the asphyxiating gases the Huns have used with such dire results. Our soldiers to wear respirators. Guy, looking quite smart again, departed at three.

Eliza dined intoxicated with the fillip of a newly appropriated velvet dress of Mamma's, snatched from the rummage heap. She was so tightly welded into it that we could scarcely unfasten it when she left. Frances, complaining of Lady Angela's[2] backbiting of Letty, said, too deliciously unconsciously, 'We were in the train and there was Annie and Nurse and Toby!' I love the idea of Toby[3] spreading scandal in the kennel. Eliza contributed rather interesting titbit of war gossip—that the only reason why there has been no Zeppelin raid on London is that the Kaiser absolutely refuses to countenance it on account of all his relations there. The Council are alleged to be very keen on its attempt. I quite credit the poor scapegoat of the resentment with the harbouring of such a sentiment.

Friday, 30th April

Mr Norton and Countess Benckendorff arrived teatime, having motored from London and seen several churches on their way. Norton is as much 'the perfect lady' as ever, and Countess B. an adorable old gypsy queen. She is very asthmatic and difficult to hear, but one takes it on trust that she is saying very good things.

Mr Balfour, Ettie, Evan, Dinah and her husband Sir Iain Colquhoun and Joan Lascelles (née Balfour) had all arrived by dinner time. It was very amusing seeing the two war brides. Joan's marriage must seem a strange episode in her career—engaged, married, and back to the front all in nine days. Dinah's husband has an enormous trench of a wound all the way down his leg, and won't be going back for a month. He is a terribly 'tigsy' man, rather good-looking in a minute, dapper way—spruce with rather 'Guardee' manner. Dinah looking very pretty and smart in trousseau. Joan looks very happy, I think, beaming passionate, reverent adoration at 'Nunckey', as she calls A.J.B.

No bridge after dinner. We sat round the drawing-room fire, quite

1. The *Gantheaume*, sunk on 26th April by an Austrian submarine in the Strait of Otranto: actually less than a third of her crew was saved.
2. Lady Angela Forbes: see index for all names on this page.
3. A son of Lady Wemyss' chow, Pina.

happily though unscintillatingly. Ettie very disfigured by short
fashionable skirt. It looked like an accident. I hair-combed with her.
We discussed war anxiety and she told me about the poor Mannerses at
Avon.[1] Talked about Sibyl and what quality it was that made her success
and popularity irritating. I give Ettie very good marks in wartime.

Saturday, 1st May

Ettie went up to London early to go into waiting. Day wet, didn't
go out all morning. Sat about in hall, writing letters, reading newspapers and in desultory conversation. Mr Balfour, Dinah, Joan and
Sir Iain played tennis in the afternoon. Sat next to Sir Iain at dinner and
got on quite well. He is quite easy when one is up against him, though
rather a non-conductor in a group. After dinner we played the game of
guessing the person thought of by asking what flower-animal-musical
instrument-shop-landscape-architecture, etc., etc., they were like.

Sunday, 2nd May

I went to church with a fairly large contingent. Mr Bateman preached
an extremely good sermon on immortality. Mr Balfour, Papa, Evan,
Sir Iain and the two 'war brides' played tennis. I did not feel well
enough to play. Talked a good deal to Countess Benck. She has a
wonderfully strong personality, and gives one a tremendous impression
of mellow shrewdness. I love talking to her, though she is difficult to
understand. She is one of the people one longs to please.

Priest came to dinner; I sat between him and Mamma—A.J.B. on
her other side. Certain amount of general conversation at our end.
Discussion as to relative merits of Charteris and Wyndham family. I
complained of the only famous Charteris[2] being a notorious villain.
Mr B., because they are Scots, took up the cudgels for them with vehe-
mence. We had the dear old hare of who amongst the company one
would suspect of murder, and Mr B. said he would like to write a
novel with me as a villainess, as he can imagine me in the most lurid
roles. I can't think how I deserve this compliment, but it is one he
always pays me. His charm is as radiant as ever. He really is in a class
quite, quite alone. Oddly enough, in spite of his divine amiability and
sweetness and easiness, I should still feel shy alone in a room with him.
I love talking to him with other people. I suppose it is that having
always known him as a child, and always being rather edited to him
by Mamma, I have never really been able to change gear and adjust

1. Lord and Lady Manners: see index.　　2. Colonel Francis: see index.

14

an independent, grown-up relationship with him. I have really scarc
ever had a *tête-à-tête* with him. I know he used to think me silent, b
he can't now as I have become quite a rattle. I can imagine ho
intoxicating he must be to meet on one's own grown up. Perhaps
fall just a tiny bit between the social and family stools with him. He
Papa, Lady Essex, and Joan played bridge, the rest of us rather feeble
letter games. I had the privilege of seeing Sir Iain's leg wound. It is
too magnificently awful—like an enormous crab.

Monday, 3rd May

Extraordinary scene with Bibs after breakfast. The shadow of the
approaching term is upon her, and she was very annoyed at the idea
of having a second inoculation which she feared would keep her in
bed for the last day of her holidays. She is extraordinarily susceptible,
and I think Sir Iain, with whom she has been having a fishing flirtation,
has rather ruffled her heart.

Everything combined made her very naughty and rude to poor
Mamma. The roles were completely reversed. Bibs, fat with rage and
sullen dignity, sat fiercely knitting like Madame Defarge, vituperating
scathing sarcasm and reproach on her meek parent. Of course, one
couldn't help laughing, but she really was very naughty. The *comble*
was when she said, 'And you only have me inoculated because you
want to see the doctor!' (There had been a lot of ridiculous chaff
about Mamma having a flirtation with the doctor, which apparently
Bibs had taken seriously.) Mamma feebly, 'But, do you think I couldn't
see him without an excuse?' Bibs, witheringly, 'Not without making a
sensation.' I rocked with laughter. Bibs remained sombre for a long time.

A.J.B., Joan, Dinah, and Sir Iain played tennis after lunch. Party
reduced to Mr B., Mamma, Joan, Frances and I. Very pleasant gossipy
dinner. Discussed Margot a good deal—Joan rather amusing about
her in-laws, the Harewoods. She is so passionately devoted to Whit-
tinghame and the whole Balfour clan that she rather shudders at the
sort of 'One of us Lascelles' note. We sat in Mamma's sitting room
and Mr B. read the tenth and last of his Gifford lectures to us. Very
interesting, though my mind too sleepy to bite all the time. He looked
very dear and benevolent with lamplight on silvery head and the
'parallels in wisdom's brow'.

I forgot to write down 'Barley Water' Norton's tactful remark to
the two war brides when sitting between them at dinner. 'It is only the
destruction of cathedrals and poets (Rupert Brooke) which matters in
this war'! Countess Benck liked Beb's poems very much.

Wednesday, 5th May

Letter from Beb by early post. He seems to be having a thrilling time aeroplane shooting, etc. He gave amusing account of how his soldiers ordered eggs for him by a charade of the process of laying them. I gather he is at Dunkirk.

Early tea and then Mamma and I motored Bibs back to school at Malvern. Lovely drive, and she wasn't so very depressed as it was her last term. Letter from D. H. Lawrence wanting to know what had happened since our expedition to Chichester.

Thursday, 6th May

Short letter from Beb from 'dug-out'. Mamma drove me into Broadway to catch the twelve o'clock. It was the most lovely—really hot—morning. Wrote a line to Beb, read papers, and began Burton's *Anatomy of Melancholy* in the train. Came to stay at Frances' house which is empty—my favourite form of cuckooing.

Friday, 7th May

Astonishingly warm in spite of thunderstorm. Violet[1] called for me in motor at twelve. Told me they had had a telegram from Ian Hamilton saying Oc[1] seriously, not dangerously, wounded. It is in the leg—really nowadays almost the news one congratulates oneself on! There is the most thrilling account in *The Times* of the landing of the troops in Dardanelles. It sounds a miraculous achievement. I would rather have Beb in France than there. I should think the fighting was quite as dangerous and the conditions much worse, and it is so terribly remote.

Tried on white skirt at Prince's. Went to Bumpus and ordered tiny Shakespeares to send out to Beb. Ordered a cake at Buzzards and then went to Downing Street. P.M. looking as mellow, serene, and leisured as ever. I gave him Beb's last letter. Lord Grey[2] was at lunch. Talked a little to Margot after. I can't help being rather amused at the gentle, rather soothing way everyone addresses one now—a sort of unspoken condolence. Margot announced the Navy had been made by Fisher and the Army by Haldane.

Elizabeth[1] took me out in motor and we did various shattering shoppings together for two hours, finally killing ourselves at Selfridges. Margot told me to order things in her name at Fortnum and Mason, so I selected delicious comforts for Beb—cigarettes, chocolate, bottled fruit, chicken galantine, and so on. Elizabeth looking tired,

1. Violet, Arthur and Elizabeth Asquith: see index.   2. The fourth Earl.

but so paradoxically pretty that I had to dewdrop her. She was delighted—she says any looks praise goes straight to her head from unexpectedness.

Saturday, 8th May

Papers full of *Lusitania*. They think 1,500 have been drowned, amongst them Sir Hugh Lane. It shows vividly how one's standards have altered—in fact, how out of drawing everything is. Very nearly as big a disaster as the *Titanic*, which loomed so large in one's life for months, and this is merely an incident, so full has one 'supped of horrors'. It will, however, arouse great rage, and one wonders how America will take it.

Bought pair of white shoes at Raoul's, and picked Venetia[1] up at Mansfield Street. She goes out to nurse at Lady Norman's hospital on Monday. She was very, very nice. We had a collation and did various shoppings.

I went home early, just on twelve, expecting Katharine.[2] She never came so I rang up and, to my horror, servants said she had started for France as they had heard that Edward was seriously wounded. My crust of numbness melted and I felt sick. Racked my brains to think of where I could get more details—the servants were incoherent.

Lunched Bruton Street—war talk the whole time. Evan white heat of hate against Huns . . . on the vermin-must-be-exterminated tack. I got a letter from Beb—still no letters from me, which makes me sad, and apparently the rations have gone wrong and the mess is subsisting on the eggs of one duck. Poor darling—and I know his appetite so well! London, I think, looks distinctly more abnormal now—more soldiers, more bandages and limps, and more nurses— quite a sensational sense of strain. Raw recruits led by band still make one cry and everywhere the rather undignified, bullying posters —very, very dark at night.

We telephoned to Anne Islington and she made inquiries about poor Edward. It sounds very, very bad—wounded in the groin in an explosion, and Sir John, Frances, and Katharine have all gone out which would never be allowed unless his condition was critical, as Boulogne is now a war area and they are very strict.

Monday, 10th May

Went to Bruton Street and, to my delight, found Mary was back from

1. Venetia Stanley: see index.
2. Mrs Raymond Asquith: Edward Horner was her brother.

Egypt. She is brown and very thin, like a greyhound, but the leanness is of training rather than bad health. She is in excellent spirits and full of amusing Egyptian tittle-tattle. Went to Albert together, where she bought herself a hat.

Went down to Brighton by 4.30. Long journey in taxi from station to Kemp Town and found lodgings recommended by Charlie Meade —disappointingly poky and not convenient in many ways. Beastly place Brighton seems—all glare and asphalt and pebbles instead of sand. I think I must go to the other part of town. Kemp Town is inconveniently far from the shops and so on, without any of the compensations of remoteness.

Tuesday, 11th May

A lovely day, and by the evening I was devoted to Brighton. Another letter from Beb—he still hadn't heard from me.

The D. H. Lawrences arrived at one o'clock and we went out on a bus and had lunch at a filthy little shop. They decided to stay the night and we engaged another little room in my lodgings. Aileen Meade arrived while we were out—we had the most ridiculous discussion about the lodgings, which exhausted us and convulsed Lawrence. I rather wanted to change, but Aileen's sentiment for Charlie's old gardener (reinforced by finding a photograph of Charlie on the wall) made it impossible for her to contemplate sending her Antonia anywhere else, so I acquiesced and decided to leave the children, at least for the present.

Mrs Lawrence rested on the sofa, and Lawrence and I took Aileen to the station. We couldn't get a taxi, and thought we should never catch the train. It was a tiring day, spent mostly on asphalt in the sun, but I found the air a wonderful tonic and felt unusually well. We all had tea with the children. The Lawrences were riveted by the freakishness of John, about whom they showed extraordinary interest and sympathy. The ozone had intoxicated him and he was in a wild, monkey mood—very challenging, just doing things for the sake of being told not to—impishly defiant and still his peculiar, indescribable detachment. We all went out with the children till their bedtime and then we returned to our lodgings about five minutes away, had a short rest, and then a dinner of whiting and cold chicken— Lawrence and I had bought asparagus, and so on, on the way home from the station. We had delightful dinner talk.

I find them the most intoxicating company in the world. I never hoped to have such mental pleasure with anyone. It is so wonderful to be such a perfect *à trois*. I am so fond of her. She has spontaneousness and warm cleverness, and such adoration and understanding of him. He interests and attracts me. His talk is so extraordinarily real and living—such humour and yet so much of the fierceness and resentment which my acquiescent nature loves and covets. He is a Pentecost to one, and has the gift of intimacy and such perceptiveness that he introduces one to oneself. I have never known such an X-ray psychologist. It is really uncanny—he gives the most subtly true analyses of people, e.g. Papa and Mamma whom he has only seen for a few moments. There is something so extraordinarily real and significant about their lives that they make one feel rather as if one had spent most of one's life on the crust of things surrounded by blindfolded friends in masks. In his talk there is none of the crudeness and occasional ugliness (the result of over-emphasis) one finds in his book, but he has passionate resentment against the existing frame and values of life. He can see nothing but fatuity in the war. I tried to argue about this at dinner and we had most interesting talk—small thanks to me. We went to absurd cinema after dinner, then broke into the children's lodgings at about ten to get my Benger's, and then to bed. I really enjoyed the day acutely, and am most grateful to Eddie for the gift of such friends.

Wednesday, 12th May

We all breakfasted with the children. They went out and we sat on in the funny little sitting room, so packed with ornaments, and had a philosophical discussion—very interesting. He is a fierce believer in the absolute and the actual, 'twice two making four' independently of the human mind. I wish I could repeat, but alas I can't.

About eleven we three walked on to the top of the cliff where it was lovely and we lay there for about two hours and had one of the talks I shall always remember, though alas I could no more record it than a thrush's song! He was most interesting and earnest about John, round whom we talked most of the time. He thinks him very abnormal and that he will require most careful treatment. He thinks he is what he calls a 'static challenge', and that his throwing of food, and so forth, on the floor is symbolic of real Descartism, the negation of all accepted authority. He said dry, conventional authority, verbal bullying, must never be applied to him. He considers Nurse exactly right for John's nature, but I'm afraid he thinks I am quite wrong and that there will always be conflict between us. He considers me not positive enough, and that John would see lack of conviction—what he wants is a simple positive nature. He thinks—rather like Whibley* calling Mamma cynical—that my so-called tolerance is really based on profound scepticism and a sort of *laisser-faire* cynicism. I tried to argue but I think he has extraordinary insight, and, of course, it is the idealists who are hard, and if everyone were as acquiescent and 'philosophical' about people as my mother and I, I suppose the world wouldn't move much. He quite alarmed me about John and rather depressed me about myself.

We went into town and lunched at Fullers. Thrilling talk the whole time. They are tremendously interested in my autobiography and all my family, and they are most skilful cross-examiners. They went off after lunch, and I returned to a very happy evening with the children.

Thursday, 13th May

Ceaseless, ceaseless, relentless rain. Had early tea and went up to London by 5.5 and installed myself at Cadogan Square, where I found Mamma. It seems so strange and dreamlike to be back there again. The house depresses me and has rather a cramping effect on my personality. Just at present I love the feeling of regeneration one gets from new people and new houses.

Sargent, Mr Balfour and Mary H. came to dinner. Sargent extraordinarily inarticulate, grumbling and growling and clutching the air in efforts to produce quite ordinary words. He and A.J.B. not a very felicitous combination. I didn't enjoy the evening. Practically exclusively war conversation with a good deal about America's attitude. Mr B. thinks they will fight and that their joining will be of great importance.

Mary and I detached after dinner and had a little serious conversation. Evan came in late, looking quite pinched with 'Hun hate'. News of the sinking of the *Goliath* by Turkish torpedo was in the evening paper—an old ship, but about five hundred lives lost. We didn't go to bed until nearly one. I gave Mamma Beb's last letters to read. Another from him arrived after dinner with curdling accounts of bullets whistling past his cheeks.

Friday, 14th May

Appalled at the prospect of picking up threads of London life. When I am feeling tired I get awfully nervously fussed at the thought of all the 'neighbours' one ought to be seeing.

Yvo came up for leave, and we went out 3.30 with Violet in her motor—she is just going off to Alexandria to see Oc. Took my shoes back to Box, who refused to allow that they hurt me. Went to Sussex

Place to fetch the baby's chair—a most embarrassing bit of furniture which had to be lashed to the roof. Too queer seeing the Pepinage[1] occupied by Belgians. They have nailed the stag's head up in the hall, and on one of the chairs Beb's funny red brief bag with large white initials is playing the part of an antimacassar! Went to Fortnum & Mason and despatched delicious comforts to Beb—pheasant, chocolate, cod-cutlets.[2] Violet in very good tonic form.

Yvo and I went to the Alhambra—not very amusing, except for two delightful mock conjurors. Yvo looks very sunburnt and well. Found letter from Beb when I got home. I had been panicky about him all day—it is curious how at intervals it rises to the surface. Edward is going on as well as possible, thank Heaven!

Saturday, 15th May

Woke up at about six again and tossed and tossed with impatience. It is a maddening habit—one's head feels so tired and dusty by breakfast time. I wish to God I was strong! I am sick to death of my body and of being always rather half-mast. The combination of ill-health and poverty is really too much of a handicap. I could contend with either singly, but it is a very formidable collaboration.

I went by myself to Prince and told him he must do something to my white coat and skirt to make me look less like Queen Mary. He is having trouble with the police as the order for internment has just gone forth. He says he is a Russian, but hasn't got his papers to prove it. Bussed from Oxford Circus to Harrods Stores and walked back home to Cadogan. Lunched with Mamma and Yvo. Rested in back drawing room. Yvo read me a little Burton's *Anatomy of Melancholy*— most amusing read aloud. We went to the Tate—I was not in very good picture digestion. I went down to Clonboy by 5.40 and spent the evening with Mary and Aunt Georgie.

Sunday, 16th May

Captain —— came to tea. He bores me a good deal. I know no one with whom one talks more utterly at cross-purposes. He doesn't listen at all. I should like to break into foul language to see if that might attract his attention. We pottered about in the garden—a great deal of war talk. What were one's topics before it began?

1. Nickname of uncertain origin for Lady Cynthia's London house—her husband sometimes called her Pepinetta.
2. Before the days of deep-sea trawlers and refrigeration cod was a luxury fish.

21

Monday, 17th May

A drenching, depressing wet day. Mary came and read the papers on my bed—appalling casualties. She had a letter saying Julian[1] has had a skull wound. Helen Mitford's husband is killed and Lord Ednam seriously wounded. Mary and I went up by 10.30 to London.

Another letter from Beb, and a very curious one from Lawrence in answer to my request for a written analysis of John's character. He calls my spirit hard and stoical—a serious indictment to which I do not plead guilty. Went to see Tonks at Vale Studio B, Vale Avenue. He has been back about a month from the hospital in France and was very full of his experiences. It was a case of duty and not of inclination and he doesn't seem to have enjoyed it very much. He was too irritated by all the squabbles and various human foibles. He doesn't 'suffer fools gladly' enough. I was very glad to see him again. His dour simplicity always rather rests me. I had been feeling very depressed in the afternoon and came away distinctly improved in spirits. We walked home together.

Tuesday, 18th May

Papers beginning to be full of the Winston and Fisher crisis. Papa had arrived the night before—very mellow. I took my black taffeta dress back to Miss North and lunched with Harold Baker.* His little house in Queen Anne's Gate is delightful, fitting and suiting him like the shell of a snail. He is, of course, very busy and had to hurry off to questions in the House. He told me he thought the Admiralty situation was very serious and he didn't think they could possibly keep Winston if Fisher went—Fisher would have such a dossier against him. Of course, Winston had been blamed for a great many things, including the discarding of courts martial, the Antwerp enterprise, and the *Cressy*, *Hogue* and *Aboukir*[2] disasters, but I imagine the main point of dissension was over the bombardment by the Fleet of the Dardanelles. Apparently this project of his was very much opposed. Of course, it was one of those imaginative, daring attempts which might succeed, and if it did would give enormous kudos to the instigator. Now it seems to have been futile and expensive, and people made sore by the appalling casualties in the landing force blame him for the delay, which they think gave the Turks time to concentrate an enormously strong defensive army.

1. Julian Grenfell, poet-son of Lord Desborough.
2. Three old cruisers sunk successively, as they went to each other's aid, by a single U-boat on 22nd September 1914; 1,459 lives lost.

I think it will be very sad if he goes. He has genius and imagination, and at the beginning of the war was enhaloed by the brilliant naval mobilisation. More than most people I suppose he has the defects of his qualities, and would always be a source of danger, pining for despotism, seeing himself as a Napoleon and inclined to be unconstitutional. A brilliant, audacious layman is bound to exasperate the experts under him, and unpopularity with the Navy is not necessarily against him, but the national confidence seems to have been gradually undermined. One wonders what they will do with him.

Bluetooth had a letter from Frances Horner with a rather bad account of Edward. He is still having internal haemorrhage. Julian is very bad, too, and cannot be considered out of danger for ten days. I enjoyed my lunch. It was the most terribly depressing wet day. I dined at 10 Downing Street. Met the P.M. going out on the threshold. He looked as unruffled as ever. Party was Violet, Mr Davies,[1] Bongie, Cis, Hugh and Nathalie Benckendorff. Very glad to see Nathalie again— she has been nursing in France for two months—we were both hungry for Cabinet gossip, but were too delicate to ask any questions, so we came away without gleaning anything, much to the annoyance and disappointment of our respective parents. Natalie dropped me home.

Wednesday, 19th May

Papa just starting to Boulogne. His description on his passport pleased me—hair brown to grey (quantity unmentioned), eyes brown, complexion fresh, face oval, nose straight.

Mr Balfour, Evan, Whibley, Tonks, Colonel Sykes, Norton, Mary and Nathalie came to dinner, and we telephoned to Countess Benck and she brought on a small drum—Lady Johnson, Benck, and Louis Mallet. I think it was a great success. I sat between Whibley and Tonks. Whibley very characteristic about Asquith and Bonar Law's speeches which he had heard at the Mansion House in the afternoon. Nathalie was on the other side of Tonks and they had a hospital talk. Colonel Sykes is second-in-command of the Flying Corps. He has a very nice bird-like expression.

Of course everyone was quivering with excitement about the dissolution of the Ministry and we tried to pump Mr Balfour as much as possible. He didn't seem to know very much about the germ and development of the crisis, but apparently a coalition government has been definitely decided on. The general impression is that he will go to the Admiralty, but he says he doesn't really know yet, only he has

1. See index for all names on this page.

given his consent to accept any post he is offered. He says personally he would prefer not to have one of the heavy administrations. He says Winston looks quite serene, and has intimated that he would like him to succeed at the Admiralty. Fisher used to be fond of Mr Balfour, but apparently is now annoyed with practically everyone, as he thinks Mr B. and the rest ought to have more strongly opposed naval bombardment of the Dardanelles, though according to Mr B., Fisher himself at the time made little if any protest. Of course he ought to have resigned then if he was so convinced, instead of waiting for results. Mr B. said he only received first intimation of proposed coalition on Monday morning. I suppose Fisher, in that call the papers made so much of, forced Mr Asquith's hand—he must loathe having to jettison any of his colleagues. It is most interesting to see what will happen.

Whibley was interesting about George Moore[1] at dinner. He says he has got Northcliffe absolutely under his spell, and that it will do incalculable harm to boom French as it upsets Kitchener and generally fans the flames already existing between them. He says Will Irwin, who wrote the brilliant account of Ypres, is a tool and a knave (Whibleyesque!) and that the whole account was faked in order to magnify French. Apparently the main divergence in the strategy of Kitchener and French is that the former is in favour of the campaign being as much a war of 'attrition' as possible, which would mean just holding on to trenches and not taking the initiative, whereas French is always eager to force things and attempt advances at the expense of the appalling casualties which are now occurring. I should imagine each point of view was natural to their situation rather than to their intrinsic psychology. Out there, monotonous endurance and negative results must be very hard to bear and the importance of keeping up the spirits of the troops must loom larger than at the War Office.

I wonder if George Moore can really be so important an influence as he is made out. Whibley really flatters him. One thing is certain and this is his genuine love and admiration for General French, but to attempt advertisement and glorification is the most dangerous service that can be paid—it is nearly always damaging to the object.

Thursday, 20th May

Adele Essex, Evie, and Venetia came to lunch. Adele had dined at

1. Not George Moore the novelist, though he was also a visitor at Stanway, but George Gordon Moore. See index.

Downing Street and was most amusing—she has a rare gift of repeating conversations. Venetia was disappointing as a source of information to be tapped: she had been away and hadn't seen the P.M. Adele said that at last the poor darling really looks tired and worried, and his bridge—always bad—was an eloquent barometer. Evie as a widow reminds one of private theatricals.

News of Edward and Julian fairly satisfactory. Edward has had a kidney removed and is going on all right, and Julian has been trephined. There were slight symptoms of paralysis, but I believe temporarily that is almost inevitable. He cannot be considered out of danger for ten days. Poor Ettie—what anguish!

Mamma went to see Mr Balfour. He is to have the Admiralty, and I'm glad to hear Fisher is to go.

Friday, 21st May

Mamma and I lunched at Downing Street, where a tremendous atmosphere of tension and distress prevails. Mr Asquith generally presents the most extraordinarily mellow serenity to the world, and is an imperturbable buffer between himself and all crises private and public. I have never before seen him look either tired, worried, busy, or preoccupied, and I have seen him weathering a good many storms now, but this time he looked really rather shattered with a sort of bruised look in his eyes, and I felt very sorry for him. It must be a fearful situation for him—the necessity of carting colleagues and the difficulty of yoking a heterogeneous team.

Margot was wildly strung up, very sad about poor old Haldane who is to be ousted and wild with Harmsworth for his attack on Kitchener in the *Daily Mail* headed 'Kitchener's Tragic Blunder'. She commissioned Mamma to enlist Mr Balfour's services in an attempt to muzzle Northcliffe. She didn't give any very coherent account of the past and, for the present, everything still seems to be in the melting-pot as far as ministers and posts go. Apparently McKenna, whom every man in the street would like to expel before anyone, with the possible exception of Haldane, is the one fixture about whom there has been no doubt. Haldane seems the only certain resignation and, of course, the small fry—and the other obvious additions are Balfour, Bonar Law, Austen Chamberlain. Apparently Curzon is regarded as an inevitable embarrassment, though terribly difficult to know where to place him, and I believe he and Kitchener are not on hand-shaking terms. What one would give to be able to eavesdrop on the first Coalition Cabinet!

It is dreadful to think how this internal crisis will rejoice the hearts of the Germans—I'm afraid they will be the only ones who will derive any pleasure and satisfaction from the Coalition. It has obvious disadvantages to the eyes of the nation and, of course, neither side can be expected to welcome it. Of course, politically, if anything survives the 'wash-out' of this war, it is a considerable sacrifice to the Opposition. They might well have been borne on the crest of the wave of resentment which surely must inevitably be incurred by any government forced to carry on a war of this kind. Now all will be tarred with the same brush of obloquy. To the Liberals, I suppose it must seem rather a confession of failure, though no vessel could really hope to weather so unprecedented a tornado, and to several it means eviction from the Cabinet to make room for others, which must bring considerable bitterness.

I sat next to Colonel Hankey,* whom I thought quite delightful, with a charming, quiet, deliberate manner. On my other side was James Dunn. We relived the 'trip'[1] and he told me about all the thousands of Canadian horses he has sold to the French Government. Bongie was there, looking like chewed string. I am astonished at Violet having been able to tear herself away from the helm at such a moment, but she has actually gone off to Alexandria to see Oc, who is in hospital there. The *Daily Mail* was formally burnt at the Stock Exchange in the afternoon—funny enough for them to have to report it the next morning!

Saturday, 22nd May

I am going to launch a ship next Saturday,[2] and on Friday I had cleverly extracted the promise of a dress from Margot by flatteringly asking her advice as to what I should wear for the occasion. She said she would take me out to choose a gown, so I called at Downing Street for her at 10.30.

She was very rouged, shrill, and overwrought, and her analysis of the dresses was brilliant and quaintly interlarded with political interjections. She is miserable at poor old Haldane having to go, whom she maintains is the best Lord Chancellor we have ever had. She was very exhilarated by the fact that she thinks she is responsible for the inclusion of Lansdowne in the Cabinet by having called on Lady Lansdowne yesterday in her frankest manner. She said she hadn't told

1. In 1909 Lady Cynthia and her mother had visited Canada and the States, where Ego had been Honorary Attaché to Bryce.
2. At the request of Winston Churchill.

Henry. She was very pleased with herself as regards Lansdowne's prestige in foreign affairs, as a valuable asset against George Curzon's encroachment. She is amazingly, naïvely personal, and continually harped back to the latter's not having asked her and Elizabeth to his ball. Lansdowne is to have a seat in the Cabinet without any administrative post, owing to health. She said the quarrels at the front between the Kitchenerites and the Frenchites amongst the generals were too appalling. No doubt she exaggerates a good deal, but I'm sure all the short leaves with ensuing gossip, etc., must be damaging to relations between the War Office and General Staff. It is awful to think of petty, private jealousies and quarrels aggravating by an ounce the appalling results of this cataclysm of history. I must say Margot was at the top of her form. She implied that she thought Beb would be killed! She thinks Violet is engaged to Bongie. She was too amusing about the dresses—I must say some of them were fair game. Finally, I chose a model to be copied in white cloth at Reville and Rossiter.

Mr Balfour came to lunch—there was only Connor,[1] Mamma and myself present. I don't think I ever enjoyed hearing him talk more, he was so wonderfully luminous and fair-minded. I wish I could write it down, but alas I cannot remember much and stray things out of their context sound so banal. I was interested to hear him discuss Haldane and his merits as War Minister. He said he had come to the War Office at a most difficult moment under Campbell-Bannerman and with a strong wave of radicalism, and that he really didn't think it would have been politically possible for Haldane to keep the army any bigger. Had he refused to concede the small reduction—for which he is now blamed—he would have been obliged to resign and, in all probability, his successor would have made far more drastic modifications. Therefore, he didn't really think Haldane could be held individually responsible for the reduction, and he considered that he had done excellent work with the Territorials whom Kitchener had certainly erred in rating so low. Anyhow, he agrees that Haldane is being very hardly used now, as he is going—not because of any errors he may or may not have committed—but as a concession to the incredible but apparently widespread stupidity which really believes him to be a pro-German.

He seemed to think Kitchener was probably to blame for the wrong proportion of shrapnel to high explosive shells, but greatly deplored Northcliffe's abuse of Kitchener. Retrospection is no use now; the thing is to concentrate all skill and energy on the present, and it is most mischievous to try and destroy that great prestige of Kitchener

1. Agent to Lord Wemyss: see index.

which is probably by far his most valuable asset. Mr B. gave a wonderfully lucid exposition on artillery and the respective functions of shrapnel and high explosive, which I was very glad to hear.

He said it was curious how very much more popular Lloyd George—whom one would expect to be such a rock of offence—was with both sides of the House than McKenna. Lloyd George appears to have a kind of licensed irresponsibility and people forgive what they, at the time, considered the most heinous crimes. Of course, he had personal charm, whereas poor McKenna is calculated to jar nearly every nerve in everybody. Lloyd George appears to have gained the appreciative confidence of the City by asking, and taking, the best expert advice in the financial crises of the war.

Mr Balfour was very interesting on what he considers the great gulf between Bismarck and the present leaders of Germany, not only in strategy but in ambition. Bismarck, he is certain, would never have staked his country on the chances of this war—even though they may have been five to four at the outset—and in his opinion Bismarck would never have hankered after 'world empire'. All he wanted was the unity of the German Empire and commercial prosperity which they were peacefully enjoying before this desperate sort of 'double or quits' gamble. He said the private Russian news received that day was better. It has been very bad lately.[1]

We had all been going to Hunstanton for the annual Whitsuntide party, of which Mr Balfour, and Evan, Mamma and Ettie, form the nucleus, but all plans collapsed in the whirligig of this last week. Finally, Mamma and I went down to Brighton by ourselves to see the children. We came to the Hotel Bristol, which is nice and quiet. We arrived about seven and went round to see the children in the Arundel Road.

Sunday, 23rd May

Sweltering hot day. Brighton is rather like the Inferno . . . it is all asphalt and glare. Mamma wrote letters and I joined the children on the beach in the morning—uncomfortable alternative of pebbles or wet sand to sit on and not a shred of shade anywhere. At 3.30 Mamma, I and John drove to Rottingdean in a fly to see Lady Burne-Jones. She was in bed and Margaret Mackail* gave John and me tea downstairs. He was blissfully happy with a garden rich in taps. I took him upstairs to see Lady B.-J. for a few minutes. She was looking rather fragile in a lovely little lace bed. Mamma and I went for a walk with Pina[2]

1. During May the Third and Eighth Russian armies were in precipitate retreat.   2. Lady Wemyss' chow.

after dinner—such a lovely night. She has been sorting and reading a great many old letters—her 'testimonials' I call them. They are so full of wonderful dewdrops and really acted as a tonic to her.

Monday, 24th May

I must say this is a most wonderful place for sleep. It is quite two years since I have ever felt at all sleepy in the morning. I have always woken up in full possession of my faculties, but these mornings I again know the almost forgotten joy of lingering on the threshold of sleep for ages after I have been called, and how I sympathise with Beb's lateness for breakfast because he is daily in that blissful state! I think it suited Mamma, too, and it was quite a nice peaceful Whitsuntide. She paid for everything at the hotel—I'm afraid I am a very expensive married daughter.

Tuesday, 25th May

We both went out after breakfast and saw the Asquith brothers in their green paddlers. She went off at twelve to stay with Wilfred Blunt at New Buildings. Hot as hell again. I rested in bed and was thrilled by *Monte Cristo*. At three got into a fly, fetched children and underwent—very successfully, I hope—the ordeal of family photography. Had tea with the children. We all staggered to the pier and I took John home in his beloved electric car.[1] Walked home, read *The Times*, and had solitary dinner.

News none too good, gas having again forced us to retire. I find it more and more difficult to read war news—one feels chronically sick. When will there be light through this awful tunnel? Curious to see what will have transpired in London. It is rather pathetic, the Admiralty, I think—exit ardent youth and enter the venerable—a sort of philosophical Cincinnatus Mr Balfour is.

Wednesday, 26th May

Got home to Cadogan Square at about tea time—found Mamma and Papa who was just back from Boulogne—he brought the horrid news that Julian is dying.

We had tried to get Bishop Furse* to dinner, but Whibley couldn't get on to his tracks, and Mr Balfour had had to go up to Edinburgh to

1. Not a motor car, but Volk's Railway: see index.

see Jellicoe, so we were only five for dinner—us three and Whibley and Lord Hugh Cecil.*

The latter looked pink and plump from flying, and was in excellent form. I really think I put him almost first as a talker and, when he is not on theology, he really isn't at all kinky or fanatic—in fact, last night I thought him extraordinarily mentally well-mannered, gentle and fair, unwrapping the subject with such art and everything in such perfect English. I like his earnestness, combined with that astonishing flavour of humour and personality about everything he says. He and Whibley disagreed on practically every point raised and Whibley was in his most violent, interrupting vein—almost a bore sometimes, as one would really have preferred the luxury of listening to Lord Hugh.

We discussed conscription—I was delighted to hear Lord Hugh still speaking against it, and maintaining the practical superiority of voluntary troops. I was afraid one's case rested mainly on aesthetic grounds. Whibley considered it pure sentiment, maintaining (as illustration), that the French fought just as well. They went all over the diplomatic aspect of the outbreak of war and whether it could have been prevented, etc., Whibley attacking Edward Grey for shilly-shallying, saying he didn't even know himself which way his own speech was going to sum up. Lord Hugh, on the other hand, maintained that the speech was an absolute masterpiece—real Mark Antony oratory—and the only way in which he could possibly have roped in various members of the Government was by first giving the case against the war and then meeting each point one by one. If anything was to blame, it was democratic government—the machinery and not the individual minister, who could not bluff until assured of the support of his colleagues. I agreed with Lord Hugh against Whibley on nearly every point. He considers the war the inevitable, logical conclusion of the *Entente Cordiale*. He told us what had been the attitude of various individuals as to going to war or not, which was interesting. After dinner he told us his flying experiences. Whibley stayed till long after twelve. He had read 'The Prussian Officer' because I had told him about Lawrence and said he had 'great talent', but he thinks he is suffering from 'over-emphasis', which is obvious.

Thursday, 27th May

Still fine, but windy and much colder. Grace[1] appeared in her welcome motor and took me to St Louis, where I ordered a white 'Mercury'

1. Dowager Countess of Wemyss.

hat to launch my ship in. Then I went to Mrs Cullen and had hair cleaned—process maddened me to desperation. Grace brought the news that Julian had died the night before. It is most tragic and one is haunted by the thought of Ettie seeing her glorious son die by inches. How can such things be endured by women? We have all been caught up into a Greek tragedy and are but gradually beginning to realise it.

I lunched at the Admiralty with the 'setting sun' minister. Saw Clemmie alone first for a little. She looks very sad, poor thing. Winston came in rather late from the first Coalition Cabinet. He looks unhappy, but is very dignified and un-bitter. I have never liked him so much. Clemmie said she had always known it would happen from the day Fisher was appointed, and Winston said that, if he could do things over again, he would do just the same with regard to appointing Fisher as he says he has done really great organising work. I think his nature —though he may be unscrupulous and inclined to trample on susceptibilities of sailors, or whomever he may have to deal with, from eagerness—is absolutely devoid of vindictiveness, unlike the half-caste Fisher who really runs amok from malevolent spleen and is now saying he will tell the Germans where all our ships are.

Winston's chief consolation was in the reflection, expressed in a glowing period, of his extreme youth. Talking of the Cabinet of the morning: 'There was I after ten years in the Cabinet, and five years in the most important office, still by ten years the youngest member!' He said this with an attractively naïve delight. He said he was experiencing the 'austerity of changing fortune' and congratulated himself on being able to extract some epicurean enjoyment from it. He seems pleased that it is Mr Balfour who is to succeed him, and thinks he will be much liked by the sailors. 'He is a great luxury', he said— rather a nice description I thought.

He was told the news of Francis Grenfell's death which moved him very much, and prompted oaths and an eloquent melodramatic outburst. It is a hard case—he has been wounded four times and now they have done for him. He got the V.C. at the very beginning of the war. Winston beamed at his little harem and said we were a much nicer tableful than the Cabinet. I had delicious looks dewdrops from them all, though I felt rather absurd in new-fashioned, full, short, black taffeta dress. Two ships were sunk in the Dardanelles this day—very sad ending for Winston. Clemmie said it would break his heart if that enterprise were abandoned now, and that one of the reasons he welcomed Mr Balfour was that he thought he would carry it out. He complained with melancholy of the leisure he would soon have— Eddie Marsh is to follow him, though he said 'there would be very little meat on his bone'. When he said goodbye he hinted that he meant to go out to the Dardanelles soon.

When I got home I found the new First Lord dining with Mamma and Evan arrived from Grace's. Mr Balfour told us of his interview with Jellicoe—he looks very interested and vitalised by his thrilling job. He told us of the torpedoing of another ship in the Dardanelles and admitted the situation there to be very, very disquieting. He feared it might become untenable owing to submarines. He greatly deplored our not having taken up Zeppelins and said he thought we made a great mistake there. He spoke very nicely of Winston—enumerated all his marvellous gifts—but said he thought he was 'predestined' to failure and vast ambition. He said he really thought Fisher was mad —apparently he threatened to 'break' everyone at the Admiralty. Praised his powers of organisation. It was very interesting seeing the two First Lords—Dash and Sagacity. Evan, of course, miserable about Julian.

Friday, 28th May

Papa, Polly and I went to King's Cross for the 2.20 to Newcastle, where he was accompanying me to launch my ship. Such a long journey.

Saturday, 29th May

Woke up feeling illish and to my despair found it was pouring with black, cold rain. It all looked depressing and dingy. It is about ten miles to Hebburn-on-Tyne, the scene of the launch. We arrived in very good time and there was a lot of hanging about, being introduced to lots of people and looking at a lovely model of my godchild ship. I got the Rowells[1] to coach me as much as possible. I was so terrified of not breaking the bottle, of doing anything wrong. I thought both the Rowells were delightful—such a nice, nervous, keen little man. After about half an hour we proceeded to the quay where the ship was. I had already been armed with a huge bouquet. The rain, which had tantalisingly stopped, began again mercilessly. The situation was really saved by Grace's white mackintosh, but one's feet got very wet and cold. A dripping photograph was taken and then there was rather a long delay. A delightful sailor, Captain Power, who is directing all the ships in this district, stood with me holding bouquet and umbrella, etc. I had a confused feeling I was being married. The service lasted less than ten minutes—just prayers and hymns.

1. The shipowner and his wife.

At the magic moment I pulled the lever and the ship shivered into life and began to glide away—then I had to hurl the beribboned champagne bottle which mercifully broke very satisfactorily, and shout, 'Success to the *Champion* and all who sail in her'—and away she slithered like a lovely, lithe animal, very fast and with wonderful grace. One's words are drowned in a cheer and it is the most intensely moving moment. When she reaches the sea she curtseys deep and settles down into her element. It is a beautiful sight and one feels such a strong sense of personality about the ship—how dreadfully I shall mind if she comes to grief!

The next function was tea and speeches. I sat between Rowell and Power and opposite a really lovely golden bowl which, with its fellow, has been given to me. Rowell made a speech proposing the health of the ship and its launcher. Captain Power responded for the ship and Papa for me. He did it extraordinarily well—beginning by saying that he could answer for the fact that the want of the power of expression was not one of my reasons for not speaking for myself. His speaking was much admired.

Rowell told me he had great difficulty with his workmen—many of the best enlisted and he suffered a good deal from slackers. Apparently the *Lusitania* proved the most effective whip. He repudiated the idea of their being overworked—a point on which apparently Margot had attacked him. Discussed Winston with Captain Power. Motored back and caught 5.20. Very much embarrassed by bouquet at the station. I enjoyed it all and liked the new people immensely. Train very late—we didn't get home till 12.30. Papa was extraordinarily nice all the time—one cannot believe he is the same person as one remembers on occasions. I have lost all *gêne* with him now. We get on very well together socially.

Monday, 31st May

Three letters from Beb all at once. He sounds really extraordinarily happy and says it is a great holiday after the Bar. It makes the whole difference to know he is enjoying it, so that one has no vicarious suffering added to anxiety. I also had a letter from Mamma giving me an awful telephoning grind. Mr Balfour and Adele were coming to dinner and she wanted a man—I tried Oliver Stanley, Cust, Curzon, etc., but they were all engaged. Evan was uncertain. He rang up to ask who was coming and when I said Adele, he said he wouldn't come. The nuances of his mourning for Julian are very delicate—he won't meet her at dinner, but apparently lunches with her himself every day?

I suppose he doesn't like being seen with her in public, as a tribute to poor Ettie.

Grace called for me at eleven and took me to Friary House, where we did a two hours 'shift' at making portions of respirators.* There is a little machine with which you chop writhing, fish-like long strips of talc into the requisite lengths. You cut through five at a time and keep them in bundles of fifty. We worked at one machine, taking it in turns to work the machine or to feed the other with talc. We did about two and a half thousand together. Any manual labour has great fascination to me and I simply loved it. It is such fun feeling a factory girl and it gave one some idea of how exciting it must be to do piece-work for money. One felt so competitive even unrewarded. I must say I was very glad I hadn't got to do a twelve-hour day—it is quite tiring. The work isn't by any means quite automatic, as one can waste a lot of precious material by 'missing one's drive' or not getting the five thicknesses quite even, and with gross carelessness, one could cut off one's finger. There were quite a lot of other people working there at this and various other jobs. How one would have laughed incredulously at a vision of what we should all be doing in a year's time if it had been presented to one in 1914—the wild tango year!

Dinner ended by being only Mr Balfour, Adele, Papa, Mamma and self. Mr Balfour, I thought, looked rather depressed. He had just realised that the insatiable Winston had grasped the Defence of London as a sort of annex to the Admiralty. He said it was quite indefensible, so he wouldn't worry about it. We had a good many harrowing details about Julian.

Lord Curzon came in at about 11.30 when we were very tired, looking brisk and happy. Cabinet air certainly seems to suit him. He says he cannot discover what the duties of the 'Privy Seal' are. Mr Asquith has secretly gone to France.

Tuesday, 1st June

Zeppelin attack on London occurred in the night. Mamma came up and told me. I was horrified at the idea of having slept through it. Mockett rumoured forty people had been killed by Zeppelins, and the cook swore she had heard the whining of wings between twelve and one, but I think it must have been retrospective imagination.

Went to Downing Street for lunch—Margot, Elizabeth, Miss Way, Colonel Bridges,* Jack Tennant, Mr Spender and Mr Nash. Bridges is supposed to have done brilliantly and is back with a wounded arm. He is a huge, fine-looking man with a slight touch of vulgarity in appearance. He told Elizabeth the bitterness in the army about the munitions is such that if the war stopped tomorrow there would be a revolution, and every member of the Government would be hanged. Margot is still hysterically inveighing against the Press. Bridges said it had done untold harm at the front by giving away positions, often making it necessary to abandon an observation post. He advocated appointment of Repington* as Press Censor, but Margot said he wasn't 'straight' enough; 'The greatest hound I know'. The London *Mail* has surpassed itself by saying Margot daily plays tennis with German officers at Donnington Hall! She was wild about it, and they all discussed whether it would be advisable to take any steps. Margot very strung up altogether.

Went out with Elizabeth, first to Debenhams, then she dropped me at my dentist. She was very darling and subdued. Dentist scraped me, but actually said there were no casualties. Hurrah! Basil[1] rang up to say he had arrived. I suggesting his lunching at Adele's the next day. It turns out that the Zeppelin bombs only killed four people and destroyed some shops. I think it was mostly at Whitechapel. Names are kept out of the Press.

Wednesday, 2nd June

Went to see Evie Rivers-Bulkeley at the Canadian Red Cross, and enlisted as visitors to wounded officers. I think it is the most embarrassing job one could possibly undertake. How will the unfortunate creatures be able to convey the fact that they don't like one, supposing that to be the case. The idea is that they are lonely having no relations in London. Evie was bustling about looking very officious.

The family motor has arrived in London. It is an open Ford with an unliveried man who has never been in London before—unfortunate, I am not at all a good geographical instructor, but the man is intelligent and studies the map hard in between, and it is a great joy to have anything. I went to lunch with Adele in it. Basil was there; his hand begins to get a little better at last. I do hope it won't recover before the war is over. Lord Freddie called for him and they went off to Francis Grenfell's funeral.

I walked round to Bruton Street and found Evan with Evelyn[2]. He was very excited about his airman friend Sykes. He had only just discovered that he had returned because Henderson had no further use for his services at the headquarters. He couldn't understand why—this is Sykes's story. They had always been on excellent terms and,

1. Lord Basil Blackwood.   2. Lady de Vesci: see index.

suddenly, Henderson said he was dissatisfied with the way things were going and offered Sykes the command of a wing somewhere out of the way. This he said he couldn't possibly accept, so he came back to see Winston and offer himself to the Admiralty for work at the Dardanelles. Winston agreed, and then came the Cabinet crisis. Evan, who is devoted to Sykes, implied that he thought it was jealousy on the part of Henderson. Duff came to see me at 4.30. We had a very nice talk. Under the Coterie* crust I think he is really a great dear.

Thursday, 3rd June

The little motor is the greatest godsend and is saving me many minutes and many shillings. Lunched alone with Bluetooth. It is wonderful how entirely without *gêne* we are now; quite slipped back to the old gear, yet without any reference to the past. I must say I do think him good to talk to. I think I have always missed that relationship subconsciously.

We had a long amusing talk about George Moore. Papa and Bluetooth plunged into the thick of all the ridiculous gossip: it is too impossibly like a *Daily Mail* feuilleton story that he should be a spy. I can't believe it. I asked Bluetooth about Sykes: he said he had got a very bad reputation for pushing self-interest and thought Henderson was quite right to send him back. I have seldom heard two such different sides to a question.

Basil came to see me at four and stayed some time. Very delightful —we discussed my intended visit to him in Ireland. He is less keen to get back to the front now nearly all his regiment have been killed. Katharine came at six, looking lovely. We talked about Haldane a good deal. Apparently the Opposition, principally Bonar Law, made his withdrawal an absolute *sine qua non*.

Friday, 4th June

Basil came to fetch me . . . we walked to the Admiralty for lunch. Eddie and Goonie Churchill* were there, and Winston came in very late from the second Coalition Cabinet. He was gloomy. Lord Freddie came to fetch Basil again. They are the most devoted brothers.

I went straight home, collected books, etc., and at a quarter to four

1. Lady Cynthia was eminently right. In June 1915 George Moore went from France to the U.S.A. on a routine business trip, but rumour got to work and he was forced to take action against an English provincial newspaper, easily winning his case. See index.

Bluetooth called for me in his motor to take me down to Brighton. He was going to stay with his sister Queenie. It was a lovely afternoon and we had a delightful drive. He has an astonishing gift for being personal, and I cannot believe we have had so long a gap in our relationship. Found children brilliantly well. Returned to my old room in the Eastern Road.

Walked to the Hotel Bristol and dined with Bluey. My spirits, God knows why, just now are very much better than they ought to be, and I felt in good form and we had rather fun. Got rather buffy on chartreuse. We discussed the Coterie, a subject on which we found ourselves very much at one. Sat in cold smoking room for some time and then he walked me home. I am glad we have made friends again, but hope that no réchauffé 'situation' will arise—which, I suppose, means that I feel it may. I wonder when and why his bitterness evaporated.

Saturday, 5th June

Started at about three to motor to Greatham with Bluetooth to call on the Lawrences. It was the first time I had ever deliberately edited them and I felt rather nervous. Lovely drive through heavenly Belloc country. Bluetooth told me he was completely baffled in diagnosis, and hadn't the faintest idea of what I was really like. It is very odd, but his company always enhances rather uncannily my rather Undinish sense of a lack of continuity in my personal identity. It is impossible to express what I mean, but it decidedly makes me feel fantastic and unreal, though not in the least devitalised—very much the reverse as far as actual spirits go.

We found our way to Greatham all right. Lawrence was strolling in the garden with Meynell, looking—I'm afraid—very ill, but very picturesque and arresting in corduroy coat, with tawny beard and those curiously significant eyes. Felt a little shy at first. Bluetooth looked rather baleful and whispered and was rather deaf, but I think it went off very well. We had tea and quite happy talk.

Lawrence's voice, with its layers of harshness and softness, is very interesting—every inch of his body talks with his tongue, and vividly, too. I love his blend of earnestness and delicious whimsicality—humour and anger—great power of resentment. Generally these two, humour and resentment, are incompatible—with him they are formidable allies. Bluetooth did like him, to my satisfaction, and he didn't much mind the exuberant Hun. We discussed the 'Ottoline' of course, and Bertrand Russell. Lawrence has taken to a typewriter—there was a war story coming to life on it.

Afterwards we were admitted into the Holy of Holies of the Meynells. He, she, Sebastian and Viola were all assembled in a room full of trophies of the élite of literature—a real little museum, calculated —if anything could—to reduce to an absurdity, Keats, Shelley, etc. A blighting, stifling cult. And, as for the family, I have never believed in the existence of such stilted preciosity. Quite incredibly like caricatures in a book—most interesting as specimens, but making one feel acutely, physically uncomfortable. Meynell himself, with a silky, reverent unctuousness, displayed literary treasure after treasure, and we had the utmost difficulty in escaping. I thought Viola looked far the most human, but probably I am partial because she said I was the prettiest person she had ever seen.

Delicious drive home. Bluey told me amusing gossip, that Jack Pease had been expelled by McKenna* from his house in the country where he was staying because he was seen holding Pamela's hand. Apparently McKenna is a monster of jealousy as well as of most other things. Bluetooth gave me quite a lot of War Office atmosphere. He is devoted to Kitchener. Very poor opinion of French, I fear. He seems to think he should be withdrawn.

Tuesday, 8th June

Motored to Downing Street from Cadogan Square for lunch. Present —P.M., very late from Cabinet, Margot, Elizabeth, and Colonel Bridges's wife. P.M. looking quite restored and serene again. He seemed to have enjoyed his expedition to France, and Beb had spent two days with him. He said he had never seen him look so well and that he was in very good form. Everyone very full of the glorious exploit of Lieutenant Warneford who, in single-handed conflict, brought down a Zeppelin. His own machine turned a somersault from the force of the explosion, but he righted himself and returned unscathed. He has been given V.C. Mr Asquith said far the most wonderful personal achievement of the war was that of the submarine lieutenant who went to the Dardanelles—apparently he has sunk eight ships.

Wednesday, 9th June

Went out at ten and worked at respirators for an hour and a half. Basil and Lord Edward Grosvenor* called for me at 1.15 and we motored in the latter's motor to Robin Hood farm, where he and Dorothy are living. Rather a delicious place. We found Dorothy looking very pretty in lovely clothes. She is going to have a baby in about three months.

Winston and Clemmie came to lunch. He still looks very glumsy and distraught, poor dear. Ned Grosvenor went back to the Admiralty at about three and the Winstons departed leaving Dorothy, Basil and me to very protracted *à trois*.

It rained on and off. Discussed suitable wife for Basil for hours. Kitty Somerset, in amusing and lovely clothes, called for him in motor at six and took him off to Reigate. I stayed the night, dining *à trois* with, I think, an extremely happy couple. He has great charm and seems much in love with 'Dorrie' as he calls her. He said the Naval Flying Corps were devoted to Winston and that they wished him back. He endorsed everything Bluetooth said about Sykes—he loathes him.

Thursday, 10th June

Bluetooth came to tea with me—rather a nice story about Lord Hugh. Bluetooth asked a mechanic how he was getting on and the man said: 'That Lord Hugh—ee's a regular 'ell-'ound!' What a compliment!

Dinner party here. Bishop Furse (rather a lion since his famous letter to *The Times*), A.J.B., Curzon, Whibley, Basil, Grace, Adele, Mamma, and self. I sat between Basil and Whibley. Basil gave me a message from Kitty to say they had disagreed on every topic except me. The implication was that they were very dew-droppy, but when pressed for a qualification, he said they accused me of having no 'sentiment'. This I hotly contested, trying to explain reserve. Rather interesting talk on 'style' with Whibley. He said Congreve and Shakespeare were far the greatest masters of prose and that amongst the moderns Synge was the only one with a real sense of 'cadence'.

When we got upstairs Mamma read aloud a newly arrived letter from Mary, describing how happily they were working in a hospital: 'I generally say "Good morning" to the officers before I settle down to the men'! Now poor Letty has got scarlet fever—cruel luck. Men came up fairly soon. I talked to Curzon. He was rather amusing about the war-born necessity of some sort of polygamy, and we agreed that widows must have babies, even if their husbands have been dead for more than nine months. Mamma's dinner technique of moving to table for a meal in the other room came into action at about a quarter to eleven with excellent results.

Bishop Furse is like the Ancient Mariner since his visit to the front, bursting to pour out his convictions to everyone. He is a huge, rather fine figure of a man, with crucifix and lovely shoes. I felt prejudiced against him, but was distinctly mollified, partly because he thought

me a 'lovely creature', but he is rather touching and has a sort of
bludgeon force about him—really rather a fine face. He would look
very well standing up in his stirrups with a mace like Bishop Odo.

I shall never forget the scene that ensued. Oh, for a dictaphone and
a cinematograph! They went hammer and tongs at conscription.
Bishop and Whibley for, and Lord Hugh against. I loved everything
Lord Hugh said, and thought his patience and manners wonderful.
The other two were so crude, and rough, and wonderfully rude to him.
They abused him like anything—luckily there was never any real bad
feeling, but tremendous noise and mutual interrupting. Lord H. clung
to the voluntary system on sentimental and practical grounds—the
others maintained it was a tin god and a fetish, and that it was the
greatest mistake to assume that the English character really required
different treatment to that of other nations. Hugh insisted on the
importance of the willing 'spirit' of soldiers; Whibley was brutal and
for the scruff of the neck system. The climax was Whibley hissing
and hiccoughing out: 'You're a damned bloodless radical of 1880.'
'No—of 1884,' (I'm not sure of the dates), replied Lord Hugh, with
great dignity. 'You're the ghost of John Stuart Mill,' yelled Whibley.
Finally the Bishop, standing behind Whibley, muzzled him with a few
huge fingers laid across his mouth. The Bishop kept saying to poor
Lord H., 'But you see, you will overlook the fact of the war,' an
accusation for which I could see no sort of justification. Lord Hugh
advocated 'discipline' like the army for the workmen. This seems to
me the obvious solution—to have free enlistment, but then to be
bound by your own act, just like the marriage laws or enlisting in the
army principle. The Bishop kept asking what the Government is
doing and why they are so slow, and repeating and repeating: 'What
we want is organisation'—which is about as helpful as when Lord
Rosebery said with such *réclame:* 'What we want is efficiency.'

One can't help being irritated by the abuse of laymen when one
thinks of the superhuman difficulties confronting the statesmen and
generals. However, I suppose people have a perfect right to criticise
without having any constructive policy of their own, only I do resent
the tone in which Whibley does it. If I hadn't known and loved him,
I should have hated him last night. We all agreed Lloyd George's
speech was a blunder. It was a most interesting, supremely comic, and
rather touching scene. They were so earnest and were so little use to
each other. I'm afraid the Bishop was disappointed and went away
unencouraged about the Government. Whibley said we hadn't a 'dog's
chance of winning the war' as things were. I loved Lord Hugh.

Friday, 11th June

Adele Essex picked me up at three. She had been to see Ettie and talked a lot about her. Apparently she is in a most remarkable state—not even of hysterical exaltedness, but of real immunity to grief of the ordinary sort. She says she feels no sense of separation, but just consciousness of his radiance and a quite unimpaired zest for life. She will not break down, wears colours, and scarcely admits she is to be pitied at all. Can it last? One feels there must be a reaction to flatness and just the daily longing. The only thing is, she has got such marvellous powers of bluffing herself that she may succeed, and then, of course, her abnormal sense of the importance of things will help. One would feel, 'What does it matter to myself, or others, if I do break down and just give up?' She will always feel it is of vital significance to keep her flag flying—then, of course, she has so many tethers to life. It is so different to Con Manners—Avon and everything was just a frame for John.

Ashmead-Bartlett,* just back from the Dardanelles, came to dinner to see Mr Balfour. There was only us four, and it was very interesting. In spite of his voice and personality, he was really rather good—crisp and clear. Mr B. cross-questioned him a lot. He gave excellent description of the submarine terror and of his sinking in the *Majestic*.[1] He had written report on the situation for Balfour and Asquith.

Saturday, 12th June

I got very dear little letter from Billy:[2]

Darling Cynce,

I loved your letter. Death selects our bravest and best; but the barrier between two worlds is so gallantly and lightheartedly crossed here by many every day, that one can hardly feel it as a separation, or even an interruption of their gallant and beautiful lives.

Death is swallowed up in victory.

We are a nation of foolish and courageous volunteers fighting against the luriest of professionals, and we are paying the price for it.

No more news now as we are just off to the trenches armed like Iron Pirates.

God keep you and yours.

Love from Billy

1. Warship torpedoed at Gallipoli 22nd May.   2. Billy Grenfell.*

Bluetooth called for me at 11.15 and we motored down to Little-hampton, lunching at Horsham. He told me, in great confidence, that Venetia is really going to marry Montagu[1] and, so that he may not forfeit his fortune, she is formally to become a Jewess. He said the poor P.M. is absolutely broken-hearted, that it is stimying all public troubles. Perhaps, if truth were known, it is really the cause of the Coalition! Margot has been trying to run Pamela McKenna as a red herring to Venetia. They motored down to the Wharf together last Saturday and then he told her, and she told Bluetooth.

We got down to Littlehampton about four. I thought it too delicious after Brighton—a real paradise for children with huge stretches of lovely sand. Bluetooth was in the Royal Beach Hotel. I dined with him there. Very pleasant evening, I think, with extraordinary rapidity. Things have reverted very much to the old gear. I do hope it won't bring unhappiness again. He told me he had never seen me look so beautiful as that night, and was very outspoken. He is the most wonderful incense-burner. An equal relationship with him would be wonderful. It is a cruel, wasteful pity that he should never have succeeded in having one. Read Rupert Brooke's poems together.

Sunday, 13th June

Dined Bluetooth. He told me confidentially that one regiment—East Lancashires, I think—have been detected making overtures for cessa-tion of fighting with the Germans opposite them. I got into bed about eleven and half an hour later heard electric front-door bell tearing the silence. It rang four times before the landlady opened the door, then she appeared with a telegram. I knew at once it must be from Beb, and read the following: 'Come London immediately. Wire train Downing Street. Splinter of shell grazed lip removing two teeth. Quite well.'

Monday, 14th June

Caught 10.10 to Victoria. I found Beb with very swollen lip and two teeth broken off—otherwise very well. Really marvellous escape— the sort of thing one must congratulate oneself upon these days. Margot came back about one—very affectionate to Beb, and his father was at lunch, also Montagu, Bongie, and Davies. Beb displayed wonderful museum of battle trophies—every sort of shell and fuse, etc. They gave us the motor and I took him to Farmer. He said he could

1. Edwin Montagu: see index.

kill the nerves and keep the stumps to be crowned instead of having a plate, which is much better. We went for a drive while he ordered a man to come and give Beb gas. I insisted on watching the operation and then very nearly made an awful fool of myself by fainting—luckily not quite, but he went an awful colour and made horrible noises.

Evan and Mary came to dinner. Beb talks extraordinarily well about his experiences and gave excellent accounts. He has had a thrillingly interesting time. I shan't write anything about my feelings at having him back because the Hun will read my diary. Admiral Meux* wrote a letter to the Prime Minister, saying General Ashton has said he heard Beb was doing splendidly. He has been recommended for promotion. Beb looks very well, though a little strained. He is excited, but I think enjoying well-earned holiday very much.

Tuesday, 15th June

Beb and I both had breakfast in my room at Cadogan Square. Could not get dressed before eleven—constant interruptions and fierce skirmishes with Beb over my diary. Went to Farmer for certificate for the Admiralty: he gave Beb a fortnight's leave.

Went to Royal Academy. Amazing to see it just the same as ever. The old sheep by lakes, historical pictures, etc. It gave an extraordinary sense of stability quite unaffected by cataclysm. Percentage of tropical khaki pictures surprisingly small I thought. Rather a clever Lavery of a military hospital—very good atmosphere, it almost made one smell the antiseptics. Certainly war doesn't seem to incubate art. I have never seen a more vapid collection.

Walked to Downing Street, meeting Jack Islington and Mr Norton. Lord Lovat, Basil, Masterton Smith, and Bongie were at lunch. I sat between P.M. and Masterton. Discussed the First Lords with Masterton —he is the brilliant Admiralty Secretary. I asked him to talk to Beb about guns, as Beb has returned with a commission from the General to 'ask for more'. Beb went to report himself at the Admiralty. I walked through the park with Basil, meeting Arthur and Gerald Balfour together. A.J.B. asked after Beb. I told him how much he wanted to speak to him, and he said he would when he dines on Thursday. Basil and I went to the New English Art Club. Very poor exhibition, I thought, with the exception of one lovely Steer and Tonks' 'Russian Ballet'. Beb and I dined together early and went to Alhambra, where there was a Gaby Deslys ballet, but we only waited for her first appearance and then came home early to see Mamma, who

43

had just returned from Stanway. Beb very interesting about his experiences, and bitter on the subject of generals and ammunition shortage. General opinion out there seems to be that it is madness to hang on to the Ypres salient.

Wednesday, 16th June

Beb breakfasted in my room. I read some of the *Daily Mail* to him, including his father's speech of the day before, in which the P.M. definitely stated that he had been informed, on the best authority, that we had not been handicapped by lack of ammunition when he made his much-discussed speech at Newcastle. I can't understand. One feels there must be some individual criminally to blame.

Papa, Mamma, Beb, and I all dined with Adele Essex: party was Ribblesdale, Fox Macdonald, and Eloïse Ancaster. Quite a pleasant dinner. We discussed the rumour that the Germans utilise even their corpses by converting them into glycerine with the by-product of soap. I suggested that Haldane should offer his vast body as raw material to Lloyd George. We played poker after dinner. I played in a syndicate with Papa, which is always unsatisfactory. The syndicate lost about a pound.

Thursday, 17th June

Dinner party at home. St John Brodrick, Madeline, Winston, Clemmie, Major Farquharson, A.J.B., Norton, and Evan. I sat between Evan and Winston. I was very tired and flat, and Winston depressed, so we didn't make a great success of it. Beb sat next to A.J.B. and talked of his guns. He is very anxious to draw his attention to their Anti-Aircraft Brigade, which is very much in need of ammunition and more guns. Apparently, Mr Balfour hadn't realised that the Germans had a seventeen-inch gun (the one that bombarded Dunkirk) nor that the naval guns had knocked it out. Beb had a few more words with him on the landing before he went, and Mr Balfour told him to write a statement of the facts to him. Mr Balfour looked depressed, too. He and Winston brought horrid news that Lieutenant Warneford, the brilliant young naval airman with whose exploit in destroying the Zeppelin England was ringing, had been killed trying a new machine in Paris. Too tragic.

Papa, Clemmie, Madeline, and St John played bridge. The rest of us conversed in groups. Major Farquharson, the Don-Soldier, is a curious man. He amused us enormously by describing an interview with Bluetooth who, he complained, treated him very much *de haut en bas* with patronising manner, quite making him feel he was being court-martialled. Winston discussed statistics of German and French population. He said we were wonderfully well off in a large class of what he called 'truculent' young men who were accustomed to giving orders, and thus quickly convertible into officers.

Friday, 18th June

Beb, with military technique, requisitioned one of the Downing Street motors, so we had a heavenly drive down to Littlehampton, arriving about six and finding children just starting out. Beb delighted with Michael who is looking lovely.

Saturday, 19th June

Beb in morning list of casualties. Picture of him in *Daily Mail* saying he was wounded in the Dardanelles!

At 3.30 Beb, John and I motored to Greatham and had tea with Lawrence. Lovely day. Greatham is in the most delicious bit of country. Went for a short walk with Lawrences, meeting a Meynell picnic. Dined hotel. Letter arrived from Basil Blackwood asking me to send him Beb's poem 'The Volunteer', which the P.M. had told Lady Moira Osborne was the best poem written on the war. I copied it out. Beb has written a revised version and was furious at my sending the old. Tried to force me to get the letter back by hiding my diary out of doors. I very cleverly—or rather, very luckily—found it. However, I did try and intercept letter, but it was too late. Beb very angry.

Monday, 21st June

Uncertain, cloudy day. We had to transfer to the hotel as rooms in lodgings were engaged. What a lot of lounge life I have had lately!

After lunch at about three we had a grotesque expedition to the photographers to have a 'Holy Family' group taken. I had sent the motor to Greatham to fetch the Lawrences and they had arrived when we emerged from the photographers. Beb disappeared, saying he must sleep, and I took them on the beach.

We all had tea there together and then went for a walk. I wanted Beb and Lawrence to have a talk, so lingered behind with the Hun. She confided her difficulties as the artist's wife to me, saying Lady Ottoline,

D.—D

etc., were horrid to her, treating her as an appendage and explaining her husband to her as being dropped straight from the sky. Lawrence and Beb had war talk, and he accused Beb of subconscious 'blood-lust' and said he knew he would be bitterly disappointed were peace to be declared tomorrow. He has an *idée fixe* that 'destruction' is the end, and not the means to an end, in the minds of soldiers.

After our walk we sat on the sands and discussed war and the German code at some length. 'There you betray your origin, Frieda!' exclaimed Lawrence on one occasion. Frieda admitted that her country-men had no sense of what the English mean by 'fair play'. Lawrence maintained that the German theory of war—though filthy—was perfectly 'logical'. This we denied. They went away at seven. Beb liked him, but I'm afraid has no room in his heart for the Hun.

Very sorry to leave the children and Littlehampton tomorrow.

Wednesday, 23rd June

Horrid east-windy day made me feel very ill and uncomfortable. Mamma and Beb lunched with Mr Balfour,[1] so that Beb could have another gun interview. I gather it was satisfactory.

Yvo arrived. He has transferred himself into the Grenadiers and so will now be living in London.

Thursday, 24th June

Yvo came in about 12.30 from his first morning with the Grenadiers. It is too funny to think of him as a 'Guardee'. He showed us his lovely sword, with the names of all the famous victories in which the regi-ment had taken part inscribed on it. He and Beb sat down to another altercation as to the rival claims to glory of their regiments.

I put on my white 'launching dress', and we three went in an open motor to lunch at Downing Street. There was a large party: Edgar, Mr Dunn, Lady Horner, an American professor, a Norwegian admiral, etc., etc. I sat next to Dunn, and on the other side was an empty place for Cis, who never came. The Norwegian admiral is a fine figure with

1. In a letter written in May 1931, in response to his mother-in-law's inquiries for 'details of his interview with A.J.B.', Beb Asquith explained: 'The reason I saw Arthur Balfour was a strong rumour at the Front that our guns were to be taken away from us for the use of the Fleet. (In those days guns were very scarce.) I remember the interview very well. He showed great interest in a new and very ingenious invention which formed part of these guns. On the main issue he was extremely kind, and I think one result of the interest was that we got two more batteries.'

a leg and an arm shot off. Dunn had brought him there, and seemed to think he was doing important diplomatic work by his flirtations with Norwegians. Apparently, they have been supplying Germany with some very important ingredients of ammunition, but Dunn seemed to hope they might be prevailed upon to desist. He is still supplying the French Government with thousands of horses every week, and says he has lost a lot of money over it. He asked me a lot about George Moore. I thought the P.M. looked depressed. I walked to Friary Court and cut about three thousand respirators. The work still fascinates me.

Beb and I dined with the Midletons. I had rather an interesting evening. At dinner I sat beside Robinson, the editor of *The Times*. I have talked to him before and found him good company. We discussed the qualifications, moral and intellectual, which make a good general. He spoke enthusiastically of Lord Roberts. He was rather amusing about 'obituaries', saying how awful it was when he was taken by surprise and had to sit up all night at ghoulish writing. He said he rather enjoyed writing them about people who were alive and well. He goes through them every three or four months, but all the same, Jo Chamberlain's the only case in which they were fully prepared.

After dinner I talked to Colonel Fitzgerald for the first time, and thought him delightful and very interesting. He talked on the fringe of shop the whole time, but I refrained from any leading questions about munitions, etc. He was very interesting about the Germans. He said the most difficult thing Kitchener had to contend with was the optimism of people as to the duration of the war, which made them always press him to act as if the issue were immediate instead of remote. He said neither K. nor he had suffered in the least from having taken the pledge.

When we got home we found Wells and Uncle Guy still with Mamma. After they went we had a conscription talk. Beb has come back passionately in favour of it, and says the feeling in the Army is unanimously that way.

Friday, 25th June

Katharine came to see me. She had been working at her canteen at Euston. She told me one very interesting thing—that the 'highest authority' quoted by Mr Asquith in his famous speech at Newcastle was not Kitchener, but French. I wonder if this is true. Her story was that, when Lord Derby* attacked Mr Asquith for his statement, the latter sent him French's letter. Lord Derby told George Lambton, and he told Katharine. It sounded plausible enough, for, of course, if it was French they would not be able to divulge it as long as he remained in command, and it would explain Lord Hugh's letter to *The Times* announcing that he would not ask his question in the House, as to whether Kitchener was his authority, and that he expected the answer to be in the negative.

Saturday, 26th June

Cadogan Square was in the throes of receiving hordes of furniture, pictures and statues from St James's Place.[1] They all looked so funny and un-at-home in their new incongruous setting. Amongst other things there is a bust of Cromwell so strangely like the P.M., both in its strength and its weakness of face. Beb had requisitioned the Downing Street motor again, so that at about 5.30 we were able to roll luxuriously down to Reigate Priory.

I sat out in the garden with Whibley a little, and then went upstairs to dress before dinner. Dinner 8.30, party consisting of Kitty, Molly, Snede, Julia Maguire, Edgar, Whibley, Lord Hugh, Captain Thorpe, Belloc, Mr Maguire, Bobby,[2] and Beb. I sat between Belloc and Whibley. Oddly enough, though I have so often sat at the same table, it was the first time I had ever actually sat next to Belloc. Knowing someone very well by sight and in the third person, before you actually experience them yourself, gives one rather a bad start I think. It's rather like beginning a book in the second volume. We got on quite well, but Whibley not having a woman the other side of him, we had to talk *à trois* most of the time. Towards the end of dinner Lord Hugh joined in, and finally Whibley and Belloc got the bit between their teeth on the topic of the corruption of politicians and there was no holding them. Belloc told me he missed George Wyndham[3] more than any other man. After dinner I had a long and very nice *tête-à-tête* with Whibbles. He and Belloc, witnessed by Edgar, sat up talking until nearly three.

Sunday, 27th June

I didn't get down till past eleven. I found Whibley waiting for me in the hall and we went straight into the garden. Poor Whibley seems rather depressed. He is feeling being a 'spectator' of the war and doesn't know what he could do. He was delightful, as he always is

1. London home of the tenth Earl of Wemyss, about to be auctioned.
2. Kitty's son. 3. Eldest brother of Lady Wemyss.

à deux, so understanding and sympathetic in thought, and so unlike his general conversation paradoxical tub-thumping. 'Genuine' is a hopelessly debased word, but he is supremely what it ought to convey to one's mind.

Heard very good anonymous description of Aubrey Beardsley repeated, 'the Fra Angelico of vice'.

Monday, 28th June

The night of the poker dinner planned when we played at Adele's. Ruby and Ralph Peto, Duff, Lady Essex came, and with Papa, Mamma, Grace, Yvo, Beb, and I, we made ten. Mary arrived from Egypt in the middle of it, and made a tremendous sensation by her extraordinary beauty, which is much enhanced by thinness or something. I have never seen her, or indeed anyone, look more lovely.

Wednesday, 30th June

Mary told me, quite undramatically, that she was by way of being engaged to Strickland. Apparently Letty, probably from over-conscientious dragoning, had entirely stymied Mary from him. No sooner was she removed by scarlet fever than they 'fell into each other's arms'. It is very exciting.

Thursday, 1st July

Katharine, looking lovely in a white hat, came to lunch with the news of Violet's engagement to Bongie. We discussed it at length, not too good-naturedly. It seems almost incestuous to marry someone you know quite so well, but I am glad really, and think she is wise. Margot is, of course, 'over the moon'. He is to remain on as the P.M.'s secretary till the end of the war. Margot is triumphantly tearing Violet round from dressmaker to dressmaker, ordering sumptuous trousseau, and about half an hour after she had been told, she pinned paper on to Violet's pincushion with elaborate list of all the presents friends were to give: Philip Sassoon—furs (skunk). Violet is terrified that she will write and levy them. Apparently the P.M. is delighted, too. Diana[1] came to call for Katharine looking brilliantly improper.

I felt so shivery and ill that I decided to go to bed. Yvo sat with me in my room before dinner. I told him about Mary.

1. Lady Diana Manners: see index.

1915

Friday, 2nd July

Parkinson came to see me in the morning, and said I had a septic throat and must stay where I was. It is curious the way I always produce an infectious disease just as Beb is going out. I felt just the wrong degree of illness—not bad enough to be torpid and resigned, and not well enough to be able to enjoy reading, writing, or meals.

There was a dinner party—Evan, Belloc, Beb, Violet and Cis. Violet came up afterwards to see me, sucking formamint. I think she is really happy and serene—just absolute security and a kind of dependence on Bongie. I do hope they will be happy. We discussed Venetia's becoming a Jewess.[1] I don't think it's a thing one ought to feel vicariously at all. Bluetooth says, in a letter I got this morning, Bongie is avoiding Montagu; and Mr Asquith has told Venetia that, if she persists, he will never speak to her again.

Saturday, 3rd July

Woke up feeling better, but with throat still pretty sore. Mary Herbert* disobeyed her mother and came to see me in the afternoon. She told me Eileen Wellesley* claims very serious love affair with Rupert Brooke saying that quite unsuspected of everyone else they used to meet in Richmond Park and in Eddie's flat. No doubt Rupert Brooke had the thoroughly polygamous instincts of most poets.

Sunday, 4th July

I sent for Parkinson early as I was anxious to get leave to go down to Littlehampton with Beb, who was longing to get away. He did not give it to me, saying I must wait another day. However, I decided to disobey orders.

Monday, 5th July

The 'Downing Street Romance' was in all the papers. We went down to the beach, but the wind made it intolerable and we returned to the pleasant shelter of our garden. Such a ghastly population in the hotel. I told Beb they represented England and were what he was really fighting for, and he nearly resigned his commission.

1. Venetia Stanley was embracing the Jewish faith because her husband would otherwise have forfeited his right to the family fortune: the ethics of this widely discussed.

John was delighted with picture-books of trains I had got for him. Michael loves Beb and cries to go to him. Beb was very happy with them. It was his last day of freedom; the next morning the horrid machine catches him again, and he is due to report at the Admiralty. He expects to be sent to Portsmouth first, to lecture to the men there.

Tuesday, 6th July

Beb went up to London by 10.10 to go before his Board at the Admiralty. I spent a rather muddled day with my luggage packed, having given up my room at the hotel. Finally I telephoned to Beb at Cadogan Square. He was out, but I had torturingly indistinct words with Mamma, Mary, and Yvo. I gathered in gaps and guesses that Beb was staying in London waiting to arrange, and for its result, interview between Arthur Balfour and Osmondson. Dined and got drunk all by myself on burgundy. Howling tempest came on. A kind lounger lent me an umbrella and I splashed my way to my bedroom in the children's lodging house.

Wednesday, 7th July

Terrible storm raging at Littlehampton. I came up to London by the 10.10. We had a fantastic dinner party. Maud Cunard, looking the most inebriate of canaries in an incredibly unbecoming ultra-fashionable short dress, the mysterious don-soldier Major Farquharson, Duchess of Rutland, A.J.B., Lord Hugh, Oswald Balfour, Joan Lascelles, Lady Ancaster, Lorraine (airman), Mamma, Mary, Beb, Yvo, and self. I sat between Lord Hugh and Yvo. Lord H. was perfect.

Yvo and I played the game of imagining all our companions were lunatics, and we didn't require to stretch our imagination—it was a most plausible conception. They all looked madder than hatters. Farquharson, we decided, was suffering from the obsession that he was personally responsible for the war; Mamma from the one that she was stopping it by bringing all these people together at dinner. A.J.B. thought he was a rabbit. Farquharson was beside Maud and rose looking a 'sadder and wiser man'. I have never known her so aggressively comic and personal. She, he, Harry Cust, and Mamma were a very funny group. Harry thought his (Farquharson's) name was 'Fox' and would address him as such, gratuitously mentioning his name in order to correct Maud in what he thought was the mistake of calling him Farquharson.

We had the usual tea party to end up with. Lord Hugh and I loudly discussed our digestions to the general amusement. We found we both woke at four, and he said he had cured himself by a certain varallette which he pressed on me. 'I'm sure you're very acid,' he loudly snapped out. Farquharson is a curious figure, rather baffling. As with Disraeli's novels, one never quite knows whether one is laughing with or at. I like him on the whole.

I forgot to record the fact that Bluey came to see me at tea time—rather depressed. I thought. He is going to sit on Commission with St John and Selborne, etc., to try and reduce expenditure at the various Administrations. He is a supporter of Von Donop. Mr Balfour had just returned from the conference in France.

Friday, 9th July

I went to see Diana about twelve. She was in bed with a broken foot, poor thing—a casualty sustained a few days ago when jumping out of Mr Montagu's motor on arriving at Brighton. She was lying really looking exquisitely gleaming in a lovely primrose, *crêpe-de-chine* night robe on a very successful theatrical bed, surrounded by flowers and air balloons. Ice-coffee, strawberries, chocolates and nectarines were strewn all around her and she was entertaining a Coterie court. Lilian Boyd, Jaqueline de Portalès, Katharine, and Felicity. The chief topic was the desirability of mothers, and the best methods of circumventing them. Lilian Boyd and Jaqueline were airing their grievances as daughters, and Diana and Katharine were giving them advice. I was rather bored at finding a group, but there was no outstaying them.

Beb and I got to Portsmouth about six, and went to Royal Beach Hotel. It seemed so funny to be back there again. We went out after dinner and the searchlights were as lovely as ever. The sea looked magical. We listened to excellent band of the Marines who were playing on the pier.

Saturday, 10th July

Beb went off to barracks and I pottered about the town and bought one or two 'bargains' at the sales. We lunched with the Meuxes, arriving late and finding the Battenbergs* munching away. I lost my head and bungled my curtsey—I couldn't remember whether they were real royalties or not. I sat between him and quite a nice French sailor. Beb and I had tea in a shop and then taxied to Fort Augustus to see one of the 'Grandmammas'. She was shrouded in tarpaulin, but looked grim enough.

We dined with the Meuxes. Mary Curzon was there looking wonderfully glittering. Her face does make most others look like grey balloons, and she certainly is the perfect fairy princess, exactly like the conventional description of them—gold hair, deep blue eyes, jetty fringe, peach complexion. It may not be a very ambitious or imaginative type of beauty, but it is perfection in so far that it absolutely achieves what it attempts. I don't think one could alter anything and keep the design. So, she has got superlative objective beauty, which must be recognised. Her looks are a statement instead of an appeal like those of more freakish beauties. I sat next to the Admiral—he was gruff and amiable. Rather flat and low poker after dinner. I won a few shillings. Then Mary Curzon told my fortune with extraordinary, fantastic old cards. I always drew the devil.

Sunday, 11th July

Cold, grey day. Wrestled with odious packing. I had a letter from Bluetooth, talking of the 'infamy' of Lloyd George in connection with Haldane. According to rumour, he is trying to snatch at the premiership.

Beb telephoned to tell me I was to come to lunch with the General. I took taxi and joined the party. Beb, very shy and respectful, delightful General, and Lady Ashton his quite nice wife. Lady Ashton and I left them to talk shop, and went up to play with rather nice rude children. General motored us to our hotel, and then I had my last desperate lap of packing and we started off to Littlehampton in motor we had extravagantly ordered. Alas, my dressing-bag stayed behind and in it every necessity and luxury for the night! Beb was determined to stay at the hotel, but it is so expensive and I finally got him to acquiesce in sleeping in the children's lodgings. We dined at hotel. Population worse than ever.

Monday, 12th July

We had a very happy, peaceful day. I had a heavenly, very rough bathe. Wind dropped and it was the most lovely night. Beb and I walked on the beach after dinner—delicious sobbing waves. He goes back to France Friday. He was offered a 'soft job' at Eastney, but refused it.

Tuesday, 13th July

We came up to London by the 10.10—still without my bag. Lunched with Mary, Frances, Guy (home on three days' leave), Oswald Balfour, and Yvo, then we all went on to matinée at His Majesty's organised by Elizabeth and Clare Tennant in aid of the Red Cross.

Very amusing audience—a wonderful bevy of beauties selling programmes and Margot like a cuckoo in a clock appearing now here, and now there, everywhere in the theatre. I counted nine changes. It was a variety entertainment. A great many recitations, amongst others, Lady Tree in *manqué* Kipling: Lewis Waller, a stirring bugle call in two purple patches out of *Henry V*; an excellent Frenchwoman, etc. Elizabeth acted a 'slight duologue' with Gerald du Maurier. I was most agreeably surprised. I thought she did amazingly well and she looked so pretty—really charming, and her dress was lovely. I think it was a real success. I sat with Oswald in the stalls and found the audience very distracting. There was an excellent farce about a woman's war committee by Knoblock—Lady Tree perfect in it. Afterwards I went on to Ruby's, where we played poker. Duff, Irene and Nancy—Beb lost what I won. Sir Edward Goschen was there.

Beb and I dined with Montagu and his bride and her family—Sylvia, Blanche, and Oliver Stanley. Dinner was leavened by Nellie and Bongie. I enjoyed it very much, but it was a trifle strained and Venetia certainly doesn't look completely happy. After dinner Bongie and Beb rushed off to enquire after Violet who, poor thing, really has got typhoid—cruel luck.

The house is delicious and comfortable. I found Montagu delightful to talk to and I think he will give Venetia exactly the life she wants when once she has taken the plunge. I felt sorry for her last night, but I feel it will be happy. Bongie is giving Violet a Lavery portrait of himself.[1] She and Nellie were very amusing about their nursing: 'Have you ever burnt a patient?' 'No, but I stuch a pin in a forehead, and it festered.' They went on just like Sarah Gamp and Betsy Prig. Beb went round to Downing Street and had a talk with his father. Woke Mary and me up at 3.30.

Wednesday, 14th July

It was the first day of the sale at St James's Place, and Beb and I looked in for a little—a horrid sight. A thick, smelly crowd of professional vultures bidding away and the Charteris family sitting in a row tittering.

1. The gift was actually Lavery's—he had offered Violet Asquith a choice of a portrait of herself or her future husband.

We dined with Eloïse Ancaster and went to the revue at the Ambassadors with her, Duff, and Mr Norton. I thought revue delightful. It was the first one I have ever really enjoyed. It was called *More*. The principal lady, Madame Delysia, had wonderful vitality. At the end she sang the 'Marseillaise' with no voice but great temperament.

Thursday, 15th July

It was Beb's last day. After tea he had a strange whimsy—he wanted to drive in a landau. So, one was ordered and we went for a dignified drive, calling first at Frances' and then at Bruton Street to say goodbye to Evelyn, but she wasn't visible. Very weepy all the afternoon. The second time is much worse.

Beb and I dined at the Berkeley and went to *Potash and Perlmutter*.[1] I enjoyed it much. The acting is brilliant. When we got home we found Mr Balfour, who told Beb he thought he would be able to produce the eight guns for the battery. Beb very pleased.

Friday, 16th July

Guy, Frances, and Mark Tennant came to lunch. Mark looks lean, but not so bad considering all he has been through. He is on leave for a few days after having been out for eight months on end. Yvo is incredibly, subtly smartened up since he has been in the Guards.

Beb and I went down to Dover by the three o'clock. On our way to the station we called at Downing Street to say goodbye. Train very crowded. We arrived 5.15 and found Dover the scene of a Shakespearean tempest. Beb went to enquire for his boat and found none was leaving Dover, I believe on account of the supposed presence of submarines. He heard there was one going from Folkestone the next day and decided to go by that.

Saturday, 17th July

We travelled as far as Folkestone together. Beb got out there and I went sadly on to London by myself. I got up at about two, and Bluetooth called for me at four and motored me down to Littlehampton. On the way we had tea at the famous Box Hill Inn, where Keats wrote 'Endymion' and Nelson and Lady Hamilton spent a night.

1. Comedy by Montague Glass and Charles Klein at the Queen's.

1915

Grey, gusty morning but in the afternoon it became blue and lovely. Bluetooth was enjoying George Wyndham's letters very much—I had lent them to him. The remainder of my 'beach' party, Katharine and Whibley, arrived by the 6.6. Its genesis was really that I should introduce Katharine to Lawrence. It was rather fun. Whibley had never met Bluetooth before, only knowing what he called his 'shut-in' face. They quite liked each other.

I was still living at the lodgings. The others had taken rooms at the hotel. We dined there in private den. Bluetooth had taken a sitting room for our party, but we went out into the garden. Whibley rather drunk and terribly affectionate. I had very embarrassing time. Tried putting my hand in my pocket, but found that was the very worst tactics possible. I am terribly lacking in *savoir-faire* of that kind, especially with the old and ugly. They all walked me home about eleven.

Tuesday, 20th July

Rather a bad night and got up feeling ill. Was breakfasting with the children in dressing gown—hair down and cold-creamy face—when, to my horror, Whibley suddenly entered the room. He went off by the 10.10 train. Bluey, Katharine and I spent the morning together quite happily. He can't get over the oddness of being with us two. After lunch I went up and rested in Katharine's room. She came up later, complaining humorously that B. had said I had so much more 'tact' than her.

We started off for our much anticipated and discussed visit to Lawrence at 3.30. Lovely day and Sussex looked too divine. We found Lawrence alone, Frieda being in London, His hair had been cut and he was a little too tidy. He gave us tea and we talked for about an hour and a half. I felt awfully shy at first and the atmosphere was a tiny bit strained. Bluey had said he felt he was going to be 'boisterous', but turned out quite silent. When we had exhausted Lady Ottoline, a topic which proved a little like bathing in shallow water, we got on to mines and miners. It ended in a Lawrence soliloquy punctuated by intelligent listening remarks from Katharine and me, and I thought he was enthrallingly interesting. He spoke with horror of the absolute deadness of the lives of miners in the new kind of highly organised mines. He was very amusing about the Duke of Portland and his 'model villages'. Katharine loved him and was most anxious to know what effect she was producing. It was a great success. She went to London by a train from Arundel. Lawrence motored there with us.

Bluey and I returned to Littlehampton. I went to children, and dined with him at the hotel. We sat out after dinner and had significant conversation about 'tact' and 'stranger'. We got locked out in the garden and had to bang at the kitchen window.

Wednesday, 21st July

Bluetooth and I started to motor back to London at twelve. Lovely drive and very good companionship. We lunched at the Box Hill Inn and sat in the garden afterwards. We relived the time at Archerfield, when Margot told me to give him both hands and him to take me for a walk, etc., and I taxed him with having called me a 'bore'. He admitted having used that as an excuse. I magnanimously forgave him.

Uncle Guy and Whibley came to dinner. Papa was in and made rather a good joke about Venetia. I was saying she hadn't had much ritual when she became a Jewess, and he said, 'Didn't she even have to propose Judas Iscariot's health?'

Thursday, 22nd July

Very funny letter from Lawrence with slight—I fear not very satisfying—dewdrop for Katharine. I quoted the following lines to her for the verdict on her and also as evidence that he is not in love with me, as she alleges, but only regards me as (God help him!) a potential instrument in his revolution.

'May I bring Viola Meynell to tea; she would like to come as she thinks you the most beautiful woman in the world. It always irritates me this talk about "a beautiful woman". There is something so infinitely more important in you than your beauty. Why do you always ignore the realist thing in you—this hard, stoic, elemental sense of logic and truth? That is your real beauty. I think I should like Katharine Asquith very much, but I doubt if she's got the quality of absoluteness there is in you or not so much . . .'

Huge dinner here. Table most difficult to arrange—so many men and amongst them so many professors. Adele, Margaret Mackail, Lady Raleigh, A.J.B., Professor,[1] Wells, Fisher, Bluetooth, Birrell, Mackail, Evan, Papa, Mary, Yvo. I sat with Bluetooth after dinner.

1. Sir Walter Raleigh: see index for all these names.

Friday, 23rd July

Stayed in bed hoping the day would seem endless with plenty of time for diary, letters, reading, and going through my poetry repertory, but somehow it melted very disappointingly.

Venetia came at one and was very entertaining. I had been to Jays with her yesterday, watching her trying on her wedding dress and trousseau, when she was in excellent form and very happy. Katharine and I not successful when we went present-hunting for her.

I dined with Frances. Dinah was there and it was very pleasant and peaceful. Mr Balfour dining with Mama, and I talked with them a little when I got back.

Saturday, 24th July

Stayed in bed all the morning. Lunched with Mamma, Papa, Mary, Frances, and Lady Angela. Discussion on favourites amongst children and we all agreed on which were the three Mamma preferred—Ego, me, and Bibs. She denied feeling any difference, but we were very certain. Laughed about the ups and downs of Papa's feelings for us, and decided each to keep a chart, like a temperature one, of his affections. Angela raucous and generally rather more like herself than ever.

Poor Mamma very depressed, having had another plan talk with Papa, who appears to want to remain on at Gosford. She finds the doubt as to the fate of Stanway life and the general uncertainty very distressing. It is very tiring being suddenly confronted with an artificial 'home'—only a home because it belongs to you instead of because you have lived there—and, of course, she adores Stanway and has just spent a year of toil getting it ready.

Sunday, 25th July

Lunched with the children, and I trespassed in the hotel garden and read *J'accuse*. Rather an interesting French indictment of Germany. The Lawrences came to Michael's birthday tea bringing Viola Meynell, who never moves without a copybook in which she enters notes for her novels. Children very demoralised by candles on cake. I felt ill and depressed, and it was the least successful of all my Lawrence meetings. There was rather a floater* going on about Ottoline, who has written to say she hasn't room for Frieda, and Frieda is furious with her. Slight semi-facetious, but distinct, friction between the Lawrences. First time I have ever seen it.

Monday, 26th July

Glorious day, as it always is when I leave Littlehampton. Came up to London by 10.10. Went hotel and changed into pink check muslin, and went to lunch with Bluetooth. Enjoyed it. He had been to Venetia's wedding lunch and said all were very calm.

Lady Angela came to dinner, swallowing chlorodyne for tummy-ache. I agreed to go to court with her the next day. She is to bring an action against her husband to get more money. Papa and Lord Ribblesdale are witnesses. She wanted a hat to wear in court, so I brought down a large selection and she bought the white one I got at Selfridges and which gives me a headache.

Tuesday, 27th July

The lawsuit was postponed until twelve o'clock and so I couldn't go. Went down by 2.10 to Taplow to see Ettie. Found her lying on sofa in her sitting room looking curiously 'unwound' for her, but she was wonderful to talk to, and later on, when we went for a walk together, seemed quite normal. I loved her. She inspires one with tremendous admiration. There seems nothing strained and artificial about her marvellous courage, just a sort of alchemy which has translated tragedy to the exclusion of all gloom. We talked a good deal about Julian, and afterwards quite natural, flippant gossip. She was full of the engagements. No diminution of zest or humour.

Mamma and I dined with Bluetooth. Adele, Evan, and Bongie were there. I thought it a success and enjoyed it. Everything well done. It is extraordinary how bachelors manage to lap themselves round with comfort and luxury, without any of the friction and worry we have with servants. Evan and Bluetooth had old-maidish talk comparing domestic notes.

Wednesday, 28th July

Had my hair waved in Sloane Street and visited Diana. Lord Rib came before I left: he had heard Charles Lister's* wound was not serious in a telegram from Harry Wilson.

Bluey called for me at 3.30 and we went to see the Mestrovic sculpture at the Victoria Museum. They are very strange, but I thought some of them really beautiful in a violent way. We picked up Frances Horner and motored her down to Philip Sassoon's place Trent, which has been lent for Edward's convalescence. Found a gloomy party— Elizabeth, looking very bilious, poor Edward very asthmatic and depressed. She had come down to see Edward, and when Katharine had got down from London she had found her playing the piano by herself, with Sir John and Edward both entrenched in their bedrooms. K.'s children were playing about—very 'chatty'. We strolled about in most lovely garden with pink pillars and flamingoes. Edward went to bed before dinner. Sir John, Frances, Bluetooth, and I dined together, then Katharine and I went up to E.'s bedroom, where we had a long reminiscence talk. His spirits seemed better.

Thursday, 29th July

Duff, Eileen Wellesley, De Grunne, and Clare Tennant came to dinner. Papa in very good form. Eileen disgusting about an amputated finger she had mislaid. She looks pretty in her nursing dress. Gambling hell—Eileen won twelve pounds, mostly off Duff the usual benefactor.

Saturday, 31st July

Mary and I were called at a quarter to seven, had hurried dressing and drove to Euston on our way to Dublin—stood in an endless queue to get our tickets. Found Basil at the station. Very pleasant, easy, uneventful journey with excellent crossing spent on deck. Basil, poor thing, very shy of our rather blatant leopard skins, tried to conceal us in the second class part of the deck. We arrived here at the Secretary's Lodge, about seven in pouring rain. Delicious little house, very clean and comfortable with pretty garden.

Sunday, 1st August

Slept very badly and was conscious of pouring rain, which continued for the first part of the morning. We got up late and our host went off to work. He came back at twelve bringing the Comptroller, a very glib and rather charmless man. We four walked to the Viceregal and inscribed our names in the book. Lunched *à trois*—nice plain chickeny food. Basil gave us sketches of all the personnel of the staff. I had a short siesta after lunch, then Basil and I looked at his commonplace book together.

The day had turned into loveliness and at half past four we walked to the Viceregal, equipped for tennis. A great deal of chaff about curtseys and court etiquette and Mary and I were in great trepidation. 'Queen' Alice[1] came in and was very sweet to us. She is pretty: such

1. Lady Wimborne: see index.

lovely, dancing, golden eyes. We were much confused by Basil's character sketches and sat patiently waiting for the wrong woman to be witty. After tea, tennis on new hard red courts.

We all dined at court. Tremendous ceremony maintained—much more than is attempted in Canada, and I suppose it is much more important here. Lady Wimborne really perfection—heaven-born manner, smile, and dimple, and most conscientious. It's no sinecure either. He rather makes one wince in this lovely, glamorous land, but he is not without the rudiments of a sort of Anthony Hope King technique. I sat next to him. He is very easy—just a fairly frank bounder. The curtseying when one leaves the room is terrifying, as it is performed in complete isolation when one is framed in the doorway. I tittered.

Basil is so nervous lest we should disgrace him—almost like Ego was when I used to come down to Eton. After dinner Mary and I sat with the 'Queen', who was most 'gracious' and expatiated on the beauties of Mary's brow. His Excellency joined us and kept us on our hind legs for some time, then 'Their Majesties' withdrew leaving us in a queer dream-like pie. The staff is a strange assembly of clowns . . . 'motley's the wear'. We got home about 11.30. We three very happy and easy together.

Monday, 2nd August

Received good 'love letter' from Bluetooth in the morning. He is writing to me every day now. Mary drove on the box of a coach to some races with a party from the Viceregal. They were away to lunch, so Basil and I were alone. After lunch he drew and I had the joy of reading aloud 'Lycidas' and a large selection of very familiar beloveds from *The Oxford Book of Verse*.

We walked over to tea at the Viceregal. Individuals are beginning to emerge for one from the staff and they look much less like each other, and are very much thawed. Lady Fingal, who lives on a reputation for wit, was there, but she was not extravagant with that commodity in my presence. Queen Alice exquisitely dressed.

We dined at court again. Large banquet of over thirty. Too amusing watching the dear old 'trouts' (as frumpy women are called here) making their curtseys. Lady Wimborne looked lovely in exquisite head-dress of ospreys and emeralds. I went in with General Friend (in command of forces in Ireland), and like him very, very much. On my other side was a darling 'funny'—a soldier.

Basil drew a delicious menu (illus. on p. 1) which I found in front of me. Mary looking lovely and I had many dewdrops for her. She sat between the Comptroller and another member of the staff, and elicited the information that they had been very alarmed at the prospect of us, as they had heard we were very well educated! and the type that asked odd questions. They said they were agreeably surprised.

I had on my gold flame dress and feared it might embarrass my curtsey, but managed all right though I could not refrain from smiling, for which Basil censures me. After dinner there was a great deal of standing about while 'Their Majesties' circulated, bestowing a few words on each guest. The band played and I was much amused.

Tuesday, 3rd August

Basil, Lady Powerscourt and I motored into Dublin. Called on Horace Plunket. 'Æ' came down to discuss scheme of books for the soldiers with Basil—a strange, unkempt, bearded genius. He took us to see his room all beautifully frescoed by him with faery figures in 'brass paint'. His writing table is the most wonderful, fantastic, earthquake disorder imaginable. One couldn't have believed it possible—mountains of tottering paper littered with writing pads, etc., pen-bed swaying on the top. He explained, quite seriously, that one must have either physical or mental disorder and he had chosen the former. Horace Plunket has a charming face, but I had no talk with him.

Basil told me he had decided to go into the Grenadiers. I think he ought to stay here where he is very useful, but of course he won't.

Wednesday, 4th August

One of the staff told me shattering news that beloved Billy[1] had been killed. I couldn't believe it, but alas it must be true. I found it in *The Times* in the evening. It's too unthinkably awful. It's the first that has been much more than vicarious to me. He was a huge delight in one's life, a real luxury, and I shall miss him more and more. It is the end of one's youth all this. Soon one will hardly remember who is alive and who is dead. In a sense Death is really becoming annihilated—the division grows narrower and narrower. Of course, every feeling is swallowed up in one's horror at the thought of Ettie and poor Willie.[2] How can they face such utter desolation, such extinction of joy, glamour and hope. I remember them so well as little curly-headed boys in white the first time they came to Stanway.

1. Grenfell.   2. Lord and Lady Desborough: see index.

Thursday, 5th August

Delicious morning. Walked round garden before breakfast. Mary and I frousted all the morning. I read fatuous novel by Florrie Bourke called *Faithfulness in High Places*. Basil returned to lunch.

I splashed across to tea at the Viceregal. Afterwards all of us, Mary, Sir George Prescott, the Comptroller and I settled down to a poker Hell. Their Excellencies and Basil were entertaining Devlin in another room. Basil came and summoned me into the royal presence, and I had about twenty minutes talk with 'Queen' Alice. She was in great distress because Basil had just told her he had definitely decided to go into the Grenadiers as soon as they will pass his hand which, alas, is ever so much better. The Wimbornes are in despair at the idea of losing him. He is so excellent at a very important and ticklish post, and they don't know who they can get as a substitute. She talked of nothing else—dewdropped him up to the skies and implored me to try and persuade him.

Basil and I went for a short turn in the motor—I drove—and then we went for a walk. I discussed the question with him, but what is the use? Of course he would be more useful to his country here, but it's not a thing one can argue about as it's not a question of opinion but of feeling. His instinct to go is irresistible, and of course one understands, though it does seem waste for him to be an untrained lieutenant. We didn't get back till eight.

Delicious evening after dinner. We all stretched ourselves on sofas round the fire—like a Roman banquet. I read 'Locksley Hall' and 'Lotus Eaters', then we relapsed into frivolous personal conversation and inquisition. We allowed Basil to ask each of us three questions about the other's biography, and he extracted list of proposals. I've never seen anyone so inquisitive. Bengers again. I'm sleeping vilely here. Took some Trional.

Friday, 6th August

Misty, muggy morning. Short walk with Basil before breakfast. He went off to work, returning about eleven in the little Ford to motor us to Cloe Guinness to bathe. Such a comical-looking little woman. We walked over lovely garden and then bathed with the maximum of comfort. A small, blue, deep bath in the house. The chill taken off the water and there were beautifully heated dressing rooms. We three disported ourselves and the house party watched us. I loved it. I wore my new green bathing dress. My third wedding ring slipped off. We couldn't see it, but I suppose they will find it next time the bath is emptied.

After lunch we squeezed into the little Ford again and went down to Dublin. Ghoulish sightseeing in old vaults where the atmosphere contains strange properties of preservation, so that one can see bodies hundreds of years old. Rather horrid. An accumulation of cobwebs like fishing nets and dozens of coffins with the brasswork still quite bright. The man who showed us round has developed the most extraordinary charnel-house voice. The whole thing made me shudder, and I felt revulsion at the idea of ever being a skull.

Dined at the Viceregal. Stickyish evening. Afterwards we stood about in such purposeless groups that in desperation Irene and I started round games for a small circle. We played 'Harrods Stores', etc., etc. Not a brilliant success, but better than nothing.

Saturday, 7th August

It rained more or less ceaselessly all day. We returned in the afternoon to Cloe to have another bathe and had the greatest fun. Cloe—alas! —whom I longed to see in the water (I so much wondered what would happen to her face), refused to make a Roman holiday for us, but her two companions joined us in the bath. The auburn grenadier girl was most unpleasantly clad in clinging Eton blue, and the old 'trout' was in thick black clothes with stays, stockings, etc. I don't believe she can ever have got really wet through. She swam silently to and fro, passing us at regular intervals like a penny steamer. We suffered from remorse afterwards, thinking we had not been sufficiently sociable in the bath. I suppose we ought to have played ring-a-ring-a-roses like women do at Brighton.

Instead of this, we rather kept ourselves to ourselves. We stayed in ages and had the greatest fun. Mary and I fought and were both nearly drowned. Basil and I did some very funny rescue work: I was saving him when we both sank like lead and swam in opposite directions to the shore. I swallowed gallons—the water was appreciably lower. We had delicious tea, and then drove off, feeling that we had used their house rather like a public place. After we got back Basil and I went for a long walk in such delicious soft rain.

Heavenly telephoning between Basil and the persecuting Florrie Bourke. He rashly embarked on saying he was reading her book (he hasn't opened it). She immediately asked him how far he had got. He appealed to me, 'For God's sake, where have I got to?' holding his hand over the receiver. I prompted him to say, 'Where the mother has an accident'. There is no mother and no accident!

Sunday, 8th August

Poured all the morning. At about 11.30 we three splashed through the park to the Zoo and spent a soaking hour there. Much amused by a keeper who, when asked what time the lions would be fed, replied with complete solemnity, 'They're never fed on Sundays—they couldn't digest it'.

It was a terribly limp, Turkish bath day, and we could hardly get home, and had to be given a dope for starting out to take our *congé* at court. We went to lunch there—finding, to our relief, that His Excellency was away for the day and Her Excellency in bed. The staff were like schoolchildren with the masters out of the room. Mary and I went upstairs to see 'Queen' Alice. She was looking too lovely in exquisite sofa clothes and a delicious lace cap. We stayed some time and she was very sweet to us. There was a large photograph of her Spanish lover by her side.

Mary went to tennis and Basil and I motored into Dublin in the little motor and spent some time in the Picture Gallery. It is a very good collection. I drove the motor quite a long time round the park with great success. We had tea when we came back. The day had turned into most lovely evening and we went out for a walk. Found a bench in the sun and didn't come back till eight. Very good talk—I am fond of him. He has real 'lovable' charm, quite apart from social charm of manner, etc. We had our last dinner *à trois*. Felt happy. He complimented us on our relationship as sisters. More morbid self-analysis, and delicious Bengers.

Monday, 9th August

Called 6.15. Not at all sleepy. Continental breakfast, reserving John Bull one for the boat. Polly went by train and a Viceregal motor took us all the way to Kingstown harbour.

Basil came on board to see us off and an amazingly funny thing happened. He was talking to us and was just beginning to think of saying goodbye—expecting bells and customary warnings—when suddenly the bridge fell with a bang and away glided the ship. Like a figure in a cinematograph, he tore gesticulatingly upstairs to the captain on his bridge, and implored him to stop the ship. It was no use. The captain said it was quite impossible, and wasn't even sympathetic.

I'm ashamed to say Mary and I laughed till we had to cling to one another swaying to and fro. He behaved angelically about it, but it really was cruel. It involved six hours wait for the next boat back from Holyhead. He couldn't send a telegram. His Excellency awaited him at 10.30, and unfortunately he had a great deal of urgent, important things to do that day. He rather minded the idea of providing such laughter to the staff—they will live on it for weeks. I was sorry, but I'm afraid I was even more amused. We made the best of it—eating a large breakfast and sitting and walking on deck. Lovely day and perfect crossing. Left him a pathetic object on the platform at Holyhead. Mary and I had comfortable, uneventful journey to London.

Tuesday, 10th August

Most ghastly day of stress and strain. By the end of it I felt as if I had lived through years of scarring life. I went round at about eleven to see how Frances[1] was. Found Dr Holland and her mother there, things having really begun at last at about three in the morning. She was too bad to see me, but they were afraid things were going to be very slow as she was having the same kind of futile pains as before. I stayed with Annie outside the door, and tried to comfort and distract her. She was very sweet. I am fond of her. She is so absolutely woman in the raw.

I lunched with Venetia and Montagu. Venetia went off to sit to Lavery, and I returned to Catherine Street. Found Annie sad, saying Frances was not getting on at all. The doctor was in with her. We listened outside the door, and realised he must have decided to act as we heard the clink of instruments. Soon—it was about 3.30—to our great relief, we heard the unmistakable sound of the baby's voice. It was an enormous girl weighing over eleven pounds. Holland said he would never let Frances wait over her time again. Annie and I went in to see the baby. Frances looked very white and sad, but was supposed to be quite all right, and in about an hour's time I went away, having seen the baby bathed, and feeling quite happy about Frances. Holland went away, too, not intending to return until the evening.

I went to see Evelyn and found her out so, by the merest chance, I returned to Catherine Street about three-quarters of an hour after I had left it, and found the most terrible commotion going on. Frances had had an awful haemorrhage, followed by complete collapse. By the mercy of Heaven, Dr Holland was in when they telephoned and got back very quickly. When he first saw Frances, he thought she was

1. Frances Charteris: awaiting the birth of Laura, her second daughter.

dead, and then he would only say there was a chance of saving her.

It was a nightmare of terror and horror. Kakoo[1] and I had to fly up and downstairs, and in and out of the room fetching ice, salt, and water, tearing blankets off beds, and filling hot water bottles. They had great difficulty in getting the douche the right temperature, and I had to go in and hold the thermometer. At first my hand shook so that I thought I should never be able to read it, but luckily I was able to pull myself together. Annie behaved splendidly, really helping. It was a ghastly sight—the bed tilted right up backwards. Poor, darling Frances absolutely corpse-white, ceaselessly moaning and imploring them to desist in their treatment. 'Don't, Keithie . . . Oh, Keithie, don't!' Really haunting. Keith[2] had tears pouring down her cheeks, and Holland worked grimly and athletically. They had to torture her, poor darling. She was only just kept alive by the injections. The whole world seemed a sea of blood and Holland was like Mark Antony up to his elbows. For hours she was in desperate danger.

It has all become confused to me; a blur of terror, ice, blood, pain, and glamorous doctors. As far as I can remember, Holland at one time pronounced her definitely better, and then she got worse and he told us to telephone for Dr Parkinson or Streatfield. Parkinson was out—Streatfield in, and he came round incredibly quickly and rushed into the arena. I don't know how much later it was that Holland said he wanted Parkinson as well. I jumped into the motor and went round to his house. Luckily he had just come in, and I drove him back at once. He sat forward like a jockey all the way, snapping out questions and with tremendous air of set determination. I believe his moral effect was most valuable: the other two were getting tired and depressed, and he seems to have rather stimulated Frances, too. Very soon she pathetically asked for some brandy and soda. Kakoo and I flew off to a chemist to procure a cylinder of oxygen, in case it should be needed. Poor Keith nearly broke down. We had to give her soup. By about eight I think they considered Frances out of danger.

I have never felt such admiration and gratitude as I did towards the doctors. In crises they have immense glamour for me, though I don't think much of them for ill-health. Parkinson stayed with Frances all night. Guy didn't arrive till 9.30, so he was spared much and she was able to see him. Poor little darling! When she was very bad she said, 'Oh, what has happened? I thought I wasn't going to see Guy again'.

I went round and had dinner at Venetia's—Montagu, Sylvia, Dorothy Henley and Gertrude Bell were there. Afterwards I went back to Catherine Street and saw Guy. Frances was asleep. I went to bed

1. Kathleen Tennant, later Lady Granby.   2. Nurse Keith.

1915

very tired and profoundly grateful. I am glad I went back as they really needed 'supers'.

Wednesday, 11th August

Rather unsatisfactory, patchwork sort of day. Good account of Frances. Went to tea at Appensodt's for an assignation with the Lawrences, but it didn't come off. Bluetooth sent his motor for me, and I dined alone with him. First 'check' since our renaissance. I was what—for want of a better word—I call 'cataleptic' and he was unhappy and wouldn't be persuaded. It was impersonal and inevitable—almost a floater, but staved off. He does turn one's thoughts inwards too much somehow. Resents the 'mirror' basis of friendship, and yet promotes it more than anyone else. I feel so much more 'objective' and, therefore, happier with B.B. Bluetooth gave me two boxes of delicious *langues de chat*.

Thursday, 12th August

Mary had two letters from Strickland saying they thought they were going to be dismounted and sent to the Dardanelles. He and she want to announce their engagement. Travelled up to Gosford by myself, arriving in a thunderstorm and finding Mamma, Letty, Bibs and the children. Bibs burst into tears when told of Mary's engagement.

Friday, 13th August

Very depressing here. The house is like a great, dead, empty cage hanging in a tempest of misery outside. Very devoid of any lived-in, home feeling—a sort of 'no-man's-ground'. Mamma miserably depressed about plans, money, and her life altogether. It makes me very unhappy and I don't know how to help her. She is distressing herself so terribly about Papa's threats to let Stanway, and the uncertainty as to the general principle of their lives in the future. Awful Connor money talks—all very difficult to understand and explain. Wrote a lot of letters in the morning and played some tennis on hopelessly mossy courts.

I went over to see Margot, who is in the Lubbocks' villa at North Berwick. She had been here the day before, leaving a wake of weeping, injured people. Both nurses mortally offended. She said John had no roof to his mouth and Michael looked like a Red Indian. I went over meaning to tell her what pain she gives and try to stand up to her, but as usual all my resolution evaporated and directly I was in the room I knew it was quite out of the question to say a word, even though she gave me several cues. Also, she is disarming. I always resent her so much more in theory than in practice.

Mary has written with adorable coolness to both her parents, telling them she is engaged to 'Tom'.

Saturday, 14th August

A telegram has arrived from Mary, saying she has had a telegram from Tom to tell her he is just off to the Dardanelles. Poor darling, I am very sorry for her. Ego, with four other officers, remains behind in charge of five hundred horses. He is furious and miserable. It is the sort of 'miss' and disappointment he is always meeting in his life. Letty's feelings are mingled relief, anger, and compassion. I think it is a matter for frank congratulations, but of course it is rather a bathos, though probably the selection is completely mechanical.

An amazing tea party, competing with and defeating Mamma's best freak entertainments at Stanway. Two incredible and quite indescribable old Scotch sisters in real pantomime clothes—like the most overdone character parts in a play—came and, to make the situation quite perfect, they were leavened by Margot. Margot was priceless, engaging the madder of the two in a vital conversation. They didn't realise who Margot was and the madder asked her what she 'thocht o' the preesent Government'. Margot returned, 'What do you think of Mr Asquith?' This was replied to by an eloquent dumb show spasm, followed by a vicious denunciation. Then there was a lot about women smoking. 'I saw a great many women—young ones, too— smoking at Harrogate.' Margot drew the madder out splendidly and she explained all about her servants. The other sister got uneasy and said crushingly, 'We will noo drap the sarvant topic,' and (with withering sarcasm), 'Vary interesting isn't it?' I'm afraid she meant to scold her on the way home.

Saw the children going to bed. John is very silent and unresponsive these days. I read Beb's letters to Letty after dinner.

Monday, 16th August

I stayed in bed most of the morning. Letty, Mamma, and Bibs motored into Edinburgh. Letty mutilated a wasp at lunch and Mamma would climb up and down the window for ever so long trying to find satisfying evidence of its death. Just now Letty is in quite the best looks I have ever seen, with Mediterranean-blue eyes and shell-pink cheeks. She has a stern sense of duty about the maintenance of good spirits and will go on reiterating, 'Are we downhearted? No!' But we are, for all that.

We all three had letters from Mary giving an amusing account of her first visit to the Stricklands. She was shown photographs of Tom at every age, which made her cry. She is very, very much in love, and of course, poor darling, is miserable at his going to Dardanelles. Weather cold and unpleasant.

Wednesday, 18th August

Exceptionally good morning post including an Ego, a Lawrence, an Aubrey,[1] and a Bluetooth. Delicious, very typical one from Ego. Lawrence's letter very long and full of bitterness and diatribe—very difficult to answer. It is so difficult to know whether he has any constructive plans which are at all applicable. I fear I am what he calls 'static'.

Friday, 20th August

Papa rather dashed at breakfast by letter from Strickland *père*, saying that he was in the same death-duty boat and couldn't afford to settle more than £1,000 a year, but that he would give an allowance to make it up to £1,500 a year, and in addition to that, Tom will have his salary at the bank. No doubt he would settle more if Papa would. These things seem always to be done on a commercial system. He must think £5,000 a very niggardly *dot* for an 'earl's daughter'. I don't think it shows they are not rich, and probably they will give them everything they want, even if they give them little on paper.

Saturday, 21st August

Lovely day. Bluetooth came over—he is staying with the Asquiths—and we went for a walk by the sea. Pamela McKenna had accused him of being 'abstracted' on the fleet expedition and said she 'knew why and that she didn't mind so long as it was making him happy—but she was afraid it wasn't'. The P.M. came in at that moment and said he had heard there had been an 'approximation'. We didn't get in till 7.15.

1. Aubrey Herbert.

Sunday, 22nd August

Wore my black-and-white gown. It was much dewdropped. Letty and I had exquisite vision of Adele in hat and stays. Really her legs are poems and, if I had such knees and feet, I feel I should be safe from all the 'slings and arrows of outrageous fortune'. They would be an unfailing source of consolation.

Mamma, Letty, and I had very hot walk to church. I liked the new minister, with his sandy head and harsh voice. Sermon rather touching in its ugliness and simplicity. Extraordinary luncheon party of some of Papa's golf cronies. These invasions are rather trying. We went up to play tennis at Craigielaw at 3.30.

We returned late to a huge tea party—Countess Torby, Lady de Trafford, Margot, and the George Hopes. George Hope is very good-looking. His wound doesn't show at all, though it has blinded one of his eyes. John had great success at the piano. It really is extraordinary how he chooses the notes and gently caresses them, all the time, making most eerie Puck faces. To my consternation I heard him say— I could almost swear to it—'I'm going to play Schumann.'

Monday, 23rd August

News of sinking of German ships by the Russians, and American rumour of success in the Dardanelles. Wrote letters and went up to tennis at Craigielaw. I played rather well, first with Letty against Mary and Mamma—a very vocal set—and then with Mrs Connor against Mary and Bibs, and finally with Mrs C. against Mr Connor and Bibs. Mrs C. provoking beyond all imagination; throwing balls in one's face when one was serving, arranging them round one's feet, and running at every ball with mouth wide open as if to swallow it.

Connor and I motored over to the Asquith *ménage* at North Berwick. We had been going at four, but Margot telephoned to say the P.M. insisted on having his golf after tea, so would I come earlier so that Bluetooth could see me. We started 3.15. Connor told me of the family finances. It appears there are £28,000 to be paid for eight years to meet death duties, etc., and Connor says he has only £5,000 a year to meet this with after Gosford and Stanway have been kept up and all the allowances to the various individuals (including £4,500 for Mamma's 'General account' and £2,000 for Papa) have been paid. He thinks it quite out of the question to attempt living in **two houses** and thinks Gosford should be shut up.

We found Margot and Bluetooth sitting on the sofa. The P.M. was in his bedroom with a novel. Bluetooth and I went out for a walk. It was the most lovely afternoon; the Bass Rock a blue spirit. I was afraid of returning to Gosford empty-handed of news so I pumped him as much as possible. The P.M. has had a long letter from Hankey who was sent out to inspect the operations in the Dardanelles. It was written on the 12th August, and in it he says that he thinks there is a 'fair chance' of success. Apparently it ought to have been achieved a short time ago. The plans were perfectly laid and success ensured, but for miscarriage owing to gross blunder on the part of Stafford and some other generals. Five are being sent home. He said it would scarcely be possible to abandon the enterprise: it would mean losing Australia, so soaked with Australian blood was the soil.

I tried to extract some of the practical (I know the sentimental) arguments against conscription. He says the main, and to his and Mr Asquith's mind the conclusive one, is that at the most there remain only three-quarters of a million more men in the country who could possibly be tapped for military service, and these will easily be secured on present system. At present we have about three million mobilised. I don't quite see how this applies to the control of labour question which is the main argument for conscription. Bluetooth denies that you can force labour in the same way that you can force men to fight. He told me Kitchener's argument against it was that you couldn't mix volunteers and conscripts, so great would be the contempt for the latter. I don't think this is very convincing.

We returned to tea. Mr Asquith came, very mellow and asked a lot about John. Puffin* had given a glowing account of his musicalness. If I were Margot I would whitewash the Prime Minister's face. He is so much attacked for callousness because he looks rosy and well. Played with the children when I got in, and then went for a short walk with Adele. She also discussed family finances with great intelligence. I like her more and more. Papa had gone away in the morning so we had no Hell, but some letter game and fairly early to bed.

Thursday, 26th August

Letty had a cable from Ego saying they had got the first list of casualties, and that Tom and George were all right.

Friday, 27th August

Letty and I started by the 9.15 to stay with Ruth Montagu at Corrievorrie-Tomatin. Two golfers arrived at breakfast just before we started, they have come to lay out the new golf links at Longniddry, which Papa and Mr Connor hope may produce a large fortune. We had quite a good journey in third-class carriage through lovely country and supported by cold grouse sandwiches.

We arrived about four and found nothing to meet us. Letty and I started to walk and were given a lift by someone staying at a neighbouring house. We were just arriving when Venetia and Bluetooth overtook us in their motor. Beauty discussion nearly all through dinner, or rather ugliness. Racked our brains to think of plain women —astonishing how rare they are. Montagu yawned like a hyena after dinner. We all wore pairs of ear-rings on approval for him to give his bride. I think she seems very happy in a bluff, robust way.

Sunday, 29th August

Still more or less persistently wet. I rather love the rain on my face— it made my skin fit beautifully—but I wish we had had one day of glowing sunshine to illuminate the hills. Montagu was at home 'resting on the seventh day'.

Wet walk with Bluetooth in the morning. Discussion on self-centredness and he elaborated the charge brought against me, i.e. that people to me were means instead of ends—that I had no objective interest in them, and only liked them as 'mirrors', and in so far as they contributed to my vanity and self-interest, etc. It was admitted that I had powers of sympathy, but that might be intellectual purely and a necessary concession. Of course it isn't really true, but it is partially. I fear, and do recognise, that I am much more *self-centred* than *selfish*. I don't think I am selfish.

I had a walk with Montagu after tea. I found him excellent to talk to. He has a certain charm—the repulsiveness is purely physical. He said he thought Venetia terrifyingly 'selfless'. Letty and I had to do most of the top-whipping at meals. Both Montagus were on the whole very unvital, and Bluetooth never makes much noise in a group.

Monday, 30th August

Still rain. Frousted over fire in the hall. Heard rather a good epigram on Macaulay: 'He overflowed in conversation and stood in the slops.'

Went out with Bluetooth, cold depressing rain and we had one of our 'bad times'. He said he was 'pessimistic' and inclined to credit the sinister conception (Frances Horner) of my character, and to think I didn't 'like' him at all—beyond the old 'mirror' way. I ought to have quarrelled with him but didn't, only he distressed me—gave me the haunting, Undine feeling again. I must make it clear that if he *does* think me such a 'horror' (for it *is* a horror), I cannot understand how he can see me, and that I do not want to accept a relationship based only on the admiration and contemplation of what he considers my beauty and charm. It must be barren—what good could it be to him? 'I think I do still love you a little, if that's any comfort to you . . .' were his last words.

Came home feeling very depressed, to find Venetia in the most extraordinary mood of apparent complete ennui and lifelessness. I do hope she isn't really unhappy. Perhaps it's health. I'm sure the marooned honeymoon, even if unpleasant, is really the most wholesome. It doesn't do to dodge the situation and each other by living in a crowd.

We went from Aviemore by train about five o'clock. We didn't get into the house till 12.30. Found very touching little letter from Ettie enclosing my last letter to darling Billy. That and a Meredith poem Ettie had copied out for him were in his pocket when he was killed . . .

Tuesday, 31st August

Took John to Drem at eight o'clock to meet Beb, who was back on 'short leave'. He told me he thought he could get an extension, as he was feeling as if he would crack up. He looks well but distinctly strained, especially his eyes. They have been having a very bad time—dysentery, poisoned water, and ceaseless tension. One of his officer friends has gone off his head from sheer strain—horrible. Beb still rather angrily pro National Service.

It is a queer party for him to come back to. Angela (arrived in my absence), Adele and Grace—Adele is horrified by Angela, she certainly is a good foil for her; Papa quite mellow.

Wednesday, 1st September

Dr Ewart came to see Beb and said he was to have a fortnight's leave.

Thursday, 2nd September

Marigold[1] and I thought we would arrange dinner table, but it wasn't at all a success and Papa didn't seem at all pleased to have Angela beside him—they had most obviously had a row and the atmosphere

1. Lady Angela's daughter.

was very charged. They played bridge, Letty did 'stunts' to us in the sitting room, and I did a vampire with lip-salve for blood on my lips. Then Letty, encouraged by Grace and most of the party, courageously (but with great trepidation) decided to cut off her hair, which is pouring out since scarlet fever. Grace was the executioner: it was an anxious moment, it is so irrevocable. She had it done *à la club-head*—Joan of Arcish, like John and David.* Luckily it waves and goes into quite a good shape. It is amusing and I expect suits her as well as anyone, but I don't know that I really like it. I think it always looks a little uncanny or unpleasant—suggestive of prison, illness or suffragettes.

Friday, 3rd September

Breakfasted upstairs with Beb—the War Lord and the War Lady in shocking morning tempers. Letty, Marigold, Mary and I sat in the sitting room after dinner. We were chatting about Ego, eloping, etc., when poor Letty suddenly began to cry in earnest. A sudden gust of homesickness for him had proved too strong for her. Mary—thank heavens—has at last had letters from Tom and is happier.

Saturday, 4th September

We went to lunch at Glenconner. Elizabeth called for us in the motor and we picked up Margot on the Archerfield Links. She was looking ghastly ill and told us horrid news of Charles's[1] death—he died on the hospital ship from his wounds. It is too awful. I am beginning to get quite numb, one can't go on feeling with anything like normal sensitiveness. He was a rare and adorable creature.

Edgar, Pamela McKenna, and Lionel Earle are staying at Glenconner. The P.M. looked very ruddy and well. After lunch he settled down to a game of cribbage. I felt ill and on edge, and my nerves were rasped by everyone. We had a little languid tennis before tea. I don't know when I have been so unhappy, in an unsatisfactory indefinite way, as I am these days.

Sunday, 5th September

In the afternoon there was a terrific invasion—the Torbys and the De Traffords came over with an enormous retinue (we were twenty-six at tea), they simply swarmed on to the tennis court. I saw there was no hope of being able to play, so I walked home with Elizabeth.

1. Charles Lister.

I was still feeling utterly wretched, and she did not tonic me out of my gloom. She is very difficult to derail—I took her in to see Grace. Tea was pretty stupefying. The de Torby girls are rather attractive, but I completely fail to detect Vi de Trafford's famous beauty. Elizabeth booms her as an example of the luscious classic, but I *can't* see it. Her face doesn't attract even my curiosity in the least, and she hasn't even got dazzle or glitter. I think her mouth is so ugly, but I hear Margot thinks it the best she has seen.

Monday, 6th September

My life still creeping a very 'broken wing', though I felt physically better all day and then worse again in the evening. I am full of self-contempt at being able to think of myself. At least the war should be a red herring, but I begin to feel a horrid numbness creeping over me. The Tragedy is so spendthrift. Either Billy or Charlie's death a year ago would have absorbed one's thoughts for ages. If one begins to see things 'in proportion' one may as well begin to die. I have never had such a down with myself as I have had all this week.

Peaceful lunch with poor Angela away. At breakfast she told me there had never been a day in which she hadn't wished herself dead —it melted me. I wish I didn't always confuse compassion and affection. . . .

Beb and I dined with the Asquiths. I sat between the P.M. and Colonel Stewart, who is commanding Hood's Battalion in the Naval Division but has been home wounded for the last two months—such a nice simple man. Poker after dinner—Beb sat up late writing poetry.

Wednesday, 8th September

Divine, sunny, warm day and I felt quite well and happy. 'Lo what animals these women be . . .' We played tennis in the morning and I lost far too many shillings to Duff. Mary was quite off her game, and Duff and Marigold smashed us.

In the afternoon we walked up to links and Beb, Duff, Letty, Mary, Bibs, and I had a divine, very cold bathe. It was anguish at first, but I loved it. Bibs terrified by an anonymous naked man who was bathing. We had tea out on the grass afterwards, real delicious basking. Beb and I walked home together. Found Grace, Papa, and Mr Mure Ferguson all very depressed—Angela having been in a vile temper and behaved like a mad child absolutely ruining their golf at North Berwick. She is too extraordinary. I have never known her as moody

Mary Elcho (later Countess of Wemyss) with her sons and daughters at the turn of the century: Ego (later Lord Elcho) and Guy (right) are behind her, Bibs on her lap, Cynthia has the chair to her right, and Yvo and Mary are seated in the foreground

Mrs Percy Wyndham (Gan-Gan)   *Grandpapa—10th Earl of Wemyss*

Gosford House in East Lothian

and uncontrolled as she has been this time. She has been pretty poison
ous to poor meek Marigold.

Very merry dinner. Angela quite recovered in temper. We discussed
how much mutilation we would accept in order to gain a million
pounds. I wouldn't sacrifice a toe, but Duff and Angela seemed to
think they would gladly be mere torsoes on those conditions. Just
before going to bed Duff and I exchanged glances at each other's
diaries whilst the leaves fluttered past. 'Angela is the bloodiest bitch
I have ever seen', was the only entry in his which caught our eye and
mind.

Thursday, 9th September

Another divine day. We expected Yvo and Mamma to arrive at Drem
at 8.30. He was coming up for one day to say goodbye to us as, alas,
he goes out to France on Sunday. Bibs went to the station to meet
them and returned disconsolately without them, and with rumours of
a Zeppelin raid in London. We telephoned to Cadogan Square and
heard Yvo had missed the train on account of Zeppelins. The poor
weary arrived at about three o'clock, full of thrilling accounts of the
Zeppelin raid which had really been an adventure. I shall never get
over having missed it—it makes me furious!

Mamma was dining with Mr Balfour in Queen's Square when the
row began. He remarked 'I am responsible, and the guns are quite
inadequate.' Mamma saw a Zeppelin quite distinctly. Our own
defensive guns made a terrific noise, and there were a great many
fires blazing and casting a lovely copper glow on the sky. Yvo had
a splendid view from a roof and missed the train because it was impossible to get a taxi.

At dinner I was near Papa and Angela, and we had a wonderful
gastronomical conversation. She does know a lot about food. We
also discussed the minimum on which people could marry with any
hope of happiness. Angela put it at £5,000. She declaimed about the
oddness of the present generation's taste for having babies! and we
all discussed how many we wanted. 'How is it you never had twins,
Hugo?' made me laugh rather.

After dinner we had a 'huddle' in the sitting room and tried to
keep our spirits up. Yvo and Mamma went off into the night at about
eleven. It is terrible Yvo's going. Poor Bibs looked too desperately
miserable, never taking her eyes off his face. She has an Evelyn
temperament—I had to sleep with her in Mamma's bed, she felt so
unhappy and lonely.

Friday, 10th September

Altogether an irritating morning, so much waiting about for each other in long passages. The amount of time thus consumed in this house is incredible. The hall being at the end instead of in the centre of the house, and the fact that there are two front doors, leads to fatal results.

Lurid Angela row. I came into the sitting room, where she and Papa were, after lunch and she said, 'I'm the most disagreeable woman in the world, do you hear, Cynthia?'

Papa: 'I really think you are'.

She (to him): 'The mere fact that you can read these'—pointing to *The Times* broadsheets—'shows that we haven't one single idea in common, and how absolutely topsy-turvy the whole thing is!'

Then she said she was going away, and I heard- 'Hugo! Hugo, do you realise I shall never see you again?' etc., etc. However, everything seemed to have settled down by the evening and now she is staying until Sunday.

Saturday, 11th September

Beb and I dined with the Asquiths. I sat between P.M. and Mr Meiklejohn. P.M. told us of the Zeppelin raid. He and Eileen Wellesley and McKenna drove about to look at the debris. Violet Keppel was there and did some brilliant imitations: she has considerable 'pig-charm'. There is an 'affair' between her and Cis, and Beb and I felt sadly *de trop* as everyone else played bridge and we were left alone with them.

Sunday, 12th September

Beb and I motored into North Berwick for him to see doctor. He gave him another fortnight's leave. Sat next to Duff at lunch—Mary was on his other side, and we had rather an amusing conversation cross-examining him as to his past love affairs.

It was Mr Asquith's birthday: we had a cake for him, and he came to tea to see his grandchildren. They presented him with flowers. Michael looked very pretty, was very coquettish with his grandfather, and had a great success at tea. John silent and absorbed in his own thoughts. Colonel Stewart photographed the three generations together. Sat between Papa and Duff at dinner. Huddled in the sitting room afterwards. Discussion as to whether 'a really nice girl' would ever be proposed to by someone she didn't mean to accept.

Monday, 13th September

Frances and Edward arrived at tea-time. Venetia came with them, and we persuaded her to stay to dinner and go by the night train to Drem. Edward looking quite well again. Frances' face the same 'scene of savage grandeur'. Venetia came and sat in my room: I found her *very* restless-minded.

Dinner quite pleasant. Papa, Venetia, Edward, and Frances bridged. I read Beb's poem and Lawrence's letters aloud in the sitting room. Venetia went away at ten to eleven. We were all delightedly amused by the idea of her travelling down with the P.M.—funny enough! It will be almost their first meeting since the breach. Mary, Edward, Beb, and I had a discussion about the Montagus before going to bed.

Tuesday, 14th September

Mamma had a wonderfully courageous little letter from Ettie. She quoted a sentence from Charlie's last letter to Laura: 'I now know that I shall not die. This does not mean that I may not be killed.'

Papa very angry at dinner because Mary let out that she had been to a party to which he didn't want her to go. He was very angry with Guy for taking her.

Wednesday, 15th September

We sat up till twelve talking—rather interesting—Edward and I, and Beb and Letty. Via Mary and Strickland we discussed love, marriage, etc., etc., and, through Edward, I gained some lights on the creed of the Coterie. I'm sure there is an insidiously corruptive poison in their minds—brilliantly distilled by their inspiration, Raymond.* I don't care a damn about their morals and manners, but I do think what— for want of a better word—I call their anti-cant is really suicidal to happiness. I am much more in sympathy with the elder generation— what one might call Ettyism—which is an object of ridicule to them. Of course, the platitude that they are 'all right individually' is true, and they are excellent company, but I do think they are unsuccessful as hedonists because I am sure they shut more doors of enjoyment than they open. I think it rather a typical thesis that it can't make any difference to your feelings whether your son be killed by a bullet or by a bus: they hold countless similar logical fallacies. Beb and Edward are most unsympathetic to one another.

1915

Friday, 17th September

Letter from Bluetooth with a little political gossip. 'Conscription' isn't dead after all. Lloyd George has decided to stump the country and, if necessary, force a November election. He is having a fateful interview with the P.M. this evening. I wonder if the P.M. will come to the simple compromise of taking the power, but not using it until it is clearly required. They might agree on that, as L.G. with all his shallow knavery is said to have an obscure feeling that he ought not to injure the P.M.

Rather amusing discussion at tea on 'heart', springing from a statement of McKenna's (called a platitude by me and a paradox by Elizabeth) to the effect that I had the most heart of the women who were in the room. Margot was amongst them, which made Elizabeth demur—Some people (Adele perhaps?) obviously feel with their head, and Elizabeth said Margot 'thought with her heart', which I think rather good.

Beb felt dizzy again at dinner. He didn't play poker with us, but sat alone writing. I lost 2s 6d. Letty and Mary were sitting in my bedroom, watching me soaking my feet in mustard and water, when Beb came in looking rather queer and said he had broken a vase. He had smashed an inoffensive vase in Edward's room, because it 'wasn't pretty'—I remembered Lawrence's statement that Beb's destructive spirit had been aroused, and that he couldn't bear 'to see a house with its roof on' and I felt alarmed. I believe the desire to smash is a recognised symptom of nervous strain from Artillery work, and I do so understand it, only one *must* drastically discourage it, for there is nothing that it mightn't lead to, and his arguments when scolded were rather unhinged. 'Gallant and wonderful soldiers were being killed, so why should ugly things survive?' Such logic might lead to the smashing of Lady Horner's face.

I remonstrated with him and he became very emotional and *exalté*, talking with tremendous feeling, even tears, of the sufferings and gallantry of the men and officers. There is no doubt that his nerves, as quite distinct from his nerve, are much affected and he must be kept very quiet. I think he feels tremendously the sense of the completely different plane in which the men at the front are living, and the great gulf between them and those at home—he has a tremendous feeling of reverence for the soldiers, and I suppose a sort of sense that the beauty of their heroism is not fully appreciated. I think this produces a sort of sub-conscious irritation and indignation against the immunity and immobility of people and 'vases' at home.

80

Saturday, 18th September

Beb very, very tired. I sent for Dr Matheson, who said he had better
stay in bed and I sat with him a lot. He read my diary nearly all day.
I went for a short walk with Edward in the morning and he told me of
the vase incident—he was very nice about it.

Papa had arrived in the morning in a very evil temper and was
horrid to Mamma again. I found her sobbing in her room before dinner.
He had again said that she must live in London instead of Stanway
this autumn and winter, so that she won't be able to have people
staying with her. Poor darling, it is vile that she should be so harassed.
Angela (I suppose) has put it into his head that Mamma 'always gets
her way in the end'. Of course, like the other crisis, it will blow over—
he only stamps his foot, never keeps it to the ground, but it is such
waste of powder!

Papa, having spat out his spleen, was very mellow at dinner. He *is*
indolent.

Sunday, 19th September

Much happier. I spent the day pleasantly between my room and Beb's,
and didn't dress until dinner time. He seemed better. I am waging a
great anti-cigarette campaign and dole him out two after each meal.
Bibs smuggled him one.

I resurrected for dinner and sat beside Edward, who was very
agreeable. Elizabeth was sparkling away to Papa. We are playing a
game of scoring each other's typical remarks. When any one of us,
so to speak, mimics him or herself we exclaim 'pip-pip'—Ego's old
catchword. Beb had his dinner in the sitting room. Mamma, Letty,
Mary, Grace, and I joined him. The others were playing bridge. We
read Rupert Brooke's poems aloud, in turn and in chorus. Letty did
brilliant imitations of the Ladies Wenlock and Wantage.

Tuesday, 21st September

Letter from Bluetooth with the following political gossip:

I understand that the P.M. is to receive an ultimatum on Monday.
It is his usual day for a crisis, but he has warning of this one. L.G.,
I believe, has reviewed his forces and comes to the conclusion that
they are rather weak. Curzon, who is both hated and suspected of
personal enmity to Kitchener, Bonar Law who has no party (it all
belongs to A.J.B. again) and is sick of politics, Carson who wants to
get out of the Cabinet on any pretext because he thinks his hands are

stained with blood of the Dardanelles. Yet I'm not so confident that the P.M. will dispose of it easily, and the suggested compromise may prove congenial to his temperament.'

I took Basil, who arrived yesterday, out at three: we sat on the bench facing the sea until five, talking and gibbetting.* Papa and Edward had a day's shooting, during which Edward distinguished himself by shooting a keeper in the ear. Beb and I took John out—he was most entertaining, reciting 'Little Black Sambo' and singing 'Strong Beer'.

Thursday, 23rd September

Basil showed me his letter to Lord Wimborne putting his case in insisting on returning to the front—very good. Lord Wimborne actually got Kitchener to send Basil a message saying he wouldn't accept his services, as he ought to remain where he was in Ireland.

Divine sunset after tea—went first for a walk with Beb and then with Basil—very tired. After dinner we played clumps* for a little—it felt agreeably reactionary—then we played an odious gambling game of Diana's called 'Mr Dodd' and a little poker. I lost £1 6s.

Sunday, 26th September

The day was wet on and off, but with a most wonderfully clear transparent view. The Forth Bridge looked as though one might touch it, and we hadn't been able to see it all for over ten days. I spent most of the morning sitting to Basil in the drawing room. It is curious how incapable he seems of drawing *from* a model, he couldn't really get a likeness at all. At the end of the morning I turned the tables and in a few minutes executed something very much more like him, though a cruel caricature, than was the net result of my sitting for hours—he produced nothing. Grace came in and drew me, too, at the end of the time, but that was a failure as well. Apparently my chin is very disconcerting, as it fluctuates between great length and extreme shortness.

One of the most lovely sunsets I have ever seen. Mamma and Basil, followed by Beb and me, walked down to the links—perfectly divine. When we got back Basil and I sat out on the terrace for a bit. He is in great agitation about his prospects, as Lord Wimborne has been very high-handed in his anxieties to retain his service and has ensured that he will not be accepted in the Grenadiers. However, he is still obstinate and intends to overcome all obstacles.

It really has been great fun this party. Diana has been in excellent form, mimicking Maud Cunard, etc., quite brilliantly. She certainly is a remarkable and radiant being. To my amusement, Basil thinks her almost prohibitively ugly, but is disarmed by her fun.

Monday, 27th September

Basil, Beb, and I left by the early train to come here to Holker Hall. Bitter cold when we arrived. To our horror, found the party having tea out of doors: Moyra,[1] Dick (with real old-fashioned gout in the foot), Gilbert Russell, Betty, and Lord Cranborne—to whom she has just become engaged to the general excitement. Moyra *is* a hardy woman. Her fifth daughter is only six weeks old and she is already leading a normal strenuous life. To my misery, I was taken straight out for a long mountainous walk in my boots with high heels in the middle of my foot, without even being allowed to see my room.

I had a good rest before dinner, which was late and unpunctual. Sat between Dick and Gilbert Russell. The latter is very entertaining. Dick very amusing about his battalion of 'physically unfit'. Apparently they are promoted according to the number of their varicose veins and the flatness of their feet. We played letter game after dinner—quite amusing. Gilbert, who is a very droll cove, made a very odd guff remark at the letter game: 'Oh, Basil always tips the butler with his mistress's I O U.' I suppose he meant 'hostess's', but he never gave any very adequate explanation of his cryptic remark.

Tuesday, 28th September

Moyra's uncanny constitution is really a serious drawback in a hostess, and she rather chivvies one from sport to sport, leaving no gaps in the day for reading the newspapers or writing letters. It is the most unpunctual household I have ever been in—I have had to wait at least half an hour for dinner each night. Moyra is very pretty and very nice, but very thin mentally and I find her rather a non-conductor. He is a great dear, but too ugly.

Basil and his queer friend Gilbert Russell, whom he is exploiting here, are very amusing together. Lady Salisbury arrived in the evening as an 'in-law'. The 'young people' look very serenely happy. They dance alone to a pianola every evening for hours, which amuses us. He is rather bloodless and, like all his race, sits on the middle of his spine.

1. Lord and Lady Richard Cavendish: see index for all these names.

1915

Wednesday, 29th September

Perfectly lovely glittering blue day. Found Basil, Lady Salisbury, and Gilbert strolling in the garden before breakfast. At about eleven we went coursing, Moyra and Basil each being the fond possessor of a dog. Numerous long-shanked children came and helped beat. We went to a lovely place by the sea. It would have been a perfect morning without the dogs and the hares.

Thursday, 30th September

Weather still brilliant. Lady Salisbury is very delightful. I like her, even her hyena laugh. Lady Frederick Cavendish,* who arrived yesterday, distinguished herself at lunch. She was sitting next to Dick— Beb was on her other side and I was on the other side of Dick. Suddenly, I heard her say in a loud voice: 'Have the Asquiths gone?' It gave me a nightmarish feeling that I wasn't there, or that I oughtn't to be. She is generally such a bright pointful old trout, too. She is the widow of the man who was murdered in Phoenix Park.

I did my very best to come down late for dinner, but it isn't possible!

Friday, 1st October

Another lovely day. Lady Frederick is a great dear. We asked her to gamble the first night and she said, 'Yes, if it isn't for money.' I managed to read the whole of Well's *Bealby* in the interstices of this day—only fairly amused by it.

Saturday, 2nd October

The glory has at last departed and it was quite a grey day. I felt quite sorry to leave. Found a peaceful, reduced party at Gosford; Mamma, Grace, and Evie. They were furious with me for not having told them of the engagement. Excellent letter from Yvo describing the great engagement in which, by a fluke, he and Bim* had not actually participated. He seems to be enjoying glamour, and talks of the joy of having his legs swung along by thousands of marching men in night marches. John was very pleased to see me.

Monday, 4th October

Bibs dined with Mamma and me. She was rather a stormy petrel and took objection to Mamma using the word 'second-rate'. As a 'treat'—

Bibs, John and I all slept in my bed. It was a very exhausting one. John woke for good before six, was exquisitely amused by the situation, and it was like having a bicycle and a puppy in bed with one. When I woke up his arms were tight round my neck.

Tuesday, 5th October

Beb got here in time for lunch. He had been staying at Downing Street and had been to the Wharf for Sunday. He hadn't got any very definite news, but I gather London is fairly gloomy as to the progress of the 'Victory'. It was typical of the swift optimism, the way Grace and the others received the news that Sunday 26th of the beginning of the advance, when Mockett came in and announced we had taken such and such a number of guns and prisoners. I knew, when the casualties came out, that there would be a groan of reaction such as succeeded Neuve Chapelle, and now it seems doubtful whether anything worth while has been achieved.

Bluetooth said in a letter: 'It is not certain yet whether the attack has failed. Both Governments, French and English, were very much against an advance, but the soldiers insisted and were confident of success.' It is damnable about Bulgaria. I'm afraid it must enormously aggravate the Dardanelles situation.[1]

The Connors came to dinner. Mamma read Yvo's letters aloud. It is his birthday today, poor darling.

Wednesday, 6th October

The first number of Lawrence's paper the *Signature* has come. I *am* amused at the sort of stuff I have been circulating. They take such an exalted point of view about the war—calling it blasphemy, etc.—that I'm not at all sure that technically it doesn't amount to treason. Certainly it might be said to be discouraging to recruiting. Poor fools, it's not a good moment in which to hope to found a new religion!

Friday, 8th October

Depressing war-gossip from Bluetooth:
'The French were to begin their second attack today—they seem

1. On 25th September the Allies had launched a double offensive in the West, achieving considerable initial successes, but the Germans were for the first time defending in depth, and the long-drawn-out failure led to French's replacement by Haig. Bulgaria had joined the Central Powers on 6th September.

to do better than us. Apparently we gassed our own men at Loos, and a whole division of Kitchener's army ran away. There is also a story that one of our generals was captured playing bridge.'

After dinner I read Beb's poems aloud. He has had an enthusiastic letter of dewdrops from Strachey who is going to publish his Artillery poem in the *Spectator*.

Sunday, 10th October

By the morning post got a splendid seventeen-page-long letter from Yvo. He writes awfully well. His writing is very difficult, and it took us ages to read aloud at breakfast. We each snatched it in turn. Mamma laboriously copied it out after tea.

Monday, 11th October

Beb and I went by early train. For once I gave way and consented to go first class. I read the whole of Lawrence's last novel *The Rainbow*, which he had sent me. A strange, bewildering, disturbing book. It is full of his obsessions about sex conflict (all the lovers hate one another) and the 'amorphousness' of actual life. Excellent bits of writing, but still too much over-emphasis and brutality. One cannot count how often and how gratuitously he employs the word 'belly'.

We are staying at Bruton Street, which I hope is no bother to Evelyn. Sometimes this perpetual 'cuckooing' gets badly on my nerves. She is away and there are only two housemaids, so we can only have breakfast and tea in.

Tuesday, 12th October

Woke up to the inevitable of my first day in London—disinclination to pull wires and start people, and yet *désoeuvré*. I talked to the housemaid and we decided that we had better get in a girl to cook. Telephoned Mary. She was happy as she had heard Tom was invalided back to Alexandria—'trench sores' and sprained ankle.

Bluetooth came 5.15—awkward *à trois* while Beb was there. I wasn't much 'fun' *tête-à-tête* either. Sybil Hart-Davis came at a quarter to six. I quite liked her. Beb and I dined at Les Lauriers. Sybil, her bereaved sister, and Iris Tree were there: a queer trio. The last-named looked very striking in black velvet with a large red leather bag. We walked home. Beb read me a very good sonnet, and 'so to bed'.

Wednesday, 13th October

Beb lunched with Strachey—I with Bluetooth. Things fairly happy. He seems dissatisfied with my letters, he showed me some of them.

He told me the Cabinet of the day before had been a very stormy one. It was the first time the question of conscription had been raised at a full Cabinet—Kitchener had gone over to pro-conscriptionists. He said the reason why the recruiting had fallen off, as it undeniably has, is that the War Office are deliberately slackening their efforts—in fact discouraging—in order to make conscription necessary. He also said Lord Lovat claimed to have evidence that Northcliffe had actually spent money on impeding recruiting—this is most interesting. If it could be proved, of course, it would be high treason. . . . Bluetooth says there are now one and a half million potential recruits, instead of three-quarters of a million, as he told me in Scotland. However, he still says there is *no* good case for conscription and that there isn't nearly enough equipment even for the present number of recruits—not nearly enough rifles, and that if Kitchener says there is, he lies. . . .

Mamma and Bibs had just arrived from Scotland, and we dined with them, Letty and Mary at Queen's Restaurant, Sloane Square. Just as we had finished and were emerging, there was a bustle and we heard the magic word 'Zeppelin'. We rushed out and found people in dramatic groups, gazing skywards. Some men there said they saw the Zeppelin. Alas, I didn't! But our guns were popping away and shells bursting in the air. I felt excited pleasurably, but not the faintest tremor and I longed and longed for more to happen. Bibs was the only member of the family who had sufficient imagination to be frightened and Letty's fun was spoilt by the thought of the children. My only words were: 'Something for my diary!'

Beb and I went straight off to Downing Street, thinking it would be the best place for the entertainment, but, alas, it was all hopelessly over by the time we got there. They had had an excellent view, seeing the Zeppelin quite distinctly, and I had been asked to dine there—cruel luck! The P.M. and Margot were out, and Violet was entertaining Goonie Churchill, Hugh, Davies, and Bongie. Jack Tennant was dining with Bluetooth and they both came round, too. We telephoned Scotland Yard to enquire if there were any big fires, as we longed for excitement, but they said there was nothing. I felt very baffled.

Thursday, 14th October

We lunched at Adele's. Louis Mallet, Lady Minto, Anne and Lord

Ribblesdale were there—quite amusing. The does spat out Hun hate and the diplomacy in the Balkans was discussed a good deal. Sir Edward Grey in that context has been compared to 'sending Parsifal to a poker party'.

I went out with Violet in the afternoon. She took me to see Dorset House—the nest preparing for her and Bongie. It's a lovely little house, with perfect drawing room. They are lucky to get it. Bongie and Violet dined with us, and we went to the cinema, *The Birth of a Nation* at the Scala. We were awfully afraid we might miss a Zeppelin call, but nothing happened. The cinema is marvellous—loathsome black horrors—it was one of the worst experiences I have ever had. The battle scenes were brilliant, but I am most haunted by the black hands coming through the door of the besieged cottage. It seemed endlessly long. One felt years older when one emerged.

I got rather a sore letter from Lawrence. He is irritated by the criticisms of the *Signature* and *The Rainbow*.

Saturday, 16th October

Went to see Elizabeth. As I was leaving I met Diana Manners on the threshold. John Simon—looking very juiceless—came up and spoke to us. I thought him sufficiently irritating.

Diana: 'Isn't it awful. Raymond is going out next Wednesday.'

John Simon: 'No, I think it's quite right. The time has now come when one can only feel sorry for those who are unable to go.'

I have written to Evelyn to ask if I could have the children here for a bit—rather minded asking. I went to see Lady Howard de Walden.* I liked her immensely. She has such wholesome charm, without being in the least commonplace. She is an unaggressive tonic: if I was playing that game about her I should compare her to a delicious soap, she really rather braces one. She talked a lot of Egypt and said she was very much in love with Ego. She had a pleasant theory that Ego had already started for Salonika, where he is going with a composite brigade. I'm afraid it is possible, as it is secret, and he might have been unable to cable the news to Letty. She and Mary go out next Wednesday. It will be too hard if she just misses him.

As I was walking home Constantine Benckendorff passed in a taxi. He stopped, drove me home, and stayed about an hour. I was delighted to see him again. He chaffed me about liking war—a scandal Nathalie had been spreading about me. He has come to London to study 'Aircraft Defences'.

Sunday, 17th October

I found my way to Byron Villas, Vale of Health, Hampstead. I found the Lawrences having tea in a dear, clean, little room. Both are in an acute state of misery. The war is driving him quite mad with rage—he just sits and gibbers with fury. He sees no hope in the country, nothing but war, and the war he sees as the pure *suicide* of humanity —a war without *any* constructive ideal in it, just pure senseless destruction.

His theory is that the nation doesn't *really* want it to stop—because of the nullity of life, as if in a sense it were the result of a vacuum. He insists that the fact of my enjoying Zeppelin raids proves that I am bored: this I deny. He admits that a kind of beauty, romance, and glamour is achieved, but insists that they are purely incidental—the sugar coating to a pill. I felt really sorry for him, it is a genuine *supplice* to him. Their rooms are delightful, but he already feels he cannot stay any longer and talks of going to America, as he says there is at least some 'hope' there. Of course he would loathe it. He came half way home with me on a bus.

Beb and I dined with Letty for a Hell—very successful little dinner in most imposing dining room: Evan, Constantine,* Diana, Lett, and ourselves. Very amusing discussion as to whom we would jettison amongst the giants in literature and art—tremendous blasphemies were bandied. It arose from someone having heard the four great painters whose claims Sargent entirely repudiated—Velasquez and Mantegna were two of them. Constantine was divine. I was glad to find him splendidly 'sound' about Dickens and Hardy. Dickens is one of my great touchstones.

Monday, 18th October

I went to Harrods Store with Bibs and ordered an ear-shield for Yvo. Beb and I dined at Downing Street. Family party: P.M., Raymond and Katharine, Violet and Bongie—Raymond with a moustache. He is supposed to be going out on Wednesday; it seems more dream-like than anyone else somehow. Katharine looked lovely and rather wretched, poor darling! I was much chaffed about D. H. Lawrence. Apparently *The Rainbow* is causing an explosion on account of its 'belly', etc., motif. His incidental 'foulness' is a great pity, because he will be read flippantly for that only—the last thing he would wish. People will read him *for* it, instead of *in spite* of it.

Tuesday, 19th October

Evelyn came up this morning with rather a bomb-shell of news that Aubrey and Mary were arriving home quite soon. As he is invalided, this means turning out.

I lunched at Cadogan Square. I can't remember who was there—it's all so blurred now. I came back, and was sitting here, waiting for Aileen and George Brodrick. I felt strangely restless and couldn't settle down to read, the telephone rang and I rushed to it, welcoming the diversion. A strange voice answered: 'I am speaking for the War Office—from Captain Charteris.' And then: 'We've got very bad news here. . . .' Even then, from some strange lack of imagination, I never guessed. I thought it was Zeppelins, or something public. 'It's about Yvo Charteris. . . . You must be prepared for the very worst. . . .'

Then I knew and rushed upstairs, and gradually the horrible pain penetrated. Oh how it hurts and how little one ever faced the possibility for an instant! Darling, darling little Yvo—the perfect child and youth. How can one not be going to see him again? None of the others could have quite emptied the future for each of us quite like him. He was the greatest luxury in one's life with his overwhelming charm—his brilliancy, sweetness, and that supernatural sympathy and understanding. One looked *forward* to him always as an ever-increasing joy. There was something so *expectant* about him, with his interest and amusement in life, it was like someone just sitting down to a wonderful banquet. How can one believe it, that it should be the *object* to kill Yvo? That such a joy-dispenser should have been put out of the world on purpose. For the first time I felt the full mad horror of the war. . . .

One might have expected it, but I had such a strong instinct that he was coming back and anticipated the fun of having him with a slight wound—such as he had joked about in his letter. Now this sheer finality and silence—a complete precipice—*nothing* one could do for him. One felt so that there must be something. Aileen arrived, and then I had to begin to think of what I must do about the others. I thought perhaps Evan had gone to Mamma himself. Aileen telephoned to him and he said he couldn't leave the War Office. Then I realised I had got to go and tell Mamma myself. I left a note for Beb and Aileen came with me. Mamma was closeted with the new governess and I found Mrs Chapin in the sitting room. She wanted to stay, but I got her to go and then poor darling Mamma came in. Of course no words were necessary, my face told her all—and I think she really expected it.

She was wonderful, quite calm after the first moment of horror. About five minutes afterwards she said something so sweet and natural, just what one feels when one is dazed: 'What a bore!' Mrs Chapin insisted on coming back and then Letty arrived, having heard the news at Bruton Street. Beb brought her. They were both shattered. Then we had to think of the worst horror—the telling Mary and Bibs. We telephoned for them to come back from the Stricklands: I think they guessed and I shall never forget their poor petrified faces. If it wasn't for Tom, I don't know what would happen to Mary. He was like a twin brother—practically her life. Letty and I went round to tell Grace: she was heartbroken. I don't believe anybody can ever have made himself more loved in nineteen years, but then—quite dispassionately—I do think he was perfect.

I went home—dined with Beb. Grace, Letty, Mary, Guy, and Frances dined at Cadogan Square. I believe it was awful. I meant to join them directly afterwards, but my head was too bad until I had taken aspirin. I went at ten and found them all gone. I went round to the Stricklands to say goodbye to Mary. She and Letty had wisely adhered to their plan of starting for Alexandria the next morning. Poor darling, she was quite frozen, automatically greasing her face. My terror is that they find Ego and Tom gone to Salonika.

Wednesday, 20th October

Oh the anguish of waking to such heartache and how immune my life has been! The extraordinary difference between people—even Billy whom one thought one was so fond of—and one's own little brother. Somehow with the others who have been killed, I have acutely felt the loss of them but have so swallowed the rather high-faluting platitude that it was all right for them—that they were not to be pitied, but were safe, unassailable, young, and glamorous for ever. With Yvo—I can't bear it for him. The sheer pity and horror of it is overwhelming, and I am haunted by the feeling that he is disappointed. It hurts me physically.

I lunched with Guy and Frances. Mamma and Bibs came. Then I went out shopping with Mamma; we bought reach-me-downs at Selfridges. Adele had lent me her motor for the day. I gave Mamma tea here. Bibs came and lay on the bed with me. Poor little darling, she is too piteous—she can't even cry! I cried myself nearly blind, which brings a merciful exhaustion. She is the most sensitive, imaginatively sorrowing child in the world and simply idolised Yvo. His photograph was always under her pillow. I said something about

Monica having lost two brothers, and she said, 'Oh, I'm sure Ickey was at least six brothers. . . .'

Thursday, 21st October

went to Cadogan Square. Poor Papa is most piteous—heartbroken and just like a child—tears pouring down his cheeks and so naïvely *astonished*. He had never expected it. I think he really loved Yvo far the most of his children, and was so proud and hopeful about him. He said he had never given him an excuse to be angry with him for a moment.

Poor Katharine came to see me in abject despair. Raymond had gone off the day before. Frances had seen him march past her house just before I got there for lunch. Katharine seems quite, quite hopeless about him, she might have just seen him into his coffin. It is all too awful.

Friday, 22nd October

Mamma called for me in the morning, and we went to Selfridges and bought hats. Bibs lunched with Beb and me. At three I called for Adele, and she took me to St. James's Palace and instructed me in bandage rolling—it isn't bad work, but I preferred the respirator job.

Saturday, 23rd October

We took John to the Zoo, and entirely failed to make him even see a lion or a tiger. He cut them dead. I wonder if there is anything wrong with his eyes. Felt in a mood of black-bitter nausea about the war. I'm afraid Lawrence's views are beginning to soak in.

We went down to Stanway by the 4.45. The pain of Stanway is in a way intense—the whole of that little passage is so imbued with Ickey. Every inch reminds one of him—sometimes as a child, sometimes as a youth. Yet, in a way, the atmosphere is healing. As Bibs says, one *knows* he is there. The way she talks about it is most wonderful and touching. She said it made her 'burst' to be here at first, but she has found a very bright little star for him.

She said: 'Ickey came and talked to me that Tuesday night. He just came and whispered to me, like he used to when he found me crying in bed at Stanway: "Cheer up, Bibs!" ' I think she is helping Mamma, she is so sentient and spiritual. She can't bear to be left alone for an instant. Mamma is wonderfully brave, but it makes one's heart ache to see her. Bibs said it was extraordinary how everything had changed. 'Stanway is different, and even John looks bigger.' Dinner was not so bad as I dreaded. Papa is miserable.

Sunday, 24th October

The London colonel sent a letter from Yvo's colonel at the Front. Yvo was leading a party of bombers in a gallant and futile attempt to take a German trench—there was an enfilading fire from machine guns and he was killed by six bullets. Thank God it must have been instantaneous! The colonel said he had the makings of a very good officer and was a great loss. The rest is silence.

This letter made Bibs sob for the first time. I suppose it made her realise the physical side. It poured and poured ceaseless rain all day. Stanway was weeping. Bibs' face all day was haunting.

The service was at six. Very beautiful and touching amongst all the people who loved him as a child. The bier stood in the chancel with a Union Jack spread over it and a laurel wreath leaning against it. The service was conducted by Bateman and Ashwin, and the Priest gave a little address. I liked it very, very much. He loved Yvo so—I knew he would do it well. He dwelt lovingly over Yvo's classical knowledge. Prew looked a magnificent effigy of woe.

Bibs slept with me. Poor little darling, it is too awful! She moaned like someone in great physical pain. She tears one's heart.

Wednesday, 27th October

Walked with Beb to see the German guns in the Horse Guards' Parade. I left him at Downing Street. I lunched with Bluetooth. Afterwards we went to Harrods, to look at writing bags for his birthday present to me. Constantine came to tea with me. His aircraft job is over and he goes to Archangel at the end of the week. He was divine—we agreed about immortality.

Thursday, 28th October

I went out by myself at about 11.30 and searched several shops for despatch boxes for myself: sent a selection to Bluetooth on approval.

Lawrence came to lunch with us—Frieda has a cold and didn't accompany him. He was in excellent form, really delightful. It is difficult to believe he can have written *The Rainbow*—I see no connection. Beb liked him very much. We had a great deal of war talk, but he is much calmer and less tortured than he was last time I saw him. He has decided to what he calls 'lapse'. They have settled to go away to Spain. I think he really dreads being recruited, which he would consider the 'supreme acquiescence to a gigantic horror', but of course he is much too consumptive. He was merciless about poor little Eddie, giving an excellent imitation of his lamenting Rupert Brooke over his evening whisky. He was brilliantly funny about the décor of this very harmless sitting room. He told me Frieda had at last abandoned the idea of her children and was very miserable.

Beb and I went to see the Zeppelin damage in Lincoln's Inn. Tonks came to tea, and then Eddie, and then Whibley: the latter two inspected their godson Michael. What a funny *levée*—Lawrence, Tonks, Eddie, and Whibbles. Whibbles stayed till twenty to eight—which upset my plans.

We dined at Downing Street. Violet, Bongie, and Cis. I went to see Margot in bed. She cried over Yvo: said she loved him better than any other boy and had wanted Elizabeth to marry him. She said: 'How could your mother let him go?'—a terrible point of view. Violet very nice.

Friday, 29th October

Beb insisted on taking me to St Paul's Cathedral, where a memorial service was being held for Miss Cavell. We didn't get in, but saw the crowd outside—disgusting, just like Derby Day!

Basil came at three. He has come over from Ireland for a few days and is staying with the Russells. Beb did some 'dentist-wrecking'.* We have only got one sitting room. Basil also came to dinner with us. Beb went out just before and bought some very good liqueur brandy which they enjoyed immensely. Beb had complained bitterly at the prospect of an *à trois* dinner, but it went off very well. Basil and I gibbeted afterwards.

Saturday, 30th October

Thick, saffron fog torturing the back of one's nose even inside the house. We just caught the 4.45 to Stanway. Train horribly crowded and I got cut off from my book. I had had a letter from Lawrence saying he had done a 'word-picture' of me in a story and warranted it was better than Sargent. I felt very uneasy, dreading a minute 'belly' analysis.

94

Sunday, 31st October

Very wet all the morning, leaves showering off the trees in golden bushels. Lawrence's story arrived by the morning post. It is called 'The Thimble'* and is extremely well written, I think, though the symbolism of the thimble is somewhat obscure. I *was* amused to see the 'word-picture' of me. He has quite gratuitously put in the large feet. I think some of his character hints are damnably good. He has kept fairly close to the model in the circumstances. The heroine is twenty-seven, the husband a sometime barrister who has become a lieutenant in the Artillery.

The Priest came to dinner. Papa read 'The Thimble' aloud.

Thursday, 4th November

I am crystallising into a sort of ritual these days here, and greatly resent any interruption to my routine. I read in bed in the morning, do exercises, breakfast at nine off raw egg and puffed wheat with Mamma, Bibs, and Sockiloff.* Bring Michael to Beb's bed, then I write till 11.30, when I push John's perambulator for half an hour. At twelve we play tennis, which I am enjoying immensely and rapidly improving at. Half an hour reading rest before lunch, and then again afterwards until we play tennis at three o'clock.

Three delightful soldiers came to tea with the sister. One charming man was a schoolmaster from Fife. One poor boy had had his leg amputated right high up—very piteous. Mamma, Bibs, and I motored the soldiers back to the hospital and attended a concert in the ward. Most delightful and touching atmosphere: most of them had such gentle faces, one felt the horror of their returning to such Hell. They sat about in groups with arms entwined like affectionate monkeys. I felt very melted and for the first time that I should like to nurse myself. One boy, who had been gassed, had a really lovely tenor voice.

Friday, 5th November

Made a Titanic effort and answered poor Lawrence's last extraordinary letter about the war in which, and with the assistance of a poem, he tries to convince me that we ought to 'down tools'. He appears to think that *I* could stop the war, if only I really wanted to! He writes wildly about the disintegrating process of war, etc., and makes rather arbitrary distinctions between *in*trinsic and *ex*trinsic evil—all eloquent enough, but I'm afraid his feet quite leave the ground.

I read a good many of Horace Walpole's letters with considerable amusement: he reminds me so much of Evan. A cable arrived from Mary saying they were going to be married in Egypt and would wait until the 20th, supposing Mamma and Bibs would come out—arriving on the 18th. Mamma doesn't seem to want to go, unless it should prove to be the one chance of seeing Ego, who thinks he will be going to Gallipoli.

Saturday, 6th November

Uncle Guy joined in the tennis. After lunch he went to inspect the hospital and we all escorted him. I can't bear the slightly criminal atmosphere that pervades a hospital. It seems monstrous that being wounded should be penalised and soldiers allowed no alcohol while civilians swill away. Their boundary is tiny: they are only allowed to walk up and down in front of the hospital unless they have an escort. All speak of Eliza in glowing terms. The one-legged boy showed me a 'photo' of his young lady, which I thought a great honour.

Kitchener's departure in the papers—what can it mean?

Sunday, 7th November

Letter from Bluetooth in which he said the rumour loudly circulated by Margot was that French was recalled and Kitchener dismissed. Anyhow, Kitchener has gone to France and at present the P.M. has taken over the War Office again.

Monday, 8th November

Beb and I motored into Cheltenham and caught the 12.30. We got to Pixton, after many changes, at about six o'clock. Aubrey and Mary didn't arrive till 8.30, both looking thin and gaunt. I think Lawrence would rejoice and say both Beb and Aubrey were looking 'chastened'.

Wednesday, 10th November

Lovely morning with beautiful lights on dead leaves and West Country hills. Aubrey went out shooting. Beb coquetted with the idea, but put it off till the afternoon and then altogether. A great deal of feudalising went on all day. Pixton is a real stronghold. Mary does it very well and loves it. She sat in my bedroom before dinner and cross-examined me on the subject of 'lovers'. She told me Lord Alex Thynne* was engaged to a Gaiety Girl—funny enough!

By the second post came a letter from Lawrence saying *The Rainbow* had been suppressed. Some reader had appealed to a magistrate and got him to ban it. Fancy taking the trouble! There is something very funny about my having godmothered the one suppressed book.

Thursday, 11th November

Beb and I went up by a twelve o'clock train, leaving Aubrey and Mary to follow. The Admiralty have issued warnings about submarines and Aubrey will not countenance Mary going out on a P. & O., so she is going to try and beg a passage on a hospital ship.

Soon after I got home Evie[1] appeared, bringing the heart-rending news that George[2] had died of dysentery at Malta. We had heard he was dangerously ill about a week before. At first I felt quite numb, as if I were incapable of feeling any further emotion, then I felt so bitterly unhappy and almost angry. Dear George—it is practically another brother, and one around whom such memories of fun and dearness are wreathed. Apart from the loss, what tears one's heart is the thought of his dying alone in a strange hospital. One has seen him through so many illnesses in sybarite homes and how loveably and childishly dependent on one he used to be. Last year, when he was at Stanway for weeks after his appendicitis, night after night Mary and I used to have to sit with him, each holding one hand until he went to sleep. I simply can't bear to think of it. . . .

Oh why was I born for this time? Before one is thirty to know more dead than living people? Stanway, Clouds, Gosford—all the settings of one's life—given up to ghosts. Really, one hardly knows who is alive and who is dead. One thing is that now at least people will no longer bury their dead as they used. Now they are so many one *must* talk of them naturally and humanly, not banish them by only alluding to them as if it were almost indelicate.

Friday, 12th November

Horrible wet fog. Beb and Mary called for me and we taxied to Hampstead to introduce Mary to the Lawrences. We felt very shy in anticipation, but it was a success and Mary really appreciated him. Our conversational *hors d'œuvre* was Ottoline, and then we got right into War in the Abstract and he was himself. It was interesting and amusing. Frieda looked wonderfully Prussian. With a helmet she would do well as a picture of Prussia. She kept alternately accusing Beb of being a

1. Mrs. Rivers-Bulkeley.   2. George Vernon.

soldier and a lawyer. I should think we stayed two hours, then Lawrence walked us to the Tube.

I am always alarmed by the misery and hystericalness of his letters —but when one sees him again one can scarcely connect the man with his writing. There is so much delicious laughter in him which he entirely extinguishes on paper. In his last letter he told me he heard I had said, '*The Rainbow* is like the second story in the Prussian Officer, only worse.' I asked who it was. And it was that little sneak Murry, who had eavesdropped on Basil and me at that water-colour exhibition whilst pretending not to recognise me.

I lunched with Bluetooth. He told me Winston had resigned and that there was talk of Mr Balfour going to the War Office. He told me a funny story of Venetia sitting in front of fire and soliloquising in a dreamy voice, 'I wonder if that old swine is still in bed.' (Montagu has a habit of going to bed after lunch.)

Saturday, 13th November

Telegram from Beb saying he was in bed at Downing Street with a chill, he thought, and couldn't come down. Very annoyed. Then a most annoying and perplexing telegram came from Margot: 'Think you had better come up tomorrow evening see Parkinson about poor Beb. Wire Parkinson what time you get up.' I couldn't understand it and didn't know what to do.

Wired to Margot: 'Cannot understand telegram. Came down here for George's service. Will come up tomorrow evening unless you wire me to come early.' It is too *tiresome*—just as I had got back here. If only Beb had come down with me on Friday. I had such a strong instinct against his stopping up. I *loathe* going to Downing Street. Damn! George's nice devoted servant Fern arrived for the memorial service.

Sunday, 14th November

I got a wire from Beb first thing in the morning saying: 'Stay for George's service. Parkinson has me here in bed, possibly for several days.' So I decided to stay.

We had just the same service for George as for Yvo, with different hymns, and the poor broken-hearted Priest made another address. He did it beautifully and all but broke down. He talked of George being welcomed by his 'foster-brother'. I talked to Fern for a long time. He was very touching—that immaculately professional butler with tears pouring down his cheeks. He said, 'You know, he was very much more than a master to me.' He couldn't bear not to have been there to look after him at the end after having 'mothered' him through so many illnesses. 'His Lordship was never much of a one to get up in the morning, but when I used to come in and tell him how late it was, he used to say, "Oh, it's all right, Fern, I'm at Stanway now." '

I got to Downing Street not much before 10.30. Found Beb in—very pale—and he told me he had had a fainting fit at luncheon on Saturday. I was horrified. If only they had told me, of course I would have flown up. I found Bongie, and then Violet came in and told me about it. It must have been terrifying. He had been looking ill all the time, turned a ghastly colour, shook all over, and fainted. Mary Herbert was there and supported him. He had a rigor and was unconscious for quite a long time, and his heart very bad. They sent for Parkinson. He says he is on the very verge of spinal neuritis. There is a quantity of cases of this kind affecting people in various ways, resulting from strain at the front. He says he must be quiet in bed for a fortnight, but that he may be moved down to the country. He is not to smoke or drink *at all*, poor darling. I sat with Violet, Cis, Davies, and Bongie for some time, and then Violet stayed with me while I went to bed—I couldn't get to sleep.

Monday, 15th November

Beb slept well, but was very drowsy and weak most of the day. I had to feed him like a baby. He is missing cigarettes, but not nearly so much as I should have feared. The room he is in is cold and passagy—very difficult to make comfortable. I couldn't make the fire burn properly and shivered there all day. Parkinson came earlyish and said Beb was going on all right. Mary came at about eleven. While she was there Margot appeared—I followed her out into her bedroom. I noticed her glance of melodramatic commiseration and the most amazing scene ensued. She began: 'This is a fearful blow, isn't it?'

I said, 'Well, I think it's really rather a good thing that it should be defined, so that one can really keep him quiet now.'

Margot: 'Ah, but do you think he *will* be able to pull himself together? I don't. Oh my poor Cynthia, you've got years of anguish before you! I know it so well with poor Lucy.'

I gasped, wondering what she meant, as I knew Beb was not suffering from arthritis. Gradually I realised her meaning—that poor Beb was suffering, not really from his experiences at the Front, but from a

99

protracted course of drunkenness. She fabricated corroborating words for Parkinson: I suppose you know what that young man is suffering from? Alcoholic poisoning!

She has an obsession about drink: her grandfather and Lucy's husband both died of it, and she has had anonymous letters about the P.M. Beb often what I call 'takes his receiver off' and is very distrait, especially when bored—as he is by her—and on these occasions has an odd, almost dazed manner. This she attributed to drink. He is just as likely to be in such a mood first thing in the morning as after dinner. I suppose what Parkinson said was, that, with neuritis, no alcohol should be drunk; that his condition was aggravated by having had it; and *even* that, supposing he had not drunk before the war, he would have been less likely to succumb. She probably suggested to him that Beb was a drunkard. Retrospectively, she always puts her own words into the mouth of her interlocutor, I have noticed this over and over again.

What I am *positive* about is that I have never seen Beb 'drunk': in my opinion his misfortune is that he has too strong a head, and is able to drink more than is healthy. She couldn't believe that I didn't realise that Beb was a regular drunkard, and was astonished to hear Parkinson had not told me. She said he had told her he was going to. She poured out a lot of novelette twaddle about my being the only person who could save him, and so on. It was altogether a horrible scene. I cried and was furious, but very inarticulate.

She said: 'Do you suppose he drinks in your house? He goes out for it, etc.' And that he often lay for hours on the sofa here. She said Mr Balfour! and lawyers had spoken to her about it. This means she has spoken to them—*damn* her! She told me of the anonymous letters she had about Henry, and said there must be some 'terrible temptation' in the family. She wished that everyone would be a teetotaller! She said she had told Henry[1] she would leave him, and she had left him at four o'clock in the morning—all sorts of megalomaniac twaddle. I must say the more I see of her, the more I entirely exonerate Violet. I felt so sore and bubbling over that I tactlessly told poor Beb. He said he had noticed Parkinson's surprise at finding a glass of untouched brandy by his bed: 'Do you mean to say you can have that there without drinking it?'

Tuesday, 16th November

I had told Violet about the Margot bother: she interviewed Parkinson

1. The Prime Minister.

when he came in the morning and so did I. It was just as I supposed, the words put into his mouth were pure fabrication, or at least the substance of what she had said to him. Parkinson shrugged his shoulders at her and said she had obsessions, but one wonders how straight he speaks to her himself. The worst of her is that when you tell her how inaccurate she has been, it seems neither to astonish nor impress her. She expressed no indignation and scarcely surprise at hearing Parkinson had denied having said what she attributed to him. She's too amazing! What makes one furious and miserable is that one knows she probably says it to many other people. It really is a shame....

Mary[1] came to see Beb before lunch and I walked part of the way home with her. I told her about the drink business, and she said she had had a row about it with Margot directly after Beb fainted. Bluey came at 6.30. I told him about Margot, and he said she *had* said something to Aggie[2] about it. Damn her! Fancy telling Aggie. Even if it were true, it would be Margot's business to *conceal* it from outsiders instead of advertising it. Mr Asquith went off to France with the 'Defence Committee'. The others dined out. Violet came up and saw me in bed. She has been very nice these days.

Wednesday, 17th November

Margot gave me five pounds. Hush money! She also lent me a motor in which I went off to Hampstead to see Lawrence. The Authors' Society want to contest the suppression of *The Rainbow*. It ought to be an amusing lawsuit. This may postpone their departure to America. They were going next week. He says he cannot 'live' here any longer. While I was there a telegram came from Morrell, asking if Lawrence would come and see him at the House of Commons about *The Rainbow*. So I drove him back to London.

Beb and I, with glorious paraphernalia of bathchair, hot-water bottle, and thermos flask went down to Stanway by the 4.45. Mamma met us at the station. Beb all right on journey. I found amazing letter from Lawrence suggesting our coming out to America. Children well.

Thursday, 18th November

Beb none the worse for his journey. He is comfortably established in my lovely room, and I am half there and half in his dressing room. It is very cold here—hard white frost—but very lovely. Told Mamma the Margot tale while I was going to bed.

1. Mary Herbert.   2. Lady Jekyll.

1915

Friday, 19th November

Amusing letter from Basil about *The Rainbow* and a kindly one from Lady Jekyll about Margot and Beb.

I got up late. Beb all right and quite serene in bed. He has sent some of his poems to a publisher. He wants them brought out in cheap booklet form.

Saturday, 20th November

Bitter cold. This was the day on which Mary was by way of being married at Cairo, and so the bells were rung here and at Didbrook at intervals all day. We kept running up to the Cockpit to listen to them. Halliwell came to see Beb and stayed with him for quite an hour. He pronounced him an 'interesting case', and seems to think it will be a long business. His spine is very sensitive.

I went and did 'clerical' work for Eliza—enjoyed the writing out of lists in an ostentatiously clear hand very much. Someone rang up on the telephone and asked if we had had any ear or arm amputations. Bibs was working in the scullery. Ettie arrived at Evesham. Mamma met her and we drove back from Winchcomb together. Evan arrived before dinner. Quite amusing dinner—discussed whether the Coalition was 'cynical' or not. Evan said Lloyd George had said to Kitty that Mr Asquith was the obstacle, and that nothing would be done until he was removed. Evan said he would sooner have Lloyd George— folly, I think. I told him about Margot.

A telegram to say the wedding had been postponed—the reason assigned was that no leave could be obtained. It's very funny, having pealed all the bells. . . .

Sunday, 21st November

Cold grey day. We had a real old-time, animated Ettie breakfast. She went to church, arriving only halfway through the sermon!

Quite an amusing discussion at lunch as to which of us were influenceable and which uninfluenceable, with many ramifications, as in which nuance it was a spike and which a dewdrop. Mamma, Ettie and I sat for some time in a tearful trio reading letters and talking of the war youths. Bibs' blank verse poem describing a family in wartime —with the youngest at the Front—written just after Yvo went out is too touching . . . real poetry of emotion.

I had a long talk with Ettie in her bedroom. She was wonderful

102

and most touching. It is so amazing the way in which she, externally, is absolutely normal in company. The same old extraordinary zest unimpaired, and the exaggerated interest in everyone and everything. One almost begins to wonder and think it inhuman, but directly she is alone with one she is just a simple, effortless woman with a bleeding heart. Tears pour down her cheeks, and she talks on and on about the boys, and yet preserving such wonderful sympathy for others—so understanding and sensitive about Yvo. One really feels great love and reverence for her. . . .

She says she thinks it illogical to be so unhappy with her conviction that they would not mind and are happy. She seems to have no qualms about immortality, and cannot account for the fearful pain of their loss. She told me she found the complete, sudden disappearance of Billy harder to bear than the long, loving farewell to Julian. One wonders —she has had experience of each. . . .

Monday, 22nd November

Sat over the breakfast table with Ettie for a long time . . . we had rather fun over the Margot alcohol business, she also read some of Lawrence's letters with great interest.

Ettie went away after lunch from Evesham. I was dropped at Winchcombe and did a little writing for Eliza. Talked to the delightful grenadier who knew Yvo and was wounded the same day. He said Bibs looked as if her heart had fallen into her feet when he told his battalion.

Tuesday, 23rd November

Bluetooth writes that he has been involved in the Margot-Beb fuss. I am rather glad. Mamma, Bibs, Pamela, and I went for a dog walk in the morning up to the old beech tree. There was quite a thick, dank fog. Besides Pina, Gan-Gan's dachshund and Uncle Guy's greyhound are here, so the dog tyranny is worse than ever. They're always on the wrong side of the door, colds are caught turning them out at night, and all through meals Mamma and Gan-Gan steadily cook for them.

An answer came from Sidgwick and Jackson the publisher to whom Beb had sent his poem, saying they would publish them at once in sixpenny booklets, giving him a royalty of a penny on each copy sold. I am totally ignorant and don't know whether these are good or rotten terms—it doesn't seem much. I expect the best way would be to publish at your expense, the initial cost could be but little. I wrote to both Whibley and the Professor asking for advice. I also got off my letter to Margot. I thought she would consider silence acquiescence.

Thursday, 25th November

I had arranged to pay a cold-blooded visit to the Professor at Oxford. I arrived about 10.30. The dear Professor met me and lamented that he had to deliver a lecture on Crabbe. I insisted on going to it, and sat nibbling ginger biscuits amongst a crowd of attentive Negroes and nuns. Afterwards we walked up to the Hangings together, had a mutton lunch, and then they both walked me back to catch the 3.8 train. They were both very dear, and it was quite a success. Their son Hilary, who has been out for ten months, has completely broken down. The Professor says penny royalty is quite as much as he ever gets, and advises acceptance of Sidgwick's terms. I had had a long interesting letter about publishing from him in the morning.

Friday, 26th November

Yvo's soldier servant Bates had written to say he had ten days' leave and could come down here. He arrived at eleven, bringing his wife. Mamma and I saw him first in the sitting room. He was the greatest darling imaginable. I have *never* seen such charm—extreme good looks and the manners of an ambassador. That rather irritating phrase 'one of nature's gentlemen' echoed through one's mind. He had such lovely tact and told us all he could of darling Yvo. 'I should like to assure you that Mr Charteris was absolutely fearless—perfectly cool— and I never saw him in the least depressed, not even as it were melancholy.' The Germans were occupying the same trench. That is why artillery preparation was impossible. Yvo's death was undoubtedly instantaneous. He said he had told him so much of Stanway. He said, what we had not heard before, that Yvo had already been hit in the arm, but had refused to take any notice of it. Poor darling, he must have had the joy of thinking he would get home with ideal arm wound. If only we had had him back just once, how he would have loved it!

Saturday, 27th November

Very hard white frost and bitterly cold. Mamma went off at 10.30 to motor over to Sudbury for a memorial service for George Vernon. She left me to the sinking ship of the Needlework Guild. The party began to assemble at a quarter to four. Grandmamma was invaluable as a peepshow. They spread out their offerings on the dining room table and then we had tea in the hall. After that, we moved to the drawing room and played the immemorial game of musical chairs. A niece of Mrs Mockett obliged the company with some songs—she had no voice. John and Michael came down. The noise was too much for Michael's equanimity at first and he howled, but soon recovered. *The* success of the evening, which broke whatever ice remained, was the glorious game of blindfolded manhunt, two people groping towards each other on the floor armed with newspaper truncheons. The Raleighs—father, mother, and son arrived in the middle and the Professor was too divine, making a Roman holiday by entering the lists against David's brisk little nurserymaid Blanche. He looked endless—like a sea serpent—and immediately made for cover and intrenched himself under the table. Blanche finally found yards of overlapping legs and attacked them with fury. It was a wild success— all the fats and all the thins roared with laughter. After they had gone I took the Professor up to Beb and they played chess.

Sunday, 28th November

As cold a day as I have ever suffered in. I had to copy out a lot of Beb's poems as we sent them off to Sidgwick and Jackson in the afternoon. The Professor and I pony-carted into Winchcomb and had tea with poor, over-worked, over-worried Eliza. We walked all the way home through lovely icy starlight. He was very dear, but talking to him is always a little like dancing blindfold—one never quite knows the whence and the whither. He is the greatest darling. More chess before dinner. The Allens came and we had a very happy dinner. Afterwards the Professor went up to chess again, and I was made to read Beb's poem. I shall get an awful reputation. I bargained with Mrs Professor that, if she promised not to say that I read my husband's poems aloud, *I* would not say that her husband insisted on lecturing to his guests. Beb continues very good and contented in bed.

Monday, 29th November

A letter from Basil arrived by early post saying he hoped he might be able to get to London for the days I was there after all. He had thought it impossible before. He said he would wire to Bruton Street. I am going up for Violet's wedding.

The Professor and I motored to Honeybourne and travelled as far as Oxford together. The train was terribly delayed at Oxford by impromptu movements on the part of troops. I thought we should never start again, and fumed and fretted over my *Life of Charlotte Brontë*. I was anxious to get up to London as, owing to the uncertainty of Basil's arrival, I had left all my plans open. At last we crept into Paddington, and I found to my annoyance that my box had been taken out with the Raleighs' luggage at Oxford. I had relied on that broken reed of a Professor and done nothing about labelling it. I did what was necessary at the lost-property office and then went home.

I found a letter from Basil saying he was coming, and soon he rang me up on the telephone and we arranged to dine together. Bluetooth came for a dentist at six. We discussed 'The Thimble'. No luggage arrived, so I couldn't change. Basil called for me, and we dined at Les Lauriers. Bad dinner with a physically unfit quail. He came home with me and stayed till about eleven. We did a little gibbeting. Very pleasant evening, ending with the welcome appearance of my box.

Tuesday, 30th November

Adele and I went to Violet's wedding in St Margaret's. *Thronging* crowd outside and everyone one had ever heard of inside. We took a place at the very back, thinking we should get a good view of the bridal procession entering the church, but they must have been morbidly punctual for we discovered that they were already invisibly stationed at the altar. I was offered a seat in the family pew, but refused, desiring to avoid unnecessary proximity to Margot. So, I saw nothing save the couple's emergence. I thought them both looking quite their best. Kakoo and Elizabeth were the only bridesmaids, in *lovely* velvet—rather Russian—ballet dresses with gold toques. Exquisite pages—Randolph Churchill, the McKennae, and the Harcourt boy. There is something terribly grim about a pompous wedding now. It seems so unnecessary and irrelevant, and one feels so remote. This is unkind because, if one were the bride oneself, no doubt one wouldn't feel one's glamour in the least impaired.

I went on to Downing Street. There was supposed to be no reception, but there was a serried throng. I felt too confused to take an intelligent interest in the presents, spoke a few dazed words to a great many people—amongst others poor Ian Hamilton, looking very broken. I had very little contact with Margot, though I could not avoid the receipt of one affectionate peck. She was swilling a very dark brown drink behind the buffet. The P.M. held my hand very affectionately, and looked at me with a tremendously charged expression intended to convey condolence on Yvo and the Margot affair. He told me he had written to Beb.

Venetia was looking a magnificent Jewess in her fabulous bird-of-paradise hat. Later I went on to her. Her abode is almost Elinor Glynish—magnificent, impersonal, green lacquer room; the bird of paradise hat; rich chocolate to drink, etc.—I felt a country bumpkin. Her bedroom is that of a courtesan. How she has changed since her old days, when she used to be so brutally careless of her person! I went on and had a dentist with Bluetooth. Conversation more or less exclusively personal. Kitchener's return seems to be creating great consternation. They don't know what to do with him. Technically he is still Secretary of State for War. When he went away he took the seals of office packed up in his box!

Basil had arranged for me to dine with Norah Brassey.* I went rather shyly, but enjoyed it very much. The object of my being put into touch with her was that she should draw me. She is extraordinarily good, and insisted on getting to work at once, so I was perched up on the arm of a sofa and she worked away furiously. She found the shortness of my nose incredible. Basil walked me home and came in and shared my Bengers. I get fonder and fonder of him, and *love* being with him.

Wednesday, 1st December

Went to the palmist Teresina in Manchester Street. Basil had had an appointment for eleven, but to my surprise she explained that she felt unable to do him that day and wanted him to return. He waited while I was closeted. It must be about nine months since I went to her before. She is a very nice and obviously shrewd woman with a good vocabulary. She said very much the same things about my family and my in-laws—all quite intelligent. She saw the blow about Yvo. She gave me a good deal of advice about the necessity of concentrating on Beb, whose development and career imperatively needed my co-operation, and she very earnestly warned me against getting too interested in my relations with another man. She obviously saw a tendency to stray and begged me not to drift, telling me I was not so well balanced as I appeared! I haven't the energy to write any more but it was all interesting. She said Beb would recover, return to the front in a different capacity, and that out of the post-war conditions opportunity would arise for important administrative work. He would not return to the Bar. She predicts the next important war date would be 27th of this month.

Basil and I went into the Wallace Collection and then to the Grosvenor Gallery to see a wax bust of Lady Cunard by the Servian sculptor Mestrovic—ludicrous. We lunched at Selfridges. I behaved outrageously, complaining of the smell of oysters and being overheard by the oyster eater, and insisting on opening a window. The rain poured in on a fat customer and she said with dignity, 'I'm eating *hot* food'. I thought it very funny and the window had to be shut.

I went home by myself. Basil had something to do, then he came back to Bruton Street and sat with me till I had to go to catch the 4.50. I have managed to see a lot of him these days—an orgy of dentistry. He came down on purpose to see me, so it was duty as well as inclination. Lord Freddie came to call for him, disguised as his solicitor in a brown beard. Got down to Stanway all right. Thought Beb not looking very well. He was voracious for London gossip. Children well.

Friday, 3rd December

In the afternoon I went for a solitary gusty walk which I enjoyed very much. I motored into Winchcomb after tea and did some work for Eliza, copying one letter out twelve times, etc. After dinner I had an experimental cigarette—rather enjoyed it.

Saturday, 4th December

A cable arrived from Letty saying Mary and Tom were being married this day. It was only on Thursday that we had got Letty's explanatory letter, saying the real reason for postponement was that Mary had been ill—sore throat and rash. They had feared scarlet fever, but it must luckily have been a false alarm. Jolly for their bachelor hosts! Letty wrote, 'We have taken every possible precaution—our hosts have left the house'. I like her claiming that precaution.

Sunday, 5th December

I went to church in the morning and found neither material nor spiritual comfort. Halliwell came to see Beb in the morning, he found him better, but says it will be a slow business. I had a letter from Basil with dewdrops from Norah Brassey, and an attack on my reserve and sphinxishness.

The Allens came to dinner. We had the old unpalling dilemma conversation. 'Which would you rather be, paralysed or die tomorrow,

Mary Elcho with Cynthia

A day at Eton in 1914: Papa—11th Earl of Wemyss—with Yvo, Cynthia (left) and Mary

Stanway in Gloucestershire, the 'oriel' window centre, gatehouse to the right

Ego and Letty, an interpretation by Sargent

Lady Cynthia with Mary and Bibs as bridesmaids

Leaving the church—Mr and Mrs Herbert Asquith

supposing by accepting paralysis you had to sign on for ten years of it?' After dinner I took Priest up to visit Beb. We tried to man our ship of half a dozen friends bound to a desert island. Priest has thirty-five necessary human beings, for whom he prays every morning—a good many of them are dead.

Wednesday, 8th December

At last a lovely day to look at! Letter from Basil at Holker, where a huge wedding party is gathering round Betty. Poor Socky[1] was rather under her cold, and was snappy and snubby with Bibs and me at luncheon. She is a champion 'non-conductor'. Finally, I was reduced to asking Bibs the date of the Battle of Waterloo, a lapse of taste for which I was greatly disapproved of by both pupil and teacher. Stayed in all the afternoon reading Walpole. Beb very busy correcting the proofs of his poems.

Just now all the news is bad and yet none of it is likely to have much effect on the ultimate issue. But it is uncomfortable to read continually of German successes and German plans for further successes. Baghdad and Salonika are both locally as serious as can be. The French Cabinet has let us in badly. They procrastinate even more than ours. They are a rotten lot, and I shouldn't be surprised if this led to their downfall. I find it ever-increasingly difficult to read the newspapers, and the last dregs of the voluntary system are rather sickening. What a farce it is —'Come along *willingly*! or we'll fetch you!'!

Thursday, 9th December

At six went into the hospital expecting to write for Eliza, but I found a delicious concert in full swing. A handsome woman—semi-professional was giving real bliss by her songs. To our horror, they sang 'When the boys come home' and, of course, I dissolved into tears.

Beb very busy all day correcting the proofs of his poems. He was very absent and unresponsive when we went up to see him after dinner, and when Mamma said something about the poems and I began looking for them he growled, 'Cincie's always fussing and furring about the room!'—just like a querulous old professional invalid complaining of his nurse. I was furious at first, but soon saw the humour of it. If there is one thing my conscience is clear of—it is 'fussing and furring'.

1. Bibs' governess.

1915

Friday, 10th December

Got letter from Bluetooth containing the following:

'*Very Secret.* The Tenth Division has been destroyed in the Balkans —it was the Irish one from Suvla Bay. It was bound to happen owing to the folly of the French. The French have behaved so madly over this that it looks almost as though they wanted to pick a quarrel with us. But others say it is only stupidity. Anyway, it will cost them 150,000 men, and Sarrail and his force are bound to be smashed up. Don't let all this bother you—it is momentary, though I admit it is depressing. It will be used by Northcliffe in a fresh attempt to get the Government out and, coupled with the Dardanelles, it may succeed. Then there is Baghdad, too, to explain. It is a bad moment for us. The Italian Navy is in hiding and the Austrians are complete masters of the Adriatic, so that we can send no supplies to the Serbian army.'

Not very cheering news. Still feeling miserably dyspeptic—hating myself and the world.

Saturday, 11th December

I had another letter from Bluetooth in which he took back the worst of his news—the Tenth Division has not been annihilated, and has a good chance of getting out.

Monday, 13th December

Mamma and I went up to London by early train. I lunched alone with Evan. He was very sweet and rather pathetic, saying he cannot endure life such as it is any more, and has determined to go into the Heavy Artillery. I suppose his present work occupies his time and not his attention, leaving him free to dwell on misery. He is very curious—he says he is so miserable that he passionately wishes *he had never been born*, yet he appears all right and I'm sure must enjoy a good many things—his wit, wine, and friends. Bad as things are, I cannot see why the Past and everything should be cancelled by the tragedy—I feel I have a Past and a Future.

Evan has been insulted by his pretty maid—too funny! She is the daughter of his cook and fiercely attacked him for having criticised the food. 'How can you know—you're not a domestic man? You're a man of pleasure and you drink champagne in wartime!' I told him it was she who was driving him into the Artillery.

Mary and I went to Lady Norah's, where I sat from five to seven.

We chatted a lot about Basil. Norah said he had implored her not to talk about him to me, as he 'valued my opinion'. I then remembered with what marked emphasis he had expatiated on Norah's misunderstanding him. I said I would telegraph, saying we had discussed him all the time. We did a good deal, and agreed his extraordinary happiness could only arise from the best digestion and the worst heart.

Tuesday, 14th December

Stayed in bed all the morning reading Buchan's excellent 'shilling shocker' *The Thirty-nine Steps*. The Lawrences were to have lunched with me somewhere, but I got a telegram to say he couldn't come—he was ill—so I lunched in. I was very glad because Dillon* came to lunch, and I thought him so very delightful—delicious charm, and he was also extremely interesting.

He began by being very funny about Carson, whose language about the Cabinet he said was quite unrepeatable. He—Dillon—was full of eloquent indictments of the mismanagers of the war. He sneered at poor old Asquith's infatuation for Carson in the summer. Apparently he (Carson) is now full of political mischief. As a typical instance of the paralysis of the Cabinet, he said the one and only thing they had unanimously agreed upon for the last months was that Kitchener must go—and there he was, still in the saddle. Dillon is still intensely, passionately against conscription. On the large question of general policy, he is opposed to our attempting to have a very greatly enlarged army, as in his opinion our finances could not possibly stand so great a strain, considering we are the indispensable money-box for all the allies. He thinks it would be much better if we undertook to provide the Russians with rifles, instead of training more possibly unarmed men of our own—thus being the financier, the weapon supplier, and the controlling Naval power. His real argument is, of course, the very strong one of Ireland. He is prepared to go to the stake for his opinion that they *would* resist conscription, that it would be impossible to apply it and naturally productive of a very bad impression were it to be omitted from the general scheme. He maintains that there is at least one-tenth of the population who would stick at nothing—amongst whom the historical hate of an oppressed people still clings, to the exclusion of any other consideration and any fears as to the future.

In order to spite England they would take any risk with the Germans. He said that the analogy between the Balkans and Ireland was very strong, so much so that the management of the Balkans should have been entrusted to an Irishman, as the only type capable of understanding their psychology. They, too, had this historical hate and were too absorbed in cutting the throats of their neighbours to care anything for the larger issues of the war. Of course, apart from expediency, he also hated conscription in the abstract: 'What is the good of overthrowing Prussian militarism if we are going to imitate it ourselves?' We had a discussion as to the ethics of assassination as a political weapon, and whether it was ever justifiable and expedient. He stuck to its being an arguable point and, after he was gone, I was amused to hear that he—with his wise, kind, humorous countenance— is supposed to have been the instigator of many assassinations in Ireland.

I visited Adele, who was full of curiosity about Lawrence and clamoured for the loan of *The Rainbow*. Bluetooth called for me and we went to my house—he wanted to see the Tonks. We went all over it, but didn't accept my tenants' invitation to tea. Afterwards we went to look at the Raemaekers—I think them works of genius. He took me back to Bruton Street and had tea with us.

Aubrey and Mary came in soon after I did and we had a long talk. They had been dining with Venetia at Coterie headquarters. He was in a state of frenzied resentment and irritation against Diana, who rasps his war nerves. He is badly physically haunted by his experience and had exactly the same expression on his face as Beb had that night at Gosford when he smashed the vase. I so understand it. Aubrey and Beb seem to have a good deal in common in their post-battle emotions. Mary and I discussed the matter till very late. She had witnessed wonderful Coterie episode. After dinner Diana ejaculated, 'I *must* be unconscious tonight!' And away went a taxi to fetch chloroform from the chemist, 'Jolly old chlorers!' Aubrey firmly removed Mary before the orgy began. She had nearly fainted at dinner—Aubrey was still persisting that he meant to return to Anzac. Poor darling, I think it was the idea of this that brought on a recrudescence of nervous emotion. Bluetooth had consulted Hankey and he had emphatically said Aubrey was *not* to go. I hope he won't.

Wednesday, 15th December

Breakfasted in bed—finished *The Thirty-nine Steps*. It is well written and quite fun, but too full of glaring improbabilities, not to say impossibilities, which do not always succeed in giving that 'willing suspension of disbelief'. The hero certainly has amazing luck.

Mary and I ordered Beb's poems at two shops—they're not out yet, and may take some time as the proofs were full of printing mistakes. One brilliant bathos, 'Aphrodite passionate and *frail*' instead of pale. Lowenfelt is said to have made his fortune by putting his money into a patent medicine and then going round and ordering it at *every* chemist, thus producing a great artificial demand for it. I am going to do the same with the 'Booklet'. I wrote to as many shops as I could remember when I got in, ordering the book to be sent to Mamma or Bibs, as I didn't want to give the same name as the author's. Bain[1] looked startled at the idea of the Prime Minister bubbling into poetry.

Thursday, 16th December

Great news of French's recall in the papers. He is given command of the home forces and Haig takes his place. Beb made me have a chess renaissance. I jibbed at the idea, but found I quite enjoyed it. The papers discreetly objective about French.

Friday, 17th December

Nasty—cold, misty day. Beb's poems arrived by evening post. They look very 'convincing'. Some ass has written 'this little booklet' in the introductory thanks to editors, so Beb had to wire to have such mawkish expression omitted.

Horrified letter from poor Basil, saying he heard Norah had been talking of him to me. What a guilty conscience he must have! Like the forty bishops who fled the country on the receipt of a telegram saying: 'All is discovered.'

Sunday, 19th December

A letter came from Phil Burne-Jones to Beb, saying he had been asked by the Editor of the *Sunday Pictorial* to discover whether he would write some verses called '1916' appropriate to the New Year. The remuneration they were prepared to give was fifty pounds! He reminded Beb that Milton had only got five pounds for *Paradise Lost*. I wish to Heaven we had kept back 'War Cataract', it would have done perfectly! I fear Beb may find it very difficult to write to order. I don't know how to coax Pegasus back into his room and wonder what atmosphere is most conducive to Beb's muse. Perhaps I ought to make him unhappy, on the principle of 'Poets learn in suffering what they teach in song'. *It must be written somehow.*

1. Bookseller.

1915

The Priest came to dinner. Papa and Beb played chess, and the Priest and I. He said I was a very good 'partner' at chess. Certainly we did each appear to be fighting against some third thing. The Priest had been doing yeoman service by ordering *The Volunteer* at several Birmingham bookshops. I said I would burn Beb's twelve presentation copies. We went into exhaustive statistics of possible and impossible profits, and suggested the Prime Minister making the purchase of the book compulsory. It might be worked on a sort of Passover system.

Monday, 20th December

Wonderful children's entertainment at Didbrook on the occasion of presenting Mrs Alcock with a testimonial (a purse) on retiring from the post of schoolmistress after thirty-five years. Papa made a good speech. Flavia Forbes recited. The children were delicious, and there was an amazingly absurd, roguish patriotic song-writer—a policeman:

> The lads in their trenches
> They think of their wenches

was the refrain of one song, and it was always signalled by a ponderous wink. I think the moment in which the author struck that very felicitous rhyme must have been the happiest anyone has experienced since the beginning of the war. Mamma's parody is:

> As I lie in my muddy ditch,
> I think of my bloody bitch.

The singer had the best irrelevant gesticulation I have yet seen.

Wednesday, 22nd December

The Priest came and played chess with Beb. Dined *à trois* with my parents, and quite merrily too. Great amusement over Mamma having had the Sacrament administered by Bateman when she was in bed— the origin of Bibs' remark: 'I have never got over seeing Mamma in bed with Mr Bateman.' I promised Papa that, if he ever was ill, I would send for Bateman without his ordering him. Papa and Beb played chess. I read dear Walpole, who gets better and better. After the others had gone up I talked to Mamma until late—about Ickey. She was very touching.

114

Thursday, 23rd December

Horrible wet day. Papa reading *The Rainbow* all day with many protestations of disgust. He has offered me five pounds for it as he thinks it would be a good investment. Beb busy over his 1916 poem. One feels terribly disinclined for Christmas, and has to set one's teeth at it. One can't cut it with children.

Friday, 24th December

After dinner I went through the usual Christmas Eve stocking ritual with a very heavy heart. Last year with Yvo and George we had indulged in all the time-honoured stocking jokes. In George's we put twenty-four celluloid babies; in Beb's twenty-four photographs of his father, and in Papa's tiny tips from each member of his family. Some very good press cuttings arrived about Beb's poems which are now fairly launched on the world.

Saturday, 25th December

Got up early to see the children opening their stockings. It was like the nightmare of a spoilt child. They had lovely things—Michael broke the Tenth Commandment and coveted John's. We got through our Christmas somehow, though we all felt sufficiently dejected and the weather added the last touch. It simply poured. We got quite wet going to church.

Bibs was horizontal with a sprained ankle, but we conveyed her to the Christmas tree at the hospital. We took John and David with us. First there were carol-singers, then the tree with Dr Halliwell dressed up as Father Christmas—a noble performance, he made jokes in 'ye olde English' for quite three quarters of an hour. John was wonderfully pip-pippish at 'enter Father Christmas'. He was altogether wildly excited and clapped his hands at each burst of applause, wriggling and jiggling about all over the room. He loves crowds. It was a nice party.

We had a Christmas dinner: Bateman, the Allens, Charles Smith, Viva, and Margaret. Terrible hitch—Mamma had promised the motor to fetch the Didbrook party and forgot all about it. We waited and waited; at last we got hold of Grant and sent him to the relief. The poor Priest had already caught the pony and Smith was making up his mind to cold duck. They were all very good-tempered about it and we had quite a successful evening—Bibs and Flavia were at the side table to dodge being Thirteen. Beb came down afterwards. Flavia did her stunts; old Smith recited 'St Crispin's Day'—really quite well—and we played games.

Sunday, 26th December

It seemed impossible to have two Sundays running, so my only religious rite was to come down to breakfast in cloth instead of in tweed, and I did not go to church. At twelve o'clock Papa and I played two sets of tennis against Grace and Evan. They won both, but we made quite a good fight. The sun made one court most unpleasant. I enjoy tennis more and more; it gives me *joie de vivre* and a sense of swift efficiency. I love the swift challenge of it and the recurring sense of triumph one gets, even in a set one loses by many games. It is the least depressing game to lose as long as one wins some points. I know nothing that spins life out so much. You feel as if you had had years of experience, so many emotions you have passed through, and behold—you have only been playing for three quarters of an hour.

Beb still writing variations on his fifty-pound poem. Evan went up by six o'clock train. He has sent in his application for a commission in the Artillery. Such a typical telegram from Margot in the morning: 'Our love to you both. Beb's poems making a real sensation. Writing.'

Wednesday, 29th December

Went up for one of my fortnightly jaunts to London by the early train. Bluetooth has sent me a bottle of the scent Aggie Jekyll was sufficiently humourless to ask him for. 'Pour Troubler' it is called— it's ridiculously expensive, but certainly rather good. I went up to London reeking all over. Mary and Aubrey had telegraphed the day before to say they would come down for one night—most unlucky to miss them—but I couldn't postpone again. Basil had stayed in London on purpose and Adele was giving a Hell for me.

Went to Guy and Frances, where I arrived in Margot's wake, and found them and Annie and Dinah all looking very flattened out by her. She is being surpassingly tiresome about the engagement,[1] and sent a well-intentioned telegram to poor Annie, imploring her not to have a 'poky wedding' in Eddie's 'small and ugly' house. She declared that

---

1. Of Kakoo, sister of Frances Charteris, to John Granby.

Henry and she would be heartbroken if the wedding did not take place from Downing Street with Elizabeth as bridesmaid. She characteristically added: 'Have told Eddie, so he won't mind.'

Annie dropped me at Cullen and I was laboriously hair cleaned and manicured. Then I went home for Basil. I stopped at Bumpus on the way and ordered *The Volunteer* for Annie. They were sold out of it, but I hadn't the nerve to ask how many copies they'd had. Basil came at 4.30 and went off to call on his mother at a quarter to six, then Bluey came. Conscription is clinched. The Cabinet all more or less sullenly agreed according to him with the exception of McKenna, Runciman, and Simon, who are resigning. McKenna—not on principle, but because as Chancellor he says he cannot possibly undertake to finance it—Runciman for the same motives. Bluetooth is more suspicious of Simon's motives, and thinks he wishes to make himself conspicuous in the favour of the Liberal Party with an eye for the future. Asquith is trying to pooh-pooh McKenna out of it. He was engaged to dine with him this evening—Bluetooth thought he meant to go. Margot had written to Pamela, asking her to use her influence with Reggie as the P.M.'s friend.

Dined at Adele's, taking *The Rainbow* in my hand. Basil, Iris, Lord Essex, Eloïse Ancaster, Adele, self, and the Lord Derby were the party. I sat between host and Duff. Host was rather 'Essex', as Ettie calls it, because he once made Mr Balfour join the ladies by the coarseness of his conversation. He told me he had asked Mrs —— if there had ever been anything between her and Sargent. She answered, 'I have *always* wanted to, but I always feel when I come into the room and see my husband that I should have to tell him, so I haven't.'

Basil, Duff, Iris and I were the only pokerers—we introduced each player having two hands in rotation. I won four pounds odd. Basil walked me home and came in to have Bengers. Alas there was none—cruel blow! We raided the kitchen, but found nothing but mutton bones. He stayed till 12.30. . . .

Thursday, 30th December

I went out to Selfridges early and did some masterly shopping—I asked for *The Volunteer*. They had had it, but it was sold out. I also went to The Times Book Club and ordered a copy—about three were lying in a little pile. They said they had sold a good few, but the saleswoman was not forthcoming, and I hadn't the nerve to press for numbers. I felt my name was written on my forehead.

I dined with Bluetooth. All went well at first. He told me more political gossip. Apparently nearly all the principal Cabinet ministers are now agreed on the small army. It was Kitchener who, quite arbitrarily, pledged the seventy divisions to the French Government. This situation may result in Kitchener going or in general changes. McKenna is firm.

Afterwards, when we went upstairs, we had a nightmare time, and I was as helplessly tongue-tied as ever I used to be. He began by complaining of our last evening together (the one I fondly thought had been so happy), but he said—though pleasant—I had talked to him exactly like a 'stranger'. He suggested two remedies for the strange distance between us—one physical one mental—and accused me of withdrawing my mind as well as my hand. I couldn't say anything or even *feel* or *think* anything, and had that awful Undine, unreal feeling I get when pressed. He tortured *me* and had that hurt look in the eyes himself that I remembered so well—I thought I was being intolerable myself. He drove me home (it was in nearly complete silence), I was very tired, but felt I must write him a letter as I had been so incompetent. I shrank from the task and—in the way one welcomes any pretext for postponement when one is tired—I rang up Basil, who was staying with the Russells. I quite forgot how late it was and the poor thing was asleep in bed, and had to come all the way down the stairs of a much-disturbed house. He told me he had decided to stay another day. Oh the relief and ease of that *un*interrogative, undefined relationship!

I wrote to Bluetooth with that absurd lack of conviction I have about my own identity in anything like a situation:

'I *am* "thinking" '—he had told me not to—'I can't help it and I must write a word. It isn't your fault, or due really to what you said tonight. As a matter of fact I was already and independently "thinking", only a selfish fear of saying something fatuous prevented my translating my thoughts into words before. As for my tongue-tiedness tonight, I don't know what you must have thought of me—or, at least, I *do* know only too well. I can't help being distressed about us, only it is so difficult to say what I mean.

'I feel, though, that I ought to try and make you *really* ask yourself whether I am going to be happiness or unhappiness in your life. Supposing what you call "formality"—be it instinctive, theoretical, or both—is inevitable and permanent between us, am I worth while to you? I don't want this to sound anything like a melodramatic ultimatum, only it is so easy to go on *un*interrogatively and I can't help feeling the responsibility. I suppose appealing to you like this is shirking it, I ought to use my own judgment and decide. My instincts are always against interrogation and definition, and you know how much happiness you give me and how grateful I am. So the temptation is to drift . . . But I don't want my vision obscured by the stake of my happiness, because even that must ultimately depend on my conviction of yours.

'You see, I *can* be happy with this "barrier" relationship and perhaps *you* can't be? Can you tell me at all how prohibitive these inevitable "barriers" are to your happiness? Forgive my clumsiness, I can't say what I mean—I am tired—but I just wanted to say something tonight. I feel so ashamed of my helplessness, and I want you to tell me whether I, who am getting so much, am giving you anything? I can't tell.

'What a moon-faced letter! Please write frankly.'

Friday, 31st December

Margot sent me £6 10s. with a funny little letter beginning: 'I wish I could give you more, but neither Eddie nor Frank has given me a sou this year. How can people like your father, etc.'

I went to three bookshops, buying a copy of *The Volunteer* at each. At Hatchards I bought the last and the man told me they had sold two lots of them yesterday—each lot would be about two dozen—so that's good enough for one bookshop. At Sotherans they were sold out and at Bains, to my glee, I saw them 'titty up' in the window.

Basil called for me to go to lunch at Downing Street. We met the Cabinet emerging. 'Hullo Cynthia,' greeted Mr Balfour, looking flushed but rather as if he had made his point. Violet was at lunch looking well and pink: Margot, P.M., Lady Tree, Diana, Venetia, Masterton Smith were the rest of the party. I sat between the P.M., who looks indecently well, and Violet. Much talk and praise of *The Volunteer*—Margot has had many letters of congratulation on her stepson. Amusing story that Birrell saw Raymond buying the last copy in a shop and overheard muttering as he left: 'I don't much care about the word "dainty" '. It is curious and rather a tribute how everyone and the newspapers all pick out different ones for preference. To Beb's delight, Bluetooth does *not* like the 'Jewels'—he said it was in a feminine taste—but in confutation Basil likes it best.

Sad muddle with Katharine and Raymond. I went to Bruton Street to wait for them and they came to Downing Street. Very sorry not to see Raymond. He has got ten days' leave. Basil followed me as soon as he could get away from endless lunch, and he stayed with me until I had to go to my train. These occasional two days in London over-excite me ridiculously. I feel so much more appetite for topical life than I ever did before—I don't know whether it's health or the threat of war. Very sorry to say goodbye to Basil. Returned to Papa, Mamma, Beb, and Christmas tree. Read *Volunteer* press cuttings—amusing and very favourable.

1916

Sunday, 2nd January

Still pouring rain. This 'unseasonable' muggy weather is making me feel terribly tired and dejected. There is no kick in me and probably no power of resentment—I don't believe I could be angry, even if a German kissed me!

I had a letter from Bluetooth, but obviously written before he got mine. He wrote:

'Things appear to be settling down. I understand Mr Balfour proposed a committee for settling the size of the army and they all agreed. Simon is the only one who may find it difficult to retrace his footsteps, having plumped against any compulsion. Margot wrote to Runciman, "How can you find it in your heart to desert Henry when Puffin has been such a friend of your little boy's!"'

Beb comes down to all meals now. I played 'potted' chess with the Priest. A friend of his has bought fifty copies of *The Volunteer*.

Monday, 3rd January

Rather colder. Mamma started the startling idea of going to the hospital as a probationer. The P.M. sent me a letter from Strachey to him, full of dewdrops for Beb. I had a letter from Curtis—the first after I don't know how many years. He has got a professorship at Dublin.

Tuesday, 4th January

Halliwell came: saw Beb, Bib's foot, and had a long discussion about Mamma's probationary scheme. He had thought in her letter it was only a joke, but didn't veto it when he realised she was in earnest. Mamma and I had an ethical discussion on 'war work' before dinner.

1916

Wednesday, 5th January

Another peaceful, pastoral day. How demoralising my cuckoo life here is. I don't even have to order the dinner or in any way pay my passage. Halliwell had said Beb was to practise his 'town' head in Cheltenham with a view to going to London, so I motored him there and made him walk up the promenade. I asked for *The Volunteer* in two shops. They hadn't got it in stock, but were sending for it.

Friday, 7th January

Got a letter from Letty saying the Stricklands had been torpedoed, and had lost everything except what they stood up in. They weren't insured. Mamma had given them a jewel for Mary. There was an endlessly long despatch from Ian Hamilton in the papers which I read in snatches at intervals all through the day—it's heartbreaking reading.

Tuesday, 18th January

The most *lovely* spring day. I have managed to finish the nine volumes of Walpole's letters. I *have* enjoyed them. I wish he were alive and would write to me. Papa and Angela arrived on Friday evening. She is very mellow and, as usual, I am getting on incredibly well with her.

Wednesday, 19th January

Beb and I came up to London by the twelve o'clock from Broadway. The journey didn't appear to hurt him. We are staying with Aubrey and Mary at Bruton Street. Aubrey is by way of going off to Admiral Wemyss in about a week: Mary is *possibly* going to Egypt. Beb and I dined alone. Violet visited us. She said the Derby Report* was an amazing bungle. He accounted for many, many more men than the census had.

Sunday, 23rd January

Lovely cold day smelling of spring. I went to call on Violet who had just spent her first night in the new house. She was out. I waited for about an hour and was joined by Eddie. He talked about Beb's poems to my relief—I feared his silence meant disapproval—he said he liked the 'Baby' and 'Jewels' best. He told me, 'Strachey thinks Beb better than Rupert Brooke, which I don't'. Violet came, we examined the curtains, etc. Eddie walked me home. Peaceful, pleasant evening with Beb—chess. We are very happy here.

Tuesday, 25th January

Beb and I lunched at Downing Street. I had asked Margot to get Strachey to meet me, and I sat next to him feeling like a sort of Mrs H. G. Wells—very much Beb's wife. *He raved about the poems.* I quite liked him.

Thursday, 27th January

My ridiculous plan of being photographed with a violin was put into execution. Hugh—thinking me raving—brought me his precious seventy-pound instrument, and after hair waving at Emile's I took it to Lafayette. It was too funny, but I didn't giggle. I didn't dare risk false action in holding the bow up. 'Now, couldn't your Ladyship hold it as though you were just coming on and smiling to your friends?'

John[1] and Kakoo were married at St Margaret's, and it really was the most movingly lovely sight. It made one cry to think they would ever be old or dead. John looked a glamorous, knightly figure with perfect technique: he held her hand and everything in the most inspired way. She looked divine in the best wedding dress ever seen.

News, alas, had come that Guy was going to France, the next day, so Beb and I went to a family dinner at Catharine Street—Papa, Mamma and Mark. It's cruel to think of his leaving that blissful home, and he looks so ill.

Friday, 28th January

Beb didn't feel up to Dublin, so I had decided to harden my heart, leave him in Mary's charge and go over for the jaunt myself. Rather flippant conduct I fear.

Polly and I travelled over, leaving Euston 8.30. Train part very pleasant: I read *The First Ten Thousand* and thought it quite excellent. The crossing was most unpleasant—there wasn't any sensational amount of motion but it must have been very well chosen, anyhow it carried its point. Polly and I and many more were sick. I got off feeling very green and plain, and was met by a motor and A.D.C.

Found His Ex, Goonie, Lady Arran, etc., at tea. Wore grey dress Mary has mercifully lent me and the great new excitement of my life

1. Lord Granby, later 9th Duke of Rutland.

—the whiskers I had bought at Emile the day before. I think they 'become' me. Venetia and Edwin are here, and beloved Birrell. Escaped to my room as soon as possible.

There were outside visitors to dinner making us about twenty-five. Everything was very regal and stiff. I was glad to have Venetia to see it in inverted commas with me. I think the Wimbornes entirely convince themselves. I sat between His Ex and Basil. His Ex badly dislocated things by talking to me first instead of the lady he had taken in, with the result of Basil being a sullen 'Mum-Charles' for some time. Awful lot of standing about after dinner until the day-boarders removed themselves. I thought my inside would drop round my feet. I enjoyed a talk with that famous charmer Sir Matthew Nathan.

Basil summoned me to 'Queen' Alice's Holy of Holies, and we three and Birrell had a very amusing, rather coarse conversation about all the English kings. Birrell is wonderfully well up in the statistics of royal bastards. He looks very happy and dissipated here, flirting away with all the ladies. He gave good imitations of King George's horror when he wrote an appeal to him to allow Lady Headfort (that most respectable chorus-girl peeress) to come to court: 'Rosie *Boote*, Rosie Boote come to my court!' 'Queen' Alice kept us up rather late.

Sunday, 30th January

Enjoyed myself immensely all day—unusually possessed by great sense of the fun and fleetingness of life. Like Margot, I should be very 'disappointed' if I were to die now. I suppose I was feeling exceptionally well, and I was taking an enormous amount of interest in my looks—it's odd how that fervour comes and goes—at least, I can't say it ever quite goes! I suppose it's largely produced by the presence of individuals. The curls have added great excitement to bedroom life.

I had woken far too early again, so I snatched a little rest before lunch, then sallied (really sallied) down in my top-hat and new purple Prince tweed coat and skirt, which is a great success. I sat beside His Ex and had a very animated conversation. I get on very well conversationally with him, but—thank God!—I haven't found real favour in his eyes and been summoned to an evening *tête-à-tête* in his sitting room. I had quite enough of the proconsular favour in Canada. Luckily I am not his type. Lady Drogheda and Lady Arran are what suits his palate. He swills brandy and is incredibly stagy. Aunt Evelyn's gorge would rise at him as a patron of Ireland. He asked me to come round the stables with him, and at three we went, accompanied by the children, Basil, and Hazelton. I had no idea such things still existed: dozens of colossal black horses, countless museum pieces in the shape of every kind of vehicle most specially designed for him, and a huge array of glittering bits, etc., etc.

As soon as was polite, Basil and I detached and went for a walk, ending up at his house, where we had tea and some reading aloud. Amongst other things, I read some of *The Princess*—a gorgeous farce.

After dinner when the royalties withdrew the mice began to play, and *The Rape of the Lock* was enacted. We pretended to cut Basil and Birrell's hair with enormous scissors, substituting hairs from a white hearthrug. Basil was horrified when presented with a handful of coarse white hairs. Finally, I had the audacity really to sever a lovely white lock from dear Birrell's head. This we took to Goonie, who is very much chaffed about him. In self-defence she gave me dewdrops from him: beauty, cleverness, charm and—best of all—that *I* appeared to like *him*. My manners must be improving.

Monday, 31st January

Basil kept his nose to the grindstone all the morning. I had arranged to accompany Birrell to lunch with old McHaffy, who is now Provost. How well I remember the embarrassing occasion on which he cut Mr Balfour dead because he hadn't given him that much-coveted post! He lives in a very good Georgian house, with pleasant perquisites in pictures. He has two formidable daughters: the principal—the fat one —really a very striking character. We had the sort of general conversation I revel in—on George Eliot, Trollope, Jane Austen, Charlotte Brontë, and so on—with discussion as to the best exponents of dialogue, etc. in novels.

As we left the dining room the striking Miss M. asked me if I smoked. Had the answer been in the affirmative I don't know what my lot would have been—perhaps the happier one of being left with the men—as it was, I was ushered into the drawing room and spent a rather steep hour with the sisters. They have a great Abbeyleix and Downing Street *culte*, and their room might have been one's own, so full was it of photographs of Evelyn, Puffin, etc. The striking sister reviews books and promised to attend to *The Volunteer*. She gave me some shocking gossip about His Ex, saying some of the ladies who had visited the Lodge said he was so fearful a bounder that they would die rather than return. I shudder to think of the scenes enacted in the sitting room. He really ought to restrain himself with the natives—it appears to be a proconsular weakness. He can't be worse than Lord Grey.

I dropped Birrell at the Castle and returned home. I was just strolling out to the tennis court when I unluckily met His Ex, and had to go for a walk round the policies in agonisingly tight boots—most unpleasant. There was a good deal of gardener traffic on the path so I wasn't nervous. He *is* a figure of fun, but rather a pathetic one. When I got rid of him, I went to the tennis, and when Basil had finished his set I walked with him and visited his office.

Goonie deliciously amusing after tea with her queen of queer faces, and her sleepy, darlinging voice, on the subject of her education: 'Darling, I can't *add*!' Birrell most amusing and amused. *The* house-joke at present is the supposed competition between Goonie and me for the rather nimble affections of Mr Birrell. She accuses me of having 'taken him from her': I deny any attempt at 'poaching'.

The Montagus went away before dinner—one misses his mahogany countenance at meals. At dinner I sat between His Ex and Basil. The former monopolised me nearly the whole way through. In fact, so great was the appearance of success, that I began almost to fear that I might be invited into the sitting room. He has a terrible way of flapping his furry eyelids at one. He talked of the mutual hatred of all women and complained anew of his lack of occupation, saying (to my astonished amusement) that he thought he had read everything worth reading. There is a disarming naïveté about him from some angles. I suggested he write his memoirs. He was feverishly interested when he heard I was writing a diary, anxiously asking if I had the 'historical sense': he wants to be assured that the Lord Lieutenant will be adequately presented to posterity. He said nearly all ladies made a confidant of him, telling him things that made his teeth chatter.

Amusing doe-talk after dinner. Her Ex is like Marie Antoinette about money. She said she supposed I must spend at least £500 a year on clothes—the whole of my income! Her wardrobe is fabulous. Birrell, looking like a mellow old Thackeray, gave an excellent illustration of the frivolity of his mind when asked by His Ex if he would come over a shell factory with him the next day: 'Shells . . . shells . . . what shells?' Thinking of the seashore!

Short haircombing with Goonie. I find her very fascinating. She amused me by saying she had once had to give Lord Wimborne a 'gifle' for importunity. She is the most *marvellous* peg for clothes. Everything looks superlatively *chic* on her—things which might appear quite dowdy on others.

Tuesday, 1st February

Woke up at six, and tried in vain to get off to sleep again. Not being able to stay asleep is worse than not being able to go to sleep. Am beginning to get tired, but so far have run most successfully on my nerves, and been in excellent spirits and better, steadier looks than for ages. It is amazing how open to suggestion I am in the way of looks: the mere vicinity of Basil is more effective than all the cosmetics in the world. I suppose all women are like that in varying degrees. I went and had breakfast with him in his little house. His wonderful powers as a tonic are a continual source of surprise to me— my spirits in his company are quite preposterous.

I had an assignation at 4.30 with Curtis, whom I had not seen since ten years ago reading-parties at Stanway when he cherished a romantic passion for me. He has a professorship at Trinity College. Basil wanted to accompany me and we had a great altercation—I, very anxious that he should *not* do so, finally prevailed. Curtis and I had tea in a little room furnished with large photographs of me: conversation mainly reminiscent. He has written a book on the Normans and is engaged in one on Ireland. I kept Basil waiting in east wind by a ticking taxi for ages; he was furious and made a good story of keeping him standing in a draught while I talked to a 'swain'. He drove me home in facetious dudgeon.

Hair-combing with Goonie. She taxed me with Basil being 'madly in love' with me, and talked much of his ridiculous quarrel with Norah Brassey about me. He says he won't speak to her again, not as a punishment but as a precaution against a 'dangerous woman'. To my amazement, she told me that at dinner the first night she had opened her conversation with Basil on the subject of that row by saying, 'Of course, I know you are madly in love with Cynthia.' He had got very red and not denied it.

She had had the most divinely comic aphasia at dinner. According to her well-nigh incredible account—sitting beside His Ex, she thought he was the Duke of Marlborough, and began talking *of* instead of *to* her neighbour. She said: 'What a pity it is about Ivor and wine and women!' She told it too deliciously—'He startled, darling.' She had to pretend she had meant Ivor Churchill, an innocent youth of sixteen.

Wednesday, 2nd February

I thought I couldn't hope to last much longer. My health and spirits suddenly fell below zero, and I was cross and tired all day. His Ex,

Basil, Mr Birrell and the Comptroller went off to Galway for a recruiting meeting at which Redmond was speaking.

Sat between His Ex and Sir George Prescott at dinner. Talked to Her Ex afterwards. To my sorrow, Goonie tells me she (Alice) finds my 'mind alarming' though she likes me—a very grievous spike. Talked to Basil after dinner. He was a real ferret, trying (and in a measure succeeding) in extracting a list of people who had been in love with me. He is wonderfully quick to talk to, a marvellous conductor, and the sort of curtseying appreciation in his voice spoils one for other companions. I believe his charm is very much in his voice.

Basil perfectly furious at having received a curt letter from the War Office, saying they have no further use for him and that he will shortly be gazetted out of the Army. He is certain His Ex has worked it somehow, and is resolved to have a row with him in the morning, and to write to the P.M., etc. Of course, he really ought to stay here. One shudders to think of His Ex unchaperoned by him, but he is adamant.

Thursday, 3rd February

Woke early again to find the weather had at last broken. Went for a walk with B. before lunch in a delicious cosmetic of soft rain. He did some more ferreting. Sat next to His Ex again at lunch. It is scarcely in one's favour, but there is no doubt that after all I have had a success with him, and his omitting to take me into his sitting room must I think be a tribute to my alarmingness. Sat next to him at dinner and got on dangerously well. To his horror on looking down the table, Basil saw him screwing one of my long red ear-rings on to his great pneumatic tyre of an ear. He said afterwards that he supposed tomorrow I should come into dinner with his watch-chain and order on.

His Ex: 'Do you like admiration?'

I (nervously): 'Yes.'

His Ex: 'I thought you were above it. Well I remember you at your first ball at Apsley House, etc., etc.'

Goonie forgot herself and sat down in Queen Alice's presence. Talked to Basil after dinner whilst the girls warbled at the piano. Goonie was taken off to the 'parlour'. Basil and I disgraced ourselves by chortling when she returned because the flowers she was wearing were *broken*, but she swore she had had no trouble: 'One *gifle* enough for him'.

Friday, 4th February

Lovely morning. Walked across to the Private Secretary's Lodge and had breakfast with Basil. Retired to bed till dinner time and decided to postpone my departure till Monday.

Resurrected for dinner and sat between His Ex and Sir George. His Ex had the audacity to talk of his poverty: I am told that 'Queen' Alice was outraged the other day because someone estimated her annual dress expenditure at only £10,000. After dinner I had some gamp talk with her—then, at last, His Ex took me off for a 'dentist'. Thank God I didn't giggle! I sat bolt upright with folded arms and jabbered politics, and there was no hint of danger. I nearly exploded when he used the actual words 'wine and women' in relation to the P.M. At about eleven he returned me immune to the drawing room and they withdrew. Talked to Basil for a little and 'so to bed'. Goonie is gone, I miss her much.

Saturday, 5th February

Sat between His Ex and the Comptroller at dinner—Her Ex still capping her own dresses. Again I was led off by His Ex. It is very oriental, the way he stalks out of the room followed by the woman, whom he returns at his leisure to the drawing room. He talked pompously about his unerring taste in poetry, colour and so on, and was rather entertaining about the 'Souls'. His manner is too funny. 'Oh,' (waving his arm and flapping his furred eyelids) 'how clever you are! You always have exactly the right word.'

Sunday, 6th February

Came down at twelve and read *The Princess* to Basil. Lovely cold day. In the afternoon we motored in the little open motor to see my cousin Florrie Bourke. Lovely moonlight drive home. Florrie's tea was very inadequate—we each snatched a hunk of dry bread and gnawed it on the way. I had a rare lapse in that 'reticence' about which Basil always upbraids me. It was about cosmetics. I told him I sometimes rouged. His utter astonishment was a great tribute to the skill with which I apply it.

We found Her Ex and all the Maids warbling at the piano when we got back. After their Excellencies had withdrawn the Maids of Honour, Basil and I had a very blasphemous impromptu miracle play. We were all in Heaven—the sofa serving as 'Abraham's Bosom'. We really were very funny. The lift came in very useful for the Ascension. Went to bed very late. Someone said: 'If Lord Basil's in Heaven they had better lock the Virgin Mary up!'

Monday, 7th February

Polly called me cruel early. Basil motored me into Kingstown. The boat left there at eight. I was very sorry to say goodbye to my wonderful tonic. We didn't get home till ten. Found Mamma, Eliza, Beb, and Olivia. Beb looking fairly well. His board have given him another six weeks before he comes up for another. Children thriving.

Saturday, 12th February

Mamma and I went to lunch with Mr Bateman. We met dear Last[1] on the way back. He asked for a gun that had belonged to George and Yvo as a keepsake. In referring to my speech, he said I was 'a chip off the old block'. He was delightful about the Zeppelins which, fantastic to relate, came quite close by here last Thursday: 'I thought there was something radically wrong when I heard them'. 'Something radically wrong' is a delightful criticism of Zeps over the Cotswolds.

Monday, 14th February

Beb and I came up to London by the twelve o'clock train. I went to see Bluetooth, who was confined with a chill. He had the loss of the *Arethusa* to tell me as a secret but, unfortunately, I had already seen it on a poster. Feeling flustered by London and rather longing to have a house of my own.

Thursday, 17th February

Had one of those thoroughly fiendish telephoning mornings, so typical of London life, in which the Present is always being ruined by the necessity of having to squint at the Future.

Basil's brother, Lord Dufferin, dined. I was very interested to see him. He is a most curious, rather haunting man with (although so different) extraordinary likenesses to B. in face and manner—really more in voice and technique—the same minuetting voice with the curtsey in the manner. He has got extremely good features, but there is a distinct look of an actor and a very strong American twang. At

1. Gamekeeper.

first I thought him distasteful; halfway through dinner fascinating, and finally I suspended my judgment. He seemed to have so many different layers, certainly he is a little uncanny.

Friday, 18th February

Beb and I lunched at Downing Street: Louis Mallet, Phil Burne-Jones, Mr Asquith's brother, Denis Mackail, Katharine and Barbara Wilson were there. I sat next to Cis who told me he was constantly being congratulated on Beb's poems, by people who think they are his. Margot was looking very well and was in her pleasantest mood. She dew-dropped my purple tweed and only insulted me retrospectively about my top hat.

Basil came at five. I had told him in the morning that I had had dinner with his brother. He was most astonished and to my amusement he had immediately rushed off to see him on the subject.

Beb and I dined with the Ian Hamiltons in their rather painstaking house. I sat between Sir Ian and the White Bear Warre.* Sir Ian looks better and talked quite normally. He and his wife Jean are enthusiastic admirers of Beb's poems. I liked the White Bear: he is very good-looking and his wife is rather a sweet. There was the most astonishing voluble gushing American woman there—Flora Guest, who had been a Mrs Dodge. 'I'm crazy about you and I like your husband, too—who was your father?' etc. She offered to come and rub Beb's spine with olive oil, and motored us home. I talked to Jean after dinner. She told me she had nearly asked Viola Meynell, but hearing her young man (D. H. Lawrence) was passionately in love with me she had thought better of it. What enormous leaps to conclusions people do take! Afterwards I talked to Mrs Guest's son, Dodge, who went out in the Naval Division with Oc, Patrick, Rupert Brooke. He has been recommended for the V.C. Sir Ian told me the Naval Division was to be disbanded. Of course they are orphans now as they were the children of Winston's brain, but it seems a pity now—they must have got so much regimental sentiment and *esprit de corps* by this time.

Dr Lawrence came to see Beb in the morning. He reported 'substantial improvement', but said he ought to return to the country.

Monday, 21st February

Mary, Diana and I went out, accompanied by Beb, to look at models with a view to borrowing clothes for me to wear at the performance Lady Essex has let me in for in so high-handed an American way. It is going to be at the Gaiety and we are to be lady buyers looking at a parade of mannequins in a dressmaker's shop. Lady E. had my name printed on a large poster without asking my leave: I suppose I ought to be angry, but I'm not really. Diana told us there was a music hall skit on her in which she is amusingly 'taken off'. We didn't find one model at Reville's which we could have been seen dead in; we went on to Lucile's, but there they only had two 'big Girl' dresses, neither of them very amusing

Basil picked me up before lunch, and we joined Papa and Venetia at the Grill Room of the Hyde Park Hotel—Papa in a rollicking mellow mood. He told such a good story of Mallam, sometime vicar at Stanway, who wrote asking if he could leave. 'Certainly,' Papa replied, 'if you can find a God-fearing man who would be suitable for the living.' Mallam wrote back: 'I have found a God-fearing man whom I think would be very suitable. He has offered me a bed, which I think I shall accept, so that I may be able to form some opinion of his wife.' We had the old 'pro-German' argument, Papa and Basil maintaining that one ought not to give cigarettes, etc., to wounded Germans—an attitude I cannot understand.

Papa, Basil and Goonie came to dinner. I sat between Basil and Aubrey. Papa still in roistering spirits. He discussed his morality with Mary, and made me tell the table Ego's story of his parents' travelling—Mamma emerging from a third class carriage with a book called *The Soul*, Papa stepping out of a first class one on to the same platform carrying a book called *Her Soul*. Hell after dinner reinforced at eleven o'clock by Duff—a vulture in pigeon's feathers—for once he actually won. I made £3 15s. Poor Papa was stung for £11.

Mary in haircombing accused me of too obvious 'preening' in the presence of admirers! Delicious postcard from Nurse: 'The children are well. Peter died last night—we miss him very much.'

Tuesday, 22nd February

Bitter cold—snowing off and on. Beb and I lunched at Downing Street. Kitchener was there—looking *so* different from the poster—and my own conception of him—*very* mossy and gentle old gentleman. Margot gave a good 'pip-pip' of her superficial interferingness, talking vehemently about Basil's selfish obstinacy in leaving Ireland and then saying, 'Are you off to *France* tonight?'

Basil came to say goodbye. He was off to Ireland. I *shall* miss my tonic.

Beb and I dined with Bluetooth to meet Hankey—Sir Maurice as he now is. The cold in the dining room after the fire went out was so intense that I became physically and mentally congealed, but even before that I couldn't boast of my great success with Hankey. He and his wife went off in the Tube in galoshes and scarves. He is a curious man—not impressive—but quite likeable. He appears to be an invaluable *diplomatic* hybrid between a soldier and a politician, and Bluetooth seems to credit him with practically saving the Government.

Wednesday, 23rd February

Still bitter cold with snow falling. Went out with Adele about clothes for her matinee. I feel more than half inclined to back out of it: it seems a brilliantly vulgar conception, a mix-up between actresses, mannequins, and 'society lydies', and open to attack on many grounds —amongst others on war economy—as the mannequins will be there as advertisements of their very expensive establishments. We went to Eros's and chose quite a pretty black model to be copied for me in pink.

Dentist with Major Bluetooth at six. He has been invited to go on the Air Council. Sir Ian Hamilton, Papa, Gwendoline, Osborne and Muriel Beckett came to dinner. Papa has just passed a sad milestone in his life: a man in a bus—about forty years old—had relinquished his seat in his favour.

Thursday, 24th February

Caught the 4.55. Found Stanway in deep snow. Telegram from Beb: STOPPED BY SNOW.

Friday, 25th February

Deep snow on the ground. I thought rather wistfully of the days when I used to pray on my knees to wake up and find it on the ground: now I'm afraid I would rather have the tennis court intact, a sad sign of grown-upness! I went to the station and met Beb, who arrived about eleven, quite happy—having spent the night like a 'carol' in a comfortable inn.

Papa did two geographical puzzles I had ordered from Selfridges— one of Europe and one of Canada. I also succumbed to their charms and learnt a little geography. One can hardly recognise Papa as the same 'mellow fellow' who played tennis in London. He and Beb played chess after dinner. Mamma very, very low. I read Arnold Bennett's *These Twain*: I can't think why it doesn't bore one.

1916

Saturday, 26th February

Still deep snow. After lunch Mamma, Beb, Papa and I went for a very deliberate constitutional. Papa in a fur cap with flaps over his ears. I walked with him and promised to ask Bluetooth if he could find a job for him. He is sadly in need of occupation. After tea Olivia, Mamma and I stumbled into one of those rare 'immortality' talks and all tentatively. Mamma seems terribly 'weaned' from life just now. She goes to my heart. I wish I could be more demonstrative and comforting.

Sunday, 27th February

Snow still falling. I walked to Didbrook with Mamma before lunch —very heavy going through snow. She talked of Yvo all the time, planning a little memorial of his letters, etc.

After lunch Beb perpetrated a most horrible atrocity. He has always been bothering about John's hair being too long and, suddenly, when I was out of the room, he hacked about two inches off on one side. He brought the hair in to show me. I rushed in and found poor John looking a figure of fun. I have seldom been more unhappy and never more angry: I wept and made an awful scene before Nurse. It really was an abominable thing to do. We had always taken so much trouble about the cutting of his hair, and he had such a good medieval club head, just what I wanted. Now the whole ear—a feature I consider obscene—is exposed, and it will take months and months for the hair to grow right again. Damn! Beb was full of irritating sophistries, not nearly contrite enough. He tried to be funny and said we could each look at the side we preferred. Poor nurse is miserable. God—I am angry!

Monday, 28th February

Still snow. There's no doubt it's a practically unmitigated nuisance. Mr Blow* arrived in the evening—a real ghost of one's past. When I was a child he was *the* Key to Heaven; now he makes me sleepy—alas! Bateman came to dinner, very typical. Papa went away in the morning, rather mortified by my defeating him in a jigsaw puzzle race. No particular news of the Verdun battle. I suppose thousands are dying each minute.

Tuesday, 29th February

After dinner I read Whibley's *Blackwood's* article aloud—real gutter-press. Blow talked a lot about his much adored Kitchener. What a curious relationship! Apparently K. is devoted to him and they are always together. Blow had had breakfast with him the day he came down here. This association or some unknown agent has had a very brightening effect on Blow. He is wonderfully improved—hope for us all!

Wednesday, 1st March

I had to go up to London to take part in Adele's 'frightfulness' at the Gaiety. The whole-length portrait of me with the violin appeared in this week's *Sketch*. I can't help thinking it was a good joke. At Bruton Street I found a letter from an unknown writer beginning: 'Hearing you are such a skilful violinist, I thought you might like to purchase an excellent violin. My wife, formerly a *German girl*, now a *French governess*, etc., etc.'

I lunched with Bluetooth. We were quite happy. He promised to try and find work for Papa. Went round to Reville's about my acting clothes: finally settled—without much conviction—on the black, gladiatorial hat, the red coat with a short umbrella-shaped Reville gown, and black patent leather boots. Had my hair waved.

Telephoned to Adele when I got home. She asked me if I would take the speaking part of Elizabeth who is ill. Like an ass, I lost my head and said 'yes'. I could so easily have been firm, but I thought it would only involve saying a word or two in chorus. It's monstrous the way I was let into this vulgar business! Adele sent round my part 'Miss Eliza Ascot'. Diana and I are girls meeting in a dressmaker's shop. I have to say the most appallingly difficult kind of thing—just ordinary colloquialisms, such as 'Oh, there you are!' It is so impossible without perfect technique to say those things naturally, and yet at the same time *loudly*. Ursula was really only declaiming, and how different that is to acting!

Thursday, 2nd March

Spent the morning in misery, thinking of the fool I was going to make of myself over my part. It was the cruellest nightmare I have ever been in. To my rage, there was an enormous audience. I had no idea of the geography of the stage or anything, but spoke my words as badly as possible—they were such brutes. I think my second sentence was the worst stumbling block.

Diana: 'So, you got my note.'

Self: 'Obviously—or did you think it was my usual subtle intuition that told me you would be here this afternoon?'

'Obviously' proved an impossible remark, and I had to cut it. None of the professionals—Ethel Levy, Lady Tree, Playfair, and so on—knew their parts or tried to put anything into them. The play really was so rottenly written, the jokes made one blush. Viola was quite funny as the frumpy Russian princess. Knoblock—the author—directed the proceedings feebly. I hope never to experience so unpleasant an afternoon. Went home in despair.

Mary had come up from Pixton and I slept with her. The household in rather a hysterical condition about us all three being there at once. Unfortunately, a new housemaid had just arrived and, thinking the present situation was the normal state, she pronounced it to be an impossible place.

Friday, 3rd March

Woke up with that terrible feeling of impending ordeal. Basil arrived from Ireland and telephoned. He is staying with that gaoler Nancy and found some difficulty in getting out of dining with her, but managed to do so. Playfair—God bless him!—had suggested coming round to take us through our parts, so Diana and Nancy and Countess Papenheim had a rehearsal at Bruton Street during which we locked Mary out of her own dining room. Playfair was very hopeful.

I went to make up at Countess Papenheim's and we drove to the Gaiety together. Then followed the worst two hours of my life. wandering aimlessly in growing panic from dressing room to dressing room, asking everyone's advice as to one's make-up, one's last inch of confidence choked by the utter ugliness of one's bedizened face at close quarters; standing about on stage, trod on by hot supers, knocked by scenery; not knowing where to go and longing to die, with that terrible feeling of being caught in a trap and the futility of exposing oneself to such misery. It was one's own fault. The things that *happen* in life are bad enough, but the things one brings on oneself!

I made an impromptu appearance in Hawtrey's play by walking behind the stage when there was a window at the back of it. The whole audience saw me and were much amused. A super was appalled and indignant: 'Oh, you can be seen there!' With a splitting head and craving for air, I bolted like a rabbit into somebody's dressing room and opened a window—the door banged to. The same super rushed in and said I had made a noise like a gun going off. At last, at last, it came to our turn! We got through it somehow, and now it is just a blue in my mind. The audience never laughed, how could they? I believe we looked quite nice, on the whole, though I expect most of us *below*, rather than *above* our average. The dumb ladies were Norah, Mrs Reubens, Muriel Wilson, Mrs Lavery, Phyllis Boyd, etc., etc.

We threw flowers into the stalls at the end as if we were trying to propitiate a somewhat chilly audience. Thank God it's over! I believe both Diana and I were quite inaudible from the dress circle. Iris Capel was unwillingly dragged on to the stage at the last moment as the Duchess said she could not allow Diana to act unless the name of some respectable girl figured on the programme. Basil came to see me after I got back.

Saturday, 4th March

Woken at dawn by the telephone, tore to it to find that I had been disturbed by correspondence involved by the servants' love affairs. It happened twice before eight o'clock. How I sympathised with Papa's telephonic troubles at Cadogan Square, where he was rung up by enquiries as to where his footman gets his false teeth!

Mary and I couldn't get breakfast until we had nearly fainted from hunger—great domestic ructions. The new housemaid who arrived on the same day as us has given notice. The edict has gone forth that Bruton Street is to have a complete rest-cure, so Beb and I lose our ideal central nest. I don't know where we can perch in London now, and I'm sure I shall never be able to keep Beb quiet at Clonboy, which Evelyn has lent to us from the 18th of this month.

Plans are perplexing, and sometimes I get very depressed about the shapelessness of my life. In spite of great war sorrow—I suppose because of improved health—I feel much more *potential* now than ever before, and the idea of a little London house of one's *own* is a well-nigh intoxicating one. However, I dare say it's just as well to have something concrete and impersonal to grumble at. I can't get really badly anxious about money, though God knows no one's future was ever less secured! One can't get really depressed when there is no long vista, nothing but blind corners.

Beb and I came to Stanway to find it still in snow. Only Mamma and Olivia.

Sunday, 5th March

Still more and more snow. I am weary of God's crude practical joke.

1916

Triumphant success of my joke—a notice in the *News of the World* saying I am one of the most skilful violinists in Society!

Tuesday, 7th March

The snow redoubling its efforts. Great expedition into Worcester to see Mary Anderson's return to the stage after a withdrawal of over twenty-five years. The entertainment was in aid of the disabled Worcesters. Several people sang and Mary Anderson acted in *Comedy and Tragedy*, written for her by Gilbert in about 1888. It really was very moving, and what it must have felt like to her, it makes one cry to think. I thought it really a *wonderful* performance. She came to life before one on the stage, getting to look younger and younger. I had no idea she had *ever* been such a good actress. I thought her really brilliant, and it was wonderful tour de force at fifty-three. She had the greatest furore any actress has ever had. It is amazing that she could have relinquished such triumph as she tasted and settled down for life at Broadway. I suppose her giving such evidence of the absence of the 'artistic temperament' is the reason I have always been told that she was never really a good actress, but owed her glittering success merely to her looks and grace. Her voice and gesture are perfect.

Wednesday, 8th March

Snowed all night. There's no doubt it is depressing. These days I feel very much reminded of how deeply sad one is. In London one is made to forget for bits of time with sharp reminders—here one *sucks* tragedy. I really don't know which is best, only I do wish I was more conscious of some *continuity*, and was less just made by my context. The thought of Verdun and what is happening sickens one. It has all become nauseating.

Great fussification going on about Bibs' confirmation. Bateman funks it and, without asking Mamma, has sprung it on the Priest. Shyness forbids Bibs to be prepared by him. Mamma told Bateman *I* had raised the question of confirmation. He was much impressed. Thank God he doesn't know that it arose from a discussion on the bareness of Bibs' wardrobe: 'Be confirmed and you'll then have a new dress'.

Sockie attacked me at lunch by asking Bibs some questions for which she had been specially crammed—the names of the Graces, the Muses, etc. Retaliation for my asking Bibs the date of Waterloo, etc. She is pathetically formal. She always asks Mamma if she may get up and, if Mamma doesn't hear, she really waits for permission. Yesterday, after Mamma had come in to lunch, she said: 'You didn't see me, but I did stand up to say good morning to you.' A solemn ritual is that Bibs must always rush to open the door for Sockie's exits. As Sockie has St. Vitus's dance and Bibs is clumsy, this involves much noise, many collisions, and some breakages. Bibs is very loyal about her, and to my mind distressingly subservient and good—morbid about being punctual to the minute for her lessons.

Thursday, 9th March

Day of terrible depression. I suppose a thaw is the most conducive atmosphere. I am distressed about Mamma. She doesn't seem to get any better. If only one could make people's *presence* as *intense* a happiness as their absence is sorrow. One should teach oneself to be as consciously glad that Bibs is alive as one is sad that Yvo is dead. If I could only canonise the living instead of the dead.

Friday, 10th March

No snow actually forward. Beb more energetic about walking and 'taking notice' of his surroundings. He and I walked to Wood Stanway in the afternoon. Margaret Smith came to tea. Apparently Viva is in considerable distress in France. She refuses to go into the hostel Angela has provided for the Buffet girls—says it's insanitary and beastly—so, at present, she is getting neither money nor board. I think she had much better find other employment if she can. Papa and Angela seem to have lost interest in the Canteen.

I read Mamma two chapters of *The Egoist* after dinner: she fell asleep. Found Bibs crying in bed, so told her she might sleep with me. She came with all her luggage, numberless relics—little presents Yvo gave her—all of which have to be severally kissed . . . poor darling little ritualist!

Saturday, 11th March

A lot more snow fell. The weather is most depressing. I frowsted all morning. I have been re-reading *Jane Eyre* with tremendous enjoyment. I still find Rochester irresistible . . . I suppose I ought to have outgrown his charm.

1916

Tuesday, 14th March

Telegram arrived from Basil saying he wouldn't be coming to Stanway till Friday. This was annoying, as I had been going to travel down with him Wednesday, after one night at Mells. Now I had to alter all my plans as I felt I ought to stay a night in London in order to see Oc, the necessity for returning to Stanway having been removed. Very cross.

Wednesday, 15th March

I went up to London by 10.30. Had to go to Bruton Street to collect some clothes to wear in the evening. It is too tiring having all one's belongings so scattered. Basil came to see me. I was annoyed at his postponement, and his visit coincided with a most awful fit of nervous depression—a real brain storm such as I have not experienced for months. Impossible to define—whirling wheels of misery and bewilderment—no God—no income—no continuity—a sense of complete insulation. Whence, what, why was I? I felt a mere mirage. It was awful, almost like madness, but I suppose only due to over-tiredness. Naturally the interview was not a satisfactory one. Basil has never seen me like that before and I could not explain.

Dined Downing Street. Visited P.M. in bed with bronchitis for a few minutes. He looked serene, surrounded by flowers and detective stories presented by various fair friends. He promised to speak to Hankey about a job for Beb. Oc is looking wonderfully well and efficient, and is very dear. We—Oc, Beb, Violet, Bongie, Margot, Oc's colonel, and a girl (an Argentine, I think) went to *Romance*, an American play. I enjoyed it enormously, and thought Doris Keane, the great American star, wonderfully fascinating and thrilling. I was quite irritated by Beb's lack of temperament in not falling in love with her, if I had been a man I should have jumped over the footlights. Her gesture is perfect; her clothes too lovely—I am quite converted to crinolines. Owen Nares coped very cleverly with a very difficult part.

Beb is staying at Downing Street. It was very funny meeting him at the theatre like old days.

Thursday, 16th March

Interviewed a cook and engaged her for Clonboy next week. Travelled back to Stanway. Basil had begged me to stay and come down with him tomorrow, but I had been dignified and refused. Mamma in better spirits. My nursery, alas, a 'bare, ruined choir where late the sweet birds sung'. It's indescribable how I miss them. They have gone to stay with Nurse's mother for a few days on their way to Clonboy.

My earring I lost at Irene's when I played poker the other time I was in London had never been found. I really can't write to Scotland Yard again. They will think me mad, enquiring for three different possessions in one week—purse, bag and muff. It *was* a bad week!

Friday, 17th March

Lovely day. Bibs and I both had 'spring fret'. Basil, Beb, and Papa came by late train. Atmosphere at beginning of dinner not quite comfortable, but it got all right. Talked about old Oxford dons, etc. Papa and Beb played chess. I read *Markheim* to the others in same room—rather a failure. I felt very flat and depressed. It is the first occasion in which Basil has not proved a tonic. I had a sort of feeling that one chapter is over, and the sort of sparkle of spring gone out of our relationship.

Saturday, 18th March

Basil and I went for a walk at three. We went up to the source of the spring, and sat on a fence by Russell's pond. Still feeling faintly the same *désenchanté* sensation, but much less so. It was a lovely spring afternoon.

I think the doctor he went to about his throat rather alarmed him about his health. Like all wonderfully illness-free men, I expect he will get nervous once his attention has been drawn. The doctor told him he had no reflexes and implied heart trouble. I think he is beginning to feel the first signs of advancing years and is a little depressed. It was a nice walk, on the whole.

Papa carried Basil off for chess after dinner. A Miss Wilkinson arrived. She is at present governess to Pamela Glenconner and, as she will be free before long, she had come on approval *in case* Mamma thought it worth removing Sockie in her favour. She is pretty and pleasing. Papa and Mamma were both charmed with her. Bibs, who is passionately loyal to Sockie, was surrounded by barbed-wire fences of prejudice, saying she didn't want a 'dressy governess with papers on literature'. Mamma and Miss W. had a talk in the sitting room.

1916

Sunday, 19th March

Pouring rain. In the afternoon conducted a dripping party to Hailes Abbey—Beb, Bibs, Basil, Olivia, and Miss Wilkinson. They were very unkind—Basil asking 'When are we going to see the Abbey?' *after* we had contemplated its certainly rather inadequate ruins. The *comble* was when he had to pay *all* our entrance fees at the museum, no one else having any money. Bateman came to tea. I read one act of *Hamlet* to Basil before dinner. He and Beb played chess, and Papa and Basil had a very eager contest in most of which Papa triumphed.

Monday, 20th March

At luncheon we all competed in the right enunciation of 'To be or not to be': very satisfactory, as we each thought ourselves best. Beb and Basil played chess. I rested on sofa, and then read two more acts of *Hamlet* to Basil in Cabinet ministers' room.

I am removing my 'base' after a visit of about six months, so I am uncomfortably busied with books, letters, and various accumulations.

Tuesday, 21st March

Beb, Basil and I travelled by the eight o'clock train. We breakfasted together. They agreed over their eggs and bacon that the tendency of war was to depreciate Woman and her significance, the cameraderie therefrom born between men being a much stronger thing than love. I put in a feeble plea for the Venus and Mars theory. Basil and I travelled third—Beb first. We did some gibbetting. It may be subjective—I can't tell. (Four lines are here eradicated by C.A.) We parted at the station—a diminution of glimpses seems the result of these last days together. I think our high water mark was during my two visits to London, but I can't analyse.

Travelled down to Windsor by 4.30. Found children had arrived all right. Evelyn has lent us this house while she is in Ireland. We have got her housemaid and a Belgian refugee, Jean Baptiste, is acting as a kind of butler. I have got my own cook and it is an appalling thought to be ordering and paying for one's own food after so long a holiday. I interviewed before dinner, and tried to be clever about meticulous war economies—'margarine', no lump sugar . . . Had a very straightforward solitary dinner and went to bed early very tired.

Wednesday, 22nd March

Very depressed and shrinking from life in the morning—a prey to one of my morbid attacks. Having for so long complained of not having a house to myself I now felt unprotected, exposed, and rather lost. Felt incapable of making an atmosphere of my own. It was a very wintry day and the house was bitter cold, which was probably what chilled my blood and consequently my thoughts. I breakfasted in bed and then came down to cope with the cook.

Took the children in motor to Windsor to meet Beb arriving at 12.42. I felt sick and torpid, and could not give him a happy welcome, but luckily he was in good spirits himself. He had spent the night at Downing Street. Of course his father has been characteristically inert and nothing has been arranged with Hankey. I wrote to Bluetooth and asked him if he could have them to luncheon to meet one another.

We went for a walk in the afternoon. He appalled me by saying that, even if the war stopped now, he would never return to the Bar but intended to become a novelist! Cheering prospect for me. Our future is indeed on the knees of the gods—most parlous with growing goblins and decreasing income. John developed a cold and stayed upstairs, and we went and played with Michael and him after tea. John has a very good recitation of 'Johnny Head in Air'—surprised to find he knew it by heart. Fish and cold lamb for dinner. Beb read me some AE. I was very toxic and went to bed early—Beb very sweet and revelling in having a 'nest' to ourselves.

Thursday, 23rd March

Snow falling again to my disgust. At six I went off to call on Miss Weisse, having had the inspiration of trying to explain John to her. I felt all the old tremor on driving up to the door. She was really very nice and very interested—said she thought it sounded 'anxious', but that it might be quite all right, and realised my great hopes by offering to take him for half an hour every day. I am to take him for diagnosis at 9.30 next Tuesday. It will be most interesting. After dinner Beb read me a little of *The War and After* by Lowes Dickinson.

Friday, 24th March

Beb and I went up to London by train soon after luncheon—this time to 'cuckoo' at Downing Street . . . reluctantly, as its atmosphere distresses me, but it was the only double perch I could find. I went

to Miss North and tried on my new dress, a resuscitation quite un-
recognisable of the lovely pink and silver brocade Adele gave me in
the summer. It has an incipient crinoline—my first—and is a great
success. The most lovely colouring—pink over blue tulle, producing
the exact effect of opal. Very becoming, I think. This cheered me a
little. Had hair waved.

Went home early and had long rest. I had Violet's room. Beb was
very skied—miles away. I took my temperature before dinner, feeling
very shivery. It was only 100 so I didn't feel justified in shirking
dinner, and what a dinner it was in wartime! incomprehensible enough
as it would have been in peace. Over twenty people—with few exceptions their only status was as bridge players. If you must have bridge,
why not have one or even two tables? Why shock London by feeding
twenty bores in order that you may have your bridge? It does seem
a great pity. I wore my new dress—great success—superlatively
dewdropped by Margot.

I sat near —— who always reminds me of little Lord Fauntleroy,
and is the *one* person I can't help averting my head from in self-protec-
tion from unconquerable boredom. My chief conversation was with
Lord Lurgan, comparatively pleasant. He regaled me with stage
gossip, having apparently been a great theatrical patron.

Saturday, 25th March

Found the Droghedas (why?) and Duff when we arrived at Walmer
Castle. Sylvia Henley who is now 'leading lady' had motored down.
Short rest before dinner—wore new gown—sat between P.M. and
Bogie Harris. P.M. talked to Lady Drogheda nearly all the time,
though the next morning he denied Sylvia's imputation of being *sous
la charme*. I must say she is a 'dainty dish'—she and His Ex *are* a
couple—a good deal of such handsomeness as she had is gone, she
has got so lined. However, I have to mourn another (almost my last)
prejudice, she seemed very kindly and I quite liked her. The husband
seems extremely nice. I was rather glad to see Bogie again. He puzzles
me. I can't gauge his brains or anything about him. He is somewhat
of a mystery. I believe no one knows his income, occupation, or love
affairs.

Two tables of bridge got to work directly after dinner, leaving
Beb and I and Bluetooth over. The latter and I went to the P.M.'s
sitting room—I can't talk under the shadow of bridge. He accused
me, to my surprise, of an 'Excelsior' tendency and of not being sufficiently earthy. I thought no one was ever less of a missionary! A few

words with Margot and Elizabeth in bedroom. Margot in good spirits.
Elizabeth is better. The wind was howling round the castle; one
couldn't believe one wasn't in a ship far out at sea.

Sunday, 26th March

Lovely cold spring morning. I came down to breakfast, which in
this household even calls itself ten, and even so the P.M. didn't appear
until everyone else had finished. Lady D. mixes her colours very
badly for a morning light and looks very garish. A contingent went
off to golf. I went for a walk with Duff—'quite enjoyable'. A report
was heard by some optimist, and we had hopes of an air attack and
collected on the battlements only to be disappointed. It is a real castle,
castellated, battlemented, and drawbridged. Inside there is a fairly
thick Beauchamp veneer—numberless Medici prints, etc.

At lunch I sat between P.M. and Lord Drogheda. P.M. sniffs and
looks bored at any mention of shrapnel or anything to do with the war.
Of course he has not bestirred himself about Beb's employment. I
must say he is distressingly lacking in nepotism. Beb met Hankey at
Bluetooth's on Saturday, but he has no vacancy for him and recom-
mends his applying to the Admiralty for intelligence work. I shall
write to Mr Balfour.

The whole party escorted the P.M. to Dover, where he and his
colleagues embarked for the conference in Paris. I rather wished I
were going, but I had pledged myself to walk with Bluetooth. The
others returned to tea—Margot in very good form. Directly afterwards they sat down to two tables of bridge and played, with an interval for dinner, unceasingly until midnight—a disgusting orgy I
thought it. Beb read me Margot's article in the *Strand*. It is some
pages from her diary, relating electioneering experiences when her
brother Eddie had stood for Glasgow. She gives a description of the
P.M., whom she then heard speak for the first time, saying how his
face made up for unimpressive figure, etc. She has been given £100
for this breach of taste.

Monday, 27th March

I went for a short walk in the garden with Bogie Harris, and at eleven
we got into the car to motor all the way to London. I sat on the box.
It was very cold and draughty. I had no veil and felt rather skinned by
the time we reached London—it is eighty miles. I went down to
Clonboy by 4.50. Children met me at station—pouring rain. Beb

arrived in time for dinner. We are very happy in our little empty nest here. It is rather a luxury to be alone again. I tried to read 'In Memoriam' experimentally aloud to Beb, but he wouldn't take much of it.

Tuesday, 28th March

Took John at 9.15 for his first interview with Miss Weisse. Most interesting. I eavesdropped in the next room. Quite a success I think. She did seem to arrest his attention a little and he confessed a wish to return to her. She played to him and tried to make him count. He came down to dinner and behaved far better than he ever has before, really seeming more a normal companion.

Wednesday, 29th March

Beb had a new book on the war which absorbed him after dinner. I read *Katharine Furze* by Mark Rutherford. Unluckily, I stayed down till after the lights were all put out. Priding myself on being like a cat in the dark, I scorned the proffered candle and ran along the passage, entirely forgetting those horrid three steps. I hurtled down them with a terrific crash. Rose feeling very shaken, with unpleasant sensations in the right ankle. It didn't hurt much at first, but about three I found myself in what seemed to me intolerable pain. I couldn't bear the bed-clothes on my foot and Beb gave me a clothes basket which proved an admirable crèche. I had an all but sleepless night, and morning found me of the opinion that *pain* was after all the *only* reality in the world and therefore the war must be stopped.

Thursday, 30th March

I sent for the doctor but he didn't come till late afternoon. He said it was not my ankle but my foot, in which I had torn a ligament. He said it was very painful (joyful hearing), and would take some time and that I must have massage. Very bored at the expense. Very, *very* cross.

Friday, 31st March

I had a letter from Mr Balfour in the evening. I had written to ask him whether he could give Beb temporary employment at the Admiralty. He said he would be very glad to find something congenial in his office, but didn't think there was anything worthy of Beb's abilities as the Intelligence Department was overstocked. He suggested his applying to French for anti-aircraft work, for which he was qualified. This seems the obvious course and I shall write a letter to General French.

Saturday, 1st April

Lovely, really warm spring day. I came downstairs hopping like a young blackbird. I'd no idea what an exertion hopping was. It's awfully tiring and shaking. Michael thought my movements most entertaining and enthusiastically encored each hop: 'Mummie dance more'. Bluetooth arrived soon after five: Stella[1]—the fourth member of our symmetrical party—was unable to come until the next morning. Talked to Bluetooth before dinner. The cook produced a very good chicken trimmed with sausage, bacon, etc., and the turtle soup (tablets from Fortnum and Mason) was a success. Our à trois family dreaded by me went off quite well.

Sunday, 2nd April

Stella arrived before lunch. She was very pleasant, if trite, and I still think her profile superlatively pretty. Beb is happy with her. They walked in the afternoon and, in lack of a foot or a motor, Bluetooth and I drove through the forest in a nice leisurely fly—really a very pleasant means of locomotion when one is free of a goal. B. very nice. There has been no return to a higher gear since that uncomfortable evening after which I wrote to him.

Took Stella to the nursery after tea—saw children in their baths. Quite successful evening. Stella told us of her African life: she appears, like a second St Francis, to have wandered amongst lions, leopards, and apes. Just before bedtime we had recourse to some gibbets, but they weren't necessary.

Monday, 3rd April

The magical weather still holding out. Stella didn't go till after early lunch. I sat out a little in the afternoon and watched the children playing blissfully in the garden—they came down after tea. Beb read to me 'The Eve of St Agnes'. Its magic perfection and sumptuous richness came to me with a fresh shock.

Beb is so happy here—absolutely content without occupation.

1. Beech, née Campbell, daughter of Mrs Patrick Campbell.

1916

Tuesday, 4th April

Thrilled by *The First Seven Divisions*, which I began reading before dinner. After dinner I read *The Newcomes* to myself, and then we played a game of chess. Beb gave me a castle. I won—I can't think why—I suppose he was experimenting, so I went to bed thinking chess an excellent game.

Thursday, 6th April

Nasty relapse to cold weather. Letter from Bluetooth saying: 'Carson —curse him—has made himself leader of the Tories and intends to lead them out of the Coalition, which will mean the devil of a mess'.

Friday, 7th April

I had a very nice letter from General French, saying he would look into the case and write again. Donald Tovey* is engaged to an Edin-burghite—a hard blow for poor Miss Weisse no doubt. She complains of lack of humour in her letters—I don't know how she could show its presence.

Saturday, 8th April

We expected Gwendoline at about three, but she didn't come (she motored down) till about 6.30, so we had rather a hanging-about afternoon. Eddie arrived about seven. He was made to travel with bottles of wine like John Gilpin, as Beb had forgotten to order it. Again no whisky, but Eddie was comforted by beer at bedtime.

We did gibbets after dinner. I *am* enjoying their revival. I can't think why I allowed them so long a slumber. About ten years ago the 'gibbeting' phase was the most marked of my life, and then Eddie and I were, I should think, almost the champion exponents of the art. We found we were still pretty good and both went to bed un-hung. Hair-combed with Gwendoline a little.

Sunday, 9th April

Gibbets again after dinner. I was unhung, but hung Eddie once with 'Where souls do couch on flowers we'll hand in hand'. Eddie told a very good child story, about a dog called Paddy run over by motor and killed. Mother hardly dared break news to child. Did so during pudding. To her intense relief, after a second's pause, the child calmly continued pudding. Later mother heard crying, and found child with absolutely tear-congealed face: 'Oh Mummie, Paddy's killed'.

Mother: 'Yes, but I told you that at lunch, darling'.

Child: 'Oh, I thought you said it was Daddy!'

I enjoyed our Sunday party. I began to think, after all, I should have enjoyed hostessing. Gwendoline is always real pleasure to me, and her company is the sweetest flattery. She has a wincing-curtseying-with-appreciation manner only rivalled by Basil, and *such* delicious daintiness of mind—quaintness without a tinge of preciousness. Eddie very dear and 'as you were', sadly bereaved, but bravely cheerful.

Monday, 10th April

Lovely sunny morning. Sat out very happily in the garden with Gwendoline. We started a traffic in dewdrops and she produced some really sustaining ones for me. She was amusing about all the gossip and surmising about Beb and me in the old days. She said the Duchess of Wellington, wishing to hold me out as a sad warning to Eileen, constantly said, 'I saw Cynthia looking too lovely, but I notice she had no very nice furs'.

We motored up with Gwendoline after lunch—great luxury. We were perching at Downing Street—tired into palpitations by the atmosphere at once. It's exactly like a scene in a farce round about Miss Way's room. Elizabeth was rushing about trying on a new evening dress with a hat on; about three telephone messages were going on at once; the hospital nurse was buzzing about (she has been converted into a sort of sub-Miss Way and seems to do all Elizabeth's telephoning, and also to be her confidante and lady's maid); Margot came dashing in and began to eat poached eggs with Puffin, grabbing at Elizabeth's dress (a present from Mrs Cavendish Bentinck) and saying it looked as if it had been bought at a Red Cross sale . . .

Puffin, Elizabeth, Beb, Oc, Cis, and I dined together and Puffin, Beb and I went to the Barrie play. There I was awkwardly placed between dear little Puffin, who thought it all lovely and sweet, and Beb, who groaned with disgust at nearly every word. I tried hard to prevent Puffin's feelings being hurt. I remember so well how one hated the attitude of 'grown-ups' when one was a child. Stella's voice sounded very pretty.

Tuesday, 11th April

I was in Violet's old room, which isn't at all bad, except that the bell is in no way connected with Polly, and I hated telephoning filtered through a butler—I am so unused to it. There was a floater because I took Miss Way's telephone book. Oh, how I 'covet my neighbour's house'!

Sat between P.M. and Puffin at lunch. P.M. was flanked by poor trumpeting Lady Reading. Lord Reading produced a most delicious pidgeon-English letter from a *babu*. P.M. told me pathetic story of the Italian speech which he had so elaborately prepared and rehearsed, only to find that the deputation were all blatantly English.

I went off early to Baroness D'Erlanger's house with Elizabeth, who had organised the 'Poets' Reading' in aid of the Star and Garter Fund. I was selling programmes, so got in for nothing. It was a most amusing idea, ten live poets reading their own poems, Birrell in the chair, playing on the 'birrell organ' as the *Daily News* remarked. The poets were Belloc, Binyon, Cammaerts, Davies, Hewlett, Walter de la Mare, Newbolt, Owen Seaman, Margaret Woods, Yeats. There were also books being sold and a Max Beerbohm inspired by the occasion. I stood on my bad foot for about two hours selling programmes— the crime of selling more tickets than there were seats had been committed, so by the time I went up there was no possibility of a chair. I went to the Green Room, where it was very comic seeing all the poets thinking over their parts. It was almost impossible to hear or see. I had to stand on my bad foot in the doorway in a howling draught. I heard an actor read Julian's beautiful poem—not very well—and then Yeats recited four poems preciously, but really rather beautifully. Wonderful to be able to do it, no paralysing sense of humour there. Belloc was making an unholy row talking to Basil in the Green Room—he complained of being the 'sport of the rich at forty-six': I heard him say his 'Doris'—very funny. Then Basil and I gave up the effort to hear in disgust, and went down and had tea together.

Wednesday, 12th April

Found Beb had established himself in Violet's old sitting room. Sat with him there and we were joined by Oc and Violet—the latter had just been sitting to Orpen. I lunched with Bluetooth. Much amused by Mrs Hughes' verdict on Margot which he told me. She had lunched at Downing Street, and I suppose not been any too well treated, and on enquiry as to her impression of her hostess said, 'Oh, a very common type in New Zealand.'

Basil and I travelled down to Clonboy by the 3.50. He only caught the train by the nails of his toes, and was in a state of exhaustion and dilapidation, following on Gilbert's farewell carouses before returning to France. They had been entertaining Iris Hoey, Peggy Curran, etc. Lord Wimborne was of the party and had begged them, because of his public position, not to mention the fact that he had driven Iris Hoey home. Basil revived under the good air and wholesome fare of Clonboy, but he complains that his constitution is breaking up under him and certainly doesn't look well.

Thursday, 13th April

Very blustering boisterous morning. Breakfasted with Basil at nine. He spread out a litter of papers on the piano and played with a little work. We went out into the forest at about eleven—rested after lunch and went out again at three. It poured unjustifiably long April showers and we got soaked—the wind was cold too—we crouched behind the copper horse and saw lovely Turneresque view all round the castle.

Children came down after tea. Beb and Basil played chess—gibbets again after dinner. Our à trois meals have really gone off wonderfully well. I suppose nobody could be easier to combine than Basil, his visit has been very successful. For once I really begin to feel that I 'know' someone, and feel at home with and yet stimulated by him. Tried hard to extract a satisfactory dewdrop for Mary H.—his attitude against them is very tiresome.

Friday, 14th April

Beb woke up with temperature—an obvious case of flu. I went up to London by the four something. Put on my opal dress and drove to the Bonham Carters with the P.M. Violet had a dinner of ten before her party—P.M., A.J.B., Barrie, Soveral, Diana, Ava Astor, Goonie. I sat next to Barrie and found it a sad humiliation. He destroyed my nerve for ages, so great a bore did he convince me of being. I could *not* make him smile and, instead of telling him about my children, I found we were discussing the cinema at unjustifiable length. I was even reduced to commenting on objects on the table—luckily there were some red bananas. Bongie was on my other side, a rather pompous host.

Before the drum arrived the supper party film was gone through, so that the dinner-party censors might pronounce whether it should be presented to the public or not. Lord Bob Cecil had started a great agitation, by saying it would be most injudicious to exhibit an account of the P.M. being displayed sitting beside Madame Lichnowsky* at supper—but it was pronounced quite harmless. I must say it was very amusing, though it was sad not to see myself.

Two years ago Barrie had given a supper party for the first night of one of his plays and had everyone photographed arriving, in the stalls, and eating. It was too comic to see all one's friends characteristically passing before one's eyes. Violet made a very good appearance; Pamela Lytton and Eddie talking in the stalls were too delicious, and Montagu was sprawling—a real Caliban—in the front row. Ruby Peto and Mary Curzon passed together, looking too lovely, and Violet was seen eating and talking with great animation. Mrs Lavery, Margot, Elizabeth—*dozens* of familiar faces—and the P.M. beside Gladys Cooper. Basil appeared and came and sat beside me—he left before the end, as he was off to Ireland the next morning. There was a Charlie Chaplin film—a disgusting dentist scene—I scarcely smiled. And then there was Barrie's *Macbeth*, which certainly is funny. It was tiring— the noise made one feel one was on a night journey, and one scarcely knew who was real and who photographs. I had some conversation with Hugh and Bogie was very attentive—I think I've had a *succès* there.

Saturday, 15th April

Margot had given me a hat of hers a few days before—too ugly to be seen dead in, and also much too small. I went into Jays to ask if they would change it, but to my humiliating embarrassment they said it must be at least three or four years old.

Lunched at Downing Street with Elizabeth, Eric Drummond, Jack Tennant, Bongie, and Co. Great discussion about Pamela Lytton. I— in my opinion platitudinously, but in Elizabeth's paradoxically— supported her claims to superlative charm, saying I should have married her if a man, etc. Elizabeth and the unnatural men there demurred. Jack Tennant admitted she had made his heart beat quicker, but didn't endorse my good opinion of her intelligence. I said, 'But, surely, you don't want a woman to be good at political economy?' —rather a floater, as that is exactly his wife's forte! The P.M., coming in late, warmly supported me, saying Pamela had had the greatest erotic success of her day and was the most accomplished 'plate-spinner'. It is bad tactics on Elizabeth's part to belittle in women just those assets she is without, scoffing at Pamela, Ruby, and other beautiful sirens.

Oc travelled down to Clonboy with me by the 3.50. Found poor

Beb in bed with influenza, but temperature already brought down by drastic sweating. Oc and I walked into the forest after tea. Very *gemütlich* evening with him. He is a great dear—genial and sane to a fault.

Monday, 17th April

Gave Oc his breakfast at about ten—early for an Asquith. We sat out in the garden until he went away at about eleven. Miss Weisse came to tea. Before getting on to mine, I let her have her head on the topic of *her* son Donald Tovey. She—poor thing—is *utterly* miserable about his engagement contracted in Edinburgh. At the best I suppose it would have been hard to bear, and there seem to be no extenuating circumstances—elderly, kittenish, commonplace, and unmusical. Miss W. had thought her one point was her Antigone-like devotion to her father, but he was now to be abandoned to lodgings. Miss W. thinks she has no knowledge that she is marrying someone *remarkable*. No doubt she will learn, but the process will be a painful one. I am really sorry for poor Miss W.

John was the next topic. She recommended musical drill of some sort, and seriously advised my taking him to a child specialist. This I had already decided to do. He is nearly five and must be taken in hand. Sometimes I feel miserably worried about his abnormality. I don't *think* Miss W. is really afraid for him *ultimately*, but of course as she says, arrested development, if only temporary, interferes with a boy's career.

I walked her all the way home to Northlands. We talked about the war—interesting enough as she was in Germany for six weeks after its declaration. She certainly is very much more pro-German than most people to whom the word is applied, maintaining that they are fighting for their lives and not for aggression. She said it was very impressive, the way the whole country geared itself for war—just like lowering the gas—every expense coolly decreased. She said she had undoubted authentic information as to the number of their soldiers at the beginning of the war—over thirteen millions gross—and had offered her information to the War Office, but been scouted.

Wednesday, 19th April

I'd had a telegram from Pamela saying rehearsals at His Majesty's at 10.30, so I went up to London early. Beb stayed at Clonboy for an extra day's convalescence so, being single, I put up at Lady Wenlock's.

1916

I went to His Majesty's and found Viola,[1] Moira, Phyllis, Pamela, Joan Poynder, and a few professional men—producers and actors. There were great discussions, Pamela honeying brilliantly, and it was decided that the performance must be postponed until the 12th—general relief.

We went through the last act once—I read the part of Hypolita in the absence of Gladys Cooper. We amateurs are all doing court ladies with one or two sentences apiece. Afterwards we all went on to Burnet's and had a clothes debate—allotting the colourings. I am going to have a white velveteen dress stencilled with gold, and green sleeves.

I lunched with Katharine who is back at Bedford Square waiting for her baby. We had plovers' eggs—a gift from Venetia. Katharine rather pathetic trying to find a parlourmaid—they are almost as extinct as the dodo.

I dined with the Montagus. Venetia resplendent in a home-made tea gown self-embroidered with beads, really extraordinarily pretty. The Parsons, Diana, a temporary soldier called Cripps,* Duff, and a nice fat brother of Montagu's were the party. I sat between the latter and Montagu—quite happy. Viola was in her most ejaculatory mood —gave Diana, Venetia, and me a very spirited account of the birth of her baby. Diana, Viola, Alan, Cripps, and I played poker—the others bridge.

Viola and Diana were giving sort of imitations of themselves— every sentence a mannerism:

Viola: 'Aaauh—Blight!—GOD'S EYE!'

Diana: *'Funny* or NOT?'

Thursday, 20th April

I went off and scoured the bargain basement at Selfridges and then, in great excitement, to Park Street for my appointment with Dr Cantley. Found John there—Nurse had brought him up for the day —he was quicksilver with excitement. I went into the doctor by myself first. He had had my letter and asked me with a smile, quite a kind one, if I had been studying psychology. When John came in, of course he behaved in his *most* eccentric way—wriggling, giggling, twitching, and making faces. Cantley stethoscoped and examined him naked, finding him physically perfectly all right. He said he was a 'neurotic' type, but would prescribe nothing, opining that he would become more normal. But saying—what is obvious—that he must now have

1. Parsons, née Tree—Alan Parsons was her husband.

some form of tuition and discipline besides Nurse—something that will control, take him out of himself, and gradually coax him more on to the same plane as his fellow-creatures. I felt rather re-assured—I don't quite know why. Nurse and I took him to Stewarts, where he revelled in a lunch of Scotch broth, ham roll, banana, and cake. We discussed his unnormality more frankly and thoroughly than we ever had before. I thought her wonderfully understanding and sensible— she *is* a dear. I left them munching and went off to lunch with Blue-tooth.

My spirits had risen and I was quite merry. He told me I had got fatter and quite changed my face again. The political corner—I suppose the sharpest—has been rounded safely apparently, and a secret session (without precedent) has been decided on. Last Saturday morning, when I was at Downing Street, Margot was very hysterical and saying they would never be in Downing Street again after the following Tuesday. She was writing a special messenger note to Lord Stamfordham at the time. Walked as far as War Office with Bluetooth.

Went to Paddington for 4.50. *Terrible* holiday crush. Got into first class carriage with Papa and Angela: Beb joined us at Oxford. Found the Montagus, Flavia, Moira, Olivia, Guy, Frances, Dinah—a motley assembly. The Montagus had motored all the way down from London —a longish joy-ride, and I suppose the Treasury are responsible for the poster 'Don't motor for pleasure'! Montagu sat between me and Mamma—he, like Venetia, Angela, and Papa sat down to bridge immediately after dinner. The rest of us had a parliament in the boudoir. Long debate on the ethics of the aristocracy selling pro-grammes and on Diana. Dinah looks too wretched—her husband has just returned to the front after curtailed leave. Venetia came to my bedroom for a little.

Friday, 21st April

Excellent joke by the housemaid. At 7.30 in the morning Mamma told her to go and tell Frances there was no early celebration of Holy Communion. Instead of going to Frances, she went to Venetia!

Mr Wu[1] is a great success here. Papa and Angela both think him 'charming'—Venetia is in good form and seems very happy now. They played bridge again after dinner. The rest of us had another parliament in Mamma's sitting room—a long war debate, Beb detailing all the evidence in favour of the war being a war of attrition, and ex-plaining that that meant extermination. Poor Dinah looked grimmer

1. Montagu.

and grimmer. Hair-combing with her and Frances—Guy had held forth on the duty of having as large a family as possible, promising me ten pounds for each baby.

Saturday, 22nd April

Watched Venetia dressing. She has become the most dainty and *recherché* of women about underclothes, and has the most lovely things. It seems so anomalous and foreign to one's conception of her. They *motored* off to Alderley at about eleven.

Beb and I strolled before lunch. Too miserable to see the awful havoc wrought by the storm. So many of my favourite childhood's trees lying low. Still feeling very depressed altogether. Sockie much shocked at lunch by a flippant discussion on the prospect of post-war polygamy: Bibs frightfully seriously distressed at the hypothesis. Letter from Connor enclosing ninety-seven pounds—my share of Ickey's little fortune. Bibs got it, too, and looked heartrending. I walked up to the Pyramid with her—a magical evening. Mamma is *miserable*—it's really like a broken heart. What *can* one do?

Sunday, 23rd April

Rather fun tennis in the afternoon—Angela and I versus Papa and Dinah, and then Olivia and I versus Papa and Angela. I was victorious each time and ended up thirty shillings to the good from Papa. Angela rather obscene in *tête-à-tête* with me on tennis court.

Monday, 24th April

After lunch Mamma spoke to me about Beb's infringement of doctor's orders, Papa having pointed out to her that he had had claret, port, and brandy for lunch. I went and abused him and, I'm ashamed to say, lost my temper and when irritated by a hopelessly *irrelevant* argument actually boxed his ears. I have never been near doing such a thing before and I was more surprised than he was. Felt very ashamed, and poor Beb much annoyed. His sophistical arguments do make one angry though. Felt rather ruffled, but played some more tennis.

Tuesday, 25th April

Angela, Dinah, Frances, Papa, and I all went up to London by early train, motoring into Moreton. We actually inveigled Papa into a third class carriage.

Went to see Pamela, meaning to catch the 3.50 down to Clonboy. She persuaded me to accompany her to a cheap theatre where Mary Anderson was acting, to try and persuade her to take part in *Ariadne*. It was a delightful performance, with such a nice, rapt audience— the seats only sixpence. We were put into a box with Mr Navarro.* Ellen Terry came in after doing a Catharine of Aragon scene. She is too delicious and fascinating—a child with such marvellous, bubbling-over vitality. It was like having an electric battery in the room, and one felt ashamed of being the slug one is. Mary Anderson did the sleepwalking Lady Macbeth scene very 'powerfully'—her voice is splendid. We went round to her dressing room. She was cordial, but all Pamela's entreaties were wasted. The reasons given—genuine enough I should think—are over-business and fatigue. Navarro's passionate devotion to his wife is touching.

Caught the seven o'clock train. Found children well. News of Dublin riots in evening paper.

Wednesday, 26th April

Real divine, piping-hot summer's day—basked in garden. Beb complains I am not always in tune with the weather, and I was in a foul temper all the morning. Miserably depressed about the present and the future.

Letter from Bluetooth saying Mr Asquith revealed no secrets (at least to him) at the Secret Session, and that the situation in Ireland is appalling—the railway and the Post Office in the hands of the rebels and Dublin Castle besieged. *How* I wish I had happened to be there! I long to hear from Basil, but fear all communication may be cut.

Thursday, 27th April

News of fighting at Katia—our Yeomanry were the troops engaged. Lord Quenington's death in the paper, so I concluded no news of Ego and Tom was good news.

Friday, 28th April

Still lovely and hot. I went up to London by 11.20, perching at Frances's empty house this time. Beb followed after lunch.

I lunched with Bluetooth. He asked me if I had had any news of Ego, and aroused my anxiety, till then inexplicably slumbering. I telegraphed inquiries to Mamma at Stanway. Pamela called for me in motor to take me to Gaiety Theatre. She asked me if I had heard any 'more' about Ego, was astonished to find I knew nothing and told me, to my horror, that he was wounded *and* a prisoner! Ego a prisoner—poor, poor darling—one can't bear to think how miserable he will be. It's too cruel, and so like his pathetic luck to be captured at his very first engagement. It's too difficult to realise. Of course from our point of view, I suppose it's the only way of securing his life. The worst anxiety is removed, but the chafe and fret for him forbid self-congratulation. I think I would go almost mad—the indefiniteness of time is so awful. I can't bear it for Mamma. I had so hoped he might come back on leave soon and that it might be the one thing which might revive her—now it may be for years and years. One will be frightened about prisoners at the end of the war, too . . .

Felt very stunned. Viola was at the Gaiety and the manager explained what they had done at the rehearsal to me. Went to Belgrave Square. To my relief, Gan-Gan had already had a letter from Mamma. Letty had cabled home. Tom is a prisoner, too—poor darling Mary, how will she bear it? Uncle Guy, Dorothy and Guy's wife were there. They think it is Germans, not Turks, who have got them. I'm sorry, Turks are supposed to treat their prisoners better.

We dined with Irene—Eddie, Willie de Grunne, Oc's young Colonel Freyberg,* Phyllis, Oc, and Moira. I sat between Willie and Freyberg. The latter's brother was on the flag-ship just sunk and he didn't know whether he was amongst the saved—didn't seem to care either. Was told of the fall of Kut. It has been a ghastly war-week. We played poker. I left off exactly square.

Saturday, 29th April

We lunched at Downing Street. Sat between the P.M. and Oc. The McKennas were there. P.M. imperturbable as ever. Telegram arrived from Ireland—laconic enough—no great disturbance reported, but military said they were unable to go and disperse rebel meeting at Wexford. Everyone thinks poor Birrell will have to go. Freyberg's brother was drowned.

Sunday, 30th April

First letter from Basil since the troubles began. It was characteristically dated: '28th Fructidor, Year I of the Republic', and on the envelope there was an immense 'Opened by the Censor'. It was a sadly discreet letter and gave me no private news.

Tonks arrived teatime, just to spend the evening—funny to see him in khaki. He is in the R.A.M.C. at Aldershot, and has found some very macabre and congenial work. He does drawings (accurate) of all the badly disfigured faces before they are treated. Had longish talk with him. I took him into the forest, which was looking too lovely in the setting sun, with young green beech trees pirouetting all round one.

Monday, 1st May

Sat out a little in the afternoon, reading Queen Victoria's letters with amusement and interest. I never realised how 'soppy' she had been about Melbourne. Beb still very busy writing. He read me some of his new poems—excellent I think. We are very happy alone here and it is excellent opportunity for dedication to the children—so much easier to see them thoroughly than when staying in other people's houses. No letter from Stanway.

Wednesday, 3rd May

Lunched at Downing Street: Diana, Venetia, and Nathalie, etc., were there. Violet, Venetia, Nathalie, and I all had on the same type of hat— toque with wreath of leaves. I liked my green and gold edition best. Margot dashed off to the House to hear poor Birrell's *vale*. I believe he reduced everyone to tears—his political sun is setting in a sky of soppy affection. I had a bad neurotic *crise*—felt ill, diffident, and miserable with *crispé* nerves. Six days a week in the garden and the seventh in London is I'm sure not the right mode of life: I think one's London and country ought to be alternative, uninterrupted blocks of time. One can't get attuned for London in a day.

I rested and then went to see Gwendoline who is in bed. Her delicious company cheered me wonderfully and we had a very amusing talk about 'lovers', as to how far we were 'gullible' and whether it was the fact, or the reputation, we liked. I confessed it was testimonials I wanted.

Thursday, 4th May

Lunched Bluetooth. He had it at a quarter past one as the Gaiety claimed me at two. He told me to buy myself a purse-bag from him. Three times I've arrived with only an envelope for purse!

1916

Ghastly rehearsal—absolute chaos—poor Viola distracted, almost in tears. No professionals turned up except the facetious Ben Webster, who is doing the Duke. The children's ballet came for the first time. They, too, have a lot to learn before next Friday. We got no forwarder with our parts. The authoress had been there the day before. Her appearance is too pathetic, the most anomalous envelope for an aspiring aesthetic soul and brain: she is half cross governess, half something out of the Irish R.M.—man's collar, diagonal tie, pince-nez, spats, sandy hair, and frown. Her voice is redeeming, very remarkable, with good diction and vocabulary. She had views as to how each word should be said. When we escaped I went with Joan to see her dress tried on at Mrs Nettleship: I have got to inspire Polly to make mine for me.

We went to *Please Help Emily*, which I enjoyed quite immensely. I always love Hawtrey. Gladys Cooper had a delicious part and did it quite well. They dropped me at Irene's: she was, as usual, having a *soirée* and had given me leave to pitch my Hell there. Led by Kelly several of them were making an infernal noise joke-singing round the piano. Irene, Eileen, Duff, Montagu's brother, Hugh, and Freyberg played very distracted poker. I won four pounds.

Friday, 5th May

Caught one o'clock train to Egham for Clonboy. Found large pile of letters, including two from Basil giving an interesting account of the surrender of the biscuit factory garrison. They are quite cut off, he has had none of my letters, and writes dejectedly. At last I had a long letter from Mamma—very darling and diffusive. She thought she had wired to me. Her letter stirred me up, and I had an acute attack of misery and cried bitterly, but—oddly enough—it was about Yvo. One's emotions are like submarines—what makes them suddenly rise to the surface?

Monday, 8th May

The telephone bell rang before dinner and, to my surprise, I recognised Basil's voice. He had just come over from Ireland for a day to put Lord Wimborne's case before the P.M. I unscrupulously decided to chuck Bluetooth, and we arranged to lunch together at the Berkeley next day. Beb read me a lovely *and* erotic poem after dinner—I went to bed happier.

162

Tuesday, 9th May

I was by way of lunching at 1.15, but on account of a damned rehearsal, didn't arrive till past the half hour. Found Basil waiting, but no table at the Berkeley, so we went across to the Ritz. We had to wait a long time there—tremendous congestion owing to Drury Lane matinée. Basil looking well, and very interesting and amusing about Ireland. He had had an interview with the P.M. that morning, who had said he wanted Lord Wimborne to resign—principally (Basil thought) in order to have the gift of the post. Selfishly, B. hoped he would have to resign, as it would solve his own difficulties about getting away, but otherwise he thought there was *no* reason why he should and he had pleaded his cause with the P.M. To begin with, the Lord Lieutenant is not responsible and he (Basil) said he could witness to his having said he did want a division of soldiers for Dublin. He told me confidentially the most amusing things. His Ex had simply *swilled* brandy the whole time, and his dutiful wife had busied herself filling up his glass and writing a minute diary of his day: '3.45 His Ex telephoned, etc.' His Ex had been superlatively theatrical and insisted on his poor secretaries using the most melodramatically grandiloquent language down the telephone—standing over them to enforce his dictation: 'It is His Ex's *command.*'

The pathetic thing was that it never occurred to him that there would be any retrospective blame. He was delighted to think he was at last really in the limelight and acquitting himself so well—flushed with importance and triumph. The first intimation of a floater was the telegram saying martial law was proclaimed and Maxwell* coming over to take complete command. He was flabbergasted and miserable. Hitherto having magnified the trouble to add to his glory in coping with it, he now was anxious to belittle it, insinuating that Maxwell was not needed. Finding his arrival inevitable, he then wanted to get everything over before he arrived by negotiating with the rebels and coming to terms. What a ghastly floater if they had surrendered otherwise than *unconditionally.* Altogether he seems to have behaved like the Emperor of Asses. I hope Basil's advocacy was better when speaking to the P.M.! He said His Ex had 'done well', then gave these amazing illustrations of his conduct. He had stridden up and down the room exclaiming, 'I shall hang McNeil! I shall let the others off, but I shall hang McNeil'—as though he were plenipotentiary. Basil said Maxwell's coming had been a great blow and surprise to Birrell, too.

Basil was away at Belfast when the trouble began: he rushed back and had great difficulty in persuading the sentries to recognise and let him through. I enjoyed my lunch very much. We walked to the Bath

Club, picked up the beloved Freddie, and went on to Bruton Street together. Beb arrived at the same time, and we all went in and mobbed Mary Herbert. Basil telephoned to Bongie to arrange another meeting with the P.M.

Wednesday, 10th May

Letter from Basil saying he was off to Ireland (Tuesday night). He had seen the P.M. again and thought Lord Wimborne would have to go. Mary telephoned a letter from Lord Howard: good news as far as it went—the badly wounded had been left behind and there was, after all, a railway quite near, so they will not have had the long, hot trek.

Lord Wimborne's resignation in the evening paper.

Thursday, 11th May

Beb, McKenna and I drove to Bluetooth's together. The rest of the party were Aggie, Pamela, and darling Birrell. Birrell had asked if he might leave it open till the last moment as he never knew whether he would feel able to face people. He looked melancholy enough, but was very sweet and amusing—McKenna too comic. I really do like him—he appeals to the fraction of me which loves Dickens. We had great fun chaffing him about the Zeppelin night, which he spent in driving about with Eileen Wellesley and the P.M., whom they dropped at Downing Street. He simply *revelled* in the badinage, continually harking back to the subject if it was allowed to drop: 'So the P.M. said we dropped him like an old sack, did he?' (delightedly). The topic occupied most of dinner.

After dinner there was an excellent stage telephoning between McKenna and Jack Tennant, each trying to postpone the reading of their Bill to a later day: 'Can't yer take the air on Monday—do,' etc., etc. Afterwards McKenna sang 'A Little Gorblimey Hat' as a stunt. He told how he recited Burke for ten minutes every morning of his life, and had cured himself of stammering by this excellent habit. Walked back to Downing Street and found Margot still at bridge, and P.M. gone to Ireland.

Friday, 12th May

Zoller came to do my hair at eleven. This time I had a big Titian plait braided with pearls round my head, and it was successful. We had to be at the theatre at twelve for final rehearsal of our scene: I made Beb escort me—he was rather embarrassed by my appearance. At last a little trouble was taken about us, and we were properly grouped—Lady Tree, Duchess of Rutland and Diana all helping with suggestions. We had picnic food, each of us having brought contributions, in a small dressing room. A Gaiety girl appeared offering to do up our faces. She bedizened me in the most ghastly way, making my face look like a mask—and a very ugly one, too—introducing a cupid's bow to my mouth, almost up to my nose. We had the usual hours of anguish, looking at ourselves with despair and taking incompatible advice from everyone. Stella Campbell rectified my face as well as she could.

We listened to some of the play from behind—applause fairly tepid—and when the time came got through our scene without disgrace. I said 'Madam' at the wrong moment, interrupting Viola's song, but it didn't matter much. I believed our scene looked pretty, but nearly everyone—I fear—was bored stiff by the play, pronouncing it hopelessly undramatic, tedious and dragging.

We went into a box to watch the rest of the performance. When it was over Eileen, Irene, Moira, and I went on to see Katharine in our war-paint. As we got into our taxi a man in the crowd said, 'You don't often see a nice bit of stuff like that'. Venetia, Diana, and Raymond were brutally candid about the play, thinking it execrable, but they are not fair barometers. It's sad to have taken part in two such failures as this and *The Latest Thing*. I went to Cadogan Square to see Mamma before dinner—my hair still smothered in gold dust. She looked very tired. I dropped her at Mr Balfour's, and Beb and I dined with Frances.

Saturday, 13th May

Was rung up by telephone just as I was starting for dentist and found, to my surprise, that it was Muriel just back from Egypt. Horrifying news! People had been to identify the bodies left on battlefield at Katia. There was none which could possibly be Ego's, but alas one the description of which corresponded to Tom. The Turks had removed their identification discs so, of course, there is a chance it may have been someone else's, but from Muriel's account I fear it is a very slender one. Soon I suppose the list of the prisoners' names at Damascus will come to London, and then, and not till then, we shall know the truth.

Met John at Dr Shuttleworth, the specialist recommended by Miss Weisse. John answered above his average. The doctor disquieted me on the whole. He said, 'You can't go by looks', and there *might* be indubitable 'intelligence' permanently without control. I feel cold terror about John now more and more often. It is just because the word 'stupid' is so inapplicable and because of a strange completeness about him as he is, that makes one despair of any reason why he should ever change. Oh God, surely nothing so cruel can really have happened to me myself? I must just hope and wait and hope.

Friday, 19th May

Went to Downing Street for lunch. P.M. just back from Ireland, looking very rubicund and pleased with his joy-riding. I sat beside a poor blinded officer who had been at the wonderful St Dunstan's institution for the blind. He was most pathetic and very nice, making one's heart ache. I had to cut up his food for him, and there was an awful moment when he thought his empty plate had got food on it.

Returned to Cadogan Square and found Mamma, Papa, Beb, and Sockie. Inexpressibly relieved to hear all our alarms on Tom's account were false. He is safe at Jerusalem on the way to Damascus. Through the American Embassy we had asked for their two names and Tom's had been cabled, but alas not Ego's. This is too cruelly disappointing. I'm afraid it is fairly conclusive evidence that he can't be with Tom, so we have no idea where he is. There seems no reasonable doubt that he must have started with them from the battlefield, since all the bodies and badly wounded have been identified. As it was a twelve-hour march to the railway, the assumption is that he cannot have been very badly wounded, but of course he may have got worse and been obliged to be left somewhere—it's horrid not knowing. According to rumour, he was at first shot in the shoulder, and so slightly that, after having his wound dressed, he was able to go back into action. There is, however, a rumour that he was wounded a second time and someone has got hold of the idea that it was in the lung. This sounds mere *gossip*, though. Mamma terribly worried, over-tired, and nervy.

Mary Herbert came in with lots of confusing Egyptian rumours. Apparently the poor Yeomanry made a magnificent fight of it, standing up against seven to one odds for about fourteen hours with only one machine gun. There was some disastrous headquarters blunder. One wounded man whom Mary Strickland visited said he heard the man next to him say, 'There goes Elcho with the white flag.' If this were true, it would prove that Ego was still well enough to be active at the close of the battle.

Saturday, 20th May

Breakfasted with darling Bibs. Took Mamma to Paddington to catch the 10.30. She was going all the way to Truro to stay in Miss Jourdain's convent for a rest. She took a crucifix as an offering. She seemed better and calmer. We put the clocks on an hour in obedience to the Daylight Saving Bill.

Monday, 22nd May

Letter arrived from Ettie enclosing one from Fitzgerald, or someone, saying Kitchener was trying to get Beb an appointment in France, so I had to confess to Beb what I had done. He was annoyed, saying he couldn't possibly accept a Staff job until he had some further training at Woolwich, as the marine guns are naval and different from the army ones. I don't know what will happen.

Tuesday, 23rd May

Beb went up to London by the 11.20 to go to War Office and arrange for a transfer from the Marines to the Royal Field or Royal Horse Artillery. Telegram from Papa saying Ego's name was not in list sent from Constantinople, but the doctor had been left at Arish with some wounded whose names were not given—I suppose he is amongst them.

Saturday, 27th May

The historic first meeting between Papa and the Stricklands[1] took place and was a great success. Mrs S.'s hats are so sad, but they are all three so nice and comfortable. Papa admired Barbara this time: she was looking very pretty. Poor Mary had had a superlatively soppy letter to Tom returned to her with the explanation that they had condensed it into four lines. It was pages and I wonder which lines they selected, one was 'My ever beloved plush-necked darling'. What fun the censor must have had!

Sunday, 28th May

Lovely day again. This break of weather is too wonderful. Goonie breakfasted in bed and then I established her writing letters in the garden. Basil telephoned to say he couldn't come by early train, as

1. Mary and Letty had returned from Egypt the previous day.

he had intended, because Lloyd George had telephoned to say he wanted to see him, so he had to go to Downing Street.

I sat out with Goonie. She does amuse me—she has a deliciously funny flavour. It is difficult to assess her brains. She speaks truth when she complains of her lack of education, and I think also when she says her vocabulary is very limited. I think the 'darling' technique must have originated from inability to find the next word. Anyhow she is excellent company. I read a Birrell essay on Lamb's letters and Beb's new poems to her, and we gossiped. Talking of Mr Asquith, she said she had lost her own popularity with the P.M. by telling him what she thought of his visit to Rome, etc. She had been disgusted by Pamela McKenna the other day who, sitting on his other side at dinner, at the moment when he was about to turn round to Goonie, had seized his glass exclaiming, 'I must drink out of your glass!' And, turning it round pointedly to where he had drunk—did so. This demonstration pleased him so much that he continued to talk to her until the end of dinner.

Basil arrived while we were having tea. He had not actually seen Lloyd George yet but was in communication and his surmise—obviously enough—is that they want to make use of him for the Irish negotiations. He is distressed, as he thought he had really escaped at last and was free to return to a military career, but feels he will not be able to refuse. He had an appointment with the Colonel of the Grenadiers the next morning, but it is doubtful whether the War Office will let him join on the score of age. There is no shortage of young men now. Another possibility is to join the Intelligence Corps, of which Gilbert Russell is a prominent member, and a third to go on a Staff in East Africa.

We went out into the forest, and sat with feet in sun and head in shade—too heavenly—stayed there till eight. He was in good form. He has become most enthusiastic Shakespearean, and knows nearly the whole of *The Midsummer Night's Dream* by heart. He does me great credit as my pupil. Goonie and Beb came in late for dinner. Basil amusing about Ireland. After dinner we both gibbeted. Goonie had never heard of 'To be or not to be'—a really ingenious avoidance. I am sorry our time here is drawing to a close. We have been most happy here.

Wednesday, 31st May

Basil came to see me after six and we sat out in Cadogan Square. Alas, he seems really to have succeeded in getting himself into the Grenadiers

—I wish he wouldn't be so obstinate, he has been offered very good Staff jobs. It seems such short-sighted affection on Freddie's part to want him to join in order to have his company for the short, safe period of training.

Bibs and Flavia came into the Square. I made a very good joke—at least I thought so. I always upbraid Bibs with her unnatural lack of enjoyment of playing in the Square. My happiest hours were thus spent. Flavia is, of course, like her in this respect and says she 'hates children'. I went up to two nice, healthy, active little girls and said, 'Would you let these girls play with you?' They said they would be delighted. Bibs was *black* with rage, absolutely refusing, and I had to make some feeble excuse about its being later than I thought. Basil came in and, as usual, telephoned to Freddie just about nothing—

Very depressed and longing to have a house.

Thursday, 1st June

Mary, Beb, and I went to lunch at Downing Street. My short-waisted check coat and skirt had a success with Margot. An unusually small party—only P.M., Margot, Elizabeth, Lord Hugh, Eric Drummond, and Violet Keppel. I sat between Lord H. and Eric Drummond. Elizabeth behaved odiously in poaching Lord H. right across the table. Poor darling, he was suffering from inadequately-bandaged boils on the neck. I asked Margot if we could come and stay—I can't say she looked very welcoming.

Basil came after tea. He had wanted to take me into the Park, but the weather was prohibitive, so we sat in the 'bed-sitter' and compared pathetic notes as to our houselessness. Bibs perfectly beastly to me—in order to punish me for the Square incident—her presence was like a silent scourge. I begged for an explanation, but she wouldn't give one till just before going to bed. She is a coquette.

Friday, 2nd June

Beb and I went to the Goupil Gallery in the morning: interesting khaki picture by Kennington which has made a great sensation—out of drawing and a very oleographic kind of painting, yet one likes it—good composition and extremely expressive face. Fantastic Futurist pictures upstairs—a green fish-like object lying in a bed painted like a child—we racked our brains for a possible title to it and found it was 'My Father's Death'.

While I was dressing Papa, with very blue face, told me our Fleet had been smashed in the North Sea and that our losses were terribly severe—very much more than the German.[1]

Dined with Venetia—a banquet—Winston, Clemmie, Wimbornes, Lord Reading, Barbara, Moira, and Cripps. All the statesmen looking pretty glummy over the news. It had happened on Wednesday and sounds fairly grave, but I gather the German losses are only conjectural. It certainly touches one's imagination with a dismay nothing as yet has made one feel. Winston very melodramatic, brooding and scowling. 'They're a terrible foe'. I sat between him and Wimborne. Conversation at first general and naval. It was difficult to know how much to talk to him—he was very distrait. He began by, 'You haven't seen me since I became a member of the Opposition'. He gave me one of his most purple, metaphorical, period-talking of his impotent watching of the mismanagement of his Dardanelles scheme after he was out of office. 'It was like being bound hand and foot, and watching one's best girl being—well, I won't say what'. He asked me to come and sit to him next morning in Lavery's studio, but unfortunately I was engaged.

His late Excellency on my other side poured out about Ireland, and his difficulties, and false position, and bad luck. He is very sad. He maintains that he could easily have squashed it by arresting all the suspects on the Saturday—he had them all under his hand—but he couldn't persuade Sir Matthew. He was not lucid, or I was obtuse, and I couldn't get any clear idea of what he meant. The men stayed down ages. We talked mostly about parlourmaids, trying to devise an original costume for Alice's.

When at last they came back Venetia, Cripps, Lord Reading, and Clemmie played bridge. Lord Wimborne nobbled me. He was very flushed and swollen with brandy, and I had an uncomfortable evening, as my style was hopelessly cramped by the very close proximity of Beb whom I feared was listening. He talked about Basil for ages—very comically—lamenting his wasted talents and philandered life: 'There he is, with better abilities than Winston, more judgment than Montagu, such charm—and what does he do with it—nothing! The folly of his going into the Grenadiers! He's got no drive, no *will* to live. Now that's what I've got, at least, the *will* to live. Etc., etc., on and on.' I gathered, buffy and obscure as he was, that I ought to use my influence and make Basil go into politics. I was hopeless, thanks to Beb, and could hardly talk at all. A newspaper correspondent called to ask if Winston could write a few words about the Fleet, as the news was calculated to dismay the ignorant public. Beb went to a 'furtive

1. Jutland.

frisk' at the Keppels, which he enjoyed. Basil went back to Ireland for two days.

Monday, 5th June

I went to see Keightley in the morning as I haven't been feeling or looking well and, worst of all, have been having speckles on my face. He showed me my blood through a microscope, it is all stagnant again instead of *bousculé*. He said injections would be much the best thing for me and, after some hesitation on account of the expense, I agreed to have a course. I have an instinct that they may prove really worth while.

Repington came to lunch to give Papa some information about Kut, as he is going to make a 'crying over spilt milk' speech in the House. He is a powerful-looking man, with a very clever face—extraordinarily German-looking, I think. He had just been to Verdun, and had seen a lot of German prisoners whom he described as an extraordinarily shabby lot, even minus fingers, etc. He remained closeted with Papa for a long time after lunch.

Beb and I went to the Academy—very tiring and rather nightmarish. Just as many sheepscapes as ever. Lavery has told a damned lie about Elizabeth, but it's an extremely pretty picture, and I think the one of his wife in black and gold is *lovely*. Margaret Smith's miniature of John is there.

Went home to receive my first, but I guess not my last, call from Bogie Harris. He came at about six and stayed a long time—quite agreeable and restful. Bunt, Duff, and Ruby came to dinner. Ruby shocked me by jokes before the servants about being 'churched': Papa said he had been 'churched' once! Papa, Ruby, Duff, and Beb played bridge, and Basil and I talked. I told him of my conversation with Wimborne, and he was considerably annoyed at the 'philanderer' imputation. Diana and Eileen appeared soon after eleven. Diana *very* lame, leaning on a stick like Lady Paget. Basil went, as he was tired after night journey, and we sat down to very late poker. I won £2 10s, but with minimum of enjoyment. I was over-tired. Ruby and Diana were both rather on my nerves and I really began to mind taking poor Duff's money. As usual, he had to deal cheques out—he's *very* patient about it—

Tuesday, 6th June

Basil called for me at ten and took me to see two adjoining sort of studio houses in Glebe Place, one of which he intends to buy. They're attractive, with one big room in each. He decided on the front one of the two—most extravagant of him to take one at all. Went home in a very heavy shower.

Had my first injection at Keightley's at 11.30. First strychnine, etc., then a large quantity of seawater collected off the coast of Ireland! and filtered through porcelain—rather painful. Lunched in with Beb, Papa, Sockie, and Bibs. Papa went out afterwards and returned shortly with blue face and said, 'They've drowned Kitchener'. I didn't even know he was on his way to Russia, and was flabbergasted. Streets full of shocked faces. Without doubt he was still a great national hero, and now he will never be a pricked bubble. Artistically he couldn't have exited better, but it is very tragic.

We dined with the Wimbornes in a lovely little house in Tenterden Street: Harry Cust, Basil, T. P. O'Connor, and the McLarens. Quite amusing. Harry Cust in excellent form. He and Wimborne had terrific argument about the right attitude towards peace terms, etc. I thought Wimborne showed far more intelligence than I had ever given him credit for, but Basil was much shocked by the sentiments he expressed. Sat between Wimborne and Cust. Got an awful flushed face—sea water—absolutely crippling pain and stiffness where I had the injection. Talked to Basil after dinner. Stayed too late by mistake, expecting someone else to give the signal. Slept with Letty. She talked all night in her sleep. I couldn't hear the words, but it sounded very worried. I slept badly myself.

Wednesday, 7th June

Beb and I lunched at Downing Street. Basil had proposed himself, but was not put beside me. I sat between the P.M. and Edward. Edward very brown from Egypt—not in good spirits. Robertson was there—rather impressive-looking. The *crêpe* bands of mourning for Kitchener looked very strange on the khaki. I noticed Beb looking ghastly green across the table, and he came out with the women. He was feeling faint and went and lay down in the sitting room. It is too disappointing, he had been looking so well—very depressed about it.

I had promised to go and help Violet sell at the great Caledonian Market Fair, so I went with Elizabeth and her nurse in the motor. Tremendous crowd seething at the market and every sort of woman selling at countless stalls. Ours was handkerchiefs, etc., and Violet, the Duchess of Rutland, etc., were selling assiduously. I was terribly humiliated at finding I was almost fainting with fatigue after an hour

Ivo Alan Charteris
Killed in Action
Oct 17 1915
Aged 19.

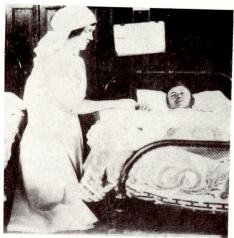

Lady Cynthia as a V.A.D. in 1917

Yvo—the last portrait

*Egypt in 1915: Tom Strickland and Mary (centre), his sister Barbara
(far left) and Letty (right)*

Beb Asquith

of it. I simply *cannot* stand. That Bovril Duchess of Rutland had been there from dusk to dawn for two days, and was obviously enjoying it immensely. I tried to sell filthy bits of jet trimming, *alleged* to be off Queen Alexandra's dress, but it didn't appeal to anyone. Diana was walking about trying to sell lovely jade-eyed kittens, etc. I *hated* it.

Thursday, 8th June

Lunched Bluetooth. He was in the depth of gloom—an awful *désenchanté* fit. Somehow it proved a foil and I went away feeling much better, having been wretched all the morning. We agreed that on *paper* my life would sound about as bad as anyone's, but he maintained that somehow I didn't really mind any of the drawbacks.

Went to Cadogan Square to meet Basil. Papa had been going to play tennis with us, but was prevented by his cold, so Lady Wimborne had engaged a professional. Basil and I taxied down to Roehampton together and had to wait there some time. At last Alice arrived, resplendent in red-and-yellow trimmed white sweater. A friend of Basil's called 'Bubbles' was there, with a bouquet of very gay, showy, Neapolitan-ice-clad young women—all lovely at a certain range and disappointing within it. Basil introduced me to Bubbles, who rather embarrassed me by saying, 'Oh yes, I heard months ago that you were a great friend of Basil's—and I'm sure you're much the nicest thing in his life'. We played in pretty fast rain, Basil and I against Alice and the professional. All played badly and inattentively. We took off our wet jerseys and had tea in the club, and then walked in the garden, which is most attractive.

Friday, 9th June

I walked to Friary Court, where I sat beside Grace, and did some respirator-chopping work—not nearly as pleasant as last year. The old ones have been returned to be cut into separate pieces for each eye, and they are covered with gas, dirt, blood, and—I should think—microbes. Everyone else had on gloves. I suffered terrors all the afternoon about blood poisoning, as I had discovered the inevitable scratch on one of my fingers.

Joy—joy and relief—a longish respite from going to Downing Street. Guy has been given another month's leave and they are going to Scotland, so Frances said we could live in her home while they were away. What luck for the 'cuckoos'! It's a delicious prospect. I hadn't realised before how the prospect of Downing Street had been depressing me.

We went to the Grafton Gallery to see the exhibition of Sargent drawings. It's a real nightmare to see so many of one's friends so blatantly depicted staring at one from four walls—I think the one of me presents the foulest woman I have ever seen.

Papa in great spirits because he had scored off Harry Cust by 'showing' him the *copy* (of the Mazzolino he has sold) as the original, and making him say how impossible it would be ever to reproduce such 'mellowness' in a copy.

Saturday, 10th June

Had to make exhausting Napoleonic plans with Polly about concentrations of luggage, etc., etc. It is too complicated moving about so much with no real base. She is to go to Downing Street for Sunday, and I have told her to leave anything I shan't want in the immediate future there.

Beb, obstinately rejecting the advice of Cowans, etc., has had himself gazetted into the R.F.A. instead of Heavy Artillery. The General told him he would go to Larkhill, a place we have never heard of, but Mary Strickland has an idea that it is on Salisbury Plain, which will be cruelly inconvenient just as we have secured a lovely nest to cuckoo in in London. Called for Mary at Cadogan Square and took her down to Littlehampton with us by 3.50.

Arrived at the hotel fiercely hungry for tea. Bed and board 16s 6d a day—much too much. Went round to see the children. Found them greatly disfigured by health—John dark chocolate freckles. Dined in *table d'hôte*—loathsome population. Sat in the 'lounge' for a bit and went up to our bedrooms early—uncomfortable beds.

Monday, 12th June

Nannie told me a lady in their house, contemplating Michael, had pronounced him to be 'just lovely'. Whereupon he had torn off his hat and said, running his fingers through his curls, 'He's got lovely hair, too.' Beb and I had a shrimp tea with them. The governess recommended by Dr Shuttleworth had just arrived, so I took her for a walk afterwards, as I wanted to describe John to her. She is quite young and seems very, very nice—gentle and intelligent. She came in with me and watched the children going to bed. John took a fancy to her and was in much his best form—really more or less normal on the surface. She thought him fascinating and I could see she was surprised. I expects she thinks I am the exact *converse* of the fatuous mother who thinks her ordinary child a genius.

Wednesday, 14th June

Beb and I lunched at Downing Street—only Elizabeth was there. She was very, very nice. While I remember, I must record two 'Margots'—Talking of Mr Balfour's neglect of distributing medals, 'Shall I tell you what's the matter with Arthur? He's got no womb . . . no womb!' And when Violet asked her if she was going to wear her hat with ostrich feathers for Kitchener's Memorial Service, 'How can you ask me? Dear Kitchener saw me in that hat twice!'

Papa, Eileen, Beb, and I had early dinner with Bibs and Sockie, and went to *The Bing Boys* at the Alhambra—a most amusing revue. George Robey brilliant. Letty, Basil, Gilbert Russell, and Ruby, etc., were behind us. I lost Papa and had an icy drive back in a hansom. Talked to Mamma a little.

Thursday, 15th June

Went in open motor to Grosvenor Square to a Mrs Leeds' house, for rehearsal of the tableaux I have foolishly let myself in for through Lady Wimborne. I am like a moth in a candle about this particular form of self-torture—each time, as with the Crummleses, it is to be *positively* my last appearance. The usual chaos prevailed. Someone called Miss Craig is supposed to be organising them, and the part of Beatrice gazed upon by Dante, with canopy held over her, was allotted to me. I must develop a goitre and a pomegranate mouth. Glad to see Diana was in the same *galère*—not that we bring each other luck. She is to be the Blessed Damozel—funny enough! Lady Huntingdon, mother of the Dublin maids of honour, is the instigator. Many people brought a sort of rummage sale of fancy dress fragments, but I saw nothing which could do for Beatrice. Vita Nicolson was there, Vi de Trafford, Violet Keppel, etc., etc. Mrs Lavery is to be the Virgin Mary, with a 'fallen woman' across her knees—Nancy and Diana were both suggested for the latter role, but didn't respond.

Dined Evan: Curzon and Norah were our party—quite amusing. Long discussion on A.J.B., as to whether he had real depth of feeling or not. Evan and Curzon both agreed they had never seen him evince it, and that his conduct during the last week has been an epitome of his whole career. His faults—that he was too logical, had too much sense of humour, and no power of imagining how ordinary people were affected. Curzon told us that, just before the Cabinet had risen on the day after the great battle, he himself had said, 'Surely the First Lord will say a few words to us about the battle?' To which suggestion the P.M. agreed. A.J.B. replied quite coldly, 'There is nothing to say to you—only a few anecdotes, and I don't suppose you would care to hear them'. They censured him for not having gone to the Naval Memorial Service, and for not having cancelled his dinner engagements after hearing the news of Kitchener's death, which nearly all the other guests had done.

Curzon went away earlyish, and Norah and Evan and I had a nice *à trois*. We tried to persuade Evan of the extreme advisability of his marrying Ava Astor, of whom apparently Lord C. still wishes to have the refusal—so annoyed did he look at the suggestion of her marrying Van Sittart.

Friday, 16th June

Went in open motor at 12.15 to Kensington Square to borrow a dress to wear as Beatrice from Mrs Campbell.* She was out when I arrived, but returned from an expedition to the Caledonian Market. What a *culte* I had for that woman once, and how terribly 'grossly her muddy vesture now closes her in'! She looked like a leg of mutton. I'm sorry to say I found her very overwhelming, too, and tiring beyond description, even for fifteen minutes. She said she hoped I wasn't 'silent and aloof', which I suppose meant she thought I was.

She asked me if I were in love with Basil. Her young husband[1] came in, and she was terribly arch with him, indulging in shy-making badinage. She kissed him on the nose before me. One way and another I did *not* enjoy my visit. It made me feel uncomfortable and phlegmatic. She got into the iron bedstead motor and wanted to be dropped at the Ritz.

Frances' bed divinely comfortable. We *are* happy here. I always thought I was unaffected by conditions, but I believe nobody is really more their slave. I'm afraid carpets and colour affect subconsciously my whole view of the Universe.

Saturday, 17th June

It was still cold, but the sun shone and the day was lovely to look at. I went to Prince and ordered kilted flannel skirt for tennis. Then we

1. George Cornwallis-West.

went to the New English Art Club—rather an interesting collection.
A *very* fine Orpen of an Arran Isle man. Two very 'pip-pip' Johns:
one of a woman with real beauty of line—considerable beauty, I
think; the other a group called 'Fresh Herrings' had more of his faults
and less of his merits. A nightmare by him of Bernard Shaw with
closed eyes! The McEvoys—*the* fashion at present—are interesting:
curious, smudgy, *line*less technique. One portrait of a girl, startlingly
like Letty, very clever. There were some amusing comics—a picture
called 'Widows' (a large group of black-garbed women, all imminently
expectant, engaged in cutting out baby clothes), also a most revolting
group of bright blue nude women.

I walked all the way home to Catharine Street where cruel fate
awaited me. I had just self-congratulatingly subsided into comfortable
sofa, with Gaskell's *Life of Charlotte Brontë*, when door opened and
Lady Florence Bourke was announced. There I was, caught like a rat
in a trap, and she sat and sat and *kissed* me when she went away. She
was much concerned to hear Basil was in the Grenadiers—wondered
why he had been so unwise and then said, very archly, 'He must want
to get away from somebody here'. Was this a hit at me or at herself?
She told me the story of the play she had just finished and given to
Mrs Pat—she said, patronisingly, she 'wouldn't mind her doing the
part of the Duchess'. At the end of the recital she said tearfully, 'Oh
yes, it's very beautiful.'

Sunday, 18th June

It *is* depressing seeing everyone in furs in June, and one gnashes one's
teeth when one thinks how short even what *ought* to be summer is.
Mary H. came to see me—still nothing doing. We deplored the lack
of 'luxe' in the details of our mother's schemes of life. She longs for
a lovely bedroom to have her baby in. Beb came in before she left.
The Duchess and Diana called before dinner to invite us to poker
that evening. The former very 'pip-pip', discoursing as to the side
you should be on in order to have a son, etc. Apparently Viola and
Alan Parsons have free fights as they hold the same theory, and one
wants a daughter and the other a son. We had a very pleasant, peaceful evening. Read Henley aloud after dinner.

Monday, 19th June

Letter from Basil enclosing one from Florrie Bourke, suggesting that
he should take her and me to a play one night when he wanted dis-

traction! We dined early with Mary S., Bibs and Sockie—Bibs had a letter in several volumes from Mamma. Apparently her Gosford rest is proving a great success.

Tuesday, 20th June

Poor Mary H. had a third daughter at nine o'clock. A disappointment, I fear—I'm sure she was really pretty confident of its being a boy. I am very, very sorry—not that I regard three daughters as an intrinsic misfortune—I don't think Papa has one too many, but the suspense next time will be dreadful.

Dined in alone. Pamela came and called afterwards and we had quite a pleasant chat. She is very shocked at Mrs Lavery doing the Madonna.

Wednesday, 21st June

A strange day of grease paint and glass-gazing. Got straight into my dress—gold dust and very mild (as for a ball) make-up. The gold dust too lovely on my hair. I should like to have it always: why not a *dorée* instead of a *poudrée* fashion? Mary S. came and we went on to Grosvenor Square together, taking Polly, as I thought she would like to see the rehearsal.

My tender make-up was soon cancelled and Mrs Lavery made me into a real deader—corpse-white, with eyebrows done with red pencil, so that close they were just gashes. I am sure on the stage it is better than black for fair people. I was whitened with liquid powder. The rehearsal was absolute chaos, and one wondered how things could ever be pulled through for that evening. The stage in process of erection; carpenters downing tools because of the quantity of conflicting orders; all the properties mislaid; Miss Craig offended; most people cross; and Handley Jones washing his hands of the whole thing. The lighting very bad.

Lunched as I was, looking like a dead vampire or Parken Thorpe, at Cadogan Square. Papa horrified by my bloody eyebrows. Dined in bed, and was at the house at about 8.30 with flouring gold hair and corpse face. Went to the dressing room upstairs, and spent the usual hours of last dabs and appeals for careful criticisms. Everyone absorbed in their own appearance and saying, 'Oh perfect, darling!' to enquirers.

Stood in a throng behind stage till our turn came. The heat on the stage was exactly like a Turkish bath. One felt the paint on one's face simply melting. I was laid on my couch, my hair disposed around me, and we were exposed three times—and, I gather, considered a success. I was thankful to be lying down with shut eyes. Went and uncorpsed my appearance, and then sat at back of room and watched remainder of the performance.

I had lots of dewdrops and felt pleasant sensation of admiration—still like a warm bath to me. Wimborne raved about my hair, and the Duke of Rutland claimed the right of a connection to pull it. Mary looked lovely. Heard Mrs Duggan discussing whether she should marry Curzon with Sarah Wilson. Collected my properties from the dressing room and went away after I had eaten—didn't want to dance. 'How lovely that *girl* looks!' were the last pleasant words I heard. Couldn't get to sleep.

Thursday, 22nd June

Went to look at the Italian War Cartoons at the Leicester Gallery—brilliantly clever. I then went to Eros, thinking I might find a blue serge bargain. Instead, I bought a black, trimmed with blue, gaberdine coat and skirt—which I didn't in the least want. Poor people should never go to sales. One buys things because they are cheap, instead of because one needs them. This had been twenty-seven pounds to copy, and I got it for six pounds, but . . .

Friday, 23rd June

In the morning we had a great excitement and revolution of the future. Beb had been waiting, momentarily expecting orders, ever since he saw the General at the W.O. who told him he would soon have instructions about going to Larkhill. He was gazetted last Saturday and we have had about twelve *last*-days. At length the orders came, but instead of Larkhill, Brighton is his destination. It is a great let-off for him, as it will be much more comfortable, and of course it is much more convenient for me, only I think it spells financial ruin. Instead of being safely marooned in a tin hut on Salisbury Plain, he will now probably want to reside at the Grand Hotel! If I can find lodgings, I think I must transfer the children to Brighton.

Hurried away from lunch to sell Barrie book souvenirs at the royal performance of *The Admirable Crichton*. Disposed of a few and saw the play quite comfortably. It was in aid of the Star and Garter Fund. Wonderful star cast: Lily Elsie a dream of beauty, making Gladys Cooper look like a kitchen maid. Saw Mrs Darell with her husband. I had a bet with them that I would go and sell a book to the King, but I wasn't allowed into the Royal Box.

Dined in with Beb. He is excited about his new move—it must be just like going to school. Mary has had her first letter from Tom, but he had already written two and there was nothing about Ego in it.

Saturday, 24th June

Beb meant to go down to Brighton by the eleven o'clock, but on the threshold of waking characteristically postponed his departure until the 1.55. I went and had my head cleaned at Mrs Cullen, fearing the gold dust might be harmful.

Gave Beb lunch at home at a quarter to one, and then went to have it with Basil at Queen's Restaurant. Then he took me to see his new house, which is in process of furnishing. I think it will look very nice. It was full of litter and lumber, the miscellaneous objects one never has the heart to destroy however many times one may decide ruthlessly to 'sort'. He showed me his old diaries with the possible, in fact probable, exception of certain sentences in shorthand. They were devoid of interest. Went to 1 Oakley Street, where he is still lodging in Freddie's absence, waited while he changed into mufti, and then he dropped me home.

Travelled down to Littlehampton by 3.50. A minute after my arrival, to my astonishment, enter Beb! A typical War Office practical joke. The object of going to Brighton was, after all, only to see his C.O.— who was to instruct him as to his next steps—and the C.O. was away till Monday. There is no training course at Brighton, so I expect it will be Lark Hill for five weeks or so, and then he will join a Brigade at Brighton.

Sunday, 25th June

Had a long talk with the governess—like her very much. She is convinced that there is nothing *mentally* wrong with John, though of course he is undeniably eccentric. She considers him superhumanly obstinate and self-conscious. Luckily, she and Nurse are getting on very well, but she said she would have a much better chance of effecting improvement if she were to have him more to herself. I agreed and devoted much thought to domestic politics, finally arranging for her and John to have their meals apart in her lodging. At present they all eat together, and naturally it is rather difficult for her to correct him before Nurse, and *constant* drilling is the only way to get him out of his inverted way of talk, etc. I really think I already see *some* improvement, and she says she is getting his attention at lessons. I told her I wanted her to stay on after July. What am I to do? I *can't* have three women for two children.

Wednesday, 28th June

Promptly chastened for my high spirits. I rang up Mamma, who had just returned from Gosford, and heard the cruelly disappointing news that the telegram about Ego being at Damascus was cancelled. It was a mistake—they had sent the wrong name, and now say it is a Lord Daniel. What they mean Heaven only knows—there is no Lord and there is no one called Daniel! Of course, it is no worse than it was *before* the good news, only it feels worse and the disappointment is very hard to bear.

I went round to Bruton Street and told Mary—she was horrified. I lunched at Cadogan Square: Papa very perturbed. Mamma very good, but I can't bear the setback for her. The Duchess is firmly resolved that Letty should *not* be told. I think it is a great mistake. Apart from the principle that things ought not to be kept back, it is almost inconceivable that she shouldn't *hear* it. Everyone knows, but not everyone can be told that she is being kept in the dark. I think she will be very hurt if she learns it indirectly.

Thursday, 29th June

Walked to Cadogan Square and had dentist with Mamma, lying on twin beds. I think she is *really* better for her Gosford rest and she is being wonderfully brave about Ego. Found there had been a strange case of Russian scandal about me and Letty—the idea being that I was going to take it into my own hands and tell her the news that evening, in defiance of her own family. What an officious Bunty they must take me for! Papa came in, regarded me with mingled respect and horror, and said, 'Well—have you seen Letty?' I was surprised. Discussed the pros and cons exhaustively with Mamma. I don't feel so positive as I did at first. Supposing we were, as one hopes, to get good news— say in six weeks, or whenever it may be? Perhaps she really would be grateful not to have been plunged back into a hell which really was making her ill. If the news is bad, I suppose nothing additional matters much. The great reason for being told everything is that, once one had detected any suppression, one's whole confidence for the future would be undermined. This doesn't quite apply in this case, because, if the news be good, then the anxiety is over and he will be safe out of the war. However, I don't see how it can possibly be kept from her long, and it is awfully difficult for Mamma and all of us to see her so artificially.

Basil and I had been planning for a long time to continue his Shakespearean education by going to one of the plays, but unluckily there isn't one on now. So we intended to go to *Macbeth* on the cinema. He called for me at 7.30, and we dined at the Pall Mall Restaurant. Discussed what quality, or possibly what lacuna, in us prevents our quarrelling—not only with each other, but with anyone. The cinema of *Macbeth* was very comic. One grew tired of Tree's and Constance Collier's stomach-ache faces. Shakespeare not really a good film author. Tiny, gloomy audience—the woman in front of us objected to our talking, surely rather far-fetched at a cinema. Basil very firm with her. Pouring rain when we got out and only a hansom to be had, in which we were soaked. Basil, after boasting—in fact almost complaining—of his good temper, lost it fairly successfully with the cabbie, who would let the glass down on our heads and misunderstand instructions, etc.

Saturday, 1st July

I don't know how to write about this awful day. I didn't expect Beb till 2.20, so had arranged to lunch with my grandmother. Was back soon after two, ran into room in high spirits. Beb said, 'I'm afraid there's bad news', and gave me an opened letter from Papa. 'The worst is true about Ego. The officer prisoners of Angora certify that he was killed at Katia . . . I have wired to Guy Wyndham at Clouds. I don't know how Letty will be told. It is very cruel and we must all help each other to bear it.'

Oh God—Oh God, my beautiful brother that I have loved so since I was a baby—so beautiful *through* and *through*! Can it be true that he'll never come back? At first I could only think of Letty, just the blank horror of that gripped me. Mamma's away at Clouds—that's unthinkable, too! Letty will occupy her for the first days, but afterwards I'm so frightened for her.

Papa telephoned to me and I went round to Cadogan Square. Poor, poor Papa! He really proudly loved those two perfect sons. He said he had been round to Kakoo—she expected John back in the afternoon and they thought he had better tell Letty. Her mother was not coming back till nine and Diana was away. We walked round to Eaton Square together and found Kakoo in. No John, and we discussed what had better be done. Came to conclusion that if John had not arrived by five, Papa and I would go round to Letty. We telephoned and found out she would be in between five and six. I went home to Beb and waited—no message came, so after five I went to Cadogan Square and picked up poor Papa. The poignancy of what followed was so inconceivably beyond anything in my experience that I don't feel as if I could ever be unhaunted by it for a minute.

Letty was alone with the children playing the piano to them. Papa went up—I waited downstairs. The music stopped and I heard a gay 'Hulloa', then silence. I rushed up and found Letty clinging to Papa. It's indescribable—it was just like somebody in a fearful, unimaginable, physical pain. Streams of beautiful, eloquent words were torn from her heart. The children were scared. 'What has happened to you, Mummie? What is the matter with you? Will you be better in the morning?' I ran up to Sparks—she came and fetched them, and brought sal volatile and was wonderfully nice and good with Letty. We tried to make Letty go upstairs, but she wanted to stay down a little.

Papa was wonderfully sweet, and she seemed to cling to him: 'Oh Papa, it can't be true! How could God be so cruel? There was no one else in the world in the least like him—no one—I have been so wonderfully happy. His beautiful face, his smile . . . my Ego, come back to me. Oh God! Oh God! It's no use calling to God—nothing is any use— nothing in all the world can help him. I'm only twenty-eight—I'm so strong—I shan't die!'

Marjorie came in, perfectly self-controlled and bracing—spoke to Letty as you would to a housemaid being vaccinated. 'Now, now Letty—come, come'. At last we got her to go upstairs and carried her to her room. Then she saw his photographs and the bed. She sent for the children—his two lovely little boys, and tried to make them understand. 'David, I want you to understand Poppa's—you remember what he looked like—Poppa's never coming back to us.' David said at once, 'But, I want him to . . .' but he didn't understand and said, 'I must go now, or I shall be late for bed'. She was afraid that they would never remember him and the children—the one platitude one clung to for her—became one of the most poignant stabs.

Papa went away and I stayed alone with her. She got quieter. John came after six and took the line that there *was* hope with her, clinging to the fact that it was not 'official'. I have *none*. Is it cruel or kind to give it to her? I think one ought to give her the evidence, but not colour it with subjective optimism at all—she is so open to suggestion. Nothing could be crueller than the way it has come. Those two months of terror in which she said, 'I tried to teach myself every day and every night that he was dead, then I was swept up into Heaven, and now . . . this fiery Hell. I'm so tired of being brave—I was brave for two months and this is my reward.'

When I went up and joined John I found—to my alarm—that he had really tonicked and buoyed her up. Perhaps it is right to stay it a *little* by tiny hope, so that waiting for clues may be some occupation, but I am sure she mustn't be allowed to have real fundamental hope. She can't have the physical shock twice. John was angry at our not having waited for him or his mother, but personally I think Papa was the best person to tell her: he even said, 'I think she's been most brutally told.' They are an astonishing family. A dear old family doctor came—she seemed to welcome him. He left her a sleeping draught.

The mother didn't arrive till past nine—I waited till then, and Letty asked me to come back and sleep. I went back to Beb, had Bengers, and picked up a nightgown. I dropped him at Bruton Street. I just ran upstairs and kissed Mary, and Evelyn drove me to Montagu Square. Got into bed with Letty. She didn't know whether to allow herself to hope or not, and kept appealing to me. I didn't know what to say. She said, 'I can't hope a chink—I must hope altogether or not at all'. That was exactly what I was afraid of. She took the draught and went to sleep after a long time. I scarcely slept.

Sunday, 2nd July

Ghastly awakening. She began moaning in her sleep, 'Don't let me wake up to this ghastly day—I don't want to wake up'. She said, 'I've had such a wonderful dream, I dreamt that he was there.' Then the full realisation came back to her: 'Oh God, make me mad—make me mad, if I can't die!' 'Come back to me just for one minute my sweet Ego, just to tell me how to bear it, I can't bear it without you to help. You must come back and see David just once.' 'Oh God, the pain of it! I'm so frightened—I can't face the long years. What am I to do—I haven't got the brains to cope with it? I don't believe I've got any brains—only a heart, oh such a heart. No philosophy, no religion. Ego was my religion!'

The agony of one's impotence to help. I'm not the right person for her—not spontaneous enough, too selfconscious. A sense of their utter futility makes the words die in my throat. She is so childlike in a way that I believe she is very open to suggestion, and could be helped by people. What she wants, I think, is Ettie with her extraordinary articulate *conviction* of personal immortality—I can't convey it. Martin was too sweet, seeming to understand more than David—not what had happened—but his mother's unhappiness. He kissed and patted her, 'There's a tear in both your eyes, Mummie.' She had ups and downs of hope. It is so difficult when she says, 'Is there any hope, Cynthia?' not to allow oneself to draw the sword out of her heart for a moment. Grace and Pamela came and both saw her. Pamela was very sweet. She said she would stay with her till her mother came, so I went to Beb. In the course of the morning they succeeded in buoying themselves up into *real* hope. I can't have any. Rested with Beb, and then we lunched at Queen's Restaurant. Went to see Mary H. at four, had tea with her. She was wonderfully perfect. Looked in at Letty, saw they had made her quite hopeful: she has resolved to go on as before, refusing to believe it. I think they are *wrong*, but what can one do?

Beb and I had early dinner and then he went away to Brighton. Not till I was left alone did I feel the full pain for myself—Letty's had parried it. It burst upon me now and I was in Hell. Mamma hasn't come back yet. There is still that to face. Grace rang up saying she had been full of hope, but it had been dashed to the ground—A friend of Evie's, a man called Cohen, has seen a man who was at Katia (he was taken prisoner and escaped), and he says Ego was wounded slightly and later returned to his machine gun—a shell burst quite near and none of those men could be seen again. If this is true, it explains his body not being found.

Monday, 3rd July

Breakfasted and wrote diary in bed. Papa asked me to lunch with him, and said he had begun to be hopeful yesterday, but the latest story had extinguished hope—though, on thinking it over, the story sounded most improbable. Of course there is no reason why one should believe it, any more than all the other conflicting rumours, only what can be 'official'—the word the Rutlands cling to now? Nothing.

They have Letty practically back to where she was *before* the good telegram about his being at Damascus, and I don't see what's to end this intolerable phase, unless perhaps Tom's first letter which may well never arrive. It is so difficult for us—they make one feel they think one a sensationalist. I can't humbug Letty. Let her have all the evidence and draw her own conclusions.

Papa telephoned to ask Cohen to come and see him at five, and

showed me a wonderful letter from Mamma and a copy of the one Ego
had written her after Yvo's death. I think it is so perfect:

Darling Mum,

I have absolutely nothing to say. When your own mother and
brother are concerned, it is futile to talk of sympathy, and the one
consolation for me is that—if any comfort is to be extracted, or if
the best thought is of any use, which of course it is—your soul is
big enough, large enough, for that purpose. The mere thought of
your tackling it strengthens me. That sounds selfish and detached,
but I have such faith in you—I suppose the misery of people like Ettie
breaks the shock. A woman with sympathy loses many sons before
her own. If anything could dwarf one's own tragedy, it is the agony
of millions of others, but it doesn't—it's the other way about. One's
sluggish imagination is stimulated and one merely realises for the first
time other people's miseries as well as one's own. The only sound
thing is to hope the best thing for one's country, and to expect absolutely nothing for oneself in the future. To write down everyone one
loves as dead, and then—if any of us are left—we shall be surprised.
To think of one's country's future and one's own happy past. The
first is capable of vast improvement—as for the second, when all is
said and done, we were a damned good family. Qua *family* as good as
Clouds. I couldn't have had more joy out of anything than I have
from my family. I'm glad we had that bit with Yvo at Hunstanton.
I wish I had seen him as a Guardsman. What letters! The first one
(thousand singing legs) perfect description and atmosphere—the
second one full of jolly thought and not the least selfconscious. Bless
him. I am so awfully sorry for Papa who loved him. Tell him how
much I feel for him. He must write his sons off and concentrate upon
his grandchildren who, thank God, exist —. I am sending this by Mary
Herbert who has been an angel. I am glad Mary C. has got Tom to
console. We will try and keep him here. I should rather have stayed
here on the chance of Balkans as Cavalry. Gallipoli is terribly dull but
unberufen very safe now, except for sickness. We have had very few
men and no officers hit since August 22nd. But the gloom, and boredom, and discomfort of life there seems the limit.

Goodbye darling—I love you till all is blue.

Ego

Began to write to Beb when Whibley walked in. I'm really glad
he came, though I suppose I wouldn't have seen him on purpose. He
was very, very dear and said delicious things about Ego. At five

Papa telephoned and said something quite definite had come from the American Embassy, so when the motor came I went round to Cadogan Square. Buckler, special agent at the American Embassy, has been round to Papa with a telegram from the Red Crescent, saying that Coventry and Lieutenant Strickland certify that Lord Elcho was killed at Katia—that's 'official'. Poor Papa very shattered, he must have hoped after all.

We wondered what to do about Letty, rang up her house, and asked for Kakoo who was with her. We told her and she begged us not to tell Letty anything until John did, and said she would go round to Eaton Square where he was. Papa and I came to the conclusion we had better go round and see him in case they shirked, poor things. Then he said he didn't feel he could face seeing John, he had been so irritated by him the day before, so I went by myself. I found the Duchess there and John was just taking down the same message from the telephone. Poor things, they tried still to clutch at straws, but I wouldn't let them. John wanted to see whether Buckler thought the Red Crescent authority sufficiently good, but I told him he had himself brought the message to Papa. They *had* to accept. I liked John again—he looked so desperately miserable. He kissed me and said how sorry he was. The Duchess quite broke down. I suggested she should fetch the doctor and take him round to Letty—I was convinced she ought to be told that night.

Papa and I went round to Bruton Street. Poor Con was with Mary —very dear: I had dinner with Mary. I telephoned to the Duchess. She said Letty had known directly she saw her face and had been terribly bad, and then they had left her with John, who seemed best able to cope with the agony part. Diana and her mother were going to sleep with her. Evelyn drove me home. Mercifully, I was utterly exhausted, so I went to sleep but couldn't stay asleep.

Tuesday, 4th July

Oh, the waking up to that desolate, desolate feeling! I went round to Letty, copied out that lovely letter from Ego and left her with it. Diana was very nice. Went back to Cadogan Square and waited for Mamma and Bibs. They were very late and we began lunch without them. Bibs' poor face so stricken and Mamma as I expected, looking physically better, almost braced—like people are at first. They kept ringing up from Letty's house to know when she was coming, so I took her round soon after lunch and left them together.

Drove home with Mamma. Violet came to see me. She couldn't

have been nicer, and said just what one wanted about Ego. Basil came
at six. I had sent him Ego's letter to read. I wanted him to know just
a little what he was like. He wrote me a very nice letter about it and I
found him very easy to see—no embarrassment. He walked me to
Cadogan Square. I dined with Bibs, Papa, and Sockie, and then went
and sat with darling Mamma for a little. She said she hoped no one
would say she was 'wonderful', but there is no other word for it.
Bibs came down to sleep with her.

Wednesday, 5th July

Went to Cadogan Square and met Mary, who had just come up from
the Stricklands. Another letter from Tom previous to the others she
has received, and for the first time writing of Ego: 'Ego was instan-
taneously killed by a shell—I was quite near him at the time. He had
been twice wounded and, just before, was looking happy and cheering
on his men with his arm bound up.' Mamma had left a note telling
Mary not to show it to Papa till she had seen her, so I'm afraid she
still thinks it won't satisfy him. I am most anxious to stop that growing
bitterness.

Thursday, 6th July

Went to lunch with Letty—we had it together on her bed. There
had been a third crisis the evening before when Mary brought her
Tom's letter, evidently there had still been a flicker of hope . . . Now
all is over for ever and she is glad to know it was instantaneous. She
was quiet now and pathetic beyond words. It is just like someone cut
in two and it makes one physically ill to see her. She dropped to sleep
for a minute after luncheon, dreamt of him, and there was a cruel
awakening. She and Mamma are to go down to Stanway by themselves
for Sunday. I suppose she feels it is better to face it soon. It can't be
helped, but I think it is bad for Mamma. For her, of course, it is a
severe physical strain to be with Letty. She can help her but she cannot
be helped by her. With Letty it takes the form more of a crisis, like
an illness which in a sense can be ministered to. Mamma is so utterly
different—no one can help her—each person she sees is, I think, an
effort and a strain. She is best left alone. Letty luckily has that wonderful unselfconsciousness and can pour out her heart to almost anyone.
This must bring temporary relief. She said Ettie had helped her.

Went to Miss North—ordered black linen dress. I walked to Bruton
Street, meeting Diana and Katharine on the way. I am looking so

ghastly that people stare at me in the street. Soon I shall be too tired to think or feel.

Friday, 7th July

Went round to see Margot at a quarter to eleven. She was very tearful and really quite nice—not saying anything really wounding. She started disparaging Letty, but I stopped that and certainly she did appreciate Ego. P.M. came in and made wonderful moved grimaces. Margot and Elizabeth dropped me home—pouring rain. Paid bills, said goodbye to servants, and went round to Cadogan Square.

Jack White came to luncheon. He used to be a friend of Ego's. Terrible embarrassment. He suddenly said, 'How's Yvo? Is he flourishing?' He saw by our faces and, luckily, before an answer was enforced, said, 'I mean Ivo—Lady Desborough's son.'

Polly and I went down to Brighton by 3.10. Beb had taken rooms in the Royal York Hotel. A note came from him saying he couldn't get away from barracks till 12.30 next morning. Found hotel much too expensive and nosed round, deciding to move next morning to another hotel (commercial and family). Poor Beb won't be too pleased. I hope I plumbed the depth of human misery alone in this beastly hotel: dead tired—the first sort of excitement gone and succeeded by the dreary, dreary stage, with sense of desolation gradually soaking through and through. Every wounded soldier here, too, seems to have one and often both legs amputated. There must be a special hospital for artificial limbs—a perfect nightmare. Had breakfast-dinner in a café, and went to bed in horror and misery.

Saturday, 8th July

Breakfasted downstairs by myself. When poor Beb arrived about 12.30, looking forward to the comfortable quarters he had chosen, he found me on the doorstep with all his luggage, just migrating to the new hotel. It is pretty dingy I must admit. What I really like about it is the advertisement for false teeth right across its front. We get bed and breakfast for five shillings each.

Beb is looking wonderfully better—quite different. We rested after lunch, which he insisted on having at the Royal York—our Paradise Lost. After tea we went out to the very nose of the pier. We dined at Princess Hotel, right away in Hove, with Mr Balfour, Evan, and Ettie. They were staying there for Sunday in order to give Mr B. a healthy holiday—the first time he has left London since he went to the Admiralty. Mamma was to have gone with them. Ettie just the same, she is the most wonderful of women. Sat with them in their large sitting room after dinner, and walked home to bed.

Bedroom pretty squalid—dirty lace curtains, the last lodger's toenails, dingy counterpane, do not help one to bear unhappiness. Strange perhaps, that they should count on such a different plane, but oh, how much they do! One really longs for a hill or a wood. Whatever happens, I feel more than ever resolved that sorrow must not be allowed to become gloom—if for no other reason than the treachery involved to the very ones we love, were one to allow oneself to be in any way the worse because they lived. It is cruel that they who gave such joy now must give corresponding pain, and all one can do in loyalty is never to suffer that they should be instrumental in any smallest way in spoiling one for life, and all the much that is left to one. At first the sheer pain obscures them, but the pain fades and their memory remains undimmed.

Sunday, 9th July

Pilgrimage to Littlehampton to see the children. John was supposed to be in a very naughty mood, but I really do see an improvement in him. His voice is much more normal and he answers more. His strange charm quite unimpaired. He has grown immense.

Monday, 10th July

Raining in the morning—I went by train to see Ettie at her hotel and had a long talk with her. Evan had already departed early that morning leaving 'Lady Desbury' to pay his enormous bill. She was very amused because, when she had told Mr B. that she and Evan had walked to Rottingdean, he had said, 'Now, what do you and Evan find to talk about?' Mr Balfour came in before I left, and we had quite a good *à trois* talk chiefly about Mamma, her health, her methods, etc. *A propos* of her plan weaving and dictating, we agreed that she didn't like completely passive submission, but, as Mr Balfour said, a 'succession of gentle rearguard actions'.

Mr Balfour had asked us to dine with him at eight so, after Beb had had a good sleep, we went off to Princes Hotel in a tram and had an *à trois* dinner. Quite a success. He and Beb talked guns. He went away by train about ten, the better for his rest, having dormoused most of the day. Beb and I walked all the way home—such a lovely moonlight night.

Tuesday, 11th July

Beb went off early and paid the bill for my squalid entertainment—
under three pounds. Went up to London by eleven o'clock. Mamma
not back from Stanway yet.

I went to Con at five o'clock—very dear, and able to talk about
John and all that happy Avon band. A delicious story she had about
Ego—that after I was married I was supposed to be having a flirtation
(Basil they must have meant), and at ball suppers, and so on, Ego was
always found sitting on my other side. Not true, I'm afraid, but a very
sweet story.

Mamma got back before supper from Stanway—that ordeal being, I
think, fairly well through. It must have been agonising, but Letty had
loved seeing all the people, Prews, Priest, Eliza, etc.

Wednesday, 12th July

Guy and Frances came to 7.30 dinner. Just as they were going, I
went down to the hall and saw a censored letter from the Red Crescent.
It was addressed to Lady Elcho, but I took it up to Mamma. As we
opened it, I saw Ego scribbled in pencil and, for a moment, I really
thought it was his *own* signature—and, for an instant, the Turkish
looked like an ill writing. It was Mamma's letter—Ego was in her
writing—sent back to her with profuse apologies from the Red
Crescent for the lamentable error they had made in giving false
hopes. . . .

Oh, that was *my cruellest moment*! I really believed and my heart
had bounded with joy for a second. That one can so hope shows how
little one has really taken it in. His being so far away, unseen for so
long, and the way the news has trickled in makes it quite impossible
to realise. With Yvo one felt one had been shot oneself, and knew it
was true with all one's senses. Ego I cannot feel physically—vividly
—only a great *dreariness* and the pain of Letty.

Thursday, 13th July

Woke early to the invariable grey drizzle. At twelve I took Bibs—
poor darling 'grim virgin' out shopping, to get her a check coat and
skirt. First we drew blank at the 'Ladies Skirt Co.' and then drove
with Mamma through pouring rain in the iron bedstead. Saw some
rather dreary possible 'Misses costumes' there, but to Bibs' great
relief, I had the strength of mind to leave the shop without buying

anything and we proceeded to Selfridges where we found something we really liked. I hope it will find favour with the family.

David and Martin came to tea—both most fascinating. Martin convulsed us by turning to Sockie and saying, in his most plangent voice, 'Why have you got your clothes on?' Ghastly thought!

Friday, 14th July

Stayed in all the morning writing letters. Telephoned to Katharine in the morning and she asked me if I would come to a night-shift, twelve till four, at her mother's munitions canteen at Hackney Wick. Accepted with alacrity and also gratuitously offered Mary's services. Felt rather alarmed afterwards—it seemed rather a lot to promise for somebody else without consulting them. I left a note breaking the news to her in the hall. I really felt she must welcome the idea—to me it seemed a thrilling adventure.

Mary was not at *all* pleased with the prospect of the night I had arranged for her. She said she had no illusions as to its being 'fun' and that she loved her bed. We had schoolroom supper and at about 10.15 started forth in aprons borrowed from the cook. I looked exactly like a parlourmaid with my black dress under the apron.

Most glamorous sight when we arrived—huge mysterious-looking buildings with sparks flying out of the chimneys and real Nibelungen noise and atmosphere. The canteen was large, airy, and well arranged. We had some time to be initiated into our duties before the rush began at about 11.30. Between one and two thousand hot, begrimed men rushed at us, presenting their tickets representing various values in provisions. Their rest time is precious, so their demands are urgent and one has to be as quick as a cinematograph. I don't know why it's so fascinating, but I simply *loved* it—it really excited me. One pours out boiling tea, snatches at cups—cakes—cigarettes—doling them out quicker than possible and trying to be conscientious about the mental arithmetic, which is sometimes almost complicated. The men, on the whole, were extraordinarily nice and well-mannered. They could so easily have bullied one into losing one's head, and they were very honest, often putting me right when I was cheating the Company: 'You'll soon learn the terms, Miss.' I was hopelessly stunned by an imperious demand for 'Opps Hail': I couldn't think what it was and had to ask three times, hoping for sudden enlightenment—finally, one of the paid helpers told me it was Hopp's ale. The scrimmage was pretty fierce at times behind the counter, and hot drops of tea and coffee fell on one's head. The tariff did not strike one as very cheap:

each cake was a penny and the sandwiches three-halfpence. The men had an hour's rest. Someone played the piano to them, then they filed out, leaving us to the most unpleasant part of our duties, picking up their plates—filthy with the debris of boiled pork, etc.—in preparation for the women's shift, who came in their blue caps at about two o'clock. There weren't more than five hundred of them, so trade wasn't quite so feverish. There was a saintly young Y.M.C.A. man helping. He had been there every day and night that week, and his bloodshot eyes still shone with an enthusiasm of good nature. When we had finished our work we were shown all over the huge factory—most thrilling. Toil-begrimed men handling red-hot icicles of shells—thousands of them—most Wellsian and awe-inspiring, and giving one some idea of the infinite trouble and expense men put themselves to in order to kill one another. I enjoyed the cold drive home.

The Memorial Service for Ego is to be on Sunday.

Sunday, 16th July

Reached Stanway at two and found party assembled at luncheon: Mamma, Papa, Guy, Frances, Evan, St John, and Letty. I had dreaded Stanway sufficiently in anticipation, but the exact way it smote on my heart was beyond what I had expected. It has always had a certain curious kind of aloofness from the world, like a place belonging in a sense to the dead—just a little like Venice, only mellowly and quite happily—now indeed it belongs to the dead, but *poignantly* so. Its spirit seems broken—lush, heavy, almost black-green midsummer everywhere, and the cricket field a jungle.

Letty went to and fro from the church carrying Ego's lovely sword, busby, and belt, and arranging flowers. We had tea and the service was at six. It was very lovely—perfect—the Union Jack with the symbols of his death on it, lovely prayers and hymns, just the people who loved him and a really beautiful address from the poor Priest who poured out his heart for the third time in nine months. It was really beautiful and, temporarily, uplifting almost out of the reach of pain. At the end the organist stuttered out the hymn to joy. Beb, Evelyn, John, Aubrey, Ettie, Evan, and the Duchess all went away directly it was over. The rest of us all went for a walk. Dear old Prew was most touching. 'Sad this—sad this—sad this, sad this!'

We dined together and then put Letty to bed. She had behaved *heroically*, poor darling, but looked terribly ravaged. Mary slept with her and Bibs with me: she mocked me for my bustlessness. It has poured and poured all day—Stanway wept with us.

1916

Tuesday, 18th July

Lunched with Bluetooth. He implied that what he had thought villainy, he now knew to have been extreme simplicity—in fact he told me I was a 'simpleton'. I said it was something common to all my family—probably subtly the result of Stanway upbringing.

When I got back to Cadogan I found wonderful surprise—a thirty-pound cheque from Evan to 'soften the rigours of the commercial hotel'. Bless him—I'm glad I praised him so much at dinner the night before.

Wednesday, 19th July

Arrived Littlehampton 12.47 and was met by both children, looking very well—Michael too lovely. I lunched with him. He has come on a lot, and talks very precisely and grammatically: 'Yes. No. I will . . . I like . . . etc.' I asked him if he would send love to Daddie—'love' means kiss to them—and he replied, 'No, Daddie got bristle'. When John cried, he said, 'I'm ashamed of zoo'.

Miss Quinn seemed very satisfied with John's progress, but I can't say there is any startling difference on the surface.

Thursday, 20th July

Back in Brighton. After I had written some letters, I went out in search of a bathing cap, thinking I should find a suitable one nearby, but I had to walk for miles and miles in grilling sun, but God forbid that I should complain of any ray of heat vouchsafed to us during this awful summer! It was delicious in the water—really warm and heavenly.

Friday, 21st July

The gentility of this establishment, the commercial hotel, beggars all description, and the landlady is the queen of snobs. I hear her talking about 'her ladyship' with bated breath, and issuing stern injunctions to the poor parlourmaid to be sure and help me first, and to mind and open the door for me, and so on.

Saturday, 22nd July

I sat on the balcony reading Byron's letters. Partook of tea in the drawing room—a rather blood-curdling experience. We all sat round balancing cups of strong tea, and a few remarks about the weather were barked out. As I went upstairs, I heard the landlady rebuking the wretched parlourmaid for *not* having 'opened the door for her ladyship'.

Beb and I dined at the Café Royal. Sat in the gardens afterwards— lovely evening after a really hot day. These days are really resting me. I am so much a creature of context that I cannot really feel and realise deeply here—my mind only skims . . .

Sunday, 23rd July

I thought one was really going to be allowed to be warm for a little while, but it had relapsed into chilly greyness again—all most disappointing. Beb enjoyed his Sunday morning lie—we both had breakfast upstairs. He read me Winston's third article in the *Sunday Pictorial*. A thousand pounds is pretty good pay for such balderdash—revolting description of the 'Great Amphibean', as he calls his country.

Monday, 24th July

I went in a tram to see Horatia Seymour and her mother. They live in Sussex Square—the 'aristocratic' part of Brighton. We had tea and then sat out in the little garden. How I *love* making friends! The initial stage fascinates me—exploring their personality, or perhaps to be honest, exploring my own *through* them—seeing myself from another angle and feeling quite free and *unlabelled*.

We talked at length on health and the war. At present she is very enthusiastic about 'twilight birth', a method of some sort of injection which renders childbirth completely painless. She wants to get it adopted in England. I rather dashed her, partly by rather priggishly maintaining that I would not like all that particular pain to be eliminated—it would take too much drama out of life—and also by arguing that it would not (as she thinks) really make a difference to the population. Women refrain from having babies from economy and from shirking the interruption to their normal lives, but surely the recollection of the pain of the actual birth never, or scarcely ever, acts as a deterrent. I can't believe it would with one in a million women. However, Horatia maintains that lots of women have told her they could never face the pain again. I find most of my friends sin in the opposite direction and commit treason to their sex by saying they found it less bad than they expected.

Horatia keeps a diary, too. We agreed how very *un*representative one's diary would be if read, what a false impression it would give.

Tuesday, 25th July

Horatia picked me up and we travelled together to London in Pullman. Drank some poisonous coffee. Horatia showed me an interesting letter from her sailor brother about the Naval Engagement. I gave her *The Volunteer* to read. To my surprise, a woman in the carriage asked if she might have it to look at. We gave it to her. Horatia dropped me at Cadogan Square. Lunched in with Mamma, Papa, Bibs, and Mary S. Mary and Mamma just returned from Clouds. Papa seemed quite pleased with his Mesopotamia speech. Went out with Mary at 3.30 and we were manicured at Harrods. Poor darling she is fairly depressed, not having heard from Tom for three weeks.

That man Howard whom I met at Lord Ribblesdale's Hell had asked me to come and see McEvoy's pictures. The latter has a studio in his house. So I went there at five in some trepidation. Howard played me a nasty trick, taking me first into a studio and saying, 'These are not the good artist's pictures, but another one's'. I was funny about the execrable daubs for about five minutes before I realised they were his own. As with many a good art critic, his practice limps far behind his theory.

McEvoy has some very interesting ones. An embryo Diana—not very promising, but how difficult not to make her blatant and chocolate-boxy! The most extraordinary version of Elizabeth—*just* recognisable, but such a morne-slink fatale *beautiful* Edgar Allan Poe woman. There were some very good pictures of people I didn't know, and a really clever likeness of Lady Sandwich.

I thought McEvoy a *delightful* man—eager, natural and amusing. He has an extraordinary Phil May fringe, and eyes on pivots like Garvin and Aubrey. We talked of Tonks. McEvoy, too, used to teach at the Slade. I liked him *so* much and should like to make friends with him.

Howard is very smooth and easy. He is manager or something of the Grosvenor Gallery, and apparently has a genius for 'picking up'. It's a large, amusing house—I enjoyed myself.

Basil and I dined at Queen's at 7.30. Enjoyed it. I came home at nine to find Mamma, Mary, and Letty sitting in the square. Poor Letty looks ghastly. They were reading letters from and about Ego —'Cut provender,' as Mamma said, 'that has got to last us a long time'.

Thursday, 27th July

Letty came and sat with me in my room after dinner. She has had an extraordinary letter from Mitchell, the officer who was sent out to identify the bodies at Katia. He still *maintains* that Ego's body could not possibly have been there. Luckily, I don't think Letty is founding an atom of hope on it—only it is torturing her. She feels sure he is dead, but this uncertainty again opens out possibilities of crawling away wounded, and so on, and she feels the mystery must somehow be cleared up. I only hope, when Tom gets Mary's letter, he will send some really decisive details—one has got past minding brutal physical facts. Letty kept saying, 'I know I'm going to die, but I just want to be finished off—like a shot animal. I must know exactly what happened, so that I can feel it with my senses'.

Friday, 28th July

Mamma went off to Brighton with A.J.B. I was dining with Basil in Sloane Square, but thought I might as well save his money by sharing Sockie's early meal. Found Freddie with Basil—he had just come up from Tidworth 'all dressed up with nowhere to go'—so we dined *à trois*. The Blackwood brothers are very facetious together. Basil and I went to a cinema in King's Road afterwards—there was quite a good Charlie Chaplin film, but the heat was almost prohibitive.

Saturday, 29th July

Beb had intended to come up to London for the night. I was going down to Brighton anyhow, in the evening, to chaperone Mamma and Mr Balfour. When I got a wire from Beb saying he wasn't coming after all, I decided to go down by 1.55. Most insufferable journey. Impossible to get a porter, and the heat terrific—so large was the mob that hundreds of extra carriages had to be put on. The loaded, so-called express stopped every moment and we were about an hour and a half late in arriving—and then it took me ages to get any sort of conveyance. Arrived very exhausted. Found children looking very well—Beb and I had tea with them. Delicious bathe at six.

Mamma came to see the children going to bed—Beb and I dined with her and Mr Balfour at Princes Hotel. Beb enjoyed his champagne, but we were all rather sleepy and depressed. They walked us some of the way home.

1916

Sunday, 30th July

Glittering, *scorching* day and the town teeming like an anthill. No signs of war, save for the poor, legless men whom Michael tried to encourage by saying, 'Poor wounded soldiers—soon be better.' There is no doubt Brighton has a charm of its own, almost amounting to glamour. I am beginning to be quite patriotic about this end of the town—Kemp Town as it is called—in opposition to the parvenu Hove, which has less character and is to this rather what the Lido is to Venice.

We joined the children on the beach—painfully hot and glaring. We took them in a boat to try and get cooler. Beb and I bathed from the rather squalid bathing-machines—perfect in the water, except for the quantity of foreign bodies.

Beb had to go back into barracks before dinner, so I went alone to Prince's hotel—Mamma and Mr A.J.B. both looking better and much 'brighter'. A very nice young secretary, Steele, dined with us before returning to London. Very pleasant dinner. A great deal of banter about 'Mamma's nest-egg'. They walked me half the way home —such a lovely green night—I was 'spoken to' twice when by myself.

Monday, 31st July

Grilling hot again. As soon as I had had breakfast, I went along to see John doing his lessons. He did his drill quite nicely, and some writing and counting all right—only somehow it gives you the impression of a *tour de force* like a performing animal.

I boldly decided to bathe off the pier as the machines were all full. I shall never bathe from anywhere else again! It was the most delicious thing I have ever done—down a ladder straight into bottomless green water. Apparently there is no risk of drowning as there is a man in a boat, a raft, a life-buoy, etc. There was a strong current taking one inwards, so I rowed out and swam back. Luxurious dressing rooms, too. It's a great discovery.

After dinner we sat on the pier, which was most delicious. Lovely lights on the water and in the twilight Brighton looked quite glamorous, and I like the teeming, happy crowds. Being here is strangely like being abroad. Poor Beb had to go back and sleep in barracks, as he has to inspect the bread at about six tomorrow. I have seen very little of him this visit. He is looking very well and enjoying rides on glorious downs.

198

Wednesday, 2nd August

Lovely day again, but not nearly so hot as there was a pleasant breeze blowing. Lunched in and then went to the station to see if Basil was in the train arriving at three. Felt very uncertain as I had had no telegram, but he arrived all right. He had wired to the wrong address. He was intoxicated with the charms of Brighton.

We went straight to the pier bathing station. The current was running much stronger and he was rowed out to the raft. I descended the ladder with a horrid, fat, flabby woman who boasted of being a strong swimmer. We reached the buoy at the same time. I was quite glad to get there and she was in a state of frantic panic—gasping and spluttering—and I could see her heart beating through her thin dress. Joined Basil on the raft: it's sometimes rather difficult to get on to and one clutches wildly at the toes of strange men—a curious relationship, the raft one. There were some rather rowdy 'town roughs' who were severely reprimanded by the boatman and accused—unjustly I think —of pushing a lady off the raft. We swam back and were rowed out again twice. I enjoyed it immensely. The more I think of it, the more courageous of me do I think it to have bathed there for the first time all by myself, knowing nothing of the currents, etc.

Walked back and drank chocolate at the 'Creamery'. After tea we did the aquarium and then went back on to the pier. We sat in chairs on its nose (very pleasant) and Basil played like a schoolboy with all the automatic machines—his spirits are amazing. We resisted pressing invitations to be photographed in those comic frames through which one puts one's head. The beach was swarming with little naked boys, making a continuous, curiously foreign, wordless, happy noise—very riveting.

We dined at the St James's. Time-honoured, but frivolously handled discussion, as to whether women felt pain less than men, their relative courage, endurance, etc. Basil very fussy about the 'foreign bodies' in his cider cup—sending all the waiters in search of a strainer. He went away by the 10.00—having, I think, very much enjoyed his day.

Saturday, 5th August

Breakfast, newspaper, letters. Went up to Horatia, partly on foot and partly on the electric railway. Quite a cold wind blowing, but hot in the sun. Certainly the weather has been very kind to me. I read about twenty pages of *Richard Feverel* to Horatia, sitting out in the garden while she embroidered. I think Meredith is *very* good for reading aloud. Beb came home to luncheon and we had it at the St James's, really a great discovery—an excellent, clean little lunch for 1s 9d, I don't know how they do it.

We got on a bus and had a very nice drive to Rottingdean, which is a dear little place—I wonder why it has had the luck never to grow. We lay on the beach by the whitest of white cliffs, a real bit of Albion, and enjoyed a 'sunbath'—Beb even dropped off. Then we explored the little village and I looked sentimentally through the gates of St Aubyn's and thought of the days when I used to come down in a Rumanian dress to see Ego and Guy competing in the school sports. We had greatest difficulty in boarding the six-something homing bus. Beb had to go back into barracks for dinner and the night. His duties have been very exacting this visit. I don't think we have ever had a better relationship than we have just now.

Horatia came to dine with me. We had a funny little feminine meal in the 'Creamery'—fried eggs and ham, ground rice pudding, coffee, and raspberries and cream. Then we sat on the pier. I do like Horatia and her company very, very much, and I really think I have cheered her a little, but I do wish I could marry her to someone. She told me Sybil Long had had a great success with the P.M. I hadn't heard of this before. I wonder if she is 'leading lady' now? My bill for the week has come to £3 19s 11d—not too bad.

Monday, 7th August

Desperate packing preparatory to going up to London for two days. Reluctantly coming to the conclusion that I shall have to make my home at Brighton, I feel and look so incomparably better there. Went up by eleven o'clock train.

Tuesday, 8th August

Called for Whibley at the Oxford and Cambridge Club and he took me out to tea in a shop. His hair was very long. If I had been an Eton boy, I should have walked on the other side of the street, as Ego used to when Mamma and I came down to Eton. He was very dear and dew-droppy. He says he has collected all the material for my special edition of the life of Colonel Francis Charteris. He dropped me home.

After changing I drove to Glebe Place, and took Basil his bathing dress. He is very amused by the embroidered grenade and motto.[1]

1. His bathing costume, 'apparently nibbled by sharks', had been lent to a friend by Lady Cynthia for an impromptu bathing party. Before returning it, they decided to have the 'heirloom' embroidered with a grenade and the Grenadier motto *Honi soit qui mal y pense*.

I threatened to rifle his bureau, as his dinner (in Cadogan Square) was earlier and more distant than mine, but he refused to leave the house before I did and so was very unpunctual. He put his Sam Browne belt on over his evening coat. I just noticed it, and then thought it might be a new fashion in the Brigade. We went together as far as our directions were the same.

Settled to go down to Brighton by the 1.55 next day. I wonder what particular quality it is that makes me so extraordinarily happy in Basil's company. On *paper*, I don't suppose I should ever have chosen him and yet, without doubt, I am happier with him—and incomparably so—than I am with any other friend, present or past. I laugh so much, much more—so that lines come round my mouth. It's so difficult to know why, or to reproduce the atmosphere, but I suppose the explanation is that it is more the laughter of real *gaiety* than amusement. That's why it leaves one happy and nourished, instead of almost tired and sterile, as some verbal wit does. I think we have both got real infectious spirits for each other. Far more inexplicable is that I should always feel prompted to write to him about anything which saddens or worries me. I suppose it is simply affection, because I don't think he is really *very* emotionally understanding—he's too sane, normal, unmoody, and healthy. I do hate his going to the Front and, alas, feel the strongest foreboding. He is very indispensable to me. I am sure a certain formality in him enhances his friendship. That he— my greatest friend—should begin letters 'My dear Cynthia', etc., is so different from the *familiarity* without any real *intimacy* that one is accustomed to, and promotes a sort of piquancy and a double, richer kind of relationship. It is difficult to define what I mean, but somehow I think it prevents his becoming like a relation or furniture in one's life.

Dined with the Bighams. I enjoyed my excursion amongst strangers, feeling free, unlabelled, and at liberty to strike out in any line I chose. Mrs Bigham is very pleasant and friendly—she eats raw roots for dinner and, I gather, goes in for fads and culture—their circle is semi-official and semi-musical. I sat beside Mr Bigham and liked him: there were two other men, a clever, excited-looking Schuster who is secretary to the Lord Chancellor, and a Mr Butler who is something at the House of Lords.

Conversation was mainly general and very agreeable. I felt in good form. Cowans came on the block. There is an Enquiry Commission sitting on him on account of the following ugly story: Lady Randolph Churchill (Black Jane) fell in love with a private and, at her instance, General Cowans gave the man a commission. Either another woman

entered the lists and captured this man, or in any case he did not respond to Jane's passion, and spleen and pique made her induce Cowans
to degrade the man to the ranks again . . . Cowans, poor man, has
the reputation of jobbery, owing to his susceptibility to 'ladies', but
this story sounds quite incredible—Bluetooth stoutly denies it.

The Bighams' house in Cheyne Walk is too lovely. I lay on a sofa
as big as a barge. When the men came up I instructed the party in
gibbets, and afterwards we had my favourite conversation about books:
fiction—Trollope, Brontës, Thackeray, Dickens; books for children,
etc. Friendly arguments and people speaking at once. I walked all the
way home: Butler escorted me half the way and then had to hurry
off to be a special constable from twelve to three. I met Basil coming
away from his dinner at the corner of Cadogan Square. Couldn't
get to sleep . . .

Wednesday, 9th August

Very disappointed to get note from Basil saying that, after all, he
couldn't get leave to come down to Brighton. Great pity, it was such
a perfect day for bathing! Later on he rang up to ask if I would lunch
with him. Decided to stay and go down by later train.

Eileen came by appointment at 11.30. . . . She has engaged herself
to a penniless artist in the Flying Corps. She only met him a fortnight
ago, staying with Nesta whom she had instructed to provide her with
an 'incense-burner', so that she might enjoy her holiday. Most romantic engagement. He used to fly over the sea every morning and drop
a bomb enclosing a love-letter at her feet. She admits he says 'tophole'
and 'ripping'. I do hope it isn't the glamour of the Flying Corps
uniform, but she seems very happy. After the war they are going to
live a Trilby life in Paris and both illustrate books and design posters.
Eileen wrote to inform her mother, forgetting even to give his name,
and she received the following priceless telegram: 'So terrible you
cannot even give name. Dreadfully afraid it might be, worst of all,
an Asquith. Mother.' This delighted me.

Lunched with Basil at Queen's Restaurant. I gave him four tiny
Shakespeares to form part of his field equipment. He was very pleased
with them. I telephoned to Sussex Place, found the housekeeper was
in, and so we decided to raid my house again. We went there in the
Tube—very good game—I pretended not to know him in the lift,
so that when he spoke to me it looked as though he were trying to
scrape acquaintanceship. People looked very shocked at an officer
behaving so badly! Got into the house, but found the keys away, so

two workmen from next door came and broke the locks. Letters all in wild disorder, dirty and burst out of their elastic bands—mountains of love letters from Edward, Bluetooth, Bones, and Billy. I am terribly ashamed to say I let B. read some of them, an action I should think vile beyond words in anyone else, but as a matter of fact he couldn't tell who they were from, *except* Edward's—and I honestly *know* he wouldn't mind a bit. I found Papa's priceless 'heavy father' letter about my engagement and read it aloud. We stayed there till 4.30.

Returned Cadogan Square. Had tea and then B. saw me off at the station—hot journey—I read the letters from Ego I had found. Beb was in the hotel—worst possible luck, we have just played Box and Cox. He has to be in barracks till Friday now.

Saturday, 12th August

Unlucky, worrying day owing to chain of circumstances. Beb had told me he expected to be on duty Friday till Sunday, so I had asked Basil to come down Saturday to Sunday, then Beb's days in barracks fell unexpectedly early in the week, so he was free. Saturday morning Beb expressed great disgust at the prospect of B. coming, saying it was his first leave for five weeks (a picturesque exaggeration), and that he wanted to go away somewhere, or anyhow be alone with me, and that he was sick of that eternal *à trois*.

A telegram from Basil saying: 'Arriving 2.15.' Beb was there and was not at all pleased, in fact he was really rather unpleasant, saying he wanted to go away from Brighton. As a matter of fact, the Asquiths couldn't put us up, and it would seem rather pointless to go up to London. His distaste of the *à trois* is rather theoretical, because we always seem to be getting on so well. However, I saw his point, but I think he was a little unjust in his reproaches, because it really wasn't my fault and, after all, Brighton is a public place. We had rather a sulky lunch at the St James and then rested on my bed. Beb was half asleep, and I went off to the station to meet Basil.

Miserable time there. The train was incredibly late, it was difficult to discover which platform it was going to arrive on, and I didn't know there were so many people in England as were thronging at that hot station—one was nearly knocked down at the gates. We tried to find a room at the Royal York and Albion, abortively, but to my surprise there was one room free at the top of our hotel. Found Beb out, which rather disconcerted me. Left note, saying we would start to Rottingdean at five. Basil and I had tea on the pier. On my return found note from Beb: 'I have been looking for you for two hours—am now having tea at the Royal York.' Not a good beginning. I found him there and soothed him down.

We three drove to Rottingdean in a taxi and bathed. It was peculiarly painful, the tide was right out and it was fearfully stony. I was better off in bathing shoes, but the others suffered agonies. However, it made us laugh a lot and was quite a success, though several gobbets of flesh were taken out of me by being hurled against rocks. Changed for dinner when we got home. Sat with Basil on the balcony for a little.

Sunday, 13th August

Banged at Basil's door at seven. We had agreed to bathe if awake. We just ran down to the beach with coats over our bathing clothes. A man, perhaps what they call a 'beach policeman', stopped me, saying it was only for men that station. I said 'Rubbish!' which, unfortunately, he overheard and was furious, threatening to send for the police and saying I must go to Kemp Town. My bathing dress was very wet from the day before and I didn't at all like the idea of going either to Kemp Town or the police station in it. However, we found the situation could be overcome by going through the technicality of taking a bathing machine and leaving one's coat. We had the most heavenly bathe—soft sand and delicious waves, exactly the right size. I *did* enjoy it. I hadn't woken Beb up—an error of judgment—but I thought he so clung to his Sunday sleep, instead he was very annoyed at having been left out of the plans.

The only train to Bognor was at 9.40—rather a bore—I had had an awfully bad night and tried to sleep in the train. I couldn't, but rested my face. The 'nest' lent the Asquiths by Sir Arthur Du Cros is a very comfortable one: hideous house, but trees in the garden, splendid sea view, and comfortable Elsinore battlements to walk on. Huge party looking like a musical comedy: P.M., Margot, Elizabeth, Violet, Puffin, Diana, Nancy, Duff, Hugh, Sylvia, Harry Higgins, Caves, and so on. Some tennis was being played on a mossy court, but I strolled about the grounds with Basil, and met P.M. with Sylvia. The P.M. shuffled partners and I walked home with him. Watched Diana, Duff, Nancy, Elizabeth, and Hugh bathing in very rough sea—Diana swam beautifully and looked dazzling—there were rafts, etc., some way out.

Had rather fun with the news of Eileen's engagement. Sat sleepily in the garden watching tennis in the afternoon and we returned by the 4.45. Beb and Basil both slept heavily in the train. Tea at the Café

Lady Cynthia

(*Above*) *Lady Cynthia with her mother, Harold Baker (left) and Ego;*
(*below*) *A brace of sou-westers: Lady Angela Forbes at a fancy dress ball*
and Lady Cynthia at Brighton

Royal when we got back, à trois on the pier, and while I went to dress, Beb and Basil went to the Metropole and had cocktails. Horatia came to dinner, bringing muslin and silver strainer for Basil's cup. Great dewdrop discussion and comparing notes as to whether all that came into one's net were fish or not. Basil forgot the time, dashed off to try and catch the Southern Belle, missed it and returned depressed at the ghastly prospect of a train which took two hours and only landed him at London Bridge. He started off again in good time for that. Our à trois had really gone off very smoothly, but Beb boiled over periodically when we were alone, and I must say it was very tiring.

Monday, 14th August

Horrid morning, first packing then unpacking at the Royal York, whither we had transferred ourselves. It is only a shilling a night more each, and very, very comfortable. Beb got back soon after six and we had heavenly bathe in enormous breakers—it had been very windy all day. Dined at the St James's—*quite* happy and all right again. Walked along the front seeing life.

Tuesday, 15th August

Sat outside hotel reading Byron's letters till one, when I went up to the Seymours. Lunched with Horatia and her mother, then we had a delightful reading aloud in the garden. It's very lovely. I do think *Richard Feverel* almost the best 'young love' . . .

Horatia took me to phrenologist, a Professor Severn. I nearly had bad giggles. He spoke his patter too quickly to be very convincing, but on the whole wasn't bad. He filled up a chart for me, the maximum mark being seven. The following are some of his verdicts on me: Size of Brain $5\frac{3}{4}$, Organic Quality $5\frac{3}{4}$, Amativeness 5, Conjugality 6, Friendship 6, Alimentiveness 5, Secretiveness $4\frac{3}{4}$, Cautiousness 6, Conscientiousness $6\frac{1}{2}$, Spirituality 6, Veneration $5\frac{1}{4}$, Constructiveness 6, Benevolence 6, Ideality 6, Imitation 6, Mirthfulness $5\frac{3}{4}$, Human Nature $6\frac{1}{4}$, Agreeableness $5\frac{3}{4}$.

Horatia and I had tea together in a shop. I had a divine, very rough bathe in enormous breakers which boxed my ears. Beb and I dined in our own hotel—he had shot an excellent grouse which we eat. Went for a walk in Madeira Drive. Very contented mood.

1916

Wednesday, 16th August

I went up to Horatia at about 11.30. Found her—as I thought—looking especially ill. We read sitting out in the garden. Lunched with her, the mother, and Cynthia. Why is the atmosphere somewhat oppressive where any three women live together alone? I told them about the grouse Beb said he had shot and—when I heard my own voice—for the first time realised the absurdity of such a cock-and-bull story, and what a gull I had been. Of *course* there are no grouse in Sussex—he must have bought it at great expense from a shop. I shall buy a salmon and claim to have caught it bathing.

Thursday, 17th August

Was called early and packed desperately—great strain. Came up to London by eleven o'clock train. I am going to Pixton for about ten days and am so afraid that before then Beb may have been moved off to Salisbury Plain, and I shall have no excuse to return to my 'spiritual home'.

Lunched with Bluetooth. He has read D. H. Lawrence's volume of poems *Amores* and was at first so much impressed by them that he nearly wrote to Lawrence to say how remarkable he thought them.

I had some conversation alone with Helen Campbell at the Bighams. She had written me an extraordinary letter to say they had been doing table-turning at Knebworth, and the name Yvo Charteris had been spelt out. When a message was asked for, the sentence 'I question duty night and day' was given. They asked who it was for, and the answer was 'Mother', and when they asked where she was, 'Ireland'. They inquired if there was anything more and 'Kiss her' was spelled out. Then Helen had been too upset to go on. She was frightfully excited and, being a believer, absolutely convinced that Yvo had really been *there*—very anxious to convince me. I don't quite know why, but the whole thing is *distasteful* to me. It gives, I think, a sad idea of survival. To be hanging round unable, though longing, to communicate and having to use a middle-man in the form of some revolting medium—No! No! *NO!* Yet it is certainly most curious. Helen was the only person there who knew Yvo, and I can swear to her sincerity.

Friday, 18th August

I am sitting out at Pixton. After the constant brace of Brighton it is like sitting in a greenhouse. Children both asleep when we arrived.

Had a talk with Miss Quinn. John has been doing his lessons well, but otherwise, in general conduct, Miss Quinn thinks he has 'gone back'. She doesn't have him so much to herself here, and is hinting that she ought to have him right away by herself somewhere. If I stay on at Brighton, I think I shall let her bring him there. I shall never have the nerve to *say* it to Nurse—I think I shall have to wait till I'm away and write it.

Sunday, 20th August

Mary amused and rather annoyed me by an account of that preposterous Nancy's behaviour at Con's dinner. She had railed at me about Basil before everyone, saying to Mary: 'I can't speak to you, you're a cousin of that little minx—she's the most awful little minx! There was I—Basil was my only pleasure in life and she took him away from me, and won't let him come and see me. She pretends to be a good woman, she pretends to be faithful to her husband, and she takes Basil away, etc., etc.' It's a boring form of humour, really. What alarms me is that I know she would do it before me just the same, and if he were in the room, too. The idea of the last contingency makes me blench!

Wednesday, 23rd August

Great bear-fighting scene after dinner. Aubrey confiscated *Spoon River Anthology*, a book he dislikes, from Mary and we had a fierce fight to recover it. Lady Carnarvon* rather shocked, I think. At one crisis I yelled out, 'Damn you!' but I hope she didn't hear that.

Thursday, 24th August

Soft rain fell practically all day—feeling awfully tired. As Aubrey says, one feels as if someone else had been for a long walk on one's legs. Sat out and read during an interval in the rain—am immensely enjoying *Barchester Towers*, it is so wonderfully in drawing.

Pleasant *tête-à-tête* dinner with Mary, followed by further orgy of morbid personalities. Speculated as to how conscious of looks-admiration one was from individuals, and tried to get our hopes or fears confirmed by the interchange of dewdrops. The game is to mention someone who gives one the sensation of admiration, and then the other has to try and remember confirmatory or contradictory evidence.

Unluckily my memory for other people's dewdrops is very short. She stayed in my bedroom till nearly one. I told her she saw life highly coloured, and credited many people with the breaking of the seventh commandment who would be astonished beyond measure at such an imputation. She said she was certain I underrated such statistics at least as much as she overrated them.

Friday, 25th August

Ettie's book about Julian and Billy came by the evening post. It is called *Pages from a Family Journal* and is riveting—Mary and I have been fighting over it. I long to read it straight through, but so far have only scanned and glimpsed. It appears to be admirably done and makes a delicious record of glorious, gilded youth. Heavenly dewdrops for me from darling Billy: 'Cynthia has been angelic to me in the absence of more puissant rivals—she really is inimitable and irresistible in face and character' and 'Ask Cynthia to Taplow—Panshanger—everywhere—she is the only woman'.

Whibley came at teatime. A very pleasant evening, gossiping about the lives, wives, and loves of Meredith, Hardy, Thompson, and other literary lights. I don't know why, but the idea of Coventry Patmore giving Mrs Meynell pearls amuses me so intensely, also the fact that Meredith married a Miss Peacock (she ran away from him) and was so devoted to his father-in-law Peacock.

Saturday, 26th August

Whibley and I discussed our fits of depression. I confessed my excessive dependence on dewdrops, which he said he couldn't understand. He spoke very tenderly of our first meeting and swift recognition, as if it had been of mutual love at first sight! Bless him, I don't believe he knows he's a gnome at all. I love talking to him. He is so different when off his dinner-table aggressive horse, really wonderfully understanding and talking the same language.

After tea he and I sat in the garden summerhouse. Alas, he waxed more than verbally tender, stroking away at my hand! His is a very inoffensive form, but how I hate it. However, I was very weak-minded—each year of seniority and each degree of ugliness makes protest more difficult—and it was not until he began to stroke my hair and cheek that I got up hastily, saying I must go and see the children.

Monday, 28th August

I went up by early train accompanied, of course, by Whibley. It was tiring to have to talk in the train, but he was at his nicest. He's very soppy about me, and got very pink when we said goodbye, saying 'I love *you* and hate the race'—we had been discussing the ugliness of the travellers.

Dined with Basil at Queen's Restaurant. We drank Lachrymae Christi—nastier than any medicine. He told me he had scolded Nancy for her abuse of me and reduced her to tears. I wish he hadn't. We sat in Cadogan Square together. Lovely night and I felt very moonlit. A great milestone in our relationship: for the first time he conveyed to me the fact that he loved me—in such a way that I could not fail to receive the message and yet with such skill, tact, and innuendo that I was spared a single moment of embarrassment. I can't pretend I'm not glad—but yet—it was all done very indirectly.

We had a long discussion on the ethics of flirting, trying to define 'flirt' in the invidious sense of the word. I held that the only unfair method was to pretend to care more than you did, and that no woman could be blamed for making herself as attractive as possible. The exercise of charm cannot be called *encouragement*, however much it may be an inducement. He demurred, saying the ideal woman in a book (not by any means *his* ideal), on perceiving she was liable to attract a man, would draw in her charms, as if turning off so much electric light. However, he agreed that practically it was difficult to apply, and that a woman could hardly be expected to (as he said) put on her biggest boots and do her hair badly if she felt a man was susceptible. Long attack on my poor heart, saying I had none or anyhow not enough ever to inconvenience as his did. Tried to dissuade him from this opinion. I *do* think there is some truth in Bluetooth's theory of 'mirrors' and Elizabeth's rather clever phrase that I regarded people as 'occupations'. I have great *appreciation* of people but, though I love the company of many people, I don't suppose I am really *fond* of many of them. Appreciation is more or less essential. However, Basil is a conspicuous exception to this rule, so it is hard that the charge should be levied by him. He took my hand for just a minute, and when he remarked on its coldness, I was able to say 'Cold hands—warm heart'. He said at parting, 'You *have* a little heart, cultivate it.' Such as it is, my heart ached a good deal and I slept badly. Excited and pleased, but worried by sense of responsibility. How I have wondered and doubted as to what his feelings were to me! It was not what is called a 'declaration', but I cannot honestly pretend even to myself that I can doubt his meaning. I only hope it will not become difficult to continue more or less on the old gear . . .

Tuesday, 29th August

Had to make a raid on the kitchen at 5 a.m. Horrible wet, cold day. Went to order spectacles.[1] Luckily the opticians keep their prescriptions. Lunched with Bluetooth. He was inclined to be critical about Ettie's book. I waxed rather argumentative—Travelled to Brighton by 3.50.

Friday, 1st September

I went to Bognor by the 3.55 with an appalling amount of luggage on which I was heavily excessed. Arrived at Craigweil carrying Beb's sword in my hand. Found Elizabeth, Bluetooth, Margot, Puffin, Goonie, P.M., Violet, Davies, and Barbara and Viola arrived later. Changed and played tennis with Puffin who is in the throes of a passion for me—scarcely took his eyes off. He is a really dear little boy, with exquisite manners of heart and head. Goonie forgot herself and asked Margot where on earth he got his 'prince' manners from.

Saturday, 2nd September

I think my in-laws' is almost the only household where breakfast isn't even supposed to begin before tea, and then it was very late. Beb, self, P.M., Davis, Viola, and Barbara were the only ones who appeared at all. I went to have a few words with Margot in bed—she managed to inflict a good many jars and jangles. I also visited Goonie's bedside and left her the Ettie book to read. She had got a letter from Birrell which she wouldn't let me read, but she owned the cap fitted when I said that, very often, one minded one's letters being seen not because of what was in them, but because of what was *not* in them. Played a good deal of tennis—was in good form and enjoyed it. Such a heavenly bathe before lunch—perfect sand and sea! My mermaid green bathing dress had a success with Margot. Rested after lunch and then more tennis.

Great ructions all day because the P.M. had invited Diana and Margot had put her off because there was no room. Unfortunately, Diana had chucked Mrs Duggan to come. Viola—one of her great

1. To replace a treasured tortoiseshell pair lost in the train the previous day.

adorers—was very indignant and at tea there was a skirmish between her and Margot.

Viola: 'It's really a dreadful thing to have done. Diana's not accustomed to being treated like that.'

Margot: 'I thought she wasn't accustomed to being received.'

Viola (who carries the role of *complaisante* wife to excess): 'Well, I expect Duff and Alan will both chuck. There's nothing for them to come for now.'

Margot: 'Chuck? Surely they won't be as middle class as to do that?'—to which Viola retorted that Margot couldn't talk, being both middle class and a chucker.

Duff, Alan Parsons, Francis McLaren and a strange man whose name I forget, a journalist I believe, arrived before dinner, and Bluetooth returned. Afterwards, Violet, Goonie, and I sat out in the garden for a bit, and then Margot called us in to witness the most amazing scene. I couldn't have believed it if I had been told about it, and even now it seems like a dream. Yeo—the goodlooking butler who used to be at Gosford—was made to stand up to the roomful, and do his really excellent stunts. He barked like a lion, made a noise like sawing wood, a brass band, cats, etc., etc.—all brilliantly done. It was funny enough to hear someone, who had just handed one the potatoes, roaring like a lion, but it was only the preface to—in my opinion—the greatest breach of taste I have ever witnessed. They made him do very good imitations of various prominent guests at Downing Street, their voices and walks—McKenna, Haldane, Lord Morley, and so on. It was a very pungent scene. The P.M. lolling in ruby glee, chuckling away at his butler ridiculing his colleagues; Margot, as though she were producing Patti, rating anybody who made a noise; and all the guests rather embarrassed and giggly. The funniest thing was the way Yeo—in his most professional, deprecating, butler voice—gave out the name (just as if he were announcing him) of his victim: 'Lord Morley' and so on. I had the rare luxury of being *shocked to the core*. None of the family—except Beb, who was horrified—saw anything odd in it, but I canvassed a good many of the other guests and they agreed with me. It seemed to me terribly symptomatic and really to shake foundations. What must that stranger have thought, and what copy for a journalist! It's awful.

Sunday, 3rd September

Wet windy morning. Tremendous excitement when I got down to breakfast. Diana had telephoned at 3.15 a.m, to say there were fourteen

Zeppelins over London and one had been brought down. Furious at not being there, and then rather alarmed, thinking there might be a ghastly mess. Davies got on to his family's house in Bayswater and heard they had slept through it; and then they got on to Downing Street and found that was still standing. It was ages before they could get an official message, and then Margot came running on to the tennis court saying, 'It's very flat. Only one Zeppelin reached London and not a cat's been hurt.'

Beb and I had early dinner and went up to London by the 8.30.

Monday, 4th September

Beb shopped in the morning. We had early lunch and he went off to Larkhill, just like a boy going to school. I remained in London with no definite plans. I was by way of going down to stay with Horatia, but didn't know which day till I knew when Basil could get his inoculation leave—the plan being that he should come down to a hotel at Brighton.

Dined with Basil at Queen's Restaurant. Sat in summer house in Square. Went home with very mingled feelings. I cannot pretend I am not glad to know he loves me, and yet I feel distressed with responsibility, and the future is difficult. How I have wondered if he really cared, and how well he has concealed his feelings! I was never quite certain. He was perfect and said delicious things and, of course, it gave me great happiness of a kind. With my accustomed tongue-tiedness I said I would write when I got home. He said he knew what I should say and wouldn't read it, but I made him promise to. Slept very badly and wrote him a long-long letter at 4 a.m.—a great effort —trying to define the situation, present and future. It was very difficult, everything seemed fatuous and like something in a novel. Not much Pepys about this part of my diaries—I wonder if all diaries are as unrepresentative of their writers as this is of me.

Tuesday, 5th September

Basil sent a note round. I was very tired after my bad night and rested. I dropped my letter at his house and by odd coincidence met him on the doorstep—Lunched with Guy, who was looking very handsome with a thin moustache. The dear Priest was staying with him, very glad to see him. I was feeling ill with pain and there was nothing I could eat.

Dined with Basil and sat in the summer house again. He was very dear and said he quite agreed with my letter. I behaved with proverbial feminine inconsistency—practice entirely divorced from theory. He told me he had been in love with Kitty Somerset for seventeen years.

Wednesday, 6th September

Lunched with Whibley at the Savoy. Was feeling ill and was a sore disappointment to him in the way of appetite: he kept plying me with unwelcome dainties. Went home to change into tennis clothes. Basil, Freddie, and Mary H. called for me and we went by Sloane Square tube to Queen's. Basil and I played together. Physically it was rather a nightmare to me: my arm—Heaven knows why—was all numb and shaky. I couldn't grip my racket and played execrably at first, my service quite, and my returns practically, gone. Guy and George Moore[1] were playing with two other men on the next court, and Puffin and Elizabeth were with a pro on another. Margot had telephoned and suggested their cutting into our game, but I thought it was rather too much. We had an amusing tea and tubed back to Sloane Square. Basil walked me home. I deposited my luggage and walked him to his house. Went in for a few minutes. He put me into a bus.

Lawrence has sent me his volume of poems accompanied by a maddish letter. He is engaged in writing a sequel to *The Rainbow*, what can it be?

Thursday, 7th September

Lunched Downing Street and played tennis with Elizabeth, Puffin, and a so-called professional at Queen's. He served whole games of faults over the net and *scarcely* got a return over—he made us quite hysterical. Margot fetched us home in motor. Poor Basil interned in barracks all day, but he telephoned to me.

Dined with Mary and Aubrey at Stratford Place. The George Lloyds were there, and the fanatic Josiah Wedgwood, and Lord Eustace Percy. I sat beside Wedgwood—he rather interested me. He was an extreme radical and is, I believe, a wonderful soldier now. He kept saying how glad he was there had been a war, and also that he wished women would fight.

Friday, 8th September

Rang up Basil and stipulated for a female escort for my lunch on guard.

1. From this point references are to George Moore, the novelist.

He promised me Brenda. Put on black chiffon, picked Brenda up at the Bath Club, and we went on to King's Guard, St James's Palace together. Brenda had cut her wavy chestnut hair short, and was looking astonishingly pretty and attractive. There was one other woman, Basil, Freddie, and two other officers. I felt a little shy, but it was quite a success. Played ping-pong after lunch. Walked all the way home. Met Evan, who had rung me up to ask me to come to lunch, saying he was off to France with machine-gun next week—great heavens!

Saturday, 9th September

Lunched with Basil at Queen's, and then walked with him to his house. Not *very* happy. Beb arrived about four, looking *wonderful* after an excessively arduous week. We dined at the Berkeley, which he enjoyed immensely, and went to the famous *Battle of the Somme* cinema at the Scala. Very thrilling and moving, and in my opinion *not* an error of taste, except perhaps the dressing of the wounds. Curious to think it will be being given hundreds of years hence . . .

Just after Brenda and I had left yesterday an order came to say no more ladies were to be entertained on guard. The end of a very old custom. Very funny that we should have been the *very* last.

Monday, 11th September

Paid expensive joke on Aileen.[1] We had discussed the awful sort of *cotillon* vanity one has about wishing to impress one's nurse with the amount of flowers received—dreading unfavourable comparisons between oneself and Ruby, and so on. I ordered lots of little bunches to be sent from General March, Admiral So-and-so, Lord Cuthbert Black, v.c., Archdeacon Rose, etc. Went home and recovered my face by rest and rouge, and put on black chiffon with aigrette hat.

Mary Herbert, Mary Strickland, and I all lunched with Guy for Eileen's wedding. She was married at St Bartholomew's, Smithfield—the *most* lovely little church, but a fearful long way to go. Her face looked pretty and I'm glad to say she was an emotional bride, not a brisk, bright one. No bridesmaids. Venetia, in her mythical bird-of-paradise hat—the one she was married in—took the two Marys, Violet, Guy, and me on to Apsley House.

It gave me a pang to think that at one's own wedding—when one felt so wonderfully *exaltée*, glamorous, and self-conscious—people were all the time being just as ribald as we were on this occasion,

1. A daughter had been born to her the previous day.

thinking of our clothes and very coolly criticising the bride's: I was jarred by our atmosphere. The Apsley House reception was strangely depressing, a bad compromise—just the wrong number of people, a great flatness in the atmosphere.

Dined with Brenda for Basil's party, then we went on to Basil's house. Norah and Hugo Rumbold played and warbled at the piano, and Basil, Mrs Darell, General Lowther and I played some rather absent-minded poker—I lost thirteen shillings. Strange sort of re-adjustment in one's public relationship a declaration makes, Basil is easier than anyone else probably. Didn't get home till past one. Mrs Darrell dropped me.

Tuesday, 12th September

Felt deathly tired all the morning with very deep ruts under my eyes. I lunched with Evan, who is very excited and *exalté* about going out to the Front. He is going as A.C.C. to Colonel Swinton (Ole-Luk-Oie)* with some new secret invention in the way of a gun. As far as I can make out, its object is to be able to go over all obstacles in some mysterious way. Apparently it can't be adequately tested here, and no one knows whether it will prove a terrific, epoch-making success or a complete failure.

Basil came at a quarter to five. I was due to see Aileen Meade at a quarter to six, so I made him walk me towards Portland Place. Found Aileen well and terrifically dressed up—she had very much appreciated my flower joke, and was pining for Lord Cuthbert Black, v.c., to materialise. Dined with B. at Queen's Restaurant and sat in Square.

Wednesday, 13th September

Here beginneth the fourth volume. I really must try and reduce my handwriting or no house will hold the complete edition.

Katharine came to see me at 5.30, looking an inspiration of love-liness, real 'beauty that makes holy earth and air', and very darling— a complete relapse from Coterie spirits to wan pathos. Very racked about her Raymond and not knowing where to turn for money. She has been leading an ultra-domestic life at Mells with her children— has only just left off nursing her baby and is pleasingly soppy about him. This reminds me of heavenly Mells story. Katharine changed her room, and the Montagus went into the one she vacated. At six in the morning the nurse, as usual, brought the baby in to be nursed and stood over Montagu with the flannel bundle for some time before she realised her mistake. In telling her story she said, 'At first I thought Mr Horner must have come back'!!!

Dined with Basil at 7.30 and we went to the sequel of *Potash and Perlmutter*, rather a burlesque but very well acted. Guy and John Granby were behind us. Basil looked wretched at saying goodbye. The change in relationship makes quite a new person in my life. I can scarcely connect them.

Thursday, 14th September

I lunched with Sockie and went down to Wilsford by 2.10 from Waterloo. I had forgotten how pretty it was. It's delicious the way the garden melts into the meadows, and the meadows into the downs. The 'cuckoos' are in luck! Beb turned up looking so well on his very strenuous routine. He revelled in a hot bath and we had quite a nice little dinner. Afterwards I read him some of Lawrence's morbid *Amores* poems. He went off about ten. The house is very pip-pip—such a strong Pamela atmosphere. I am in the blue tulip room.

Friday, 15th September

An eremite's day. How seldom have I ever had a completely solitary day! It was quite an experience, and one that I enjoyed. After lunch I sat out re-reading *The Vicar of Wakefield*—most lovable of books. Then I wrote to Katharine, Raymond,[1] Pamela, and Horatia, and began to write in a pretty book a Shakespearean anthology—purple patches out of each of the plays. A very detached day—not even a newspaper. Perhaps something tremendous has happened?

Saturday, 16th September

Letter from Basil in the morning, postponing discussion of the question to our next meeting. Misty morning which brightened into the most lovely day with real hot sunshine. I established myself in the 'stone parlour', a very nice out-of-door shelter with writing table and couch. I wrote up the children's books, added largely to my Shakespeare anthology, and began to read Southey's *Life of Nelson*. After lunch I read the whole of *The Rivals* with great enjoyment. I had no conception it was so witty.

Beb and I went for a delicious walk before tea through lush meadows along the brown, swirling river in which fat trout were lurking.

1. He was to be killed in action before receiving this letter.

Lovely brown shoulders of downs in the distance, and I longed to go to them, but Beb, after hard week, was not panting for exercise. I am enjoying these peaceful empty days here. If only it were June instead of September, and I were approaching my twenty-second instead of my twenty-ninth birthday. I am haunted by the sense of evanescence lately—feel the horizon shutting down on me. The future used to be so absolutely shoreless, like infinity.

Sunday, 17th September

Large post brought to me in bed. Funny letter from Evan, apologising for the anti-climax of his still being in London, and one from Basil, wretched with a bad cold. Very amused and indignant to discover, amongst a huge pile of bills, one solitary receipt for a subscription from Beb to the Lost Cats' Home—an inexcusable impulse of philanthropy.

We had an early tea and then went out. We left our little, lush, sheltered valley and struck straight out on to the downs. Seeing Stonehenge looking small and insignificant in the distance, we felt obliged to walk to it across country. I suppose it was just under three miles, but very rough going, and we got soaked. All the military camps are an extraordinary sight—miles of red huts defacing the spaciousness of the downs. There is generally the hum of an aeroplane in one's ears, and altogether one might be just behind the lines.

Monday, 18th September

I found the orthodox way to Stonehenge—a lovely grassy drive. Walked miles seeing nothing alive except hares and aeroplanes. Such a magically lovely evening. My heart nearly burst with the beauty of it. How much more one feels it when quite alone!

I wrote to poor Nurse in the morning, sending her the bombshell of my decision about removing John.

Tuesday, 19th September

Heartbreaking day. Came downstairs in high spirits, opened newspaper, and saw in large print: LIEUTENANT ASQUITH KILLED IN ACTION. Darling, brilliant, magically charming Raymond—how much delight and laughter goes with him! It seems to take away one's last remains of courage. One might have known that nothing so brilliant and precious could escape, but after each blow one's hopes revive, and one reinvests one's love and interest. Now I feel I have really relinquished all hope and expect no one to survive. Katharine is the most awful thought—a nightmare horror which makes one's brain reel. I have always dreaded it for her, even before there was a war. She seemed 'fated', and I always felt she would be the worst subject conceivable—hopeless and utterly beyond anyone's help. Poor, poor darling, lovely Katharine! There is nothing one can even say to her. Miserable day, hating the solitude I had hitherto loved.

Wednesday, 20th September

We were called at an unearthly hour and Beb went away. Another letter from Basil by second post. The Grenadiers are sending out a draft of twenty-one officers to replace casualties and he says he is certain to go with the next batch. Prospect terrifies me—felt miserable altogether. Spirit rather raised by lovely walk towards Stonehenge which I took after tea. Rest of the day spent at my anthology, and bolting food and books. Interested in a Life of Abraham Lincoln. What a marvel of a man!

Thursday, 21st September

When I came back from walk on the downs, at a quarter to seven, I found Beb already arrived, having motored all the way from the Wharf in the Government car. Rather an abuse of petrol, I can't help thinking. He had spent the night at the Wharf with his father. There were literally thousands of letters and telegrams arriving every hour from all parts of the world. The P.M. had motored over to Mells to see Katharine when he got the news. According to the only report received. Raymond was shot in the chest while advancing. He walked on a little way and then fell down and died. I suppose he was shot through the lungs.

Beb and I strolled through the garden a little. He was in a very darling mood. After dinner he read bits of my anthology aloud. He and the newspapers are very full of the prowess of the 'tanks', as the Tommies have christened the new great armoured caterpillars which go through, or over, all obstacles. Of course, they must be the invention Evan was going with. One wonders whether they haven't been precipitate, and whether it would have been better to have a much greater number as a real trump card before laying it on the table. No doubt now the Germans will be able to copy them and, at any rate, will find some counter to them before long. They must really be very violable. Anyhow, they seem invaluable as a tonic and joke to our men.

Friday, 22nd September

Beb was called at 6.15 and went off to his camp. Donne's poems, sent me by Whibley, arrived by first post. Letter from Basil by the second. He says Mark Tennant has been killed, for which I am most awfully sorry, and that the casualties in the Guards have been extra-ordinarily high. He also said he didn't believe the much-vaunted 'tanks' deserved all the credit they had been given, and he heard they had failed entirely on the Guards' front. Dull grey day. Stuck to my routine. Wrote out reams of Shakespeare, finished Life of Lincoln, and trudged the downs spouting poetry. Beginning to tire of my own company a little. Am not growing on myself. No news of poor darling Katharine.

Sunday, 24th September

Delicious day. Beb did about four hours work at different times and I finished my anthology. We went for a stroll in the morning and the afternoon, and such a lovely walk in the evening. Turning to the left instead of going on to the downs, we came to a perfect view of a village clustering round the lovely bend of the river. I have never seen Beb look so well and good-looking, and I don't think we have ever been happier together. I don't know how I could bear his going to the Front again. My nerves have gone to pieces utterly.

Monday, 25th September

Beb returned to school at cockcrow. I had a vile journey up to London. Frightfully slow, crowded train, and sitting vertically in third class carriage with soldiers standing on one's feet as well as sitting on one's hands. Very tired when I got up at nearly three.

After early tea I went to Catherine Street. Frances was out and I waited about an hour and a half for her. Poor darling, she looks very shat-tered. The circumstances of Mark's death seem particularly cruel. . . . He had had such prolonged torture, hating every minute of it, and owing to bad health (he hadn't been sleeping at all), he was just coming home to go on a staff. He got through the battle all right, and had gone across to another trench to congratulate his brother-in-law, Ian

Colquhoun, on both their escapes; on his way back, Ian saw him blown to bits by a stray shell. That wonder fire-eater Ian is said to have killed about thirty Germans with his own hands, the three last with a club. Apparently one of the tanks let down the Guards terribly when they relied on it, as it fell over and left them exposed. The casualties in the brigade have been too appalling. They say headquarters were hit, and that is why the lists are coming in so slowly. Lord Lascelles, who is back with a broken arm, saw darling Raymond dying in a field station. He was under morphia. I dined with Basil and we sat in the square. Lovely night. I was, as he said, 'unsatisfactory'.

Tuesday, 26th September

I lunched with Kitty, our first meeting after a very long interval. She has got a delicious little house in Regent's Park for only £140 a year, and has done it very well indeed, I think. The drawing room has shiny black walls, and cushions made out of old ball dresses. Bobbetty and Betty Cranborne were there—she is just going to have a baby.

I walked from there to Miss North and from there to Bruton Street. Mary and I talked much of Raymond. She said the P.M. had reported on poor Katharine as we feared, saying she was quite 'inaccessible' to any sort of comfort. Aubrey came in from an interview with H. G. Wells, and we three went to an exhibition of very striking paintings by Nevinson. Walked and bussed home.

Dined with Basil's friend Jeffie Darell. Conversation rather crude after dinner. Jeffie complained of her smart black jet dress (Bradley) being too tight. They made me try it on and as it fitted she gave it to me, also a pink *crêpe-de-chine* nightgown which was tight for her. As I won £1 17s at poker it was a profitable evening. Basil walked me home. Alas, poor jester Bim has been killed, too. The news came only today. That's the fifth grandson for poor Gan-Gan.

Wednesday, 27th September

My birthday. Alas! I have entered my thirtieth year. Grim thought. Basil remembered and sent round a note. I lunched with Bluetooth who, poor dear, is utterly crushed by Raymond's loss. Gusts of hate against Margot, were, however, distracting him a little. She had rung up his butler and told him to tell his master that she was very surprised that he hadn't written to either her or Mr Asquith—a wonderful instance of her egotism. I wonder if she expects Katharine to write to her first. She wrote to Anne saying, 'I was in love with Raymond for ten years. Finding he didn't care for me, I began to abuse him which I now regret.'

Basil called for me, we picked up my luggage at Cadogan Square, and he saw me off to Brighton from Victoria. He is to follow on Friday. Found Horatia and her mother at home when I arrived to stay with them at 18 Sussex Square.

Friday, 29th September

Florry Bridges and her sister came to tea. Florry had been at the Wharf when they got the news about Raymond. Before the end of the evening Margot was asking someone to show her card tricks, and Florry showed me the most awful letter she had written to her the next morning, asking her to go to Handley and Jay and see which had the best *crêpe-de-chine* dress—cut and style—so that she could order it on Monday. I went to station to meet Basil, who arrived at 6.40. On the way up in the fly he told me he is to go to France next week— a horrible bit of news.

Saturday, 30th September

Horatia and I both slept vilely again. Very, very tired. I can't think why 'Dr Brighton' has so signally failed this time: there must be some spell of ill-health over the house. I breakfasted downstairs with Basil. He had obviously got a chill on the top of neglected influenza, and was, I think, feeling desperately ill and—for him—very torpid. He is very unaccustomed to feeling ill, and has a terrible theory of 'keeping up', so probably is unduly depressed when he is not feeling well. I persuaded him to be inoculated. A nice khaki doctor motored us down to a hospital in Hove where, after an interminable wait, another doctor with a German name gave him a double dose—double because he had had enteric.

Sunday, 1st October

Impossible to get a place in a Pullman, so we came up by the much more leisurely 5.08, in a frightfully crowded carriage. Basil's health began to improve, and I dropped him at Glebe Place. He was dining with Freddie, who he now hears is to go to the Front as well, but arranged to dine with me at Queen's instead. There is no doubt it is getting much too fashionable.

Slept better. Heard nothing of Zeppelins. One was brought down north of London.

Monday, 2nd October

Basil telephoned, and said he had been to a half-crown doctor in King's Road who had given him a tonic. Unfortunately, he has to go all the way up to the north of Ireland to say goodbye to his mother—a real exercise of filial piety, for he isn't fit to travel and has a terrible lot to do.

I dined with Mary and Aunt Evelyn at the Hanover Restaurant. Felt terribly tired and depressed. Sylvia was there with her husband, and Maud Cunard came in with Beecham, both looking disgusting.

Tuesday, 3rd October

Weather as bad as ever. Papa played golf with Arnold Ward. Poor dear, he is terribly *desœuvré* in London—reading novels in the morning. Mary and I went and sat in Cadogan Square together—both very miserable. She is very dejected at Aubrey's departure[1] and indeed I think all our nerves are shattered. She said she thought Aubrey had good battle, but bad battlefield nerves—a good distinction.

I went to see Basil at five. Found him looking much better. Had tea with him and stayed till he had to start off with his luggage. Freddie is going to Ireland with him—a great alleviation. His room looked delicious. I do mind his going terribly, terribly. He is indispensable to me.

Arranged that Evan, Mamma, Papa and I should all dine at the Hyde Park Grillroom. Mamma returned from Scotland looking fairly well, I think. Papa in great facetious spirits. Poor Evan went to France for a week and found he wasn't wanted. Swinton, to whom he is attached, has been badly treated and left behind. Evan dropped me at Portland Place to see Muriel who is going over to Paris. How she has circumvented the immoral rule that no woman with a husband at the Front can go to France, I don't know!

Wednesday, 4th October

I went to Miss North, taking the black dress Mrs Darell gave me. It does not suit me. I will see if it fits Horatia who is in want of a black

1. To Salonika.

dress. Came home, changed into black chiffon, and went to lunch at Downing Street. Margot has not altered her technique one jot: luncheon tables as full as ever and the Wharf full for Sunday. I sat between Eddie and the P.M. Juliet Duff was on the P.M.'s other side —I do think her the ugliest beauty. Poor P.M. looks very, very sad. He deplored Basil being in the Guards and said it ought to have been absolutely forbidden instead of only made difficult. Certainly it oughtn't to be left to their own choice whether people with brains like Raymond should go on a Staff. Appalling as the waste is, no individual can put it even to himself that he is too potentially useful elsewhere to throw away his life as a Subaltern in a function which anyone else could fill equally well. But, if the Staff needs an individual's brains, it ought to come as a direct command. As it is, no one sensitive will go on a Staff now, so invidious has it become, and all our intellect is being chucked away in the trenches. Cis was there, with a moustache, as he has been in England all the time. He has, of course, been made a captain. He made poor Davies, who was sitting beside him, blush purple repeatedly by saying he was going to tell me what Davies had said of me. He let him off till the end of lunch, however. It was that he was 'drugged by my beauty'. Amused by hearing that Wimborne is now called in Ireland, the 'Rebounder'.

Mamma and I and Papa dined with Evan in his lovely rooms. He had just had the most outrageous letter from Margot about Raymond, saying that he, too, was like Raymond—without enough nature, warmth, and glow.

Thursday, 5th October

Breakfasted upstairs with Mamma. Went to the Arlington Street Hospital for officers at about twelve o'clock. Mamma met me there. Diana, Letty, and Phyllis Boyd were all there beautifully uniformed. I believe Diana is wonderfully efficient. The hospital really looks very nice. I want to come up from Brighton every other week and under-study Frances and Phyllis.

I lunched with Maud Cunard who was looking an amazing Guy Fawkes. There was quite a large party, but I had a few words with her first, during which she told me Basil was the man she loved best in the world, that she heard he was desperately in love with me, and that she would get him stopped from going to the Front—really, as if she could! I sat next to an interesting Italian diplomat and had rather a good war talk. Harry Cust came in on my other side looking very dissipated. Someone said the Speyers ought to be seized as Germans on which he said, 'I don't want to seize Lady S.' He also said he loved the infamy which shone from my every feature.

Friday, 6th October

I lunched at Queen's Restaurant with Brenda, Freddie, and Summie. They are the happiest and most comfortable trio to be with; certainly she is a clever little woman and amazingly attractive and pretty. Poor Freddie is pretty depressed at the prospect of going out. I like him so much. He has a great deal of Basil's charm without his brains. They dropped me home in Summie's little motor. Beb arrived back from his terribly severe week in a sodden camp at Okehampton. I had to break it to him that he must make his own plans for the evening, as I was dining with Basil on his last night. He was rather pathetic about it, but good.

Basil had had an awful day of rush with photographers, lawyers, etc. He called for me. We tried to get into the grill room of the Hyde Park, but it was so full we had to go to the Restaurant where the food was bad. Nancy had again been bullying him about me, trying to find out who he was dining with and whether I had been the object of his going to Brighton. I went to Glebe Place with him—it looked disconsolately half-packed-up—divan, Oxford suit. It was awful saying goodbye to him. At the best I shall miss him terribly and I am so dreadfully frightened. What I would give to know I should see him again! He was very pleased with the lock of hair I gave him. He dropped me home. I promised reluctantly to go and see him off at the station.

Saturday, 7th October

Beb and I breakfasted together. I took a farewell note round to Basil's house—just missed him, so it was given to his servant to take to the station. Went to Dress Agency. The train was 11.55. I started in good time. About five minutes before reaching the station my taxi passed the draft—nearly three hundred magnificent men almost all over six feet, marching along with women hanging on to them—Basil marching at their head, very upright and military, with that strange look of self-surrender that particular position gives.

I found Freddie at the station and he took charge of me. Soon the draft came swinging in. I have never seen such a magnificent body of men. Certainly the standard of the Guards hasn't gone down at all. There was a crowd, and we were kept back by policemen while the soldiers went on to the departure platform. Basil saw us and smiled as he marched by. After a time, relations and friends were allowed on and we found Basil. Jeffie Darell was there to say goodbye. Baroness D'Erlanger was there, too, with Hugo Rumbold. I had a good many last words with Basil with such a lump in my throat, but thank God I didn't cry! Lord Francis Scott and lots of fine-looking officers were there to see them off and one heard all the 'Goodbye, old Basil—the best of luck's'. Nothing could be more dramatic and moving. He was glad I came so it was a good thing I went, but never again! Jeffie wisely took me away before the train started. The send-off cheer would have finished me.

She dropped me at the Berkeley, where I lunched with Beb. He, I, Grace, and Letty went down by 1.45 train to Stanway. Letty and I third class. She looked desperate as we approached the familiar country near Toddington. Stanway hurts a good deal now.

Tuesday, 10th October

Bibs came into my room soon after seven and did her physical exercises before me. I have never seen such stress and strain, such cracking of joints, gasping and groaning. In this, as in everything else, she is morbidly conscientious and will repeat a particularly strenuous exercise if she thinks she hasn't done it quite fairly.

She and I bicycled into Winchcomb—a great expedition. It was very hard work. My front tyre was quite flat. It seemed uphill all the way there, and the wind was violent and in our face. I had to walk a great deal of the way. I loathe struggling uphill. Bibs fussed the whole time about getting home in time for lessons and to my irritation, when we got to Winchcomb and found it was a little late, insisted on driving home in the motor which happened to be there. Either she is terrified of Sockie, or else she has got fatty degeneration of the conscience! I sat with Eliza for about twenty minutes and then bicycled lonelily home. Grace played with me and Michael, and then came to see him in his bath. He is being the greatest joy to me these days. Grace and I dined early with Bibs and Sockie. I read two Boyd Cable war stories to her while she did her old patience. I think them quite excellent.

Thursday, 12th October

Called at seven and went up to London by early train. Lunched with Bluetooth, who told me of the rumour that the Germans are going to fight their next naval battle with gas. He had been at the Wharf the last Sunday, and had a good story of Margot expostulating with Keynes for not playing tennis: 'I must teach you, you're an ass not to play. Think of your bridge—if you didn't play you wouldn't know a cat.'

Went down to Brighton by 3.10. Found Beb comfortably established in the Royal York.

Friday, 13th October

Financial panic. Supposing Beb did not go to the Front for some time. I realised that a prolonged comfortable visit to the Royal York would inevitably involve bankruptcy, so I took advantage of poor Beb's absence to move precipitately into the unutterable squalor of a bed sitting room at the lodging house John and Michael stayed in.

Saturday, 14th October

Beb turned up at lunch time, having been ordered to bed with influenza or rheumatic chill. An illness at the lodging house was out of the question—much too squalid—so shamefacedly we were obliged to return to the Royal York. I don't know what the staff there must think of us—repeating the same manœuvre. I wonder which one of us they consider the lunatic.

I couldn't face the expense of living at the Royal York myself, even if I could have coped with packing again, so I shall continue to sleep at the lodgings. My plight is pretty ridiculous: Beb lying at great expense in the middle of the town—John at one extreme end —the comfort, warmth, and cleanliness of Horatia's house at the other —and myself sleeping at a fourth house and eating anywhere else.

Sunday, 15th October

In spite of absurd situation the day was really one rather after my own heart. Reading Congreve aloud to Beb in his bed in the morning and Meredith to Horatia in hers in the afternoon. Harry Preston, the notorious owner of this stage-patronised hotel, visited Beb and showered contemporary fiction on him. I went up to Sussex Square for lunch—had it with Horatia's sister and the children. Read Trollope to myself after lunch while I rested—I am what is called 'making myself at home' in the house, and then went up and actually finished reading *Richard Feverel* to Horatia, great triumph!

Monday, 16th October

Went long bus ride to call on the colonel's wife. She was out, but I had tea with him and she came home before I left. He's a nice old buffer. I summoned up my courage and asked if he had any idea when Beb would be likely to go out. He said not before six weeks and it might be much longer. Home to Beb. Practised him in the Morse Code. Groped my way to the Creamery and dined on ham and blackberry and apples. Went up and sat on Beb's bed: he read me some poems by Gibson and pronounced me a leprechaun.

Tuesday, 17th October

Got up early and had breakfast downstairs in little, empty sitting room. Went across to Beb—temperature sub-normal. We read some *Jorrocks* aloud. I can't understand why it is loved by people who, like Basil, don't like Dickens.

Went up to Sussex Square through pouring rain about four. Found Claud Russell* with Horatia. He is very comfortably quartered in a large country house about seventeen miles from here attached to some Hussar regiment. I asked and received a bath—most welcome form of hospitality. I can't face the one at the lodgings. Came down and had tea and quite a pleasant *à trois* talk with Horatia and Claud. I wasn't frightened of him this time. I do think him extraordinarily good-looking and almost caricaturishly well bred.

Wednesday, 18th October

Hurried across to Beb as soon as I got out of my Durban squalor. Picked up the *Daily Mirror*, which was lying on his bed, and was just screaming with indignation at Philip Sassoon having been given the Légion d'honneur, when my eye was caught by a picture of Beb surrounded by the following information: 'Lieutenant H. Asquith has been appointed by the Attorney General to the office of Junior Counsel to H.M. Customs and Excise. During the war the duties of the office will be discharged by Mr Giveen.' Beb had not yet received the letter on the subject from F. E. Smith, so was very much surprised and thought I was joking when I read it out. He thought it meant £2,000 a year in fees, but when F. E. Smith's letter came he said it was only £150 to £200. However, it is a rung on the ladder and, from that point of view, very important. However, any allusion to 'after the war' to me rings like a joke in doubtful taste. I can never look round so blind a corner.

1916

I had a letter from Aunt Evelyn suggesting John and his governess coming to Abbeyleix. Accepted with alacrity—I think it is an excellent plan.

Friday, 20th October

Sharply cold day. Lord Alex came down on 'business' and called at one to take me out to luncheon. We went to the St James's. He was very agreeable and wonderfully susceptible-looking, wincing with appreciation—a trick I always enjoy, I must admit. He had written a faintly 'flirtatious' letter. We discussed Ettie's book—inevitable topic. He told me Sidney, in a crowded restaurant in France, had rushed up to Philip Sassoon who was sitting at a table, and genially exclaimed: 'Hullo, Monsieur le Decoré!' Upon which, Philip, purple in the face, rose and without a word rushed out of the restaurant. As Basil had warned me, Alex said darkly that he would be going out again in ten days. We sat long over lunch and then he went off to tip his nephew Evelyn Baring, who is at school here.

Beb and I went house-hunting together over various genteely-named and dingily upholstered abodes. Found nothing very satisfying. The best rooms were owned by a woman looking too like a murderer. Harold Russell, the eldest and only married member of that famous family, was spending the day with Horatia. Pity her two best friends should be married men. She brought him to tea. Alex came, too, and Beb and I entertained them all in the spacious lounge of the Royal York. It was great fun. I thought Harold most delightful and amusing —droll is the word for him. Everything he says has flavour and idiosyncrasy. He is obviously nicer than Gilbert—I should think the most human of the family in some ways. I felt really drawn toward him. We discussed our diaries exhaustively as he writes one, too, so there were four diarists—an unusual convocation.

Beb told the story of Sir Edward Grey. About a fortnight ago Sir Edward dreamt that the ghost of Joseph Chamberlain appeared and said to him: 'In modern times two men have been shouted down in Parliament; the first was Alfred Lyttelton in the Chinese Labour debate; the second was the P.M.; the third will be you on the fall of Bucharest'.

Saturday, 21st October

Horrid morning, packing and tipping. We went up by the Southern

Belle. We lunched with Grace and stayed comfortably in her house until it was time to catch the 4.45 to Stanway.

Sunday, 22nd October

Such a painful east-winded day. In the afternoon Beb, Whibley, Bibs, and I frousted over the fire in the library and played the morbid game of choosing our crew of six bound for perpetual residence on a desert island. Bibs very candid. She is terribly indignant and disgusted at poor Whibley having taken advantage of her pigtail and bestowed a kiss on her when he arrived.

The Allens and Bateman dined. Our two clerics—surely the best in England—were in excellent form and we had a hysterically laughing evening. Poor Priest nearly went into a seizure at one moment—most alarming. I hope it won't be a joke of mine which finally kills him in a heart attack. He threw a bombshell at the table by announcing that Stanway water produced madness and goitres, laying alarming statistics before us. This led to many jokes and we all agreed to take the pledge and abjure water. Whibley delighted with our parsons. I wish I had been here the Sunday before when a most ridiculous stage archdeacon (archbishop or archbeacon Mamma always called him) came here for the Mission. His sermon was denunciatory, and he said only one in six Society ladies ever instructed their children in religion. At dinner Papa asked where he got his statistics, and he replied from 'monthly nurses'. Grace made a poem about it. The Rev. Eustace told us that, in the afternoon, he had seen a magnificent stag at the top of the Cockpit. He had thought it must be a vision, but the choir-boys confirmed the evidence of his eyes.

Monday, 23rd October

Wrote a joke letter to Bateman at breakfast—it was not sent. What would he have said and done had it been? I long to know. Once, when Mamma was coming to dine with him, he wrote about three letters to ensure Mary's presence as a chaperone! This was my letter:

Dear Mr Bateman,

Some relations of my mother's have turned up unexpectedly and the house is very full. I know you have a spare room and it occurs to me that it might not be inconvenient for you to put me up for a night or two. Unless I hear to the contrary, I shall turn up after dinner tonight. I shall not bring a maid *A bientôt.*

C.A.

Tuesday, 24th October

Mary's twenty-first birthday. A lovely spring-like day. The Smiths, Allens, etc., all came and we played Ring o' Roses, Nuts and May, etc. After dinner I read them some of *The Rosary* aloud. Aloud it is a roaring farce. We all declared we must adopt 'soft, white lace at the bosom'.

Wednesday, 25th October

Letter from Basil. He says the 'strand' is always on his heart—blessed sentimentality! I went for a walk with Adele. We discussed the relationship between Basil and Nancy. I asked her if she had been there on the occasion when Nancy so vehemently abused me at Con's. She said she hadn't heard it, and all Nancy had ever said to her was, 'That Cynthia's the most amusing little devil: I don't wonder Basil likes her'. I was reading hard to finish Wells' war book *Mr Britling Sees it Through*. It is very clever and registers so many of the different phases of one's war thoughts and emotions. Mamma, Mary, and I all went to tea with Eustace Bateman (temptations of St Anthony, we called it) who was entertaining a dreary clerical couple.

Thursday, 26th October

Lovely day. Very sorry to leave Stanway, sad as it is. Beb had to return to Brighton. We left by 10.30 stopping at Oxford, about which Beb had an *accès* of sentimentality. We lunched with the Raleighs, driving out in a hansom. They were very dear. He walked us back into Oxford by the Ferry Path and we visited Balliol. Oxford has a melancholy beyond all expression now. I thought of the whirling Commem days—at any rate we couldn't have danced with more fervour and *carpe diem* spirit, even if we had known what the near future held. Went to London by 4.25.

Explored that other stratum of society by dining with Jeffie Darell again. The party was Jeffie, her husband (home on leave from the Guards' Headquarters Staff), Gordon Leith, Cuckoo Belville, K. Norton, Gilbert Russell and a man called Mortimer Jones. We played very confusing, chatty poker. I ended 21 up. The atmosphere was just the same as last time—everybody was a 'blithering idiot', a 'dirty dog', or an 'old boy', and on saying good night the joke of the man saying 'I will see you in a horn' to the woman was typical of the humour. Distinctly good-natured all of them, and I didn't feel in the least uncomfortable as a fish in strange water. Amused by story Alex told me of Lutyens, the architect, who after lunching with the King said, 'I'm not much of a fisherman, but if I had caught him, I should have let him go'.

Saturday, 28th October

I had arranged to meet Alex and Gilbert Russell who were going down to Brighton. We had a very comfortable journey and I quite enjoyed my 'Elsa', as we used to call being the only member of one's sex. They are a pair of comedians—Gilbert is a very loose talker with the word 'mistress' for ever on his lips. We played the analogy game: Alex gave Gilbert *pâté de foie gras* and a sleepy pear—both excellent.

They dropped me at my new hotel and then joined me for lunch at the St James. I tried to get Beb but he wasn't in barracks. I offered Gilbert money for my lunch and Alex said, on his declining it, that it was the first time he had ever seen him refuse money. The stinginess of the Russells is a standing joke.

A letter from Basil came in the morning. I saw Horatia's little married sister whose husband is with him. She had been cheered by an officer telling her that the King had been furious at the way the Guards had been decimated, and refused to allow them to be sacrificed again. They were not in an emergency to be put in the hottest place, and were to be quite out of it for a long time. I don't suppose this would really have any effect.

Sunday, 29th October

I lunched with my two middle-aged roués, Alex and Gilbert, again and we had a very prolonged and amusing *à trois*, which, considering a painful sore throat, was rather a feather in my cap. Gilbert was pretty loose in his conversation. After a long discussion as to what they would expect from their wives, I came to the conclusion that it would be my duty to warn any spinster or widow they might be thinking of honouring with a proposal. They had the highest ideal of domesticity combined with the cynic's complete trustlessness. They would not suffer any friendship with other men, and would on no account allow their wife to dine at a restaurant with a man. 'After all,' said Gilbert, 'I have never dined alone with a woman without making some sort of assault on her and why should I expect other men to be different: it's all a matter of opportunity'. Apart from any question of jealousy, they held that a man-friend must inevitably subtract some of the cream of a woman's attention from her husband. No one could write two best letters a day, and the lover always had an unfair advantage.

Wednesday, 1st November

Conscience told me I must do some war work, so I went up to Sussex Square and Lady Seymour introduced me at the depot and I was instructed in the art of swabs, sitting between rather grim Brighton ladies in caps and aprons. It looks easy and is really very difficult, and I felt very humiliated by my clumsiness. I wasn't at all good: my instructress kept assuring me that the 'knack' would come to me. I hope it may.

Thursday, 2nd November

Another letter from Basil, announcing his birthday and asking for *Adonais* and *The Hound of Heaven*. For a few hours the sun shone by day and the moon by night, so my spirits rose accordingly and once more I liked Brighton.

I was lunching with Claud at the Royal York. Beb was free, so I told him and he joined me. Claud's close-fistedness is a classical joke. To our surprise he insisted on paying for our lunch—emphasising that he was doing so. However, he had to borrow thirty shillings in order to be able to pay for his taxi, so he didn't do so badly after all. I wonder, was it borrowing? I shall watch the post with great interest.

Sunday, 5th November

Alas, Claud has sent a cheque for thirty shillings, thus bereaving me of a story for the preservation of which I would gladly have paid thirty shillings! I am writing to Basil every day—it is no trouble and one can guess how one would long for letters out there.

A terrific gale raged all day—a really bad one, so that by evening it had become mythical and one was told of overturned buses, blown-in shop windows, and so on. I went all the way to Langdale Road to lunch with Florry Bridges. She told me Margot (talking of Peter Flower and his physical attraction) had often said, 'I slept with him every night—every night of my life—everything except the thing itself'. Carton de Wiart has been wounded again but only quite slightly. Fancy an eye and an arm already lost, and two other wounds! Beb and I dined at the Royal York. He is good-looking again. It is uncanny to be so *journalier*.

Monday, 6th November

I bought myself a sou'wester outfit at Hannington's—coat and hat—and shall now defy the elements. Had my constitutional bathe[1] followed by a cup of chocolate. Beb came home for luncheon and we went to the Grill Room under the Albion, rather a discovery. Rested reading Byron's letters. Walked up to the depot and made swabs for two hours. Got on better. The women workers are not attractive. One wonders what on earth they do when there is no war. Oliver Stanley has come to Beb's barracks and he dined with us at the St James's. Afterwards we went to the cinema. No letter from Basil for several days. I wonder why.

Wednesday, 8th November

Met Claud Russell by assignation at the Royal York at 3.30, and spent the remainder of the afternoon with him. I enjoyed his company. He played with the penny-in-the-slot machines on the pier, of course only attempting those in which his skill, strength, or luck might restore him his penny. However, he did pay my pier toll (with the air of one who gives an opera box), and he gave me tea at the Royal York. At last a letter from Basil—sent by hand—he says mails have been interrupted. He, too, had had no letter for a week and I have been writing every day.

Friday, 10th November

Had a very good swim in the morning. Great blow to hear the ladies' bath shuts at the end of the week. There is a circular one next door for mixed bathing—much better bath, but can I face 'mixed bathing' indoors? It seems totally different from alfresco. I shall have to try and find some fantastic hour when there will be no one.

Monday, 13th November

Nasty thick fog, tasting almost like a London one. Stayed in bed, only coming down for tea. Letter from Basil saying, alas, that they are moving. I hope not to the front of the Front. Read Trollope's *Can You Forgive Her?*—there are no clergyman portraits, which are his forte.

In the morning I at last wrote to Lawrence, whom I had never

1. At Brill's baths.

thanked for his book of poems he sent me about two months ago. Oddly enough, just as I had sent my letter, one arrived from him—very pip-pip—still accusing humanity of fighting as an end in itself, implying that the thing was an orgy rather than a sacrifice. I wrote again, expostulating with this view as eloquently as I could. He asked me why I hadn't sent him Beb's poems.

Tuesday, 14th November

Got up late. Alex came down for the day to see me. Beb was back for luncheon, so we three had it together at the grill room. Then Alex and I spent the afternoon walking up and down the pier, very happily. He is good company, distinctly amusing as well as comic. The almost melodramatically serious way in which he suddenly asks one about one's plans or anything is very funny. Anyway, chin or no chin, he succeeded in making me feel quite pleased with myself.

Beb and I walked to Sweetings, but finding it shut, we had dinner at the Ship. He has been told to get inoculated this week—rather ominous. By the last post came a pencilled line from Basil saying they were now in the area of discomfort—mud and awful din all round them. This depressed me. I am so afraid they will use the Guards in this advance. His being away has been a dull ache all these weeks, and now it will become a pain, and I am getting panicky. Today I have a strong sense that he is in it. I had so hoped they would stay quiet where they were till after Christmas.

Wednesday, 15th November

Bluetooth arrived at 4.10. I met him at the station. We tea-ed at the Royal York and then went for a walk along the front. Lovely evening. The first real wintry day, making one feel clean and exhilarated. Bluetooth full of political gossip. London appears to be seething with intrigue and politicians behaving like 'politicians'. Lloyd George is hand in glove with Carson and Winston, and they are doing their best to unseat the P.M. and throw out the Government. The other night of the Nigerian vote of censure there was a very narrow squeak, and the Whips were frantically summoning the supposed supporters of the Government. They rang up Lloyd George's house and his wife naïvely said: 'He is out, but I know where he is—he is dining with Carson.' This created great scandal—Carson being prime instigator of the vote of censure, and Carson turned up for the division and Lloyd George did not.

Their plot is to unseat the P.M. and Lloyd George is to be Prime Minister and Winston is to go to the War Office. They are credited with having 'got at' Bonar Law, and their boast is that they will be in office in a month. Bluetooth thought it just on the cards that they might succeed, but that if so they couldn't hold their position for more than a month. I asked him if he diagnosed Lloyd George as pure knave, but he gives him credit for sincerity in as much that he really thinks himself a Chatham with a divine mission to save the country, therefore holding any means which will put him in power justifiable. He says he is loathed by all the Liberals now—in fact he is only popular with the dukes, an amusing whirligig of time. He is hated by the army. When he was in France, he thought he would suck up to General Foch by praising French artillery at the expense of the English, which he said was rotten. Foch was disgusted by such toadyism and telephoning to Haig told of him, describing him as a *sale cochon*. Notwithstanding any awkwardness arising from this recognised intriguer, Lloyd George and the P.M. have just gone to France together.

Thursday, 16th November

Bitter cold day. East wind shivering through everything. Letter from Basil saying they were moving again, probably to even muddier spheres. I do pray they won't be used in this advance. Bluetooth thought they were only employing county troops. Up to London by 9.45 and down to Stanway by 4.55. I am in Mr Balfour's room, which I hate. Very uncomfortable bed.

Friday, 17th November

Bitter cold day with torturing east wind. Everyone disfigured and discoloured. It was a moot point all day as to whose nose was the reddest, mine, or Mary's. Long letter from Basil describing horrible scenes of desolation through which he was marching up to his knees in mud. Two men had to be dug out of the snow. Beb, Mamma, and Letty all came by 4.45. Letty looking a shade better. Mamma in good spirits. Beb's arm very stiff from his inoculation. Poor Beb very cold in the night. I had to be unselfish with hot water bottle and eiderdown.

Saturday, 18th November

Basil mentioned the late man drill in a letter I got from him this morning, and I made a riddle—my first and probably my last. I asked it all day and darling Michael dutifully learnt both question and answer. 'Why is a mandrill's wife like an officer?' 'Because they are both mandrillers.'

At dinner Beb dangled Aubrey's dewdrop to Mamma's daughters, i.e. 'I think Mary is the most beautiful woman I have ever seen—but I would much rather look at Cynthia.'

Sunday, 19th November

Lots of snow on the ground and nasty slush falling. Letter from Basil saying, alas, that he was going into a 'ditch'. I had so hoped they would be kept right out of the trenches for a long time, and it is a great disappointment. Felt very depressed about that in church—and I'm getting into terror about Beb going out, and then Michael is so piercingly sweet and in every way wonderful, that I have a pang of fear each time I look at him. Tearful in church but, as Beb says, I am very Aprilly and I was in high spirits at luncheon—so much so that Mr Bateman said: 'Lady Cynthia's looking so wicked today.' He and Gan-Gan had such a delicious flirtation. I like the story of the German who, when asked if he thought this war would do any good, said: 'It has already done good: it has taught the French to pray, the Russians to be sober, and the English to fight.'

Monday, 20th November

I went for a walk with Mamma at twelve o'clock. She told me she is intending to go to a spiritualist. She is agnostical about it, but thinks perhaps one ought just to give a chance to the theory that the middle-man may still be necessary for communication—more on account of Yvo than Ego. She feels he might want to. For the first time I told her about Helen's table-rapping. I asked her what she would think of my having a baby, and she encouraged me to do so. It has lately come to me rather strongly, the feeling that I ought to give myself a chance of starting one before Beb goes out. If he were not going, I should naturally wait till next May. I am in no immediate hurry—am anxious to do some strenuous war work and would like to have a baby born in the winter. But, in the circumstances, I have a superstitious feeling that one ought not to postpone. I think it is largely the extraordinary delight Michael is to me now. I feel that, whatever happened, life could not be anything but thrilling with such a child. The nursery seems the only solution—I would so love to have a daughter. So, I really think I shall condemn myself, though it does require some strength of mind. Teresina said she thought it doubtful whether one ought to have a baby on account of nerves during a very anxious time, but I don't agree, and personally I feel a baby would always steady me.

Letter from Basil by the evening post which plunged me into depth of depression. It was written on the sixteenth, and he was just going into a first line trench for a spell. Afterwards they would work their way back through second-line and reserve trench. Miserable all the evening. Mamma read some of Oliver Lodge's *Raymond or Life and Death* aloud.

Wednesday, 22nd November

Went up by early train. Beb and I dined at Downing Street, the two over from a three-table bridge party. I sat between Duff and Jimmy Rothschild. The latter is considered to have potent queer charm, but I didn't feel it much and he seemed to prefer talking to Lady Tree. After dinner I talked to Pamela McKenna and liked her much better. After five years' sterility she is going to put herself under the obstetrical knife.

Directly men came out, Beb and I returned to Bruton Street (where I was 'cuckooing') for my poker Hell. Brenda and Diana were dining with Gilbert at the Ritz and they all came. It was very successful as far as I was concerned as I made sixteen pounds, but Mary H. forgot to provide any drink or food. Gilbert looked desperately dry and dislikes the game. Duff came late. There was a cooking party in the kitchen and some sausages were produced.

Brenda had not heard from Freddie for six days and was rather worried. Apparently his company must have gone into the trenches before Basil's, and I suppose communication is impossible in spite of Basil's hope. The silence when one knows they are in is very agonising and the worst of it is, that by the time a letter reaches one to say they are out, one will know they are in again. I am very, very frightened about Basil.

Beb went back to Brighton by the twelve o'clock train. He was rather jarred by the big Downing Street bridge dinner—and the contemplation of the men who will survive the war, Jimmy Rothschild, McKenna, etc. Margot was not in mourning.

Thursday, 23rd November

Mary H. and I breakfasted in bed together and she read some of my letters. She said she was sure Alex's ambition was to cut out Basil, and was prepared to bet that he would make love to me. Venetia called for me at twelve. She had just had an Aaron's operation—more from sense of duty than any strong maternal craving, I think. We walked to the Arlington Street Hospital together. Found Letty, looking very ill, sweeping a floor. Diana hooked on to Venetia and me, and we walked out together. United I found them rather tiring and bewildering. Amazed by Diana's snack at twelve o'clock at Stewart's. She ate foul meat pastry pies and rococo cream cakes with both hands, and incredible speed, for five minutes. Congratulated her on her digestion.

Had a dentist with Adele, probably for the last time in the lovely context of Bourdon House, from which the Duke of Westminster is evicting her in February. She had had a pretty good letter from Margot (who had never written her a line about her husband's death): 'I am terribly sorry about the house and I can't understand it. We have all had bad knocks—do come to the Wharf for a Sunday; we are small parties and all in mourning'.

Mary and I dined with Alex at the Ritz, the other guests being Mark Sykes and Duff. I was alarmed at encountering Mark Sykes at last: he was a well-known spectacle to me but there has never been any intercourse. However, I found him most unalarming and excellent company. Conversation was after my own heart—a Dickens paean. Sykes and Duff seemed to know him verbatim. Sykes has a curious likeness to an enlarged Wells. We took the whole party on to the Benckendorffs who had asked us to dinner—Evan and Juliet Duff were there. Our party played poker with Jasper and Nathalie. I won £1 8s. Poor Mary, as usual, lost heavily—even losing with fours in her hand. The Ridleys dropped us home. Mary and I indulged in a reminiscent conversation, foolishly kept up till three o'clock.

Friday, 24th November

Lunched with Kitty. She very much admired my black velvet costume, the war economy I am so proud of—one skirt with a day and evening top to it. Kitty very dear to me, but very inconsecutive in conversation, perching on a thousand topics.

Bluetooth's dinner, the nucleus of which was Frank Mitchell and self, was transferred to Downing Street. Oc had note from Freyberg, the hero of the Naval Division which has done such great deeds. He is back with four wounds and recommended for V.C. The note was a frenzied appeal to Oc to stop the terribly erroneous puffs of him in the papers. Frank Mitchell, who is in the Press Censorship, was appealed to, but wasn't very helpful and Oc went off to see Sir Frank Swettenham about it. When he came back I talked to him whilst the others played bridge. He is a dear. He was curtly ordered on to the Staff just before he was invalided home—according to Margot, because Haig thought the P.M. must be shielded from further personal blows.

Saturday, 25th November

We went down to Brighton by 5.55. To my joy, I found a prodigiously long letter from Basil. It was written on the 21st and gave a most gruesome account of their spell in a first-line trench—horrible conditions of exhaustion, mud, and wretched trenches filled with three-week-old corpses. Very heavy shelling, but mercifully few casualties owing to the mud—only thirteen wounded and two killed in Basil's company. Awful seven-mile walk back through dreadful mud and on the slippery wooden walk they call the duckboards, floundering and tumbling along in the dark with their heavy loads until the men were completely exhausted—and this after three sleepless nights! It made me pretty miserable, but it's something to know they are out for a few days. I have an awful, gnawing anxiety about Basil—it is always floating in my mind and sometimes reaches extreme acuteness. I felt so absurdly secure about Beb generally: was it instinctive, or only because I had then no experience? I am dreadfully frightened about Basil. Each letter I feel may be too late, and I rush to post it.

Tuesday, 28th November

Very cold, but I adhered to my ritual—bedroom exercises at 7.30, then running to the swimming bath. Great physical and moral glow. Beb came in on his way back to barracks and said me the newly finished poems he is just sending to Sidgwick and Jackson for publication with *The Volunteer* ones in a bound book. He said them very well.

Friday, 1st December

Cold and fine—swam before breakfast. I am becoming habit bound. Alex came down for the day. He called for me 12.30 and we went to the Albion Grill Room: Beb joined us there for luncheon. We were determined on a walk on the downs, so we went in the Dyke Road tram to its terminus and then took to our legs. We must have walked quite six miles altogether. It was very cold, but very delicious and it made me feel well and happy. We talked a tremendous lot and this new friendship is really a pleasant addition. He is so much less pompous *à deux* than in a group, and I can't help liking him. I think he likes me a good deal.

Saturday, 2nd December

Went to station on foot and met Beb, Mary H. and Oc off the 6.40—had a very happy, amusing evening. In defiance of the convenances I put Mary and Oc both up unchaperoned at the Royal York. Naturally enough, they were given adjacent rooms. This has made an excellent standing joke for our Sunday party. The maid who showed Mary her room smilingly informed her that the 'gentleman was next door'. Altogether I don't know what the Royal York staff think of us.

Beb and Oc very full of the political crisis—the acutest there has yet been. Oc is a great darling. I am so glad to find he is not at all deaf from his ear perforation.

Sunday, 3rd December

Beb and I breakfasted with Mary and Oc in order to regularise their position—the unorthodoxy of which became an invaluable joke. The waiter asked whether our breakfasts were to go on Oc's bill as well as Mary's—there was no doubt in his mind about hers.

We played the fool on the pier and went to the tourist's whole hog by being photographed with our heads through burlesques. I was the head of a woman sponging Oc, and Mary and Beb were done in the same situation. We dined at the St James's—very amusing conversation. Have never seen Beb in such good form. Very 'loose' too, chaffing Mary about her 'turgid passions'. We all made autobiographical confessions of past susceptibilities and, in inverted conjugal style I twitted and upbraided Beb with incurable faithfulness and single-heartedness. He tried desperately to prove his dogdom, but I dissolved his evidence.

Monday, 4th December

Oc, Mary and I travelled up to London by the eleven o'clock. When Oc had to register at the hotel he had to give 10 Downing Street as his permanent address—tempting to Providence during the present situation. Read the papers in the train. Really the *Daily Mail* has been too foul these last days. Mr Balfour is simply called 'old Balfour' and referred to as a senile driveller. There was a paragraph headed 'An

Asquith Flag Day'—I hoped it was a suggestion for an Asquith benefit collection, instead of which 'Indignant' (or whatever the signature was) suggested that everyone against Asquith should buy and wear a red flag, thus painting England red.

The autobiographical nature of our conversation the night before led me to confess to Mary that I had been very much in love with Oc in Dresden. She promptly told him. Dear Oc, he was so embarrassed —even at so posthumous a declaration—that he nearly twisted one of the tails off Mary's sables. However, he was able to murmur, 'Not more than I was with her'.

I was, by arrangement, dining and going to a play with Alex. I hoped he was going to ask two other guests, but he told me on the telephone he hadn't got any. I would rather have been chaperoned, but I didn't demur. We dined at Queen's. He had made no theatre arrangement, so we just went to a picture palace in the King's Road. Walked there—icy cold. He is a funny fellow—such careful phrases, one feels he is waiting for a possible cue to fire ready-made ones off.

Tuesday, 5th December

Lunched Bluetooth—he was very sad about Bron[1] and perturbed about political situation. He seemed still to hope that the P.M.'s resignation might be averted. He said, rather reproachfully, that Montagu had secured his position with both parties. He twitted me again with my (according to him) reputed incapacity for loose talk.

I was dining early with Oc for his last night, but he telephoned to say dinner was postponed until 8.45 as the P.M. was in after all and the theatre was abandoned. It was great luck for me to dine at Downing Street on so historic a night. The atmosphere was most electric. The P.M. had sent in his resignation at 7.30—a fact I was unaware of when I arrived and only gradually twigged. Oc, the Crewes, Eddie, Cis, and Elizabeth and Margot were dining.

I sat next to the P.M.—he was too darling—rubicund, serene, puffing a guinea cigar (a gift from Maud Cunard), and talking of going to Honolulu. His conversation was as irrelevant to his life as ever. Our subjects were my mandrill riddle (which Beb had told to a startled party the other day), and this wonderful brand of cigars. I asked for one to give Beb for Christmas and he gave it to me. Cis afterwards offered me ten shillings for it. I had a great *accès* of tenderness for the P.M. He was so serene and dignified. Poor Margot on the other hand looked ghastly ill—distraught (no doubt she was, as

1. Lord Lucas: see index.

she always claims, 'rumbling')—and was imprecating in hoarse whispers, blackguarding Lloyd George and Northcliffe.

When we first came out Elizabeth, Lady Crewe and I had an *à trois* —Margot joined us. When the men came out she, Mr Asquith and the Crewes played bridge. Violet came in, bringing with her Mr Norton and Sir Ian Hamilton—the latter to say goodbye to Oc. Of course, the whole evening was spent in conjecture and discussion— most interesting. I tried to absorb as much as I could, but I am not quick about politics. I gathered that, before dinner, Mr Asquith had said he thought there was quite a chance of Lloyd George failing to form a Government at all. The Tories—in urging him to resign— had predicted such a failure. In any case, most people seemed to think that any Government he could succeed in forming would only be very short-lived. Of course Lloyd George would greatly prefer Bonar to be Prime Minister, in order himself to avoid incurring the odium of responsibility. The King had sent for Bonar but, of course, it would be very difficult for him to accept the office on the terms which had made Asquith resign it. The King is alleged to be very terribly distressed and to have said, 'I shall resign if Asquith does'. The prospective attitude of the Liberal ministers was discussed. Everyone was convinced that not one of them would take office under Lloyd George, with the possible exception of Montagu. Bluetooth had assured me that the latter would, but nearly all the Asquith family repudiated the idea. George had been a very wily, foxy cad, and the Government whips must have been very bad, as apparently the P.M. was very much taken by surprise.

It had been a well-managed plot. According to Margot and others, Northcliffe has been to Lloyd George's house every day since the beginning of the war, the imputation being that George feeds him with Cabinet information, telling him the next item of the Government programme, so that he is able to start a Press agitation, and thus gain the reputation of pushing the Government into their independently determined course of action. It was said that the F.O. was really Lloyd George's ambition, and during the last weeks he has been going to the Berlitz School and reading histories of the Balkans. I believe the French like him, but he is loathed in Russia and Italy. He has had to cart Winston—whose exclusion was, I believe, one of Bonar's conditions. Certainly one cannot imagine a crazier executive than George, Carson, and Bonar, Of course, it would virtually be only George.

Was it my last dinner at Downing Street? I can't help feeling very sanguine and thinking the P.M. will be back with a firmer seat in the saddle in a fortnight. I only hope to God he is—disinterestedly because I really think him the only eligible man. Incidentally, what could happen to all our finances I daren't think! Certainly it is a most painfully interesting situation—deeply to be deplored at this juncture I think—and it's rather disgusting that such seething intrigue should survive war atmosphere.

Oc saw me off in the tube. Very sad to say goodbye and he had a tear in his eye. Lost my head and passed through Charing Cross three times owing to political excitement. Got home very late. Talked to Papa. The P.M. said *The Volunteer* was incomparably the best war poem.

Wednesday, 6th December

Alex called for me at a quarter to three and we went to see McEvoy and his paintings. Rather shy. There were a great many portraits in hand—a most lovely one of Goonie—a really thrilling picture. Alex dropped me home. He was really off back to the Front the next morning. How self-conscious one feels at these goodbyes! I wrote him a *vale* letter when I got home and the next morning he telegraphed from Charing Cross: 'What a perfect letter'.

Beb came up in great excitement, having secured two days' crisis leave. He lunched at Downing Street. A great day of intrigue and Buckingham Palace interviews. Beb said he would come to Cadogan Square at five. I waited with growing irritation, as I had altered my afternoon plans on his account, but he didn't come till past six. Then I had to tell the housemaid to make up a bed for him. We dined with Guy and Frances. Michael Tennant was there. The lay political talk bored and irritated me. Frances and I had a John talk. Beb, of course, went to Downing Street after dinner. I walked home. Feeling ill, tired, depressed, and cross.

Thursday, 7th December

Beb and I lunched at Downing Street. Found Margot at the top of the stairs, looking ghastly ill and in a great state of mind, saying it had only just been remembered that the Connaughts* were coming to luncheon and that they were thirteen. She had asked Cis to have his in bed, as he had for the last week owing to influenza, but he refused to be complaisant. I offered to go and she said, 'No, you will help— you will play up. What one doesn't want is these great blocks of silent men—Bongie, Beb, Cis—they never utter.' Maggie Ponsonby was there, Lord Grey, Davies, Violet and Bongie. I sat between the Duke and Bongie. The Duke was charming: he is the only gentleman royalty, with manner and presence. He boasted of his daughter-in-law's nursing prowess, saying she had herself amputated a finger—a shocking bit of royal licence. The P.M. wonderfully unbroken by the storms of state. I have got quite a lump in my throat about him.

Went to see Venetia at 4.30. She said Montagu had had dozens of frenzied letters from Margot full of insults: 'I hear you are going in with them—where is friendship? Where is loyalty?' However, poor dear, he is not going in with them, though I believe suffering tortures in refusing. Apparently he is *sous le charme* of Lloyd George and could quite well go in with him as regards his own intellectual conscience, so it is a real sacrifice to personal loyalty. Surprised to hear Mr Balfour was going to the Foreign Office.

Bombshell of news—Frances says Elizabeth had been to see Kakoo, bringing with her a young man to whom she announced her engagement. He is one Gibson,* an American diplomat, clever they say but quite impecunious. I always had such hopes of Elizabeth. This is really too much. To marry an American is bad enough—but a poor American! Margot hates Americans and is doing her best to dissuade Elizabeth, and there have been many tears. So the political was not the only crisis at Downing Street. It's the last straw at this juncture—Libby Gibby—what a name, too, Gibson! Heard a good name for Montagu, 'Shylock the merchant of Venetia'.

Saturday, 9th December

Returned to Brighton by the 4.30 yesterday. I went to tea today with Florrie Bridges whose husband, General Bridges, was there on leave. They were having tea and with them—great excitement—was the hero of the war, Carton de Wiart. He is wonderfully undisfigured by his Nelson wounds—loss of eye and arm—and I rather fell in love with him. Very good looking, with great distinction—hands and gentle languid manner—certainly most attractive.

Tuesday, 12th December

Letter from Basil saying, alas, that they are just going back into the trenches. Lawrence sent me some typewritten poems which he proposes to 'inscribe to me'.

Wednesday, 13th December

Another nasty dull day. Beb went a-hunting. I stayed in bed until four. Cis visited me after luncheon. We had tea together at the Royal York and a longish talk afterwards. It is true about Elizabeth's engagement to Gibson. Margot is bitterly opposed, accusing him of being alien, aged, and lame (he is only about thirty, and the only evidence of lameness is that he doesn't play tennis). Her material advice is a good pippip; 'There is no reason why you shouldn't be on cousinly terms without marrying him—why marry him? I was on cousinly terms for years.' I have always thought Cis is the best Margot raconteur there is.

Beb returned rather 'bean-fed' from his hunting and we had early dinner at Sweetings. Cis was convulsed with amusement at Beb's manner in ordering 'Lob-ster'. We agreed afterwards that he was the 'oddest' man we knew, and compared notes as to his strange, unacknowledged moods, in some of which (as far as contact with others went) he was as though in a padded room, and one was hammering vainly—as if against thick felt. He was in one of his funny moods of manner this night. When he came to bed he said a very good poem to me—just composed—so no doubt the throes of composition accounted for that particular 'bead'.

Friday, 15th December

Bitter cold in London—I felt chilled to the heart and profoundly depressed. Lunched with Bluetooth. Mingled our depressions. He had been down at Walmer. Said P.M. had asked him whether he thought there would be any harm in his making Bongie a K.C.B. Discussed their finances. It is funny the way all the ministers have taken to their beds. I don't believe Lloyd George will ever get up again. It looks like sheer funk. Having talked with eloquence of a patent medicine of the 'vigorous prosecution of the war', it's no joke to have to begin to put it into practice.

Went to Cadogan Square to see Mamma just up from Stanway. She was going down to Brighton for the night to see Mr Balfour.

Saturday, 16th December

Mamma had asked me to meet her at a séance in Tavistock Square at eleven, with a man Aunt Pamela had taken to her. I went, disliked it, and acted—according to the medium—as a screen, owing to scepticism and nervousness amounting almost to hostility. It wasn't even a good exhibition of telepathy, and I thought the whole business unpleasant. The poor man got hopelessly on the wrong track about me, thinking my husband had been killed.

Went to see Freyberg, v.c. in his hospital at Park Lane—splendid animal. Eddie came in while I was there. Freyberg said he loved Oc better than anyone else on earth. Ghastly fog. Caught the 3.10 by mistake at 4.20 and arrived at Brighton two hours late.

Monday, 18th December

Horrible cold, grey morning. The thing I mind most at this new hotel is that the coffee is never more than tepid. Real hot coffee for breakfast makes one much more ready to face the day. I couldn't stand the cold of the house either, so I migrated to the froust of the Royal York to do my writing. I suppose it is really stealing coal, but we have spent a good deal of money there.

Beb went up for the day to see Mary H. and his publisher. I had a telegram from Claud saying he was coming over to luncheon. We met at the Royal York and lunched there. He stayed till after dinner and we got on very well, I think, waxing quite confidential and comfortable. He spent a good many minutes of the day counting his change, but actually stood me luncheon, tea, and dinner! This time it was the first day of the 'limited courses' regime, so it was an auspicious time to begin entertaining. I took him to Professor Severn who was most flattering to him. He obviously thought I was 'keeping company' and had brought my suitor on approval. Claud studied his chart very carefully afterwards.

Thursday, 21st December

Emerged dazed and helpless at Victoria to find dearth of porters. Amazed to hear, 'Good morning Lady Cynthia', and to find Claud had come to meet and help me—a real knight errant. He wrestled efficiently with the porter, luggage, and dropped me in a taxi at Cadogan Square. I was astonished and grateful. I think he is maligned. I am finding him rather lavish about 'treating'.

Had hair waved. Lunched with Bluetooth, who was very depressed, finding everything 'weary, stale, flat and unprofitable'. Went to see Colonel Freyberg, v.c., at three. He explained his trench-storming tactics—excellent they sound. He gives each man a map, thus making them independent of officers in an emergency. Then I had to pick up luggage at Cadogan Square and catch 4.55. Found Stanway in deep snow.

Sunday, 24th December

A very orthodox Christmas Eve so far as appearances went. Real Christmas card snow, but with what maimed rites it came to us. It was dreadful. The whole place seemed to ache. The children perforce dragged us through all the old paraphernalia, and poor darling Letty kept up most valiantly until the evening. I didn't go to church—I can't have two Sundays running. Guy very busy making snowmen and a snow house, and Letty worked with him like a Trojan all the afternoon. Mamma threw 'Jack o' Stanway' out of the window for the children. He was thrown into a rug—a very successful entertainment. It's wonderful how much energy and spirit she throws into catering for the grandchildren. Beb was in great travail all day, bringing forth new poems and revised versions of old ones. I midwifed him as much as I could and we went for a very nice snow walk before tea.

The Allens came to dinner—oysters and woodcock—and we talked of food all the time. Afterwards, with very aching hearts, we went through the old stocking ritual—bending over the children's cots like the best. Letty was valiantly persevering for the children with set teeth. I hung up her stocking. This touched her very much—she thought it would be her first Christmas without one—and led to a complete breakdown, poor darling! She sobbed and sobbed, and it was heartbreaking. She pulled herself together again and went downstairs to decorate the hall. She is wonderfully plucky. We were all red-eyed by the time we went to bed. Found five pounds from Grace in my stocking—surprising and pleasing.

Monday, 25th December

Woke up very early to have the fun of seeing Michael open his stocking. He dormoused for a long time and kept me hanging about, but when he did wake up he was most satisfactory—shrieks of joy: 'Another handkerchief!' and so on. His cot looked too delicious packed with treasure. We took all the children to church. They were wonderfully good. Michael's only disappointment was that he very naturally thought the offertory bag was an extra Christmas present.

The Allens came to dinner again. Mamma convulsed us all by suddenly saying, 'Mr Allen, I hope you are eating nuts'. I don't know why it was so funny. The poor Priest had one of his awful laughing fits and I was afraid he would die of a heart attack. We christened him and Mrs A. 'Mr and Mrs Squirrel Nutkin'.

Tuesday, 26th December

Great adventure! I did a day's nursing at the Winchcomb Hospital from eight to eight. I went in some trepidation, but I hadn't realised the tremendous psychological effect of a uniform. Directly I stepped into the ward I felt an entirely new being—efficient, untiring, and quite unsqueamish—ready to cut off a leg, though generally the mere sight of a hospital makes me feel faint. It's wonderful how right it puts one with the men, too. I feel so shy as a laywoman, but was absolutely at my ease as 'Nurse Asquith'. I loved hearing myself called 'nurse' and would certainly go on with it if I were free. I felt all the disciplined's fear of the Sister and the experienced V.A.D., and most terribly anxious to acquit myself well.

First I was put down to wash an oilskin table. It looked so clean at first, and appeared dirtier and dirtier under my attentions. Then I washed all the lockers, etc., etc. The morning in my memory is a long blur of mops, taps, brooms, and plates. The unpleasant moments are when one can't find anything to do. One can't bear to stand idle and yet one feels a fool when one ostentatiously attacks a quite irreproachable counterpane. My most serious breach of etiquette was that I spoke to a soldier while the doctor was in the ward. We had a meal of cocoa and toast and butter at 9.30, to which I brought a ravenous appetite. It seemed an eternity to 12.30 when we had our lunch.

There really wasn't enough to do. Most of the cases were trench feet—quite raw, a horrible sight. I assisted at the dressing of them, feverishly obeying curt orders. The men were delightful. One of them, an Australian, said he had thought I was my sister when I first came in, I said, 'We are not really much alike,' and he said, 'But your figures are very much the same'. Eliza, the Sister, the V.A.D. and I had lunch together. I had my two hours off, two to four. Made lots of beds after tea, tidied up lockers, etc., etc. Had a long chat with the Australian. Only got tired in the last hour. The dug out, as they call the outhouse where the taps and so on are, is very uncomfortable and cold. Got home at 8.30 feeling excited, wound up, and very well. Far less tired than after an ordinary London day. A telegram came from poor Bones, asking for news of Ego.

Friday, 29th December

A thorough, thorough thaw with the usual effect on the spirits. I am reading the diary of Marie Bashkirtseff for the first time. It makes this one seem sadly insipid and impersonal. No doubt writing it in the form of a journal prevents it being at all an emotional review of one's life, but I'm sure if I exercised discrimination and only described peaks in my life I should never have the energy to write at all. To write about every day automatically is really far less effort.

Sunday, 31st December

All went to church. Papa read the lessons. Walked up to the Pyramid with Mamma in pouring rain. Guy had to leave to return to military duties after tea. The Allens came to dinner, and I gibbetted with the Priest. No one sat up deliberately to see the New Year in, but we were awake.

What a year! Will the next be better?

1917

Wednesday, 3rd January

Went to Cadogan Square and then on to lunch with Bluetooth. Thanked him for the little gold wrist watch he has given me for Christmas. I should be puzzled to have to define our relations nowadays. Since the midnight letter I wrote him there has never been the slightest demonstration. Everything is comfortable and unexciting—no volcanic sensation even.

I went down to Brighton by 5.35. Beb had taken rooms at the Royal York, having—as he said—secured special terms for an officer. His 'special terms' turned out to be only a reduction of about one shilling each a day, and it is much, much too expensive for us, fourteen shillings a day. I irritated him by talking money at dinner. His attitude is very difficult and tiresome, since he will confuse necessary economy with stinginess—as unfair as calling hunger greed. He talks highfalutin' nonsense about it and taboos the topic. I was very overtired and we had a ridiculous quarrel in bed all about nothing. I sobbed and couldn't go to sleep for ages.

Thursday, 4th January

Beb had ordered a fly for me at a quarter to nine and I was driven right up on to the downs to see Beb's guns practising. It was gloriously beautiful up there and I enjoyed it. Beb looked very soldierly and professional. I didn't get back till 12.30 and felt wonderfully ozoned. Beb came back to lunch. We are so comfortable here. It does make such a difference having hot coffee for breakfast and a warm lounge. I wish we could stay, but we oughn't to, alas!

We dined in—happy evening.

Friday, 5th January

Beb went away for the day shooting. As temporarily we are on inclusive terms, I lunched in. I must say this hotel is wonderfully comfortable after our long experiences of squalor. I am trying to negotiate for reduced bed-and-breakfast terms. Of course, for that one pays far more in proportion to what one does for inclusive terms, but I can't bear to think I am not gaining anything when I have a meal out. The best would be inclusive terms with a reduction for every lunch and dinner we were out for. I asked if this would be possible. The office girl asked Mrs Preston, who said she must have a 'chat' with Mr Preston,* so we are no forrarder yet. I think it's a very nice hotel. The people are all friendly and civil.

Saturday, 6th January

Swam before breakfast. Went a-shopping—bought a blouse. Beb returned and we went to the Metropole to lunch. The course restrictions involve a great deal of mental arithmetic at meals. One is only allowed two courses, but some things only count as half a course. Beb and I went to Professor Severn and I listened with amusement while his head was told. He said Beb had a 'Scotch' head—would he were Scotch about money!

Beb was on duty, so I had one of my little Creamery dinners and went straight to bed. I am in best looks. Marie Bashkirtseff is always apologetic when she makes a similar entry in her diary, but why should one be? Today I could really pass a great deal of time very happily just looking at myself in the glass. It's extraordinary how one's whole outline seems to alter, as well as complexion and eyes.

Sunday, 7th January

Gilbert telegraphed: 'Motoring down with Nelke to lunch with you if convenient.' I was amused and pleased at the prospect of seeing the bride. Claud was coming to luncheon anyhow.

Gilbert looked happy—rejuvenated and much less corrupt. She is a German Jewess—pretty full face, quite refined, and very well and correctly dressed. She has a very nice voice and manner, and is very gentle, feminine and friendly. I really cottoned to her. They seemed very happy. They have only known one another for seven weeks and Gilbert had never seen her parents until he went on appro as prospective son-in-law. The father is an enormously rich City man; there are no sons and only one other daughter, so Gilbert has feathered his nest well.

We lunched at Sweetings. Great deal of matrimonial chaff. They both asked me for tips. In my letter to Gilbert I had threatened to tell

her of the very high standard of conjugality he professed to expect
of his wife. She said I hadn't put her off. In spite of his heiress in the
bush almost in the hand, at the end of lunch—we had all done ourselves
well—Gilbert said: 'Claud shall pay for this meal, we have given him
two luncheons'. Claud ruefully submitted, saying he wouldn't have
had two kidneys if he had known. A comic waiter upset a bottle of
water over Gilbert. He took it in excellent temper. It might have
caused such an explosion as would have put her off the marriage!
They motored away at about three.

I put on my sou'wester and Claud and I went for a longish walk in
the rain. He intends to start a diary and has commissioned me to buy
him a book. After tea in the lounge we went to the Palladium cinema
—good film. He went away by 8.25 train.

Wednesday, 10th January

Great excitement. We went to the Hippodrome. Heard the renowned
Bottomley* speak a few straight words from the 'shoulder', as it is
called. What a scoundrel he looks, but he does speak well! He is
staying in this hotel and looks too revolting at close quarters. A large
photograph of him occupies the place of honour in the hall with the
inscription: 'To my great little friend Harry Preston.'

Thursday, 11th January

Pouring and blowing—so cold it was difficult to get oneself out of
bed. Letter from Gilbert to say he was coming to stay here on Friday
till Sunday. He is not bringing his Nelke. He wrote: 'I hoped you like
my girl: she liked you immensely.' 'My girl' amuses me.

Very disappointed to get a letter from poor Basil saying they were
going to be sent back into the line, just as they were securely counting
on a well-earned rest and the prospect of leave. It's too cruel! He
commented on Gilbert's engagement and said he supposed the 'fear
of loneliness would drive him to it, too'.

Friday, 12th January

Beb and I lunched in the Grill Room of the Albion. He had been put
through the gas chamber—tear shells and asphyxiating ones. He reeked
of it and his eyes were still watering. When I got home I found Claud
in the lounge. He was on his way up to London and I walked him to
the station. I suggested his coming to see his brother on Sunday and

got the rather nettled reply: 'I don't know why you should think I was coming to see Gilbert and not you.' He asked us all to lunch with him at Sweetings on Sunday.

Saturday, 13th January

Lovely morning. Beb went off early for another day's shooting, I wrote letters and went out for a walk with Gilbert at twelve. He seems in a really nice state of soppyness and happy as any boy. He maintained to me that financially he would be a loser, because though she would double his income, she would assuredly more than double his expenditure.

We lunched at Sweetings together. An acquaintance of Gilbert was there, and he stared at me wondering whether I could possibly be a German and a Jewess. Gilbert desiring air without exercise, we took a taxi and drove over the downs and home by Rottingdean. Unfortunately, it snowed and was rather dark. Had it not been for the Nelke topic, I think I should have been rather hard up. I like him, but don't really find it very easy to talk to him alone. He is certainly funny, but in a rather restricted area, and there is no doubt I'm not good at obscene talk. I can, if necessary, be fairly coarse with women, but it does not come easily with men. Yet I am as incapable of snubbing coarseness as I am of initiating it!

Sunday, 14th January

Stayed in bed until dinner. I read *East Lynne* until my eyes ached. Claud sent me up the beginning of his diary[1] to read—a circuitous way of conveying dewdrops, in fact almost a 'declaration':

'Saw Lady C. for the first time these many years without a hat on —she looked none the worse for that. On our walk she wore sou'-wester oilskins—women's attractiveness does not increase in proportion to the cost of their clothes. Did not want to see anyone this time in London and saw no one—was looking forward to meeting Lady C. the next day at Brighton. She gives me the impression of being a *femme inattaquable.*'

I was much amused.

Tuesday, 16th January

A letter from Basil saying he was being sent off to some hospital on

1. Lady Cynthia had bought him 'a superior exercise book at Boots' and had had great difficulty in finding a place where they would fit it with a lock.

account of his bronchial cold. It sounds desolate—destination unknown, no letters, no papers—but I am very glad he has gone to a respite of warmth and rest.

Was lunching with Beb in the Albion Grill Room when Claud came mooching in. I wasn't certain he was coming to luncheon, but sure enough there he was and he stayed till after dinner. Beb does not like him at all—finds him uncanny and distasteful. I think he is rather 'voor'.*

Wednesday, 17th January

Packed hard, and left the dear Royal York to catch the 2.20. They presented me with a box of chocolates—'one of our souvenirs'. Shall I return to Brighton? I feel the chapter is closing.

Thursday, 18th January

Dined with Colonel Freyberg, V.C., at the Carlton Grill Room. Eddie and Irene were the other guests. We dined nominally at 7.15, but Irene was ages late as she is kept at hospital till 7.30. Her energy is miraculous. Freyberg's sleeve is covered with gold braid. He has a ghastly red trench in his neck, is very deaf in one ear, and cannot move his arm. In spite of this, he succeeded where others failed in winding up Irene's little car for us. It generally breaks a few young men's front teeth nightly I should think. She drives it most efficiently in the dark. We went to Harry Lauder's musical play—the first time I have ever seen him. He certainly is extraordinarily lovable—marvellous geniality. His son has just been killed and it is terribly moving when he sings a sort of 'when the boys come home' patriotic song. Eddie wept. He and I discussed Lawrence, who wants to get to America, where he thinks he will be able to publish his books, and has appealed to us for advice and assistance. After the play we went on to Irene's hoping for poker, but alas no players turned up. Freyberg dropped me home. I liked him very much.

Friday, 19th January

Still bitter, bitter cold. I went down by ten o'clock to spend the day with John at Clonboy. Felt alternately cheered and depressed by him. Got back to Michael at about six. Beb returned with disconcerting news that the 'practical joke' department of the War Office is dissolving his Brigade at Brighton. No one knows what will happen.

Just before dressing for dinner, while Beb and I were standing beside Michael, the house was shaken by an explosion. To me it sounded like a small bomb very near. As a matter of fact it was a huge explosion right outside of London in a munition factory. We thought it was a bomb dropped by hostile aircraft, but even with Michael there I couldn't squeeze up any alarm. When I went upstairs a few minutes later I found Polly gasping on a chair and she gasped out, 'Oh my lady, what did you do in the bath?' She thought the geyser had blown up and hadn't dared come down to look at the scalded debris of her mistress.

Saturday, 20th January

A day of great irritation and annoyance. I telephoned to poor Beb, whom I had billeted for one night at Bruton Street, and he said he was ill with a feverish cold—most inconvenient as we were due that afternoon at Panshanger. Made poor Beb as comfortable as I could. Ettie telephoned to say she did want me by myself and I caught the 4.39 from King's Cross.

When we arrived[1] at about seven we found Ettie, Evan, Norah, the Ancasters, and the Professor and Lord Desborough.

In spite of the hour we were given tea and Ettie was the tuning fork to a conversation which destroyed all chance of a face rest for me—I needed it, too.

I have only been to the house once before when Lady Sassoon had it. The dining room is almost awe-inspiring—the pictures magnificent, but I can never look at them when I am talking and eating. I know I shall leave the house having seen nothing. I sat between Lord Desborough and the Professor at dinner. Poor Lord Desborough is most piteous. He looks like some great animal who has been struck on the brow, neither wanting nor expecting conversation. He said naïvely to the Professor and me, 'You know, Billy was a very intelligent child. He used to ask such funny questions. One night I went to see him in bed and he asked several questions quickly: "Do rhinoceroses make a gruff noise?" "Do fishes laugh?" and so on'. We (Lord D., Patrick, Eddie and I) played poker. I lost £1 10s. Ettie and the Professor talked; the others bridged. I did not enjoy my evening—was tired and in one of my morbidly humble moods.

1. Lady Cynthia had been joined in the course of the journey by Edward Marsh and Patrick Shaw Stewart.

Sunday, 21st January

Bitter cold day, but I have never known such a fiercely heated house. Ox-roasting fires and hot pipes. I had a congested face all the time. It was queer being at a real Saturday to Monday party again—really very much like a pre-war one. We had an old-time Ettie-ish vivacious breakfast. She, the Professor and I had quite a long *à trois* first. We discussed features, coiffures, etc.—always comic with a man and Ettie, in these matters, is little more knowledgeable than a man. The Professor remarked that I should be 'very ducky quite bald'—a theory I cannot endorse.

When the others came the Charles Lister book was discussed. Patrick's lynx eye had detected a great many errors he wished to have corrected for the second edition. We all laughed over the cruel thing about Mrs Benson—'Mrs B. comes tomorrow, which is a pity'.* How could he have left that in if there were any bowdlerising at all? No foul abuse would be so bad as that mild resigned statement 'which is a pity'. I don't see how she can ever 'come' anywhere again. I should have thought suicide would be the only possible course! The casualties of the explosion now seem not to have exceeded about three hundred. The day before rumour put it at two thousand, and Eddie had been told that 'the Thames was full of arms and legs'.

It was difficult to get time even to write a letter but I escaped to my bedroom for a bit. Never has a house so completely baffled my bump of locality. I never knew whether I was going to the bathroom or into the Professor's door. Instead of going to church, a party conducted by Lord Desborough went over to see the German prisoners. There are about a hundred of them in the park and they work in the woods. I was not allowed to talk German to them. The specimens I saw were of the meek-and-mild type, not at all 'blond beasts'. They had rather ignominious identification marks in the form of a blue disc patched somewhere on to their backs: it looked as though its purpose was to afford a bull's eye to the marksman if they attempted to escape. I walked home with the Professor, and he talked very nicely of Letty, for whom he has a great feeling. He thinks her street-arab Cockney humour, combined with pathos, very attractive.

We got home just in time for luncheon. I sat between Lord Ancaster and Lord Desborough, and suffered tortures of civility strain in having to attend to my neighbours when I longed to join, at least orally, in the general conversation on Keats, and so on. They contended that Sophocles was the only poet about whom nothing could be said. Evan maintained there was really nothing to be said about Milton, but we then laughingly remembered that the Professor had written a book about him. Patrick, to my amusement, blushed like a girl on finding the whole table listening with forks poised to him holding a literary argument with the Professor. Whenever I was particularly interested Lord Ancaster would embark on his skating experiences in St Moritz, or Lord Desborough would for instance, *à propos* of Milton, inform me that the poet's mother was buried at Taplow. I know no greater tax on one's manners than to have to lend an attentive face to one's neighbours when one's ear is in the possession of one's *vis-à-vis*.

Eddie and I went for a walk after luncheon. We discussed the expediency of marriage for him and the loneliness of bachelor old age. He said he really was a bachelor by policy, not like many from mere accident. If he could be given the choice of falling in love with a willing spinster or not, he could choose not to. At tea Evan told me Eddie had proposed to Juliet Duff, but I am almost certain I do not believe it. Over the meal we discussed Flecker—tremendous incense was burnt at his shrine, and I am glad I loved his poems so much three years ago. We played galloping old maid with Imogen. She has grown very pretty—has extraordinary technique and charm and is very much dressed. After that, the Professor read aloud to us extracts about Swift from the memoirs of a Mrs Pilkington—very delightful.

This time I secured a very good face rest before dinner and came down looking and feeling my best. It wasn't even an effort to listen to Lord Ancaster and Eddie was on my other side. Norah gave me a dewdrop from what she called an 'admirer'—'Nature tore up the receipt when she made Cynthia's face'. It turned out to be by Basil: I shouldn't have guessed, it doesn't sound like his style.

The same lot of us played poker—very merry, chatty poker. I felt lively, amused and amusing—a very distant cousin to myself of the night before. Incidentally, I won £6 10s. Afterwards I was seduced into sitting up with Patrick and Norah in her sitting room. They said I looked more 'guileful' than ever. I left my five-pound note there and had to go back to retrieve it in dressing-gown and my hair down. Rather an abandoned scene: Patrick toying with my tangles and rapturously exclaiming, and Norah—full of gay wit and charm as ever such a wonderful verbal bacchante. We laughed a lot and I went to bed shortly before two, too much wound up to go to sleep. More irrationally up in spirits than I had been down before.

Monday, 22nd January

Lord Desborough, the Professor, Eddie, Ettie, and I had an early breakfast. Amusing conversation on the present time amazing post-ponement of age, or rather of middle age, for women. Ettie and I agreed what a terrible jar it was the first time one was told as a dewdrop that one looked young. They said I didn't look married and that they would take me for about twenty-four, my face being too 'accomplished' for less than that.

The Professor, Lord Desborough, and I all went up by the 9.50—bitter cold. Lord Desborough was quite interesting about his Niagara swimming feat. The Professor told fables, and I edited him with his Crabbe anecdote which I love: Nervous young man to cultured lady at lunch, in desperate attempt to converse: 'Do you know Crabbe's *Tales?*' Lady, feverishly clutching at conversational straw: 'Have crabs' tails?' Man, frantically: 'I should have said *read* Crabbe's *Tales.*' Lady, still hopeful: 'Have red crabs' tails?' Man falls and remains in total silence.

The Professor and I went to Selfridges—in an emporium I am with excitement, as he aptly said, 'like a dog in a rabbit warren'. It is bitter, penetratingly cold and the pavements are covered with icicles of slime. Walking is beastly.

Irene, owing to cook's illness, gave her dinner at the Berkeley: self, Freyberg, a Mr Fairfax, the Comte de Noailles, Duff, and Bettine Stuart-Wortly. I sat next to Freyberg. He interests me enormously. I love his lack of humour, his frank passion for fighting and his unconcealed dread of peace. Life appears to hold no other interest for him. He wonders what he will do when it is all over. He maintains the human element is just as determining as in Napoleon's day—just as much scope for a military genius. I wish he could be given command. Duff as usual was drawn away by Diana. She was dining with Venetia and he denied that he was going there but—to our amuse-ment—soon after he left, Venetia rang up to ask for him. A complete give-away!

Tuesday, 23rd January

I lunched at Baroness D'Erlanger's—exploring expedition. Alas, for the bereavement of another prejudice, I quite liked her! I went home to wait for Freyberg, with whom I had a dentist appointment. He came at 3.30 and we had a longish talk. He does interest me and gives me the impression of a potentially really great soldier—in the Napo-leonic sense rather than the V.C. hero. He seems to have so many of the qualities—lack of humour, chafing ambition, and a kind of admirable ruthlessness and positive self-reliance. He knows when to quarrel with a superior and when to get rid of an inferior, and un-hesitatingly takes his cue. He has an elaborate system of espionage over his potential officers, but claims lightning intuition as to the merit of the candidates. There is a sort of directness, bluntness and inter-personal finesse, an absence of inverted commas, and what Severn calls 'approbativeness' about him which is very refreshing. I suppose the Coterie would call him a bore, but so they would most of the dead whose biographies are worth writing and reading. He boasted of the way he is hated by envious rivals and jealous superiors in rank. There is a distinct grimness about him at times, and his sort of snubness of face is anomalous, though it is a strong face. He said he hated pain and would rather die than go through his recent suffer-ings again, hastily adding, 'But I suppose that is selfish', with a delight-ful unselfconsciousness.

I was taking Michael to tea with Dorothy, and he dropped me there in a taxi. There was a little baby party upstairs—Betty brought the future Lord Salisbury, aged three months. A real little Cecil, looking all ready to make a speech. As usual, each mother's eyes were glued on her own offspring and the children completely insulated.

Wednesday, 24th January

I lunched at Bruton Street: Mary, Aubrey, Margot Howard, Lord Newton, and the very nice-looking General Macdonogh, head of Intelligence in London. Bluetooth was there, too.

Michael called for me and I took him to the Colonial Office to see his godfather Eddie said explanatorily, 'My godson,' with some embarrassment. Then I took Michael to Frame's first dancing class. Such an amusing sight. Poor Michael longed to join in, but he is too young. Felt flushed with self-consciousness about him—longing for everyone to appreciate him. It's ridiculous to care so much. I don't know how I shall ever get through life as a mother.

Had tea with Gan-Gan and went down to Brighton by 5.40. Beb had acquiesced to my proposal of returning to a cheaper hotel.

Thursday, 25th January

Beb turned up at 7.30 with horrid news that the blow had fallen, and he was ordered to Forest Row next day. I don't know what it will be like. It isn't far from here and, anyhow, I shall still have Claud for a neighbour—it is only eight miles from where he is stationed.

Good joke of Claud's—and no stingy one either! When I gave him his diary he said, 'I'm not going to pay you for that book, but I will give you something useful in return. What is your size in gloves?' He implied that he would give me penny for penny in value with meticulous honesty. I expected two pairs of gloves, the book having cost 7s 6d. What was my amazement, when I opened the boxes he had brought, to find one dozen white washing gloves, one dozen beautiful suede ones, and a handsome fur-lined pair thrown in, too! Well done, Claud!

Friday, 26th January

Really miserable at leaving dear Brighton. I have loved the life there and feel the ground has been cut away from under my feet. I believe the air and so on has spoilt me for life anywhere else, and I don't know how to lead any other sort of existence any longer. Packed sadly before luncheon at the Royal York, about which I have a strong sense of home.

We went up to London by 3.40. Claud appeared, to Beb's great irritation. I sat with him and a brother officer in a Pullman carriage: we had tea and gibbeted. Claud invited us to come and stay at Audley Square, which I should have liked to do, but Beb preferred 'independence' at Brown's Hotel, Dover Street. I was too shy to thank Claud for the gloves in public, and so rang him up from Cadogan Square. Diana Russell sent a note endorsing his invitation to stay— I longed to accept, but Beb was firm. I could not sleep—tossed and tossed in misery. Had real *nostalgie du pays* for Brighton, feeling that one breath of ozone would heal me.

Saturday, 27th January

Colder than ever—real effort to get out of bed. Beb and I went to the National Gallery. Very interesting lot of pictures there collected by Sir Hugh Lane. We dined at the Berkeley and went to see *The Aristocrat* together—a naïve, but enjoyable play. Successful evening. Eddie was bridling in the dress circle with Juliet Duff and Ivor Novello.

Letter from Basil, saying, alas, he was shortly returning to his battalion! He quoted a dewdrop from Claud: 'My greatest pleasure is Brighton for tea and a walk with Lady Cynthia, whose acquaintance was new to me, but whose many qualities I believe you have appreciated almost since you were middle-aged.'

Sunday, 28th January

Cold still intense. It is alleged to be the coldest spell since the sixties. By verbal and written request, I called on Claud again. Spent very pleasant three-quarters of an hour with him. He is very sad at Brighton being over—I can't realise that tragedy yet.

Beb and I dined at the Ritz with Gilbert: our party was dear little Nelke, Osbert Sitwell, and Clare. The latter was very pretty and very much the young 'married woman' talking glibly of 'cocottes' and capping Gilbert's risqué stories. I was 'animated' and in good form— we had fun. Great facetiousness about suggestions for a comic wedding for Gilbert and Nelke. At another table the Montagus, Frances Horner, Diana, and Duff were dining with Edward. We flattered ourselves that their dinner was being dank and that they were envying our hilarity. Pretended to cut them, sailing past with averted eyes when we went out, but we returned to talk to them.

Gilbert thought the following story suitable to regale his fiancée and their guests. A wife, suspicious of her husband and their pretty parlourmaid, determined to seek confirmation of her suspicions. One night she got into the parlourmaid's bed. Sure enough, she heard footsteps approaching, and a man entered the room. 'Ha, ha! I've found you out!' she exclaimed in sorrowful triumph—to find it was the butler!

Monday, 29th January

Had breakfast latish. Felt I oughtn't to leave Michael on Gan-Gan's hands much longer, so I wrote a note to Grace suggesting her having Michael as a paying guest—anxious as to her reply. A good deal of telephoning this morning. I have forgotten my London technique and the amount of one's life spent in planning for the small remainder of it seems appalling.

Beb and I lunched with Evan at Claridges. Eddie made our fourth. I thought the decorations—new—extremely effective and very becoming to the many beauties who were there. Evan very delightful. Discussing war psychology, he said he found everyone more stupid, slower at the uptake, since the war. I haven't observed this. Ross was there, *à propos* of whose invitations his wife said, 'Well, the upper classes can't be very particular.'

Beb went off at four o'clock to Forest Row. I tubed to Hyde Park Corner and called on Grace, whom I found in bed with pleurisy, in a delicious white rabbit jacket. She was delighted at the prospect of having Michael—a great relief to me. I think they will be very comfy there. So soon as her water-pipes have thawed, Michael will emigrate from his great-grandmother to his great-step-grandmother—a masterly bit of billeting.

Tuesday, 30th January

Went shopping with Mary H. She advised me to 'go easy' about poker, saying there was a certain spikiness in the atmosphere, 'passing the hat round' sort of feeling. It astonished me. I explained how very much in inverted commas my whole poker stunt was. She agreed.

An icy dark walk to Queen Anne's Gate to dine with the Montagus: party was Goonie, Gilbert, his Nelke, Hugo Rumbold, Duff, and Sybil Hart-Davis. I sat between Montagu and Gilbert. A subdued dinner heartening up towards the end—very little table-talking, mostly whispering. Beb very silent and unresponsive between Venetia and Nelke. I feel just like a mother watching a debutante about him— vicarious self-consciousness is very agonising. There was a bridge four and the rest of us—Venetia, Beb, Hugo Rumbold, Duff, Nelke, Gilbert, and I—sat down to baccarat. Not at all my fault (I even went so far as to propose clumps). I have always hated baccarat before, but I must admit I became rather a convert, though I still think poker much more socially amusing. Beb made a vast pile and then left it to me as he went off to see Aubrey. IOUs. of seven pounds and more flew about, and a shocking amount of money changed hands. I ended up forty-four pounds to the good. I don't think I won myself. Much more money changed hands than at poker. I should very much have disapproved of such happenings had I not been there myself. Patrick joined in late and 'bought the rabbit'.

Letter from Claud bemoaning the fact that his Brigade is also to be broken up, so I shall not have him for a Forest Row neighbour, after all. I'm very sorry.

Wednesday, 31st January

Snow falling in large flakes. Freyberg and I had arranged a morning walk on the telephone, but when he arrived at about eleven we decided in favour of fireside fun. He was not feeling very well—had an access of giddiness while he was with me. I reminded him of his promise to tell me about his childhood, but he said he didn't feel in the mood for it. He was very delightful—talked of ambition and so on. It is interest- ing to get the newcomer's impressions. He is surprised by the lack of reticence in London society. I was amused by one delightfully un-selfconscious betrayal of his expectations when he said, 'This war has taught one a great many lessons; one will know what to do when one is in command in the next one', implying his future Napeolonic authority. I enjoy exploring him. I have got extraordinary zest for human being intercourse just now—could spend the whole day in interviews. Is it in spite of, or on account of, the war?

Beb and I went to lunch with Frances Horner to meet the ex-P.M. The McLarens were there and Montagu. The P.M.—I cannot dispense with that address—was very sweet, but rather *piano*. I sat between him and McLaren. The latter not in harmony with my mood. Michael came round to see his grandfather. He looked very sweet, wasn't in the least shy, and said, 'Have you got a present?' Gan-Gan had brought him and she drove us all on to Madame Tussaud's: Michael enjoyed it. Then we took him to tea with Mary's three daughters at Bruton Street, and we had tea with Mary. Patrick Shaw-Stewart came in looking rather despondent, having failed so far to get a job at the War Office. He doesn't want to return to Salonika at the expiration of his fort-night's leave, meaning to return to the Naval Division sometime, but being anxious for an interval of London fun.

Thursday, 1st February

It was snowing steadily in the morning, and I think it was an act of great devotion on my part to walk and bus all the way to Tite Street, Chelsea, to see Horatia. They have only got one sitting room, so her mother and we two had an *à trois*. It was not worth the getting there and back.

I lunched with Irene: Patrick, Eddie, Willie de Grunne, and Felicity were there and I sat between Eddie and Willie. I talked to Patrick across the table and we had a reminiscent conversation.

Whibley came to see me at Catherine Street at 4.15. We had tea with Frances and then I took him on to Grandmamma's, as I wanted to see Michael. Risked taxi-ing with him, with logical conclusion of very trying demonstrations: 'I love you, I love you', with much hand-squeezing and ear-stroking. Poor dear, I wish he wouldn't! Whibley and Gan-Gan talked sweetly together about George. Then Whibley insisted on seeing me home and it was worse than ever. For the first time he actually got in a kiss—though only a graze, just as I was getting out.

Rested and put on my opal panier dress to dine with Gilbert at Audley Square. I had boldly borrowed Grace's motor, an untold blessing. The house was surprisingly warm and the food ample. The party consisted of Gilbert, his bride, Diana Russell, General Lowther, Osbert Sitwell, Norah Brassey, Bluetooth and another man: I sat between Gilbert and Osbert. Gilbert started an odd general conversation, half in form of an inquisition, into everyone's washing technique—how often did they soap themselves from head to foot and so on. He said his enquiries had taught him that the majority of women soaped twice daily, the majority of men but once. I found Sitwell quite agreeable to talk to—he told me he read every night of his life till three or four in the morning.

Bluetooth placed himself beside me after dinner. It was the first time I have talked to him thus, sitting in a circle for ages, and somehow it tickled me. He rather pined for his bridge. Osbert Sitwell was à trois with Gilbert and Nelke, and looked rather uncomfortable. I felt obliged to rope him in. The Russell bus dropped Norah, Bluetooth and me home. It is funny to see everybody struggling into their galoshes after dinner.

Saturday, 3rd February

Frost as relentless as ever. Mary Herbert called for me and we walked and tubed to my house in Sussex Place to try and excavate for my skates. I had no inclination, but my sense of duty about pleasure is strong, and I felt I must make an effort about skating. Polly was still laid up. I looked at piles of dusty band-boxes until my heart sank and I gave up the search.

It was the night I had long since arranged to take Freyberg to dinner with Norah. Mercifully he called for me in a taxi as it is quite impossible ever to get one here. Norah has taken a little house in Wimpole Street. Freyberg and I went to the wrong number and walked boldly in. Halfway up stairs the parlourmaid asked us if we were expected. We found the right number afterwards. It's a tiny, little joke of a house. We found Norah looking very lush in fancy dress and Evan. Amusing, imaginative food. Freyberg was rather overwhelmed by Norah's fantastic volubility. She didn't 'draw him out' and he was silent at dinner, but quite happy of course. I hoped we would have talked his 'shop', but there wasn't a word until Norah and I left him and Evan in peace and then, no doubt, they had a great bout of it. Evan made a delicious great floater at dinner. It was very cold and he said briskly, 'Shall I shut the window, Norah?' and, on looking round, found it was firmly shut. We four played poker. I am getting rather bored by the 'Mrs Poker' jokes about me. By great luck we found a taxi, and Freyberg chivalrously insisted on driving me home. He took off his gloves and made me put them on with a manly tenderness worthy of any Ouida hero. Guy had come up for the night. He was very long-suffering about finding me still in occupation of his room.

Sunday, 4th February

Poor Polly resurrected and went to Sussex Place and found my skates, and Pamela gave me a voucher for Regent's Park skating club and drove me. I wore my purple tweed and three-cornered black hat—pronounced a good skating kit. It snowed hard all the time, and I was suffering too much from the pangs of envy of Irene to enjoy myself much. She is the real 'Ice Queen' and looks a poem—I should love to be an Ice Queen—Diana, Edward, Margot Howard de Walden, Letty, and Mary H. came—the skating nobs. We were the duffers. Princess Patricia was there, looking really a dream of beauty. She has infinitely improved, having lost that pneumatic look about the face— far better-mannered, too. I skated round with the dear old Duke, and Norton, and McLaren, and McKenna. I wish to God I were good —as it is, it's a doubtful joy!

Walked out to dinner in Frances' snow boots feeling just like Lucy Gray. Deep snow and still falling. Luckily, I had only to go to Queen Anne's Gate for *tête-à-tête* with Bluetooth. Long discussion after dinner of 'love of life'—he maintaining life not worth while on the whole, I contradicting.

Monday, 5th February

Dined with Freyberg at the Berkeley: party was Freyberg, Eddie, Irene, and a young airman who had been in the Hood Battalion. We went to a most enjoyable Hawtrey and Baby Barnes play. Had hot coffee at a cabman's place afterwards. Freyberg drove me home. He took my hand in the taxi to see if it was cold and held it for some time, in what spirit it was impossible to judge. I said goodbye to him and wished him luck. He passed his Board next day and hopes to get out at once. I am glad I have made friends with him.

Tuesday, 6th February

Sad occasion at Catherine Street. Poor Ian Colquhoun's last night before returning to the Front. He, Dinah, Michael, and their father

The Pre-Raphaelite mood   *With Michael in 1916*

A fancy dress occasion—Michael as a harebell

Basil Blackwood illustrates his letters—D. H. Lawrence and dinner with Lady Cynthia

dined here. Alas, great domestic crisis—poor Frances' cellar quite empty and no coal to be procured for love or money. The phenomenal cold still worse than ever and now we can't even 'keep the home fires burning'. We all shivered and had goose flesh, but we got through the evening very well with the help of silly round games. I was as facetious as possible. Old Frank convulsed us all by saying he had once kissed Lady Jekyll behind a haystack. Poor Dinah terribly on the rack. She has had a cruel time.

Wednesday, 7th February

Breakfasted in fur coat. Frances went to the hospital. I had my hair waved and then wrote in the nursery, it being the only room with a fire. At last we are beginning to feel the pinch of the war in material things. What a long time it has taken! It has been an exclusively emotional experience for most of us, but these last days each hostess's brow has been furrowed by mentally weighing meat, bread, and sugar. Frances says the allowance of sugar is larger than what she consumes, on the other hand the meat allowance would mean a reduction by one half.

I lunched with Mamma, Bibs, and Sockie. Poor Mamma is having a bad time at the dentist, and was dreadfully restless at lunch—she walked miles and miles feeding the dogs. She discussed my finances, saying she thought she could give me £100 a year during the war, but wondered which would be the best way—she would like to feel she was helping towards Beb's insurance. I think it had better be given to me. It is much better that Beb should not feel any richer—the poorer he is on paper the better.

Thursday, 8th February

I found Beb established in an inn, rather than a hotel, in Ashdown Forest—quite small, but nice warm sitting rooms which are all right if their emptiness could be guaranteed. We are sharing one bedroom upstairs and I had rather an attack of claustrophobia while I was unpacking. Before I had completed my weary task, the punctual Claud arrived, having taxied over from Maresfield—Beb very bored at his advent. We had tea and then went an *à trois* walk through extreme cold and lovely 'seasonable' landscape. We went to Beb's camp—very picturesque: 'Timber Town' it would be called in a cinema drama. Claud had lunched with the Duchess of Marlborough at Brighton on Sunday and said she had provided six courses. When

Goonie arrived to stay with her, the Duchess bade her choose one out of the six spare rooms, and she found that a fire had been lit in each one in case it should be chosen! Enjoyed being shocked over this impious extravagance. Claud warmed himself in front of the fire for a few minutes, and then departed after his unbroken *à trois*. I wonder if he regretted his taxi fare.

Beb and I had quite a good dinner and then established ourselves in the best of the two sitting rooms. We are trying to bluff people into the impression that it is our private room. I have made a litter of bags and papers in it, and try and look as proprietary as possible. Unfortunately a ghastly bounder of an officer—late of the A.S.C., now to be a gunner—came in with his wife and talked to us. He is much concerned as to whether he will lose his second 'pip', as he calls his star. I hope he will. Early bed—this air makes one drunk with sleep.

Friday, 9th February

Beb came home to lunch—almost distressing to me as the mess in camp is so miraculously cheap—only sixpence a day. Pleasant frowsty evening reading *Dombey and Son* and writing letters. The light is very bad for reading—distant guttering gas. For once, Beb wanted to go to bed early. Neat note from Claud informing me he had left for Tidworth. 'And so the curtain rings down. I hope it wasn't a one-act play'. I am sorry he has gone.

Saturday, 10th February

Thaw definitely set in I think. Beb and I went to tea with a brother officer and his wife, the Smallwoods—she was lively and gossipy. On my saying I liked Brighton, she said, 'Oh—I understood you were never there. I thought you only came down for one morning every month.' This amused me: obviously the gossip was the London Society woman who only paid flying visits to her husband. Linchman, another brother officer of Beb's, appeared with his wife at dinner: I see in this little cheek-by-jowl place I am going to have a real taste of garrison life. Afterwards they came into what I consider my sitting room, and we conversed. She had been told of a very nice house with a ready-made cook in it available for two guineas a week. It had several rooms and we began to coquette with the idea of taking it between us four. An interesting experiment to share a house with complete strangers. They seem very nice and I believe it might work quite well.

It seems so incredibly cheap. It is about a mile from the camp—a slight drawback, but after all, that's not very far. The woman seems efficient and I hope she would do all the housekeeping.

Wednesday, 14th February

Beb returned from his morning's work with news that his B.E.F. leave would begin on Monday, and that he would go to France either Monday week or Monday fortnight. We go to Egham Saturday.

Sunday, 18th February

Foggy, muzzy day. Got up with rather speckled spring face. We all breakfasted together. There were war scones made with barley instead of wheat—very good. I took John out from eleven till nearly one, and very exhausting I found it. I don't wonder his governess needs a siesta. Beb walked with us nearly as far as the Copper Horse.

I went for a walk with Evelyn after luncheon, and had a long John talk. She thinks his governess (in spite of some faults) is doing good work, but thinks it essential to have someone else in charge of John, a governess not being capable of the two functions—the mental training, and the dressing and undressing, and so on. She advocated Polly.

I was feeling deadly depressed and bothered. On paper certainly I can make out a desperate case. The sore past—two war terrors—the sickening worry of John—bad health—a load of debt—and now, last but crushing straw, I must give up Polly to John. Evelyn told me I ought to be with John—so I ought and so I will, a great deal. I shall go down Fridays to Sundays, but I must be in London a good deal. In the circumstances I can't sit in the country alone with John. It only makes me ill with distress and I don't think I'm very good for him. I must do some war work in London.

Monday, 19th February

We lunched at Bruton Street. Aubrey was in mufti: he has got a civil appointment as Parliamentary Secretary to the Duke. Evan and McEvoy was there. McEvoy is going to paint Mary, and brought several very rough sketches as suggestions for poses. He said to me, 'You must let me draw you some day: I should so love to.' Is this an invitation? Aubrey gave me some dewdrops from Evan who, defending me against my old enemy Lady Crewe, had said to her: 'My niece can walk round ninety-nine out of a hundred women, and you are one of the ninety-nine.'

I joined Beb at Michael's. He acted as balm to me, and was piercingly sweet. He calls Grace 'Silver Knob' in return for 'Copper Knob'. We had 7.30 dinner with Mamma, Bibs, Sockie, and Grace—I took a copy of Beb's poems just printed. Mamma very tired, looking at me with great love and pity. I said Cust was looking after the 'propagation', meaning 'propaganda'. I was very much bitten with Grace's suggestion that I should learn to drive and use her car as a taxi.

Tuesday, 20th February

Horrible, wet, dank day. I don't know what has come over me these days, but I have got a complete mental or nervous collapse, akin to a kind of madness. Such ghastly depression—life seems a sheer nightmare, every prospect a horror, every retrospect a pain. Pangs of the past and fears of the future, with terrible lassitude. Generally I have snapped my fingers at the facts of life, and my worst unhappinesses have been for undefinable causes—subjective and morbid. Now for the first time I feel the 'fool of circumstance'.

Friday, 23rd February

Found Aileen Meade at Bruton Street when I looked in to see Mary, and she drove me back to the hotel and stayed some time. She and Mary H. urged me to take some tiny *pied-à-terre* where I could be on my own with Michael, and I am coming to the conclusion that I must have a home, but it's so difficult to find and I can't afford it. Mary has great insight.

Saturday, 24th February

I reached the climax of my pathos by dragging all over London carrying Beb's field boots, trying to get them mended. He has orders to report at Southampton on Monday, so he is really off: we expected it as he has received the laconic telegram: 'Your name is on the slate', from Forest Row. We settled to go down to Clonboy to see John, and to go to Southampton together on Monday. To Chesham Place, had tea with Grace and said goodbye to Michael. He made himself almost cruelly sweet: 'You will come back and see me soon, won't you?'

Monday, 26th February

I decided to abandon going to Southampton. I didn't feel physically
up to it, and it is at best a doubtful policy. Beb and I went to Waterloo,
and found special train for Southampton was leaving at 11.50. Mamma
was there with chocolates and cigars, and Mary and Evelyn. After
saying goodbye, they tactfully withdrew, leaving me to give Beb
hot coffee. I didn't stay till the train went.

Dorothy and I, the two grass widows, dined alone and had a nice
peaceful evening. I was tired out. She was very nice—very forlorn
without her Ned, a real case of all her eggs in one basket. Her house
is wonderfully comfortable—real pink, unimaginative *luxe*. A very
bad preparation for a 'decayed gentlewoman' in search of a three-
guinea flat.

Tuesday, 27th February

Felt rather better. Gone to the Front is better than going. Breakfasted
in bed. Mary called for me in her motor and we went flat-hunting
together. Saw ghastly homes—over fish shops in dreary districts. My
spirits sank and sank. When I read an advertisement I always visualise
spacious rooms, and I feel sick and claustrophobic when I see the
reality. We saw one five-guinea one, not at all bad, with telephone by
the bed, good cupboards, and at the mouth of a tube. The woman said
she might 'come down'. I don't know what I ought to do, and as I
can't even afford a flat, I'm not sure that taking this might not be a bad
middle course—almost as well go into my own house! Either means
certain insolvency, and the sheep I should be hung for would be very
much superior to the lamb. Mary and I began almost to retch, and
very glad we were to return to Mayfair.

Wednesday, 28th February

Bluetooth much distressed by a wail of a letter from me and was very
kind and sympathetic when I called at Queen Anne's Gate. I confided
in him about John for the first time. Dorothy called for me in a motor
angelically hired for the purpose and, with Michael and Nanny, we
went flat-hunting. I took her to the possible entresol one. Nanny
approved very much. I can quite imagine living or dying there, but I
think five guineas is too much, as it might be called a basement.
Unfortunately, the woman said fifteen people had been to see it that
day—perhaps she was bluffing. Dorothy very dear and helpful, but

her dainty appearance is particularly unbecoming to humble flats. The pursuit makes me a socialist. One gets terrible vistas of human life.

Thursday, 1st March

Nasty, foggy day. Dorothy and I started out house-hunting at about 10.30. I wanted to see as many as possible, since I had to make an offer for the basement flat, if I came to the conclusion that I wanted it, before five. I went to Letty's house and telephoned to the agent from there—actually committed myself to offering £4, and he said he would telephone.

Friday, 2nd March

Rang up agent in great trepidation to find out whether my offer was accepted, but he hadn't got on yet to the owner. Had woken up at five again and read the whole of Edith Wharton's very clever book of short stories. Went to see Horatia, who is staying at Sybil Long's— oh, the joys of a central situation!

Telephoned palpitating to the agent again, but still no news. Claud came for a dentist. We talked and gibbetted. I think he is rather in love with me. Dined alone with Dorothy, and we had a tremendous discussion on 'flirting' and topics in its environment. She maintained that any sort of intimacy with another man was incompatible with an entirely happy marriage—that the latter must of necessity be completely absorbing, a *métier* for a woman leaving no spare time of interest over. In fact, that there should be no crumbs worth anyone else's picking up. I tried to contest this desperately: in theory I think it wrong and economically false, but in practice I must own the happiest wives are the friendless women. It is difficult to combine. I couldn't make out whether she was talking at me or being rather tactless. It was quite interesting to hear so distinct a point of view. There is no doubt her love for her husband is a consuming religion. I like her very much.

At tea-time the agent rang up to say the flat owner would accept my offer for four and a half guineas. I stuck fiercely to four guineas and the agent acquiesced, so there I am—saddled with a basement off Baker Street! We can get in on Thursday—too exciting. I am trying to screw the Sussex Place rent up to ten guineas instead of seven. If they accept it will be a great help; if they refuse I shall have to come to an appalling decision. Shall I turn them out, risking a failure to re-let, or shall I climb humiliatingly down from a mere bluff?

Saturday, 3rd March

Bought *The Cornhill*, containing Katharine Tynan's article on 'Two Brothers—Lord Elcho and Yvo Charteris'. It is very simple and soppy, but inoffensive, giving excellent extracts from their letters.

I took Michael to a fancy-dress party at Venetia's. We walked. These days I am very virtuous about abstaining from taxis. Very nice party. Winston was there—Goonie, Clemmie, Diana, Duff, Viola, Alan, and so on. Clemmie's eldest child is a most beautiful boy— Randolph Churchill.

Sunday, 4th March

Beastly day with agonising, disfiguring east wind. Mamma and I had planned to visit my flat, but the tiresome woman refused to stay at home to let me in or to leave the key with the porter, so we were baffled. Claud visited me here at Cadogan Square at 5.30, and poor Mary Strickland complained of being excluded from the only room with a fire. He and I discussed people who were 'spectators' in life. We agreed we both were. Also discussed the Russells' lack of social success. Dined with the Montagus—the only other guests were Osbert Sitwell and Alice Wimborne—extraordinarily happy evening. Very amusing discussion as to what popular people were 'bubbles' to us. Alice drove me home.

Tuesday, 6th March

I joined Mary Herbert, who was trying on at Revilles. She and Miss Rye, the charming vendeuse, very much admired my old off-the-peg Selfridge black dress, which I have had embroidered round the neck. It is a success. Mary taxed me with Claud, and asked me how I 'liked him as a lover'.

Wednesday, 7th March

Claud and Evan dined. The former looked like a great cat in a dream. I sat in Papa's room with him after dinner. I think he wanted to make some sort of declaration, but found me—as he wrote in his diary— *inattaquable*. As it was, he only succeeded in telling me of a physical defect—too strongly marked line of nostril on the side of my nose. He implied that, when he first saw me, he could scarcely notice anything else, and he had been amused when I had said the fault of the Horner family looks was their lack of any such line. I asked him if he had thought any criticism like Pierpont Morgan's complaining of some other man's nose 'being small and the same colour as the rest of his face'. He told me I was in very good looks, but that he hadn't thought much of my looks at first and had had an argument on the subject with Gilbert. He said he supposed he would never know me well enough to call me Cynthia. and asked me whether I supposed he would have fallen in love with me if the Brighton life had continued for months. It doesn't sound much, any of this, but his manner made it a distinct *passage.*

Thursday, 8th March

Very unsavoury morning of house agents, solicitors and insurance companies—interviews with various representatives—signing of agreements, cheques, etc. I inspected the fire damage at Sussex Place.[1] It is luckily not very serious, but the poor tenants were in sad distress, as the kitchen fire couldn't be used. Miss Schmidt was in tears, too, about my threat of re-letting the house. I immediately climbed down from ten to eight guineas.

Alex, back on Parliamentary leave, telephoned asking if he could see me. I said I was engaged all the afternoon in pushing Michael in his perambulator from Chesham Place to Baker Street. He said, to my great amusement, that he would push the perambulator and we arranged an assignation in Hyde Park. Unfortunately there was a confusion between Hyde Park Corner and Hyde Park Gate, and we never met. Alex claimed to have searched for hours.

When I arrived at my new house, I found Letty and Mary having a furniture mania in my drawing room—very sweet of them. Letty brought some azaleas, too, and bits of stuff to drape horrors. I was not going to stay the night, as I thought it best to give the nursery party time to settle down. Had tea with them and left them very happy —Michael intoxicated with joy over the flat. We got our provisions from Selfridges.

Friday, 9th March

Woke up very excited at the prospect of installing myself in my flat. Very busy all the morning telling Polly what I wanted to take, and so on. My base for books, clothes, etc., has been Cadogan Square for a long time now and it's no joke transferring it. It's like moving an Army Corps, though I'm not taking absolutely everything.

1. A fire in the kitchen had burnt a hole in the dining-room floor.

Alex drove me to my new home, where I found the nursery party having tea. It was a bitter cold day and my spirits were a little dashed by the rather charnel-house atmosphere and the unlived-in appearance of my drawing room. I call it my basement—one doesn't feel subterranean, but there is no denying that one does go down instead of upstairs. Michael was in wild spirits, pattering about the passage and being very officious—dusting, ringing bells, etc., etc.

Claud came to see me at six. I had to see him, unsettled as I was, because he was just going off to Dublin where he is now stationed. He was very nice and helpful about my room, both with his mind and muscles. We moved all Letty's and Mary's arrangement and things began to look much better. I am lucky about the black *moiré* curtains and covers. Pretty cushions will look nice on them. Claud called me Cynthia for the first time, rather dramatically, 'Cynthia, I must go now.' He said he had been told I was a very 'unflirtatious' woman, and that he believed it. I asked if he considered it a dewdrop or a spike and he said 'a tremendous dewdrop'. When he said goodbye he raised my hand and kissed it twice fervently. The end of the second act, as he said. I wonder when the third will begin. He told me he had left me some money in his will in case he should be submarined.

Nurse cooked me a scrumptious whiting quite perfectly and I enjoyed it so much, and felt a real sense of peace creeping over me in my *gîte*. Very busy until late—furniture mania-ing, arranging papers, etc. Nurse too delightful and helpful. We took down the ugliest pictures. Bedroom quite comfortable, but I was too excited to sleep and had a vile night.

Saturday, 10th March

After writing letters I went to Sussex Place and did a lot of looting. Nearly broke my arms staggering back with books, and so on. I sent Winnie to fetch other things after lunch and it begins to have quite a home aspect now. I hung up Tonks' pastel of me. Nurse, in the intervals of her many activities, contrived to cover two cushions for me. She is a treasure. Her cooking is excellent. I think we are going to be very happy.

I went all the way by Tube to Queen Anne's Gate and lunched with Bluetooth. Afterwards he showed me all the letters I wrote to him during our first acquaintance. He had warned me so strongly of their badness that I was almost agreeably disappointed. Returned by Tube, and we had tea in the kitchen all together. Then I entertained Michael for an hour in the drawing room.

Alex came when Michael had gone to bed and stayed a long time. Discoursed on the difficulty of arranging one's life in London—how to protect oneself and one's time without too much ruthless elimination. Alex is very *embonpoint*. He asked if he might come again the next day. Funny that I should have three dark admirers about forty-five years old. Mercifully, I had another evening alone. Coped with letters and went to bed tired. How difficult it is to keep abreast, even before one has begun one's war work! Heard from poor Beb that he has influenza.

Monday, 12th March

A lot of telephoning in bed. Michael said, 'Mummie, you mustn't keep on telephoning all the morning.' Mary sent her motor for me and, after shopping at Selfridges, I drove to McEvoy's studio to see her portrait. She is being done full length in tweeds in a rather dramatic pose. I think it looks quite hopeful. I told her it would do well for a poster advertisement for the work she has undertaken in relation to the 'Women on the Land'. McEvoy works in a tiny studio piled thick with the hundreds of portraits he has on hand at the same time. Each time he sees me he repeats how much he would like to paint me, but I must be wary and make quite certain that he means at his expense, not mine. Sybil Hart-Davis was under the impression that she was sitting to Nicholson because he admired her, and great was the consternation when he sent in a huge bill to her husband.

Dined alone with Bluetooth—very agreeable evening. He elaborated his theory of my 'simpletonhood'. After eleven I went across to Venetia's house having been bidden for poker. Found Neil Primrose and Scatters Wilson* awaiting their host and hostess, who had been dining with Winston. Mary and Goonie came with the Montagus, and Diana, Patrick, Duff, Osbert Sitwell, Phyllis Boyd, Frances Horner, Mrs Arkwright, and Lord Stanley trickled in. We sat down to an oyster, baby potato, and champagne orgy. I sat between Osbert and Montagu. After a long, quite amusing supper, Osbert, Diana, Phyllis, Lord Stanley and I settled down to poker. The others all played bridge. Alas, we played till 3.30—arrant folly which was all the more appreciated by me because I lost my five pounds. Wished I had gone straight home from Bluetooth's.

Mrs Arkwright drove me home. Found the outer gate of the flats locked—awful panic that I was shut out for the night, but mercifully after some time a porter appeared to respond to my despairing bangings on the door. One of my predecessors appears to have been a lively lady. Her telephone friends keep me quite busy and on Sunday night Nurse was woken at 3.30 by loud pealing at the bell. Trembling, she opened the door, and a man's voice said, 'Is that you duckie?'

Tuesday, 13th March

Walked and bussed to Bruton Street for lunch. Overtiredness, anaemia of the brain, or something, gave me odious symptoms. I couldn't focus my eyes. It was as if the lower part of my vision couldn't work, for instance, I could only see the top of people's faces right. My head swam and at luncheon I thought I should faint. As in a nightmare, everyone seemed miles away.

I sat next to H. Fisher, whose delightful face and conversation were, in the circumstances, rather thrown away on me. Drank port and felt a little better. Juliet Duff was there, and King Hall of Naval Intelligence, whose bright little face beams out intelligence. He looked very blue about one of Mamma's protégés.

Wednesday, 14th March

I lunched at Cavendish Square, the first time I have seen my in-laws back in their old nest. Asquith looked well, but I didn't sit beside him. Margot very preoccupied. I was between Scatters Wilson and Oc: and Barbara and Viola, and Elizabeth and a general were there. Gossip conversation after lunch.

I went off earlyish to the Gilbert-Nelke wedding. We were not asked to the church, but went straight to the house. I was too early —found only a sister of Osbert Sitwell waiting. Gradually the wedding guests trickled in: Brenda, Goonie, Venetia, Sybil Hart-Davis, Jeffie Darell, Alex, Phyllis Boyd, and so on. Finally the bride and bridegroom appeared. She looked really delicious in quite the most lovely wedding dress—a shimmering soft-as-satin brocade. Gilbert showed his spirit unbroken. There was a large child running about the room and, intercepting my and Brenda's eyes, he hastily said in an explanatory tone, 'That's not our child'. It made me laugh. Maud asked me to come up to her bedroom while she changed. There were about six of us spectators, and wonderful mouth-watering sights we saw in the way of underclothes, etc. Real imaginative *luxe*. I am always envious of the bride's trousseau. They went gaily off.

Alex and I had arranged to go on and see the Epsteins. They are very interesting—a wonderful head of a tiny baby. He dropped me home at my flat. Played with Michael. Claud arrived at six. He had

telephoned in the morning to say he was already back on leave—
rather an anticlimax after our sentimental goodbye. He thought he
had got a week but, on arrival, found a telegram recalling him next day.
Michael, uncannily attracted by him, would insist on dragging him
all over the house to see gas stoves, and so on. I think his charm is that
he doesn't cater to children with voice, face, or manner, but talks to
them quite normally. I have never known Michael so fascinated. Claud
dropped me at Portland Place for dinner. Passionate hand-kissing on
saying goodbye in taxi.

Thursday, 15th March

I dined with Con—the house gives me a heartache. Con, Hoppy,
Anne, Jack Islington, Lord and Lady Kenmare, Duff and the Ormsby
Gores were our party. I sat between Billy Gore and Duff. Gore is
working with Milner. He said something about being extra busy on
account of the Russian Revolution. Instead of jumping at this *bonne
bouche*, on which he no doubt expected to dine brilliantly, I let it pass
—thinking it was, as usual, something which had escaped my notice
in the newspapers. I am always so topically ignorant. As a matter of
fact, his news was the terrific, historic affair of the last three days,
about which there had been no breath. A great epoch-making revolution, the Tsar's abdication, and so on. Con and Lady Kenmare made
up for my shortcomings after dinner. He must have thought me
deplorable and I like him so much.

Sunday, 18th March

Made my postponed journey to Brighton. Michael very busy helping
me pack. I left the room for a few moments to find my box filled
with every possible portable object—towels, fire irons, etc. He was
rather hurt when I took them out.

I am staying with the Seymours. Horatia was in bed, but I lunched
with Lady Seymour, and arranged that she should be a Mrs Pipchin
and board John and his two attendants. It will be much nicer for them
than lodgings, but it will not be for long as she is probably going to
let her house. Then I think I shall try and send them to Eliza's cottage.
I really can't afford lodgings and the flat. Dined alone with Lady
Seymour. She is terribly delicate on the subject of money and couldn't
negotiate with me as to terms. Horatia was the agent next day and I
agreed to pay £4 10s for everything.

Monday, 19th March

Nasty, blustering, grey day. Reported great advance in the newspapers. Cavalry actually said to be in open action. I wonder how much it means, and whether there have been ghastly casualties. I'm so afraid Basil must be in this fighting.

Tuesday, 20th March

Mrs Bridges, damn her, had told me there was a train to London at eleven! I had an awful scuffle to get packed, and dashed down to the station to find there was no train until 12.25. Much annoyed. I hate the joins of life—so large a part of mine seems spent on station platforms.

I went straight to Cadogan Square from Victoria and had a late meal there. Papa blue and poor darling Mamma looking very worn and harassed. I'm afraid London life is sheer treadmill for her. Ordered uniform for Pamela's hospital at Harrods.

Dined with Mrs Belville. She was rather subdued and 'undirty dogging'. I sat between General Lowther and a little Jew—owner of the *Daily News*. To my amusement, Lowther told me I had got Gilbert 'talked about' by lunching with him that day at Brighton just after his engagement. An officious scavenger of a woman had gone to see Lowther about it: 'Do you know he was seen lunching alone at Brighton with a very pretty woman?' Everyone seems to like Lowther very much. I don't quite see his point, but there is a sort of robust jollity about him. He talked very crudely of the trials of a honeymoon. Cowans was there and Evelyn Fitzgerald. Lady Sarah Wilson and Jeffie and K. Norton came in after dinner. I won £3 8s at poker. The Becketts were, too.

Wednesday, 21st March

Bitter cold again. Intermittent falls of snow. Claud sent me a ghastly newspaper photograph of myself headed 'Helping the lads' with 'There's one here who needs you'. I got up after necessary writing and telephoning. Bussed to Selfridges and spent practically all my poker earnings on boots, torch, socks, and comestibles for Beb. Had a delicious snack lunch with the nursery party followed by half an hour's rest, after which I had to put on my white uniform for Pamela's[1] hospital. Felt rather a fraud as we only do pantry work. The shift is from three to five, ideal hours.

1. Lytton.

There are supposed to be four of us: Moira Osborne, Pamela's little sister and a rosy girl and myself. We cut bread with a fascinating machine in a very nice blue pantry, boil eggs, and so on, and then take the teas round to all the bed-ridden men in the wards. Finally, we have to wash up the mugs. It is frightfully cold downstairs, and one's feet get frozen—otherwise, quite pleasant work.

Dined with Juliet Duff: Aubrey, Mary, Evan, and Adele were the party. We played poker and I lost fourteen shillings. Evelyn Fitzgerald was to have joined us, but he didn't get away from one of those ridiculous 'Ark' dinners given since the war (why?) by Lady Londonderry, the 'Enchantress Circe' as she is styled, at which all the men have animal nicknames. They take place every Wednesday, and strike me as absurd—Cowans, I believe, the nucleus. I forgot that Lord Ribblesdale made one of our party. He had a bad cold and kept saying '*Je souffre.*'

Thursday, 22nd March

Very cold day. One's hands were 'yellow and black and pale and hectic red'. Michael very sweet in the morning. He picked up Yvo's photograph and said, 'Who's that soldier?' When I told him, he said, 'Was he killed? That was a drefful pity! He's got such a nice face. Is he in Evvun? Would he like me to write to him?' I wrote and actually got in an hour's Motley. Went to lunch at Bruton Street in my uniform. Shrieks of amusement and admiration from Aubrey, and the rest.

Dined with Bluetooth. Mary sent the motor and I called for her at Bruton Street where our mothers were peacefully dining together. How we wished we were! The dinner was—host, Belloc, Aubrey, the Parsons, and Diana. Diana and Belloc were the only two who got an innings at all, and by the end of dinner we were all fielding for Belloc. He recited his verses and was very delightful. I have never liked him so much, but I was not enjoying myself—'spring fret' or something. I think I am really too sore for Diana's boisterousness. Good soldier story. The young son of General Stuart-Wortley drawled out to his men, 'Father says you are to point your guns this way,' and his men shouted, 'And what does Mother say?'

Friday, 23rd March

I went to lunch at Cavendish Square, was early and had a conversation with Margot in her bedroom. She suddenly took a medical interest in me and looked at my tongue, eyes, and throat. She practically reproached me with my calmness while Beb was at the front, expatiating on the rumblings of her stomach on the hypothesis of Henry or Puffin being out. We talked about John, which produced a blue-purple flush on my poor cheeks.

The Keppels were at lunch and Diana. Margot rather obviously raw inside—very snappy to poor Mrs K. Household atmosphere very electric. The P.M. didn't say a word on the question of Beb standing for Parliament.

At four I went to see Freddie Blackwood in Mrs Samuelson's very nice-looking hospital in Grosvenor Street. He has had pneumonia and, poor dear, looked so delighted to be back. He said they had a hellish time. I love his manner—very reminiscent of Basil, whom he gave wonderful military dewdrops, saying he couldn't have possibly endured these months without him. He said he looked very ill.

I had been congratulating myself all day on the fact that I was not dining out. There was to be no scramble into clothes, no nose-powdering, no taxi-ing, and I was just going to subside into my bed with an egg dinner on a tray, looking forward to a delicious read and an early sleep. Then, the telephone rang and Duff asked me to join a dinner party at the Ritz given by Scatters. I resisted for a long time—said I would consult the looking-glass, and after doing this twice I re-iterated my refusal. But it seemed churlish and middle-aged, and when Duff said he would come and fetch me, I gave in. I scrambled into black velvet, did what I could to my tired face, and with great success.

I thought I was looking my best and Duff endorsed my opinion. Found huge party at the Ritz: Papa, Montagus, Lady Crewe, the Neil Primroses, Lord Wimborne, Phyllis Boyd, Mrs Arkwright, Patrick Shaw-Stewart, Jimmy Rothschild, Scatters Wilson and Frances and Diana. It was a meatless day. All the same it was quite a good Belshazzar. I sat between Patrick and Duff. Patrick told me he was in love with four people and, therefore, pretty busy: I found out three—Diana, Phyllis Boyd, and Julia James. I believe him to be quite incapable of specialising. Enjoyed my conversation with Duff very much. Felt tremendous reinforcement of mutual appreciation. We agreed that his friends were loose talkers and low livers, and that the blushing, shockable, formal, elder generation had been the ones for living and loving. He deplored this. I said it was always an alternative, and quoted the classic example of Swinburne. He told me a delicious example of Margot's inconsequence. Talking to him of Venetia she said, 'Of course, she's a Jew. Both Lord Sheffield and Lord Carlisle are Jews'. Duff asked which was her father, and Margot said, 'Neither'.

Mrs Arkwright looking lovely. She does grow on one. The only thing I don't appreciate, though it is considered a great charm, is the 'mane' of dusky hair on her neck. Lord Wimborne was in terrific form, flapping his funny lids at Diana, Phyllis, and Mrs Arkwright. One can't dislike him. It was a free and easy party—entwined arms, and everybody else's darling. Two bridge tables and a poker table for self, Duff, Patrick, Diana, and Phyllis Boyd, Jimmy Rothschild, and Frances. I lost £2 15s. Supper of eggs and bacon, etc. I sat next to Duff again. The parentage game was played a little. Patrick— Uriah Heep and Bernard Shaw; Eddie—Tom Tit and Sappho; and Diana—Voltaire and Venus. I didn't get home till three, having left my brooch and muff as well as lost money, but I'm glad I went— 'something for my diary'—Lord Wimborne asked us all to stay the night on sofas.

Saturday, 24th March

Deadly tired after orgy. Two letters from Claud in the course of the day, one beginning 'Beautiful Cynthia' and the other 'Sweet Cynthia, perfect and adored'.

Sunday, 25th March

My beau Whibley called for me to take me out to lunch. I evaded the kiss of greeting which he calmly tried to bestow and got off with only the hand. We lunched at the Café Royal. He talked lyrically of my beauty, which he said was 'like genius', and of his love for me.

I was really firm with Whibley, who wanted to taxi me home. I insisted on walking—economy was my pretext, but my real reason was another one. I went so far as to allow him to give a discharging shilling to one he had called. He walked me all the way home. He is a great dear, but I do wish he wouldn't take my arm even in Regent Street.

Mr and Mrs Gilbert Russell called on me—looking very happy. She has already acquired that subtle 'married' look never acquired by me. We tried to teach Gilbert to read poetry with the aid of my commonplace book.

Went by bus to family supper at Cadogan Square. Whibley had put himself on to the meal, and Charlie, Madeline, and Letty and Adele were there, as well as Connor, Frances and Letty. Sacheverell Sitwell came to eat, but left immediately afterwards, being confined to barracks on account of the rumour of invasion which has been exciting us during the last twenty-four hours. What can have given rise to it?

Monday, 26th March

Still bitter cold with falls of snow. Spring is very reluctant. I lunched in my uniform with Irene: Eddie was there and the George Lloyds. Russian gossip talk. The story goes that the amazing Rasputin used to cover his fingers with jam and the ladies of the Court, including the Tsarina, used to lick it off! No explanation of the invasion rumour. The Guards have been confined to barracks for the last three nights.

Dined Cavendish Square. Very nice little party: the Bongies, the Herberts, Elizabeth, Oc, and Léonie Leslie. The P.M.—I can't not call him that—is looking so wonderfully well and almost beautiful, very venerable. Bless him. We played ridiculous games of Pounce after dinner.

Tuesday, 27th March

Enormous budget of letters: four from Basil and two from Beb. Basil reproaches me with falling off in my letters. Mary Herbert came to see me after her day's work and held an inquisition as to my 'lovers', 'declared' and 'undeclared'.

Wednesday, 28th March

I went in my uniform to lunch with Phyllis. I 'bussed', of course mud-spotting my white dress. Pamela's insistence on pure white is very extravagant, it involves a clean dress practically every time, and one's laundry bill will be inflated beyond all recognition. The egg drama was more complicated than ever. One man gave me nine—one of them broken. Even my paltry two hours' service tires me. Irene's double life is more of a mystery to me than ever!

Beb writes that my block of flats 'is the most notorious place for Miss So-and-so's'. He says I should change my home and ask Humbert's[1] advice—he must think me terribly adaptable to environment!

Thursday, 29th March

I was caught in a heavy hail storm on my way to Fortnum and Mason to order some fun-foods for Beb, and only got back just in time to change into my uniform and go out to lunch at Bruton Street. I have blossomed out into the out-door uniform—dark blue *crêpe-de-Chine* veil and the orthodox cloak. It is very becoming, but I feel self-conscious in it and walk in terror of being called on for a street accident.

1. Lady Cynthia's lawyer.

What could I say, but 'Give him air'? Very nice lunch at Bruton Street, just Mary, Gwendoline Osborne, and McEvoy. McEvoy crystallised his offer to paint me and took out his very overcrowded engagement diary and booked me for 9.30 next Thursday. I am very glad.

Friday, 30th March

Lunched with Michael and then went to the hospital. There were four of us on the shift this time, so we were able to move with dignity. I find even I am relatively methodical and I did a lot of organising—reforming the hopeless egg chaos. It was rather a nightmare. There had been five operations in the top ward. Apparently dead men kept being brought in on stretchers whilst I was handing the jam round.

Sunday, 1st April

An Arctic April. No semblance of spring in the bitter-blasted first day of the month here in Brighton. I breakfasted upstairs and then took John out in the garden until lunch time—very tiring. He and his governess lunched with us: he behaves very well at meals, and gazes at Lady Seymour just like Paul at Mrs Pipchin.

Tried to read after luncheon, but Lady Seymour was very disposed for chat. She has an interesting, handsome, cadaverous face with very fine eyes. She was reminiscent. We talked of the Alfred Lyttelton book I was reading, and she was able to supply gobbets of gossip about various people mentioned in it. She told me how she had once met old Sir Charles Tennant and his wife years before their offspring took London by storm, and described her as an ultra-common little woman, who boasted that the apricot tarts consumed in her nursery cost a pound. What a mysterious thing that generation of brilliance was—what an interesting study for students of heredity! Margot always humorously says: 'My mother was a lady.'

I had a talk with John's governess after dinner. I feel more and more despairing about any real change in John. Improvement in behaviour means little to me. It is an awful shadow over my life. I may forget and be merry, but happy I can never really be while it is there. Why? Why? Why? is all that rises from one's heart and brain.

Monday, 2nd April

Very stormy night. Terrific noise in my room and I was at length obliged to drag myself out of bed to try and soothe the window. No letters by first post but one from Claud by the second: 'Dear Cynthia, I am glad the silence was audible, but there is nothing to report, nor much chance of seeing you whom I love.' He is not tautologous.

I took John out in the garden after lunch, having bought him a ball. He has quite a good idea of kicking. After tea Lady Seymour and I had him in the drawing room. Have been through the accustomed cycle of feelings. First miserable despair, with almost horror, then his great charm intervenes and I become soothed, almost reassured. Lady Seymour very nice about him. We get on very well together. I am really rather fond of her. After dinner, at her request, I read half Dickens' 'Haunted Man'. Beloved Dickens. As usual he warmed the cockles of my heart.

Tuesday, 3rd April

Snowed in the night. Lovely sunny, cold morning. John and his governess took me to the station in the bus and John looked strained and pale. He minds my going very much now. I went to Cadogan Square and ate the remains of Sockie's and Bibs' lunch. Shopped at Harrods.

It was the evening of my long-arranged dinner and play with Duff. He did things *en prince* and sent a hired motor to fetch me. We dined at the Carlton Grill Room. I must say he is agreeable to talk to, but I suppose he isn't a born *cavaliere servente*. He said he dreaded becoming a 'Bluetooth', surrounded by palliatives and missing happiness. We had an interesting talk about murder and suicide, and a certain amount of personalities, trying to discover any common denominator in attractive women. We went to the Ambassadors. Morton was brilliantly amusing in a French farce. He is a genius. Loved it. John and Kakoo were in the stalls next to us. Duff dropped me home—hovered round with would-be fondling hands and pressed for another meeting.

Wednesday, 4th April

Letter from Basil implying he would accept a post with 'responsibility' if it were offered now. He wouldn't accept the ordinary, empty, staff thing he is likely to be offered, and it must be soon or else it would be too near the offensive. At present they have gone back for a six weeks' rest. I telephoned to Freddie and we consulted as to what could be done in the way of wire-pulling. I suggested his trying Bridges.

Went to my hospital. Mamma met me there with the startling news that Lord Roberts was coming to inspect us! It was Lord French, accompanied by his A.D.C. John Granby. I caught John kissing one of the parlour ladies in the pantry, but luckily it turned out to be Kakoo. French is very 'royal' and came into our blue pantry and embarrassed us all by thanking us for our services, just as though we were straight out of the trenches. We felt foolish.

Thursday, 5th April

At last, a real, lovely, glittering, glimmering spring day! I felt buoyant. At ten I put on my Fortuni tea-gown, mounted a bus and went off to my first sitting with McEvoy. He lives miles away in the Grosvenor Road, but luckily there is an excellent bus connection. I get off a No. 2 at Victoria, and a No. 24 takes me to his door.

I had had a terribly bad night and feared I might be disfigured, but luckily I looked all right. He began a small watercolour of my left (certainly my best) profile, and was enraptured with his work. I think it is quite promising—hopelessly pre-Raphaelite though—I had rather hoped for a new version. He is a dear, and very agreeable to talk to, though I find it very difficult to hear what he says in his squeaky voice. His very small studio is piled thick with half-finished portraits. He is much too 'fashionable'. I can't believe it can be good for his art to paint so many people at once. What a pleasant life! His favourite hobby, his principal pleasure for a highly lucrative profession. Paid to do what he would pay to be allowed to do—and the days passed in the company of, on the whole, very agreeable people. He seems to realise how fortunate he is. He loves discussing his models, but is really pretty guarded. He never abuses, and though lavish with dewdrops, never really raves about any individual—at least never gives anyone the palm.

My father-in-law was the next appointment in his crowded day. He is doing a good thing of him. The picture of Mary promises to be lovely, but I don't think it very like. I like his running, detailed commentary on one's face: 'I do like the modelling of your nose—that's lovely! What a wonderful colour your hair is—each lock a different shade! How long your lashes are!' I sat for about an hour-and-a-half. He works quickly and talks nearly all the time.

I lunched with Bluetooth. He was in much better spirits and we had rather fun. He had spent the last Sunday at Blenheim, where Diana had been making her debut. Lord Wimborne was of the party and the Duchess of Rutland, considering it a house of ill-fame, had presented Diana with a revolver and charged her to be sure and say at tea-time, in a loud voice, that her maid always slept with her! Mrs B. was to have gone, but Lord Ribblesdale vetoed it at the last minute. Lord Wimborne is said to have given instructions to have the locks removed from the doors!

Walked to my hospital. Kakoo and Betty were on my shift today. I thought I had got over my squeamishness, but was ashamed to find I felt as sick as ever at seeing poor Thomas who had just had both feet amputated. He was just coming round, moaning horribly, the bed-clothes propped right up revealing the two poor bound stumps. It made me feel very ill. Fancy the painful return to consciousness, and instead of knowing one had a baby, to know both one's feet were off. Ugh!

I tea-ed with Dorothy, and Gwendoline Osborne drove me home. I dined alone with Mary H., going and returning by bus. I am really getting very good at cheap locomotion. Think of the distances covered this day without one taxi!

Friday, 6th April

To my astonishment, woke up to find heavy snow falling. It had been so hot the night before. It is characteristic of my diary that I have never alluded to America having at last come in.

Very agreeable lunch with Duff. He told me of the cruel April Fool played on Lord Wimborne at Blenheim. They gave him a summons to breakfast with Lloyd George, the very circumstance he was longing in vain to bring about. He thinks he has a solution of the Irish question and he is also afraid of being *dégommé*.

Duff dropped me at the hospital. I enjoy my work there more and more. Poor Thomas looked ghastly ill, suffering from shock. Pamela flits from bed to bed being 'sweet'. I went round to Bruton Street when I got away. Michael was in excellent form as I pushed him home. I told him I had been boiling eggs: he was humiliatingly sceptical as to my efficiency—'You boil eggs!' My dinner in was no disappointment—delicious. First I wrote letters, then had dinner in bed—boiled egg and bread-and-milk, and then finished *A Sentimental Journey* and read half *Othello* out of the copy of the first folio Whibley gave me.

Saturday, 7th April

Kakoo, Moira, and Pamela herself were my fellow-workers at the hospital. Afterwards I went round to Bruton Street, and had tea and a thrilling talk with Mary. Astonished to hear my marriage was much canvassed, and by many thought unhappy and detached. How astonishing are impressions given and taken—and I thought I was proverbially 'uxorious', was almost anxious to soften that impression! It bears out the theory that you cannot have any friendships with men without people drawing the inference that you are detached from your husband. Obviously, from what Mary said, I have been considered in love with Basil. We discussed the difference between people—why some were immune from all gossip, though one couldn't put one's finger on any distinction between their conduct and that of those of the victims of gossip and conjecture of any kind. I suppose it depends a lot on the man. Some are known not to 'waste their time'. Of course, people always precipitate things. No one would believe that Basil had made no sort of declaration until a few months ago—but then I know I am particularly difficult to make love to, and of course outsiders don't know this. Why is one allowed to waste, or at least to spend time on a woman, and not allowed to spend as much on a man without being considered 'in love' with him. It is ridiculous!

She said the Asquiths' opinion was that I neglected Beb, didn't try and make the most of him by sufficient 'taking in hand', and that I thoroughly lowered his spirits and vitality. It is too comic, only it makes one angry. As a matter of fact, it is always in his family that I suffer from feeling Beb underrated.

Heard amusing story of the Curzons. He told her that her black garb, donned for the Duchess of Connaught's funeral, was not sufficiently deep mourning, though it was pitch-black. She said, 'I haven't got anything else, except my widow's weeds'.

Sunday, 8th April

I met Duff at Pagani's and lunched with him. This sudden *plaît* with him is funny after such long standing on the threshold. I find him excellent company—very good at both people and book discussion. He is just going off to Scotland for a week with the Montagus, Diana, and Scatters, and possibly Patrick. Diana and Scatters are now inseparable, a curious alliance.

Tuesday, 10th April

I dined with Violet and went in time to have a greatly appreciated bath. Cis dined, too. After dinner, Violet and I had a certain amount of gossip talk. I think her a brilliant raconteuse. This is a good 4 a.m.

pencil note of Margot's to Elizabeth's maid, 'Can't you do anything to improve Miss Elizabeth's appearance? She looks as if she slept under, instead of on, the bed.'

I had a letter from John's governess saying she would leave at the end of the month she was so disheartened by all the changes—all no doubt because she and Polly cannot work together. It's very disappointing.

Friday, 13th April

Mesopotamia Flag Day and Mary H. had undertaken the selling at Claridges. On me fell the task of arranging the luncheon tables, and I myself invited McEvoy, Eddie, and Willie de Grunne. I wore my lovely old black-and-white cloth dress and my aigrette hat. Michael was delighted and exclaimed, 'Oh, what a smart little Mummie!' I had great fun telling Brenda that old men—about whom I knew nothing—were millionaires and watching her ply all her arts. McEvoy was watching the scene with great psychological glee. It was a great success.

Monday, 16th April

A long letter from Basil and two from Beb, asking for chocolate, fresh vegetables, and so on—had to dash out to Selfridges and order things. Claud came at six. He is home on a week's leave. He stayed till a quarter to eight. I put on my black velvet and dined with Mrs Belville. Sat between General Lowther and Gordon Leith: Ava Astor was there, Ethel Higgins, and Lady de Trafford, Evelyn Fitzgerald, the editor of the *Daily Express*, and another man. Very disappointed to find there was no poker. Evelyn Fitzgerald talked Margot and politics to me after dinner. Gave tremendous eulogy to the Old Man— I hear he is very dewdroppy about me.

Tuesday, 17th April

Lunched alone with Claud in Audley Square. He was very typical, trying to mend an electric torch all the time. He told me Mr Balfour has gone to America to confer and advise, the first I heard of it. He also told me there had been an uproarious Republican meeting in London—a fact successfully suppressed in the Press. With Mr Balfour go Lord Eustace Percy, Eric Drummond, and General Bridges. I should think Mr Balfour would 'leave a very good impression in

America'. He is certainly very unlike an American. Did some gibbets with Claud. I must confess I felt him very much in love with me, but there was no trouble. He addressed me as 'beautiful Cynthia', but was otherwise agreeably formal. He showed me a short cut to my hospital. Poor Thomas, the man who had both feet amputated, had died on Friday. I'm afraid it must have been a case of mis-management.

When I got home found a letter from Freyberg which told me Oc has again been snatched away by a Staff on the brink of taking the offensive. How furious he must be! I went by bus to Margot Howard de Walden. I was introducing Tonks to her and we had the most delightful little dinner, just four with Steer. It was a really nice evening. They were both such dears. I liked Margot more than ever before. We agreed to preside over a Coterie of Artists. Tonks abused me for having my hair parted at one side, instead of down the middle. Said I must stick to my early Victorian type and ought to wear my hair in a coarse net. It is hard to be such an anachronism. After dinner we sat so happily by a log fire. Somehow we, as Puffin would say, 'dropped into poetry'. I shone in quoting, but was honest enough to confess it was with the 'sweat of my brow' that I knew so much by heart and not easily, as was suggested. I was pleased by Margot's story that once she and her husband, without realising it, were three weeks on end without ever leaving the house. Finally, their butler suggested that it might be a good thing for them to go out. Tonks and Steer walked me to a No. 2 bus.

Wednesday, 18th April

Pouring rain in the morning and I had to be at McEvoy's at 9.30. Stood waiting for a bus with room for ages, but finally gave it up and went in a taxi. McEvoy had a bad cold and wasn't quite himself. I think it must have affected his eyes because he kept raving about my eyelashes, which I have always felt to be my weakest point: they are neither long, nor dark, nor curly. Can it be the form of nerves which prompts me to admire my friends' ugliest hats?

Claud came in to see me sitting. His slow manner made me nervous at first, as I thought McEvoy would like a more prompt delivery of dewdrops, but as it happened he took a great fancy to Claud. The latter was looking through a collection of sketches, and I enquired who the 'nice old cup of tea' was. Rather to my confusion, McEvoy replied, 'That's my mother,' but it wasn't in the least a floater.

Dined alone with Claud. He is skilled in dumbly conveying his emotion. We did some gibbets. He took my hand on the pretext of telepathic assistance. He showed me albums full of amusing photographs of the family as children and youths—some of the Blackwoods, too. It is such a funny room, like a museum. There is even a machine for producing electricity. When I asked if I might use it, he replied, 'It is unnecessary—there is plenty in the room when a person of your magnetism is in it'.

I went back in the bus and called on Violet, still patiently waiting. She is taking a deliciously womanly, almost Dickensy, interest in her layette and showed me lots of tiny treasures. Bongie had actually bought some clothes himself in Paris—too touching. He walked me home and came in to see the flat. This must have finally murdered my reputation with the porter. Awful blow—a letter from my Schmidt tenants to say they must give up the house in a month. Blue ruin unless I can let it again at once.

Thursday, 19th April

I lunched at Bruton Street. Evie was there and an Irishman. They talked of the German cadaver factory which arouses such pious horror. I can't help seeing a certain magnificence in it. Freddie Blackwood called for me and we went to the Grosvenor Gallery Exhibition together. There are fourteen McEvoys there: I can't believe it can be right for him to be so prolific—they can't all be legitimate children.

Dined with Bluetooth. Small party: the Gilberts, Goonie and Ivor Churchill, a most delightful boy, wonderfully like his mother to look at and so intelligent and charming. I loved him. Gilbert was entertaining after dinner. We cross-examined him and debated as to how he could be so happy considering that, according to his own confession, he was without any tastes or hobbies except food and drink. He seemed to have no keys and yet claimed—and rightly—an unusually large share of enjoyment.

Friday, 20th April

McEvoy got on well, I think, with the watercolour and announced his welcome intention of doing me in oils as well. Nannie brought Michael to see me and Freddie came. Not recognising the portrait of Betty Cranborne, he said firmly that he didn't know her—unfortunately, the next moment she herself came in, and greeted him as an obviously near and dear friend!

Lawrence came to see me. He has not moved from Cornwall for over a year, so it had been a long interval. He looked better. I still found great interest and vividness in his face and voice, and he wove the most interesting theories round the John mystery. He thinks him the logical conclusion of generations of frustration and conforming to an unreal plane. The result being that John is quite off the plane I have violated myself in order to remain on. He is certain his state is spiritual not mental and a case for exorcism, and said I could cure him by getting off the false unreal plane of 'buses, Lloyd George's speeches and so on, to which I was now clinging. He said the first time he saw John he had noted the revolt in his eyes, the subconscious antagonism. He believed he could help. He talked about the war—assured me Beb wouldn't be killed if I didn't want him to be and reproached me for 'subscribing to the war' to the extent of working in a hospital.

He said he had not made a portrait of Ottoline in his new novel. His woman was infinitely superior, but the Morrells were so furious at the supposed lampoon that Morrell wrote—inconceivable as it sounds—to the publisher, asking him to come down and identify the character as his wife, and Ottoline asked Lawrence to return an opal pin she had given him. Fancy calling in that worm of a publisher as detective!

Saturday, 21st April

Stayed in bed late and wrote to Beb, Basil, and Alex. Had a letter from Basil from the Ritz in Paris, where he was enjoying two days' leave. Freddie is trying hard to get him on to a Staff, but I'm afraid he is going to be obstinate. Lord Derby has written to Haig about him.

Went round to see Violet. I lunched at Cavendish Square. My little adorer Puffin was very pleased to see me. Margot taxed me with having said she had asked for Oc to be taken on the Staff. She was rather 'hen-a-hoop' and pleased with herself for having told McEvoy he couldn't draw. P.M. not looking very well—very dear. He asked after John. I did gibbets with Puffin.

Went by Tube to Bluetooth, dined with him and took him to the great movie *Intolerance* which, as the papers say, 'leaves the spectators gasping'. It is an incredible thing—such a *mélange*—great stories each seen in snippets, now a glimpse of the Crucifixion, then a man being hung in America, alternating with scenes from Babylon and the Massacre of St Bartholomew. The Babylon pictures were spectacularly marvellous. Diana and the Montagus were in the same row, and Claud in the Russell box with his brother Harold and a daughter. I enjoyed it very much and Bluetooth was delightful all the evening. He drove me home in a four-wheeler.

Sunday, 22nd April

Sleepy in the morning. Telephoned to enquire after Violet and found her baby had been born at five that morning—a girl. I went round to see it at once. Quite a nice little brunette—plenty of hair. It's eyes were shut, but the 'sockets', as Keithy said, were very large. Left a note for Violet.

Lawrence came and we took Michael out. He pushed the pram. Michael's hair and his beard were a perfect match. We looked a funny sight. We went to the Zoo and enjoyed it very much. Michael deliciously happy and exhibiting a surprising knowledge of animals. He liked Lawrence very much. He was being delightful and whimsical. How amazingly unlike he is to his books, in which there is no gleam of humour!

I went by bus to dine with Claud. He gave me delicious whiting. Claud very amorous. It is difficult to snub any liberties he chooses to take because his 'drollness' is a sort of armour and I couldn't help laughing when, on my edging away, he said, 'I suppose you think I shall put my arm round your waist, though why you should think anything of the sort I don't know', and he had just done so. His languid effrontery makes me laugh and somehow it is inoffensive. He has considerable charm for me. He walked me all the way home.

Monday, 23rd April

Found a note from Freyberg saying he was back for one day, and could I lunch with him at the Berkeley. He was looking wonderfully well, and literally glowing with joy and exhilarating self-confidence. He had just got his Brigade. It was really delicious to see a man so happy. He kept on exclaiming. 'You can't understand what this means to me. I am only twenty-seven, therefore eight years younger than any other Brigadier. I've been put over thousands of heads—my command is now five miles long and what's more, I feel fully competent for the job.' He enumerated all the counts under him with the tenderness of a child for its toys. He smote the table with his fist until the Berkeley rang and said solemnly, 'I promise you that if they give me what I ask for I shall be able to take any position.' I was touched and impressed by him. He spoke with tears in his eyes at his pain at leaving the Hood Battalion, and of how his men had cut off his buttons as souvenirs— said he meant to run his Brigade as intimately as he had his Battalion and his firmest resolve seemed to be to quarrel with the generals. His brigade is composed of London Territorials, as yet unbaptised by fire, and he is to be under General Gough to whose support he owes his promotion. Of course it has been much opposed on the ground of his youth and there is no little bitterness. He explained how ruthlessly he eliminates any officer falling short of his standard. He said he had backed himself to be a brigadier within the year eleven months ago, and thinks he will have a division in a year if the war is still on. When it is over he has got the eighteen-month job of superintending the evacuation of France—after that, he intends to go to Mesopotamia or wherever he hopes there might be fighting. He ate Homerically, laying down his fork to exclaim: 'How I love fighting!'

All this sounds melodramatic and vainglorious, but it is completely inoffensive, so unselfconscious and simple is he in his complete self-confidence. I really enjoyed seeing him and am very glad he wished for my company on his one day. He was a wonderful contrast to Lawrence in point of view. I felt very much sympathy with both. I wonder if it is a good thing to be so fluid.

Claud came before six, stayed while I dressed for dinner, and dropped me at the Carlton. He told me he hadn't liked my voice at first but had got used to it. Wondered whether he would have fallen in love with me ten years ago. He is a queer lover. He complained of loneliness in London—said he only wanted to see me. Very agreeable dinner with Duff. Conversationally, we suit each other perfectly. We went to the cinema afterwards. He is appearing to be in love with me now. Told me he liked being with me better than anyone else—tried to be demonstrative in the taxi but, as with Claud, I escaped with kissed hand. He pressed me to dine again with him, suggesting each day in the week. I pleaded engagements and then going to Stanway. I don't want to get into the way of doing nothing but *tête-à-tête* dinners.

Tuesday, 24th April

I dined with Claud. He was on his best behaviour and didn't 'tease' me at all. He walked me all the way home. I had left my umbrella in the taxi the night before and telephoned to Duff to ask if he had it. He couldn't find it at the cinema and sent me a lovely new one with a tortoiseshell handle—very sweet of him and such impressive promptitude, initials and all!

Wednesday, 25th April

Slept badly and woke with heavy cold. Mercifully I had Mary's motor to take me to McEvoy and wasn't so very late for my 9.45 appointment with him. I was rather disappointed to find he had washed all the colour out of it again. He congratulated me on the feather in my cap of having shared Freyberg's one lunch with him—said it would arouse great jealousy.

Thursday, 26th April

Woke up feeling very disfigured by my cold, but I had to go and sit to McEvoy at 9.30. He was rather tired and out of spirits, felt baffled by the watercolour and began, I thought, a brilliant oil sketch. He took a great fancy to the little brown Mercury hat I had rescued from Scotland Yard after leaving it in a taxi, and made me wear it. He kept saying what a wonderful model I was.

Went to lunch at Cavendish Square. F. E. Smith arrived under the impression that he was lunching with Lady Cunard. On seeing the room getting thicker and thicker with Asquiths, he became suspicious and said, 'I am lunching with Lady Cunard, aren't I?' He rushed off when enlightened as to the situation. I wore my pretty pink Kosky hat. Michael came round afterwards. I had been dreading the Margot ordeal and no doubt Nurse was in the same boat, but she found nothing to say against him. Moira told me an amusing story of Lady Wolverton. The latter, thinking the time had come to economise, got into a bus. She sat beside a woman who kept loudly sniffing and she asked her aggressively if she hadn't got a handkerchief. The woman replied: 'Yes, but I never lends it in a bus.'

Frances, Aileen, and I had arranged to go to *Damaged Goods*, the play for 'adults only'. Aileen called for me in her little motor and we dined at Catherine Street. Guy and a brother officer, a Captain Gough, were there. They tried to dissuade us from going. Frances and Aileen were very half-hearted, but Dinah and I were determined to stick to our plans. We all went, but Frances and Aileen went out after the first act. Dinah and I sat it out, and I must say I was quite interested. It isn't in the least artistically good—a sheer tract—but I didn't feel it boring and I should think it may be useful. It is, of course, unavoidably unpleasant, but I don't think gratuitously so, though crude and unconvincing in places.

Friday, 27th April

Spent most of the morning tidying up my drawers, having become self-conscious about them as Polly's arrival approached. Had a really depressed letter from poor Basil. He seemed utterly bored with being a platoon commander out of the trenches, and only wishing the attack would begin.

Mary H. sent her motor for me and I called at her awful labyrinth of an office. We both went to lunch with Margot Howard de Walden, Augustus John, and Steer came. I had never met John before. He is very magnificent-looking, huge and bearded. His appearance reduced Margot's two-year-old girl to terrified tears. I like him but felt very shy with him. There was a certain malaise over us. Mary and I both exhibited our faces, hoping he might want to paint us. He is doing a portrait of Margot and at one time asked her to sit for the 'altogether', saying she had such a perfect artist's figure. It is more convenient to have an artist's face.

Steer is a sweet. He once very delicately asked Margot if she had ever seen Mary without her clothes, saying she had such beautiful bones and he was anxious to know if they were continued throughout. Margot once asked John how many wives he really had (he is rather a mythical figure), saying she heard he was a most immoral man. He indignantly replied, 'It's monstrous—I'm a very moderate man. I've only got *one* wife!'

Spent the afternoon at house agents, trying to dispose of both my town properties. I dined with Claud—wore my yellow taffeta which is greatly admired. Had a good many *passages* with him. Luckily his whimsicality generally makes it easy to laugh it off. He *would* caress my foot which was on the sofa. When I took it down he begged me to put it up again, saying he promised not to touch it again as long as he might just look at it. He then took my hand, saying he supposed he might touch that, as long as he didn't look at it. He kissed my foot when he was doing up my shoe. He asked me if I believed he was in love with me, but withdrew, saying it wasn't a fair question. He said he thought I was sceptical about his love, and said perhaps I preferred the word 'moppy', as he will call soppy, as being less serious. He presented me with the most gorgeous white and red Spanish shawl—too lovely—but I think I must be careful with him. He walked me home and telephoned to me when he got back.

Saturday, 28th April

Polly brought John to lunch in the flat. It was tantalising and painful. The two boys looked so delicious together and one felt poignantly what fun one ought to be having with them. Michael was so sweet, trying to entertain John and offering him his toys one after the other.

'Will you play ball with me? No?' John knocked him down. Poor Nurse looked very wistful and it made us unhappy.

Nannie cooked us a delicious lunch. We had early tea and Polly, John, his governess and I went down to Stanway by the 4.55. Found Papa, Mamma, Mary Strickland, Bibs, and the Montagus.

Sunday, 29th April

A lovely spring day. It made one feel limp but it was very delicious, and it's a great gain not to have purple hands after about nine months of them. The daffodils are lovely here. This reminds me of a wonderful passage in a letter from Lawrence: 'It is much best for you to go down to Stanway. The spring is here, the cuckoo is heard, primroses and daffodils are out in the woods, it is very lovely. I feel that the buds as they unfold and the primroses as they come out, are really stronger than all the armies and all the war. I feel as if the young grass growing would upset all the cannon on the face of the earth, and that man with his evil stupidity is after all nothing—the leaves just brush him aside. The principle of life is, after all, stronger than the principle of death, and I spit on your London and your government and your armies. Pah! What are they, Lloyd George and Haig and such-like *canaille*? *Canaille, canaille*, the lot of them—also Balfour—old poodle that he is.' I like the poodle climax.

I went to see Venetia in bed after breakfast. She doesn't eat any and sleeps late. It was the anniversary of her engagement, and Montagu had given her a lovely ornament. On her bed lay a long letter from him. It began: 'My most precious darling.' We played tennis, Venetia and I against Mary and Montagu. We won.

After tea Mamma, Mary, Bibs, Montagu, and I walked to Cromwell's clump, up that heavenly 'primrose path of dalliance' to Hailes. It was a lovely evening, but socially rather an ordeal. Mamma and Montagu aren't happy together. Bibs had the sullens. The Allens and Bateman came to dinner. Eustace in supreme form. He was wildly excited over my beautiful Spanish shawl, which I wore draped round me, and very intrigued to know how it went on. Venetia nearly stripped me in an effort to explain. Naturally, there were a great many St Anthony jokes after he had gone.

Monday, 30th April

Montagus went away early. Lovely day. Great picnic on the 'primrose path' of Hailes Wood: the Allens, Bateman, Mamma, Mary, Bibs, and

1917

I. Divided our rations very carefully. Mr Allen collected crumbs in an envelope to take home to his dogs. Both priests were very happy— Bateman incredibly playful. He tickled me with a straw when I tried to go to sleep and made me say 'God!' but he didn't seem to wince.

Tuesday, 1st May

Twenty-five wounded soldiers came to tea and lay about happily on the grass, looking like large gentians. They picked daffodils and had sausages for tea. Read a little Keats to Mamma and Mary before going to bed. Feel very unhappy about Mamma, poor, poor darling.

Thursday, 3rd May

Mary and I travelled up to London yesterday. Went by my two buses to McEvoy this morning. He worked first at the oil, then at the water-colour, rapidly effacing any resemblance to me in either of them. His funny little wife with a Phil May fringe and a goitrous neck was there.

Friday, 4th May

Put on my tennis clothes and went by Tube to Baron's Court to play with Scatters, F. E. Smith, and Venetia. Lovely morning. It was terrifying tennis—a very high standard of play. I played with Scatters, who is the best, and we gave them half fifteen. We each won one set. Scatters is all over the court—wonderfully active. F. E. played an odious 'man at the net game' and pulverised me into sending the ball straight into the lion's mouth time after time—or, in trying to avoid him, I sent it gaily out. Scatters would shout minute directions as to the exact spot where I was to place my return—disconcerting when, as was often the case, I was wondering whether there was an off-chance of my getting it up at all. We all drove back to London with F. E. and then Scatters took me on in a taxi. He took me into a flower shop and bunched me exuberantly—a lovely growing rose, masses of daffodils, and a carnation to wear. He is a funny ebullient bounder, with his blue eyes and hoarse whisper. 'Well, angel, how are your finances?' was a typical remark he addressed to me.

Went to see Violet—very appalled by her beauty, her skin is trans-figured. She was very nice and happy. The baby is terribly pretty, Ottoline, looking like a nightmare, was there when I went in.

Lady Cynthia in her 'agency' hat

Lord Basil Blackwood

Augustine Birrell

Lady Wimborne

H. H. Asquith

Venetia Stanley and her pet bear

Aubrey Herbert

Raymond Asquith

Put on my goldfish dress to dine with the Leeds. Quite a big party
—Lord Hugh, Eddie, Hugh, David Henderson, Raymond Green,
McEvoy, Mabel Montgomery, the Duchess, Moira, and Gwendoline.
The Osbornes gave me wonderful looks and wit dewdrops from
McEvoy, and he came and talked to me. He is a most delightful man,
an artist in flattery. He told me of his dream of founding a sort of
guild in the country and producing tapestry, and so on. He offered
to drive me home. Eddie hooked on to us and insisted on taking him
by Tube to his house. They came into my basement. McEvoy didn't
think much of the Tonks and said, 'There's still a chance for me'.

Saturday, 5th May

Was dining and going to *Hamlet* alone with Duff, but Diana, Letty
and Alan Parsons hooked on to us, to Duff's ill-concealed annoyance. We dined at the Savoy and went to *Hamlet* late. I had had no
time to rest and was tired. *Manqué* evening, except for the play which
I loved seeing. It is gorgeous, though the 'quotations' make one almost
shy. H.B. Irving is good in the pathetic and melodramatic parts, but
too old, heavy, and inflexible for the lighter, failing in the satiric parts.
His face is nice, but not sensitive enough. Hamlet's should be as the
surface of a pond and he should have such lightness. The rest of
the cast were all pretty bad. He has cut it a great deal, but fairly
skilfully.

Monday, 7th May

Had the utmost difficulty in getting on to my bus at nine o'clock to go
to McEvoy. I fought like a beast, but others fought more successfully
and I failed to get on three consecutive ones. Arrived late at the studio.
McEvoy's paintings of me are certainly Penelope's webs. When I
began this sitting the oil painting of me was nearly full face, half an
hour later it had been turned away to three-quarter face, and by the
end of the morning's work it was dead profile. McEvoy seemed rather
overtired and nervy. He has been called up for re-examination before
a medical board. He implied that he would be glad to fight, but as
there was no chance of that he hoped he would be left to paint in
peace, rather than put in an office.

I dined with Mary H. Hugh and Alan were the other guests. We
went on to a war charity concert at Lady Cunard's. It was such a
long time since I had been to a Mayfair crush—extraordinary to hear
such a gaggle of geese again. Margot Howard sang well but nervously,

and was abused by her cruel teacher Olga Lynn, who herself gave an exhibition of great technical skill. Birrell, old sweet, sat beside me groaning with music boredom. He asked me if Margot's voice was what you called a 'su frano'.

Tuesday, 8th May

Felt very tired, ill and despondent in the morning, very conscious of my heart beating—a sensation I hate. Docketing my bills, which took me most of the morning, was not a cheerful occupation and I didn't have the nerve to add them up.

Claud came at 6.15. Michael annoyed at his being in mufti. He stayed till after eight. I told him I was going to write my diary and he said, 'I suppose you will write, "I thought he was never going away".' He expatiated on the theme of how much more beautiful I was than he had at first thought. He asked me if I admired myself. I said I did, very much. On cross-examination, I found he was prejudiced enough to have preferred me to adhere to hypocritical cant and say 'No'. Dinner in bed. Read *Bleak House*. Had a glowing letter from Freyberg saying, 'Life is very sweet just now'—also a very good new battle poem from Beb.

Wednesday, 9th May

Lunched with Freddie and Brenda. Bobbetty and Betty were there. Brenda had been bunched some delicious plovers' eggs. Freddie seemed very depressed. I suppose he is dreadfully anxious about Basil, afraid of the Guards going in soon. Went to the hospital. They are taking rations seriously now and we are not allowed to give the men more than three slices—it goes very much against the grain.

Went and had tea with Claud. He gave me a Belgian necklace and apologised for having 'teased' me. Rested. Dined with Mary H. and wore my Spanish shawl with great éclat. Brenda was astonished when she heard whom it came from. I sat next to that delightful Ivor Churchill, whom I had invited. He is a darling. Freddie, Brenda, Ruby, Alan, and Duff were the rest of the dinner and Margot H. came afterwards. We played poker, I coining £4 9s. Mary had a good telephone message from Miss Way—would she bring three bad bridge players with her to the Wharf on Sunday. As a matter of fact, it was a mistake for 'was she able to play bridge enough to play with three bad players'.

Thursday, 10th May

Maddening morning. Was disconnected from the telephone owing to
the previous tenant not having paid her bill. All my expostulations
with the controller were in vain—they refused to reconnect me until
they received the cheque. It was just like having one's tongue cut out.

I went round to F. E. Smith to pick him up for tennis. He showed
me his library, immense and magnificent. We taxied down to Queen's
together. He told me that it was, as I surmised, to me and not to Beb
that he had given that post.[1] He is a magnificent bounder, and I can't
help liking him. His appearance is like something in a novelette—
the Zeppelin-like cigar always in his mouth and the reliefs of good
living on his face. We found Scatters and Rosie Boote (Lady Headfort)
waiting for us. I was amused at the *galère* I found myself in. Scatters
and I played together and won two very stubbornly contested sets.
He is amazingly active—all over the place and very difficult to play
with. He takes practically every ball, and when at last one has to tackle
one, one's hand and eye aren't in at all and out they go.

Dined with Claud, was very happy with him and able to cope with
what he calls his 'teasing'. He kissed my fingers one by one. He walked
me home.

Friday, 11th May

Evelyn and Mary Herbert called in the little motor at 9.30 to take me
to McEvoy's. Mary's driving rather alarming. He worked away at
his Greek coin rendering of me. Alex came in, and Dorothy and
Aileen. Walked away with Alex, who is home for three days' Parliamentary leave. We went as far as Victoria, where I mounted a bus,
and he went off to the continuation of the Secret Session begun the
night before. He said Lloyd George had made a most feather-brained
speech, saying there was plenty of food in the country—no cause for
alarm—with many of his statistics flagrantly wrong.

I lunched with Gilbert and Maud. Claud was there and we went
off together. He waited for me for ages outside Kosky[2] and then
we sat in Hyde Park for some time. He was by way of returning to
Ireland that night.

Saturday, 12th May

I had been dining with Claud, but Brenda persuaded me to bring

1. See p. 227.   2. Milliner.

him to dinner with Margot Howard de Walden. Prince Leo had had his excellent regimental band up to play for the entertainment of the Canadian officers Margot had had to tea. The band were sleeping in the stables, so she thought she would make use of them and got up an impromptu dinner/dance.

Claud came rather unwillingly. I sat between him and Summie, and so had an agreeable dinner. We were about fourteen: Brenda, Moira, Mrs Higgins, Letty, Prince Leo,* Freddie, and a sprinkling of diplomats. A good many more people came in after dinner. Margot sang to the band, divinely—it was quite a different thing to her performance at the concert. There was a good deal of dancing. The music teased my heart and it seemed a mockery of an old times dance. One looked for vanished faces and winced at the mushroom growth of strange men. Letty revolved round the room with her tragic mask of a face. What a mistake the 'business as usual' attitude is!

It was rather an inchoate evening. As a non-dancer, one didn't quite know what to do. I spent most of the time keeping Claud in a good temper until late in the evening Freddie and I got up some poker. Alex and an anonymous young man played with us. I ended up square. Letty outraged poor Alex's feelings by addressing him as 'Fatty'. Margot's patriotism was such that not one bite of food was given. People were holding their stomachs with hunger and there was a good deal of murmuring. Alex, wishing to drive me home, prevaricated when Jeffie Darell offered me a lift in her motor, and accepted when he discovered I was going with her. She was facetious about it. It was about two when I got home. In the morning I had a letter from Basil saying he really thought there was at last the very near prospect of leave for him. Hurrah!

Sunday, 13th May

Stayed in bed. Went through my poems. Bibs visited me, and I said 'Allegro' to her. Lunched in my dressing-gown with the nursery party. Went back to bed again, getting up in my yellow taffeta to receive Alex at five. He stayed a long time. Mary H. scarcely takes my word for it any longer that he doesn't make love to me. Certainly it doesn't accord with his reputation, but, though he lays each day of his leave at my disposal, I am grateful to say he has so far not given me one moment's embarrassment.

I dined with Claud at the Curzon Hotel. We walked there from his house whither we returned after dinner. He makes love to me continuously, but doesn't offend me or ever seriously embarrass. He has a certain amount of magnetism for me, but I have no fear of its being 'fire' I am playing with. It's curious how much more capable of mild flirtatiousness I have become lately. He took me home.

Monday, 14th May

Letter from poor Beb saying he had neuralgia, toothache, and an abscess. He hoped to see a dentist the next day, but feared the nearest was twenty miles back. Had lunch in dressing-gown with Michael and stayed in bed all day. Went to the Savoy for early dinner with Duff. Brushed my hair back off my forehead and wore it 'without a path' as Michael says: surprised to find it suits me very well.

Duff and I went to see *Ghosts*—very well acted. How horrible it is! There could be nothing worse than the mother watching her son's brain softening. I think the *comble* is when the wretched man says the words 'softening of the brain' always make him think of 'cherry-coloured velvet'. Argued with Duff as to whether it was a tract or not. We walked home and then were lucky enough to find a taxi. Nearly all the buses are off owing to a strike. Duff said that Nancy Astor went in for all the follies that flesh is heir to, and that poor Elizabeth is a 'bludgeoning bore' who left him feeling his head was 'bowed' and she was 'bloody'. At my door he was anxious to be affectionate in both word and deed, and made me laugh by saying, 'I hate that horrid old chaperon of yours' when the old porter bustled up with his keys to let me in.

Tuesday, 15th May

Mary H. took me to Halkyn Place in her little motor. We discussed Alex. What an amazing man he is! His relationship with me is very strange when one tries to reconcile it with what one hears about him. He places every day of his leave at my disposal, and comes and sits with me for hours, but with the most extreme formality and decorum —he has never so much as touched my finger. I suppose my evident embarrassment alarms him prohibitively, and yet he considers my conversation and friendship worth while on the other plane and so keeps to it. Thank God for that same alarmingness!

Thursday, 17th May

After a month's drought it was pouring and pouring with rain, and I got soaked walking to Evan's. Ettie and Ole-Luk-Oie (Colonel

Swinton) were lunching with him. I thought the latter a most delightful man. He has a charming shrewd face and talked very well—an extremely easy stranger. Had a great argument as to the ethics of the *Cadaver Anstalt*. I saw Ettie off at Paddington: Nancy Astor was in the next carriage. She leapt at me and said, 'I do so want you to try Christian Science for a time'.

Dined at Ava Astor's. It was a huge dinner—quite prehistoric it seemed and there was no nonsense about rations. The rooms are rather lovely, but such 'reception' ones—purely for entertaining. One can't imagine them as the scene of anyone's private life. I had a bad attack of collar-bone-necklace nerves. I sat between the Comte de Noailles and Winston. The latter was in excellent form—he spoke lyrically of Freyberg and reiterated through clenched teeth, 'Mr Britling hasn't nearly seen it through yet.' He continually exclaimed, 'How clever you are!' Lord Charles Beresford, the Ronald Grahams, Joan Poynder, Clemmie, Evan, old Lady Paget, Moira Cavendish were amongst the other guests. There was bridge. Joan, Noailles, and I got up poker which we played joined by dummies. I won about thirty shillings.

Friday, 18th May

Claud had announced his return to London (his soldiering seems a farce) and came to see me about eleven. I took him round to my house to fetch some books. It was looking very nice and I was swept on a wave of homesickness. Started reading 'Adonais' to Claud—dropped him at Audley Square and lunched at Cadogan Square. Converstaion with Mamma afterwards. She told me of the terrible Campbell McInnes melodrama. He has become a raving drunkard and she[1] is going to divorce him. She has just been packed off to Clouds with her new baby. Fancy he and poor, tiny, little Phil[2] had a ghastly struggle at Rottingdean and Phil actually downed him!

Went to the hospital. Pamela was there. Discussion in the pantry as to the relative charms of Lord Blandford, Ivor Churchill, and Ivo Grenfell.* Pamela commissioned me to keep Ivor in hand until Daveena was ready to marry him. There was an awful horror in the ward—a poor man dying with a broken back.

Ivor Churchill had invited me to dinner and poker, and I went to Sunderland House and his mother, Lord Blandford, he, Goonie, Edgar, Wolkoff, Fox Macdonald, Moira Osborne and I had dinner in a gorgeous marble room at the window of which children of the proletariat were flattening their noses and kicking up a row. At intervals

---

1. Later Angela Thirkell, see index.   2. Sir Philip Burne-Jones.

they were chivvied away by footmen. It was a strange junction of east and west and smacked of pre-revolution. I sat between Fox and Lord Blandford. The latter is, I think, a very nice boy, though not such a finished manikin as Ivor. Moira, Wolkoff, Blandford, Ivor and I played some very amusing, enjoyable poker at which I won £3 6s. I wore my black velvet and unparted hair. All approved of the latter. A very pleasant evening—either of those boys would do admirably for Bibs.

Tuesday, 22nd May

Lunched at Cadogan Square—Mrs Pat Campbell and Mabel Montgomery were there. Mrs C. disfiguringly fat. She was going to recite at a hospital and gave us a dress rehearsal. It was a battle poem about heroism at Soissons and was really curdling. She did it well bringing tears to our eyes.

Monday, 28th May

Duff and I were to have dined together, but we were both conscripted into the Parsons' dinner for dear old Birrell. It was a very successful little party, only Parsons, Duff, Diana, Birrell and I. A bold experiment undertaken—might have been a grim failure but came off very well. We each in turn read aloud a purple patch in literature of our own choosing. Diana reclined on a couch à la Madame Récamier and was in excellent face and lovely dress. Viola and Birrell read Lady Gregory's 'Workhouse Ward' together in brogues admirably. Duff, in the best ecclesiastical voice I have ever heard, read some perfect Thomas Browne. My choice was 'The Bishop Orders his Tomb' and the 'injurious time' bit of Troilus and Cressida. Amused Birrell by referring to Basil as 'Dufferin's boy'. Duff drove me home—proffers of affection successfully daunted.

Tuesday, 29th May

Basil rang up first thing in the morning. He had arrived unexpectedly at night. Mistook his voice for Freddie's. He is staying with Claud, funnily enough. Terribly oppressive day, finally expressed by violent thunderstorm while I was at the hospital. Very excited by prospect of Basil coming to fetch me. He came at three o'clock looking very brown, wonderfully well, and not a day older. I felt very shy. We had tea at Gunter's and then went to the flat.

Dined with Claud at the Curzon Hotel. Basil, knowing his secretiveness, asked him where he was dining. Claud said he would have answered, 'With an old tutor', but Basil's manner made him suspect a joke so he answered truthfully. He walked me home, rehearsing my 'decalogue' for him.

Wednesday, 30th May

Much cooler after thunder. To McEvoy at 9.30. Basil came at a quarter to eleven. Didn't like either of my pictures. We lunched together at Claridges and had great fun. We were appalled into hysterics by the entry of old Lord Brassey. He comes into the room bent double, supporting himself on a sort of trolley with wheels, and it took him quite half an hour to 'gain his seat', during which time all eating and conversation is suspended. It seems to me amazing to think it worth going to Claridges otherwise than on one's feet. I believe he does it nearly every day, and I suppose M. Charles (prince of head waiters) only whispers in a church voice behind his hand, as he did to us, 'Poor Lord Brassey.' Claridges had recently become the most fashionable place in London. Is this due to Charles or to Lord Brassey's comic turn?

Basil very *intrigué* about my relations with Claud and Alex. I pitied poor Alex for having to pretend to like Dickens—he walked me to my hospital. Picked up Claud on my way to dinner with Mamma and Whibley at Cadogan Square. Very pleasant dinner. Basil joined us afterwards, after having dutifully dined with his mother. He and I rushed rather rudely out of the house, without saying goodnight to Whibley and Claud, so as to escape their company. We had the good fortune to find a taxi, and he took me home and came in for some time. Gave him some Bengers. Seeing him again has not been a disappointment. He thinks my new coiffure an improvement.

Thursday, 31st May

Have let myself drift into a very false position. Feel I am cheating and don't know what to do. Lunched at Evan's with him, Dorothy and Basil—fireworks of chaff between Evan and Basil. Dined with Basil at the Berkeley and then went to his house in Glebe Place. I often wish we were back in the undefined phase and miss my old friend.

Friday, 1st June

Very distressed and worried, also very tired having slept badly, so I

stayed in bed late. Lunched with Michael. Basil called for me after-
wards and we went to see Eddie at the Colonial Office, and then to see
McEvoy's pictures at the Grosvenor Gallery. Basil converted to him.
Had tea together at Gunters.

Dined with Jeffie Darell, Basil, Freddie, Brenda, Gilbert, Maud,
and Prince Leo. Brothers Blackwood and Gilbert in music-hall turn
vein. I was feeling rather tired and dank. We went to *Zig Zag*. Excellent it was. I delighted in George Robey. Jeffie's motor took us home.
Basil insisted on coming in with me when my door was reached at
11.30. I don't think he ought to have before Prince Leo and Freddie
and Brenda, but I was too shy to expostulate. He stayed some time.

Saturday, 2nd June

Very tired. Got up late. Basil came to see me before luncheon. He
was going down to Cliveden for one night—a small concession to
Nancy's avidity. I upbraided him for his moral cowardice. Went to
hospital where there was a plague of eggs. Claud called for me and
came home. He was distressed because he had a spot on his nose and
was also in low spirits, but he said, I 'did him good'. He stayed long
enough to give the cure a fair trial at any rate. I read him 'Love in a
Valley'—new to him. Dinner in bed—a respite I was glad of.

Monday, 4th June

Stayed in bed most of the day. Picked Basil up at Audley Square
and took him to dinner at the Montagus. It is funny his staying in the
same house as Claud, and involves a lot of telephoning to one number
on my part. Large dinner party. I sat between Lavery and Alan Parsons.
Poker—ridiculous scene. Basil, in protest against Diana's autocracy,
insisting on shuffling the cards against her orders. A shiver went
through her court, and she and Alan sent him to Coventry!

I didn't enjoy the dinner very much. No taxis available. Basil
took me home in the Tube and stayed some time.

Tuesday, 5th June

Stayed in bed until after lunch. Went to see Claud. Mamma came to
us for tea. Dined early with Moyra Cavendish: party was her, Dick,
Basil, self, Eddie and Adele. Parlourmaid came in quaking with fear,
the potatoes rattling in the dish, and informed us that the postman had
told her the worst raid yet known was then in progress over London.

The women behaved well. We went to the revue *Cheep*. No one appreciated it much except Eddie. Moyra had electric car and Basil was firmly dropped first so he wouldn't come home with me.

Wednesday, 6th June

Have been in terrible plight of being nearly a whole month without a diary to write in. It will be a grim grind to write it up from my mere jottings on odd bits of paper—and it will be but a cursory account of this bit of life.

I was to have sat to McEvoy this morning, but chucked and walked in the park with Basil instead. Went to 'see life' in Rotten Row and was amused by meeting my two sisters—Claud turned up and was mercilessly chaffed about his mossy clothes by Freddie. Took Basil to lunch at Cavendish Square: it was a Stars and Stripes lunch—the American admiral, and so on. Basil had got out of his Nancy dinner, but I suggested and he agreed, that he had better dine alone with his Freddie and come on to me afterwards.

Went to tea with Claud. Freddie came in and looked embarrassed. Dined with Duff at the Carlton—excellent talk. He drove me home and I put on my Spanish shawl to receive Basil. He arrived very late and must have murdered my reputation with the hall porter. He stayed for a very, very long time. He was shocked at the gift of the shawl and lectured me about having tea in Claud's house.

Thursday, 7th June

Basil's last hectic morning. I met him at the Berkeley to give him early lunch before going to the station. Drove there in a taxi—he was armed with a fishing rod which looked re-assuring. I had written him a very difficult letter that morning, which I gave him to read after he had gone. It was not so poignantly dramatic as last time since, instead of taking out a draft, he went in a Staff train. Jeffie turned up and Claud —I thought it was pointless to stay and went off before they got into the train—Claud drove me away and we lunched together at the Curzon.

Friday, 8th June

Lunched with Whibley at Kettners. Driving away, he made the most passionate declarations to me. It really is too inconvenient—I like him so very much as a mental companion and don't know how to cope with the present situation. I don't believe he is in the least conscious of being a gnome, but sees himself as a *jeune premier* and my resistance the result of native prudishness merely. The next day he wrote me an incredible letter about 'the golden afternoon in Piccadilly' when there was nothing else in the world but me.

Went unsuitably dressed in Spanish shawl to a very comic dinner of Mamma's: Dr Cobb, Evan, Wells, Schreiner, and Adele. I thought Cobb looked an evil man of God, Schreiner was very heavy in hand, Wells deliciously amusing. Mamma gave Evan and me ridiculous giggles by addressing Cobb as Hobb. Mamma had hired a coupé for him, so it was arranged that I should drive him to his Kensington home and then take it on. Evan said, 'You'll be hobnobbing all night.'

Saturday, 9th June

Tonks paid me a long visit at 5.30. Told me that Eddie had—I am quite certain unconsciously—deeply offended him by appearing to slight a heart's blood picture of his. He alleged that Eddie had not even thought it worth commenting on, and had held a book up to his face while Tonks was showing it to him—he was quite vindictive about poor little Eddie.

Tuesday, 12th June

Still extraordinarily hot—a wonderful spell of weather. What a June! but I wish we could have saved up the weather for our seaside July. I lunched at Cavendish Square: Bobbetty and Betty were there, and I sat beside Louis Mallet. The dear Old Boy[1] was delighted with Oc's great success as colonel of the Hood Battalion—he had just been awarded a clasp to his D.S.O. and his father handed the King's letter of congratulation all round the table with proud sniffs.

By some lucky chance, I then paid an impromptu call on Nathalie. With her I found a young Russian woman who was looking for a house with a garden and near a Tube. I immediately whipped her off to 8 Sussex Place and she expressed great appreciation, and said she would take her husband to see it the next day. Delighted to have hope of letting it again.

Wednesday, 13th June

Sat to McEvoy at 9.30. While I was in his studio a very serious air-raid took place. He, however, robbed me of any war perquisite of excite-

1. H. H. Asquith.

1917

ment by telling me the guns I heard were only a rehearsal. It was not till I got home and saw Nurse that I realised the raid. Michael had been woken out of his sleep in the park and harangued the crowd in the following wise words: 'People shouldn't stand about in gwoops. It's very dangerous to stand about in gwoops. If I was frightened I wouldn't stand in a gwoop—at least, I might put my foot in one.' McEvoy urged me to write. Why he thinks I have either ideas or words I don't know.

Thursday, 14th June

The Russian lady came to see me. To my great relief she has decided to take the house. We arranged that the husband should come and have a business talk with me the next morning.

Friday, 15th June

A shy, unattractive young Russian arrived at 9.30 about the let of the house. We agreed that we must have a solicitor to draw up the agreement, and I went off to see Humbert in his office, feeling proud of transacting lovely business. Humbert looked very blue at the idea of Russians (I suppose they are all liable to awake to complete insolvency any morning), and insisted on references and a house agent being responsible for the inventory. He also winced at my present address.

I lunched with Evan in uniform, Mr Balfour and the Duchess of Marlborough making up the party—London is full of rumours of Evan's engagement to Adele. I feel completely sceptical about it. What a wrench it would be to give up his perfect rooms and have to go and live with three women and pool his plans—I feel if he does marry it will be as a provision for his old age, not to improve the present, so I think he is more likely to want in theory to marry a younger woman.

Dined at Margot Howard's—a huge party turning into a dance with songs. A gloom was cast over the early part of the evening by the fact that poor Prince Leo, who was to have been at the dinner, was in bed upstairs screaming with pain. He had hurt his leg in the Bath Club and was clamouring for morphia and hands to hold: Brenda and Margot had to spend a lot of time with him.

The dinner party, as always nowadays, assembled in broad daylight and cruelly unbecoming it was to most of the women. I hated the first part of the evening—feeling tired, shy, and a depressed Rip

312

Van Winkle—resenting the new generation and poignantly reminded that my own was dead. But I cheered up, played poker, and finally enjoyed myself very much.

I was cheered by the delightful companionship of Ivor Churchill—that amazing, straight-from-Cartier paragon of precocity. We sat together through Norah Phipps' long break of songs and enjoyed ourselves. I said, 'It must be fun to hold a room as she is doing,' and he said, 'It's you who are holding me, not her'. He and I and Venetia drove away together. Mary H. chaffs me with 'cradle-snatching' and talks of my 'lover of seventeen'—a rumour I do *not* want circulated. Disparity of age is a point on which I am sensitive. It might be urged that my 'lovers' are on the old side, and that this looks like an attempt to bring down the average. This generation seems more conspicuous in beaux than belles. One looks to see how Ivo Grenfell and Ivor Churchill are looking tonight more than at any two girls: Yvo's beauty on this occasion, in dark blue Guards' uniform with a flushed radiant face, was really riveting and he and Bettine dancing together were really a sight for the gods—perfect Adam and Eve.

Saturday, 16th June

Went down to Stanway with Mamma by 9.50. It was unbearably hot in the train. Angela McInnes is a pathetic refugee here: a singing husband having brought her an ordeal of misery, she now has decided to divorce him. Mamma and I took her five-year-old son for a walk with John in the Sling after tea. I wept tears of anguish over poor John—it is so tantalising seeing that other boy. It was so hot we had dinner out of doors.

Tuesday, 19th June

Lunched with Margot Howard de Walden. The Freddie Blackwoods were there and Duff who has been, as he says, 'allowed' to go by the Foreign Office and, as the ill-natured say, 'combed out'. He is joining the Grenadiers, but has to go to a cadet school for three months first. Freddie looked indecently gleeful when he heard. Margot—bless her!—told me I could order any dress I liked at Wilson's sale and put it down to her. I chose a lovely grey-and-gold chiffon classical evening dress.

Thursday, 21st June

I had tea with Maud Russell and went to the Poets' Reading with her.

Gilbert Murray was there and made a flippant speech in what I thought was very bad taste, making the already trembling poets *writhe* with self-consciousness. He laid down the axiom that all good poets were bad readers. Poor Turner, a khaki-clad, quivering figure who was the first to break the ice certainly didn't prove himself disqualified from being a good poet. The only word I heard was Popacatapetl—but it came in several times. Drinkwater read ambitiously, and rather clerically—I liked his poems. Walter de la Mare was attractive to eye and ear. Hewlett I thought very tedious. *Far* the most lovable was little Davies who read delicious poems very sweetly. I felt him to be a real poet and when one sees him one loses any lingering impression of artificial, strained simplicity. He is so obviously nature-inspired and not a retailer. Yeats was the stage poet—a pale hand checking a lock trained into rebellion—a cathedral voice and a few editing remarks before delivering a poem.

It was not very full this year. I enjoyed it, though weary before the end, because I was in the front and could hear without effort, but most people seemed to think it a puny performance. In theory it ought to be so thrilling, but somehow it doesn't seem to be done in quite the right way, and one longs for a Tannhäuser to break up the decorous meeting. It lasted two hours.

Friday, 22nd June

Dined with Mary Herbert—a particularly successful and delightful party. I sat between Lavery and Eddie, both of whom were struck by Aileen Meade's extraordinary resemblance to me. Brenda was there in an outrageous dress—shorter than anything I have seen off the stage and drawn tight under her outlined behind. Margot Howard de Walden and Mrs Lavery were the other women, and the rest of the men were Freddie, Lensky the Russian singer, Bluetooth, and Aubrey: others came in after dinner, including Diana, Venetia, and Willie de Grunne. Lensky sang beautifully and so did Margot. I sat on a sofa with Bluetooth, who exclaimed at my beauty and said he couldn't believe I was the same woman who had lunched with him. Apparently my face had in the interval changed from its 'biggest' to its 'smallest'. Lavery was also struck and, in the middle of a song, leaped out of his chair and said, 'You must get McEvoy to paint you just like that in your present pose.' I felt inclined to say, 'Why don't you paint for yourself, John? Every woman was looking her best. Why does that sometimes happen?

Monday, 25th June

Great excitement putting on the new dress Margot gave me. It's a lovely one and suits me very well. Ivor, who fetched me to dine with him at the Carlton, said it was the best he had ever seen. He took me on to Margot's great concert party. It was a real success, an enchanting evening. Edwina sang wonderfully, but I was more thrilled by a wonderful cello player, Suggia. She is too fascinating to watch: when not playing her face is evil unredeemed by beauty, but as she plays something comes into her face, and she is rivetingly beautiful—amazingly expressive—a real half-Medusa/half-Madonna head with snake hair. Someone has cleverly said she looks as if she were 'committing adultery with her cello'. I sat with Willie de Grunne through the music and then there was a buffet. Afterwards, informal singing and dancing, during which I sat with Claud who had been dining there. He was half seriously, half jestingly, debating whether he wouldn't leave off seeing me.

Tuesday, 26th June

Called for Claud and we sat in the park together. I was engaged to go to tea with Lady Ancaster and he accompanied me. She was full of gossip, saying Lord Wimborne was to leave Ireland on account of some very grave private scandal.

Friday, 29th June

Dorothy Grosvenor and I travelled down to Willowhayne, East Preston, Worthing by 1.55 from Victoria. The house is ours until the end of July. We didn't get there until past five. We were a little dashed by the intense cold, the hardness of the beds, the austerity of the chairs, and the general depravity of the furniture, and I was prohibitively tired, but I mean to make a success of it.

Monday, 2nd July

I began reading Forster's *Life of Dickens* and was enthralled by it. It is a great joy and relief to find he loved his characters as much as I do, and felt bitterly bereaved whenever he finished a novel.

Tuesday, 3rd July

The 5.30 post brought a letter from Basil with the following tantalising information: 'The Divisional General offered me the post and office of Staff Captain to the Second Guards Brigade. Now that is a thing I would have liked to have accepted, but I felt it impossible to do so in view of the near approach of *der Tag*. I am sure you will understand the position and see how impossible it is to do otherwise. I don't say I refused without misgivings. I did so unhesitatingly, but with regret. I tell you this privately—please do not speak about it. I might get a cheap burst of credit from people who aren't in my position and don't understand the difficulties of accepting. I don't deserve credit and don't want it. I particularly don't want to be used as a stick to beat the Staff with because he despised the Staff. The truth is very much the reverse. I long to take it, and would jump at it greedily in other circumstances. It is idle *offering* people jobs. If one is wanted to do particular work one should be ordered to do it.' Dorothy told me Maurice* has said the Air Service General, Trenchard,* was very anxious to get Basil on his Staff. I wonder if there is any hope of that coming in the imperative. I fear not.

Thursday, 5th July

Two letters from Basil, in one of which he wrote: 'I have got a rather disagreeable and dangerous little bit of patrol and reconnaissance to do on a certain night this week. I hope it will be over when you get this letter. I didn't tell you until I thought it would be. I think it will be all right, but it is no good blinding oneself to the risks. One has to take them into account and, if anything goes wrong, it will be difficult to extricate oneself—but even then not impossible.' This threw me into a fever of apprehension and I had the worst attack of war-nerves I had had for a long time. My tooth, which had given a few premonitory twinges the day before, gave me a raging pain and I spent a wretched day. I went for a long solitary walk in the afternoon to try and get away from it. Dorothy gave me a potent sleeping-draught and I got quite a good night's sleep.

Friday, 6th July

Decided I must go into Brighton to see a dentist. After luncheon, just as I was going to start walking to the station, a telegram was handed to me. I knew without any doubt that it was from Freddie and read: 'Very sorry to have to tell you Basil missing after trench raid on 3rd. No further news. Freddie.' I think I quite hopelessly accepted the worst at once and felt utterly smashed and as though the world were emptied of a vitality.

Got through to Brenda on the telephone. She told me the raiding party had been divided into two. The ten men of one party had returned *without* their officer, whom they said they had lost in the dark. Basil and his ten men had none of them returned—all missing. I suppose this is more hopeful as they may have been all cut off and taken prisoners. Somehow I can't *feel* hope—the evidence doesn't affect me.

I feel he has gone out of the world. It was he and his wonderful spirits that had done so much to carry me through these awful years. Now I don't know what to do—what to think. Life seems a huge bore. I wish I could tell him how much, how inexpressibly much, I am going to miss him. Anything which made me laugh, anything which troubled me—both alike—made me want to write to him at once. I say I have no hope, and yet I don't suppose I *really* believe him dead for a moment.

My difficulty is I can't imagine him a prisoner. The best news we could have is bad enough. Poor, poor Freddie. Brenda said it was dreadful to see him. I sometimes thought I must have paid my war-toll, but there is no limit. My life seems a succession of bludgeonings. My head ached badly from crying and I fell asleep on my bed without meaning to. Woke up and found the gas on at about one o'clock.

Saturday, 7th July

Went to the post office in the morning and found it placarded with news of a serious air-raid in London. Thirty aeroplanes was the report. Sat about in the garden and had lunch with Dorothy. She was *very, very* dear and understanding. Food choked me. We went by the 2.40 and had a broiling walk to the station escorted by the children. The journey seemed endless.

I went to Cadogan Square for dinner. Mamma and I sat in the square and she was very darling to me. Unfortunately, we got entangled with Grace on the telephone and had to go round and hear exactly what she had felt during the air-raid. She was at the Academy with Evan at the time. A bomb actually dropped in Mount Street.

Sunday, 8th July

Lunched in with Dorothy. Waited about, too restless to read or write, for Horatia's visit. Her sister has as yet not heard from her husband Selby Walker—Basil's captain—*since* the raid. A great many steps have been taken to get news of them, supposing they are prisoners. The other officer is a Roman Catholic, so they have wired to the

Vatican; also the Queen of Spain has been applied to, as well as Princess Pless and a German man who knew Basil. Beyond that there is nothing to do but wait. I can't make out *how* much I hope. It is so difficult to imagine, to visualise, anyone one knows well as a prisoner —anything else is easier, alas! If he *is* alive, what a wonderful crop of dewdrops I shall have to give. Mary H. said, 'He was the biggest thing in the war,' and I hear there has been more sorrow in the Guards over his loss than anything else since the beginning of the war—they simply adored him. How battered and smashed I feel. After each bludgeoning I feel there is going to be no escape—that it's going to be just everyone that matters—but then hope revives and one re-invests in the survivors. Evan said the only way in which life could be made livable was to regard it as something quite insignificant. But one is too young for that and life, after all, is a pretty long business. Some sort of very vague but secure religion—quite unformulated—makes it all bearable for me. Would it be easier if one hated the Germans? I feel them—poor devils—to be our wretched allies fighting against some third thing. The whole thing *must* be the means to some end, and that no political one.

I dined at Cadogan Square: Mamma, Evan, Guy, Frances, Letty, Bibs, and Sacheverell Sitwell. I wore a lovely blue Fortuni tea-gown of Dorothy's she had given me. I regret more and more having missed the raid. There are a good many anecdotes about it. Eileen Scott's nurse fainted—dropping the baby. A man with a lost head telephoned wildly to the exchange, 'I want my wife. Where's my wife? Where's my wife?'—giving neither name nor number. Poor little Martin was very frightened and refused, quite rationally, to be reassured, saying: 'But when they come with bombs they do kill people. They killed my papa.'

Monday, 9th July

The morning post brought me a very piteous little letter from poor Freddie and I telephoned and arranged to lunch with him. I have never known anything like the love between these two brothers, or seen one grown-up person so dependent on another human being as Freddie was on Basil. One never saw one without his telephoning to the other and arranging some assignation, and they wrote to each other every day. Freddie showed me such letters as there were: it seems a strange story and, as usual, the evidence is conflicting. Lord Cavan's report had given the more hopeful news that Basil's men were all missing with him, but the letters from the C.O. and Selby Walker reported that *all* the men of both parties had returned without their officers, and had apparently given no coherent account of how or why they had lost them. There was one gossipy story from 'Bubbles' (Bagot-Chester) to the effect that one of the men had seen Basil shot, and later looking into the shell-hole into which he fell, had found him gone—this would, of course, imply his having been taken up by the Germans alive. But, alas, these stories quoted from privates are absolutely unreliable, and this one doesn't tally with any of the rest of the evidence. Freddie couldn't understand the affair at all, but thought what probably happened was that Basil told his men to stay where they were and wait for him, and crawled on by himself to reconnoitre. The men waited, kept communication open all night, and finally returned. In his letter the Colonel refers to the damned affair as 'Basil's little stunt'. A cruel thing happened with poor old Lady Dufferin. They wired telling her the news and later on sent another telegram saying, 'Have told Nellie'. This was miswritten, 'Safe—tell Nellie', and she wired joyfully back.

I had tea with dear Letty and saw Ego's two darling boys. Had a good talk with her. There is a *great* deal of beauty in her nature and mind. She showed me a very touching letter from poor Smallbones. She has been made very happy by a dewdrop from Ego found in an old letter to Mamma: 'She is a little Puritan with the glamour of a Bohemian'.

Tuesday, 10th July

Had my hair waved and took my tooth to Sir Francis Farmer who sentenced the nerve to death. Went by appointment to have tea with Ava Astor. She was very nice and, of course, talked much about Basil saying he had a 'beautiful character' and 'of course, he adored you with his whole being'. Talked to Dorothy at bedtime. She had been spending the evening *tête-à-tête* with 'Uncle' John—Lord Revelstoke. He had told her he had once been very much in love with me when I was a girl, but knew it was no use approaching me on account of Beb.

Wednesday, 11th July

Sat to McEvoy early in the morning. I was feeling miserable and I'm afraid my face must have looked it, but he made my watercolour very lovely I thought. I had decided to have John up to turn some more stones in the way of doctors, and he and his governess had arrived and were lodging at Bruton Street. I tried to cut his hair—with no

1917

success. He is no better and alas, alas, it is a nightmare to me to be in the room with him now. I must struggle against this.

Friday, 13th July

I lunched alone with Freddie, who was tortured by a headache. I think he quite quenched my rather strong hopes about Basil by showing me a letter from Bubbles about that unfortunate affair of the third. He writes: 'A private gave an account which, I am very sorry to have to say, I believe to be the correct one! It was that Basil, and two or three men, had run up against a German who fired point blank at Basil, missing him twice and the third time hitting him fatally. He fell forward and remained motionless.' Of course, privates often mistake officers, but as there was—alas!—only one, how could he in this case? I suppose there is just a chance that he was unconscious, not dead, but it is a tiny loophole. Yet, it is an odd story. Why couldn't the men shoot the German and look at Basil? Why did they leave him? It convinced me at the time that he was dead and I broke down again for the afternoon. It is too much for me all at once. God what a week!

Saturday, 14th July

Went to Farmer at 9.45 and had my tooth finished. I had decided to return to Willowhayne. Dorothy is not allowed to travel[1] and remains in London, but I think it will be much better for me to be there and have a look at myself alone—I am only living on nerves in London. It is merely postponing.

I got down about seven. Michael gave me a very sweet welcome. I went on to the shore after dinner. There was one of the most gorgeous sunsets I have ever seen and I felt a kind of peace settling on me.

Sunday, 15th July

The post has become a bitter pang. I cannot believe that I shall never have another of Basil's letters. He has been a very great deal of the wind in my sails for the last five years. It is a hard thing to lose one's tonic these days.

Monday, 16th July

Another lovely day. I am curiously intermittent—incapable of

1. She was expecting a baby.

320

sustained emotions of any kind—and all day I felt a curious numbness and cessation of sorrowing—so much so that I was shocked by myself, but of course it is only a lucid interval. The pain will return.

Tuesday, 17th July

Letter from Brenda saying in his last letter Penn held out a tiny ray of hope, as another private reported that he had seen Basil go on crawling *after* the shots were fired. Not much in itself, but showing one must really discount all the men's evidence, as not one agrees with another. I finished the *Trojan Women* after dinner. Re-reading *Jude the Obscure* to myself—a wonderful book.

Wednesday, 18th July

A pouring, blustering day succeeded to a hurly-burly of a night. My four last letters to Basil were returned to me. This brings a bitter pang of realisation—I longed for him to have read them.

The silence is cruel. It is the first bereavement in one's *daily* life I have known. The boys were intermittent—he was an uninterrupted serial. Everything makes me realise how I miss him—nothing which is without an association with him—a whole language gone.

Friday, 20th July

Delicious day. I had a letter from Freyberg in which he wrote, 'Life is wonderful and sweet'. I am glad someone finds it so. Adhered to practically the same routine with the addition of a bathe before lunch. We got through a good deal of *Tess*, which I am reading to Horatia. The astonishing poetry of the book has come again with a shock of revelation. It is more beautiful than I remembered.

Saturday, 21st July

Wore my Spanish shawl at dinner. Horatia was flabbergasted with astonishment when I told her it was Claud's gift. It led to a discussion on what presents one would and wouldn't accept from men. She said she had once refused a diamond heart. I don't think I have ever been offered jewels of any value. We agreed that we couldn't take clothes, or be seen in a dressmaker's shop with a man, which reminded me of Phyllis Boyd shouting, 'Come and help me buy a bust-bodice' to Michael Tennant in Bond Street.

Three days without a letter from Beb.

1917

Sunday, 22nd July

Another lovely day, giving me health and freckles. I had a long, long letter from Mamma, who has been coping with John and heckling his doctors, and so on. It made me ashamed and feel I must appear a disgraceful mollusc and as though I had run away from London. As a matter of fact, I have waited post by post for a letter from Dr Hysslop, and meant to come to London if it raised any point for decision. But she has been to see him—my consolation is that she does really *love* heckling doctors and is far more competent to do it than I am.

As far as the news went it was good, as Hysslop thought May's treatment rather good than bad and was quite prepared to prescribe at the same time—apparently there is no danger of any clash. He will give John some preparation of thyroid.

Got a letter from Beb saying they had been badly gassed and had lost some men owing to defective respirators.

Thursday, 26th July

Last day at Willowhayne, Horatia and I ill and depressed. I felt quite sad at leaving my temporary home. It has been a great rest, because—with my odd power of detachment—I have made it into a sort of parenthesis, and got *outside* my own life to a certain extent. I almost obliterated my identity in the temporary context—felt a sort of suspension of emotions.

Friday, 27th July

I had a frightfully hot and disagreeable journey, reaching Victoria at about a quarter to two. Met Margot, Elizabeth, and Oc in a motor and they picked me up. Oc back on leave looking very war-worn. Margot very bedizened—a painted skeleton. Elizabeth wan and lovesick. Frances tells me her young man—Gibson—has never once written to her since he left the country about six months ago. Elizabeth's interpretation is that so Quixotic is he that he feels in honour bound to 'keep away' because he is confronted with consumption and a financial breakdown—this doesn't seem very plausible.

Monday, 30th July

I went to Teresina. She exclaimed when she touched me, and said she had never seen so 'shocked' and 'scorched' a hand, and that no one could have a blacker bit of life than I was now traversing. This was very satisfactory and rather comforting. She at once saw both my present pains: held out *no* hope about Basil—seeing just a blank—but implored me not to accept the medical opinion as to John and said she was positive it was only a *temporary* trouble and that it was very important for me to keep hopeful and not to 'turn against him'. She saw what a loss Basil would be and, what with that and Beb being away, said I had a time of great loneliness and emotional blank to go through. I might have a great many nominal friends but was nearly always a 'spectator' with them. This is true. Basil and Beb are the *only* two men who have really got inside my life. However, she said I had courage and would 'come up' again. She raved about Mamma, as she does each time, but deprecated her dabbling in spiritualism. She said Papa ought never to have been a father—a godfather yes, but a father—no.

Wednesday, 1st August

The post brought me the following letter from Brenda: 'Isn't it too thrilling? Freddie has just heard from Colonel Fielding that a German officer prisoner reports that at the beginning of the month they took two English officers and a private prisoners and, as far as he knows, unwounded. So we have every reason to believe they are Basil and Gunnis. . . .' I wonder how much one ought to accept this. I gather Freddie is absolutely confident. I daren't be that, but I do think it is a very strong presumption.

I went to sit to McEvoy at 9.30. When I got back Pamela Lytton rang me up on the telephone and offered me a part in a new play *Dear Brutus*, by Barrie. She said it would be lucrative. Perhaps it is my duty to my children and my creditors to accept, but I refused: however, she said she would come and see me about it next day.

Dined with Ava Astor and wore my grey-and-gold dress. A large dinner party: Papa, Maud Cunard, Ian Hamilton, Lord Hugh, Eddie Marsh, Adele, Venetia, Lutyens, Mr Balfour, and so on. I sat between Lord Hugh and Eddie—quite a nice dinner—but I was tired. Maud Cunard in very good form afterwards, trying to prevail on Mr Balfour to sign her divorce law petition, and asking him to make a speech in the house beginning, 'Though a bachelor, I am in favour of polygamy . . .' The rumour was that the Government was tottering to its fall. Eddie told me he had begun a third volume of Georgian poetry and wanted to include 'The Volunteer'.

Friday, 3rd August

Brenda came to see me. She says Freddie is now *completely* confident.

I don't quite know what I feel myself—strong hopes certainly, but no security. What I can't understand and don't like is that, after giving the facts on which Freddie relies, the Colonel said at the end of his letter: '. . . so there is an off-chance of their being all right'. An 'off-chance' seems such a very modest way of putting it.

Saturday, 4th August

Had the motor to take me to the station, and Polly and I went by the ten o'clock. We had the most awful journey—everybody in England seemed to be going to Minehead. Owing to luggage regulations, people now carry their portmanteaux in the carriages: there wasn't even room to read and boxes were put on one's lap. I arrived at Pixton after four and, to my relief, found all the adults—Mary H., Margot Howard de Walden, my father-in-law, Alan Parsons, and Hugh—had all motored to Minehead. Rested.

We had an amusing dinner. I whipped myself up into quite good form. The Old Boy was very mellow and sweet, and talked a lot about his sons. He was pleased with Michael.

Monday, 6th August

The P.M. spent a happy morning with a Rhoda Broughton. He is superlatively mellow—in delightful form at meals. We did a little war-work by cutting belladonna leaves. The heat was roasting and I took back any wish to 'work on the land'. Mary and the P.M. motored to golf at Minehead—Margot and I went for a good two hours' walk. I enjoyed it, and we talked an enormous deal. We accused Mary of having bottled our mutual dewdrops, thus betraying that she didn't want us to like one another *too* much. We punished her by discussing her exhaustively, but I don't think we said anything she would mind. We agreed that, whereas Sybil was an ordinary duchess-snob, Mary was a Coterie-snob. We discussed whether her imagination *was* lurid —as I say it is—in the sense that she sees life more like a novelette than it is. Talking of rumours, Margot assured me that though she had often heard the question of whether *I* had a lover discussed, the unanimous opinion always had been that I had *not*.

Tuesday, 7th August

The P.M. and Alan went off at 9.30, the former leaving a Collins* for Mary and a note with twenty-pound cheque for me. I lay out in a hammock after luncheon, and Margot sang to Mary's accompaniment. We three had a very interesting talk about wealth, its obligations, privileges and penalties. Margot almost cried in discussing some of its more painful aspects. We observed that we three represented three quite different grades, and we wondered how we should acquit ourselves if we could be shuffled. We drew lots—Margot pulled my 'basement', I Pixton, and Mary Seaford House. I said that the acquisition of sudden notorious wealth would worry me till I was ill: the knowledge that my taste was the only obstacle between me and being the *best*-dressed woman in England, with the most beautiful furniture, and the best cook would make me *feverish* I'm afraid. We also had a heated discussion on the ethics of taste arising from the question of whether I ought to have accepted Barrie's offer.

Wednesday, 8th August

I read Hodgson's poems in the morning, and 'The Widow in the Bye Street' aloud to Mary and Margot after luncheon. I don't know whether it *is* literature, but certainly it is a most effective 'assault and battery' on one's emotions. I still think the verse beginning: 'Oh, how his little face come, with bright hair', terribly moving.

Friday, 10th August

Whibbles arrived after tea. He told us that, when it was suggested to Sarah Bernhardt that she should act the part of Hamlet, she asked what happened to him at the end of the play. She had acted Ophelia for years and years, but had never taken the trouble to read beyond the third act. He said she did Hamlet very well, because she didn't understand a word of what she had to say. Whibley repudiated Masefield *en bloc,* saying he was no better than a hymn with reiterated ugly words substituted for holy ones—just a sham and a trick.

Saturday, 11th August

Whibley in very good pip-pip form at breakfast—explaining to us that Bonar 'Jaw' was a German Jew who read Dante whilst buttoning up his braces buttons. A new man arrived—Captain Lane—A.D.C. (gent help, as the Americans would say) to Smuts. We had the most extraordinarily comic political debate after dinner. Lane I thought was a nice gentle bewildered gentleman, blinking at Whibley's vituperations. I got quite 'fierce' and attacked the latter repeatedly, trying to find out if there *was* any philosophy behind his apparently quite crude man-in-the-street attacks.

Monday, 13th August

Whibbles and Captain Lane left early. Lane was a fairly ponderous man, with a great hero worship for his chief, General Smuts—and they are both terribly shocked by the English public man's habit of week-ending. After dinner I started reading Webster's *White Devil* to Mary, but Primrose's[1] presence in the room made it impossible, and we fell back on the last two acts of *Antony and Cleopatra*.

Tuesday, 14th August

The rain has got into my brain and I can't write either diary or letters. It is too dismally depressing this weather, apart from its destruction of the harvest—*Gott mit uns?* We went canoeing in the morning— rather fun. Mary and I very nearly upset. We were all three terrified by several animals: one bustard, one horse, one cow, one stag.

Wednesday, 15th August

I went off to Mells for two nights to see Katharine. I found her with her children. Her hair has turned very grey. Her little Julian is a darling with fair curls. He 'slits' his eyes like Raymond. We sat talking in the garden and had a very cold bathe in the swimming bath after tea. Jack Horner joined us at dinner. We talked of the Asquiths' indignation at Montagu's so-called 'ratting'. Margot was vehement about it, saying 'Venetia ought to leave him'. She wrote to Katharine about it, and when she in her answer defended Montagu's conduct, complained bitterly to Bluetooth of the letter, saying that when she had shown it to Henry[2] he had said it must be a 'forgery'. I think that's a brilliant Margot.

Thursday, 16th August

The one fine day was only a flash in the pan. We awoke to as grey a morning as ever. Katharine gave her children lessons for two hours in the morning, during which time I wrote letters. Then we had a long talk over the fire. We discussed the pros and cons of publishing letters. She says Raymond's to her and Bluetooth are so marvellously good

1. Nickname for Aubrey Herbert's youthful secretary.   2. H. H. Asquith.

that she feels they will have to be published some day. But, of course, they couldn't possibly be published for a very considerable time without a *great* deal of bowdlerising. She is, on the whole, in favour of just collecting them and leaving them until after her death, but many people urge her to make a selection at once and have them printed for the benefit of his friends while his memory is still green.

I had a long haircombing with her. She lifted the veil and revealed such a depth and intensity of suffering as made one feel one could never be happy while she was alive. It was so difficult to find *anything* to say to her—it seemed presumptuous and impertinent to offer any of the things one does to other people. She admitted that, had she been offered the choice of whether she would buy her ten years happiness at the price of the suffering now involved, she would do so, but she said she would have tried to teach herself to live a little more on herself and not so exclusively on another human being. I think what she says is true, that you can roughly divide human beings into two classes, one of which *live on themselves* (however much they may love), and the other who live on some other person. I suppose I really belong to the first category—persons are luxuries to me. She regards the remainder of her life as a bad debt to be discharged. What makes me feel so hopeless about prescribing for her is the recollection that she wasn't happy *without* Raymond, even before he came into her life. It needed him to reconcile her to life. She is a haunting thought.

Saturday, 18th August

Frances told us a good Queen Mary story at breakfast. Going round a hospital, she was struck by a fair-haired mother with a very dark baby. She commented on this and returned to the woman's bedside again after completing her round, saying: 'His father must have been very dark—wasn't he?' To which the woman breezily replied: 'Sure Ma'am, I don't know—he never took his hat off'.

Katharine drove me into Frome, starting me on my journey of about six hours. At Pixton I found this telegram: 'Arriving London on leave August 19th. Beb.' A surprise—I didn't expect him until Monday. The last train up to London had gone and there is no Sunday one, so I was stranded and couldn't get up. I wired to Bruton Street suggesting his coming down here for the first part of his leave and advising him to wait till the Monday morning train as the night one was so bad.

1917

Sunday, 19th August

At about 5.30 a call of 'Cynthia' interrupted my dreams. I sprang up, wide awake, and found Beb who somehow had got a motor at Taunton and had broken into the house. We talked till nearly seven and then he fell into a heavy sleep. He seems all right—not a bit deaf anyhow— but says his 'guts' are ruined, and that he has had a sort of dysentery all the time. Very full of his experiences. I haven't seen him in a good light, but I really think he is all right.

Monday, 20th August

Beb slept on till after twelve and had his luncheon in bed, then walked down to the Weir with John and me. After tea we sat in the summer house and he talked a lot of the war, very interestingly and picturesquely. He has had a ghastly time, both for danger and discomfort—continually in such smells that he had to puff a pipe ceaselessly or be sick, and never coming out of the line for a proper rest. He is undoubtedly *exalté* and exhilarated by some aspects of the fighting, but on the whole is very, very war-weary and, I'm afraid, *loathes* the idea of returning. But he is in good spirits and I see no shadow of a return of his former illness. I think this proves it to have been the effect of one particular explosion and *not* strain and tension. He has had far more of the latter this time.

Tuesday, 21st August

Beb and I breakfasted in bed. We took John for a drive in the pony cart and sat in the garden after tea. Poor darling! He is already beginning to watch the hands of the clock. Ten days seem a terribly short respite after so long a hell.

We were amused by a typical telegram from the Wharf: 'What day do you come here? Please bring six gallons of petrol which you are entitled to.' A good use to put your soldier son to! Beb has never heard of this perquisite. I wonder if it exists for unmotored subalterns.

Friday, 24th August

Beb and I went up to London at twelve o'clock. Mary and I had fondly anticipated weeks of *tête-à-tête* life, with time to read the Bible aloud. How it has all crumbled away! Beb and I put up at Cavendish Square —he has sentiment about his old home. Of course, we were put on different floors. I left Polly at Pixton to take John out. Beb and I dined at the Berkeley and went to *Three Weeks*—an excellent bad play.

Saturday, 25th August

Beb and I breakfasted downstairs. I had my hair waved and then we went out together. I took him to see my flat. We lunched at Cavendish Square and went down to the Wharf by the 3.20. The party we found consisted of the P.M., Margot, Elizabeth, Puffin, Ruggles-Brise, Spender, Sir William Tyrrell,* and Dunn. Violet and Bongie are occupying another house a few yards off: it has the most lovely garden. I haven't been to the Wharf since it was enlarged. It is now the most lovely bijou residence—*exquisite* taste (though too like a shop)—but at what cost I wonder? I sat beside the P.M.—very mellow. He thinks Beb looking well. Bridge, of course, after dinner: I was left over with Bongie, Beb, and Spender—not much fun.

Sunday, 26th August

Got up in my Septimus yellow, which met with full measure of Margot's approval. The little flapper who waited on me called me with the stern ultimatum that 'breakfast would be cleared at 10.30'—however, some of the party sat over the table until 11.30, while I was gibbetting with my enamoured little brother-in-law. The Old Boy, Puffin, Elizabeth and I played the general information game at luncheon. Puffin is always trying to find musical 'teasers' to stump his father with.

After lunch Beb and I went over to Violet's garden, and sat under a tree for over an hour in extremely heavy rain. We then joined a symposium in her drawing room—her, Bongie, Dunn, and Spender. The latter was very interesting about journalism and the personality, mentality, and tactics of Northcliffe. He says he employs vast armies of men with notebooks who go and listen in public houses, and report on the tone and appetite of the moment for which the papers must cater.

When the men join us after dinner, bridge immediately begins. Beb and I went and sat in the barn. Violet joined us later and we had war-talk. Beb urged arbitration. I haircombed with Elizabeth. Listened to the Gibson rhapsody. At last she has had a letter from him. She seems completely confident that things will come right in spite of the consumption of lungs and purse.

Monday, 27th August

Beb behaved very characteristically. The evening before he had been very firm about the necessity of going up to London by the early train, but when I had scrambled up and everything had been hysterically packed, he came into my room and said it was so lovely a day that we must stop and go on the river. We decided to go at one o'clock, and a taxi and early lunch was ordered. On the river we went, and very lovely and peaceful it was—perfect balm for poor shell-teased Beb. There was no new factor in the situation, but Beb suddenly announced that he must now stay until after luncheon. I made a fussy protest, but submitted. He talked very well about his experiences at luncheon—and what is odder—Margot listened very well. I have never known her so nice and so unpainful as on this occasion. Puffin insisted on gambling with me at *rouge et noir*—I won over a pound.

Our train was very late, and we didn't reach Cavendish Square and the surly odd man until 6.30.

Tuesday, 28th August

Beb's last day. We lunched in together. Afterwards I took him to be photographed by Swaine. Swaine—knowing me of old—tried to exclude me, but I went firmly in. I endeavoured to make Beb look less like a dog on trust—of course he giggled when told to say 'Hulloa'. We drank chocolate at Gunter's and then drove to McEvoy's studio. Beb was immensely impressed by McEvoy's art and liked my watercolour very much. We went to *Zig-Zag* together and enjoyed it enormously. Poor Beb—he is dreadfully depressed at returning to Hell. He loathes it in theory and practice, with curious reservations, and passes into a sort of ecstasy at the impressiveness of it.

Wednesday, 29th August

Beb had his breakfast in my bedroom at 6.15 and, after a dramatic farewell, went sadly off to Victoria Station. Great was my amazement when, about an hour later, I heard him call 'Cynthia' outside my door. No boats were running, owing to the gale, and instead of sending them to kick their heels at Dover they charitably stopped them at Victoria, bidding them return at the same hour on the following day. So, here was an extra impromptu day dropped into our lives. Going is in some ways so much worse than gone that, at first, I rather wondered whether the reprieve was worth while, but he was able to enjoy his day and I am glad he got it. He went to see Eddie at the Munitions Office. We lunched with Gilbert and Maud. Claud, to my surprise, was there. Beb was shy and awkward, and I had a bad bout of vicarious self-consciousness. We went to War Cinema at the Scala. There were some very interesting German propaganda ones which had been intercepted on their way to neutral countries. The sinister spiked helmets made me feel that, even yet, the Germans must win. We came home to tea and had a very nice dinner and evening together.

Thursday, 30th August

Beb went off early again—this time not to return. I sat to McEvoy from ten till twelve. The water-colour is finished, and Margot Howard de Walden says she will buy it and give it to me. The oil I sat for all these months is now a washout. He has taken off my hat and recommenced. He exclaimed about the mystery of my face, saying 'Why can't I get the delicacy and sensitiveness of your face, when it's there for all the world to see!' To my amusement, he was for once unguarded in his abuse of a 'patient'—mainly I think because his sitter had abruptly chucked an appointment.

I lunched with Bluetooth. I have never known him so nice. He walked me to Selfridges—stiff with selfconsciousness because (as to my amazement he explained) he thought my appearance was so conspicuous that every passer-by *must* stare at me. I proved this was not the case. It was great fun seeing him in a 'calico Hell'. He asked me what I wanted for a birthday present. I said a fur for my neck and we went upstairs and chose a white fox—thirteen guineas it cost, I'm afraid.

Ivor came to dinner with me. He is a charming creature. I feel really fond of him and we have great mutual understanding. We compared notes on identical fits of depression and on insomnia—greatest of bonds.

The news of poor Francis McLaren's death from a flying accident was in the newspapers. I never thought to have put him in a category with Icarus.

Friday, 31st August

Sat to McEvoy again, this time in my love-in-a-mist blue teagown, greatly approved of by him. Papa picked me up there and drove me home. Bluetooth advised me to write to Evelyn Fitzgerald about Beb's seniority and I did so, and the P.M. said he would speak to Cowans, who is going to the Wharf for Sunday. When Beb was transferred from the R.M.A. into the R.F.A., Colonel Fitzgerald told him he could retain his seniority, but he has *not* done so. Promotion in the R.F. is so cruelly slow, and there are so many senior to him. I don't suppose he would automatically become a captain for ages and ages. It is rather hard when he is so much older than most of his brother officers. So many people seem to be jobbed. I wish he could be.

Saturday, 1st September

Polly and I went down to Sunningdale to stay with Jeffie Darell by the four o'clock train: found Jeffie, Brenda, and Freddie. I went for a walk with Brenda. It is now over two months since Basil has been missing, and none of the many wires pulled has brought any news of him. She, however, told me what I hadn't heard before—that they had been able to search the ground and had found no trace of them. This makes it more rational to go on hoping. Claud arrived before dinner.

Sunday, 2nd September

Fine, but cold. I breakfasted with Claud and Freddie. Brenda and I later talked about Alex. She gave me an amusing account of his famous 'assault' on her and told me that, the other day, a recently widowed friend of ours whom he had been persecuting played a trick on him by pretending he was suggesting marriage: 'Very well Alex, you are quite right, our friendship has gone on so long—and I think it's very nice of you to come back to me now I am free'. Terrified, he rushed from the house and never went near her again.

We also discussed and compared notes as to the fantastic habits of another friend of ours. I am very glad we did this. Obviously it is a peculiarity of his, as our experiences seem very similar. To give a very typical example, he once stuck a knitting needle into Brenda—really hurting her—and recently here he had, with the room full of people pricked her arm with a pin. We agreed that, just because it was so remote and fantastic, his method embarrassed one much less than the ordinary normal love-making; and yet, it was just because of its strangeness, very difficult to check, as one had no precedent or clue. What etiquette book instructs Mrs X what she should do when Mr Y bites her arm?

Brenda told me about sadism (unknown to me) and said he was much interested in it. It is a kind of perverted sexuality, which makes men want to inflict pain on the women who attract them. It is a recognised vice. The question is, is there anything really morbid about him which might get worse if unchecked, or is it just a stunt? What makes us a little anxious is the obvious distrust of him implied by other men. Brenda said that she once, in all innocence, mentioned the knitting needle incident to Summie and that he looked disgusted. Obviously such behaviour suggests more to men than it does to us and perhaps we ought to be careful.

We quite alarmed one another, and began to be haunted by visions of being suddenly carried upstairs when on a visit and plunged into a boiling bath, or being disfigured by one of his morbid whimsies. We agreed that any fears seemed at moments so unreasonable, so well-balanced was his mind in conversation, and so strong was the admixture of gentleman-ness and almost prudishness of a kind. However, my blood began to run cold when she quoted a remark made when she had told him of a cut finger. 'Did it bleed much? I do wish I had been there to see it.' I had visions of Dracula. Can he really be a little mad, or really morbid? Certainly there seems to be something uncanny about him. He does inspire aversion in strangers. Brenda said he had one day really frightened her. Looking green and strange, he had seized her neck, saying 'Do you know, if I pulled your neck a tiny bit further back I could break it now?' We came to the conclusion that, for his own sake, his peculiarities ought to be severely snubbed. He had once written an angry letter to Brenda complaining of her having accused him of 'pouncing' to someone: Brenda had not done so and, of course, he cannot be accused of pouncing in the Alex sense of the word. One never feels any fear of his even insisting on kissing one.

Monday, 3rd September

Lovely day. Stayed in bed to write up my diary. I am coquetting with the idea of taking a thirty-shilling a week job at the Admiralty, in which case I think I shall bicycle to and fro. I had rather heroically decided on quite another form of war work and signed my own warrant for another baby. I weighed all the pros and cons, thinking it was only a case of making up my own mind, but to my astonishment it was not to be.

I went up to London by the 2.17 train. Ivor called for me and took me to Claridges for dinner. He walked me home. I wonder if he fancies himself in love with me. I really don't know.

1917

Tuesday, 4th September

Walked with Claud: I am much more conscious of his sort of flat-footedness than I used to be. Lunched at Seaford House and came down to stay with Violet at the Mill House. The garden was looking delicious. I was amused and rather horrified to hear that Margot has forced Lady Boot (wife of the cash chemist) to buy the place, ostensibly for her grandchildren, but really for Margot as an annex to the Wharf.

Violet and I had a very nice *tête-à-tête*. I felt fond of her and we had a good talk. She is marvellously painfully absorbed in the baby and has been through great anxiety about it. During our hair-combing I was horrified to see a nightmare monster of, I suppose, some sort of spider creeping on my wall. I was astonished at my display of femininity and became quite hysterical. It was so huge—I could scarcely believe I was in England. To sleep in such company was out of the question —what were we to do? Violet made heroic efforts to catch it in a shroud, but its eight legs were terribly swift and it always evaded her. Finally, feeling like 1st and 2nd murderer, we had to collaborate with fire irons and at last the deed was done. But, never, never have I felt so convinced in the survival of personality after death. I *know* that creature was not finished by my shovel.

Wednesday, 5th September

We had an evening much disturbed by telephoning to London and discussion with the overwrought Nannie, and heard that Edgware Road was in ruins from an air raid. It is getting beyond a joke—I begin to wonder whether I should have Michael in London.

I was interested to hear from Violet that, when in the early days of the Gallipoli expedition she had said to Kitchener, 'Winston certainly deserves great credit for instigating and pushing this scheme through all on his own,' he had strongly repudiated the claim of Winston's undivided responsibility, saying he had always been strongly in favour of it himself and that, as an oriental psychologist, he naturally recognised the enormous value of the moral effect.

Saturday, 8th September

Arrived at Glynde to find Anne Islington, Ivor Churchill, Joan Paynder, and Maud Cunard sitting out in the garden. It's a place with real magic—a lovely grey courtyard and amusing variety of architecture. The outlook is on to bare shoulders of downs, but everything was veiled in a curious mist. Maud was looking more like an inebriated canary than ever. I love her slight concessions in the way of country clothes! She was in amazing, startling soprano-soliloquy form and has come on immensely since I first saw her—she's a priceless woman —like most of the great laughter-raisers, she often doesn't know when she is being most amusing and sometimes blinks with astonishment when one laughs at her sweeping absurdities. She fell upon a volume of Donne's poems—new to her—and read 'The Flea' aloud and thought him some poet: 'Do you know Donne?—he's a most lecherous poet.'

I went for a short walk with Ivor (looking wan and exquisite in country clothes), then we had tea, during which Maud eclipsed herself. She protested how she hated a *tête-à-tête* with either man or woman— naturally what she likes is co-called 'general conversation—which means her soliloquising to a large audience. Not only did she detest being *alone* with a man, but she emphatically maintained that she never *had* been. This startling statement was repeated at every meal. Thomas Beecham's name was always on her lips, and she is full of the coming opera season for which, by the way, she is giving me a box—great fun. She attacked my father for not giving me more money, saying she would write to him on the subject—a threat which filled me with horror and I implored her to desist. The conversation was switched off to Ivor's father who, as she told his son, was intelligent without being intellectual. She talked of Nancy with comic detachment, saying she liked her because she was a 'good mover'.

Eddie, Novello, and Wolkoff arrived by a later train. Novello— composer of 'Keep the Home Fires Burning'—is one of Eddie's *culte*, and inspired great hostility in Wolkoff and Ivor Churchill, the latter called him Lady Rocksavage. I had never stayed in the same house with Wolkoff before, and got to like him better. I have always tried to say it was his projecting teeth which put me off, but—to be honest —I know the obstacle is that Hart-Davis told me in Venice that he didn't admire me at all . . . so incapable am I of being objective about people.

I rested before dinner. The electric light isn ı put in yet and I found it very difficult to do my hair by two candles. I wore my grey-and-gold which was much admired. Maud made us all mannequin before her. She is very amusing about Oreste, the great beauty specialist to whose hands she has now entrusted her face. I don't know quite what he is doing to her, but she is getting that curious pneumatic look which doctored faces acquire. If I couldn't look better than Maud, I think

I would be contented to look worse and not take such infinite trouble. Oreste is alleged to work miracles. He takes tucks in women's upper lips and reefs in their double chins. I love the story about him and Ava Astor. Maud was raving about his skill to her and she repudiated any knowledge of him. Maud then said to Oreste, 'I have got such a beautiful friend, Mrs Astor, whom I want so much to come to you—but she won't.' Oreste flamed with fury and said: 'If Mrs Astor—whose face I have made for the last twenty years—denies me, I shall deny her.' He refused to attend her for three weeks and so she had to go to bed until he relented.

I sat between Anne and Eddie at dinner. In the drawing room Maud gave me giggles by talking about Ivor's 'dear little sympathetic hand' and seizing it. She calls him and Wolkoff the 'troubadours' and loves them much. We played bad, inattentive poker while Novello played and sang—Wolkoff writhing under his performance. It was the most lovely night with a blood-red moon and we went out into the garden. We heard a breathing ghost—great stertorous gasps—I don't know what it can have been. The mystery was never solved. I was moonstruck—had a banshee phase and frightened Joan by making weird faces and noises. Slept very badly.

Sunday, 9th September

Joan and I breakfasted with the four men. Ivor dramatised his meal with skill, making us take great interest in what he ate and drank. It was quite a healthy John Bull breakfast, but his customary one is a cup of chocolate and two peaches, which I think a triumph of exquisiteness. He looks exactly my idea of the princess in the pea-under-the-mattresses story. He and Anne went to church—she armed with a volume of Shakespeare. I read Eddie's commonplace book, and with him and Joan listened to Novello's playing and singing.

We all went out before lunch and ate figs and peaches. I felt braced by the air and impelled to take repeated leaps into a haystack. Tennis in the afternoon on a very soft grass court. My green crocodile shoes much admired. Wolkoff and I fiercely contested sets against Ivor and Joan. In the intervals Anne gave us heavenly imitations of Margot. Maud kept up to her concert pitch all day, or at least, all of the day during which we saw her. But, her technique is to stay in bed—presumably under grease and doing all her plotting and writing—till about a quarter to two, when she comes chirruping into the dining room exactly like a canary just out of its cage.

Ivor Churchill and I went out together after tea. I felt a curious constraint with him and I *think* he wanted to be sentimental, but he only got as far as accusing me of being 'stand-offish, cold and formal'. How do all other women behave? What is the accustomed technique? He said he wasn't happy.

Sat between Ivor Churchill and Novello at dinner—the latter is at any rate very easy to talk to. After dinner Anne told card fortunes and a Mrs Carstairs did palmistry, and there was a little dancing. It was a miscellaneous evening. I even did a little gibbeting with Eddie. We sat up late, and then Eddie, Novello and I were so hungry that we went on a kitchen raid in search of biscuits. Amongst the Margot anecdotes was her saying to the butler, on receipt of a telephone invitation to go over to Blenheim for lunch, 'Tell them I would rather *die* than come.' I like this story of a foreigner: '*J'etais à Londres. J'ai vu le beau monde, et le demi-monde, mais je n'ai rien vu d'aussi immonde que ce M. Alfred Monde.*'

Monday, 10th September

Lovely hot morning. All the men went off early. I breakfasted in bed. Went out and stole fruit in the garden with Joan. Anne joined us and then Joan (I suppose by instruction) left us alone together. Anne and I sat down together under a wall. Her witch-blue eyes and yearning chin are vividly stamped on my senses. She began, 'Cynthia, do you think Basil is alive?' went on: 'Would it make you very unhappy to know he wasn't?' and then: 'Because, you know, he isn't.' She showed me a letter from Freddie: he had had a telegram from the Crown Princess of Sweden saying Basil had been killed at Buesinghe, which is the name of the place where he was missing. This must be accepted as final—it has come at last.

In theory I didn't have much hope, but the gulf between the tiniest doubt and this stark certainty is *much* greater than I expected. All the same, I am grateful for this long phase of uncertainty. I don't know how I could have borne it all at once. I do think that being a little weaned from daily intercourse *before* one knows for *certain* that it is never to be renewed is a gain—it helps to strengthen my already strong impression of the distinction between something which is merely *inaccessible* and something which is lost. To use a hackneyed expression, I have felt him so 'close' to me all these weeks. He has been dead all the time; so why shouldn't that feeling always continue?

It is difficult to express but I feel I can go on regarding it as though one's *capital* were unimpaired, but one weren't able to touch any pocket money. Thus I mean to keep the wealth of his love to enrich me always. I *refuse* to admit extinction. But, day-to-day life isn't much fun without pocket-money.

Tuesday, 11th September

Telephoned to Brenda in the morning. She said Freddie was being very good. Margot Howard de Walden does things in grand style: she sent her footman to take all our rail tickets. The train was 2.0 to 6.20 and Michael, Nannie, and I had a most luxurious journey in a first-class carriage. Bitter cold when we arrived at Chirk. It's a real, battlemented, castellated, drawbridged castle—lovely country. Party only Margot, Olga, a little boy, and that darling Steer.

Wednesday, 12th September

A cold, wet, blustering day. Had a dear little letter from poor Freddie, thanking me for mine. He was very pleased with my expression of Basil 'putting the wind into other people's sails', and sent me two photographs of him. He said, 'Basil would like to think that I saw a lot of you, so I hope I shall . . .' I also had a perfect letter from Mary Herbert. Had rather a bad fit of crying before tea.

Thursday, 13th September

The musician Cyril Scott swelled our party at dinner. He is an angular aesthete, with hair brushed from brow to nuque, and a fancy tie and collar. I didn't take to him, but I must say it was *divine* lying on one's back on cushions in the so-called chapel while he played on a magical organ. Sometimes it would sound too far away to be in the same world, and it conveyed a sense of triumphant imperviousness, as if nothing could really matter. The flickering firelight was very becoming to the listeners.

Saturday, 15th September

After writing letters, I sat out reading Conrad's *The Shadow Line* until driven in by rain. At luncheon Cyril Scott discoursed on the seven types of humanity—Venusians, Jupitarians, Mercurians, Lunarians, Saturnians, Martians, etc. I was diagnosed as a Lunarian—some of their qualities being dreaminess, imaginativeness, and turned-up noses.

After lunch we went for a ride with Margot's nice khaki rector uncle. I was much more comfortable in the habit Mary S. has sent for me and begin to feel quite at home in the saddle again. The uncle dewdropped my riding. Mary Herbert arrived before dinner. We listened to the organ in the chapel again. To my great amusement when Mary complained of a cold in her head Cyril Scott, claiming to be able to cure her, firmly seized her nose in his musical fingers and kept his grasp on it for quite ten minutes. When Margot said she had indigestion, he went to his room to fetch a silver fork, with which he scratched the back of her hand. I shall take care what pains I announce. Short hair-combing with Mary. She is tired and rather resenting the human beings here—minds Cyril Scott's manners and deplores a sort of lapse into 'commoners' on Margot's part.

Sunday, 16th September

A physical set-back let me fall into the depth of misery. If only I were a little more backed-up by my health, I *know* I could bear my sorrows well enough. As it was, I felt overwhelmed all through the day and *terribly* detached—miles off the earth—just what Johnson calls 'a gloomy gazer' on life and human beings. We took the children to the kitchen garden (two miles distant from the house) in the morning and had orgies of fruit.

The uncle and two officers came over for luncheon. In the afternoon we had very hot tennis. It tired me. Steer and Oggie rolled down a grass slope, giving me my happiest moment in the day: I shall never forget her flesh-coloured cylinders of legs! The uncle took us into the dungeon—a nightmare of a place. The soldiers stayed to dinner and we had music in the chapel again—during which I cried a good deal—the eyelash stuff running into my eyes and hurting infernally. At Steer's suggestion we went for a walk before dinner. He is a darling and I enjoyed our quiet talk.

Tuesday, 18th September

Basil does leave a bewildering blank. My spirits are leaden. I came to breakfast with purple eyelids. We rode at eleven. Mary was on a newly-arrived racehorse labelled by the trainers as *not* a suitable hack for ladies. I disliked it at sight—its tongue was out and it looked a vicious brute with a cold misanthropical eye. It kicked and kicked ceaselessly, obviously from malice not from high spirits—its spirits are low. Poor Mary did not (as Guy Carlton would say) 'vacate the pigskin', but she had a very exhausting, uncomfortable time. She and Margot nearly had a serious quarrel. Margot is only a beginner and Mary said she shouldn't ride the horse, as it would certainly kick her off; Margot, on the other hand, insinuated that she could manage it better than Mary, and that the latter's teaching had been inadequate. The question is: Shall Margot be allowed to experiment? And, if so, would Mary rather she were killed, or would she rather the horse were quelled by an exhibition of superior horsemanship? It's an awkward dilemma.

We played tennis again. We all remarked that Scott *never* picked up a ball either for himself or his partner. Mary, not seeing he was in the room, shouted, 'Well, did Cyril Scott take a lot of your fat off?' When she discovered his presence, the only explanation was the true one. He said his heart was weak and he was forbidden to stoop. Poor fellow—but how much better it would be to explain!

Wednesday, 19th September

At meals Cyril Scott gave us some of his strange creed of yogis, astral planes, and so on. He made us laugh by telling us of a man who got dysentery for twenty-five years because he was chased by a bull. The superman head butler, an awe-inspiring beetle of a man, took us round the cellars and plate chests. Never have I been so made so sensible of RANK. When I heard all the ushers and grooms addressing him as 'Sir', I felt I ought to take my shoes off. It's a wonderful survival this place. How Polly must revel in it! I'm sure it's balm to her bruised soul.

After dinner we practised yogi attitudes, and Cyril Scott did an astonishingly good stunt of an old clergyman preaching. I am very much enjoying Boswell's Johnson. Thank God I have the reading habit! What should I do without that bolt hole?

Thursday, 20th September

It gets worse and worse. I did know how *fond* I was of Basil, but I don't think I quite realised how much of an inspiration and occupation he was. Diana arrived, straight from the High Court. I am not up to her *glare*—I prefer more of a mental twilight—her exuberance is too much of the electric light.

Steer asked me to go for a walk. It poured with rain and I discovered he had never been out in the rain before and regarded it as a huge adventure. I love that man more and more. He is so comfy, with an infallible sense of humour.

Heard a good 'Margot' from a letter to Venetia, on the latter saying they couldn't afford to take the Mill House: 'If Mr Montagu would eat less, lower his gambling stakes, and drink paraffin, he would be a much richer man.'

Friday, 21st September

A lovely day. Oggie and Diana joined us at breakfast in amazing dressing-gowns. We sat out on the lawn—read a little *South Wind* aloud and each tried to paint a landscape under Steer's patronage. Captains Festin and Davies came to luncheon and Mary and I played four very amusing games of tennis with them. I gambled and won eleven shillings. It was disgraceful how much my play improved when we had money on. Margot is very ill and in fairly acute irritation against Diana. A quartette arrived for the week-end. I suppose it's a questionable point in wartime whether it isn't too much of a luxe to pay them a hundred pounds to come down here and play to a handful of people who could all hear them in London. I sat between two of them. They were very shy and common. It was a great luxury taking one's music lying down on sofas—a real Roman Empire touch. Margot, Oggie, Mary and I had arranged to sleep out and Hugo Rumbold joined the party. Diana and Alan came and tucked us up. Hugo Rumbold was incredibly funny doing a ward 'sister'—he was very vulgar, talking of bowels, obstetrics, and the 'bottle' for Captain Belcher—but irresistibly funny.

At about one o'clock we were still very wide awake when I suddenly saw a flare of light and then, to my amazement, and delight, rocket after rocket went up into the air just in front of us. Oggie (who was in a crib) wailed 'I can't get out—I can't get out', and Diana immediately popped her head out of the window. Whose joke was it?—danced through one's brain at once. First I suspected Diana and Alan, then Hugo, and then I remembered that Captain Festin, etc., had said they were expecting a Zeppelin raid. But the fireworks were obviously ascending, not descending. Hugo began talking very melodramatically about 'For God's sake, keep the women quiet!', and murmuring about an escaped German prisoner. Steer came looming out and between them they drove us in. Oggie was on the verge of hysterics—Margot apparently petrified—and Mary talking rather big in a quavering voice about going to the stables to call the men up. We had a wonderful 'meet' in Diana's bedroom—she in glittering demi-toilette, rouged and powdered, Alan dressed all but his tie; Steer a study in Jaeger; Hugo in a 'fancy' dressing gown; I in a ragged pigtail, and all of us in various degrees of nakedness and disorder. Scott—a wonderful mauve apparition—was found in the passage. Every conjecture was bandied about. Zeppelin? We must have heard it? Escaped prisoner?—wouldn't the searchers come and warn us before fireworking on our tennis court. Practical joke—whose? The officers? Alan was *positive* it could not be a practical joke as it would be serious offence under the Defence of the Realm Act. Each in turn was accused of being *au fait* either because they did or did *not* exhibit fear. My imagination failed me—and I was as cool as a cucumber and happily amused—only I was very puzzled. All was quiet and we went out again. We saw lights unnoticed before. (We afterwards learned they were quite normal.) I saw a light moving in the garden—but it disappeared. It was huge fun —Margot was in a hysterical condition. Finally we left Oggie and Alan in Diana's room and the rest of us congregated in Margot's bedroom—she getting between the sheets. I fetched brandy—and Scrubb's ammonia as refreshments. Steer had delicious giggles. Altogether it was a perfect sight and farce. It was then that they confessed to me that it *was* a joke and that I was the only person in the room who didn't know—but that Diana, Oggie and Alan were in the dark and—what is more—were never to know as Margot said Oggie would never forgive her for having allowed her to be frightened. It was the rector uncle and Captain Festin, etc. and had been planned for weeks. I must say a most successful and excellent joke. Margot and Mary acted wonderfully—I thought them terrified. They perjured themselves etc. Margot confessed to me by saying: 'We arranged it with them and they want to come in and have a drink.' The climax of comedy was reached when Captain Festin was brought in covered with mud from crawling in the garden and bringing with him another officer, a complete stranger, who was introduced to Margot in bed. Oggie was then heard coming along and we had to conceal Festin in Mary's bathroom. I stayed and slept with Mary for what remained of the night.

Saturday, 22nd September

Diana announced herself bilious and stayed in bed till after luncheon. She was in a wonderful green chiffon confection and held a levée. Even Cyril Scott was at her bedside—why admit a stranger? I deprecate the bedroom habit. She was in great difficulty as to the composition of a telegram to her bereaved aunt Lady Robert Manners.

Mary and I went for a ride together. We discussed the ethics of wartime entertaining in relation to Margot. I think the role of the notoriously rich is a very difficult one in wartime. People are quick to say private stinginess is cloaking itself under the pretence of patriotism. Viola arrived in the afternoon—looking wonderfully large, loose, surprised, and disordered. She fluctuates between Botticelli and German looks. She sang in the chapel to the organ. Diana stitches away busily at a glorification of a blanket she has invented for herself. I don't believe she leaves a moment of her life unused. Dear little Willie de Grunne arrived before dinner. He spoke to me very nicely about Basil. Hugo Rumbold appeared brilliantly, horribly, subtly disguised as a Russian—an opaque grey with a built-on-to nose. He had that awful pâté de foie gras look of a depraved foreigner. I sat beside him and he did the most brilliant stunts all the way through —talking in character first in Russian English and then in Italian English. Diana acted as Impresario giving him his cues. The quartette played to us again. Diana lay glimmering on a sofa with Alan clasping her foot all the time. Mary was travelling up to London by a train leaving Chester at an unearthly hour. Margot and I were foolishly determined to escort her. A hired Ford car had been ordered but there was a ridiculous mistake and instead of that the luggage van came round—a sort of Black Maria minus seats, springs or much air. However we stuck to our plan and had an excessively uncomfortable drive—but it was rather fun. We left poor Mary lying down in the ladies' waiting room and Margot and I didn't get home till three o'clock so there was a second very short night!

Sunday, 23rd September

Woke as usual—but stayed in bed late. Willie made one of his best pigeon English remarks at luncheon: 'A simple night in a foreign bed makes me quite tired.' The four sporting officers, perpetrators of the practical joke, came over to luncheon and kept up with a vengeance giving a surprising exhibition of skill in acting—simulation and dissimulation. They coolly denied any responsibility but let fall clever hints as to there having been something up about which they were not allowed to tell us. They laid it on very thick to poor Oggie whose trepidation increased and increased. She was afraid there might be unexploded bombs in the garden. It was the only topic all the way through luncheon. I got quite bewildered as to who knew everything and who knew partly, and I had no conception people could lie so well. The only remaining butts completely in the dark were Diana, Alan, Viola and Oggie. Willie and I went for a long ride in the afternoon. We found divine views and I enjoyed it very much. He confided to me that he had one and one only great romance in his life.

He had been madly in love with and engaged to a lovely girl who was subsequently forbidden to marry by doctors. We came home to a late tea and found the night raid discussion raging. Alan withered me with scorn because I said I was certain it was a joke—utterly poo-poohing such a possibility. Diana had rung Lord French up on the telephone but the beloved rector uncle had the call stopped. Margot, without confessing her own implication or official cognizance, tried to convey her certainty as to its being a joke to Oggie—but she refused to receive the impression—and got into her head the idea that Margot was trying to suppress a scare. The rector, Hugo, Steer and I had a conversation round Margot's bedside as to the best denouement. We were all getting alarmed as to what reception the joke would receive from the butts. The officers were very uneasy and begged us to preserve the mystery until after they had had their dinner. Margot still clung to the determination that Oggie must never know that she was in the joke all the time. More and more lies had to be poured out—Oggie was prepared to bet anything on its *not* being a joke—Margot laid her a thousand to one that it was; but even this failed to convince her. We sat through dinner in great excitement. The rector was called away to the telephone and came back and told the others they were all summoned back to the camp. They all got up with blue faces and sloped solemnly away. Alan with pale triumph said, 'Well Cynthia— I suppose you think this is a joke too: you *are* an extraordinary woman.' A note was then brought in to Margot—she read it aloud: 'We have to apologise for having made a wanton attack on the castle at a quarter to one on Friday night.' A very artistically wound-up practical joke! It couldn't have been better done.

However, the situation became damned uncomfortable—Viola went brown, Alan green with rage. We were so terribly anxious that the officers' feelings shouldn't be hurt by any sense of floater. Diana was *gorgeous*—generously acknowledging the excellence of the joke and redeeming the situation by her energy and address. The Parsons were—I regret to say—very rude. When we women went into the drawing room one of those quite incredible doe-scenes occurred.

At the time one could scarcely credit one's senses and now it seems incredible that such things could have been said. Viola and Oggie both tearfully clamoured that it was the most awful breach of taste and talked with wild confusion about jokes about death in wartime— frightening women and children, etc. Viola gave an incredible exhibition of lack of humour and hysterical-mindedness—I think she minded her Alan being made ridiculous and kept reiterating that his 'good mind' had thought it dangerous and that he knew about the possibilities of local raids because he saw all the telegrams. The worst of it was that she claimed *me* as an ally, saying, 'I know Cynthia feels it too—I saw her face when the telephone message came.' This I had firmly to repudiate. She reached her climax by saying, 'It's our German blood Oggie—that makes us feel differently to that lot— the spirit which makes such a thing possible to English officers couldn't possibly exist in Germany and that is why they are winning the war!' Was there ever so preposterous a remark? Oggie was stung to the quick by this mutual claim and said she wished she *had* had someone killed in the war. We tried to point out to Viola that it was not for *us* to dictate what was good war taste to much-decorated war heroes. If it appealed to *their* sense of humour it was full justification. Someone said if Margot and Cynthia who have both got their husbands in the trenches, don't mind why should others be more sensitive? Oggie was much more reasonable as to the men's part, but poor thing she was bitterly hurt with Margot, saying she could never forgive her for having deceived her and allowed her to be frightened for so long. Finally poor Margot rushed sobbing from the room. Diana and I revived her with brandy and powder. I suppose more successful practical jokes involve tear-shed—but never have I seen such a tragi-comedy as this. The leer and lurch it has developed in darling Steer is too wonderful. When the men came out the concert began. In the middle of it poor little Oggie rushed sobbing from the room. Diana was magnificent, thanking and applauding the perpetrators profusely. I love that old sport of a rector. Fancy, he tells me that after the explosions—when I went out to reconnoitre with Alan—I actually touched his face where he was crouching in the dark. Hugo and Willie were convulsed at my account of the doe-scene. We cheered the officers when they left and I hope they were easy in their minds—I'm afraid Alan rather damped them—they asked Margot to stop his tongue as he might do Captain Festin (the only permanent soldier amongst them) harm. We had some songs when the quartette stopped. Finally, large gathering first in Margot's and then in Oggie's bedroom with ceaseless recriminations, explanations and Jeremiads. Diana was flitting about looking dazzling in a very transparent, bright green, night-dress. Some more good English from Willie—'Goodnight Virgins' to Margot and me.

Finally poor Oggie I believe (this was after I went to bed at two) had practically a fit. She had taken a good deal of medicinal brandy in the course of the evening. Margot had her to sleep with her and a reconciliation was effected. God what an evening! I wish I could have written a proper account of it!

Monday, 24th September

Stayed in bed all day with visits from Margot, Diana, and Viola and Oggie. The joke was dropped as a topic of conversation. Poor Margot very tired. She complained of Oggie's henpecking. They had a great 'stunt' on all the morning—dressing up in armour etc., and being photographed in scenes. I was amused to hear from Margot that Steer was very tired by the high pressure—stunt-weary and irritated by Alan, who apparently left him to do all the fetching and carrying for the photography. He made a sort of declaration to Margot when she was sitting to him—saying he liked her better than any other woman and wished he were a foreigner like Willie so that he would have the nerve to kiss her hand. She was very touched. I wrote a good many letters in bed and read Johnson.

I sat between Hugo Rumbold and Steer at dinner. I like Hugo very much—having had a faint prejudice against him before—his manners are refreshing after Alan's complete lack. Margot had a week's *tête-à-tête* with him and is very fond of him. He made her a declaration, but took her hint and gave no further trouble. We played the analogy game after dinner. I was tired. All I can remember is for 'illness if any?'—'glands' for Hugo; for 'street'—'Baker Street' for Mary; for 'fruit'—'custard apple' for Diana; for 'appurtenances'—'favourite nail-brush' for McEvoy and 'favourite sponge' for Steer.

Tuesday, 25th September

No 'stunt' in the morning. Everybody stayed in bed late. At lunch the American newspaper on Iris Tree was quoted. It's a good bit of journalese—'Actor's daughter—genius too—eulogises Ford in verse form.'

I watched Steer painting Margot. He *is* a darling that man—we teased him urging him to matrimony. He made a delicious remark about Mary: 'It's funny I'm so fond of Mrs H.—but I haven't ever dreamt about her.' Played table football with Alan, Viola and Diana. Read 'Trial of Mrs Maybrick' aloud to Viola. Played with Michael after tea. Oggie and Viola came to see him in his bath and Margot looked in with a woman whom she introduced as Mrs Lovat. She had told us a neighbour was coming to stay for one night. I didn't look at her very carefully—she struck me as dark and rather handsome. I found a note from Steer suggesting a walk. Very much flattered I scurried down. It was late and I was tired so I proposed taking our walk comfortably sitting on a sofa in the billiard-room. We had a delightful talk. Scott came in and exclaimed about the newcomer Mrs Lovat's size. I hadn't been so specially struck with it. The rector-uncle, Davies, Festin and a strange officer came to dinner. I sat between Festin and Scott and was irritated by the latter's obvious absorption in 'Mrs Lovat' who was sitting just opposite. He scarcely took his eyes off her. I didn't take very careful stock of her—I thought her clothes rather tedious and was conscious of *faint* hostility and dimly registered her as a 'man's woman'. I wasn't much struck by her voice when she leant across the table and said 'I hope you are going to let us have some music, Mr Scott.' As I left the dining room Diana whispered, 'It's Hugo dressed up.' At first I thought she was jestingly commenting on a likeness—but sure enough we were up against another practical joke and a very brilliant one. Hugo had said goodbye to us all after luncheon and had driven off to the station with empty boxes. Oggie went with him and bought a wig—he slunk back into the house and put on first Margot's day and then her evening clothes. It was a miracle—his figure was perfect, his feet quite unnoticeable, and his décolletage very enviable. On closer scrutiny I found he made an amazingly attractive woman—lovely gentle languid sad eyes and such a pretty mouth. His walk and general technique were quite admirable. Certainly he is a most remarkable actor. The only person who recognised him was Cyril Scott. He was in it all the time so I feel less mortified by his inattentiveness at dinner. The funny thing was that Viola fell wildly in love with Hugo in this guise—she said she had never felt such passion for anyone else but Alan. Hugo wants this joke *not* to be talked about—as he thinks it would do him no good in the Guards—it would be considered too typical, considering that at the age of twenty-one when he was Cavalier to some lady he went abroad with her for six weeks disguised as a lady friend of hers. This story is true: the garbled version is that he went with Lady —— as her maid. We played a little bad poker—I lost 10s. Diana and Viola did some very good imitations and Steer—to my surprise—a *brilliant* one of George Moore. Terribly late going to bed again.

Wednesday, 26th September

The London flat seemed incredibly small and squalid after the castle. Luckily, Michael is no snob and was delighted to be back. I had my dinner in bed and what Jeremy Taylor calls 'sat on my bundle of thorns'. Polly is on board wages at Cadogan Square. I suppose I ought really to send her away.

1917

Thursday, 27th September

My thirtieth birthday—the *femme de trente ans*. It's sad, but I am thinking about it very little. Ivor Churchill came at 12.20 and took me in the park, and to see the huge shell-hole in the Green Park just behind the Ritz. All the windows at Wimborne House were broken by it.

Saturday, 29th September

Letter to Beb and diary *before* getting up is my present morning technique. Michael walked to Selfridges with me and there I took the great step of buying a bicycle, having decided on that as my method of transport in London. I rode it home in triumph and found it delightful, and much less alarming than I anticipated. Of course, there is only about a third of the traffic there used to be and one can always dismount to cross Oxford Street or to meet any crisis.

I rode it to Audley Square, and Claud and I lunched at the Curzon Hotel. We talked of Johnson and wondered whether a really assiduous Boswell couldn't collect quite a good show of sayings from almost any of us. He turned up again at about seven and suggested our dining at Canuto's in Baker Street. There had been an air-raid warning, but the 'all clear' signal had come through. However, as we were finishing our dinner, a terrific row began. A nervous waiter was infuriated by our nonchalance. I was *delighted* at last to come in for a war perquisite. It is very difficult to restrain one's sight-seeing instincts. I couldn't help standing in the doorway. We saw shells bursting like stars and heard them whistling through the air, and all round the 'cold, fruitless moon' there was a wreath of white puffs of undissipated smoke. I couldn't hear anything that sounded like a bomb anywhere near. What made the terrific row was a huge gun in Regent's Park which coughed and coughed—I do find it a strangely exhilarating sound. The streets were quite empty, and most of the people in the restaurant bundled down into the cellar. There was a very comic middle-class dinner party anxious to show their coolness by facetiousness and cracking joke after joke: 'Let's have all-clear soup' was their happiest effort.

I wasn't frightened about Michael because I could see there was nothing in that direction, but I wished I had been in the basement. We—perhaps foolishly—walked back to it before the raid was over. We found Michael fast asleep in his pram in the passage, which is quite safe from anything except a direct hit. He never even woke. Nurse said some shrapnel had fallen on the window, and I suppose the raid must have gone on for nearly an hour and a half. I rang up Belgrave Square. John had been taken down to the dining room, but had returned to bed. Claud stayed late.

Sunday, 30th September

I was to have picked up Claud at Audley Square, but felt too exhausted and made him meet me at Canuto's instead. We played the analogy game at lunch: I gave him 'damson' for fruit. He came back to my flat till he had to go to catch his train. I felt very annoyed with myself for what occurred. Being tongue-tied, I must write him a letter.

Monday, 1st October

My machine and I covered a tremendous lot of ground this day. I got very hot and tired—I *wish* I could tell Basil about it and what good pictures he would draw! I was dining with Tonks and had determined on the great adventure of bicycling there—I started at seven so as to have a chance of arriving before the raid began. It was too dark to be pleasant and I didn't enjoy myself in the King's Road. Just as I was leaving it, a policeman flew past with the cry: 'Air-raid warning: TAKE COVER', and there were friendly shouts of, 'You'd better get home as quick as possible, Miss.' The sudden silence that falls on London is wonderful: all the traffic ceases, and the streets magically empty—the whole population swallowed up into the houses. I didn't know the way and, as it was too dark to read and there was no one left to direct me, my position was rather unpleasant, but I got there in the nick of time, *just* before the firing began. It was funny, sitting down calmly to dinner with Tonks and his sister to the accompaniment of such an orchestra. They are quite blasé, having been in London for all the previous ones. The noise still exhilarates me. We stayed in the dining room—it being the most sheltered part of the house. It was a very much more desultory raid than the preceding ones, going on intermittently for about three hours—there were long intervals of complete silence. It was nearly eleven before Tonks would let me start and then he insisted on walking as far as the Brompton Road with me.

Tuesday, 2nd October

Oddly enough the raid that had seemed so much less effective had been the worst and the damage achieved was near where I was. Bomb in

Ebury Street, Eaton Mews destroyed, and Chelsea Bridge on fire. Felt tired and depressed—the prospect of getting up in my squalid, cramped surroundings is so uninviting that I postpone it.

Very sorry to see in the papers that Freyberg has been wounded again—I do hope not badly, but have heard no details. Whibley called for me to lunch: an air-raid warning had just been given, but we ignored it and went to Canuto's, and nothing came of it. His ardour and attentions were most trying. I wish he wouldn't quote Donne and call me 'his Newfoundland'. He said: 'Will you promise to love me some day?' I believe he really considers himself eligible.

Wednesday, 3rd October

I have a great plot on with Oggie. I have determined to try and get on the cinema stage anonymously—a great decision. I hope for a lucrative escapade. Oggie has asked the experienced Madge Titheradge to help me, and arranged for me to go and see her. I am very excited.

Bicycled to Pamela's hospital. What must I look like on it in uniform! Hated work at the hospital, feeling slack and listless. The poor men have been terrified by the raids, and they have had to make a ward downstairs.

Thursday, 4th October

Pouring rain. I stayed in all the morning and went through some of Basil's letters with a view to sorting them. I found it very heart-rending—it gives one so many fresh stabs. I began reading Thomas Browne's *Religio Medici*—what sumptuous prose it is!

I went to see Freyberg in Bryanston Square Hospital. He looks very white and subdued. Poor fellow, before he went out last time I remember his saying he would rather be killed than wounded again —he has been through such terrible mills of pain. Now he has been hit in *five* places again by a shell bursting at his feet—right through the lung for one, and he has a hole the size of his fist in his thigh. He is riddled like St Sebastian. I believe he's been hit everywhere except in face and head, so he's really had amazing luck not to have lost a limb. He said he'd take poison if he had to have his leg off. He refused to be taken away for a day and a half after he was hit, as he wanted to see the attack he was then engaged on carried through to a successful finish. His men didn't know he had been wounded until it was over.

He loathes being in bed and, of course, chafes and frets at the interruption to his brigadiering, which he *adores*. He was very sweet: he took my hand and thanked me for coming—I told him my cinematograph escapade and he was much amused. Together we concocted a name for me—'Sylvia Strayte' of poker significance. I then had to go and see Madge Titheradge during her matinee at the Haymarket. Her dressing room was wonderfully typical—a screen pinned all over with telegrams of good wishes for her last first night and dozens of signed photographs. She was very nice and said she would write to two managers about me. She warned me it would be very hard work—probably ten to seven business.

It was my opera-box night: I took Mary Strickland (up for one night) and Barbara and Steer. We dined at Green's Restaurant and hired a brougham for the evening. I enjoyed *Ivan the Terrible* much. I like noisy operas. Steer came in and saw and admired the Tonks pastel of me.

Friday, 5th October

Laid the foundation stone of Michael's education by taking him to a Montessori class at Miss Richardson's school in Westminster. All the other infants were out of London on account of the raids, so he was all alone. It's rather sweet—the room with the little white chairs and tables—and he *adored* it. It was simply ideal play—a very thickly-sugar-coated pill if, indeed, there be any pill at all, and looked like the most demoralising spoiling. He was allowed to seize one plaything after another out of the cupboard, flying from joy to joy like a bee in a herbaceous border, but I daresay there is more method than one detects and, anyhow, it's great fun for him. He is to go every morning at ten. It will be an awful bus effort. I *wish* it wasn't so far. He was too comic—such keenness and Ettie technique.

Saturday, 6th October

Visited Freyberg again. He talked interestingly about soldiering. I love his love of it. He said how strong his position was as a brigadier who had been through the mud of this war as a subaltern as it produced a rare alliance of practice and theory.

I had tea with Freddie and Brenda in the funny little Mayfair mews they are occupying. She was looking very pretty; he—poor darling—plunged in misery and very ill. He sits up late every night writing a memoir of Basil. He told me General Bridges had a little lion as a mascot, and when he recovered consciousness after his wound, he is alleged to have said: 'I hope the lion got my leg—he hasn't had a square meal for days'.

Monday, 8th October

I lunched alone with Brenda. She told me Freddie is very anxious to have a Memorial Service for Basil. She bemoaned their prospects of becoming head of the family and said her dread had always been possessions *without* money, and now she saw that fate imminent and herself buried in Irish country life.

Put on my oilskins and went to visit Freyberg again. He speculates a great deal as to whether he will be killed or not. He told me he could quite easily go four days without sleep.

Tuesday, 9th October

To my astonishment, after a mutual cut in the Queen's Restaurant, I received a letter from Augustus John asking me to come and sit to him. I went to his studio in Mulberry Road, Chelsea, at 10.30, taking some clothes on approval, but he chose to do me in the black serge dress I arrived in. He has a most delightful studio—huge, with an immense window, and full of interesting works. The cold was something excruciating, as his stove wouldn't work, so my sufferings were intense and I felt myself becoming more and more discoloured. His appearance is magnificent, straight out of the Old Testament—flowing, well-kept beard, hair cut *en bloc* at about the top of the ear, fine majestic features. He had on a sort of overall daubed with paint, buttoning up round his throat, which completed a brilliantly picturesque appearance. He was 'blind sober' and quite civil. I believe sometimes he is alarmingly surly. Unlike McEvoy, he didn't seem to want to converse at all while painting and I gratefully accepted the silence. He talked quite agreeably during the intervals he allowed me. He made—I think—a very promising beginning of me sitting in a chair in a severe pose: full face, but with eyes averted—a very sidelong glance. He said my expression 'intrigued' him, and certainly I think he has given me a very evil one—a sort of *listening* look as though I were hearkening to bad advice.

He told me he is shortly going out to paint at the Front. Except for the cold, I enjoyed my sitting, though I can't say I feel *at ease* with him.

I went down to Crowhurst by 5.50 to stay with Tigsy,[1] who is spending his holiday there.

1. Ivor Churchill.

Wednesday, 10th October

The Duchess of Marlborough went off to London early, leaving us to a whole day's *tête-à-tête*. It was a lovely cold day. I love Ivor's company, but occasionally I was a little anxious as to how much he was enjoying mine, and I *believe* he had the same uneasiness. We went for several short walks, talked a great deal, and I read *A Midsummer Night's Dream* aloud in a tigsy hut. He complimented me on my reading. He told me his plan for collecting quotations from their own works from every good contemporary author. He has got a gloriously bound book for the purpose. I have a good mind to do the same thing.

The Duchess came back in time for dinner. In a discussion on air-raids Ivor rather wittily said in their praise that they 'made one forget everything—including the war'.

Thursday, 11th October

Disappointed to find no communication from the cinema agents. Dined with Willie de Grunne at the Ritz. I was taking him to the opera, it being my box tonight, and was much impressed with the appearance of General Foch who was dining there. To my surprise I greatly enjoyed *Faust*.

Friday, 12th October

Changed into my black velvet and taxied through the rain to lunch with Maud Cunard: the little canary was wound up very tightly. I don't know why, but I was miserable. I had one of my fits of shyness and morbid self-depreciation—once so frequent, now much rarer. Ivor was beside me and I felt he didn't want to be—I daresay it was purely imaginary. On my other side was a very ugly brother of Thomas Beecham's, who has just bought Lympur.

Very distressed to hear Mells House has been burnt down—poor Katharine! I splashed to Canuto's through the rain and dined with Claud. He came back to the flat. We had quite an interesting speculative conversation on immortality—I claiming 'intimations'.

Ineffectually, flabbily angry with Claud and myself.

Saturday, 13th October

Had a very disagreeable bicycle ride to Augustus John's studio. It came on to rain and I arrived wet and disordered. He was very agreeable. I don't think he improved my picture. I lunched with Mary at Queen's Restaurant which is full of happy Basil associations for me.

I regretted having accepted Mrs Hunter's invitation to Hill Hall, but went down by 3.35 train. She told us anecdotes of George Moore, amongst others his replying to an *ingénue* of seventeen who asked him if he were married: 'No, I have always preferred adultery.'

Sunday, 14th October

When I came down I found it was the most lovely autumn day— quite perfect. There are two admirable tennis courts and I played well with a strange racket. There was a men's four which was treated with sacramental seriousness. Mrs Hunter was very severe on anyone who even stood up during its playing.

I had Ronald Storrs at lunch. I had had a prejudice against him, partly due to people who didn't like him and partly to those who did. However, I was bereaved of another prejudice. I still think him devoid of any personal charm, but I must own his company is wine to me. More and more do I love *vitality* and accord it very, very high marks: this he has in a superlative degree, united to great appreciativeness. Then personally I love the quoting habit by which he offends some, and he is full of literary tags and anecdotes which I always like.

I like the story he told of Sardou, who was a unique monopoliser of table-talk. On one occasion the only remark made by anyone else was a contribution from a stranger, during the momentary respite afforded by Sardou's unpleasant habit of gargling with the water in his finger-bowl—it was the only chance of getting anything in edge- ways. Sardou's comment on the bold stranger was *Quel bavard, ce jeune homme!* He also told us that, after two men had toiled fifteen years over deciphering Pepys diary, they discovered the key to the cipher had been lying on the shelf all the time.

Storrs was selfishly, insultingly anxious for a practical monopoly of music and desirous to exclude the 'Comus rout' and set them down to cards. He wanted to sacrifice me as a decoy, but I firmly established myself on a sofa and Scott played the most wonderful Wagner Bovril —first *Tristan* and then *Meistersinger*—a really wonderful perform- ance. Elizabeth would stay down with the men, making great play with a new diamond bracelet left her by Prince Bibesco's brother.

Monday, 15th October

All the others went early. I breakfasted with Mrs Hunter and sat about

until my 11.40 train. We discussed Elizabeth—she found her dreadfully tiring. I adore this story of Maud Cunard: on being asked if
Thomas Beecham's lecture had been interesting, she replied, 'No, it
was dreadfully dull—terrible! I shouted to him, "Speak up Thomas
Beecham—speak up—so that you can hear how dull you are!"'

Found a worrying letter from Lawrence saying his house had been
searched and they had been forced to leave the prohibited area of
Cornwall. He announced his arrival in London and said he had hardly
a shilling in the world. I went to see poor Freyberg. The wound in his
thigh had gone septic and he had to undergo an operation on Friday,
and was looking and feeling very miserable and ill. I do pray he won't
lose his leg. I felt dreadfully sorry for him. He asked me to put my
hand on his forehead.

Papa rang up—said Angela Forbes must see me. A fearful howdy-
do—she had been ordered out of France by the Adjutant General on
a (according to her) trumped-up charge of drunkenness. She suspects
discharged workers. They wanted me to try and get Mr Asquith to
see her and advise. Very loath to do this, I suggested Bluetooth with
his legal and War Office knowledge as an alternative. Papa approved
of the plan. I tried the telephone again and again, but couldn't get on.
Told Angela I would ring him up in the morning, and try and arrange
an interview. She was looking very distraught.

Tuesday, 16th October

Dear Bluetooth meekly turned up for lunch at the Hyde Park Hotel.
Angela was looking pretty bad. We got through our meal all right,
then went up to her sitting room and sat there till four whilst she
poured out her grievances. Bluetooth was a good listener and quite a
judicious adviser. It really appears that she is being treated badly.
Undoubtedly, she has done admirable work—she was mentioned in
despatches only a month ago—and now she is to be dismissed at the
dictation of personal enemies without any inquiry into their evidence.
She would welcome any inquiry and claims that she could produce
innumerable witnesses to vouch for her sobriety. But, of course, the
Adjutant General is omnipotent and she could easily be banished
without an explanation.

We were shown the correspondence with Lord Derby—Papa had
written him rather a scorcher—and we speculated as to what petticoat
influence with him might be worked upon. Bluey was inclined to
think that if they threatened questions in the House, probably they
would be only too glad to drop the matter and leave her to live in

France in peace, suppose she voluntarily (as she was anyhow contemplating) gave up the management of her canteens. If threats are
unavailing, Papa intends—and looks forward to—making the Hell
of a row in the House of Lords . . . a dénouement I devoutly pray may
be averted!

D. H. Lawrence came to see me at five, looking very gaunt. Last
Friday the police searched their house, took letters to Frieda, and told
them they must leave at once. It is hard for him. In Cornwall he lived
so cheaply and healthily, and he will have to go on paying for the
house there. His health doesn't allow of his living in London and all
the money he has in the world is the *prospect* of eighteen pounds for
the publication of some poems all about bellies and breasts which he
gave me to read. People should either be left in peace *or* interned at
the country's expense. I promised to do what I could in the matter,
but doubt whether it will be much—after all, the woman *is* a German
and it doesn't seem unreasonable.

Wednesday, 17th October

Fearful wet morning and I had a most unpleasant bicycle ride to John's
studio. He worked away at my picture, but hasn't introduced any
colour into it yet. Like McEvoy he sits to paint: he mixes the paints
on his palette with very vigorous sweeps of his brushes, and sometimes
steps back and looks at his painting and his model in a big looking-
glass.

Angela came to see me at six. She seemed to think her affairs
were going better and that Lord Derby showed some change of
front.

Thursday, 18th October

Went to McEvoy at 9.30. His flow of facile, sympathetic chatter was
a great change after John, and his running compliments were as cheering as ever. He told me I was like a Madonna by Whistler, and that I
had more sense of humour than anyone else—also gave me Tonks'
dewdrop to the effect that I was the only one of that whole lot worth
anything. I told McEvoy my Sylvia Strayte scheme. He was absolutely horrified (which I took as a great compliment), considered it
the most awful desecration imaginable, and warned me of white
slavery and blackmail.

Bicycled to lunch at Cavendish Square. Margot told lurid tales of
Lloyd George's cowardice during the raids: she said his appearance

of terror was such that two typists fainted at the mere sight of him, thinking some appalling disaster must have taken place.

Sunday, 21st October

Bicycled to lunch with the Laverys—all the way to Cromwell Place. Eddie was there and the sculptor Mestrovic. I saw the portrait of my father-in-law and thought it good—dignified without being too stern, and not too mellow—yet agreeable.

The Lawrences came to tea. I was really glad to see her again. To quote Hugo Rumbold, she is a 'hearty' woman and there is something warming about her. At first we were rather constrained, and they complained of my being so saddened and grown-up, bewailing the expression in my eyes—and Lawrence looked very sore and sulky— but in time we all warmed and brightened, and were quite happy. Eddie came in to see them for a few moments, and they told him their sad tale. We were not able to hold out any hopes of their being allowed to return to Cornwall. Their exclusion seems so very reasonable. At present they are living in a room in Mecklenburg Square which has been lent to them. When Eddie left, Lawrence said, 'There is something nice in Eddie after all.' Apparently he has been lowering with contemptuous dislike towards him lately. He described his hatreds for people and said there were certainly not more than eight people in the whole world with whom he could bear to spend two hours—all the rest made him ill. He knew at first sight whether a newcomer would ever be a possibility and generally fell in hate. They deplored my incapacity to hate and my constant 'trafficking' with people. Poor little Eddie winced when they told him how much older he looked. It doesn't sound as if they had been very pleasant, but I felt very fond of them.

Wednesday, 24th October

Woke up to terrible morning misery. The dreary detail of the John tragedy blackens life. One can never dismiss it from one. It is a past, present, and future nightmare. I loved my idea of that baby more than I have ever loved anything—and it was just something that never existed!

Lunched with Whibley. He was back from his joy-ride in France. The French Government had asked him to *rouler en auto* at their expense. He had been shelled and was full of his experiences. He brought me a Verdun medal—a rather lovely one—with 'On ne passe pas' as inscription.

Papa showed me the Angela dossier. Apparently the evidence had been collected by the Advocate General from a malignant worker Miss ——, who had been discharged for drink. These are extracts from her letter to another worker, sent to Angela by the recipient:

'Louise and I told him all we knew and he asked us to write to the others, so I'd be awfully glad if both you and Betty would write on a sheet of paper and sign, enumerating any incidents you know of—such as swearing words used by Lady Angela, any occasions on which she was not sober, and the way we were treated in the canteen. You know the sort of things they would want to know, and you will be doing a public good by helping to stop the woman. You needn't mind what you say, as they know all about her, but it is essential they should have signed evidence.

'Don't forget anything you or Betty know about her morals.'

Thursday, 25th October

Took John to see Forsythe, the brain specialist recommended by Katharine. Mamma came to assist me. He said it was not at all a usual case. If something had gone wrong *before* his birth, then nothing could be done, but it was *possibly* a case of what he calls introversion when training might help. He is going to read my book about John for data, and will look out for a governess for me. In the meantime, I must get another hospital nurse.

Friday, 26th October

I went to tea with Muriel and groused to her. Carton de Wiart came while I was there and I was recharmed by him. He said it was hard that Bridges should get £500 a year for the loss of his leg, whilst he gets practically nothing for the loss of his arm and his eye, as it occurred while he was only a captain. He is general now and—I suppose—would have got £1,000 had he already attained that rank when he was wounded. Bridges got £1,000 blood-money down as well.

Dined with Alex at Canuto's and we went to Barrie's *Dear Brutus*.

Saturday, 27th October

Lunched with Mamma at Queen's, and then we and Guy and Frances, Mary S. and Barbara went to *The Thirteenth Chair*, a really admirably exciting play—we enjoyed it immensely. A murder is committed in the dark during a seance and one has to guess who did it. Mrs Campbell

was excellent as the medium. We went to her dressing room afterwards and found her in great spirits. Her happiness has disfigured her,
as it keeps her too fat, but it is wonderful that she should have found
it to so great an extent. She calls George West her 'golden pheasant'.
She came back to tea with us at Catherine Street.

Telephoned to Horatia. She has had a great stroke of luck, having
met a fabulously rich American Jewess of nineteen: she is lonely and
has asked Horatia to live with her at Claridges. She has come over to
do war-work.

Sunday, 28th October

Alex came to say goodbye at twelve. He was returning to France at
1.50. He has been very nice this leave. I have seen him every day, but
am still complimented or insulted—as one likes to take it—by his
making an exception of me.

I bicycled to Mecklenburg Square to lunch with the Lawrences. They
have had a very handsome bed sitting room lent to them, but they are
both pining for their Cornwall cottage. They cooked an excellent
omelette by the fire, and we lunched off that plus sardines and pears.
He was sore and aggressive, but accused me of being even gloomier. As
a matter of fact, I am feeling much better after my temporary collapse.

Freyberg's bedside atmosphere was a very sharp contrast. He has
been awfully ill. They feared not only for his leg for his life. He is
much better now, though chafing at the prospect of another two
months at least in bed. Claud came at six—no teasing. He is depressed
by the indefinite prospect of military life at Clacton-on-Sea. It is so
long since we had an air-raid that I begin to feel I only dreamt them.

Monday, 29th October

Most lovely morning with blue atmosphere. I went to Augustus John
whose outline looked slightly blurred after the bout of which I suspect
him, but he was very amiable. He volunteered a wish to see Lawrence
—which was just what I wanted—so I shall try and make him come
to my next sitting.

I lunched with Horatia: she told me a good Russell story. Once,
walking home with Harold, she complained of feeling faint. Greatly
agitated, he exclaimed: 'Wait a minute—and I'll stop a bus!' (This was
before the days of taxi shortage.)

The Italian debacle[1] is awful. Things seem blacker than ever.

1. The Battle of Caporetto.

1917

Tuesday, 30th October

Bicycled in oilskins to McEvoy. It was greasy and windy, and I made a long detour. I arrived a very windswept, rain-washed model. McEvoy was very rattled. He has been asked to paint for the Admiralty. He worked at an *utterly* pre-Raphaelite version of me, hands uplifted in the type of clasping a crystal, a pomegranate, or even a pigeon. It is a bore to be such an anachronism. His running, enraptured stream of dewdrops is a great change after John. 'Lovely hands! Oh! It's too wonderful, etc., etc.'

I bicycled to Grosvenor Gardens to lunch at the American Chancellery with Elizabeth. A man called Davis was our host. Seldom have I had so unpleasant a meal. The basement was stifling, the meat uneatably tough, and the twangs deafening. I had an impossibly ill-mannered American on one side—Lord Lytton the other. When Elizabeth sat down she announced that she had been treating a headache with brandy all the morning: she then proceeded to drink three glasses of red wine, followed by two of port and three cups of coffee. I like this story of Lord Curzon. The new Lady C. said, 'George works so hard and sits up so late. He often doesn't come to bed till 2.30, but stays down writing out the menus for the servants in his different country houses.'

Bicycled to Freyberg. He was pining to be on the Italian front— he seemed much better.

Wednesday, 31st October

Lunch with Pamela Lytton. Hankey was there; he gave us amusing accounts of the linguistic difficulties at the Allied Conferences. He said the *only* common language of some of them was German. The War Cabinet had been buried that morning with the Zionists. What fun if Montagu and Venetia are forced to go and live in Palestine! I like the name given to the Jewish regiment—the 'Jordan Highlanders' and their motto is 'No advance without cover'.

Went to Berkeley Street to see Katharine—Edward home on fire leave. Their ten thousand books were rescued from the burning house, but unluckily were much damaged by rain. Margot's telegram of condolence, referring to Mells as 'my honeymoon house' was brilliantly typical.

Was woken at one by an air-raid. Michael won his spurs. He sat up in his pram in the passage with very bright eyes and kept up a running commentary. 'That was a big gun—it must have wheels. They are very low. Oh no, I couldn't go to sleep with such a row going on. I *do* like the noise of the guns.' It went on for about one and a half hours.

Thursday, 1st November

Bicycled to John's studio. John began a new version of me, in which I could see no sort of resemblance to myself. The Lawrences turned up. I thought it just possible John *might* add another to the half dozen or so people whose company Lawrence can tolerate for two hours. It was quite a success. John asked Lawrence to sit for him, and Lawrence admired the large designs in the studios, but maintained an ominous silence as regards my pictures. He charged John to depict 'generations of Wemyss disagreeableness in my face, especially the mouth', said disappointment was the keynote of my expression, and that what made him 'wild' was that I was 'a woman with a weapon she would never use'. 'Let the dead paint the dead.' 'Who is that bird?' was his only comment on Margot Howard de Walden's portrait. He thought the painting of Bernard Shaw with closed eyes very true symbolism.

Saturday, 3rd November

Visited Adele who has had an operation. She was exquisitely laid out on one of the Gosford Chinese beds. She said that at the Cabinet the other day Lloyd George had said, 'Does anyone know a Lady Cunard? She is a most dangerous woman.' A great many of the most constant visitors—Curzon, Balfour, Milner, Winston—were, of course, present but not *one* spoke up. What a chorus of cock-crowing there should have been!

I visited Freyberg. He had been feverish again and can't sleep, poor fellow. On the pretext of their being cold, he took my hands and held them the whole time I was there. I acquiesced. Dined with Pamela Lytton: Barrie was there—asked on purpose to help me, but threw cold water on my cinema plan. Mrs Campbell sent a beautiful golden tortoise-shell cat called Algy to Michael. He is so delighted with it. Algy appears quite happy, but has gone on hunger strike.

Sunday, 4th November

A *lovely* day. I bicycled to John's studio. He went on with his second picture of me and made it—I thought—rather lovely and quite like.

He introduced extremely good movement into the pose, a kind of rhythmus, such as he gets in his big designs. Bicycled home via the Fulham Road, and the Lawrences came to lunch with Michael and me. We had sardines and cold beef. I told Michael I had seen Mr Selfridge in a box at the opera. I couldn't think why he was so amused and delighted, until it struck me that a 'box' conveyed something very unusual to his mind.

Telephoned to Pamela Lytton. She said she and Barrie had gone on discussing the cinema question, and he said that if I was really determined, he could give me addresses, and could even help me very much by having me put into his *Admirable Crichton* which is going to be filmed—unfortunately, not for some time. On Pamela's advice I wrote to him asking for his assistance.

Tuesday, 6th November

Bicycled to McEvoy early. He was so delighted with the colour of my vaguely purple coat that he decided to paint that instead of the blue Fortuni tea-gown. He thought it helped to give my impression of extreme 'juvenility' which he wished to convey, and expatiated pleasantly on my extraordinary quality of freshness, as of a landscape newly washed by rain—dawn—and so on.

I lunched in with Michael and then went off to the Palace Theatre for the Angels' Tableaux—I was doing the Madonna in the Fra Angelico Annunciation and Michael a Sir Joshua cherub. I got through my tableau all right and I was told I looked well, but to my fury they scratched Michael's because the scenery wasn't ready, so I got him and Nannie placed in the dress circle where they could see. Margot was just in front and attacked Nannie furiously, saying it was cruel to have him in a theatre—adding characteristically, 'He isn't more than five is he?' Maud Russell drove us back in her landaulette. Hazel Lavery came, too. She gave some good Margot quotations: 'Why do you neglect your boys so? I *never* see you with them!'—she hasn't got any, and 'Why are you losing your looks so soon: you aren't forty yet, are you?'

I dined with Ivo Grenfell at Canuto's—he is a vision and very sweet, though not clever to talk to. He says he will go out soon. How unthinkable for poor Ettie.

Thursday, 8th November

Sat to John. His servant announced me as 'Lady Sinister'. Picture still looking very well. Bicycled to lunch with Stella Beech in Kensington Square. Had a long talk with her. Poor thing, it is a terribly hard life! She is trying to live on about four pounds a week, with a child and her husband's bills to cope with. Her stage career seems very hand-to-mouth and her luck very bad, as the plays she is in nearly always come off at once after they have let her into all the expenses of a season ticket, gloves, stockings, etc. For some inexplicable reason, her mother won't allow her to use the name Patrick Campbell, which deprivation greatly reduces her salary. An amazing woman—she threatened her own daughter with legal proceedings.

Read through hundreds of Basil's beloved letters in bed.

Friday, 9th November

Lunched with Lady Salisbury. Kitty was there: her boy Bobby in the Coldstream is back on leave. She had a ridiculous story that the mobile guns used in London during air-raids were German. Lord Colum Stuart suggested that the Irish should be conscripted to fight in Italy on the plea of the Pope being in danger.

I had an appointment with Freddie. He is distressed about Basil's will—he left everything to Freddie's little Basil, but had expressed a wish to Freddie that certain possessions should be given to friends. As he had not written down any directions, this cannot be done. Afterwards I visited Ivor's bedside: he was much better after his appendix operation and very sweet again. I have been concsious of an eclipse in our friendship, but it seemed quite all right again. I brought him *The Rainbow* to read.

I dined with Duff at the Criterion and we went to *The Yellow Ticket* together. He was a good cavalier and provided a brougham for the evening. He has just finished a very uncomfortable course of training, during which he was treated just like a private—had to make his own bed, clean his own buttons, and so on. Now he begins life as an officer in the Grenadiers at Chelsea. He looked very brown and well, and we enjoyed each other's company. I have seldom enjoyed a play as much as *The Yellow Ticket*—a real, satisfactory melodrama, with enough to make one laugh, too. I *rocked* when the villain suddenly opens the folding doors and reveals a large double bed to the terrified gaze of his victim. I was amazed by Gladys Cooper—she looked too lovely, and acted very, very well. The play seemed very tactless towards the Russians—I don't suppose it would have been allowed before the rebellion.

1917

Saturday, 10th November

Lawrence came to lunch bringing chocs for Michael. Not a satisfactory meeting. I was torpid. Visited Freyberg, found him much better and thrilled by a book he is writing on tactics. He showed me lots of maps, about which I have *no* intelligence. He told me they cost him two pounds a week.

Claud had telephoned to say he was up for a few hours, so I told him to come round: war talk—he could be called a pacifist, even a pro-German.

Sunday, 11th November

Tonks called for me and we dined at Canuto's. He had bad luck about the food—everything he chose had been 'used up', and the climax was when he asked for a liqueur, only to be told it was too late. Otherwise, we were very happy and we had a long talk over my gas-fire. We discussed Freyberg and Lawrence. He didn't look at all pleased when I told him I was sitting to John. He is a jealous god. He is probably just going to become head of the Slade which will give him quite a good assured income.

Monday, 12th November

Bicycled to McEvoy, and he went on with me in my purple tweed coat —my bicycling stunt has given him an out-of-door conception of me. His painting *is* a Penelope's web—this day's work rather spoilt a very promising beginning. He says I have the most 'deceptive face', my profile's so inconsistent with my full face. He and John had compared notes on my difficulty. The photograph of the water-colour has come out very well.

I lunched with Whibbles: he insisted on going to Pagani's, which turned out to be a longer walk than he thought. He has got an outbreak of gout on his finger, but insisted on its being an anomaly and begged me not to think of him as a 'gouty old man'. He brought me his new book *Political Sketches* and bunched me with lovely carnations. He will *unarm* me, even in the streets, and kept reiterating, 'I love you—I love you'. I visited Freyberg and found him sitting up for the first time. Again, on the pretext of their being cold, he took my hand and he kissed it when I said good-bye.

I bicycled to dinner at Cavendish Square—only Margot, Old Boy, Blackwell, Sylvia, and Bongie. Dinner topic was criminology—finger-

The Countess of Wemyss

A. J. Balfour in his first car

Ettie—Lady Desborough

Charles Whibley, a portrait by Sir Gerald Kelly

Chirk Castle: Lady Cynthia 'rolls' Olga Lynn and Steer

Stella Patrick Campbell tells Lady Cynthia's future

prints and so on. Asquith said he remembered seeing five pirates hanging in London when he was a boy. They played bridge, leaving Bongie and I to conversation. I like the Army order which was issued: 'The Portuguese are not to be referred to as "ruddy geese", but as "our ancient and illustrious allies".'

Tuesday, 13th November

Horatia called for me at 11.30 and we went by Tube to Basil's Memorial Service at St Martin-in-the-Fields. I dreaded the ordeal unspeakably. I hate crying in public and I *can't* restrain tears. However, it was all so beautiful that, though painful, I think it was well worth while and I am glad they had it. The service was beautifully chosen—the only blot being a dreadful little verse printed on the programme:

The brightest gems of valour in the Army's diadem
Are the V.C. and the D.S.O., M.C., and D.C.M.
But those who live to wear them will tell you they are dross
Beside the final honour of a simple wooden Cross.

They sang 'Mine eyes have seen the glory of the coming of the Lord'— such gorgeous words, and the Grenadier band playing with muffled drums was wonderfully moving. I thought how Basil would have laughed at the doggerel verse. The whole thing was difficult to associate with him and yet it shattered me. Nancy was just in front of me, which again made me smile *with* Basil.

I lunched with Bluetooth, who is just going off to Canada on an Air Board mission, then did some shopping for Beb at Selfridges. Dined with Yvo Grenfell at Canuto's. We called for the Lawrences and took them to the opera. Maud has sold my little box and given me a big one, and I filled it with the most comic concentration of human beings ever seen. It gave me *fou-rire* to think what a funny sight we must have been—the Lawrences, Augustus John, self, Ivo, Oggie, and a little fat, tenor friend of hers. The most piquant features were the conjunction of two red beards and of the young guardsman to the Pacifist's Hun wife. She would talk about the war to Yvo and tell him how very much smarter the German regiments were! She was draped in a Chinese shawl and Lawrence had trimmed his beard for the occasion. John was quite amiable and said he wanted to sit where he could see my profile against the light. The opera was *Aïda*, and very well done, but I found my companions very distracting.

1917

Wednesday, 14th November

Bicycled to Augustus John. He finished my picture. I think it very good. I passed Freddie riding at the head of his company in Hyde Park: we exchanged grins. I talked to John about the cinema and he thrilled me by saying that Griffiths was going to do *Morte d'Arthur* in *England*. Of course, that would be just my chance. My medieval type could at last be turned to some account. I must get on to him. John said he hoped I would sit to him again when he returns from France. He also hinted that I should take up the career of a model.

Went with Mary Herbert, Aubrey, and Lady Carnarvon to the Grosvenor Gallery. McEvoy's water-colour of me looks very pretty. Diana and I hang side by side, and one withering woman, in a significant voice fraught with 'Birds of a feather' innuendo, exclaimed '*Friends!*'

Thursday, 15th November

Mrs Colefax had asked me to dinner about ten days before—such long notice that I felt obliged to accept. Indefatigable lion-hunter as she is, she always does a double-bluff bait—if one fish is caught, he generally finds the bait which caught him has slipped off the hook! The Laverys were at dinner and one or two more, and afterwards a large drum trickled in. To do her credit it was really a very successful party and I am glad I went. Musicians played and war-poets read their works. Just after we came up from dinner, two young men came—one very shy, the other to all appearances very much at his ease. The former was Siegfried Sassoon. He was in khaki: at first I only noticed his sticking-out ears and obvious embarrassment, but a closer scrutiny revealed great charm and a certain sweetness and grave strength in his countenance. I felt much drawn towards him, but had no conversation with him. Nichols, on the other hand, was twice introduced to me by the zealous hostess and we spent the remainder of the evening side by side. He was a thin alert face and is quick and agreeable to talk to—he expressed great admiration for Siegfried, both as poet and soldier. They have both had shell-shock. For Siegfried, he claimed astonishing valour. They each read some of their own poems. Nichols raptly and passionately, as though absolutely carried away on the wings of his own poetry and quite oblivious to his whereabouts, and Siegfried in a terse, laconic style—each manner was suitable to the particular matter. Siegfried's have a brilliant, grim irony—Nichols' I have always thought very good. Vita Nicolson was there. Nichols said he had just been writing a slashing criticism of her poems. I went down to a war collation with him, and we discussed a mutual friend in Lawrence. He is conscious of Lawrence's strange charm, and thinks he writes like an angel, but deplored his obscenity and the obsession of the 'symbol'. He regards Frieda as a disaster and thinks she is the morbid influence. I argued this point. He said Lawrence would be furious with him now and accuse him of 'glorifying war'.

Friday, 16th November

Mary H. wired me to meet her mother and we went to the Grosvenor Gallery together. She almost wept with grief over the portrait of Mary. It is the most lovely colouring certainly, but I agree with Evelyn that it is quite uncharacteristic of Mary—flaccid, with nothing of the beautiful 'swift creature' Evelyn sees in her. Also, it seems to have glaring faults: one arm is all out of drawing (one can't see where it comes from), then the mouth is neither Mary's mouth nor an improvement on it, the lips are coarse and shapeless. Margot Asquith is right— he can't draw, and I'm inclined to agree with Evelyn that there is a great deal of the trickster about him. She also bewailed the flatness of Mary, said it wasn't a woman's figure at all. It's tragic, and it's she who has got to pay for it, too, poor darling! I must say, seeing a quantity together, I had rather a down with McEvoy.

Saturday, 17th November

A very strange dream-like day. I wonder will it prove a milestone in my life? I lunched with McIntosh (the young officer who said he could help me on to the cinema) and Serena (he belongs to the Italian Administration and is no relation, but a very great friend of Serra's?*— I don't know how his name is spelt—the cinema agent). We had hoped to motor down to Catford, but no such luck! We had to go by tram, or rather trams, as we kept getting into the wrong one. Neither McIntosh nor Serena had ever been in a tram before. People are beginning to feel the locomotive pinch of the war more than any other. Catford is as remote as it sounds—it took us a good bit more than an hour to get there and my heart sank at the idea of daily peregrinations.

At last we arrived. First we went into a room downstairs ornamented with large photographs of cinema stars. I wondered whether Sylvia Strayte's would ever be amongst them. Serra was introduced to us—he is a nice-looking, gentlemanly man—and there was also

a fat, burly man—a manager of some sort. Then we were taken
upstairs to the studio which is *immense*—like a vast greenhouse. A
bedroom scene was screened off and a woman was 'featuring' in a
night-gown. It was like the Tower of Babel—everyone shouting in
some foreign language. The 'operator'—a very pleasant fellow—is an
Italian and there is a very nice half-Greek woman manageress who
looks after the clothes, etc. The electric light is terribly dazzling.

I was then submitted to an awful ordeal of self-consciousness. The
operator told me to walk on—very happy and insouciant, laughing—
then my attention was to be drawn by some noise and I was to look
as though I saw my best friend in very distressing circumstances, and
to express horror—finally settling into great grief and sobs. It was
terribly difficult, so different from acting—no cue, no signal as to
duration of transitional expressions, the distress quite undefined—
whether carriage accident, air-raid, or making love to another woman.
The operator made me do it about three times, correcting me—telling
me not to look as though I were swallowing something in my mouth—
and then he photographed me. All our party were watching—it was
awful. They said I did it very well, but I felt such a silly and, unfortunately, I wasn't in at all good looks—pinched, with purple
pockets under my eyes. Then they took a 'close-up' of me. I had to
stand quite near the camera and again change from laughter to sorrow.
I believe these close-ups always give the subjects the most awful
shock—the face comes out like a picture of the craters of the moon.
I wasn't properly made up—only blacked under the eyes—but they
said the photographs would show how I ought to be made up.

Two men actors were there: one a very familiar cinema type, suitable
to either the burglar or the family doctor, the other would I suppose
be the *jeune premier*—perhaps I shall soon be doing passionate love
scenes with him. There are bonuses for certain incidents—two pounds
for every fall and so much for jumping into water, but I'm afraid there
is no compensation for the infliction of a kiss. I imagine the situation
is that, after we have seen the photographs of me, they will make me
an offer. I feel dashed by the difficulties and grind of getting there. It
will be an awful life, but I think I must try it, though I think I shall
certainly stick out for ten pounds a week. If they will give me seven
pounds (as McIntosh thought), I'm sure they would give me ten
pounds. I should have to be available there from 10.30 to 6 every day,
though not necessarily wanted, and it would be impossible to make
any other plans. One is engaged for a film, which takes four to six
weeks. The awful thing would be if Beb arrived on leave during my
engagement.

Tuesday, 20th November

Had a letter in connection with Barrie film production of *The Admirable Crichton*. I rang up Serena to ask if photographs were ready and told him I had had another offer. He asked me to come to dinner on Friday, and said he was sure Serra would let me know by the end of the week. Telephoned to Joan Capel[1]: she said McIntosh had given a very favourable account of my studio performance. Dined with the Lawrences for the opera—sardines, cold beef, and mixed business. Miss York— a chic poor American, like a drawing in *Vogue*, with straight whiskers —came with us, and Nichols and Ivo Grenfell joined us. Miss York designed the cover for *Wheels*. I adored *Seraglio*: we were in the stalls instead of our box. Went home in the Tube. Lawrence seems much happier.

Wednesday, 21st November

Visited Freyberg who was back in bed, relapsed after a luncheon at Cavendish Square. He had sat next to Ettie and complained that her conversation hindered him from eating. Someone had sent him a £200 platinum watch—for which he expressed the most unreasonable regret.

Evening papers full of a great 'victory'.[2] Tanks and cavalry are said to have penetrated the Hindenburg line. I wonder how much it means.

Thursday, 22nd November

Went to Selfridges and sent a joke toy watch to Freyberg as a rival to his £200 one. I lunched with the Bighams, arriving late on my bicycle. Osbert Sitwell was there and a Chilean couple (the Gandarillas) —the woman fringes in the background of McEvoy's water-colour of me. We discussed the German scheme for 'secondary marriages'. I hear joy bells are to be pealed for the Flanders victory. All my superstition revolts at this.

I dined with Venetia, sitting between Ivo Grenfell and Cardie Montagu. Nellie Hozier was there and Papa and Norah, and Rosemary* and Diana and Lutyens, etc., etc. I was amused to meet my double, Rosemary—I have actually been mistaken for her. She is very attractive, with her snub face and slap-dash voice—very in-loveable. We

1. She had introduced Lady Cynthia to McIntosh.
2. The Battle of Cambrai on 20th November.

compared ourselves feature by feature. We played an amusing spurring game with race-horses. Papa took the bank and raked the money in, and Nellie referred to him as 'that old rascal'. I lost, but he carried me. Papa has begun to be a special constable with baton and belt, but as far as I can make out his duties will only keep him *inside* Buckingham Palace.

Friday, 23rd November

Bicycled to Leicester Square to see the cinema agent about the *Admirable Crichton* film—certainly *he* won't jeopardise Serra's claim to be the 'only gentleman in the cinema world'! I felt indignation surging up when he asked me to remove my hat and looked appraisingly at me, as one might at the points of a horse. I don't think I could bear to work for him.

I tried on at Septimus and then visited Brenda, who is recovering from an operation in a nursing-home in Manchester Street. Prince Leo had just given her a lovely tortoise-shell toilet set. I went to join Michael at tea at Katharine's. She wasn't there and when I went up to the nursery the Nurse took me out of the room and showed me a note from the poor darling, saying that they had heard Edward had been killed and she had gone round to her mother. Oh God, the unutterable cruelty of it! Katherine's one anchor in this world, and he has been so wonderful to her since Raymond's death—and poor, poor Frances! Dear Edward—I wish he hadn't gone so much out of my life these last years. He seems almost the last link with my youth. What a perfect companion he used to be in those years of girlhood which are now like a sort of luminous mist in my memory—he, Raymond, Katharine and Ego all so interwoven. Soon there will be nobody left with whom one can even talk of the beloved figures of one's youth. I felt stupefied with the thought of this new load of misery crushing down on the already broken—but so curiously dried up and sterilised myself. Have I no more tears to shed? I feel I am growing more and more detached and self-sufficient.

I dined with my new friends the Serenas, going there by bus. The object was to meet Serra who made our fourth. He is a charming little man, too much of a 'gentleman' I can't help feeling to be a good businessman. Dinner was funny: whenever the Serenas had any difference of opinion they burst into voluble Italian in cockatoo voices. After dinner the situation became embarrassing, as Serena kept trying to coax us up to the fence of the terms topic and we were both too shy to *entamer* it and kept beating about innumerable bushes.

Occasionally the two men broke into Italian explanations to one another. I had told them of my dealings with the other agent and I saw they were very anxious to secure me. Finally, they—or rather Serena—asked me point-blank *what* I would come in for. I suppose I might easily have asked for more, but I thought I would begin modestly and said ten pounds a week. To this he assented with alacrity, and told me that I must understand that, of course, I would get much more on another occasion. He said he would give me a bonus, even on the first film, if it were a success—and they both hinted that it would be in my power to make the ball thus placed at my feet a very big one. He is very anxious to raise the cinema standard in England and hinted that I should be able to help him with ideas, and taste, and have in time great scope. He assured me I should have no difficulty in writing scenarios for which he would give me £200. The new film will not begin until after Christmas, and if nothing intervenes, I have really decided to launch Sylvia Strayte then. On Tuesday I shall see my photographs—a thrilling prospect! I like Serra very much, and I believe it might prove a very interesting enterprise.

Saturday, 24th November

Went to see Horatia at Claridges, and she came with me to see the private view of John's exhibition. Nannie and Michael joined us there. My portrait is very much admired: I don't quite know what I feel about it myself. Sometimes I got glimpses which I loved, and then again I would see it Chinese and freakish. I am not at all sure it isn't rather a great picture, whatever it may be as a likeness. Nurse was deliciously appalled and indignantly disgusted. Michael was sweet: 'It's a little like you, Mummie, but not very like you—and he hasn't painted your watch!' He couldn't get over that gross omission.

Dinner in bed. A crisis of misery. I find I can soothe my mind by concentrating hard on visualising black over-arching sky, and it was as though I were sleeping out of doors—a sort of feeling of infinity and immensity descends on me and releases me from my life and myself—leaving me with not exactly indifference but a sort of immunity.

Sunday, 25th November

Awful storm of wind and rain and snow. Visited Freyberg. We played the game of what commands he would give the women he knew: Lady Carnarvon got a battalion; Mary Herbert a company; I was condemned to an A.D.C.-ship—not for suspected cowardice, but because he knew I should get killed at once.

Claud came to see me at seven. Either he has, or he wishes to give the impression that he has, cooled off. He isn't nearly as assiduous as he was.

Monday, 26th November

Sat to McEvoy. He was enthusiastic about my John portrait. He is still my only keen opponent on the cinema questions. We had an argument about it. He was looking terribly tired. I wish he wouldn't dine out every night and paint all day. Freyberg came to pick me up. It was the first time I had seen him dressed and walking about. He really looks wonderfully well considering, though he is pretty lame and has a slightly hurt look all over him. His constitution must be amazing.

Took Claud to see both my pictures at the two exhibitions. He thought the John like, but a gross caricature. I was acutely conscious of Claud's shortcomings and had such a burst of missing Basil—*longing* for his perfect company. It was always such fun going to see things with him. Thank God I so fully enjoyed it at the time! I'm bored—life seems a treadmill with punctuations of agony.

Dined at Cavendish Square. Oc was there with returning voice—he is going to get a brigade. I told the Old Boy of my cinema plans—he took to the idea like a duck to water.

Tuesday, 27th November

I went and had some treatment from May. When I got home at five I found my tea party, Whibley and the Lawrences, had been assembled for about half an hour. They looked very funny, but they got on well together. Whibley liked them—I haven't heard their verdict on him yet. We talked a lot about the cinema and agreed all to try and make our fortunes by writing plays for it—I said I would get hold of a manuscript of a 'scenario' to ascertain the technique.

Picked up Norah shockingly late in a taxi and went to dinner with Ava Astor. A huge, pre-war Belshazzar—Norah Graham, the Asquiths, Seymour Fortescue, Evelyn Fitzgerald, Ribblesdale, the Laverys, Mrs Keppel, Lord Colum Stuart and so on. I sat between Lord C. and a French diplomat just arrived in London after being stationed five years in Russia. Discussed cinema career with everyone. After dinner the majority bridged. The Laverys, Ribblesdale, and I

talked by the fire. Father-in-law was *deus ex machina* and dropped
Norah and me at our respective doors. He had a motor *without* a gas-
bag—How? Why?

Wednesday, 28th November

At last it was the long-awaited evening on which I was to see my
cinema pictures. Mme Serena was ill so I found myself dining alone
with Serra. He was quite nice—very nice really, though his limping
English makes rather a barrier. We dined at the Carlton Grill Room.
I must own I was thankful there was no one I knew there. Afterwards
he took me to his office and then, in a little tiny theatre, we saw the
bit of film in which we figured. I was disappointed in my looks, but
then of course I hadn't been made up—and it was a bad print and a
very small screen—I thought my acting quite good. It's too funnily
uncanny seeing oneself. My walk was too quick.

Thursday, 29th November

Lunched with Mima Ormsby-Gore—Bobbety[1] and Betty were there
—and Aileen Meade joined us afterwards. When I got home, to my
surprise, Freyberg was announced and I found him in the drawing
room. Whether what followed was premeditated or not I don't know
—there was a leading up to it in conversation, during which perhaps
I could have nipped things in the bud. I don't know how it happened,
but suddenly there was an explosion and I found myself involved in
the most tremendous melodramatic scene—like something in the
Sicilian Lovers. Again I felt that strange, detached, spectator feeling
and my old dumbness was as bad as ever. I blame myself bitterly for
my passivity—inexplicable to me—I can only infer it to his habit of
command. I found him terribly difficult to cope with, though his
suit only inspired contemptible Narcissus feelings in myself. I do like
him very, very much, but would never imagine myself in love with
him. I should never have allowed this declaration and I don't know
what to do: I don't believe he is convertible—not a possible subject
for a 'sentimental friendship'—and I don't want to sever all relations
with him. But it's unfair playing with fire when one knows one is
dressed in asbestos oneself. Oh, the worry of it! Where I'm afraid I
cheat is that I find it impossible to give the plain, brutally truthful
negative answer to, 'For God's sake, tell me you do care a little for me!'
If I could inflict the temporary anguish of telling him I was quite

1. Cranborne.

indifferent to him, he would go right away and soon forget all about me, but my silence allows him to hope that the barrier is only scruples —not lack of inclination.

Drove to dinner with the Francis Scotts. Lord Francis told me he had orders not to send Ivo Grenfell out, but he thinks the parents know nothing of such a measure having been taken. I'm afraid Yvo will make a tremendous fuss when he realises and manage to get out somehow. Automatically he would go with the next batch. I took Freyberg to Norah's poker party: we played for some time and he began to look very white. He drove me home and I foolishly allowed him to come in, thus letting myself in for the most awful difficulties. Went to bed very tired and upset.

Friday, 30th November

Had a very amusing letter from Alex, expressing flabbergasted horror at my cinema project. I wrote to tell Beb about it—rather rushing my fences and not appearing to think he would object. I wonder how much he'll mind—a great deal I'm afraid.

Visited John at Cadogan Square and then went on to tea with Augustus John. His gypsyish wife was there—in Bohemian clothes. She is hard-mannered rather, but quite likeable and very beautiful. Symonds was there, looking startlingly like John's portrait of him, and a very comic Japanese artist, making us giggle with his English and the ritual of his manners. I quite enjoyed it, and John was *most* amiable to me. He is just off to France.

Saturday, 1st December

Went down to Brighton by 11.40 to spend the day with Freyberg. He met me at the station. He is staying at the Royal York, but we drove straight to the Metropole for luncheon. He was looking better and had a fine appetite. With his youthful face and the insignia of his anomalous rank (his medals and preposterous number of gold stripes), he is very conspicuous and much stared at—obsequious deference from the waiters. I insisted on taking him to Professor Severn, the phrenologist, but he was hopelessly out about him, marking him *low* for self-esteem and concentration. Freyberg's contemptuous indignation was such that he threw his chart into the mud directly he got out of the house. Twice it was picked up and returned to him. We went to the Kitchener Hospital to have his wound dressed. We had tea at the dear Old Royal York, then I made him go and rest while I read in the lounge. We walked to dinner at the Metropole. He told me of his wonderful swimming exploit in Gallipoli, when he swam for four hours and landed naked and alone, and crawled quite close to the enemy's trenches and lit torches. His eyes shine and he becomes poeticised talking of military adventures, and I was touched to see his eyes fill with tears once when he was talking about his men. I find him very, very attractive.

He drove me to the station to catch the 9.40. He made love to me all day—with simplicity and sweetness, and I don't know what to do. Several times he said he thought he had better not see me any more, and I suppose I ought to take him at his word: it is the candle that should withdraw, the moth cannot, but it would require considerable unselfishness on my part. I should hate to give him up altogether—conscience tells me I should. He kept asking me if I would have married him had I been free. I enjoyed the day very much—injudicious as it was.

Monday, 3rd December

Sat to McEvoy—felt quite distressed about him. He is going out so much too much—it's really demoralising. He looked quite exhausted and claimed to be a 'moral and physical wreck'. I begged him to take an occasional evening at home, and try and read: he says he has lost the capacity.

Lunched in and had to go off to the Albert Hall for the Tombola the worst of all the horrors of war. We, the Seven Ages of Women—Self (carrying baby); Erlanger child (flapper), Sonia Keppel (debutante), Diana (betrothed), Ruby (mother), Belgian woman (queen of the household), and Baroness D'Erlanger (old lady)—dressed and made up in the most preposterous discomfort in a curtained-off space. Water had got into the gas and we had to manage as best we could by the winking light—one's face would be illuminated for half a second and then darkness would again resume its sway. Basil Gill (as Old Father Time) had to recite the most appalling doggerel verses—one for each of us—and one by one (me first, carrying that damned baby) we had to walk through columns on a stage before a dense, gaping crowd. Never have I felt so great a fool!

Ava Astor drove me home. Mary Strickland, Oc, and I dined with Freyberg at Claridges. Mamma called for Mary and took her off; Oc, Freyberg, and I sat and talked—discussing marriage, and so on—then we dropped Oc at the Manners and Freyberg insisted on coming into the flat. I oughtn't to have let him, but he commands me like a

subaltern. I had an awfully difficult time with him. He stayed till
1.30.

Tuesday, 4th December

My morning was unpleasantly spent in tearing up papers, etc. in my
flat. I *hate* deménagement and am really sorry to leave my comic little
temporary home. I lunched at Cavendish Square, taking Horatia. Sat
between father-in-law and Algy West. Margot dewdropped my new
green Septimus dress but cursed us all for being such sticks at the
Tombola. She said I should hold up my baby and kiss it—such a
course would bring the house down! I'm sure dignity is my only
chance. We had to go and do it again, and this time at any rate the
light for dressing was better.

Went by Tube to dine with the Lawrences at Earls Court Square.
They have had an overwhelmingly, glisteningly clean flat lent to
them by a Mrs Gray, in which Lawrence looked very out of place in
his corduroy jacket and grey-white canvas shoes. They gave me an
excellent dinner and we had a very pleasant evening. He said the world
as it was 'bored him in his legs and arms', but he is obviously *much*
happier and saner for his visit to London. He said I was the 'vainest'
woman in the world. We discussed the disintegration of family life
and general collapsing of the moral sense resulting from the war. Of
this I am very conscious. More and more one is inclined to take *short*
views and grasp the bird in the hand. My last night in my cellar.

Wednesday, 5th December

Polly came and packed very grousily. Michael and Nannie went off
to Stanway. Winnie goes temporarily to take charge of John to save
the expense of a hospital nurse. I went to stay one night at Seaford
House—lunching with Margot and Lord Howard de Walden. Freyberg called for me there and we dined at the Trocadero, and sat
till late listening to music. He interested me enormously. He has the
stamp of a high calling which I have hardly ever recognised in anyone.
I believe him to be a genius. He said he would 'do his damndest' to
forget me when he went out. I have never had the type of admirer
who hates the 'yoke' and I respect him for it, and yet he wants the
friendship side of the relationship and complains of loneliness. But I
don't think he should be degraded into the role of a 'sentimental
friend', even if it could be more than that—which is out of the question
—he could never 'share a woman'. This he said: he also often says it

would never do for him to marry, he considers it ruin to a soldier's career in peacetime. I adore his consuming ambition, and long for him to get a division. He would be comparatively safe then. As a brigadier I'm afraid he exposes himself as much as any subaltern. I am so afraid he may get broken by fighting with some stupid superior —he would never obey what he thought a mistaken order. He swears suicide if he is either maimed or a failure. There is a distinct touch of the melodramatic in him, but I don't mind that, and I like his grimness varied by startling gentleness. He continually asked me if I thought he had better come to Stanway—which I thought unfair.

Thursday, 6th December

Was woken at five by guns—another air-raid at last! I like them with my dinner, not with my dreams, felt sleepy and bored. Mary S. and I travelled down to Stanway by the 4.55; it's an awful journey nowadays and we arrived dead tired after 8.30. I hadn't seen Bibs for *months*—she has grown in every dimension immensely.

Friday, 7th December

Mary went off early to nurse. I visited Mamma after breakfast: she has got a secretary—a Miss Wilkinson—who seems a very nice, unobtrusive, helpful person. Each member of the household has their week's ration of sugar in a glass bowl with their name on it.

Mamma, Olivia, Bibs and I drove into Winchcomb in the funny old four-wheel pony cart: at about six we started driving home and came in for a blood-curdling adventure. Some boys were playing with fire in the street, and I suppose that—combined with the criminal carelessness of the man who had harnessed her all wrong—started the pony off and she wheeled round the corner and was off at a headlong gallop down the pitch-dark street.

I remember realising that it was a case of real running away. Mamma was driving, but as soon as we knew what had happened Bibs and I seized the reins and hauled at them with all our strength. The cart lurched and swayed horribly, and sparks flew out of the pony's hooves. I didn't see my past, but my interfered-with future: I can remember almost saying: 'There, I knew something would stop my cinema career! Sylvia Strayte's face will be smashed.' At one time Mamma said, 'Shall we jump out?' Bibs and I shouted 'No!'—it was soon after that we got to a hill and I remember the instant of astonished joy and relief when I felt the tension of the reins slackening and realised the

animal was going to stop. We none of us hoped for such a denouement
—we had only wondered *how* we should be upset. In an instant we
had a huge, excited crowd round us: they were very funny—the horrid
boys obviously bored by the flatness of the climax, the women
hysterical, and the spokesman of the men was saying we were 'Four
heroes!' He piqued himself on his sensibility: 'It gives one a think to
see someone run away with—one wonders what's going to happen
to them in the end.'

The adventure was broken to Mary by someone asking her if 'she
had seen her family lately', but she was very calm.

Saturday, 8th December

I took Michael for a drive in the donkey-cart. Little Cockney that he
is, he says: 'This is a very quiet place with nobody about—I wish
we could have an air-raid or something.' I had a séance with Angela
before tea. She exclaimed against the immorality of the girls of the day!
I wonder why I get on so well with her. I think she is socially improved
on the whole, but she is being too brutal about Sockie and ever abusing
her before Bibs.

Sunday, 9th December

I don't know what has come over me. My morning insomnia of so
many years' standing has given place to heavy, heavy sleepiness,
reminding me of my schoolroom days. I had the utmost difficulty in
leaving my bed.

Angela and I played comic tennis against Papa and Bibs. The
net broke and Papa, feeling energetic and gallant on the court as he
tried to mend it, said with irritation, 'Where's that lazy Mary?' 'Lazy
Mary' having left the house at seven to toil for eight hours at the
Winchcomb Hospital!

Went to church—lessons most mellifluously read by Papa. Angela
made me shy at luncheon by saying before Sockie, 'The one thing I
couldn't be is a governess!'—very bad taste. I have been revelling in
the fun of Rabelais for the first time. I can't think why I've never
sampled it before.

Tuesday, 11th December

Mary and I and Mrs Allen travelled up by early train. We met Dr
Halliwell who was taking up his son Basil to be decorated at Bucking-

ham Palace. I told him about Sylvia Strayte and thought I saw a gleam of joy at the prospect of my making money. I'm afraid Beb can't have paid that bill I sent him.

Wonderful family party—picnic dinner at Cadogan Square and on to *Dear Brutus*—self, Guy, Frances, Mamma, Bibs, Mary, Herbert, Mrs Allen, Margot H. Usual crises about motors and taxis. Papa convulsed us all by appearing, looking like a policeman in a pantomime, in his constable's uniform and we dropped him at Buckingham Palace. I liked Barrie much better this time—infected by Mamma's and Bibs' enjoyment of it. Mary begged me to come to Pixton and I arranged to take Freyberg there instead of his coming to Stanway.

Wednesday, 12th December

Sat to McEvoy. He was looking very ill with a cold. He was painting a Russian-Canadian V.C. who has personally killed fifty Germans. What with him, Freyberg, and *all* the naval V.C.s (whom he had just been commissioned to paint) he will be able to make a real study of the type and see if there is any common denominator among them. Whibley came in and we went into the John Exhibition to see my portrait. Unfortunately it had gone away to be reproduced. It gave me quite a shock not to see it on the wall—like looking in a glass and seeing no reflection.

Went with Mamma to the Poets' Reading at Mrs Colefax's. Somehow it was ever so much better than Elizabeth's Parnassuses— smaller, more *intime*, and above all *shorter*. All the poets were young and most of them had fought in the war. It was very moving. I liked Nichols enormously, with his bright, intensely alive, rather stoat-like face. He read again in the same intensely passionate dramatic way: I like it, but a great many people don't. As well as his own, he read two —as I thought—very beautiful poems by Sorley who was killed at twenty years of age. Gosse was in the chair and acquitted himself quite well. Three Sitwells, all looking very German—Osbert, Sacheverell, and Edith—all read from their works. The author of 'Prufrock'[1] read quite a funny poem comparing the Church to a hippopotamus. There was a young man called Huxley,[2] and a very remarkable, fierce, rapt girl called McLeod who read her own clever poems beautifully. Siegfried Sassoon didn't appear, but his poems were read by this girl. Mamma was very much moved by the war poems. I was very, very glad I went. Dined with Freyberg at the Trocadero again and

1. T. S. Eliot.   2. Aldous Huxley.

we went on to play poker at Ruby's—I won £3 2s. Freyberg took me home and found his way into the hall with me.

Thursday, 13th December

Went out early for desperate shopping at Selfridges—an exhausting morning. Lunched with Mrs Lavery: Freyberg, Lady Randolph Churchill, and Mr Lutyens were there. I find Hazel rather a rattling hostess. We went up to the studio: it is funny to see a portrait of a friend as the Madonna—the gold of her dress seems to me a masterly bit of painting. It is a triptych and is going to some church in Ireland.

Saturday, 15th December

Freyberg arrived—Mary H. cross-questioned me about him yesterday. He did the great man unbending stunt with Gabriel with great success and a new pest of a puppy was christened 'Frizby Caesar'. He told me all was well with Oc as far as Betty was concerned—she had confided in him walking home from a dinner at the Leeds the night before. He had been extolling Oc and she said, 'I am very, very fond of him,' which was a cue easily taken, so he said, '*How* fond?' and the tale was told. She said, 'I know people think I have treated him abominably, but I couldn't help it—I didn't love him before.' I suppose, if Oc hadn't been recalled, all would now be settled and the Old Boy would have had to stomach a lowering of the average of beauty amongst his daughters-in-law. It's very wonderful that he should prefer beautiful paupers to plainer heiresses. The second post brought me a letter from Margot Howard de Walden enclosing a £200 cheque as a Christmas present. It gave me quite a shock, but such an agreeable one! It is most angelic of her.

So far from being a gooseberry, Mary went to the other extreme and felt too ill to come to dinner, thus leaving me to a very long *tête-à-tête* and exposing me to a veritable *tir de demolition*. It is true that I read him all the purple patches out of *Henry V*, but it was only a postponement. However, all was not lost—I locked my door.

Sunday, 16th December

Slept badly after agitating evening and woke to swirling snowstorm. Mary resurrected and joined us after breakfast. Freyberg inveighed against the Georgian Poets and reproached me for holding a brief for Siegfried Sassoon. I maintained that, having fully demonstrated his personal *physical* courage, he had earned the right to exhibit *moral* courage as a pacifist without laying himself open to the charge of cloaking *physical* cowardice under the claim of *moral* courage.

Freyberg is very uncompromising in his condemnation and, with some justice, says it is offensive to come back and say, '*I* can't lead men to their death any more'—it implies a monopoly of virtue, as if other officers *liked* doing it because they acquiesced in their duty. He thought the poem called 'The Hero' caddish, as it might destroy every mother's faith in the report of her son's death. Certainly Siegfried Sassoon breaks the conspiracy of silence, but sometimes I strongly feel that those at home should be made to realise the full horror, even to the incidental ugliness, as much as possible.

We had an orgy of military shop from Freyberg—hours and hours of it. I must say he never bores me. It interests me to see him sitting there with his, in a way, boyish snub face with its extraordinary, almost grim, determination and feel his ambition and energy and practical ability is working away like machinery all the time inside him. He has the shortest nose almost I have ever seen on a man, great breadth of countenance with very rounded outlines everywhere— his frame gives great impression of strength and almost *expresses* swimming. He's quite good-looking full face, but how impossible it is to describe anyone's appearance! He's got a nice gentle voice, and I'm glad to say has got himself out of saying 'Pardon'.

He told us of an extraordinary case of a man who got his wife to forge letters saying he was the only survivor of eight sons. On the strength of this, he was taken out of the line, but subsequently he slightly wounded himself in order to get home and the whole fraud was discovered. We went out for a short walk in the snow but, being bareheaded, he found it too cold, so we soon returned to froust. At his request, I read *Julius Caesar* to him in the afternoon. His appreciation of Shakespeare is a revelation to me. Mary had a tea party of women on-the-land workers—rather jolly girls, one of them with ring-worm. We all had tea and crackers together. Freyberg's sugar-hogging was given a free rein. They stayed for hours and hours— Freyberg and I sought peace in Mary's sitting room, but the two children fastened on to us and insisted on being entertained. Gabriel, showing herself a real daughter of Eve, sat cosily in Freyberg's lap, toying with his V.C., and stroking his hair.

Mary chaperoned us this evening and we finished *Julius Caesar*. Freyberg gave rather an amusing account of General Marx's method of making himself 'felt'. He has a disagreeable technique of his own, but Freyberg credits him with great ability: he greeted Freyberg with, 'I hate you bloody gallant brigadiers—what the devil do *you* know about training men?' Freyberg told me Ian Hamilton (at dinner the other night) had said I was 'the most beautiful creature in the world'.

Monday, 17th December

Freyberg went off by the early train. I stayed in bed, sending him a note to say goodbye. We made him count his individual wounds: he has had twenty.

Tuesday, 18th December

Mary and I talked a lot about John in the evening, and she was most darling. I gathered someone had been critical of me, and had said she couldn't imagine not concentrating on him if he were her child. I said if I believed him to be really curable, I would never leave him, but I had long really inwardly realised the hopelessness of the case and determined to keep the cruel sorrow within certain limits—not to *allow* it to blacken the whole of life for me, but to keep myself sane for Michael, and the best way to do that was to fix one's thoughts as much as possible on the latter.

Wednesday, 19th December

I got home for tea—found only Grace, Mamma, and Bibs. Michael and I played in Mamma's sitting room: she has invented a wonderful 'magic' game. I read poems aloud to Mamma and Grace out of the anthology called *The Muse in Arms* sent me by Beb and containing poems by him and Aubrey. I taxed Mamma with having thought I was in love with D. H. Lawrence two years ago—this I had gathered from Mary Herbert.

Thursday, 20th December

Very cold, but still and lovely. I breakfasted in my room, and read and wrote. Mamma came and furniture-maniaed in it. She had edited Sylvia Strayte badly to Grace and she had been pained, but I made it all right. Grace is very happy and serene here—plays patience and scribbles after dinner. We are chaffing Mamma about her generalisations and indictments on 'people', and I'm afraid both Grace and I belong to 'people'.

Saturday, 22nd December

Mamma very worried by a letter from Papa in which he seemed to be contemplating chucking his 'special' constable job. I'm afraid he finds it much more boring and unpleasant than he anticipated, and therefore characteristically begins to think it 'rot'. The Priest, having tricycled to and from Stratford-upon-Avon, came to tea—and Mrs Allen.

Sunday, 23rd December

A bombshell! A letter from Beb to say he expects to get Paris leave 10th to 18th January, and summoning me to be there by the 7th. So much for poor Sylvia Strayte's career—by then it ought to have been in full swing. I *do* wish he could come here instead. I long for him to see Michael, and this Paris jaunt will be so fearfully expensive. I am already quite flustered at the prospect of my journey. I feel *quite* incapable of finding my way there by myself. At the best, it takes two days nowadays. I don't in the least know what steps to take about passports or anything, and feel hopelessly helpless. I wrote to Margot Howard de Walden and Brenda for tips about hotels and so on. Bibs thought I meant the plural of 'tip', and didn't seem in the least surprised! Beb wrote the most comic and pathetic letters appointing a rendezvous with him at the Ritz Hotel and at the Arc de Triomphe day after day at certain hours in case of any hitch. I am haunted by the thought of his shivering in vain at the Arc de Triomphe whilst I am stuck at Havre with lost purse and passport.

Breakfasted with Mary S. and Bibs, and we held an inquiry as to why Bibs read so little. We found her life was entirely different from what ours had been in the schoolroom. Being surrounded by all of us, she is perforce much more in daily life, instead of standing on its threshold with books for realities. Her leisure is unnaturally either occupied in playing with our children, or in bolting in and out of our bedrooms. She *never* has any of the so-wholesome period of schoolroom alone with a governess. I am determined to try and have a fixed daily reading-aloud for her benefit, so before tea we started *Martin Chuzzlewit* in Letty's bedroom.

Monday, 24th December

A thawing, drizzling day. The Old Boy sent me fifteen pounds and also, in a letter, told me the sad news of poor dear Oc having been badly wounded again just after taking over command of his Brigade. What bad luck! And it sounds bad, too—compound fracture of both bones above the ankle: P.M. wrote, 'However, they hope to be able to save his foot'. I *do* hope he won't lose it.

I packed up parcels after tea, and after dinner we had the usual bedroom marauding parties, but none of us had the heart for any of the time-honoured stocking jokes . . . once the old passage seemed so impregnated with darling Ego and Yvo. Christmas has become a melancholy milestone for us, but luckily the men of this house-party (who are all under six years) take a glorious joy in all the old rites. Michael was the most satisfactory Christmas child imaginable: he refused to have the fire in his bedroom lit because he was afraid Father Christmas might burn his toes coming down the chimney.

Bibs was wonderful with her presents—one for every servant and all beautifully done up in fancy paper and labelled. She kept putting the wrong parcels in the various stockings, so our labours lasted far into the night. I had a sad little hair-combing with Letty. She has been so valiant this year—no breakdown like last Christmas Eve—and energising all day over the house decorations. My heart aches for my little John: one turns for salvation to the nursery and that is 'the most unkindest cut of all'.

Tuesday, 25th December

Nurse called me at 7.30 to see Michael opening his parcels: the vicarious enjoyment was very great. Most of the family went to early service. I joined them at a late breakfast. Found a gorgeous enamel fountain pen from Freyberg. Great excitement over an anonymous present to Bibs—a lovely, and very costly-looking star-sapphire Grenadier badge brooch. Mary and I, whom Bibs compared to Cinderella's ugly sisters, suspected an admirer and we pretended we thought it should be returned to the shop. Mary said she would pack it up, and my present from Freyberg and a bead necklace given to Mamma by her dentist! This all three daughters agreed was really going too far. Grace had given me five pounds in my stocking, Letty one pound, and Bibs one pound, too, to buy gloves with. I think it's too sweet her tipping me! Mary gave me some lovely bedroom boots and Mamma is sending for a white bunny coat from Ortons.

Wednesday, 26th December

Mamma and I motored Mary to Apperley to stay with her in-laws.

Mary and I both felt sick in the motor. Instead of eating less, we are eating *more* chocolates than at any previous Christmas. There are three boxes in the house and, with the sense that they may be the last we shall see, they are greedily passed round the table at every meal.

Thursday, 27th December

Pushed Michael over to Didbrook, reading *Black Beauty* on the way, and we paid a very successful call on the Priest—he was playing his concertina. He pushed the pram all the way home, and Michael mercilessly heckled him as to how a dead horse was conveyed to Heaven. Walked with Mamma before luncheon. She had had a letter from Papa saying he couldn't abide London and meant to come and live here—this must be entirely so as to be able to plead enforced absence and shirk his constabulary duties!

Another turn of the kaleidoscope—I was sitting writing my daily letter to Beb when a telegram was handed to me, sent from Portsmouth: 'Arriving London on leave. Will go to Stanway tonight if possible, stay there. Beb.' I met the last train and, sure enough, he arrived, looking thin but really well, I think. They are just moving to another part of the line. He brought some military dewdrops in his pocket.

Space for dewdrops[1]

He revelled in bed, bath, and the 'calm of Toddington'. He coughed for hours at night, keeping us both awake.

Monday, 31st December

I had a telegram from my cinema agent, whose glittering name is the Marquis Guido Serra, saying several scenes of the *Slave* had got to be photographed and they didn't know yet when the new production would begin.

Beb and I walked up to the top of the New Hill and back via Coscombe. It was one of the most lovely-looking days I have ever seen. Beb is in very good form—in good, lean looks and very keen and eager—seething with indignation against the Government and the 'hate campaign' of the civilians. He is ashamed of the way England brutally snubs every peace feeler, and reiterates that, either we should negotiate or else fight with all our might, which he says would mean

1. So marked in the MS, but never filled in.

doubling our army in the field. He speaks with rage of the way we are not nearly up to strength at the Front and says it is to a large extent merely a paper army. In existing circumstances a military victory is quite out of the question until America can really take the field, which will not be for years—and he thinks all the lives now being sacrificed are being wasted, it's like going about with a huge bleeding wound and doing nothing to bind it up. Thank God Beb isn't in the House of Commons! I should never have the moral courage to face the reception given to the kind of speech he would make.

1918

Thursday, 3rd January

Lovely bitter cold day. Beb went on lugubriously maintaining that we should negotiate and got rather annoyed with Mary and me. He told an amusing story of the melodramatic general, Hunter Weston. Once, when he came to inspect a battery, one of the men was drunk, so that an officer wishing to screen the man said, 'That man is a corpse,' and had him duly carried past on a bier covered with a blanket. The General—with a fine gesture as it passed—shouted: 'I salute the noble dead.'

Friday, 4th January

Beb and I travelled up to London by early train. We stopped at Cavendish Square and had an interview with Miss Way. She said they didn't know whether they would be able to save Oc's foot or not yet. We heard Lloyd George had lunched with Asquith the previous day. We went to take up our quarters at the Connaught (pre-war Coburg) Hotel—quite nice, and very central, just out of Berkeley Square. We lunched there, then Beb went off to the War Office.

I telephoned Freyberg and was dreadfully sorry to hear Patrick Shaw-Stuart had been killed. Poor Patrick—everybody settled *he* would *not* be killed. No one ever looked forward to his life more or coveted a glorious death less. Freyberg very sad.

Natalie and Whibley dined with us in our hotel. We discussed German atrocities. When Beb was judiciously trying to disentangle the evidence and be fair, Whibley exclaimed, 'But I don't want "truth": I'm not looking for Truth—I'm looking for Malice.' I think 'malice' *is* at the bottom of a much deeper well for most English people. I liked this story of Whibley's: an Englishman threw a bomb into a German trench, and when he went up to it, found he had killed seven out of eight Germans—'Lucky swine!' said he to the surviving German, as he firmly stuck his bayonet through his body.

After tea we separated and each had a dentist by gas-fires—Whibley very affectionate.

Saturday, 5th January

I took Beb to see my Augustus John portrait: I think it has real beauty from a distance and a wonderful rhythm. We lunched with Freyberg at the Berkeley before he went off to lecture on 'tactics' at Cambridge. He was, I thought, looking ever so much better—wonderfully alert and his animation had all returned—I thought him much handsomer than I ever had before. Beb was, as I feared, a little shy at first, but he soon got happily on to shop and he was charmed with Freyberg. The latter had just had a letter from Oc. Poor dear, he seems very wretched—great pain and wondering whether he hadn't better have his foot off. It would anyhow take six months to heal and then might leave a very stiff ankle. No prospect of his being moved back for a long time I fear.

Whibley had asked me to bring Freyberg to lunch with him on Monday. I said he wanted to see whether Freyberg would make a good Military Dictator after the war: Freyberg said he would chuck his lunch engagement and come, and I looked forward to being liaison officer between two such specimens. Freyberg and Beb wailed in unison over the incompetency and senility of most of the Army generals.

Beb and I went down to the Wharf by a three-something train. Found Edgar, the 'Bower Bird', at the station: he was much amused and interested in Sylvia Strayte. Horatia brought her little American girl Miss Kahn down—Margot, to my shame, having asked her blind directly she knew Horatia was living with a rich girl—she is expensively and unobtrusively dressed.

Beb and I were put up in the Mill House, which involved wet crossings to the Wharf for meals—Jelly d'Aranyi* had preceded us and we found Mrs Derenberg a fellow inmate. The latter, the 'Puma' as she used to be called, played the piano to us after tea with *supreme* skill. Margot inveighed against us all to Horatia: 'Look at all those blocks! Look at Cynthia's face—it never changes—did you ever see so expressionless a face? No music in her! She wants to be gossiping. And look at Beb and Henry—he wants to be talking all the time!'

When we sat down to dinner I heard Margot hissing in Edgar's ear, 'You have always been with us on our great historical occasions.' She was in great excitement, saying that Lloyd George, Edward

Grey, and the rest had all agreed, and their terms are 'very reasonable'. She thought hostilities would cease very soon.

Margot settled down to bridge as soon as the men came out; Puffin, Miss Kahn, Miss Copland (motoriste for P.M.), and I played poker—I lost seven-and-six; and Beb and Horatia played chess—but he was so excited by Lloyd George's statement of war aims speech that he had to read the evening paper through the game.

Walked back to the Mill House with Keynes. He is an ugly devil, but said to be a financial genius. Talking of the discomforts of skating, he said, 'I wonder, if we could only walk for one day in the year, whether we should do it all day'.

Sunday, 6th January

Nearly perished of cold in the night and very sleepy in the morning. Breakfasted downstairs. There was Church conscription, as it was National Service day, and we mustered in great force. At the porch Margot kissed Horatia and said, 'I'm afraid you thought I was angry with you this morning'—Horatia having entertained no such thought. I felt it was too much to be asked to express gratitude for all the blessings showered on us during the past years: I did not join in any of the responses. Horatia and I retreated to Mill House to write our diaries over the fire. The P.M. came over in 'search of solitude', but he found a Comus rout and withdrew to light a fire in his bedroom.

At luncheon Elizabeth told a story of Granville Barker coaching an actor by giving the instruction, 'Try and look as if you had read Shelley in your youth,' which Barrie capped by saying, 'Try and look as if you had a younger brother in Shropshire.' Gibbeted with Puffin in the terribly congested district of the Wharf, got claustrophobia and took Beb for a walk in the rain. We agreed the atmosphere was strangely jarring to war nerves. I do think his father is amazing. He is devoted to his sons and it seems so odd that, after Beb has been out for five months—liable to be killed at any moment—he should not address one word of enquiry to him, as to what he has been doing and where he has been. I suppose it is part of his habit of optimism—that he likes to blink facts and avoid being confronted by anything unpleasant, just as he avoids what he calls an 'unpleasant novel'. Beb rather feels it, as it is always soothing—at least generally it is—to talk about one's experiences. I think the Wharf atmosphere really hurts him.

Margot was in rattling form at tea. Talking of Kakoo's second baby not being a boy, she said she didn't think the Rutland family was one which should be perpetuated. Wet walk across to dinner. I wore my Spanish shawl—it was much admired. Beb said he objected to my wearing such a gift from a 'lounger'—quite an explosion about it!

I sat between Margot and Elizabeth. The latter was very typical—complimenting herself in her steadfastness to the absent Gibson and saying: 'I haven't even side-tracked into any serious flirtation, though oddly enough I very nearly have during the last two months.' He had sent her a Christmas cable: 'Love and blessings', but apparently never writes to her and she proudly said she had never missed a mail. I think it's a ghastly situation. The poker contingency went across to Mill House: we had quite an amusing game—I won five shillings, and was in my best face, feeling well and vivacious. Margot tipped me four pounds Christmas present.

Monday, 7th January

Found a telegram at the hotel saying Freyberg couldn't lunch, so Whibley, Beb and I were *à trois* at the Café Royal. We had quite good talk arising out of the Peace Terms speech. Shopped and went to tea at Cadogan Square. When I arrived, found a letter of about fifteen pages from John's new governess, written after she had finished my diary. She passionately insisted on the paramount importance of my own belief and love as regards John, and my faith in his curability. I had better copy her letters into the children's book. She really altered my attitude of mind. It is a relief to have someone who will scold one. John was delighted to see me.

Mary Herbert, who had come up for one night to see Beb, dined with us and Freyberg: Beb and Freyberg talked shop. I am not clever at technicalities, but they have a strange fascination for me and I can listen for ever to them and all the mysterious initials and statistics involved. There was a great struggle to procure port, as it was after 9.30 when the order was given, but Beb acted with commendable firmness and finally prevailed. Mary and I talked—Beb and Freyberg sat on and on, but finally I roused them and got Beb to walk Mary home, thus leaving me and Freyberg to a dentist. I had thought him looking wonderfully well, and was very sorry to hear that he was constantly fainting—had even done so just before dinner—and was dreadfully depressed. He had tears in his eyes the whole time, lamented Patrick and said he envied him and had no wish to survive. He complained of his real loneliness. I was very much touched, but felt very powerless to help him. Beb is tremendously appreciative of him—charmed.

Freyberg expects to go out on Thursday to take over Oc's Brigade. While Mary was there I suggested he should give his V.C. into Gabriel's custody while he is at the Front. She has a wild *culte* for him. He brought it in its case.

Tuesday, 8th January

Had insomnia from hunger—the cold was awful, too. Fell asleep again about seven and when I awoke it was 9.30. Stayed in the lounge writing. Beb and I were both famished and enjoyed a huge breakfast. German papers fleering at our Peace Terms. We lunched at Claridges with Freyberg—more shop.

Went to McEvoy to see Freyberg's portrait. Very disgusted with it: a wooden body with bland, meek, milk-and-water countenance—stripped of all character, nothing of the bulldog breed—more like the Prince of Wales. Criticised it boldly and got him to darken the face and raise the cheekbones. Drove home with Freyberg—very Sylvia-ish. I can't understand myself in this context.

Wednesday, 9th January

Beb and I lunched with Venetia. Old Sheffield was there and Meikle-john—Meiklejohn is more difficult to concentrate on than anyone in the world. Lord Sheffield and Beb had great statistic talk. The latter was very dissatisfied with his rations: 'So this is my lunch?' was his comment on the macaroni and egg which was all Venetia had been able to muster. Beb took me to the great War Museum at Burlington House—a wonderfully grim show.

Went round to Cadogan Square for tea. Polly and Miss Leighton had started as ill as possible: Polly already calls her that 'ridiculous woman' and Miss Leighton complains of her hostility. Claude Russell rang up, but it was too late to see him.

Friday, 11th January

We travelled back to Stanway by the 1.40 yesterday, finding Evan and Ettie in the train. She is feeling very ill, but is more deliberately and ostentatiously vital on account of that, though less communicatively so.

I went for a lovely walk up on the hills with Beb, during which we discussed philosophy. Mr Balfour's speech led us to a Peace Terms discussion at luncheon. I maintained my old argument that a draw would reduce the chances of another war, as everyone would be so exhausted and nauseated, and the fact that no decisions could be reached by a huge modern war would be some way towards being proved. Ettie insisted on a 'victory'. She went to bed after lunch and slept till teatime, when she came down full of energy and jumped on me for saying 'I wish there weren't so many poets'.

Papa and Angela arrived in the evening—Papa in his mellowest form. We had very amusing flippant conversation, talking of Grandpapa's courtship of Annie Tennant. Ettie said, 'What a wonderful lover! How *could* she have resisted him?' which was received with shouts of, 'She didn't!' It made me laugh when, *à propos* of the special train he took to pursue her in Italy, Ettie said ruefully, 'He must have been very different from you'—looking at Evan.

Saturday, 12th January

Mary Herbert arrived soon after luncheon. We had had a beauty competition conversation in which she had been rather tepidly canvassed by Ettie, who took our breaths away by the audacity of the Ettyism which made her greet Mary with the words, 'We have just all been saying that we would rather look like you than any other woman.'

Papa and the rest were in brilliant form after dinner with Ettie tuning-forking away. They were extremely amusing about the Grandpapa marriage drama, and told the episode of his getting shut up with Grace in the sitting room and having to kick the door down. That was when she stayed there as 'Miss Blackburn' after they were married! When the butler, Frederiks, heard the news, he said, 'It's those damned Lytteltons!' and fainted.

Sunday, 13th January

Papa read the lessons in church. We had a very riotous lunch. I have never seen him or Ettie in such brilliant form. She 'unveiled' him as an Egyptian mummy most amusingly. We had more very funny talk about Grace, and played the game of inventing titles of books people might have written—the idea being to give the most anomalous, the one it would be most surprising to hear they had produced. *Aunt Tina's Bible Stories for Tiny Tots* was given to Papa; *Three Girls and a Horse* to Mr Balfour, and I gave Mamma *Who to Know and Where to Go*. Everybody denied the inappropriateness of the one chosen for them—Mamma was quite piqued by someone giving her *Talks about Chaps*.

The Allens came to dinner. Papa's letter to the papers about food controller Arthur Yapp was read aloud—it is very witty. A most uncomfortable floater interfered with our digestions: Alex said to Ettie, 'Wasn't Bibs' title for Lady Angela good?'—which had been *Ragged Homes and How to Mend Them*. Unfortunately, this was overheard and Papa and Angela immediately clamoured to know what it was. Ettie, with steel audacity, lied before us all and said she hadn't heard it, though she knew that we knew that she knew. Bibs left the room without telling, but after fatal hesitation and importunate pressing Letty finally blurted it out. Had it been lightly told at once, it wouldn't have mattered, but after the hesitation it was most painful and embarrassing—nothing but a clown act of pulling the cloth off the table could have saved the situation. It fell heavily—Angela's face quite withered and she and Papa both said they couldn't see the point. Priest blushed scarlet. It was horribly double-edged, the housebreaking inference—which I don't suppose she would much mind—and the raggedness of her own home. Once the dud shell had fallen we all displayed great tact and skirted out of the situation.

After dinner we played the analogy game—rather a milestone in Angela's life. She had always had a prejudice against 'intellectual games', but won her spurs, and played ever so well and with enjoyment. We all agreed as to the marvellous improvement which has taken place in her. She is the real war profiteer. She herself alleges that it is the work which has made her so much nicer.

Monday, 14th January

Ettie and I were deep in conversation about Gösta Berling, and for what sum we would 'give ourselves', when Michael rushed up with a small silver egg-cup and peremptorily shouted, 'Take that, and be sick in it!' His power of suggestion was so great that Ettie began to feel sick and even *she* lay down before dinner.

The beloved Professor arrived before dinner, looking more like a Blake drawing than ever. I love the way his eyes signal the thought which his tongue is shortly going to voice 'coming over', and he has such a delicious giggle in his eye. After dinner really brilliantly amusing games were played. First Ettie unveiled me as a Renaissance statue; her float voice in pointing out the 'lascivious contours of my cheek' was admirable. Then Beb unveiled Evan as a ceramic of Helen of Troy—*far* the best thing of the kind I have ever seen. He really was brilliant, reaching his climax when he bared Evan's shirt-front as Helen's famous breast, delicately pointing out the curious and un-

common formation grotesquely represented by Evan's two studs
(: instead of . .)! We rocked with laughter. The Professor and
Letty then did an excellent Hamlet and Ophelia to Beb's judge.

Tuesday, 15th January

Ettie had to go up by early train and so Evan was carried off bound
to her chariot wheels—I wonder if he wouldn't have loved to stay
and talk to the Professor. Pages and pages of Barriesque sentiment
from John's governess, comparing John to Peter Pan and me to Wendy.
I got up late and took the Professor for a short walk before lunch. He
wore a rug instead of a coat, and it looked just like a Sir Walter
Raleigh cloak. I told him about Sylvia Strayte and he promised to
write a scenario with the right part for her.

After luncheon—in an *à trois* with him and Letty—my question,
'Do you miss Ettie?' led to the most interesting discussion on her.
'Miss her? No,' he replied, 'I *never* miss her—I'm glad to see her, but
I never *miss* her—because you see she's never a rest.' I said I thought
she was just one of the people one might miss in absence more than
one enjoyed in presence; Ettie being *such* a tuning-fork, one might
feel in the dark—as if the electric light had been turned out—and when
it was turned on it might make one blink. He said he didn't need a
'tonic', and that his quarrel with her was her constant 'battling'
against life, her swimming against the current—precisely the 'steel'
qualities in her which Letty and I had been admiring and enjoying.
I had even thought I must make an effort to emulate her and I must
say it was honey to hear the Professor's disapproving dissection of
her. How she would have minded what he said!

I said that I thought, before the war and its weight of personal
suffering had fallen on her, one might have been irritated by her
stubborn gospel of joy and attributed it largely to health and personal
immunity. But that, now she had earned the right to preach and
practise, her determination to go on fighting with broken tools and
to save what was still worth keeping was wholly admirable and most
valuable. This he admitted, but when I said I envied her capacity
for intimacy, he strenuously denied it and said that her deliberate
activity made her mechanical, and prohibited any real friendship or
the finest companionship—his great point being that she never
'blossomed', and that that was what he valued. When, in his compari-
son of us, I denied the dewdrop that I was natural he said, 'No, you're
not natural—you're Nature.'

The Professor has just re-discovered Dickens—having not touched

Henry Tonks, by Margaret Smith

Papa—11th Earl of Wemyss

Eddie 'St. Sebastian' Marsh

'The Professor'—Sir Walter Raleigh

Sir James Barrie

Lt.-Col. Freyberg, V.C. C.B. D.S.O.

Barrie's room in Adelphi Terrace

him for years and approached him critically, he has now found himself caught up in a flame of love and admiration. At dinner he said no one should read him between childhood and thirty or forty—certainly *not* in college days. The discussion led to his reading us heavenly bits out of *Our Mutual Friend*, chiefly those relating to those masterpieces the 'Wilfers'. Beb's sick, dainty face led to a fierce discussion between me and him, which inducted the Professor into some very good talk about beloved Dickens. I said he was my principal touchstone about people, and that I should never have married Beb had I fully realised this dreadful lacuna. Beb said, with a sort of pride, that at Oxford they had considered Dickens something scarcely to be mentioned, and he accused us of being on the wave of the counter reaction. This annoyed me—as at every age I have read and revelled in him from pure hedon-ism—I maintained that no one would feel obliged to admire him from literary snobbishness, as they would Keats. He gaped at me when I said that, whatever his faults of style, I ranked him with the real giants —with Shakespeare, in fact, because he had above all the quality of wealth, and love, and sympathy—and I also claimed the Homeric quality for him.

To my joy, the Professor was an eloquent ally and said Dickens was a 'howling swell': that he had suffered from mispraise—which had produced the reaction against him—that by his contemporaries he had been liked for the comic and the sentimental, and that now the tide of true appreciation had thrown him right up amongst the giants. He spoke of his 'heavenly homeliness', his exuberance and amazing richness, and proved how false and superficial the charge of 'unreality' was. To Beb's inquiry he maintained that Sterne was 'thin' beside him, Meredith nowhere, and Thackeray *pour rire*. In fact he said he had 'eternity'. He considers *Great Expectations* the masterpiece and that, even from the point of view of 'style', the description of the marshes was as good as anything.

It was interesting talk and I wish I could record it. I enjoyed getting heated, and Mamma told me to 'put two bits of Beb on the fire'— meaning coal. I made the Professor promise to 'testify' his con-version to Dickens. I think he might write something delicious about him.

Wednesday, 16th January

There was a very heavy fall of snow during the night and we woke to find the world enveloped in it—about nine inches according to the retainers. Alas! A huge branch of the tulip tree, and one of the beautiful

1918

Scotch firs had been brought to the ground. The dear Professor, at the last moment, just as Grant[1] was rather sulkily fidgeting at the door, decided to assume he was snowed up and stay another day. Lettie went on a salvage expedition to knock the snow off the loaded branches.

The Professor and I spent most of the morning worshipping the hall fire. *A propos* of Margot Asquith, we discussed selfishness and egotism. He distinguished them well by saying a pig was selfish and not egotistic: egotism means self-preoccupation and admits the possibility of any amount of self-sacrifice.

Food encroaches more and more as a topic for table talk. We are very short of butter and jam and so on, and how we all enjoy our food! So far we still press the only scone or whatever it may be on our neighbours: it will be interesting to see when this formality is dethroned by natural instinct and 'after me' frankly takes the place of 'after you'. Beb certainly feels he is under-nourished under the home regime, but it is wonderful how Papa's looks have improved under rations. His 'muddy vesture of decay' is wonderfully *less* gross.

I frowsted all day, reading *Splendeurs et Misères des Courtisanes* when not otherwise employed. The Professor sat in the 'booky room' with me before he went out and remarked that I was 'the most comfortable furniture in the world' and that he 'wouldn't go to Heaven unless I were there'. 'Now, Lady Desborough could never be "furniture",' he added. I asked if one could possibly be both—meaning tonic and sedative, and he implied that I was by comparing me to a fire always ready to be blown up. I suppose one criticism of Ettie from the man's point of view might be that she was electric light, to which he hadn't got the control of the switches in his own hands.

Thursday, 17th January

Beb and I came up to London to spend the last two days of his leave at the Connaught Hotel. Miss Way told me on the telephone that they had telegraphed to us at Stanway telling us to come and stay at Cavendish Square. I suppose the wires are broken. Beb preferred to remain at the hotel.

Beb and I dined in alone. At about eleven he went to see his father. He gave him fifty pounds. They had had a Secret Session in the afternoon. The situation seems most serious. The Germans have brought forty divisions over to the Western front and he admitted our lack of reserves.

1. Servant.

398

Friday, 18th January

Complete thaw—quite hot and muggy—fearfully tiring. Beb went to interview Dr Forsythe about John. We lunched at Cavendish Square. Margot, in another gorgeous new dress, was going off to a *thé dansant* at Lord Curzon's. I sat beside Eric Drummond and we talked of the growing comedy of rations. He claims to be already suffering the pangs of hunger. Maud Cunard was in marvellous form, holding the whole table—even Margot listening quite silently. She browns the covey, shoots away the whole time and occasionally really hits the target. She explained what she would do if she governed England— her main reform would be to have music in all the parks, and make *everyone* dance on beer. She inveighed against the 'police gazette' school of poetry—Masefield and so forth—and said Beb was a real beautiful poet like Keats.

Saturday, 19th January

We were not called and both overslept ourselves, so I had to have a hasty breakfast and dash off to McEvoy's. Unfortunately, I took my tweed coat (the purple one of his bicycling conception of me) off by mistake and sat down in my white blouse. He was struck by the effect and insisted on painting me in that instead. I wonder if any canvas has ever been through so many vicissitudes as this one. It began with the hatted, Greek coin effect and then—via two different teagowns— came to the tweed, and now it is all cancelled again. Sad with the result of this sitting. It's strangely coarse, the drawing of my face. He will do it on too large a scale. Beb picked me up.

We lunched with Evan. Beb enjoyed his pâté de foie gras, burgundy, cigars, and brandy. Lord Hugh was there—very nice, he sang the praises of alcohol and inveighed against Lady Cunard, whom he complained was just like a child—adding 'I hate children!' Evan discussed whether he would be justified in leaving his job with the tanks and returning to the Bar. He said he thought he *was* the round peg in the round hole, but asked himself whether it was at all necessary that that hole should be filled. He read us his account of the 'Tanks at Cambrai'—very interesting—and described the two men who were respectively the brain and the heart of the Tanks.

Lord Hugh kindly took Beb off to the War Office to try and wangle permission for him to go on the Staff train the next day. It is typical that the Staff should roll away in Pullmans after luncheon, whilst the regimental officers are rattled off at five in the morning. At the War

Office Beb was told he would have to have a warrant from some official saying he wanted to see him in the morning, thus providing exemption from going by early train. We threw ourselves on Eddie's mercy and he was most angelic, taking Winston's name in vain, and in his beautiful hand wrote: 'The Minister of Munitions wishes to see Lieutenant Asquith at eleven o'clock on Sunday morning.' Beb and I went and had tea at Rumpelmayers.

Sunday, 20th January

Beb and I had early lunch and I took him to the station. Felt something more like a presentiment at parting with him than on any previous occasion. Miserable, gloomy afternoon—pouring with rain. The gloom, gaunt-cold, dirt, size, and discomfort of Cadoggers struck me even more than I anticipated and I fell into an awful crisis of depression, not lightened by John and his governess. Papa and Angela came in, Angela saying she wanted to go on the cinema stage and seeking my assistance.

Claud Russell came to see me at six. He is completely at leisure just now, having been left behind by his regiment which has gone to Ireland. He thinks it *may* be due to his talking pacifism at the men. He was no use to me—only made me long for Basil.

Monday, 21st January

Gan-Gan horrified over my Augustus John portrait. I took my bicycle from Seaford House—found it revived my spirits wonderfully. I am becoming anxious about my cinema prospects. I can't understand Serra's strange silence, so I motored to his office—he was out, but I left a note asking him to ring me up.

Tuesday, 22nd January

Woke up at three and couldn't get to sleep again for ages. John's governess pressed about twenty-five sheets of letters into my hand— a great portion of it was in rhyme (her jungle jangles she calls it). It had been written in a rage—she said at three o'clock in the morning— it must have been the intensity of her thinking about me which aroused me from my slumbers. It was an indictment (for which she remorsefully apologised) . . . what amused me was her indignation over the books I had asked her to order for me at the library: Keats' *Letters*, Morley's *Recollections*, and Balzac. She wanted to know what on earth they had to do with my sons? She has had a letter from Mamma saying she thought she had found an ideal farm for John a mile from Stanway.

Very sentimental talk with the governess before she went home, in which she told me how she longed to die. I compelled myself to kiss her for which she has been dumbly asking all these days. Poor dear, she has such a craving for affection. Poor Oc had his foot taken off last Saturday. It's horrid—but I believe he was in great pain before.

Wednesday, 23rd January

John and his governess walked me as far as the park, and then I bicycled to Mrs Cullen's to have my hair cleaned. We met Papa and he gave John fourpence. He is constantly giving him little tips and is being very sweet to and about him. I had written a long letter to John's governess, having felt incapable of responding to hers by word of mouth. Mine was not a success. She wrote to me three times in the course of this day! I lunched with Freddie and Brenda at Claridges to say goodbye to Freddie, who is going off to—what he calls—the 'Le Touquet Salient'.

Tea with John—he really is improving. Papa and Angela came in much elated over her good press—Papa saying the affair would turn Derby out!

Thursday, 24th January

Mamma and I lunched with Mr Balfour—his brother Gerald was there, Nellie, her mother-in-law, and Bob Cecil. Poor Mr B. said he was very ill and wouldn't be able to keep on at his office. As usual, we had amusing food talk.

I had my interview with my agent the Marquis Guido Serra. His silence and the delay is explained. The poor man had been called up for military service!

I dined with Ava Astor—Adele, Norah, Goonie, General Bridges, Evan, Aubrey, Lord Colum Stuart, and an unknown man in uniform. I sat between Aubrey and General Bridges. The latter had got his artificial leg on but—poor man—disagreed with me when I said Oc would be better off with an artificial than with a stiff leg. He minds a lot I'm afraid. He forgot who I was and, à propos of Angela's case, said how funny her getting 'two of her old lovers—Ribblesdale and Wemyss' to speak for her was!

1918

Friday, 25th January

I bicycled off directly after breakfast to sit to McEvoy. At one time the picture became lovely—far better than it has ever been before—the effect of the white blouse was most successful and it became wonderfully moonlit and insubstantial-looking, translucent and strange. I wish I could have snatched it away from under his brush at its best moment, because when I left he was far advanced towards spoiling it. The muddy vesture of decay had grown much grosser, and somehow he had hardened and coarsened the whole thing again. He bewailed the great difficulty of painting me—marvelled at my extreme flower-likeness saying I was like the 'inside of an orchid'.

When I got back to Cadogan Square, I found Angela eavesdropping outside the door of the room where Buckmaster* was discussing her case with Papa. Apparently he almost gave the whole day to them. I called for Claud and we went to a cinema of Lord Kitchener's life produced by my agent. It was not good—too much powder with the jam. Claud was very flat-footed and lymphatic. No one is a more powerful foil to the memory of Basil. I wonder why he no longer invites me out to lunch or dinner. Is it increase in parsimony or decrease in affection? I returned to tea hoping for peace, but was invaded by Papa and Angela. Buckmaster had got Lord Derby to agree to say something in the House which satisfied Papa—but left poor Angela raging. She was wretched.

Elizabeth called for me and we went to dinner with her rich Rumanian lover, Prince Bibesco,* who lives in a delicious house in the Grosvenor Road. He is handsomish—like a black tulip, ultra-foreign —rather inarticulate, but making up by almost witty gesticulation. Desmond MacCarthy was our fourth: I find him most *delightful*—a nice, plain face—very appreciative and great flavour in his talk. Elizabeth's mental, physical, and moral archness was beyond all description. I have never seen anything to touch it and sometimes I didn't know which way to look. She kept rallying her lover on his crossness, insinuating it was the invariable effect of her *troublante* presence, and there were incessant and provocative references to and quotations from Willie Tyrell, Eric Drummond, Eustace Percy, and Hugh Gibson. I have never known her quote herself quite so much.

She and Bibesco played—she with epigram and he with gesticulation—the game that they were a couple who had separated after nine years of married life: McCarthy and I were puzzled and embarrassed spectators. She engineered a *tête-à-tête* with him after dinner. McCarthy and I found ourselves alone in the drawing room. When they joined us we played games—analogies and so on—during which Bibesco lay on the floor cuddling Elizabeth's feet. His own conversational powers are rather elementary and he is obviously naïvely dazzled by Elizabeth's fireworks. He has an amiable habit of registering people's conversational successes, or even attempts, by shouting out 'Good!' to the startled talker, exactly like the partner at tennis who shouts 'Well tried!' to one's every stroke. I enjoyed the evening very much. He gave us the most delicious dinner, and Elizabeth went off with a Spanish shawl and a bottle of peerless Benedictine. She told me he is going to leave the whole of his fortune to her.

Saturday, 26th January

I went for a walk with John. When I got in I found Buckmaster with Papa and Angela. He is a charming man, with such a delightful, clever face: he asked after Beb. He was trying to smooth Angela into contentment with the statement Lord Derby has agreed to make. I think it was much better than I would have expected, but Angela was far from satisfied and wanted to fight. I wish Papa and Ribblesdale weren't both going to speak: it is so very comic. Lord Derby is going to give the centralisation of all canteens as the impersonal explanation for shutting her down, saying it is no criticism of the great zeal and ability she has shown, and that the War Office is *not* responsible for the wild rumours afloat and that they hope she may find other work.

Sunday, 27th January

One of the most lovely spring days I have felt. Met Willie de Grunne outside St George's Hospital and we went for a walk in Hyde Park together. He was very 'pip-pip'. 'Oh, it is dreadful how much I adore you today: you do agitate me so! It makes one quite happy to be in the neighbourhood of such a person as you.' We talked a little *Welt Politik*. He is incensed at the spreading pacifist atmosphere in this country, thinks Mr Balfour quite *usé*, and is very anxious for him to go—he would like Asquith, stripped of his family, in his place.

Monday, 28th January

I telephoned to Frances Horner about Bluetooth: she thought he was a *shade* better, but he is very gravely ill—unconscious most of the time. His family assembled at Liverpool, so she and Katharine came away. I was lunching with Whibley, but Evan suggested my taking him to Mount Street, so we went. They drank some peerless white wine—the name of which I forget—and some of his famous Old Brandy, with religious ecstasy. Their church voices, the tenderness of their eyes, cannot be described: I felt a shut-out Philistine. Evan edited his brandy by saying, 'I know you to be a soldier of the true Cross, so I give you some—but I must turn away my eyes while you help yourself.' His exquisite room seemed like a church to Drink, and when we rose from the dining-table, we said, 'Let's go into the Brandy Chapel.' We had great fun. Whibley said how anxious he was for Mr Balfour to be Master of Trinity. Evan took up the idea enthusiastically and said he thought him too broken down for the Foreign Office. They were amusing about the general perfidy of Gosse.

Tuesday, 29th January

Papa said Angela was almost off her head and begged me to ask Asquith to see her, thinking it was certain he endorsed Buckmaster's view. I very reluctantly complied and sent a note round. I was going down to Taplow for the day to see Mamma who, I am glad to say, is having ten days rest there. Ettie and Willie conducted me to her suite —through about three swing doors—and I asked, 'Why on earth are you keeping my poor mother like a sort of Glamis monster?' I thought her looking really better and she is very happy. I hoped she would be able to discover the mysteries of Ettie's system and organisation of life, but I don't think she has gleaned much. She read us some very amusing letters from Mary and Bibs—the *Chroniques Scandaleuses* of Stanway. I read them what Papa had given me, as he was very anxious for Ettie's opinion, the draft of the procedure in the House of Lords agreed to by Lord Derby. This is it: 'Lord Ribblesdale will ask the questions and will be followed by Lord Wemyss. In their speeches they will not attack the War Office, but they will be at liberty to eulogise the work of Lady Angela and to make reference to the necessity, in the interest of military discipline, of the centralisation of the control of huts.' After they have spoken, Lord Derby will reply in the following terms:

'The noble Lord is quite right in saying that in the interest of Military Discipline it is necessary that the control of Huts in big Military Areas should be centralised, and this is gradually being carried into effect. I quite recognise the valuable and difficult work done by Lady Angela and the closing of her canteens was not intended in any way to reflect on her management of the huts, or upon the zeal and ability she has shown in discharging her onerous tasks. I understand Lady Angela is prepared to take up other work and I should regret if this incident should interfere with her doing so. I hear of many wild rumours in regard to this case—and for these, I beg to assure the noble Lord, the War Office is not responsible. I hope the incident may now be considered closed, and these much-to-be-deprecated rumours should cease.' After this Lord Ribblesdale will answer in the following terms:

'I beg to thank the noble Earl for the statement he has just made, and to accept it on Lady Angela's behalf as a settlement of her case. While no one will I think consider that, in view of the nature and extent of her work for the soldiers, the noble Earl's appreciation of her services erred on the side of exaggeration, I am ready to admit that in view of the circumstances which have necessitated this discussion of her case, the noble Earl's tribute is not an ungenerous one. Lady Angela and her friends would, of course, have preferred the investigation she has repeatedly pressed for, but she recognises that the exigencies of the service, the critical state of public affairs, and the expense of these inquiries render it extremely difficult for the authorities to grant them.'

Ettie thought it *very* good, much more of a concession than she anticipated, and she agreed with the rest of us that Angela would be mad to 'fight'. We showed it to Lord Desborough and asked him to give an unbiased 'man-in-the-street' opinion and his verdict was just the same. Ettie wrote a soothing syrup letter for me to take up to Angela.

It was a lovely day and we went out in the garden before luncheon. At luncheon we discussed the Master of Trinity plan for Mr Balfour. Ettie and Mamma agreed in thinking he would *hate* it, and laughed at Evan's making a bed for him. I suggested a place for Evan as history teacher at Cheltenham College for Girls. We discussed childhood reminiscences. Mr Balfour's were too pathetic: the only thing he remembers is having very tired legs after walking.

Lord Desborough, Ivo, and Imogen went out to shoot our dinner —Mamma, Ettie, and I played tennis: I played well. Afterwards Ettie and I had a delicious walk. We discussed 'lovers' and their compatibility with happy marriages. She said she was not monogamous in the strict sense of the word, and had never been in love in the way which *excluded* other personal relations. To be at her best with one man she must see a great many others.

Evan arrived at ten, followed by beloved Lord Hugh. We played a letter game and then had amusing talk till dinner time. At dinner Lord Hugh delighted me by snapping out from between his bat ears, in a discussion on the symptoms of oncoming years—'I am moving towards a tranquil animalism.' I had the brilliant idea that he should have lessons in Russian with Sockie and he acquiesced—what a piquant couple! In spite of all entreaties, I obstinately insisted on returning to London by the 9.56, instead of staying the night. I was well punished. In about half an hour the lights went out and then we stuck at Acton for about an hour and a half listening to the Hell of a bombardment. I was alone in a cold dark carriage—not frightened—but very bored. At last we moved on to Paddington and then I went by underground to Sloane Square. All the lights were out and lots of poor children were encamped on the platforms. I didn't get home till about two. The raid of the night before had been severe—the air-raid shelter at Bottomley's office having been shelled.

Wednesday, 30th January

Shared a taxi with Papa and he dropped me to dine with Claud. I was taking him to Adele's party, where I had been asked to play poker. Typical Russell joke, a huge pompous printed menu of some years ago on the table: two soups, two entrées, two everything. We got on quite well, but our relations *have suffered* a sea-change.

Thursday, 31st January

Brenda offered to let me her Mayfair mews cheap when she goes to Paris. It would suit Michael and me very well—the only consideration being that it is very jerry-built and one might feel anxious about Michael in air raids. The Monday night disaster to the shelter shows nothing helps with a 'direct hit', but the question is whether it is worth considering the different nuances of protection afforded from shrapnel and splinters. Not to have one's child in London at all seems to me almost like keeping him in the country for fear of the traffic—unless of course the raids affect their nerves. Anyhow, he will remain at Stanway for the present, and I will see how things develop. Perhaps the raids will become much more formidable; perhaps our barrage more effective.

Friday, 1st February

I lunched with Tonks—a sketchy lunch of two raw eggs and some oatmeal biscuits—before sitting to him. He began a pastel of me—he claims to have entirely mastered the medium since his former effort just before the war. The two would do an advertisement of 'before' and 'after' for the use of militarists or pacifists. He told me about Lord Clanricarde, whose pastel done from memory after death, we had so admired in the New English. He was the fabulously rich old man who left Lord Lascelles a huge fortune—a disgusting old miser who wore a priceless pearl tied round his neck on a bit of string. His verminous old cloak was sent to Tonks to help him with the pastel. Tonks was delighted with his beginning of me and, chuckling sardonically, said he hoped it would 'annoy McEvoy'. He raved over pastel as a medium, reproved my use of the word 'softness' in its praise, substituting 'delicacy'. I found him very reposeful to sit to after the fevered McEvoy—he is so concentrated, so untentative, painting so few pictures, liking so few people. His jagged, cadaverous, Round-head face expresses such *certainty* of taste—value and standards. He talked interestingly of painting, considering Michael Angelo to be the greatest swell—talked of his 'sublime surety'. Amongst the English, he gives the palm to Turner whom he ranks undoubtedly as one of the few 'great minds' in painting. Talking of Augustus John's failure with Margot Howard de Walden, he said she had no 'aspect'—so true. He doesn't like my John portrait.

Mary Herbert visited me, and talked of her own uneasiness about Aubrey who contemplates remaining at home now. She would rather he returned to his job in Italy, as she is afraid of the sort of Welt Politik speeches he might make in the House, and doesn't want him to get into a false position with the Labour Party.

Just remembered a delicious story of an old lady in the workhouse at Taplow. She said, 'I'm ninety-six, but Sally says she wouldn't take me for more than ninety-three,' and (of her daughter who deceased at the age of seventy), 'I always knew I should never rear her!'

Saturday, 2nd February

Bicycle through the rain to sit to Tonks. I was feeling dyspeptic and cross. Talked of the difficulty of preventing one's life from being overrun by friends to the complete destruction of leisure. He said he was quite deliberately *complet*, like a hotel. He didn't want to make any new friends, any more than he wanted more furniture in his room. He was pleased with his work on me, but I hope he will subdue the roses in my cheeks. He commented on the funny way I suddenly brought my mouth, as it were, to 'attention', and I promised to let it 'stand at ease'. Alex came to pick me up. Tonks told him not to look at the drawing until he stopped working: how different from McEvoy's feverish dragging forth of canvasses, with the eager inquiries of, 'Do you think it will come?'

Angela told me Mr Asquith had seen her, and said he had been very nice.

Sunday, 3rd February

A horrid wet morning. Bicycled to McEvoy at ten, and he went on with my picture. I think it is better than it has ever been before. The 'moonlit' background is lovely, but the lips are much too full. He didn't alter them at this sitting, but I hope he will. I feel him depleted and nervous—too busy—without sufficient leisure to build his next thought. The mind will go out of his art. How right Tonks was when he said all artists ought to eat badly, or suffer from some such drawback, so that they shouldn't go out too much. Alex came in and his silence, after contemplation of the picture, made me very nervous.

Alex walked me home—and the bicycle—I saw Papa's amused face looking out of the window when we reached the front door. He is in travail with his speech. In the hall I found a whole copybook full of the most vitriolic abuse from John's governess. She accused me of 'living in a "soul room" with the four walls all made up of "Self", and of preferring to sit for horrible portraits, which show all the evil in you and *none* of the good, and smooth friends who flatter you, to the tiring company of your own son.' However, she ended, 'You, whom one must love so dearly.'

Bicycled to lunch with Frances Horner—the first time I have seen her since Edward's death. It went to one's heart—the poor old boy looked bowed down and stupefied with grief. Venetia was there, Katharine, and Lord Haldane. Heard Margot had selected Con, of all people, to rejoice to over the welcome 'chaos' the country was falling into under Lloyd George's guidance.

Elizabeth called for me and we repeated our quartette dinner at Prince Bibesco's. I enjoyed my talk with Desmond MacCarthy. I find his mind wonderfully agreeable. We discussed egoism, and tried to define the distinction between an egoist and an egotist. We also had rather fun about sense of humour, which he thought a grossly overrated quality—obviously only cultivated in self-defence, *faute de mieux*. In Heaven it wouldn't be needed, any more than tact. He was interesting about the critical faculty, opining that one need *not* worry about it functioning *while* reading, but wait till the tide has gone out and then look for the marks in the sand. He said people who went to a play with him, hoping to hear bright criticism straight from the

Mint, were much disappointed, as he never began to dissect until two days afterwards.

My Spanish shawl was much admired.

Monday, 4th February

Walked to the Local Food Office as I wanted to make enquiries about meat, butter, and margarine coupons, but there was a huge crowd and I didn't go in. There are huge queues outside the grocers' shops in the King's Road.

Visit from Horatia: she told me Lord Dufferin was dying. Alex called for me and we dined at the Café Royal with the Laverys—Claud, Gilbert, and Maud completing our party. I find Hazel Lavery a bore at a small party—at any rate a non-conductor to me—she never listens and entirely checks my flow. We went to the New Gallery cinema: there was an excellent Charlie Chaplin film and a very long drama, *The Life of Rasputin*—rather disappointing considering its possibilities. Tubed and walked home through pouring rain escorted by Alex—the Tube was *packed*. Found a letter from poor Oc, characteristically saying little of his own condition, but telling me Freyberg's wound had reopened.

Tuesday, 5th February

Carefully left time for letter to Beb, diary, newspapers, etc., but my morning was wrecked by poor Angela, who came in and poured out her woes. She is miserable. Lord Derby, in spite of the words 'I should regret if this incident interfered with her getting work', absolutely refuses to allow her a worker's pass.

We picked up Angela's friend, Barbara Powell, at the Hyde Park Hotel and took her with us to the House of Lords. Ladies are much more comfortably off there than in the House of Commons—one can see, hear, and smell. Atmosphere strangely sleepy after the House of Commons. The peers are a scratch-looking lot. Grace was up in the gallery—looking very grim—Con and Adele beside her. I felt self-conscious and giggly. Lord Ribblesdale spoke first—not very effectively—but then he was leaving the eulogy for Papa and wasn't allowed to attack the War Office, so there wasn't much for him to say. Papa spoke with great eloquence in his best sanctimonious cathedral voice. The Lords either had great control or else they didn't see the absurdity of the situation. Derby did not back out in any way. He said exactly what he had agreed to.

1918

Dined with Alex at Queen's Restaurant—meatless again. Quite interesting talk on War Psychology. We went to cinema in the King's Road to see the famous Mary Pickford film *The Little American*. It was wonderful, but unfortunately we missed the sinking of the *Lusitania*. We walked home. Alex still the same to me—a song without words—tender-eyed, and importunate for meetings, but never a word. . . .

Wednesday, 6th February

Angela sobbing down the telephone to Papa—quite distraught, poor girl. Lovely morning. Walked with John and his governess. Ordered a pair of stays. Bicycled against wind and time, and arrived late and tired for lunch at Cavendish Square. Sat next to Mrs Sidney Webb who froze me with her grim talk about the 'Classes'. She said after the war there would inevitably be either the establishment of the 'Equalitarian System' or else complete anarchy. The 'governing classes' had been completely 'shown up' by the war, and it was a mistake to expect the people to be too war-weary to rise in their wrath. Visited Claud— he was much more *empressé* than he has been lately and invited me to dine. I agreed to come on Tuesday if back from Stanway.

Friday, 8th February

Travelled down to Stanway by 1.40—the journey seemed endless. Poor Sockie had received the letter giving her notice: she has taken the blow angelically.

Saturday, 9th February

I went for a walk with Tommy Lascelles before tea. He spent several weeks at the Avon Tyrell convalescent home for New Zealand officers. Once, when Lord Manners had to expostulate with them for getting drunk, one of them said, 'I'm sure I'm very sorry to have got drunk in a Peer's house.' Poor Bibs came home with the most comically tragical face—she had lost the hounds immediately after the meet, only to meet them again on their way home with five masks. I don't believe she will ever smile again. We read some *Jane Eyre* aloud after dinner.

Wednesday, 13th February

I travelled up to London by the eleven something, feeling oh! so ill

410

and depressed. Tea with John and his governess—John certainly looked worse again. Papa came in. He said Angela is going to do Lady Hamilton in the movies with her own name for £100. Everybody is very full of Repington's arrest. Aubrey has just made a pacifist speech —Alex said it was very good.

Saturday, 16th February

Dined with Alex at Queen's—whitebait, soup, and macaroni. I told him what a blighting influence his spikes had exercised over my youth. Just as we had finished dinner, the waiters announced 'Air Raid Warning' and sure enough we heard whistles and 'maroons'. We walked home—to Cadogan Square—through streets already emptied save for a few bustling people. We sat in a fireless room. The guns lasted a very short time. There was one loud noise which Alex announced to be a bomb—we afterwards heard it had fallen in Chelsea, killing an officer, his wife, and three children and breaking all the windows in Chelsea Barracks. I read *Urn Burial* aloud through the barrage and then selections from *The Muse in Arms*. After a long silence a man passed along the street wailing 'All clear . . . all clear'— a curious new street cry. It was about twelve o'clock. I never knew any man so importunate to be with one, and so little importunate when he is with one as Alex. We haven't even got to Christian names yet.

Sunday, 17th February

Alex called for me at four and we went off to see a play given by the Pioneer Society. It's a ridiculous bit of chicanery—the censorship being dodged by calling themselves a 'Society' and having tickets on the subscriber system. The performances are always on Sunday. Found Oggie there and she told me *La Femme et le Pantin* was an unspeakably improper book. I remembered it as the name of the book there was such a row about Hugh giving to the Lewis girl. As a matter of fact, it turned out not at all bad—threatening in tone, but nothing actually very shy-making. The scene where the girl dances naked was very well managed with a screen. She acted extraordinarily well and I enjoyed the play. The clothes were good and the sunny guitar-twanging sort of atmosphere well suggested. The huge theatre was *packed*. It was nearly eight before it was over. Alex conducted me home by Tube and I had dinner in bed. Read Keats' letters to the accompaniment of another air-raid.

1918

Monday, 18th February

Alex turned up at a quarter to twelve and we drove to the Tate. We were surprised to see crowds pouring out and wondered at the public's sudden appetite for art, but we were told by a burly policeman that it was the Ministry of Pensions office and that our entrance was neither permissible nor desirable!

I lunched with Frances Charteris. Margot had sent for her to say, 'Your father has made me very unhappy. Poor Cis feels it very much, too. I cried all night when I heard he had only given Cis fifty pounds —you know how Cis loved Kakoo, too!'

Papa came back from Stanway. Michael had met him on the door-step all by himself and said in a loud, clear voice, 'Lady Angela isn't here!'—I dined with the Curzons why, I can't think. Such a snob party—nearly all Viceroys—the last they give before they are really in the grip of rations: Lord Crewe, Lord Hardinge, the Lansdownes, the Salisburys, Lord Farquhar, and so on. I sat between Cowans and Salisbury, and ate a delicious dinner to the accompaniment of a very brisk air raid. No one turned a hair, except perhaps Lady Lansdowne, who occasionally made enquiries about the cellar. Cowans was in great heat against Rhondda, regarding the food shortage as desperately serious, but maintaining that it had all been quite avoidable. Lady Curzon's face is busily camouflaged, her conversation briskly banal— surely she will be greatly in the way at his debating society parties at Hackwood?

I am almost certain I have started a baby. I did *not* wish it—but, if it is so, I should be more than reconciled. Under those circumstances a blessed sentimentality envelops me—but it's bad for Sylvia Strayte.

Tuesday, 19th February

Met Mary at Bruton Street and we went to the Marquis Guido Serra's office. He was in the same state of fuss and uncertainty. As he didn't know whether he was going to be a soldier and I didn't know whether I was going to have a baby, our conversation was perforce rather vague as to future plans.

Wednesday, 20th February

Brenda called for me and I went back to luncheon with her. We had a delicious chicken Summie had smuggled from France. She told me about her trials with Prince Leo—how desperately bored she had been by him for two years and how at last she had lost her temper and told him so. Now she had—she *hoped*—made a final rupture. It was Freddie who would never allow her to drop him and she had taken advantage of his absence. And the 'world' condoles with Freddie on his wife's flirtatiousness—it's an excellent example of how these sort of situations are *mis*-seen! Brenda's fear is that Leo will relapse into morphia, and that his doctor will hound her to his bedside as he did before.

Owing to rain there was no raid. They say that not *one* German aeroplane left its country last Tuesday—all that terrific barrage was due to a false alarm!

Thursday, 21st February

Great telephone trouble. Papa's latest breach of telephone etiquette was to smear the receiver with shaving soap. Nasty blow through the post. The Voyevodskys are leaving 8 Sussex Place on the 19th March, so I have to resume the misery of House Agencying.

Alex walked me to Manchester Street for my appointment with Teresina. She prophesied tremendous artistic and financial success in a dramatic undertaking which would take me abroad, but saw a temporary hitch—which I interpreted as the baby. She talked a lot about Beb; saw him very potential, but with 'disappointing' element which she felt I was feeling at present. She counselled me not to encourage the poetry side of him too much, as it was only a side-track to his real career, and said after the war I must push him into some congenial public position; he would not return to the Bar. I arranged for her to see John.

I was amused by the following letter from Augustus John at the Front:

'I didn't send the photographs: it was the indefatigable Kneustub (fair, frizzy, fat) and it was also he—not me or at my instance—wrote you about your portrait. Damned officious! Of course, I never dreamt of you or anybody *buying* that portrait. I hope you don't think I did it with any such motive. I'm sure you don't—well—of course. Do you know I was considering the problem of writing to you when your letter came and it's no longer a problem. Why ever *was* it I ask myself? I received your letter this morning—on the point of going up to a place on the line where I have been all day. A divine day with a per-petual blue, unsullied but for quaint blossomings—miniature imita-tions of clouds—which appeared without warning in the Empyrean in the neighbourhood of our flying machines (or *his*). (But, for God's sake, don't let me become a war-bore!) I saw there an almost perfectly good lady in her grave, with the top knocked off it (she had her stockings on).

'I confess I haven't started that diary yet. The truth is I funk it! I am in a curious state—wondering who I am. I watch myself closely without yet being able to classify myself. I evade definition—and that *must* mean I *have* no *character*. Do you understand yours? You, who *have* one! To be a Major is not enough—clearly now if one were a Brigadier-General say—would that help to self-knowledge if not to self-respect? . . . I am alone in what they call the 'Château' in this dismal little town. I am very lucky, not having to face a *mess* twice a day with a cheerful optimistic air. When out of the Front I admire things unreasoningly and conduct myself with that instinctive tact which is the mark of the moral traitor. The good sun makes beauty out of wreckage. I wander among bricks and wonder if those shells will come just a *little* bit nearer. So you have come towards Chelsea and have found, I hope, the kind of flat you wanted. Does the cinema still attract you? There's no knowing when I'll come across—maybe soon. I look forward to seeing you so much. I wish I could see you right now, for at this hour your hair, which comes out so fiery in the photograph, must be *down* and I seem to feel it. I pull—and there's no head at the other end. I hope you'll write to me again soon, and so help me to withstand these khaki influences. I want to paint you again. *Gute nacht.*'

Strangely elated in spirits—felt as if walking on air—glamoured by Teresina and so happy about my baby. Complete conviction of immortality and lapped in love from the dead.

Friday, 22nd February

So, I am not going to have a baby after all. Felt in really deep mourning—so surprised, and so disappointed. I had become far advanced in sentimentality and now I feel the ground knocked from under my feet as far as plans go. I must reconstruct my life. I must try and find a second string to my cinema bow.

Tea with John and his governess. She told me a lot about Gertie Millar's life. When she was well launched on her theatrical career Monckton had put a pistol to her head, saying, 'You either marry me or live with me, or else I break you at once.' She had married him and stuck to him for twelve years. Finding another woman in the house one day, she left him at once for ever. Then came the Duke of Westminster—again she left him because she discovered he was keeping Pavlova, when she had believed herself to be the 'only woman'. She is now in love with some man who adores her and is waiting to marry her the day Monckton dies.

Saturday, 23rd February

Stayed in bed and was busily going through my repertoire when
enter Evan, who had come to see Mamma, but stayed talking to me
for over an hour. He was very delightful. He said he thought Mrs
Keppel must be making up for deficiency of food by having recourse
to spirit. The other day she had lurched up to him at a party, trumpeted
out, 'Lady Desborough is the cleverest woman in London'—and rolled
away. Evan is revelling in idleness before he returns to the Bar. Mamma
arrived back from Gosford—in good spirits.

I lunched with Gwendoline and Moira Osborne, and had *beef,*
cream, and butter—the very last meal in anyone else's house. Beef
goes to my head now. We discussed the best type of looks for looking-
glass satisfaction and had a great discussion on wrinkles—under-eye
pockets, and so forth—comparing our symptoms in the glass. I
preached rouge to them both—particularly as *medicine.*

Monday, 25th February

Alex came to say goodbye—he goes back to the Front tomorrow. I
shall miss him. He sent me a telegram from Southampton: 'Please
write to me today.'

Papa and I dined at the Hyde Park Grill Room, before he went off
to Gosford to stay with the Connors. He gave me one of his coupons
which produced a very slender wing—a quarter of his whole allowance for a week. I must say it's very small—I shall to all intents and
purposes become a vegetarian. As I have all my meals out and shall
no longer find any meat at my hostesses' tables, I suppose—if I wish
to continue carnivorous—I must consume my ration at breakfast. I
don't mind a bit in theory, but perhaps it may affect my psychology.
I don't want to get *milder*—if my temper *improves* I am done for.

Thursday, 28th February

Bicycled out to luncheon with Prince Bibesco. I had asked him if he
would subscribe anything to D. H. Lawrence, and he had asked me to
come and discuss the matter as he wanted the money to take the form
of getting his book published. Told to ask a lady, I drew Horatia
and the delectable Desmond MacCarthy made our fourth. We had an
excellent lunch, preceded by cocktails and followed by peach brandy.
We discussed the possible publication of Lawrence's novel *Goats and
Compasses*. Unfortunately Desmond MacCarthy, who might be helpful,

takes Lady Ottoline seriously as a friend and wishes her protected from the pain the (according to him) obvious lampoon of her would inflict. Apparently the Morells actually threaten a libel action in the case of publication. Desmond MacCarthy spoke of Lawrence as indisputably a genius, but *no* artist. He *is* a good talker. I found it difficult to concentrate on Bibesco—he 'puts me out of action' socially.

Violet came to tea to see John. She was very nice and then I had a wonderfully happy seance with John's governess: it was impossible to believe she was the same woman as the one of the feverish scenes. Violet told me of the King's visit to Oc's bedside—he came to decorate him. Enjoyed another evening in bed—these two blank evenings have been a great gain towards possessing one's soul. I have loved reading *The Rudiments of Criticism* by Lamborn—a key to poetry recommended by the Professor and Ettie. It's a dear book.

Friday, 1st March

March has proverbially come in like a lion—a cutting wind teased and disfigured one, and moaned round the house in the approved Adelphi fashion. Papa arrived back from Scotland, having been quite happy with the Connors. There was a terrible governess squall over Polly. . . . I have much more leisure in my day since Alex's departure.

I had two raw eggs in bed for dinner, and then resurrected to go by underground to a party at Mrs Colefax's where McEvoy was my salvation. It was very typical—an impersonally compiled anthology of writers, painters, actresses and musicians. The latter stunted and Madge Titheradge recited—like Lewis Waller. I wish music didn't make me feel so mischievous—wanted to break out in the crudest manner, and could hardly resist pulling down Nora Bigham's hair. She was looking so intense. One should lie down as we did at Chirk— I *hate* these chairs. I felt as though on a night journey. I bolted some biscuits and rushed off to catch the train with McEvoy. He insisted on seeing me home to my door. Papa is more mellow than ever.

Saturday, 2nd March

Bicycled out to dinner with Guy and Frances. Pamela Lytton came in afterwards with her embroidery. She told us of the wild excitement fluttering all the girls over the Prince of Wales who, 'unbeknownst' to the King, has taken to going to all the dances. So far, he dances most with Rosemary and also motors with her in the daytime. No girl is allowed to leave London during the three weeks of his leave and every mother's heart beats high.

Sunday, 3rd March

I have got a very violent reading fever on, and would like hours and hours in which to browse. I am Keats-drunk: other poetry—except for Shakespeare—compared to him seems thin and drab, velveteen to velvet.

Tuesday, 5th March

Bitter, bitter cold. D. H. Lawrence up for two nights. Came to see me at 11.30. I thought him looking well—not his gauntest—and he was in good talking form. He has got about twenty pounds together now, so the wolf recedes from the threshold of his door. I asked him about the novel *Goats and Compasses*. He told me it hasn't been published in any form, but is now in the hands of Beaumont, whom I remembered to be Yvo's little publishing friend. Lawrence thought he would gladly publish 'privately' —(which means by subscription—a piece of chicanery on the same lines as the Stage Society) provided someone would guarantee him from any possible loss. Probably it would sell well. I promised to try and induce Bibesco, and to interview Beaumont if possible . . . 'Bunty pulls the strings'.

I have never known D. H. Lawrence nicer. He crashed on to the war, of course, complained that it is fighting one machine with another and, therefore, futile in result beyond expression. I gave him a photograph of my Augustus John. He says it has achieved a certain beauty and has 'courage'—the McEvoy water-colour he condemned as 'sweet'. Discussing modes of life, he said he really preferred living without servants and sharing the housework as they are doing at present—a 'household' oppressed him. He would like £200 to banish worry—*no* more. He *said* Ottoline no longer minded about the book (I wonder if this can be true) and that she was anxious to see him again, but that he was unwilling.

I bicycled to lunch with the Pollocks in Kensington. A hen party —the two girls, the mother, Norah Graham, and Lily Elsie. The latter's little flower face is *too* lovely and such a perfect 'Odol smile'. The likeness between her and Kakoo is extraordinary. She was very quiet—demure and sweet.

Claud called for me to dine at Queen's. He announced biliousness as an apology for inadequacy as a companion, but I have never known him nicer. I took him home and we sat by the fire and discussed the war—a good many eavesdroppers would have called us 'Pro-German'.

Wednesday, 6th March

Bicycled to sit to McEvoy at ten. Whibley attended the sitting and his conversation rather retarded McEvoy's brush. We discussed blackmail and journalism—whether most of the London *Mail* was just shooting in the dark. They have just said, in 'Things we want to know'—'How long Mr McEvoy will take painting Teddie Gerard?'—and there is no idea of her sitting to him! 'Why was Lady Cynthia A. so bored at Mrs Cazalet's concert?' was in last week, as Claud—who had been sitting beside me—rather ruefully pointed out.

McEvoy and Whibley compared notes on the fatuousness of art and literary criticism, the latter quoting one of the comments on him after his last book: 'Mr Whibley has frivolity without humour, and cleverness without intelligence.' One article had said he invariably wrote with a quill pen. I threatened to write to the London *Mail* and say McEvoy always painted with a toothbrush and asked his patients to bring their own. We had quite fun. McEvoy is wonderfully quick and responsive—like a machine in which, after paying your penny, the bell always rings.

I lunched at Cavendish Square. Margot had on a highly unbecoming Red Indian hat. The dear Old Boy sat between his two daughters-in-law. He was just off up to Fife. It was said that shops had telegraphed to the Food Controller asking if they should bury their rotting meat! I had a minute snipe—wished they were served like whitebait. Elizabeth told me Bibesco had told her he didn't want to see her any more. Whibley called for me and secured his desired taxi-cab, and firmly carried me off to Regent's Park. The lovely spring day had gone to his head, and he was more enamoured and importunate than ever— telling me in lyrical terms how happy I made him and clamouring to know if I would 'ever love him'. We discussed D. H. Lawrence. He is against publication of the novel, but says he could probably get him £100 from the Literary Fund, only he thought there should in that case be a tacit understanding that he should write something— and that, not inevitably censorable. Agony from my patent-leather-imprisoned toe. We had tea at Rumpelmayers.

Home to John: his governess has given me some beads which I wore. I chucked dining with my Russian tenants, refused to chaperone Elizabeth, and was looking forward to a herring in bed, but Papa asked me to dine at the Hyde Park and I acquiesced. A really good Charteris incident occurred. A man came up and asked me if I had 'returned from France'—seeing I was not Lady Angela he retired discomfited! Perhaps it's better than that she should be mistaken for his daughter!

Madame Voyevodsky came to see me. Poor things, they can get no money from Russia and are living on the pay he gets for his job here, which comes to an end in May. They are moving into a tiny house in Chelsea. I told her to let the rent for the last month stand over if convenient. Dined with Jeffie Darell in Bruton Street and she sent a brougham for me—excellent dinner. We went on to theatre. I thought Lily Elsie ravishing. Everyone considered her singing greatly improved under Oggie's tuition.

Saturday, 9th March

Had a letter from D. H. Lawrence enclosing the manuscript of a collection of poems he proposed publishing and—with my approval —'inscribing' to me. If I agreed I was to take them to Beaumont, with whom I was also to discuss the prospects of the novel. They are mainly (thank Heaven)! *not* erotic—ironical glimpses at aspects of the war—with very little rhyme or rhythm about them.

I bicycled off to Charing Cross Road to find Beaumont. He used to be a great friend of Yvo's and I have often intended to visit him. The shop consists of two very small rooms lined with books—a few old ones and all the new poets—De La Mare, etc., in little, funny bindings. He is a very fair, flaxen, fresh-complexioned, quite boyish-looking man. I don't quite know what I felt about him. I began by alluding to Yvo—after he was killed Beaumont wrote quite a nice thing about him and sent it to Mamma. We then discussed the book: he had only just seen Lawrence for the first time and was full of amazement at him. He is emphatic that his name must not appear in connection with Lawrence's book in the event of its being published—so is Bibesco!—and so am I. In fact I'm not sure that I want even anonymously to godmother it in any way. I doubt whether its printing will do either Lawrence or the world any good—*commercially* Beaumont's opinion was that it would be a success. The cost of printing would be approximately £370—the sale of a thousand copies would bring in £550. It would have to be done without any name of printer as it might mean prison. We agreed that the only course was to get the manuscript and let Bibesco read it for himself and make up his mind whether he wishes to proceed in the matter or not. Personally I don't feel very keen about it. Beaumont said that of course parts of it had merit—but it was worse than *The Rainbow*.

1918

Sunday, 10th March

Foggy morning. Walked with John and his governess. I met Aunt Madeline and talked to her for a bit. She said Cynthia Hamilton was considered the likely Princess of Wales. To Audley Square for tea with Claud. The Prince of Wales came on the *tapis* again. Trotter said he had met Princess Mary at a *thé dansant* and she had said, 'We don't reverse.'

John's governess and I—at her suggestion—did planchette after I got home. It wrote briskly, answering my unspoken inquiry as to who the force was by 'I am Blackwood'; a question as to whether John would get well by, 'Your dearest hopes will be realised'; and giving a lot of typical (to spiritualism I mean) sentiments, such as 'I love you more than I could on earth' and so on. I had dinner in bed—felt strangely happy and *exaltée*—why? 'You approach the most critical points in your development—beware of the pitfalls of intellect' and words to the effect of 'Think less and pray more' were scribbled by the pencil! Ugh!

Monday, 11th March

Lunched with Bibesco—the same quartette—Desmond MacCarthy and Horatia. We had quite amusing conversation on oaths and the derivation of words. I told them 'love' in tennis-scoring came from *l'œuf*. He rushed upstairs, returning in triumph to show me I was quite wrong, and that 'love'—thinking I meant it in the ordinary sense of the word—did *not* come from *l'œuf*!

I had a *tête-à-tête* with Bibesco. What an amazing man! He took my hand, on the old palmistry plea, and said, 'Desmond and I have been having a discussion on you. We diametrically disagreed on the point of whether men *vous avez fait de la cour* or not. It was plainly intimated which opinion he had held. He said he wanted to be friends and wanted me to 'trust' him. He asked how Elizabeth had edited him to me, saying, 'I suppose she told you I was madly in love with her?' He complained of her lack of reserve. I *think* he is cooling.

I went back to see Bluetooth for the first time after his bad illness and we sat in the square. His eyes are in even deeper caves. He is staying with Frances Horner.

Tuesday, 12th March

Mamma and I dined with Frances and Letty in Catharine Street. Letty told this food controller story. A farmer, accustomed to feed his household on one sheep a week, wrote to enquire whether he might kill one as usual. The reply was: 'Better kill half a sheep.' They went on to a concert. The brougham took me home to dress, and then I picked up Claud and took him on to Irene's dance—her 'dash for the throne' we called it, as the Prince of Wales was expected. I said I didn't dance when she invited me—I think it unseemly while Beb is actually at the Front—but I agreed to come in search of poker. Claud and I sat on a sofa and watched for ages. It was quite amusing, but how old-fashioned it makes me feel. I do hate the teasing catastrophic music thrummed out by those leering Negroes, and I can't believe the stuttering, furtive, modern dances can be as much fun as our valses—no *élan*, no abandon. Certainly they aren't as becoming. My sympathies were sharply aroused by a wretched, very plain girl dressed in a curtain who wall-flowered all the time. Claud is too extraordinary. He recognised no one—I asked him if he had known me when I passed him in the street, and he said he had—but then, of course, I was on my bicycle. I said I supposed he wouldn't if I happened to pass on a tricycle! I talked to Willie de Grunne and De Noailles and, just before leaving at 12.30, saw the Prince of Wales dancing round with Mrs Dudley Ward, a pretty little fluff with whom he is said to be rather in love. He is a dapper little fellow—too small—but really a pretty face. He looked as pleased as Punch and chatted away the whole time. I have never seen a man talk so fluently while dancing. He obviously means to have fun.

Wednesday, 13th March

Bicycled to McEvoy's—found him still at breakfast and had some coffee with him. He was more *ereinté* than ever. He is very busy painting rich Yorkshire factory owners, and so on. He improved my picture beyond recognition this sitting—my nose cut itself. Robert Nichols came in and stayed till the end, looking like a startled stoat. He talked a lot: he hopes to start a new *Review* through Heinemann; we skimmed over the Sitwells, and he said he thought Osbert—unlike most of the poets—*had* got something to say, but he considered him inarticulate; and we agreed that Lawrence was 'gibbered' by the war —all egotists are, I think.

Lunched *tête-à-tête* with Bibesco at his earnest request. He obviously wishes to play a large part in my life and took pains to convey the fact that he was cured of Elizabeth. He spoke quite condescendingly of her—deprecated her lack of reserve—but still claimed 'eloquence and wit' for her. He was *very* personal and ultra foreign, the 'Do let's talk about you' technique, with leading questions about erotics: 'Is your husband *follement amoureux* of you?', etc. He told me I was a darling and that he loved me, and complained of my 'squirrel' shyness when I edged away. I must say I rather liked him—he has a sort of mental sympathy. I see he means to make love to me. He shocked me by one remark: he was complaining of my hurrying away and in badinage said, 'You wouldn't want to go if I were Nichols.' I said, 'He wouldn't want me to stay'—and he said, 'Isn't he in love with you because you are not a boy?' Ugh!

John's governess very full of Gertie Millar's first night in *Flora*.

Thursday, 14th March

Mamma and I lunched at Cavendish Square—a 'lion' (whose books I don't know) called Walpole. We went on to Christie's to see a wonderful collection of Blakes which are just coming up for sale. They were just lying about to be handled! It was very difficult to get at them and I found Lady Ottoline Morrell and her long-haired party very distracting—Blake draws a queer crowd. Evan and Goonie were the only other fellow-creatures there. I longed to see the drawings in peace. Heard the Duchess of Rutland was furious with Diana because the Prince of Wales didn't dance with her at Irene's.

Wednesday, 20th March

Asking for trouble, I lunched alone with Bibesco—I have never been laid siege to by a foreigner before. The flowers and the chocolates are agreeable perquisites, but otherwise I can't say I like it much. His 'good advice' was that I should write instead of doing the 'movies' —he advocated something on the lines of a nameless diary. The 'squirrel' code had to be used a lot. He pawed dreadfully and kept promising *not* to kiss me. He tutored me and tried to hypnotise me into saying, '*Antoine, je t'aime*'. Finally he came to the conclusion that I was a 'baby' and a 'chou'. He told me Desmond puts me on so high a pedestal that he thinks, 'no man would dare to make love to me'— very anxious to know how many had, and to try and make me take him seriously. He tries to interpret my letters favourably—uphilll work I should think—and sent me lovely violets in a black bowl in the morning. He told me he had shocked Elizabeth in the early days of their acquaintance by asking her if she was *vierge*, and that she knew nothing about the physical relations. He asked me what I thought of physical love and, of *course*, told me I wasn't 'matured' yet—the marble was there, but the sculpture not emerged from the block. He wishes to undertake the job, but I'm afraid I can't oblige him.

Thursday, 21st March

Bibesco rang up and began telephoning nonsense about 'To be rich spiritually meant *giving*': he wishes to be my tutor in life—bird of prey that he is. Papa was in the room and I cut him off in the middle of a flowery sentence. In the course of the day he sent round a note saying, 'When can one telephone?' Ivor Churchill called without warning, but I was already undressed and unable to see him. I was sorry—it's so long since I saw him. He has neglected me.

The 'Offensive' has really begun—'*Nun geht's los*'. What are we in for?[1]

Friday, 22nd March

A day of the most amazing beauty—really hot. Fancy having to seek for shade in March. The spring sparkle in the air was wonderful—it seemed incredible that that hideous tomfoolery in France should be going on under the same sun. Such a day should lead to fraternising between any armies. I had to go and buy a straw hat.

Claud, Maud and I walked to Christie's, where Raeburns are being sold for vast sums. Maud and I shopped together. We jostled against the Prince of Wales who was sauntering down Bond Street all by himself. Went home very tired. The huge manuscript of Lawrence's unpublished work called *Women in Love* had been sent to me and I began to read it. I chucked Violet and dined with Claud at the Hyde Park Grill Room. Then we came home and *he* read *The Yellow Book* aloud. Very happy evening. I had such a pathetic letter from Freddie—a wail about his loneliness without Basil.

Saturday, 23rd March

The nightmare of the battle now raging oppressed me all day like a heavy weight. I have never been so haunted by the war and, as far as I know, Beb is in the neighbourhood of St Quentin where things seem to be worst. The papers give one a very bad impression—and the German communiqués are generally fairly truthful. I felt very sick at heart. Stayed in for dinner and read *Women in Love*.

1. In a haze of smoke, gas and fog, the British had attacked from the Somme to Cambrai after a barrage from six thousand guns.

1918

Sunday, 24th March

Stayed in bed reading Lawrence's rather nightmarish work. It is interesting—painfully so, and full of extraordinary bits of stark writing, but what it is all about and *why?* It seems a *mis*application of such a wealth of strenuous analysing and writing. Surely he is delirious—a man whose temperature is 103?—or do I know nothing about human beings? It is all so *fantastic* to me and 'unpleasant'— morbid to a degree. I don't know *what* to think about it.

Mary S. and Barbara came to tea with me—Mary in a new seven-guinea hat! She told me Oc and Betty were engaged! He had just asked me to go down to Brighton with him. I wish I could have, but I couldn't leave my last lap with John.

Battle news bad as far as I can make out.

Monday, 25th March

Ivor Churchill came to see me when I was dressed for dinner at 7.30. He was amusing, but I don't like him as much as I did. Irene had told me to bring a man to dinner, so I had secured Nichols—he called for me and we all three drove to Portland Place together. Nichols was a great success, and amused me awfully about Beaumont, the little publisher. Once, when Nichols had given him a long poem (his best work he thinks) and, at any rate, the fruit of great labour, he simply remarked: 'I like that.' I sat between Ivo Grenfell and Nichols —Ivo is the greatest darling. After dinner we played poker and Nichols was left to do his bit down poor Lady Wenlock's trumpet: he proved himself a champion trumpeter. They had a very long *tête-à-tête*. I lost eighteen shillings. Willie de Grunne came and joined us—very gloomy about the war news. Frances reported that General Foch was very blue. I have no news of Beb since the 19th. I have never felt so frightened about him before. Frances said poor Dinah was in an awful state—Ian's regiment are said to have had a very bad time and been surrounded. She was going to sleep with her.

Tuesday, 26th March

Fall of Bapaume in the papers. *Nothing* from Beb, but a very dear letter from Freyberg exulting in the battle he was then fighting— I am glad someone enjoys it—and saying he was just writing to say how much he valued my friendship after the war. I feel anxious about him, too.

Wednesday, 27th March

No news of Beb. Dined with Claud at Queen's Restaurant and came home afterwards,and he read aloud to me. I felt rather ill and shivery. Bibesco has sent me a book *De l'Amour*. I am amused to see he has marked the passage: '*La violence qu'on se fait pour demeurer fidèle ne vaut guère mieux qu'une infidelité.*'

Found a parcel of clothes from Eloïse Ancaster. Weeks ago she had sounded Dorothy as to whether I should 'mind' her sending me some clothes. Dorothy had been a good friend and said she was sure I wouldn't, without even adding 'judging by myself'. I had been living in hopes and began to think I must jog her by sending some of my own, when at last they came—looking apparently brand new. A most *lovely* hat with delicious yellow spotted veil, a gorgeous fur-trimmed velvet coat, two blouses, and a lovely petticoat.

Thursday, 28th March

Bicycled to McEvoy's. Couldn't resist wearing Eloïse's very becoming hat in spite of rain. McEvoy practically finished the picture. I *do* like it now. I sacrificed a hair-waving and stayed till nearly twelve. Put on my new rich coat and went and flaunted it before poor Dorothy whose mouth watered. It made me feel so rich that I kept the taxi ticking!

There was a ghastly crowd at the station—my box was too heavy and, for the sake of form I had to undo and perfunctorily take out a few objects which I carried loose in a nightmare parcel. Letty joined me at the last moment and we had a very crowded journey to Stanway with men standing on our feet. I read *A Diary without Dates*—wonderfully gripping, pitiless and true, and so vividly written. Nichols says it is the only good English thing of the war—bar Siegfried Sassoon. I'm told Ivo Grenfell is raising heaven and earth to get out to the Front. He had a terrific scene with Lord Francis Scott, his colonel, *clamouring* to go. Lord Francis said he had the very highest orders *not* to send him and couldn't possibly. Ivo asked if it could be done at his parents' request. The cruelty of the situation if Ettie has really deliberately to effect it herself! Slipped into my Stanway self—felt it coming over me half way in the train. Had a panic when I arrived: thought Papa looked flustered and saw a telegram in which I (mistakenly) imagined I saw my own name—thought it was Beb.

Friday, 29th March

Such a lovely spring day. Evan got a wire from the Ritz saying they had found important papers in his room and asking for instructions. He was appalled and said your sins always found you out if you didn't tip the housemaid. Papa did his bit in the afternoon, digging in a flower-bed for quite half an hour—during which process he unearthed three baby rabbits. He got on the Roll of Honour, then subsequent lumbago!

Saturday, 30th March

Evan read an admirable address by Gosse after lunch whilst we lay on sofas in the hall. He told us an American officer had said to him: 'I assure you, Captain Charteris, Mr Wilson is going to make this war a *personal* matter.' We fetched in those unfortunate rabbits and the efficient Letty undertook them. They filled Evan with disgust and we suggested that the ceramic Helen of Troy should be their foster mother. Mamma had a letter from Poor Annie Tennant saying her Edward is 'missing' in Mesopotamia. Bibs brought a rumour from Winchcomb that Montdidier had been recaptured. Polly came from London, but brought me no letter from Beb.

Monday, 1st April

Remembered the excitement of the April Fool's Days of my childhood and felt sadly 'grown up'. I sent a message to Michael to say I had grown a moustache in the night and he crept into my room full of apprehension. I also revived my old joke of inking a face on my knee and pretended it was a baby—to the huge delight of the three children. All three rabbits have died. Michael says 'they lived as long as they could'. I read *Black Beauty* to him in the hall whilst David and Martin did a puzzle and Evan continued his desultory reading. He is like a bee in a herbaceous border, sipping a little honey from so many books in turn. He is ostensibly studying a book on electricity in preparation for his Marconi case, but he finds it a hard nut to crack and flies for relief to Hardy, Lamb, Dickens, *The Child's History of France*, *The Wonders of the World*, etc. He told me Dickens' only comment on Wordsworth, after a meeting had been elaborately arranged between the two literary stars—'Rum old cock.'

Tuesday, 2nd April

A letter from Alex saying he is back in London with a slight wound in his left arm. What luck for him! Muriel wrote telling me not to be too anxious about getting no news from Beb as, owing to the trains being bombed, the field post was held up, and *no one* had had a letter from the Army for ten days.

Papa has started a learning by heart stunt. He has been busy with Swinburne's 'Proserpine'. He heard me say 'The Ancient Mariner'— to the despair of the chess players—himself recited passages from it, and threatened to give a performance of it in the village. He has got the most wonderful concert reciter's technique. He is in the most wonderfully mellow mood—and the wonder is that it has lasted for months and months. It is funny to see him slipping into the role of 'Grandpapa'.

Wednesday, 3rd April

Evan was to have gone off early in the morning for a tryst with Ettie at the Wharf. I blundered into his room to fetch a book and was astonished to find him in bed. He claimed a 'liver', but had very pink cheeks and bright eyes, and I thought we ought to get Halliwell to give him a certificate of ill-health to save him from a row with Ettie.

We played tennis in the morning. Mamma went off early to nurse at the hospital and brought lots of soldiers home to tea—such nice men—most of them wounded in the first day of this attack.

At midnight Mamma discovered Bibs in the hall, kneeling bolt upright with a poker in her hands. She was looking for a cat and saying her prayers to save time!

Thursday, 4th April

At *last*, a field p.c. from Beb, just saying he was all right. It was dated 24th. I drove into Winchcomb with Bibs and Michael to go on duty at the hospital at four—in Mary Strickland's place. First I had tea with Nurse Stott and another nurse, then I took temperatures. I was given three thermometers to keep going at once. Committed a farce-act— to the delight of my family—I forgot to shake down the thermometer after it had been in the mouth of one feverish patient. I then gave it to the man in the next bed and wrote down *his* temperature as 102°. Seeing his cucumber-cool face expressing astonishment, what I might have done struck me, and I took his temperature again and found it normal! Roars of laughter! I had already written it down on his chart and had to scratch it out with a penknife. Then I took part in a huge whist drive. I hadn't played for thirteen years and was very astonished to find I had won the ghastly second prize. When it was over the men had their supper and when we had tidied up, the Sister—*such* a delightful woman—did the dressings. I went round with her, holding the bowl. To my astonishment and humiliation, I suddenly found I was feeling *faint*. It was very subconscious squeamishness because I didn't know I was feeling disgusted, and I think it must partly have been due to the heat of the whist drive. I had to leave the ward for a few minutes. Felt very ashamed of myself.

Saturday, 6th April

A proverbial April day with heavy showers. Frousted all the morning —writing a good many letters and gobbling Balzac. A milestone in Michael's life. I took him to see Papa catching trout with worms. He crushed me to the earth by saying, 'You talk too much. It isn't so much *what* you say Mummie—and I like your voice—but you talk too much, too much, too much. Talk sometimes—not all the time.' The Halliwells—*père, mère et fils*—all came to dinner. I played my first game of auction bridge (perhaps a milestone in *my* life) with Mrs H., Mary S. and Alex. Evan is struggling with Briefs, and finds himself much out of legal practice after his military interlude.

Sunday, 7th April

Very wet day and ever so much colder. We had the fished trout for breakfast. We were all very hungry before—and afterwards—and talk fluently of food. We each have our own sugar and butter rations labelled. There is no doubt someone gets at my butter!

Monday, 8th April

Papa, Alex, Bibs, and I played tennis. Papa had a 'sinking' which he was very funny about. It drove him to the port bottle. I told him 'sinkings' were what made people take to drink. It was a revelation to him. He had always thought drunkards only drank from sheer greed of the taste of wine, and now said he would never be hard on them again. He indulged in a lot of sweet moralising on the subject.
   Played bridge with Mamma, Sockie, and Alex. I find I love it.

Friday, 12th April

Morning of tennis and Balzac. Ten soldiers arrived at three and we

428

had a most successful afternoon with them: tennis, alfresco bridge, fishing, high tea, and daffodil storming. They were such a delightful lot of men. A very bad war telegram arrived and threw us into depth of gloom: Merville captured, etc., etc. *Acharné* cut-throat bridge between Mary, Papa, and me—I like confiding bridge, Papa plays rattlingly fast. We considered ourselves allies against him, but his superior skill, luck, and chicanery won about seven pounds from both of us, but he will have to tear up our cheques. Zeppelins came rather near in the night. Nannie claims to have heard them.

Tuesday, 16th April

Bitter cold and a deluge of rain. Sorry to leave Stanway. In spite of the devastating battle, it's been a nice bit of peaceful family life. Papa has been such an angel and I have enjoyed Balzac, tennis, and bridge. Polly and I had a long cross-country journey to Pixton—I absorbed in *The Green Mirror* by Hugh Walpole and very philosophical about the chilly hours spent in waiting rooms. Arrived to find the ground well covered in snow. At Taunton I had got an evening paper reporting the loss of Bailleul—Oh God! Oh God!

Wednesday, 17th April

Awoke to the familiar moist atmosphere of Pixton: the old-fashioned chintzes, the inevitable photograph of the late Lord Carnarvon—there is one in every bedroom. Breakfasted in bed and re-read that most unpleasant of books *What Maisie Knew*. Came down and wrote. Mary as busy as someone in an office all the morning—a procession of gardeners, and so on. Read a little *Pickwick* to Aubrey and Mary after lunch.

Discussed Winston and his rhetoric at dinner. Aubrey had been disgusted when he had said, 'I feel I've got a man's blood on my head,' by Winston exclaiming (with, as he says, exultation), 'We've all got that!' Aubrey bitterly indicts him for Gallipoli. I tried to defend him. We chaffed Aubrey on the hypothetical situation of the Prince of Wales falling in love with Mary. He made a declaration of *un*accommodatingness.

I got a letter from Beb written on the sixth saying all his guns were practically knocked out, but none belonging to his battery had fallen into the hands of the Germans.

1918

Thursday, 18th April

Mary and I rode in the afternoon, rather a road-ride as she had to pay calls. We passed two or three groups of German prisoners on the road. I hope it wasn't prophetic, but for the first time I felt something akin to horror and fear at the sight of them—hitherto I have only been conscious of compassion, but on this occasion it was quite different. I hated passing them, it made me so self-conscious. It's difficult to know the right etiquette—one oughtn't to obviously either look or *not* look. Mary wanted to speak to them in German, but I think if one were a prisoner working in Germany one would resent a few words of dog English flung at one's head.

Bluetooth arrived at six—bringing a thirty-shilling bottle of crème de menthe. Alcohol of all kinds is becoming very precious. He told us of General Gough's visit to the Wharf, and was full of titbits of gossip which he daintily disgorged at dinner. I was amused by his account of a bridge row at the Wharf. Margot said, 'You're a liar,' to Mr McKenna who, on receipt of this insult, rose from the table and entering the next room carried his young wife straight upstairs. Half an hour later Margot went up to Pamela (Pamsky's room) in tears and said how much she regretted such a quarrel, adding however, 'But you do agree with me he's the greatest liar, don't you?' And when Pamela replied that she considered him the most truthful of men, her retort was, 'Then all I can say is that you are a squaw wife.' Before breakfast the next morning the Old Boy padded across to the Barn to see Margot in bed and cold cream and told her, whatever the possible truth of her assertion, one couldn't publicly call a guest a liar. Margot wrote a grovelling letter of apology and bridge was resumed. Bluetooth reported Asquith as very pessimistic about the military situation, partly owing to General Gough's very bad report of the French.

Mary cross-questioned me as to my *motive* in writing this diary. We played cut-throat bridge with Bluetooth. I had bad cards, but I played quite respectably. I can't help talking though—keeping up running comments and saying unforgivable things such as, 'Shall we double?'

Friday, 19th April

Such cruel cold; one felt as if one were eating ice. Oc sent on an excellent letter from Beb. Derby's departure from the War Office in the papers. How pleased Angela will be. They call him 'Genial Judas' in the Army.

Saturday, 20th April

Cold—cold—cold. Bluetooth came down very late, but we met over the last fragments of yesterday's brawn. I had a letter from Beb written on the 15th. He had been marching—marching—marching—right up to the north I suppose. I also had a letter from Augustus John, announcing his return and saying he was in a state of great mental confusion and would like to see me, as I was 'reposeful and calm' in addition to other things—also a Bibesco and a Lawrence, asking for news of his manuscript and of the Literary Fund. After all, Beaumont has shied at publishing his poems.

Alex arrived after lunch with a practically recovered arm. I was very glad to see him: his ready, punctual laugh is reassuring and it's a comfort to have someone who doesn't whisper. We went out for a walk in soft drizzle. It struck one as much warmer out of doors than in the house, where the fires are lamentable. He had been wounded on the third day of the retreat.

Saturday, 27th April

Bicycled to McEvoy's at ten. Unfortunately Pamela Lytton had told him that my picture in its *excellent* last phase was 'cruel'. Open as he is to suggestion, it was all in the melting pot again. He was rather worried about his life. The War Office wish to give him a Commission and entirely command his services. He feels it would be wrong to refuse, but it is rather hard to have to give up £10,000 a year, as he is now making, and get about £1,000 as a major.

I lunched at Cavendish Square, sitting between the Archbishop of Canterbury and Juliet Duff. Margot was grotesquely rouged and in another gorgeous new dress. Great excitement over the Air Service *crise*. Went down by 4.50 from Waterloo. Aileen Meade on whom I am billetted for Oc's wedding, met me and drove me to Tothill, the very nice little house she has got for the summer. It's about a mile from Avon.

Monday, 29th April

Ettie told a delicious story of Hoppy.[1] He had gone in a state of utmost concern to Con and told her that, when inspecting Betty's trousseau, he had said, 'Surely, darling, these nightgowns are rather thin?' To

1. Lord Manners.

which she had replied, 'Oh yes, but it will be all right because I shall wear my combinations under them.' What was to be done?

Tuesday, 30th April

The longest day to look back on I ever remembered. When I went to bed it seemed like three days since breakfast, but such good days, and such a wonderful lot of eating in them!

Disappointed to find it was a grey and draughty day, but still, it was a great thing that it shouldn't have been actually raining. We found the morale at Avon really very good, though Betty said she was feeling sick: I advised her to take her face out of circulation for a bit and withdraw until it was time to dress—but she remained in our midst in mufti. There was a great scurry arranging the presents, all the hag aunts bustling about—a very amusing scene and one's consciousness of the undercurrent of Montagu and Capulet feeling added to the piquancy. Aileen and I took as much trouble over our dressing as though we were brides ourselves. I wore my new black dress and was quite pleased with my appearance.

The wedding was a poem—really lovely and most touching—much the nicest I have ever seen and it made one think all London weddings indecent. The little chapel was most beautifully decorated —the arch of may was a dream. One felt that no one was there who wasn't really interested. The bridegroom was a brilliantly topical figure, and he stood so well on his one leg, without even a stick, though it made one tired to watch him. The bride looked astonishingly above her average—really delicious—and the sun emerged just in time to gild her hair as they walked out under the arch of New Zealanders' swords whilst children strewed gorse petals at her feet.

Margot gad-flyed wonderfully little in church. To the general consternation, she had unexpectedly turned up at Avon an hour before the wedding. Ettie had found her in the hall hissing to poor Hoppy—who stood by helplessly rubbing his hands—'I never knew such a house, the draughts are killing me! How *can* you live in such a place?' Ettie heroically tired her out by walking her to the chapel. We went back to the most wonderful pre-war meal and I ate till I was blue —there were actually solid things like ham! Betty and Oc sat beside each other at the wedding breakfast, she still looking wonderfully pretty, and she cut the cake with his sword. As they motored away to Cranbourne, the New Zealanders mustered and did a Harikro wuh?— some wild cry which curdles one's blood.

Ettie and Ivo came to Tothill with us where we fell on a gorgeous

tea: I have never had such a food orgy day. Eventually Aileen motored
Ivo to Brockenhurst to catch a twelve-something train, with Willie de
Grunne escorting her. I was just going to sleep under *inches* of cold
cream when, to my consternation, I found both Willie and Aileen
sitting on my bed. Willie said soothingly, 'Oh, all my sisters use cold
cream!'—which didn't soothe me at all. They were full of a forest
fire they had witnessed. Half asleep, I was dimly aware of Willie
toying with my pig-tail and pouring cold cocoa down my throat,
ejaculating, 'I am so glad my father can't see me now!' Why his father
should have objected, Heaven knows—it was much more important
that Aileen's father shouldn't have witnessed the scene.

Wednesday, 1st May

A muddled morning waiting for Ettie to call for me on the way to the
station. Finally her maid and luggage arrived, and we raced for the
train and just caught it. We succeeded in travelling first with third-
class tickets: Mrs Lionel Rothschild was in our carriage. We bought
some dry-as-dust buns and tried to imagine the currants.

Back to cold, gaunt, uncarpeted Cadogan Square. Tremendous day-
after-Christmas feeling. Dear Ivo came to see me. What a darling
he is, and what a continual feast he must be as a son! His beauty is
really very great, the real poetry of a youth's looks, and he has delicious
manners and blushes. He talked of his distress at not being sent out,
and is going to make a determined struggle for which he intends
to requisition the co-operation of his wretched parents—a Grand
Guignol situation. Whilst we were at tea the housemaid came in and,
to my surprise, said, 'A gentleman wishes to see you, milady.' Enter
the most awful individual in a top-hat. He looked frightfully embarrassed. I was completely at a loss—lost my head and laughed
feebly. After an interval of blinking, he stuttered out, 'Is it Lady
Asquith?' and then, 'Might I have a word with you in *private*?' I
followed him out of the room and did my best to put *him* at his ease
when he had said, 'I am so sorry. The maid shouldn't have taken me
upstairs, but I didn't think you'd like me to give it to you before the
gentleman—the truth is, I have got a summons for you!' Poor man,
how he suffered, and I didn't know how best to convey my indifference. 'A gentleman to see you' sounded like nasty sarcasm. Yvo
and I laughed and I told him it would make a good postscript to Ettie's
story of my taking him to the opera with Augustus John and D. H.
Lawrence. It was for a wretched fourteen-shillings bill!

1918

Thursday, 2nd May

Bicycled to McEvoy at my usual hour. Found my portrait in quite a new phase—all blue and white, like a Della Robbia plaque. McEvoy much exercised in mind as to whether he should become an R.A. or not, Lavery and the rest are importuning him to do so. He seems to think he would immediately develop a white beard and red eyes if he acquiesced. I daresay it is partly fear of Tonks which withholds him—he would certainly think it reprehensible apostasy, though from *what* the apostasy is, I don't quite know. Alex came in and did great harm by saying, 'I should do her true profile'. My second eyelashes were immediately painted out.

Mary H. visited me at Cadogan Square. Then, after two eggs, I went to my assignation with Augustus John. It was lucky I took the raw egg precaution, because he gave me nothing to eat—only strong tea to drink. He seemed very pleased to see me and asked me to sit again. He was sent home from France at the beginning of the offensive and now he is confronted with the task of painting a forty-five-foot canvas for the Canadians—having had to take a new studio for the purpose. Complained of his lack of a sense of continuity in his identity.

Ivor Churchill—the *petit maître* as Alex calls him came to see me at seven. He was very nice indeed—feeling ill poor dear—and having quite lost faith in Mary's power of improving his 'soul-box'. He complained of having entirely lost the faculty of reading ... very sad at the age of nineteen!

Friday, 3rd May

I was by way of lunching with Mary, and found a message saying she was at the Bath Club. Alex took me there and stayed and lunched with me, Mary, and Venetia. We saw Steer at a table, and Mary and I each wrote him an R.S.V.P. letter to tease him—writing is such an agony to him. Returned to Bruton Street with Mary, and Steer came round. We were alarmed by his appearance—I have never seen so much ballast in the way of flesh so quickly thrown overboard. He must be *stones* lighter and he would do well for a poster to encourage the Huns in submarine warfare. He really looked ill and wretched. He said he thought some of Beb's poems, which Tonks had read to him, were 'first-rate'.

Alex called for me and we dined at Queen's Restaurant (Heaven knows what its waiters think of me!), and went to *The Playboy of the Western World* at the Court Theatre. I don't think it acts as well as it reads.

Saturday, 4th May

Tête-à-tête lunch with Bibesco—chicken (not to be sneezed at nowadays!). He complained of my still being on the defensive with him, and accused me of having no *amitié* for him, adding that any Frenchwoman would regard his request for such a commodity as an insult. He said he feared I wasn't as 'discreet' as he—that Baroness D'Erlanger had rung him up on the telephone and said: 'How about Cynthia Asquith?' and that Brenda had taxed him with being in love with me.

Sunday, 5th May

An awful day of wetness. Willie de Grunne called for me and took me to High Mass at Westminster Cathedral. I love its misty vastness. How lovely it will be when it is all mosaiced! Music lovely—but the genuflexions and mummery very disturbing.

Desmond MacCarthy called for me and we discussed his friend Bibesco and his strange love for Elizabeth. He said he had accused Bibesco of 'trying to make a *chef d'œuvre* out of a pique'. Elizabeth had told Bibesco: 'I don't understand you. You treat me half as a mistress and half as a nurse.'

Monday, 6th May

Off to the John front at last—a bun lunch at Paddington, tea at Oxford, and a second one when I arrived at the farm—a very farinaceous day altogether, and supper was scones and jam plus one egg.

Tuesday, 7th May

John's birthday—I don't know what to think of him. At times I was telepathised by his governess's confidence—at others fell back into despondency. Somehow or other she has taught him to read quite a lot. I got a letter from Freyberg exulting over the delight of a tremendous battle—ten days without sleep.

Thursday, 9th May

John and his governess took me to the station—it is an ordeal behind me. Arrived at Stanway for luncheon found Mary S., Miss Wilkinson, and Sister Orde—the night nurse I was to go on duty with. My apprehension was fully aroused by Mary's gruesome stump talk . . . of course, I have come just after a very bad amputation.

I rested and motored over to the hospital with Orde in a blue funk, feeling the mixed sensations of a 'new boy', a night traveller, and an actress on her first night. There is a sort of supper meal at eight, but I didn't have any—I washed up the things and stood about. Lights are put out in the ward at nine o'clock, and occasionally one walks round the dim lantern-lit room. It is rather creepy—surrounded by all those huddled forms sleeping aloud. The porridge is put on early and has to be stirred all through the night, and one has to stoke the furnace. When there is nothing to do we sit quite comfortably in the little sitting room talking, reading, or writing. The queer anomalous meals are great fun in the setting and the eating: at about twelve one has what I suppose represents lunch (something is left in the larder in the nature of eggs, sardines, and so on, and one drinks what one likes, such as Horlicks, tea, cocoa, or coffee) and at four one has a delicious meal of porridge and so on—the porridge is far the best I have ever tasted.

The pet and the interest of A Ward now is poor little Harris, who has got his leg off right high up. A few days ago he had to have a lot more taken off his stump and he has nearly died of haemorrhage ever since. He is much better now, but still a very bad colour. He is such a darling—so brave and always smiling. It's still very painful—pray God I never have to see that stump naked!

My first night was eventful. At about eleven there came a knock at the door. In burst Nurse Ewing, who is alone in B Ward (where they are supposed not to have bad cases). She was white as paper and told us one of her men (obviously a case of bad shell shock) was quite unmanageably walking in his sleep—thinking he was at the Front, poor fellow—hurling missiles about in the delusion that they were bombs and labouring under the impression that his companions were Germans. He was 'hollering' like anything and Nurse Ewing said she couldn't be left alone with him. Away went Nurse Orde with her, leaving me quite alone in that snoring ward. I was in terror lest Harris should have a haemorrhage or something, but after a time they—to my intense relief—returned.

I went back under blazing starlight at about five, quite revived by delicious porridge and tea. Talked to Orde till about six when we call the men and the bustle begins. Breakfast has to be got ready for them and I take washing materials round to the bedridden ones. After their breakfast the dressings are done, at which I have to help, holding bowls and running to fetch things of whose whereabouts I have no idea—one feels anxious and foolish. A wag—Matthews—is a wonderful helper and enjoyed bringing boiling hot fomentations: I didn't mind the three dressings at all—the wounds were quite inoffensive. My only trial was attending to poor dear Harris. Thank God we didn't undo his stump! But we had to wash him and pull the draw sheets. The slightest movement is agony to his stump and it made me feel sickish, but I was able to function all right. We had screens round us. He was so sweet, and when we left him in peace, spent ages with the brush, comb, and glass making his hair curl. They are a delightful lot of men. My favourite is a K.R.R. called Morris, who does beautiful elaborate embroidery with an admiring audience standing round— one man seems to do nothing all day but thread needles for him. They are very friendly to one—ambitiously facetious a great many of them: one joke is to ask one to start the gramophone when one creeps round the ward in the dark. I felt my identity disappearing into 'Nurse' and my one absorption was to satisfy the Sister and please the men.

I felt excited and not in the least tired at eight when Mary arrived in the pony-cart which was to drive me home. I *am* glad I decided to do this. My self-esteem is much reinforced.

Wednesday, 15th May

Another piping hot day. These May days are indescribably beautiful. Dr Halliwell had given me a sleeping draught which I gulped, hoping to fall down like Juliet—I woke at three and then went off again until I was called at six, when I was fearfully sleepy.

On this morning I felt I won my spurs. I emptied my first bed-pan and had to see Harris's stump uncovered—his dressing having slipped off during the night. As usual the bite was not as bad as the bark. I did a good farce-act during the dressings whilst cutting a strip of plaster. I got my hand hopelessly stuck in it like a fly on flypaper. The dressing was delayed for several minutes whilst Sister and Stevens extricated me.

Thursday, 16th May

A letter from Beb in which he casually mentioned having had a small splinter in his arm—adding no damage done. To my surprise, a few minutes later I got this telegram: 'Lieutenant Asquith K. Brigade slightly wounded—remaining on duty. Secretary, War Office.' I had quite a nasty turn, as 'War Office' were the first words I read!

Tried to sleep without it, but was driven to drinking my sleeping draught at twelve. I woke at two, but fell asleep again and was only semi-conscious through a violent thunderstorm. I went off in the car and did a lot of ironing which I found quite pleasant exercise. Idled from three to five—my leg fell asleep if nothing else did.

Terrible bereavement in the morning. My beloved Stevens (an edition de luxe of Sam Weller), got up in khaki instead of in blue and went off in grand style singing, 'Why am I dressed up in khaki?' and shouting, 'I'll spit on the Somme for you, boys.' He gave both me and Sister verbal Collins with the manners of a Philip Sidney. With him also went nice funny Smith, so excited at seeing his children after five weeks' absence, and also Deans, the philosopher of the waxed moustache, whose dreamy platitudes I have found very soothing. I could never have believed I could have grown so fond of strangers in a week, and my V.A.D.-ship was almost disgraced by tears. It's horrid to know they are going via George Robey back to the Front. This experience has given me a great up with humanity. I am amazed at the standard of charm and manners, and their sardonic humour— above all, their niceness to each other, their 'best of lucks' to the out-going ones give me such a lump in my throat.

Extract from letter from Mary Herbert:

'Today I am deeply depressed, mainly weather, partly the domestic effects of Aubrey's vote on the Maurice affair, which caused us to sit up till two every morning discussing its immediate and ultimate effects, the degradation of politics, and the valuelessness of life after four years of war—all of which come heavy on the nerves in combating them. The crisis has really had enough psychology for once. I think Aubrey did right, but it had a curiously large effect, his whole constituency in arms and people almost cutting him in the street, while I was railed at across the Ritz dining-room. Bongie appears to have led the "Old Gang" into a mess again, ably assisted by Margot, who went up and down Bond Street like the Ancient Mariner clutching at mannequins, commission-aires, friends, taxi-drivers, policemen, and whispering to them the good news of their return to Downing Street.'

Saturday, 18th May

Took a sleeping draught, hoping to secure a good sleep in preparation for a busy night with Grace,[1] but—to my disappointment—I woke up in two hours. I came down to tea and sat in the hut while Mamma, and Mr Balfour (who arrived with Papa yesterday) and the others played tennis. Went into Winchcomb in the sidecar of Grant's motor bike, very dusty and flying.

Found Grace quite come round from a successful operation, but

1. Nineteen years old and a golf pro, he had had an operation for rupture the previous evening.

feeling very wretched, sick, and in pain. One of us had to sit with him all through the night and we took it in turns. I had alternately to dab him with vinegar, fan him with the *Daily Mirror*, and assist him to be sick. I *wished* I could put more conviction into my voice when I said, 'You will soon be better.' I remembered the Hell of my own appendix operation and felt very sympathetic and futile, longing to give him morphia. The smell of stale ether was sickening and it was rather a nightmare night. I felt a little creepy sitting alone in the dark ward with him and all those snoring bodies, and I got very tired. At first the ward was very hot and then it turned cold. My vigil from three to five seemed an eternity. It hurt him dreadfully when he was sick and all I could do was to hold his curly head. He was very sorry for himself—but very good. I was touched by his asking me if I wasn't tired. I *was* glad when porridge time came.

Dear Overton[1] had distinguished himself in the afternoon by falling through a skylight. The 'proper joke'—as Morris says—of it was that he hadn't played tennis (so as not to uncrease his trousers) because his 'young lady' was coming to Winchcomb to see him. His affairs had reached an acute crisis because he had been carrying on with another 'young lady' in Winchcomb, and was embarrassed to know how to square her now his official one had arrived. I afterwards heard that his second string saw him in the lane with his first string and cut up terribly rusty, poor thing. She went so far as to mutilate his photograph—sticking pins through his eyes and so on.

Sunday, 19th May

Grace was going on well, but seemed very hurt in his feelings. It was almost impossible to wring a smile out of him. Sister and I sat out. It was the most *lovely* warm moonlight night, and the starry sky wrought its usual reassuring effect on me. I finished reading *Under the Greenwood Tree* to the Sister and we made lots of swabs. I did two dressings by myself in the lovely surgical gloves—felt rather clumsy, but Sister stood at my elbow and prompted me—I did Overton's arms and Wilding's toes. I burnt the fomentation cloth.

Monday, 20th May

The dear Priest came to have breakfast with us, bringing his own sugar and bread. I read him Beb's letter to Oc. Went into Winchcomb in

1. An 'attractive scamp' who had nearly been caught playing billiards at 10.30 the previous night when he should have been in bed by nine: Lady Cynthia warned him of the Sister's approach and he 'skedaddled'.

the Scarlet Runner. A melodrama night. Sister and I had been sitting out of doors for about half an hour when I said, 'I'll just go and see what those gentlemen are doing,' and strolled round the ward. What was my horrified amazement to find Grace's bed empty. I couldn't believe my eyes—rubbed them and looked under the bed—and flew back to Sister with the news. She was in a fearful state, rushed into the lavatory, tore the poor whimpering wretch off the seat and dragged him back to bed. The castor oil acted all the time and we had a fearsome mess to clear up. Sister was furious with him. He had got everything he needed within reach and a knock on the wall would have brought us to his side. I don't know why he did it. I shall never forget the sight of Sister leading him back holding his intestines in.

Wednesday, 22nd May

Woke up at four, so came down and joined a very successful soldiers' party. Huge whist drive in which Papa, Evan, and Mr Balfour took part. I won the booby prize. My last night on duty—uneventful, except that the heat was so appalling that we sat with our tongues hanging out, and I was very tired and sleepy. Sister Orde went off early leaving me in charge. Had it not been that I am returning in a fortnight, I should have felt very sad at leaving the hospital—as it is, bedtime is rather a pleasant prospect. I have *loved* it, to an extent that puzzles me. I quite understand one's liking for the human interest side of it and the absorbing, feverish desire to satisfy the Sister and please the men, but I rather wonder why one enjoys the sink, tray, Lysol, bustle side of it quite so much.

Thursday, 23rd May

Went to bed for two hours and got up for luncheon. Talking of the 'Old Gang's' charging Lloyd George with never listening to what soldiers said, Mr Balfour quoted Lloyd George as saying: 'I remember Mr Asquith saying he had never met a soldier whose brains he would dream of using in the Cabinet—and this with a Cabinet containing Hobhouse!'

Evan told us Lady Randolph Churchill is going to marry quite a young man called Porch. I had a letter from Desmond MacCarthy in which he described the last air raid—a tremendous one—the new feature of which was that the worst crump came *after* the reassuring tootle of 'All clear' signal. It was wet more or less all day. I sat out in the hut and indoors with Evan after tea, and he read me snatches from the *Lives of the Chancellors*. He and Papa are wonderfully mellow: we call them the Cheeryble brothers. We played some Pelman games at dinner—remembering figures and cards. Extraordinary how they excite vanity. Mr Balfour snapped out 'Somebody talked' when he broke down over the four cards—a silence in which you have could heard a pin drop having been maintained. I went to bed early and— reverting to normal habits like a new bit of elastic—slept long and soundly.

Friday, 24th May

Miss Wilkinson went on duty for one night and brought me home dewdrops from Orde who extolled my head, memory, and adaptability, summing up by saying, 'she ought to be head of a large institution!' Papa gave me the shock of my life by telling me I should find the telephone disconnected at Cadogan Square as he hadn't paid his bill. To my intense relief, I found this wasn't true and telegraphed triumphantly to him, 'Considerable activity in progress on Cadogan Front.'

Dined with Bibesco and met Desmond, and to my great interest, Enid Bagnold—authoress of the *Diary Without Dates* which I so greatly admire. She is quite pretty in a fairly ordinary yellow-haired, fresh-complexioned way—*not* remarkable-looking, but quite a good talker and an appreciative, stimulating listener. To my surprise, she gave me very good dewdrops from Nichols.

Wednesday, 29th May

The most terrific telephoning bout cutting out my day. This double life of alternate, sharply contrasting fortnights has many advantages. One can concentrate for a bit on London, frittering with a clear conscience and no misgiving as to wasting one's life.

Got my bicycle out of Selfridges, went to the dentist, and then to sit with Violet. She told me her side of the ridiculous Pixton imbroglio. She and Bongie were all packed up ready for Whitsuntide when Lady Carnarvon got a panic about their going there, just as Aubrey was settling up with his constituency (who considered a vote for Asquith and Maurice a vote for an ignominious peace), and sent for Bongie and asked him not to go. Violet—naturally enough—told the story to the Wharf, and Margot wrote Aubrey a furious letter accusing him of shirking and not seeing things through. This he missed—owing to his going to Albania—and Mary took up the cudgels.

We also discussed Bibesco and his strange obsession about statistics of virginity. I was amused by his description of his great friend ——, 'Well, you see, the thing about her is *qu'elle n'aime pas se coucher seule.*' We speculated as to the link between him and Desmond, wondering whether—in spite of Desmond's obvious conventional delicacy before women—it wasn't, after all, what Birrell calls 'bawdy talk'.

Lunched with Jaspar and Nathalie at the Ritz. Lady Salisbury was there, and the Greys, and Willie who, poor dear, looked in an advanced stage of botulism. His war news, which he gets from the French Secretary, was as bad as possible. I am lost in stupefied admiration of the Germans. They have achieved a quite invisible concentration and attacked *exactly* where all our tiredest troops had been sent to rest![1]

Bicycled to Miss North and then to have my hair cleaned. It was another of these marvellously joyously beautiful May days and my spirits rose and rose. My conscience kept smiting me when my brain reminded me of the horror—worse than ever—going on in the same sunshine, but it was of no avail: for some strange reason—chemical, I suppose—I felt wildly exhilarated and full of defiant joie de vivre. Why? Why? Why?

Papa returned, but only for one night. *Nothing* will dislodge him from Stanway. It is a funny phase. I tell him he will be accused of air-raid panic. Bluetooth came to see me, and we sat in the Square. He gave me, to my surprise, such dewdrops from Margot, including that I 'couldn't come into a room without making everyone else in it look common and rather ridiculous'.

Dined with Claud—Maud and Gilbert being there. Told I was looking my most beautiful, with the sort of sheen one has just occasionally: felt Claud falling back in love with me. Gilbert very funny at dinner on the conventions—startling in his theories—again saying if he saw any woman dining *tête-à-tête* with a man in a restaurant, he immediately asked himself if he were her lover. In short, that it wasn't done, except by the *declassée*. Jolly for me, and funny enough, considering how often Claud and I have dined together! We assured him he was quite behind the times and generalising on men from his experience of himself, but he laid down cast-iron standards for Maud.

Thursday, 30th May

Another gorgeous, blazing day expressing supreme indifference to

1. Ludendorff's attack on 27th May on the Chemin des Dames sector north of the Aisne: the Germans achieved a breakthrough to the Marne.

humanity. I went and sat to McEvoy. The picture again entered on quite a new phase, in fact I was even put in another room. McEvoy is painting aircraft pictures and is motoring down to Epping to observe flying by night. The beauty of the day gave me unstifleable spirits, and I could not believe in the *reality* of what the sight of Chelsea Barracks—with those grim sacks hanging up for bayonet practice and the groups of magnificent men drilling—called up in one's mind.

Bicycled to Claud's and we went to see the Orpens together. I was much impressed by them—certainly works of genius—the khaki portraits of Trenchard, and so on, are magnificent. Tea'd with Claud, and then home to read that crude book *The Pretty Lady*. Dined with Bibesco—a quartette, Desmond and Violet. The two women always sit facing the men at his strip of a table. Violet had perhaps a slightly leashing effect on him, but he went very far out of his way in an attempt to convict General Gordon of unnatural vice. War talk after dinner —Violet and Desmond taking a very grim view of the situation, Bibesco straining after optimism.

Friday, 31st May

The marvellous break of weather still continuing. Felt ashamed of my almost indecently good spirits. Tried to quench them with the newspapers, but it was no good. Events have got too big. I can no longer digest my personal nor the national experiences. Temporarily the war has lost all reality for me.

Went by appointment to see Augustus John at eleven. He was looking wonderfully well, quite bright-eyed. We got on very well, and I felt much more comfortable with him than on any previous meeting. He hasn't begun his forty-five foot canvas War Picture yet, but is just about to. He said he would show the beginning of it to me, and me only. Later on in the day he rang me up and begged me to dine with him.

Desmond MacCarthy called for me and we spent a memorably delightful evening, first dining at Queen's and then sitting in the Square until nearly twelve. I must say I delight in his company. You could scarcely find two men more different and yet, ridiculously enough, there is something in talking to him which faintly reminds me of Basil. It is, I suppose, something in the responsiveness of thought, voice, and laugh which they have in common. Between talking to them and to othess is something of the difference between dancing on a floor hung on chains and on an ordinary one. We talked a lot about Margot, of whom he is ultra-appreciative, having mainly only heard her brilliant criticism of dead lions. I warned him of the day when he would hear her on living friends. In the square we had an interesting talk on the war. He accused me of aesthetic greed—how right he is! We discussed his reputed 'pacifism'. He edited Bibesco to me—seeing him very *couleur de rose*—with a purpose I think, as he wishes him to have some sustained personal interest amounting to an obligation, which he says he lacks since the death of his adored brother. I deprecated his 'foreignness' and the barrage of personal questions put up by him, such as 'Are you a mistress or a wife-woman?' 'Whom do you love best in the world?' and so on.

A meet on the pavement. We found Letty, Mary S., and Mamma in her dressing-gown—all outside—owing to a policeman and a light the house in Cadogan Square was displaying.

Saturday, 1st June

I lunched with Bibesco. It was much better than on any previous occasion. He said I was only beginning to get through the 'damned foreigner' conception of him. He has some psychological discernment. He is right when he says that it isn't long since I left off being a Maeterlinck woman and became a real person. He has occasional quite good flashes of wit and some of our talk is interesting enough, though too much interlarded with personalities, such as '*Tu es très chou*' and over-technical appreciations of one's charms. He ended up with '*Vous voulez que je vous aime? Pas même ça?*' He said his remark about General Gordon had been a deliberate test of Violet's suspected 'enfant terribleness'. He considered Mary S.'s beauty austere. He told me Elizabeth's strange confidences as to the statistics of her kissing experiences, and deprecated her 'promiscuity'. We agreed it was a great aesthetic error to debase such coinage, but he said there was also the danger of running to the other extreme and being a miser—a cap he wanted to fit on my head.

I expected Maud Russell to tea, but she didn't come, so I enjoyed peaceful solitude until I went to Tonks to have dinner with him in his kitchen. George Moore and Steer came in after dinner. First George Moore laid down the law in very technical art criticism, and then he was rather funny about Lady Randolph. I suggested that perhaps she liked the idea of being known as the 'one white woman in Nigeria' instead of the one black one in London. He said he could only account for how they would spend the evenings by a reapplication of the principle of the Arabian Nights, she regaling him with the recital of one of her amours (Moore claimed two hundred lovers for her) nightly—and the collection would be known as the Nigerian Nights. He then proceeded to, on the whole, fairly boring blasphemies about all my beloved novelists, maintaining that *no* English writer of fiction had any 'seriousness of mind'. In *Tom Jones* he would only admit of a certain gusto; the other novelists—with the exception of Jane Austen, who within her narrow limits *was* an artist—he described as no better than 'chaperones' and 'valets'—Dickens, of course, was dismissed as a mere buffoon and Scott was *pour rire*. He is writing an 'Imaginary Conversation' between himself and Gosse on this theme. Tonks congratulated me on being such a 'quick change artist'.

Sunday, 2nd June

Blazing day. Still in hectic spirits—a happiness with its roots in nothing. I suppose it's partly the hot weather—I never before realized how material I was. A touch of the east wind would put the war back on my nerves. I am in glowing looks. Have never seen myself in such brilliant face, especially by daylight.

Lunched with Adele. Mary Herbert came, a poem in pale pink. We had our luncheon in the garden. Of course we waded in the Billing* cesspool. What with my name, my acquaintance with ——, and my relationship with Lord Alfred, I expect to find myself in the box at any moment. The cruel thing is that, to the public mind, the mere *suggestion* of such things is in effect the same as though they were proved. Adele said the shop-women sort of strata were saying, 'We always knew it of the Asquiths, and we're so glad they're being exposed.' Margot, of course, attributes the whole thing to a political anti-Asquith plot— to make it impossible for him ever to return to office—and I should think there is a good deal of truth in this theory. Adele told us all about Lady Randolph. Porch has been madly in love with her for five years: she said she is not in love with him but suffers very much from loneliness and wishes for a companion. She says, 'He has a future, and I have a past, so we should be all right.' She asked her sister Leonie if she thought they looked very absurd together and the reply was, 'Oh, you look as if you might over-lay him at any moment.'

Ivor Churchill called for me and we had a very pleasant sit out in the park. He was in very good spirits and form. Tea with Claud— of course discussed Billing. One can't imagine a more undignified paragraph in English history: at this juncture, that three-quarters of *The Times* should be taken up with such a farrago of nonsense!

1918

Monday, 3rd June

Less hot and rather windy. Sat to McEvoy. The canvas which began by bearing a Greek coin is now covered by an Italian fresco in the blue-and-white phase. I despair of his ever finishing it. He gave me tremendous dewdrops from Augustus John, whom he complained would talk of nothing but me through the whole of an evening they had spent together. He said I was the most beautiful thing he had ever seen, especially when I arrived on my bicycle.

I lunched at Cavendish Square—to my disappointment Mr Asquith wasn't there but Margot, Sir Charles Russell, Sir Edward Henry, and Lord Stamfordham. Of course the Billing trial was discussed—poor Margot greatly incensed, but fairly rational I thought. Lord Stamfordham said he understood the whole of the Royal Household were in the 'Book'. To my horror, Sir Charles said there was no chance of a conviction against Billing. It is monstrous that these maniacs should be vindicated in the eyes of the public. What an Alice in Wonderland cast! Billing, Father Vaughan, Marie Corelli, Lord Alfred Douglas, etc. Sir Charles considered Lord Alfred might well be at the bottom of a great deal of it. Why that lunatic is at large, Heaven only knows! Sir Charles was in the old Oscar Wilde-Lord Queensberry case and says that, ever since, Lord Alfred rings him up on the telephone about once a week and pours a torrent of filthy language into the receiver. He once let his house to a respectable old lady who was much upset by this custom. Sir Charles naturally urged Margot to make no effort to force herself into the box: Billing would, of course, ask if it were true she had a German governess in the house after the war, and if Sir Ernest Cassel stayed with her, and all kinds of irrelevant questions —just as he would ask Mrs Keppel about her relations with King Edward.

Margot screamed out about the whole odious system of espionage under Lloyd George. How far it is true, or whether she has a bee in her bonnet on the subject, I don't know. She says there is always a secretary in the Square to watch her comings and goings, and that when she entertains the blinded soldiers from St Dunstan's and helps them into their taxis, a photograph is taken and published under the heading, 'Mrs Asquith says goodbye to her pacifist friends.' Poor Margot, her indiscretions so are naïve, so childlike, that they ought in themselves to furnish a certificate of innocence. Where there is so much smoke there couldn't be fire. She told us what I had never heard, that the woman who swore to having seen her at Fortnum and Mason's sending a parcel to a German prisoner—and then retracted, saying she must have mistaken Dardanelles for Donnington Hall—was the present Lady Curzon, then Mrs Duggan. There has been an article in the *Vigilante* accusing the wives of Cabinet ministers of lesbianism.

Went to an amusing Hawtrey play, *The Naughty Wife*, with Charles de Noailles (our host), Elizabeth and Eddie Marsh. We went empty and nearly fainted with hunger and thirst, especially as there was a tantalising amount of eating and drinking on the stage. Afterwards we went by tube to the Ritz for dinner and had wonderful food in Charles de Noailles' sitting-room. Elizabeth in great epigrammatic energy, defining 'cocottes' and describing Oggie Lynn as a 'traveller in liaisons'.

Tuesday, 4th June

Mamma returned in the course of the morning: she started a terrific furniture mania—ran up and down stairs all day—producing a noise like six children playing hide and seek. I bicycled to lunch with Bluetooth, found him very dejected about the Billing cesspool—thinking it will do untold harm. He said the soil was well prepared for the evil seed and that rumours of what came to us as fantastic shock had been rife in the mind of the public for years. Scandal—as to Maud Allan and Margot—had been started and widely diffused by the suffragettes. Once in a big shop, a showman, exhibiting a specimen of furniture and decoration, had said to Bertie Stopford, 'This would make a nice little Lesbian bower for Mrs Asquith—wouldn't it?' We agreed that it was monstrous of Fripp to give such evidence. I attribute his attitude largely to reprisals on Margot for her manifold professional libels on *him*. When he was about to operate on my appendix, Margot telegraphed to Mamma. 'For God's sake don't have Fripp—damndest ass in London.' Asquith, bless him, is so out of touch with the stupidity of humanity, and will not bother about the mud thrown at him. We wondered whether any advice would have made any difference to such indiscretions as having Sir Ernest Cassel at the Wharf, and so on.

Bluetooth has been disqualified for an expected job because he voted against the Government in the Maurice matter: on the other hand, Bongie is secretary to Weir (head of the Air Force) on the express condition that he is 'free to intrigue against the Government'.

Violet came to tea. I think Billing and Bibesco between them have at last completed her education and extinguished her as an *enfant terrible*. During her visit Papa came in and announced that the monster maniac Billing *had* won his case. Damn him! It is such an awful triumph for the 'unreasonable', such a tonic to the microbe of suspicion which is spreading through the country, and such a stab in the back to people unprotected from such attacks owing to their best and not their worst points. The fantastic foulness of the insinuations that Neil Primrose and Evelyn de Rothschild were murdered from the rear makes one sick. How miserably conducted a case, both by that contemptible Darling and Hume Williams! Darling *insisted* on having the case out of rotation.

Wednesday, 5th June

A thunderbolt fell from the skies in the shape of a telegram from Eliza saying we were not wanted at the hospital. The anticipated convoy hadn't arrived and so we are to wait until we are sent for. I felt the ground cut away from under my feet. I was looking forward to the peace and beauty of Stanway, and had taken all my London irons out of the fire—it seemed such a grind to have to put them in again. Cynthia Asquith was to have died and yielded to Nurse Asquith, and I felt very disinclined to resuscitate her and improvise a London life. Besides, I had taken London at the pace of a sprint thinking it was for so short a time, and was too tired for a longer run. I felt quite staggered at first, so did Mary S. Went to my first bridge dinner. It was at Bluetooth's. We were Adele, Mr Asquith, Margot, Geoffrey Howard, Ronald Graham, and Blanche Serocold. I played with my preceptor Bluetooth against the Old Boy and Blanche. We won five shillings in spite of inferior cards.

Thursday, 6th June

Sat to McEvoy. He again twisted me into another angle. Whibley lunched with Mamma and me—our first meeting after a long interval. We sat out in the square afterwards. He was quite subdued about the Billing case and we talked over all its absurdities. Whibley told me Mrs ——, the witness who claimed to have been shown the 'Black Book' by Neil Primrose and Evelyn de Rothschild, was originally employed by Maud Allan as a detective to find out what Billing knew and he had won her over as a weapon on his side.

Dined with Pamela Lytton—the McEvoys and Barrie were there. The McEvoys and I were lucky enough to catch a taxi at Victoria and they dropped me home.

Friday, 7th June

A telegram came for me from Eliza saying the convoy was arriving tonight: Mary S. and I came down to Stanway by 4.45. What Papa, in his famous recruiting speech, called the 'calm of Toddington' descended on us. Heard amusing Lady Cunard story. Filson Young, the shilling-shocker novelist once came to lunch with her and found his books lying thick on her tables. He remarked that one was missing and she said she hadn't been able to get it from the book shop. He hurried round and indignantly asked why they hadn't provided it to Lady Cunard. They said, 'Lady Cunard—why she had all your books up yesterday and returned them in the afternoon.'

Saturday, 8th June

My first day in hospital. A convoy had arrived the night before— twenty-three new cases and they were all in bed, so we had a very heavy day. I spent the morning in the 'slums' washing bandages, etc. Nearly all our old favourites are gone. We didn't finish till after 8.30 and then we had to have our dinner, as there is to be no cooking at Stanway.

Sunday, 9th June

A veil seemed to have lifted between one and all the new men. Suddenly their individual personalities began to emerge, and one felt the almost tearful tenderness one had for the old ones. Grace giggles at every sight of me and says, 'I'm thinking of that night, nurse.'

The men are wonderfully well fed, I must say, and the new lot seem agreeably surprised by the fare. One told me he has been in a trench hospital where they only got *one* meal a day and that was cabbage water.

Monday, 10th June

A day of crisis and emergency. Both nurses in B ward and several men down with influenza—Mary had to take charge of B ward. It's a great bore being separated from her and it makes things much less amusing. I must own I got woefully tired: after lunch I wrung out the bandages, hung them up to dry, polished all the chairs in the ward, cleaned the gas-globes, sewed blue stripes on coat sleeves, and collected trousseaux out of the cupboard for the men who were to get up. What exhausted me was the bedmaking after tea. I thought we should never finish. Yeats—the nice man with gassed eyes—had an extremely good-looking red-haired wife to see him. To my delight, he told me they had been engaged since he was nine!

Eliza gave an enormous overdose of quinine to all the nurses as an antidote to influenza.

Thursday, 13th June

Very understaffed—and I had to tear round. Nurse —— is a very good-natured little thing, but always breaking, dropping, knocking herself, barging into beds, spilling, or swathing herself in festoons of treacle. The men roar with laughter over her continued mishaps and so does she. All her pocket money must go in paying for her crockery casualties. We muddled the diet at lunch and Sister—whose fault it really was!—apostrophised us as a lot of h'asses. It's very difficult not to giggle at her determined transposing of h's—she *never* forgets to do it. She got very over-excited at lunch about the 'hair-raids and the hu-boats'.

A ghastly afternoon of blanket baths—such a strain on the brain! Some of the men had to be washed in bed, others given the where-withal and left, and others had to go to the bathroom; some had to be rubbed with methylated spirit in one place, some in two, and some not at all; and some had to be given clean top sheet and clothes, some clothes not sheets, and so on and so on. Nurse —— went off and Nurse Jeanne (the little Belgian who got engaged to an Australian in the ward) had just come and knew nothing about the men, so I had to do all the staff work. All went well, except that naughty Hopkins—a gas gastric case—who should have been washed in bed, went off and had a bath on his own hook. Giving the blanket baths is rather difficult and I got tired of washing black toes.

Friday, 14th June

A very busy morning at the sink. Strange how quickly I have grown reconciled to the word 'pus': hospital joke—'The doctor opened the wound and puss ran out.' Horrible business washing it out of the tiny tubes which go into Sergeant Dovey's hand. Deluged myself with his bath and had to stay wet all the morning.

Mary enjoyed our afternoon of idleness immensely. We sat out in the hut. *Delicious* dinner in bed—trout, eggs, asparagus, and straw-berries. Tried to give one another dewdrops without words by guessing which of the men particularly liked us.

Monday, 17th June

Very sorry to see Freyberg reported wounded in the papers. I do so want to know whether it is bad or not—I haven't heard from him for some time.

Grim scene in the afternoon. Captain Charles paid his monthly visit to 'mark out' the men. He is a very upright figure, with good-looking hawk profile, Maxim-gun voice and manner, and steel fingers —brings an extraordinarily strong atmosphere of militarism into the ward with him. The change in the men is amazing. I could scarcely recognize the familiar shambling figures in the erect automatons.

Thursday, 20th June

I felt very sorry when the time came to say goodbye to the men. Delighted to overhear Yeats saying to Turner, 'I *am* sorry Nurse Asquith is going away for a fortnight, she's very nice.' I am glad I have achieved my fortnight of day duty. I felt convinced I should be interrupted. I think one reason that makes me like it is my entire lack of shyness with the men. It is the *only* human relationship in which I haven't been bothered by self-consciousness.

Friday, 21st June

Up to London by 11.30. Dined in with Papa, Angela, and Flavia. Poor Angela quite in her worst form. She is again in deep trouble with the authorities—her Ambulance Convoy being held up—and she was very hoarse and indignant. Flavia is *the* most provocative-looking flapper.

Saturday, 22nd June

Went to McEvoy feeling rather ill and looking very well. He said I had brought him quite a different face and painted it again. It's really rather maddening that there should be nothing to show on that canvas after a year's work on it. I found him Major McEvoy of the Marines— in *very* new khaki with a most obviously undrilled chest. He squeaked out dewdrops. I lunched with Bibesco and we had our usual fencing game. I told him he worried too much about getting to the 'roots' of things, was too much of a naturalist in his contemplation of human beings. He continued his analysis of me, said I was what the Americans call 'an impossible proposition' (meaning for the purpose of erotic attack), that I had many different facets in my personality which were not co-ordinated—'*Ça le rend très difficile.*' He begged me to kiss him, and called me an *avare* when I refused. I repudiated the charge of miserliness—like most men he talks as though the alternatives were between 'se donnering' to *him* and a nunnery, 'chanting faint hymns to the fruitless moon'. They always seem to forget the possibility of monopolies, and attribute a woman's refusal to a love of abstract chastity, rather than to lack of love for them—or love for another. He quoted Ninon de l'Enclos, '*Ça me coûte si peu, et ça lui donne tant de plaisir.*' He said—what he had written—that henceforth he could only see me alone. He is much wittier than I realised at first. He walked me most of the way home.

Augustus John had asked me to dine with him any evening and, after some considerable mental tossing up, I agreed to and we met at Queen's Restaurant. In his letter he wrote, 'Last time I saw you, you looked so beautiful that I felt quite embarrassed.' He was, I'm sorry to say, rather bloodshot-eyed and thick in speech, but behaved all right and we had quite an agreeable dinner. He glared admiration. He asked me if I would sit to him again and I agreed to on Tuesday. He said Margot Asquith had told him his first attempt was too 'dramatic'.

Poor Papa is distracted by Angela's troubles.

Sunday, 23rd June

Went to recover my bicycle from Brenda's garage, and then to visit Maud Russell. Found her, Gilbert, and the boy baby a very happy party. A very pretty ten-day-old baby. Gilbert had already presented him with a teddy-bear and was rather perturbed at his lack of intelligent interest in it.

I lunched with Guy and Frances. I never regretted a kiss so much as the one bestowed on Guy—he had obviously got Spanish flu and a day or two later the whole household went down with it. Went to the Berkeley Grill Room to dine with Brenda—her new friend Barrie was the nucleus of the party.

Little did I think this evening was destined to be a milestone in my kaleidoscopic life. We went to the mews and all very happily sipped some wonderful old rum, a few bottles of which had been discovered in the Clandeboye cellar. Towards the end of the evening, when Barrie and I were slightly detached from the rest of the party, I heard his little Scotch voice saying to my astonished self. 'Why didn't you answer my last letter? I could easily have put you into *The Admirable Crichton* cinema, but I'm really glad it never came off—I didn't really approve of it for you. But, if you would really like to do some work, I wish you would come and help me. I used to have a woman who was a great help to me, but she left to do war-work three years ago, and since then my papers have been getting into a more and more chaotic state. I don't want "efficiency"—I should dislike anybody with a type-writer who could do shorthand, and there are very few people I can bear to have in the room with me for long. It would mean as little or as much as you liked, you could come twice a week or every day.' I gapingly realised that he was inviting me to be his Private Secretary and stammered out something about 'nursing'. He said, 'Well, anyhow you might as well come and see me, and let us have a talk about it.' This I readily agreed to, and we made an appointment for five o'clock on Wednesday. Summie drove me home.

The idea of myself as Barrie's secretary made me rock with laughter and will amuse me until I die. I told Papa and he was very much in favour of it. If I act as a filter to his sentimentality, I shall ruin him.

Monday, 24th June

Dined at Cavendish Square. It was like *The Voysey Inheritance*—an enormous unleavened family party: Mr and Mrs Oc, Mr and Mrs Cis, Mr and Mrs Bongie, and Mrs Beb—Margot went off to the opera. At the end of the dinner, Mr Asquith aroused our excited anticipation by rotundly beginning, 'Now that I have got you all assembled, I should like to consult you.' We thought at least he was going to ask our advice as to the advisability of his accepting a peerage, or on the re-distribution of his income, but we might have known better! It was that an American had sent him five dollars to buy a Bible to send to the Kaiser, and he wanted to know what he ought to do with the dollars.

He and I were just collecting our bridge quorum when Margot rushed into the room and sat down at the table, so I was one of the few people who have ever seen them playing together. Betty and I were partners at first, but he cut for partners again at the first possible opportunity, and Margot and I played together. He was very much in the typical vein of puffing his cheeks, shooting out his upper lip, and saying, 'I've got two sons, one daughter, three daughters-in-law and one son-in-law here—do you see them? Three daughters-in-law, and one son-in-law—two sons and a daughter.'

Tuesday, 25th June

Lunched with Bibesco in good spirits and looks. He elaborated his

avare charge—called me 'poor rich Cynthia', said my being 'virtuous'
was no more credit to me than my not drinking port, that I didn't want
to *faire l'amour*, but that I did want to have people in love with me.
He approved my simile of one form of flirtation being, 'Come into
the fire with me—I happen to be dressed in asbestos.' He said I had
different, quite unco-ordinated personalities, cut off like reels in a
cinema—'*Ça vous rend très difficile*'—and, complaining that there
was no *modus vivendi* in our relationship, '*Ou vous allez vous donner a
moi, ou vous allez m'aimer*' . . . a dilemma I refused to acknowledge. I
told him of Barrie's offer and he said, 'I will give you a shilling more
than what he offers'. I must say, I do think he has got almost uncanny
skill as a psychologist. I recognise myself in his versions as I do in
many of Balzac's pages. He is a very efficient liaison officer with
oneself.

I sat—or rather, stood—for Augustus John. Oh, the agony of
standing! I have never done it before. He made I thought a most
promising beginning, full-length in beige-and-green stockingette suit
with bright green hat. Mr Balfour was dining with Mamma—Papa
laid a nasty trap for the poor man by dining in with Angela, who was
thirsting for his help in the lamentable mess she is in. Desmond
MacCarthy called for me and we walked to poker with Iris. I was very
tired and didn't enjoy it. I lost £1 7s and Desmond (I am sorry to say)
£4. He was much in favour of the Barrie scheme, said it would be just
play, and that all Barrie wanted was someone to sympathise with him
over the chaos—not to convert it to cosmos.

Wednesday, 26th June

Went to John again. Felt very ill standing and began to sway. The
excitement of London after the hospital interlude has upset my equilib-
rium and I am sleeping very badly. John and I agreed to introduce my
bicycle into the picture—I shall be leaning on it. I think it will be
such fun: it would do for a poster advertisement for a 'Sunbeam'.

Went in great trepidation to my appointment with Barrie. His room
in Adelphi House Terrace is the most enchanting I have ever seen—
huge—with windows on three sides commanding the best possible
view of the Thames, and enormous ingle-nook fireplace with seats—
lovely, full book-cases—and a kitchen. A room in which you could
do everything—sleep, cook, eat, read, or play cricket.

The little man greeted me friendlily and we sat down to tea. I
poured it out and spilt it over his chair—a good omen I feel sure. I
was so afraid we might both be too shy ever to *entamer* the subject

we had come to discuss, but it was all right and he described what my functions would be. I should have to cope with his correspondence (I suppose he gets hundred of letters from silly women asking *what* it is that 'every woman knows'). In time I should be able to act as a filter and exercise my discretion as to what could be burnt, what answered by me, and what should be seen by him. I should also have to tease him to send cheques to the bank, etc., etc. He showed me his 'best' and his 'worst' drawer, which I shall have to tidy—the worst containing a welter of dusty papers which had burst their elastic bands. Very delicately, he mentioned my salary, by describing my functions and saying 'the services of a woman who did that would be worth four or five hundred a year to me'—of course, preposterously good pay for one who has *no* market value as a secretary.

The wonderfully good thing about it is that he is out of London for the whole of the school holidays (often at other times), and he wouldn't want me every day, but two or three days a week. It's a very soft job and I think it would be too silly not to accept. My family urge it strongly on me. His shyness is infectious to me, but I expect we shall conquer that, and his apparent moroseness is most misleading. He showed me photographs of the five boys he had adopted—the sons of the woman whom he loved. He took me on to the St James's Theatre where we saw the rehearsal for his children's ballet *The Origin of Columbine*. It is enchantingly pretty. David, Martin, Anne, Helen Asquith, and Christopher Tennant are all in it.

Dined with Mamma and Grace, and walked Grace home—she was very much in favour of the Barrie scheme.

Thursday, 27th June

Sat to McEvoy. Gave him my Barrie news. He quite approved and said, if I chose, I could turn him into a great political influence and dominate England. He said he would ask Princess Mary to be his secretary.

A very pleasant evening at Bluetooth's—he, self, Evan, Belloc, Masterton Smith, and Juliet Duff being the party. Unfortunately, before I had had time to edit it myself to Bluetooth, Evan blurted out the Barrie news. Bluetooth was almost sick with disgust—Juliet very envious. Evan was in excellent, boyish form—he and Belloc discussed wine in the most ultra-religious tones. After dinner I read joke Ella Wheeler Wilcox's poems aloud and Belloc trumpeted out enthusiastic praise of my reading. Then we read some *Trivia*, which Belloc appreciated, saying he had got the rare stop-short gift. Bluetooth walked me home. To Pixton this weekend.

1918

Sunday, 30th June

Letter from Beb saying, unless leave is stopped, he will arrive in London on the 5th—the very day I am due as Nurse Asquith: I wrote to break the news to Eliza. Mary H. and I picked belladonna before dinner. She said I shared with her mother the gift for investing myself and my appurtenances with glamour and predicted that I should be a legend to my children as her mother had been to her. As an example, she said my 'bicycle was my Pegasus'. I agreed that I was very subjective, but said it cut both ways and that my bicycle, if it was my Pegasus one day was my *pillory* another. She told me Diana took a very gloomy view of the Montagu marriage now, opining that Venetia—having essentially 'married him for her days rather than her nights'—was now (after her interval of grass widowhood) tortured by real repugnance and that Edwin appeared plunged in gloom.

I like the following description of Barrie in Desmond MacCarthy's letter: 'I am so glad you have taken that situation. I am not so positive a psychologist as Antoine, but it seems to me that I believe I have fancied that you like being adored—in that being no great exception. A Dulcinea is a necessity to Barrie. Sentiment is only irritating to an onlooker, and when it is combined with playfulness and real kindness and springs from a cold detached heart, it is a delicate tactful thing delightful to receive. Barrie, as I read him, is part mother, part hero-worshipping maiden, part grandfather, and part pixie with no man in him at all. His genius is a coquettish thing, with just a drop of benevolent acid in it sometimes. But you will soon know him much better than I do who only do it by conjecture . . .'

Wednesday, 3rd July

Just before luncheon precisely the same symptoms as yesterday came on, only much worse. My temperature went up to 102°, and all the afternoon and evening I felt as wretchedly, humiliatingly ill as I ever have in my life—bursting head, painful pulses, aching legs, sick, burning with cold shivers. I tossed and groaned.

Mary and I agreed we must alter our plans. She, Beb, and I were all going to the Wharf for Sunday, but we telegraphed to Margot to say we couldn't and I wrote to Beb ordering him down here.

Thursday, 4th July

Letter from Beb saying, 'Mind you don't get influenza for my leave, keep yourself well segregated.'! Temperature kept about a hundred all day.

Saturday, 6th July

Was woken at about 6.30 by Beb's unexpectedly early arrival—
wonderfully well and in good spirits. He has been at G.H.Q. for ten
days now—Bongie's brother got him the job. He says it's complete
peace and further from the Front than England, but quite hard, very
long, office work. He has been made a captain. He has brought back
an extremely interesting journal of the retreat from St Quentin full
of beautifully drawn maps. Without doubt, he's an enthusiastically
keen soldier. He had a little sleep and then we spent most of the day
in the garden. The weather, the leisure, the garden, the view, the smell
of England—is all sheer bliss to him.

Saturday, 13th July

Beb and I only arrived at Paddington just in time to get with Mary
into a preposterously over-crowded carriage on our way to the Wharf.
Beb and I had rooms in the Mill House (really nicer except for the wet
walks in cold slippers), it is more human—less Chinese and stark.
No Margot, which seemed very queer. The McKennas, Diana, the
inevitable Hun (represented by Mrs K.), Elizabeth, Hugo Rumbold,
a debutant Somers Clark (an effeminately good-looking young man
friend of Elizabeth's), and a Mrs Harrisson—a neighbour war widow.

I like McKenna. He is such a 'Sunny Jim' and ripples on so easily.
I enjoyed my bridge, though I had rather bad cards and lost. McKenna's
serious rubber was played in the rather grim little bridge room—a
room which couldn't be used for any other purpose—and I played in
the bad rubber with the Pip-Emma (I love that name of Beb's for his
father!), Pamela, and Mrs K.

Sunday, 14th July

Awoke to the rather grim consciousness of pouring rain. Splashed
across to the Wharf for breakfast. Mary and Diana very wisely kept
to their beds nearly all the morning. I got rather claustrophobic in the
little room, with people sitting about as though exposed on trays. One
is at too close quarters to one's fellow creatures and can't see them in
the right perspective.

Beb had bad attacks of nervous irritability and my work was cut
out smoothing him. He doesn't worship war like Freyberg, but seems
to fall between two stools—though he is intellectually disapproving,
it yet pre-occupies him to such an extent as to put him out of sympathy

with other contexts. Of course, the Wharf is potted civilianism, and he gets thoroughly jarred there.

The Pip-Emma enjoyed making everyone guess my new profession. After a few moments gaping astonishment, McKenna melodramatically exclaimed 'I've got it!' and then told me that I greatly resembled Mrs Davies—Barrie's *prima donna*! She had wide-apart eyes and a crooked smile. Great discussion on my career—should I Cynthia Barrie, or be Barrie-ised? Hugo Rumbold did some excellent imitations after lunch —General Brancker, McEvoy, a Russian, and an Italian. It *is* very funny not having Margot darting about the Wharf. Heard such a good story of her going to Mrs Greville's to levy cream for Puffin's strawberries. Finding her out, she went downstairs and carried off all the servants' butter, giving the odd boy a signed photograph of her husband!

Monday, 15th July

Beb and I decided to remain on at the Wharf until Tuesday. I spent most of the morning struggling with a trunk call to Desmond MacCarthy. The Pip-Emma and the little war widow sat out reading their own books in two cheek-by-jowl chairs.

The dear Professor came over to luncheon. The Pip-Emma had had a letter from him in the morning in answer to the suggestion that he should stand for Parliament, in which he wrote, 'I don't think Parliament is my line, and—oddly enough—I don't know which is my party.' I told him about Barrie. He approved, but feared I might kill the goose with the golden eggs by curbing his sentimentality. He is personally very fond of him and thinks him a genius who has never grown up. Glorious Dickens talk at luncheon.

We had the Professor on our hands, as the Pip-Emma motored Mrs Harrisson away, and in the circumstances the best course seemed to be to migrate over to Norah's. Beb was, I think, quite happy there though he didn't—alas!—shine. What I suffer from vicarious self-consciousness! If he *were* a bore, it would be different—one would accept it and become resigned—but to see someone disguising, travestying, himself is too tantalising! We went in a boat together after dinner and then had a very delicious evening alone together in the Mill House. Beb was at his very darlingest and we were very happy. We were much amused to find a copy of *Trivia* fiercely annotated by Margot, who has thus written a *Trivia* of her own round it. She is fiercely hostile, finding it affected and futile—'Terrible tosh' and 'Tragic tosh' are her descriptions of two of his little efforts and there are many scathing remarks in the margin.

Tuesday, 16th July

Went up to finish the last dregs of poor Beb's leave in London. His travelling efficiency since he has become militarised is amazing. We returned to Bruton Street and found Mary H.—Beb has had two wives nearly the whole of this leave. We were lunching with Whibley at the Café Royal and I had asked Brenda to make a fourth. She was looking a very pretty poppet and Beb was delighted with her. Whibley iconoclasted a good many tin gods for her. He fulminated against Lytton Strachey, condemning *Eminent Victorians* as mere journalese, and complaining of his total lack of grammar.

I went round to see Mamma. I had a headache which she treated very effectually with some of Dr Keightley's 'peace-powders'. Had tea with her and Lady Plymouth. Desmond MacCarthy called for me, and he and Mary Herbert dined with Beb and me at the Café Royal. The old struggle between the keen play-goers and the devout diners was renewed—finally Mary and I went on leaving them to follow. We went to 'London's greatest thrill'—*The Knife*—a really good flesh-creeper with very clever acting by Kyrlie Bellew in the part of the drugged girl. Walked home to Bruton Street and Desmond stayed talking delightfully until twelve.

Wednesday, 17th July

Sat to McEvoy in the morning. For some mysterious reason he is pleased with my portrait in its present phase. It is infinitely less good than in any previous one—very wooden—quite unlike and quite ugly. Beb came in—very shy. He and Mary and Gabriel and I all lunched at Cadogan Square with Papa, Mamma, Angela, and George Montagu —no fun. Poor Angela had noisy hysterics on the landing afterwards about her wretched troubles. Papa is nauseated by her case. He has had little else to think about for nearly a year now. Mamma said, in a delicious verbal muddle, 'It's no good unless they can get at Kew-Joo-H., Berlin'—meaning our G.H.Q.!

Thursday, 18th July

Beb and I lunched with Oc and Betty, and went to a charity matinee of *Nurse Benson*, which I enjoyed. In the box opposite us were seated Queens Alexandra and Mary, and Princess Mary. I was surprised by the prettiness of the latter—she has a lovely complexion. *She* laughed very little, but her mother *rocked*.

We walked to Cavendish Square for dinner. Oc and Betty were there and Lady Paget. There was a family drum—Mrs and Mr Cis and Bongie joining us—so we couldn't join Mamma's salon at Cadogan Square as we had contemplated. There were two serious bridge tables (Margot and Elizabeth playing against Tony Rothschild and Cardy Montagu), and all the younger Asquiths and their wives played childish card games such as pounce and old maid—a sight which surely would have melted the heart of a Billing!

Friday, 19th July

Beb went off by the Staff train at 12.25. It made all the difference to know he was only going to 'Kew-Joo-H., Berlin'—as Mamma would call it. The platform was teeming with blazing, burly generals—most of them very second-rate looking.

Visited Sybil—she said she was persecuted by invitations to the Wharf, and that Margot had just asked her to come for a week in September to play bridge with Puffin! There was a great deal of Barrie chaff—Lady Barrie! Played Bridge—assisted by Venetia, mercifully. I liked Scatters: he and Barbara drove me home. Either the scandal as to him and Venetia is—as I believe—purely legendary, or he is the most consummate misleader, because we discussed Venetia in the taxi and he diagnosed her as a jolly 'Long-haired chum' not 'out for a fling' —and quite out of the siren class and argued the point with Barbara who disagreed. But, I can't understand Venetia's strange burst of beauty.

Saturday, 20th July

John and his governess met me at Eynsham at about five. John looking pale—temporarily, according to her, owing to digestive trouble—but huge and sturdy with great footballer's legs. His expression much better—at least he wears his best one much more continuously. I was astonished by his reading, and the great thing is the delight he takes in it and the wish to show off his accomplishment. He picks up a book directly and starts off like the Ancient Mariner, and when he is alone in a room he reads to himself. He puts mechanical toys together very well too. He is very, very darling and so loving—much less hysterical.

Tuesday, 23rd July

Hot rain poured in torrents from a grey sky the whole morning. The

Duke of Rutland has really been an intolerable nuisance—we haven't had a day's peace since his prayer for rain. Mamma was bothered by the new cook's fantastically high books—I was afraid such excellent food was not got for nothing. There is a bad financial crisis on, and they want to let this London house, but I don't think they will ever find a tenant.

Lunched with Bibesco. I had some very typical passages with him. He taxed me with inordinate vanity and said he was angry with me— he wouldn't say why, but his meaning was sufficiently obvious. He admitted he had no use for 'friendship'. He told me Desmond had reported favourably on his evening with us. He had enjoyed the 'contemplative' Beb and said I was 'witty'. Went home—established myself at my writing-table, added up my bills—I'm afraid they come to about £300.

Wednesday, 24th July

The day of my début with my employer Sir James. He had written to me to tell me to come at eleven and I went—my heart in my mouth. I found the little man pacing up and down his room with pipe in mouth and dirty fingernails. To my relief, I found myself much less shy than before, and I believe we shall soon be very comfortable. We talked irrelevantly for a bit and then I found myself occupying *his* writing-table (apparently he does all his work at night), and he showed me three or four letters—very typical ones I should imagine— one from a lunatic woman, a request to translate *The Little White Bird*, a suggestion that Barrie should write a preface to something, and so on. He indicated how they should be answered and, after about one or two seconds stage-fright, I drove my pen fairly confidently. He signed two and I signed the others. He asked me what name I had chosen. I said 'Sylvia Greene' and, to my surprise, he answered, 'No, not Sylvia—any name except Sylvia—Greene will do very well.' I sign my letters C. Greene, so that even my sex isn't disclosed and, in the case of lunatics, etc., I am to write on St James's Theatre note-paper so as to close the correspondence. I wondered vaguely at his objection to the name of Sylvia. In the middle of dinner that evening, talking of Barrie, a panic thought struck me and I asked Madeline if she knew what Mrs Davies' name had been. My worst fears were confirmed when she answered 'Sylvia'. What a damnable chance that I should have stumbled on that name! How *dreadful*! I *pray* he didn't think it was intentional.

It would be much easier really to be secretary to a very red-tapey business man—as it is, I feel *I* shall have to initiate all the method, instead of merely carrying out instructions to the best of my ability. There is no plant for a secretary. I don't know how to begin. We tore up a few 1914 papers together and shook our heads over the chaos in a drawer, but when I suggested coping with it, he said, 'Oh no, that would take a long time.' Then we took a lot of photographs out of a little chest and put them back again, having great difficulty in shutting the lid down again—we had to sit on it. This was the extent of my labours. I don't believe he'll ever be able to do any more work—it will take him all his time to cut mine out. A man came to interview him about something connected with the Coliseum. I was introduced as Miss Greene and felt ridiculous, as though I were in a charade. I had a strong feeling of unreality all the time, but was quite happy and he was very, very nice. He had put up five Eton boys that night. He showed me where I could 'wash my hands'. I am to begin regularly at the beginning of September. I hope we shall come to some business-like arrangement about hours. I asked him if he could give me any rough idea, but he only answered, 'Oh, we can have the hours to suit you.'

Ghastly trouble getting a taxi to go out to dinner to meet Charlie and Aileen—we went on to the Hippodrome—*delighted* by Harry Tate.

Thursday, 25th July

Still the same atrocious weather—violent, drenching tropical storms followed by gleams of brightness. Sat to McEvoy. He has the most supple intelligence and sympathy I know. We discussed how some people might amuse without adding to one's happiness, so failing to make one like the universe more: he said that I was the one who made him most excited about the world.

Went to lovely opera the *Coq d'Or* with Willie de Grunne. Mercifully, we got a lift in a motor through the pouring rain, Oc and Betty joining us in the box. The clothes and decor were the loveliest I have ever seen. The four of us had supper and Willie and I had the good fortune of a hansom to take us on to poker. Too tired to enjoy it, terribly fretted by the detail of life.

Friday, 26th July

Took my bike to John and we both sat, or rather stood, to him. He told me how tremendously under the spell of Burne-Jones he had been, and how distressed at finding himself in love with a woman who was not at all his type. He had corrected himself by Rembrandt, but he still recognises Burne-Jones very considerably, whereas he rejects Watts with a distaste for his 'parsonic mind'.

Saturday, 27th July

Hair cleaned and waved. Bored—bored and worried. Was going to stay with Jeffie Darell and did the farce act of toiling by bus to Paddington when I should have gone to Waterloo!

Sunday, 28th July

The first fine day since the 'damp Duke's' fatal proof of the efficacy of prayer. Overcome with sleep when I went downstairs to go for a walk with Freddie. We were out together for over two hours. He is a charming child. We are no longer *any* use to each other about Basil. That he is not going to call his own little Basil by his name illustrates his present attitude towards his grief.

I sat beside Brenda at dinner—Freddie and Summie both having had to go up to London—and both then and in a late hair-combing we had a great heart-to-heart. She longs for a *cause*—a motive, an enthusiasm—just as I used to at eighteen, and feels like a ship without a rudder. She complains of having just a very receptive mind, which makes her sympathise with every kind of person, but remain outside and detached from any interest.

Monday, 29th July

Went to Augustus John. Instead of continuing the big bicycle canvas he began a small head of me—very good, I thought—but with grass-green eyes and scarlet hair. He took me to his other studio to show me the beginning of his great War picture. It is all sketched in, but without any painting yet. I was tremendously impressed. I think it magnificent and it rather took my breath away—splendid composition, and what an undertaking to fill a forty-foot canvas!

Tuesday, 30th July

Mamma and I and Miss Wilkinson and servants travelled up to Gosford, sitting bolt upright in a third-class carriage. I rode my bicycle to King's Cross and Connor met us at Edinburgh and motored us out.

I haven't been to Gosford for three years and look back to that visit across what a gulf of melodrama. Then the war was still not much more than academic to me and John was a happy baby. Yvo came up for one day before going to the Front. The house is semi-shrouded and most of the electric light supply cut off. It is strange and creepy to be here again, where so many smells and sounds are so full of associations with the various phases of one's development. I expect to come across Grandpapa at every turn in the passage.

Wednesday, 31st July

We have all decided to live as much of a routine life as possible. I am going to aim at breakfasting punctually at nine, then give Michael lessons for half an hour or so, then 'private life' for letters and so on till 12.30, when we read *Martin Chuzzlewit* aloud for an hour in Mamma's room. I read Mike a chapter of Mackail's *Biblia Innocentium*, then tried to make him copy my ABC, and then we made and read little words with the letters (word-making and taking game). He is extremely quick.

Thursday, 1st August

Fine soft rain falling all the morning. Adhered rigidly to the same routine, with the addition of an hour's Greek history. *Martin Chuzzlewit* is being a great success. Played tennis with Flavia, Bibs, and Miss Wilkinson: Bibs and I won, then Miss Wilkinson and I beat Mrs Connor and Lettie.

Walked down to the sea with Frances after Michael went to bed. She told me Pamela Lytton had originally suggested Goonie to Barrie as a secretary, but he had said he couldn't possibly stand her. I thought the thing was probably due to Pamela. Walked by the sea with Mamma. She is very much perturbed by all the problems of her life—the upkeep of Gosford and so on. It is a very difficult situation. This great block of stone seems to me very still-born. It has no living atmosphere.

Saturday, 3rd August

Mamma's birthday and Michael's to be jointly celebrated at tea. Kakoo was bringing her two daughters and little Ivar Colquhoun over for the afternoon. To the trepidation of mothers and nurses, Margot announced her intention of coming over with the North Berwick contingent. She and Elizabeth, Kakoo and the babies arrived at 2.30

to our horror—we didn't expect them till three. Margot and Mamma had a long dentist and at 4.30 we all assembled round an enormous tea-table. It was the most amusing and interesting sight to see so large a collection of the youngest generation.

Margot was wonderfully typical. She fell on Letty's cream ration and devoured it, even scraping the jug out with a spoon. She then proceeded to deal personalities round the table like a pack of cards. 'David—yes, beautiful—but he doesn't look clever. How immoveable his face is—indigestion—fatigue—ought to take paraffin!' 'Frances how thin Anne's got!' and then, in a hoarse whisper to her new nurse, 'Laura's dying—I saw that the moment she came into the room.' To Letty: 'Little Ivar Colquhoun's got more passion and character than all the rest of the children put together.' To me: 'Bibs is looking very pasty. I thought she was going to be pretty the last time I saw her.' To Mamma: 'The Brigadier *would* turn in his grave if he saw the way these pictures are hung.' She said—to Frances, who had as nearly as possible died at the birth of each of her children—'You are the strongest woman in the world for having babies, you ought to have one every year!'

In his bath Michael said, 'I don't want that new parson (person) for my Grannie—Grannie Wemyss is enough.' Mamma's birthday present to him of a Red Indian tent was the wildest success.

Tuesday, 13th August

Great excitement amongst the flappers. Flavia says Don—the airman who has twice flown over here, and whom she and Letty and Bibs had gone to tea with on this afternoon—has proposed to her. This is exciting enough to darling Bibs, but the real *giddying* thrill to her is that Flavia tells her that Daly (Don's friend) has confided to him that he is 'sweet on' Bibs. That is the exact, odious expression. When asked if it was 'serious' he said 'yes', but probably he will not 'speak' because of Bibs' youth. It is very difficult to cater tactfully to Bibs on this matter—first to remember its glamour and importance to her, and not dismiss the whole thing as a joke. She is thrilled, delighted, and only half-credulous—and *very* anxious that one shouldn't think her school-girlish, taking it over-seriously, or telling one from the boasting motive. One has to convey that one thinks the reported 'seriousness' of the young man's state quite plausible, and yet not belittle the drama by saying too much. 'Why not? It's quite natural—I was proposed to when I was fifteen, and so on and so forth.' She was too sweet and funny.

Sunday, 18th August

Walked to church. I felt rather soothed by Kirk, but Bones[1] fulminated against the service, and analysed his atheism on the walk home. The pain inflicted on animals appears to be the stumbling block between him and faith in a beneficient power.

Tuesday, 20th August

Walked with Bones before lunch. He has angelically been wading all through my soppy children's biography because he wants to make a précis of John's case to send to a doctor friend of his in Austria. He has spoken to Papa on the subject of Ego's letters, which he is very much for publishing. He told me—what I had never heard— that before I was married, he had wanted to make me his heir and then commit suicide so that I might benefit immediately, and had only been deterred by Ego!

Thursday, 22nd August

Papa spoke to me about the publication of Ego's letters—Bones having boldly approached him on the subject and received the impression that he was hurt at our not having discussed the subject with him. He is squeamish about publishing, but his mind really seemed very fluid and open to influence on the subject. We agreed that Bones would like to do it himself as a labour of love and he wasn't averse to the idea.

Long hair-combing talk on John's governess with Mamma. My last letters seem to have incensed her, and she is writing rabidly to Mamma as well as me. She really is *impossible*, but also indispensable. Mamma too angelic. She is a blessed being—a witness to God if ever there was one.

Friday, 23rd August

Very, very sad to leave Gosford, Michael, and all my family. It has been a very delicious time, or at least the sample of a pattern of something which was going to be very delicious, leaving one—like everything else—with the sensation of an uncompleted circle. It's hateful to be back in London.

1. Richard Smallbones.

Saturday, 24th August

Beb arrived at 3.30 in great spirits at having got a little holiday. We had early tea and went into the Square. Dined at the Carlton, where I was greatly distressed at the cost of champagne. We are very well off in empty Cadoggers.

Sunday, 25th August

Breakfasted on the landing and enjoyed a peaceful morning, only disturbed by the dire discovery that I had *lost* a poem Beb had sent me. He had no other copy of it and was reproachful. I felt terribly Fanny Brawneish, but mercifully he was able to reconstruct it. He is very much astride of Pegasus this time and read two lovely poems to me. I took him to lunch with Bibesco—suffering oh *such* pangs of vicarious self-consciousness (Bibesco subsequently twitted me on my shyness as an impresario)—but it was an unanticipated success. Bibesco was *charming*—quite *unrisqué* in conversation and never even calling me Cynthia. Beb exhibited himself most favourably. Desmond and his wife Molly were there, and we had a very agreeable time sitting over the table until 3.30. There was something funny about my meeting him *with* his wife for the first time coinciding with Bibesco's first glimpse of Beb. We had a certain amount of soldiering shop, tactfully nurtured by Bibesco, and Beb was in good form. Desmond complained of Mr Balfour not reading the necessary official papers. Touched on topics, amongst others, whether the lover of animals would or would not give a fly to a spider. Desmond told a story of a Boy Scout who, remembering he had not performed his requisite daily good deed, jumped out of bed and gave the canary to the cat. Bibesco wrote to me: 'Beb is a dear, and very clever—I wish I had a lawsuit on. Lucky Cynthia.'

Monday, 26th August

Good spirits and enjoyed a peaceful day. I like this detached way of taking London. Beb had a conference at the War Office in the after-noon. Evan came to tea with us, and he and Beb had a brisk tank talk. Beb thinks Evan unduly elated by our present successes and is appalled by Lord Hugh's uncompromising speech. We dined with Oc and Betty. Poor Oc—still takes his new leg off with great relief in the evenings. They shocked me by lighting a fire. We discussed Bongie— Betty complaining of Oc's exaggerated opinion of him. She and I

agreed he was on stilts due to chance association with Asquith—
without which he would never have attained such eminence as he has.

Tuesday, 27th August

Bibesco passed our front door in the morning. I being uncoiffe'd hid
behind the door, and he—being unshaven—hurried on. I telephoned
to him and he told me he had just had a letter from Elizabeth announcing her engagement! Beb and I dined at Queen's—I was indulgent
about Beb's extravagance concerning a ten-shilling grouse. We went
to the great Griffith's war cinema *Hearts of the World*.

Wednesday, 28th August

Beb and I went round to Bruton Street to see Aubrey and Mary.
Aubrey has just returned from his last job (he does have a patch-work
rug of a war), and had had his bud-shaped head shaved and looked
like a German mouse. I never saw such a sight. If Beb had returned
looking like that there would have been murder or suicide. Mary
lunched with us at Queen's. I took Beb to Charing Cross and back he
went. We have been extraordinarily happy these days. He has never
been such a darling before.

Received a summons for the next day from Barrie—a disappointment, as I was looking forward to a few hours of leisure in an empty
house. The struggle to read will be worse than ever now.

Went to Claridges by two buses to dine with Evan. We were a
party of five with Lady Drogheda, Lord Islington, and Grimson, a
good-looking American with just the right degree of twang who is
Pershing's representative here. We had quite fun. Lady Drogheda
crude, arch, and easy. Evan told a good story of a Conscientious
Objector he had to cross-examine. Evan (after much probing): 'But,
supposing you saw a man violating your mother—what would you
do then?' Man (without a glimmer): 'I should do what I know my
mother would wish, sir—nothing.' Chaffed a lot about the Curzons.
It was alleged that before marriage Lord C. had made Mrs Duggan
sign an agreement promising not to marry again, as he couldn't bear
the idea of a successor. During their engagement he used to send her
one of his speeches to read every day!

Thursday, 29th August

Felt in a terrible breadwinning bustle merely because I had to be at

Barrie's by eleven! Breakfasted downstairs punctually at nine and then tried to get letters and diary done before starting. More frantic recriminations from John's governess. Her last charge is that I used a phrase about her to which 'even Delysia' wouldn't have stooped—'the excrements of your brain!' She had misread *excitements*.

It takes me twenty minutes from door to door to get to Barrie by Underground. I found his favourite ward Michael with him—a delightful Eton boy. The work I did was easy enough—it is only socially rather difficult, because undefined. I don't quite know when to go, when to talk, when silently to work. There was a not over-formidable pile of letters. I devised my own method—opening them and giving him a précis of each: he either told me to destroy them or roughly intimated how they should be answered. In my own shorthand I scribbled notes on them, and then while he read his newspaper, I became C. Greene and wrote about twelve—taking such as were to be signed to him. I wrote one to George Robey. There were heart-rending ones from actresses, clamouring for engagements, sending photographs, etc. I got a blue flush from excitement, but all went well.

Lunched with Brenda and Summie. She told me poor Claud has been court-martialled—and was kept under detention for weeks. The charge was that he had gone up to London without leave—brought against him out of mere malice (he is, as is to be expected, very unpopular in the Mess). He refused to be Captain and really had no duties, so his absence didn't matter. A clever counsel got him off with flying colours, but he is transferring to another regiment. Of *course*, he ought to return to the Foreign Office, instead of cloaking his indolence in stay-at-home khaki. He called for me and walked me home. He seemed very tired and dispirited, repudiated his reputation for wealth (saying he had only £300 to spend), but he bought me some lovely white grapes—to my surprise. Mary Herbert turned up. I gave them tea. Claud obviously wanted to tell me his troubles, and sat on and on hoping to sit Mary out. I longed for him to go.

Bones came at 5.30. Went by Underground to dinner with Bluetooth and had a very pleasant *tête-à-tête*. He walked me home. He told me Birrell had been ecstatic in his praise of my reading aloud. Birrell and Belloc—two good testifiers.

Friday, 30th August

Same routine, arriving punctually at my work. On this occasion the youngest of the boys was in the room. I wrote one letter—to the Marchioness of Dufferin: 'Madam . . . Sir James Barrie has asked me to say he will be delighted to dine with you on the 31st August. He is particularly glad that Lady Cynthia Asquith will be of the company. Yours faithfully, C. Greene. P.S. Sir, I understand that some of the famous Dufferin rum will be in use on this occasion. For Sir J.B.' Then I asked for a duster and tackled the great cave of chaos. I tore up seven wastepaper-basketfuls of old papers—thick with the dust of ages. He said I knew much more than expected. I came provided with red tape and elastic bands—a thousand of which I spilt in the Tube. He asked me whether there was any difference between a rector and a vicar; what debentures were; and whether sponsors were required in the baptism of adults.

Saturday, 31st August

Woke at four and couldn't get to sleep again. Bicycled to my work for the first time. I didn't feel the lack of policemen (they were all out on strike) and I didn't know how to take advantage of their absence, which seemed unimaginative. The younger Davis boy was in the room when I arrived. I tackled another cave stuffed with thousands of letters from Michael. I suggested getting boxes and arranging them in chronological order. Tore up letters from Pamela Lytton and Violet. Barrie talked a lot, and I *can't* hear what he says.

Bicycled to lunch with Bibesco. We had witty talk, but he was too medical and devastatingly logical, upbraiding me for my selfish 'virtue' and pitying me for lack of temperament. He told me Elizabeth was miserable, Hugh having just broken to her the news that his doctor had told him he oughtn't to marry. Went to Augustus John. He went on with non-bicycle picture—making a *monster* of me. I was feeling very tired and looking plain after a bad night, so had a long rest, but it didn't have much effect.

Desmond MacCarthy called for me and we dined with Barrie and Brenda, who was entertaining my employer. It was just us four and we had an excellent dinner and were very happy. Barrie delighted. I like his story of the policeman who, when some officious person told him he was afraid two people were talking German in the street, replied: 'Well, perhaps it's the only language they know.' Heavy rain came on and Desmond and I splashed home. He stayed a long time, keeping me sitting in wet feet. Compared notes as to our 'well-readedness'.

Monday, 2nd September

Bought a box for Barrie's Michael's letters. Went by Underground.

There was practically no new correspondence to cope with, but rather tiresome arrears in the shape of numberless American royalties. I had to collect them (and they will have to be preserved), add them up and turn the dollars into £.s.d. I got rather bewildered. It would be so easy if one were alone and undisturbed, but the little man in the black alpaca coat prowls up and down like a caged animal and occasionally addresses a remark to me. One is at as great a disadvantage as when one's dentist makes conversation. Once I have done the arrears, I should think there would be very little work. I don't know how much to get in the way of furniture—I don't like to arrive with a box every morning. Bussed home. Egg lunch.

Bicycled to John at 4.30. For the first time, to my alarm, he made what I supposed was an advance—clutching me very roughly and disagreeably by the shoulders. I shook myself free and there was no recurrence. I think he had been drinking. I got very exhausted standing —almost fainted. Bones called for me and we dined at the Savoy. Went to *Nothing but the Truth*. He went every length—even kissing two girls to procure me some chocolates. Great difficulty in getting home, but luckily it was fine. I am very fond of Bones.

Tuesday, 3rd September

Barrie put me at another writing table. I went through a small pile of letters. There wasn't much—a *schwärm*-ing appeal for signed photographs from two schoolgirls, etc. That done, I tackled what I call his cipher—a little notebook in which he has in the most illegible handwriting jotted down addresses. I had to decipher them and write them down in a new address book. Some quite impossible ones I marked with red chalk and must appeal to him about them when I have finished, but I don't expect he will be able to read them himself. I must have invented some friends for him.

Tea with Betty. She had been at the Wharf for Sunday. Poor Elizabeth had gone up to London to weep alone. She had had ten days bliss with her Gibson, who had then gone to his doctor and said he had absolutely prohibited his marrying and only given him a year to live. A most extraordinary business. Why didn't he go to his doctor in the first place? Why won't he see another one? Betty said all at the Wharf were full of praise and pity regarding Gibson and were shocked at her cynical suggestion. Poor Elizabeth, I'm very sorry for her.

Con called for me in a brougham and took me to dine at her little Soho restaurant. Adele, Billy and Mima Gore, a portentous, limber-jawed American called Wells and Eddie completed our party. I didn't enjoy it. I can't listen to Billy Gore: he was full of well-tabulated information—just back from Jerusalem.

Wednesday, 4th September

Woke up again at about five. Read a whole Maupassant before I was called. It was wet so went by Underground. Michael D. back, but he was just going off to the country again to write an essay on 'The Song of Solomon'. Sent in a lot of cheques to Barrie's bank and retackled his illegible address book—rather boring. He said 'Damn' once, but not 'Damn you'.

Dined with Bluetooth—Eddie Marsh, Adele Essex, and McKenna were there. Bluetooth in a cloud mood. Played bridge—Bluetooth watching and I nervously appealing to him for help. Lost twenty-five shillings to Eddie. Galsworthy's and Compton MacKenzie's new books discussed—all the easier for me owing to not having read them. McKenna spoke up very nicely for Elizabeth. I suppose I am tired from lack of sleep, but anyhow I have got a bored treadmill feeling about life just now. The colour seems to have gone out of everything. I'm looking pinched.

Saturday, 7th September

Stayed in bed mixing my intellectual drinks—Barrie and Maupassant. Gwendoline Osborne visited me—very delicious—she said she hoped I would 'get Barrie under my thumb'. I complained of having no thumb. Desmond MacCarthy visited me at 6.30. We looked at my commonplace book. I was surprised by the poems he didn't know. Dined with Bones at Queen's. What can the waiters there think of me? He said how much he wished he had never met Ego and me—and maintained that all through life the game was *not* worth the candle. Bridge lesson. My first Barrie-shirking. I telephoned and wrote to excuse myself.

Sunday, 8th September

A rare experience—an entire day completely alone. I enjoyed it very much. Read *Sentimental Tommy* and two volumes of Maupassant, and went through my by-heart repertoire. Very light meals. Fell asleep early.

Monday, 9th September

Went to my work by Underground. I am getting well into the habit of reading en route and took *Love's Cross Currents* with me. Wrote several letters for Barrie, one to a poor man who wanted some advice on 'The Ascent of Parnassus'. Was amused to read one from a friend saying: 'I'm glad about Lady Cynthia—I hope she will be useful. I'm glad she's young and pretty.'

Dined with Bones at Hatchetts and we went to *Eyes of Youth*—getting soaked by heavy rain on the way. A crude bad play, but very enjoyable and giving great scope to Gertrude Eliot's admirable acting. Bones burst into raptures about the wonder of my face and its extraordinary ever-ever-changingness for which it could only be compared to the sea. Aubrey said Alex had called me 'a cross between a moonbeam and a Persian cat'—curious dewdrops!

Tuesday, 10th September

Finished with that third oubliette of Barrie's. Visited Mary at Bruton Street. She and Aubrey are having fearful difficulties with their constituents. In addition to thinking him a pervert and a pacifist they now say, 'How is it that once a prisoner he contrived to escape?' The answer being 'The Hidden Hand'. They consider an election in November a certainty now. Dinner in bed and more Maupassant—a diet which is a little disagreeing with me.

Wednesday, 11th September

Tackled an appalling dusty chest of Barrie's in which were crammed any amount of manuscripts in unimaginable confusion. My ambition is to discover *Peter Pan* which the Red Cross begged for the other day. He is almost certain he has destroyed it, but I came across one page. It was irritating work—they are so illegible. The Australians have invited him to visit troops in France which gave me an opportunity of suggesting what Grimson had urged me to—a visit to the Americans. He rose so readily to this bait that I regretted not having tried before. I must communicate with Grimson at once.

Desmond MacCarthy was to have called for me early but telephoned in agitation to say his mother had rung up, summoning him because one of her maids had locked herself up in her bedroom and they couldn't get any answer out of her—and feared suicide. Naturally he was detained a long time, so I went to Queen's and began dinner joined by Mary S., down from Scotland. Finally he arrived from his Grand Guignol. He had—heart in mouth—entered the room by the window and found it empty! The girl had locked her door and gone off—

where no one knows. We sat in Cadogan Square after dinner. He recited two poems he had learnt with great trouble, fired by my book. Told me stories of Henry James. No further ground covered in our relationship.

Saturday, *14th September*

Found my first fire this year crackling in Barrie's room—great morale effect. Lunch with Whibley at Queen's. He used to play cricket in Barrie's authors' team and told me a lot about him. Told me the story of the cabman who, with the irritating habit of his trade, when told to drive to Waterloo futilely queried, 'Waterloo Stytion, sir?' 'No, to the battlefield you bloody fool,' was the answer.

Travelled down to Haywards Heath to stay with the Osbornes in a hideous hired house called Lydhurst. I chose the largest and ugliest room and enjoyed a rest before dinner. Willie de Grunne arrived and was in great spirits with his harem of 'cuckoos'. Devonshire cream at every meal—too delicious—and exquisite cookery. For the first time for at least three weeks I was in my best face-form, perfectly comfortable (my face very seldom is) and looking my best. Somehow we turned Willie on as a psychologist and forced him to analyse our characters. I was *astounded* by the shrewdness he displayed. I had no idea such intelligent observation was always going on under all that nonsense camouflage. We plied him with every sort of question— making him compare our share of every virtue and vice. In rebutting a charge of cynicism, I said I never laughed when I was by myself— 'What, do you never laugh at your face in the glass?' exclaimed Willie. He made me laugh, too, by saying when discussing the reserve I claimed, 'Ah—if you were not shellish you would be like ten Lady Angelas: you would roll over the world!' We had such a funny evening. Ages since I have enjoyed myself so much.

Sunday, *15th September*

Stayed late in my bed, then joined Willie and Moira who musicked all the morning. He sang some most delightful French songs. I like his expression 'inconvenient' (*inconvenante*), and also his way of calling men 'vanitous cocks'. We all went for a walk in the afternoon. After tea—such a tea—Gwendoline insisted on reading extracts from my diary: she said she would never be able to read anything else. Delicious music after dinner.

Tuesday, 17th September

Came up by an after-dinner train yesterday. Woke up to find an *immense* blister on my arm like a huge topaz or a jujube. I must have burnt it on my hot-water bottle—extraordinary that I shouldn't have felt it. To prick or not to prick?

Went to Barrie—quite a lot of letters to write—no time to do anything else. Bones bicycled there with me. Very distressed to hear he has *not* got the commercial secretary job he was counting on. Poor dear, he's very disappointed. I offered to write to Mr Balfour and try a little wire-pulling. Sat to Augustus John. He was gloomy. Visited Margot H. and tried on dress at Miss North's.

I was to have dined with Moira, but at 7.15 Willie told me on the telephone that Alex had been killed, and I was much too upset to go. I'm miserable about it, and feel completely sickened and discouraged about life. He had come to be a real alleviation to me and I was relying on him more and more—his interest—spirits—his gift of entering into the detail of one's life—his appreciation of Michael—I feel bitterly bereaved and oh so weary and bored. He had been splendid in the war. I hoped he might soon sheathe the sword—and now! I'm glad I gave him so much of my time. Oh, I *shall* miss him! I was so looking forward to his approaching leave.

Wednesday, 18th September

Slept very badly. Now this new bludgeoning has fallen, I wonder why I wasn't happier before. If only it could be revoked I would feel so rich now. Went to Barrie feeling very wretched. I took him a note from Margot inviting him to Chirk and he accepted for Monday (I am going on Friday) as he likes music on the terms I described—lying down in the dark and so on. He is not musical. Talking of people talking to him about his books, he said he got rather tired in America of being told how much they liked his *Prisoner of Zenda*. He told me Michael[1] admired my clothes.

Stood to Augustus John. He has quite abandoned his uniform and wore butcher's blue this time. Visited Claud—he was quite nice, very sorry about Alex. Dinner in bed.

Thursday, 19th September

Barrie-d. Lunched with Mrs Patrick Campbell at the Savoy where

1. Barrie's ward.

she now lives with George West. She was in good form. Told me not to pander to Barrie's shyness—attributed his gappiness to use of drugs. Terrible ordeal—went to see John and his governess in their new flat in Chelsea. It's surprisingly nice for the price. John looked well and was very sweet, but I see no sign of fundamental change and feel very sick at heart. Was going to bed in sulky misery, but Desmond persuaded me to dine with him at the last moment and I am very glad he prevented me from turning my face to the wall. I enjoyed it—sowed seeds of doubt in his mind as to his infallibility as a psychologist.

Friday, 20th September

Desmond sent me round two books early in the morning. Barrie was far more chatty than he has ever been before: he came and sat on the window sill by my writing table and told me stage stories for ages —quite amusing. Claud called for me. He is working hard to get Brenda, Diana and me to persuade Margot to invite him to join us at Chirk.

Snatched a hurried lunch at Paddington—practically nothing but mustard—and got into a carriage with Brenda and Barbara McLaren. Arrived at 6.30 finding Bluetooth, Diana, and Alan on the platform. Oggie and Margot completed the ranks of the women. After dinner we played a sort of general information game, which ended in what I think Margot regarded as 'showing off' on the part of Diana and me as no one else contributed. Suffered agonies of cold.

Sunday, 22nd September

Walked up the hill with Bluetooth. I continued with my demonstration of capacity for 'looseness'. We had fun. Rested after lunch enjoying *Sylvia Scarlett*. The musicians are the most delightful children with amazing *joie de vivre*, and they begged for a fancy dress dinner. I, Bluetooth and Barbara felt utterly disinclined—but I am glad to say we were swept into the stream—it was one of those unaccountable successes. I took the responsibility of Bluetooth and rehearsed him in cloak and armour before tea. I lent my Spanish shawl to Barbara —and did my old Ophelia stunt with hair, straw, and a very good grey dress found here. We all assembled for dinner and a wonderful sight we were. Oggie—beyond the dreams of Aubrey Beardsley— as a bijou Hamlet; Margot—a guardsman (sheer Vesta Tilley—but not so shy-making as I feared); Diana, a lovely lady of the M. Beaucaire style—her dress brilliantly improvised; all the musicians excellent grotesques, and Brenda perhaps the most attractive thing I've ever seen—a black and white page boy with such perfect legs. But the real curdling success of the evening was the discovery that the toad-like butler and all his assistants were in fancy dress—a cohort of grisly parlourmaids or nuns in towels and aprons. It was the funniest sight I've ever seen, because there was never a *glimmer* on their faces and they functioned formally as ever. What they looked like carrying and handing round! After dinner it was very dream-like and I, who haven't taken the floor for six years, was surprised to find myself stunt-dancing about with all the rest. The first violin, Defauw—a ghastly sight in a yellow wig—fell in love with me, said dancing with me was *enivrante*, toyed with the tangles of my hair, which he compared to flames, and even went so far as to ask me to *bite* off a piece of chocolate for him! I have never seen people so happy as those four men—they did admirable stunts. Little Miss Sparrow looked charming in *quartier Latin* costume. Bluetooth was immensely amused and looked superb as a Roman soldier. It was dreamlike, but yet I enjoyed it. We ended up with a fairly obscene hair-combing arising from discussion of Dr Stopes' *Married Love*, a book Diana is quite a missionary about. Didn't go to bed until past two. It was a great *tour de force* when the musicians pulled themselves together and played serious music in their ridiculous guise.

Monday, 23rd September

Walked with Bluetooth in the morning—we never had a completely fine day, but there were good gleams. Found this orgy of music was disagreeing with me—unless one is sufficiently musical for it to be an intellectual occupation I'm sure hours of just having one's emotions teased and tickled is demoralising and exasperating to the nerves. On a foundation of happiness I daresay it would be all right, its effect being just to dramatise my own thoughts not to give me any new ones. On my foundation of sorrow it seemed just to serve to take the skin off several wounds and for the first time I felt the germ of resentment, a wish to hit back at something. Certainly there was something like a nerve storm amongst the women on this evening. We all felt strangely depressed, and Oggie who had lain for hours on a sofa *fondu en larmes*—when asked to sing what she thought an inferior song after Margot had sung two of her favourite ones—suddenly made a tantrum scene springing to her feet exclaiming: 'In future I shall always take the biggest peach.' It was very funny. Poor darling, she exercises every privilege of the artistic temperament. We then had a ridiculous scene in the long gallery—with its rows of armoured figures it struck the impressionable musicians as ghostly—Defauw the little first violin said he wanted an 'impression'. I did one of my melodrama screams and terrified him out of his wits—he went white as a sheet. I then went what I used to call 'moonstruck'—had the sensation of leaving my body untenanted and liable to become possessed. I acted a looney, terrifying Oggie and Margot into annoyance. Temporarily they really disliked me, complaining of my uncanniness. It was a morbid scene, and Diana 'willing' Oggie wasn't a very pleasant sight. Very late going to bed again. Barrie was to have arrived in the evening—his train was met and I was horrified at his non-appearance —fearing I had misled him as to train. To my intense relief the next day brought a telegram explaining his absence.

Tuesday, 24th September

Diana and Alan went away earlier—their absence really left the party more happy and peaceful I think. We were very happy with the darling musicians, who really give one a lump in the throat with their simplicity, gaiety, and geniality. Samuel, the pianist, is the least attractive —he is rather fatuous with dark hints as to his psychical powers. He has very good 'stunts' but with his grotesque appearance it is difficult to be certain whether he is performing or not. He might always be doing his drunkard or idiot in the train. Doehaerd,* the celloist, with his jade love-sick eyes only talked French. He came and sat beside me at nearly every meal. He talked a good deal about 'les femmes' and delighted me with a phrase about Brenda. Discussing what I considered the exaggerated thinness *coquetterie* of the English I suggested her as being possibly 'trop mince'. 'Non—non je ne crois pas—elle est bien. Je crois qu'elle aurait des "surprises agréables".' Defauw the Belgian violinist (my admirer of the fancy dress evening) is a dear little comic —all on wires—bubbling with spirits and conviviality. Doehaerd convulsed us by saying of him 'C'est un grand séducteur: méfiez-vous'. Tertis, the English viola, is an angel of mellow goodness—it oozed out of him impregnating the air—he *couldn't* see evil and one really feels a better woman near him. Few people have touched me so much. They all adored Margot, Brenda and me, finding us *ravissante, simple,* and *distinguée*. I envied Margot being able to make such dear people so happy. They enjoyed the champagne, etc., and really warmed the cockles of one's heart. Miss Sparrow (Sylvia) the little violinist aged about twenty-eight, has great charm. Bluetooth beetlebrowing and continually collapsing into giggles made an incongruous figure in the midst of this Alice-in-Wonderland party which was completed by the arrival of Joseph Holbrook (exercising too many privileges of genius —dirt, not dressing, deafness, beard, and rudeness) and Murray Davey who is the most fantastically operatic figure imaginable—always pirouetting and carolling, and looking with his Mephistophelean beard exactly like the conventional adulterer in a French novel—the one pictured in shirt sleeves, hair brushes in hand. They didn't come till Wednesday—delayed by the railway strike. I am writing these days long afterwards and they have merged in my memory.

Wednesday, 25th September

Gladly availed myself of the railway strike and didn't return to London. Bluetooth departed—only to return stuck by strike. We sat out in the garden and had a long introspection talk—complaining of my 'camouflage'. I suggested how awful it would be if, in the perfunctory discharge of my possibly mechanical friendship, I gave myself away by writing to him and saying 'I wish you were here'. It might easily happen to someone who runs friendship like an office. Joseph Holbrook read a book through the music and was rebuked by Margot.

Thursday, 26th September

Tertis was made to miss his train by a clever ruse. He was told there wasn't another one, so I gladly recognised the impossibility of going up in the afternoon myself. It was wet all the morning. Bluey and I had our usual outing after lunch. We *crept* as he was feeling a little ill. There was an evening concert in the village which we all attended. I prompted (a sinecure) the Harold Nicolsons in their sketch and pretended to sing in the chorus of Oggie's patriotic song. We had supper when we got back and then an evening of stunts. Defauw did some excellent ones—an acrobat, a cock, an elephant, and so on, and I had a great success with my purring, owl hooting, seal bark, duck drinking, etc., noises. I even did a Channel passage for 'Ladies, only'. Joseph Holbrook put his head on my stomach in an unavailing attempt to hear my purring.

Friday, 27th September

My thirty-first birthday. The most unobtrusive one I have ever had. I left Chirk at last escorted by Defauw and Tertis. They were excellent couriers getting me corner seats, tea, porters, and a taxi. Our train was two hours late. Mrs Tertis had come to meet her husband: she is older than he—plain, but transfigured by oozing, genial goodness just like him and they conveyed the impression of the happiest atmosphere possible. Dined with Bones at Queen's and played dreary poker at Iris's, losing three pounds.

Saturday, 28th September

Found Barrie with a very bad cold and a great accumulation of letters. He seemed pleased to see me—read letter from the Professor in which he wrote 'I hope the adorable Cynthia—who is very good *and* very clever, is with you.' Lunched with Whibley at Queen's and he drove me to the tennis court in St John's Wood. He was terribly amorous— the worst of it is that he is interrogatively *expectantly* so. He even said, 'I'm sure you will love me some day.' Very bothered by him. Claud visited me. He had actually gone so far as to get into the train for Chirk and then changed his mind. He read me some of those enchanting Chinese poems. Letter from Lawrence saying he has been put into Grade B that I *must* get him some work under the Ministry of Education. Delightful evening with Desmond MacCarthy—dining at Queen's and then sitting here till twelve. Had such good talk about the sham psychology of modern novels, my disease of emotional catelepsy and poverty—the non-gossip talk one has with him is so refreshing after Bluetooth, etc.

At this point, after a few more days of light-hearted entries, the diary breaks off with the sudden, sad realisation of the real meaning of the approaching Armistice. On Monday, 7th October, Lady Cynthia wrote —on the verge of a brief nervous breakdown:

I am beginning to rub my eyes at the prospect of peace. I think it will require more courage than anything that has gone before. It isn't until one leaves off spinning round that one realises how giddy one is. One will have to look at long vistas again, instead of short ones, and one will at last fully recognise that the dead are not only dead for the duration of the war.

The Volunteer

Here lies a clerk who half his life had spent
Toiling at ledgers in a city grey,
Thinking that so his days would drift away
With no lance broken in life's tournament:
Yet ever 'twixt the books and his bright eyes
The gleaming eagles of the legions came,
And horsemen, charging under phantom skies,
Went thundering past beneath the oriflamme.

And now those waiting dreams are satisfied;
From twilight to the halls of dawn he went;
His lance is broken; but he lies content
With that high hour, in which he lived and died.
And falling thus, he wants no recompense,
Who found his battle in the last resort;
Nor needs he any hearse to bear him hence,
Who goes to join the men of Agincourt.

Herbert Asquith

The Gibbetters' Hell

INDEX

Index

running forward to do so that Beb
was hit by a flying splinter from a
shell burst. His leave was nearly
due, and so he was sent home.
Later he suffered severely from
shell shock. Besides 'The
Volunteer'—actually written in
1912—he wrote other poetry,
collected in *Poems* 1912–33, and a
number of novels, of which *Roon*
is possibly the best, and a memoir
Moments of Memory which includes recollections of his war
service and has maps based on
those mentioned in the diary. For
a number of years he worked on
the editorial staff of Hutchinson,
and is remembered still as a
cultured, likeable and very 'gentle'
man), xii–xiii, xvii–xviii, 6, 7, 8,
9, 10, 12, 15, 16, 18, 20, 21, 22, 27,
29, 33, 38, 42, 43, 44, 45, 46, 47,
48, 49, 50, 51, 54, 55, 69, 74, 75, 76,
77, 79, 80, 81, 82, 83, 85, 86, 89, 90,
91, 92, 93, 95, 96, 97, 98, 99, 100,
101, 102, 103, 105, 107, 108, 109,
112–13, 114, 115, 116, 119, 120,
123, 124, 125, 132, 133, 134, 135,
136, 139, 141, 142, 143, 144, 145,
147, 148, 150, 151, 152, 153, 155,
158, 159, 161, 164, 165, 166, 167,
168, 169, 170, 171, 174, 175, 177,
180, 182, 183, 184, 185, 186, 189,
190, 191, 193, 195, 197, 198, 200,
203, 204, 205, 206, 210, 211,
212, 214, 216, 217, 218, 219, 224,
225, 226, 227, 228, 229, 230, 231,
232, 233, 234, 235, 236, 237, 239,
240, 241, 243, 245, 246, 247, 253,
254, 256, 257, 258, 262, 263, 264,
266, 269, 270, 271, 272, 273, 278,
281, 283, 285, 290, 291, 294, 302,
303, 305, 319, 321, 322, 323, 327,
328, 329, 330, 331, 332, 348, 365,
368, 374, 379, 382, 383, 385–6,
389, 390, 391, 392, 393, 395, 396,
397, 398, 399, 400, 409, 413, 421,
423, 424, 425, 426, 427, 429, 430,
431, 434, 437, 439, 456, 457, 458,
459, 460, 461, 467, 468

Asquith, Herbert Henry (1852–1928:
nicknamed the 'Old Boy', 'Pip-
Emma', and 'P.M.' Liberal Prime
Minister 1908–15, he headed a
Coalition May 1915–Dec. 1916,
and was created Earl of Oxford
and Asquith 1925. Possibly the
'Pip-Emma' needs explanation. In
the First World War the twelve-
hour clock was in use and to
ensure distinction p.m. would be
said—according to the communica-
tions alphabet—as pip-emma, the
joke is the simple one of 'P.M.'—
for Prime Minister—being expressed in this army way), xi, xii–
xiii, xviii, 16, 17, 23, 25, 27, 34, 38,
41, 42, 45, 47, 48, 54, 58, 72, 75, 76,
77, 79, 80, 81, 87, 89, 96, 100, 101,
102, 106, 111, 113, 114, 115, 117,
119, 123, 130, 131, 142, 146, 147,
152, 153, 154, 159, 160, 162, 163,
164, 166, 168, 169, 172, 189, 200,
204, 210, 211, 218, 220, 223, 228,
235, 239, 241, 242, 243, 244, 245,
266, 279, 283, 285, 291, 294, 311,
324, 326, 328, 329, 331, 355, 357,
364, 365, 372, 373, 376, 380, 383–4,
390, 391, 398, 403, 404, 408, 418,
440, 441, 448, 453, 457–8

Asquith, John (1911–37: eldest son
of Lady Cynthia). In addition to
her own diary, she kept diaries for
her two children, the one for John
being written partly as an aid to
doctors in studying his case: in the
complete version of her own diary
the references to him are fuller
and more frequent, but have been
cut as too personal and painful),
xviii, 4, 7, 18, 19, 20, 22, 28, 29,
51, 68, 69, 71, 72, 74, 75, 78, 82,
84, 85, 92, 93, 95, 105, 115, 136,
145, 148, 155, 156–7, 165–6, 171,
174, 180–1, 190, 194, 198, 207,
217, 226, 227, 257, 271, 272, 280,
283, 286, 287, 294, 298, 299, 313,
319–20, 321, 323, 328, 329, 349,
357, 358, 374, 376, 382, 384, 392,
396, 399, 400, 401, 402, 410, 411,

Index

Index

Index

Index

Index

Cavendish, Rt. Hon. Lord Richard
'Dick' (1871–1946), 83, 84, 309
Cavendish Bentinck, Mrs, 151
Cavendish Square, No. 2 (London
home of H. H. Asquith), 279, 282,
285, 294, 297, 310, 311, 328, 329,
330, 356, 364, 372, 376, 389, 398,
410, 418, 422, 446, 453
Cazalet, Mrs, 418
Cecil, Lord Hugh (1869–1956: cr.
Baron Quickswood 1941. Youngest
son of Lord Salisbury, he was
stirringly associated with Winston
Churchill in the leadership of a
group of able young Conservatives,
the Hughligans. He had joined the
Flying Corps), 30, 39, 40, 48, 51–2,
169, 301, 323, 399, 405–6, 467
Cecil, Lord Robert 'Bob' (1864–1958:
cr. Visct. Cecil of Chelwood 1923),
153, 401
Chamberlain, Sir Austen (1863–1937:
Secretary of State for India 1915–
17), 25
Chamberlain, Joseph 'Jo' (1836–1914),
47, 228
Champion, H.M.S., 33
Chapin, Mrs. Hester, 90, 91
Chaplin, Charlie, 154, 197, 409
Charles or Charlie. *See* Lister, Charles
Charles, Captain, 451
Charles, Monsieur, 308
Charteris, Anne (eldest daughter of
the Hon. Guy Charteris, she
married in 1932 Shane, 3rd Baron
O'Neill, who died 1944; in 1945
2nd Visct. Rothermere; and in 1952,
after a divorce, Ian Fleming the
creator of James Bond, who died
1964), xviii, 4, 455, 465
Charteris, Colin (1889–92: third son
of the 11th Earl of Wemyss, he
died of scarlet fever), xii
Charteris, Cynthia. *See* Asquith, Lady
Cynthia.
Charteris, Hon. (Sir) Evan (1864–
1940: sixth son of the 10th Earl of
Wemyss, he was a barrister at the
Parliamentary Bar, took silk in 1919,
and was knighted in 1932. During

the First World War he was
originally with the Coldstream
Guards, was Staff-Captain Royal
Flying Corps in the summer of
1916, and transferred to the Tank
Corps until the beginning of 1918.
He was a King's Messenger, and
Lady Angela, a connoisseur in using
them for her own urgent messages,
regarded him as 'the most detached'
of these couriers, whose task in
wartime was often hazardous. In
1930 he married Lady Edward
Grosvenor, daughter of the 5th
Earl of Kenmare), 5, 6, 13, 14, 17,
20, 23, 28, 32, 33–4, 35–6, 44, 50, 57,
59, 89, 90, 96, 102, 110, 116, 175,
176, 189, 190, 193, 194, 214, 215,
217, 218, 222, 223, 238, 258, 259,
260, 264, 267, 271–2, 275, 282, 305,
306, 308, 310, 312, 317, 318, 393,
394, 395, 396, 399, 401, 403, 404,
405, 415, 425–6, 427, 428, 440, 441,
455, 467, 468
Charteris, Frances (died 1925: a
daughter of Frank Tennant, she
married Guy Charteris, q.v., in
1912), xvii, 4, 11, 13, 15, 16, 17, 54,
55, 58, 66–7, 68, 91, 92, 116, 157,
158, 159, 160, 165, 173, 176, 191,
193, 223, 243, 244, 266, 268, 269,
283, 284, 297, 318, 322, 327, 358,
379, 412, 416, 420, 424, 452, 464, 465
Charteris, 'Colonel' Francis (1675–
1732: Whibley, as the author of *The
Book of Scoundrels*, was persuaded
by Lady Cynthia to write a book
on the Colonel, but research revealed that he had not been quite so
black as political prejudice painted
him in a volume entitled *Twelve Bad
Men*. And so, though he had proved
the type of the profligate for Pope
and Hogarth, he was abandoned as
a suitable subject. One feels he did
his best—the reference books list
him as only a self-styled colonel,
and the catalogue of his sins includes
cardsharping, theft and fraud, with
the final touch of a charge of rape,

Index

Index

(d. 1921: nicknamed 'Black Jane'. The beautiful Jennie Jerome had married in 1874 Lord Randolph Churchill, q.v., by whom she became the mother of Sir Winston Churchill. After his death she married in 1900 George Cornwallis-West, whom she divorced in 1913, and in 1918 Montagu Porch, qq.v.), 201–2, 380, 440, 444, 445

Churchill, Rt. Hon. Lord Randolph Spencer (1849–95: father of Sir Winston Churchill), 106

Churchill, Hon. Randolph (1911–: son of Sir Winston Churchill), 275

Churchill, (Rt. Hon. Sir) Winston, xi, 6, 22–3, 24, 26 fn., 29, 31, 32, 33, 34, 36, 39, 44, 45, 98, 133, 170, 195, 234, 235, 242, 275, 278, 306, 334, 361, 400, 429

'Cis'. See Asquith, Cyril.

Clandeboye (home of Lord Basil Blackwood in County Down, Ireland), 452

Clanricarde, Hubert George, 2nd Marquess (1832–1916), 407

Clare. See Tennant, Clare.

Claridges, 264, 291, 308, 333, 359, 371, 375, 393, 401, 468

Clemmie. See Churchill, Clementine.

Cliffe, Polly (maid to Lady Cynthia who had always, according to the social rulings of the day, to accompany her mistress when she went out before her marriage. Lady Cynthia referred to her as 'a lugubrious bodyguard with an unrivalled capacity for falling on the thorns of life', but her role had its problems, since her charge had 'often slipped her collar and chain' by hailing a hansom to make her escape in. She afterwards remained with her mistress for many years, as Lady Cynthia's servants tended to do), 7, 11, 32, 65, 125, 132, 152, 162, 174, 178, 189, 258, 267, 268, 271, 276, 291, 297, 298, 299, 324, 329, 332, 340, 347, 376, 393, 416, 426, 429

Cliveden (country home of the Astors, on the Thames, 3 miles from Maidenhead, in Buckinghamshire), 309

Cloe. See Guinness, Cloe.

Clonboy (country home of Lady de Vesci near Windsor), 21, 139, 142, 147, 152, 153, 154, 155, 159, 162, 257, 272

Clouds (country home of Lady Wemyss's father, the Hon. Percy Scawen Wyndham, in Wiltshire), xiv, 97, 182, 196, 306

clumps (the father and mother of 'Twenty Questions' or 'Animal, Vegetable or Mineral'), 82, 265

Cobb, The Rev. William Frederick Geikie– (1957–1941: rector of St. Ethelburga's Bishopsgate), 311

Colefax, Lady Sibyl (a niece of Eliza Wedgwood, and wife of Sir Arthur Colefax, she was celebrated as a hostess), 366, 379, 416

Collier, Constance, 182

Collins (a 'thank-you' letter for hospitality received, named after the Rev. William Collins of *Pride and Prejudice* who wrote an unquoted masterpiece in the line. They were a dreaded task for the tyro in country-house visiting and there was the lingering dread that an unscrupulous hostess might read it aloud at breakfast to entertain her remaining guests the day after one's departure. Lady Wemyss was an unrepentant sinner in this respect), 324, 438

Colquhoun, Dinah (a daughter of Frank Tennant, she married in 1915 Sir Iain Colquhoun, q.v.), 13, 14, 15, 58, 116, 157, 158, 268, 269, 297, 424

Colquhoun, Sir Iain, 7th Baronet of Luss (1887–1948: he served with great gallantry in the Scots Guards), 13, 14, 15, 220, 268, 424

Colquhoun, (Captain Sir) Ivar, (8th Baronet of Luss) (1916–:), 464, 465

Comedy and Tragedy (W. S. Gilbert), 140

Index

Index

Index

Viceroy of India by the annexation of Burma. She was a great traveller and did much for the health of Indian women), 319

Dufferin and Ava, Terence Temple-Blackwood, 2nd Marquess of (1866–1918: second son of the 1st Marquess, whom he succeeded in 1902), 132–3, 409

Dufferin and Ava, Freddie Temple-Blackwood, 3rd Marquess of (1875–1930: fourth son of the 1st Marquess). *See* Blackwood, Lord Frederick Temple-.

Dufferin and Ava, Marchioness of. *See* Blackwood, Brenda.

Duggan, Mrs Alfred, 179, 210

Du Maurier, Sir Gerald, 54

Dunn, James (1875–1956: created a baronet 1921. Born in New Brunswick, he became a barrister in Canada, founded the banking firm of Dunn, Fisher & Co. in 1907, and became president of the Algoma Steel Corporation, Ontario), 26, 46, 47, 329

Earle, Sir Lionel (1866–1948: Permanent Secretary to H.M. Office of Works 1912–33), 75

East Lynne (Mrs. Henry Wood), 256

Eddie. *See* Marsh, Edward.

Edgar. *See* Speyer, Sir Edgar

Ednam, Lord (later 3rd Earl of Dudley), 22

Edward. *See* Horner, Edward, and Glenconner, 1st Baron

Edward VII, 446

Edward VIII. *See* Prince of Wales

Egoist (George Meredith), 11, 12, 141

Egremont, 3rd Earl of, xv

Eileen. *See* Orde, Eileen

Elcho, Hugo Francis Charteris, Lord (1884–1916: nicknamed 'Ego', eldest son of the 11th Earl of Wemyss, and holder of the courtesy title Lord Elcho. Educated at Cheam and Eton, and at Trinity College, Oxford, he was Hon. Attaché to

James Bryce at Washington 1908–9, then read for the Bar and was thinking of standing for Parliament when war broke out), xii, xviii, 3, 7, 58, 61, 69, 70, 72, 75, 81, 88, 96, 134, 159, 160, 165, 166, 167, 180, 181–2, 183, 184, 185, 186, 187, 188, 189, 191, 193, 196, 197, 200, 236, 248, 275, 319, 370, 384, 466, 472

Elcho, Mary. *See* Wemyss, Mary

Elcho, Violet (Lady Violet 'Letty' Manners, second daughter of the 8th Duke of Rutland, married in 1911 Lord Elcho, q.v., and in 1921 Guy Holford Benson), 3, 6, 39, 68, 69–70, 71, 72, 73, 75, 76, 79, 80, 81, 87, 88, 89, 91, 108, 124, 167 fn., 172, 175, 177, 181–2, 183–5, 187, 188, 189, 191, 193, 196, 197, 223, 225, 235, 238, 247, 259, 268, 276, 284, 301, 304, 318, 319, 384, 395, 396, 425, 426, 444, 464, 465

Eliot, George, 127

Eliot, Gertrude, 473

Eliot, T. S., i, 379

Elsie, Lily, 179, 417, 419

Epstein (sculptures), 279

Eros (dressmaker), 135, 179

Essex, Adele (d. 1922: a New Yorker, Adele Grant, married the 7th Earl as his second wife in 1893), 5, 6, 15, 24–5, 33–4, 35, 39, 41, 44, 49, 57, 59, 71, 72, 74, 80, 87, 91, 92, 112, 116, 117, 133–4, 135, 137, 146, 230, 238, 282, 284, 309, 311, 312, 323, 361, 401, 406, 409, 445, 448, 471, 472

Essex, George Devereux de Vere Campbell, 7th Earl of (1857–1916), 6, 117

Ettie. *See* Desborough, Ettie

'Eve of St. Agnes' (Keats), 149

Evelyn. *See* De Vesci, Evelyn

Evie. *See* Rivers-Bulkeley, Evie

Eyes of Youth (play by Max Marcin and Charles Guernon at the St. James's), 473

Faithfulness in High Places (Lady Florence Bourke), 63

Farmer, Sir Francis Farmer (d. 1922: dental surgeon, with much experience in restoration after gunshot wounds), 42–3, 319, 320

Farquhar, Horace, 1st Earl (1844–1923: Lord Steward 1915–22), 412

Farquharson, Bt. Lt.-Col. Arthur Spenser Loat (d. 1942: a classical scholar and lecturer in philosophy at University College, Oxford 1899–1914, he had been attached to the General Staff, War Office, on mobilisation), 44–5, 51, 52

Faulkner, Miss C. M. (born in 1882, Nannie Faulkner was in the service of Lady Cynthia from 1911 and much loved by her children), 174, 273, 293, 299, 334, 338, 362, 371, 376, 429

Faust, 353

Felicity. *See* Tree, Felicity.

Fern (servant to George Vernon), 98–99

Festin, Captain, 341, 342, 345, 347

Fielding, Colonel, 323, 324

Fingall, Lady (wife of the 11th Earl of Fingall, a former State Steward to the Viceroy of Ireland), 61

First Seven Divisions, 150

First Ten Thousand (presumably *The First Hundred Thousand*, war sketches by Ian Hay, published 1915), 125

Fisher, H., 279

Fisher, John Arbuthnot Fisher, 1st Baron (1841–1920: Admiral of the Fleet. First Sea Lord 1904–10, he was recalled in October 1914 to replace Prince Louis of Battenberg, but resigned over the Dardanelles issue 1915), 16, 22, 24, 25, 31, 32, 57

Fitzgerald, Colonel Evelyn, 47, 167, 281, 282, 291, 331, 332, 372

Flavia. *See* Forbes, Flavia.

Flecker, James Elroy, 260

Fleming, Ian, xviii

floater (period slang for 'bloomer', presumably because such embarrassing slips in conversation or behavi-

our remain persistently difficult to thrust into oblivion), 58

Foch, Ferdinand (1851–1929: Marshal of France, largely responsible for the victory of the Marne, he commanded on the N.W. front Oct. 1914–Sept. 1916 and became Chief of General Staff 1917), 235, 353, 424

Forbes, Lady Angela (1876–1950: Lady Angela St. Clair Erskine was a daughter of the 4th Earl of Rosslyn, and in 1896 a shared passion for hunting led to her marriage with Jim Forbes, then heir presumptive to Sir Charles Forbes, 5th Baronet of Newe in Aberdeenshire. Her reply to his proposal had been, 'Yes, if I may have your chestnut horse', and by 1904 they had agreed in a friendly fashion on separation. After their divorce in 1910 an allowance was made to Lady Angela through her trustees, but her expenditure soon outdistanced it and she borrowed on the security of her jewels with her husband as a willing surety. When the time for repayment came, she was unwilling to part with any except her least favourite emeralds, and her husband claimed to set the sums he now paid as surety on her promissory notes against her allowance. She disagreed and the case was heard in July 1917 before Mr Justice Shearman, with Lord Wemyss making a brief appearance in the box. Lady Angela lost, the judge remarking on 'a very ill-advised action' and also on the extreme courtesy and gentlemanliness of their matrimonial disagreement until 'someone advised the present course of action'—one imagines his eye rested on Lord Wemyss In 1914 she was invited to go to Dr Haden Guest's Paris hospital —in the Hotel Majestic—where the casualties of the retreat from Mons were being treated, all bad cases.

Index

Unprepared, except for a few first-aid classes, she stood the ordeal well and was assigned to taking notes in the operating theatre until qualified staff could be obtained. Then, moved by the sight of a crowd of unattended wounded on the quay at Boulogne (suddenly turned into a base), she decided to open a canteen. Her British Soldiers' Buffets at Boulogne and Etaples, affectionately known to the men as Angelina's, were started on £8 of stores she characteristically ordered from Fortnum and Mason and supported by her newspaper appeals for supplies and a genius for organising. Her peccadilloes, which she zestfully described in *Memories and Base Details* consisted in saying 'Damn!' in the hearing of a visiting clergyman while she was serving ten thousand men with tea and sandwiches at five o'clock in the morning, and in washing her hair in the canteen (the official objection seems typically to have been moral rather than hygienic, but there was no hot water anywhere else that winter and, as Lady Angela sensibly told the Adjutant General, it was either that or go dirty). The absence of an official inquiry confirms her claim that her troubles were caused by her opening her buffets at any time of the day or night as they were needed, instead of adhering to fixed hours approved by the other officially recognised canteens, and that when her competitors forced her to start making charges she made a swingeing profit (promptly redistributed to service charities), whereas they floundered in debt. And, of course, whenever she cut her red tape she was certain to stand on officialdom's tenderest corns to do it! Officialdom had its revenge: balked in attempting outright closure, it secured the same end by refusing to allow back into France any member of her staff on sick or home leave. The letter quoted in the text was written by a worker Lady Angela had summarily dismissed, and came into her possession when forwarded by the loyal addressee: Lady Angela sent it on to Lord Derby to illustrate the methods being employed against her, but he merely changed his attitude from 'friendly justice' to 'official aloofness'. Her interview with the Adjutant General was bolstered into being the 'inquiry' she wanted, and only the inspiration of Lord Buckmaster devised the eventual compromise charade in the House of Lords which saved all faces.

Lady Angela now took up with enthusiasm the organisation of a convoy of cars for the French army, but alert officials created every imaginable difficulty over permits for the drivers. She rushed back to England to clear matters, her boat exploding a mine on the way over, only to find the drivers had become discouraged by the long wait and dispersed. Meanwhile, G.H.Q. craftily telephoned that she should not be allowed to return to France, but they had forgotten that she was a civilian, not subject to military rules, and with the aid of Mr Balfour Lady Angela made a triumphant entry into Boulogne. The victory was not exploited, however, for Lady Angela found life 'inconceivably dull' *en civile* and made up her mind to go home. There she redeployed her forces, and the residual funds acquired through her canteens, to start on a scheme for training war veterans for resettlement),

Index

Goschen, G. G. (son of Sir Edward), 12, 171

Gosford House (principal seat of the Earls of Wemyss in East Lothian, about fifteen miles from Edinburgh. Its size contributed largely to Lady Cynthia's dislike for it—our illustration shows only part of one wing—but in design, contents, and grandeur of setting, it is one of the jewels of the North), 4, 58, 68, 71, 72, 84, 97, 112, 178, 211, 361, 415, 463, 464, 466

Gosse, Sir Edmund, 379, 404, 426, 445

Gösta Berling (Selma Lagerlöf), 395

Gough, Captain, 297

Gough, General Sir Hubert (1870–1963: commander of the 5th Army 1916–18), 296, 430

Goupil Gallery, 169

Grace. *See* Wemyss, Grace, Dowager Countess of.

Grace (patient), 438–40, 449

Grafton Gallery, 174

Graham, Norah. *See* Brassey, Lady Norah.

Granby, John Manners, Lord (1886–1940: son of the 8th Duke of Rutland, whom he succeeded as 9th Duke in 1925), 125, 182, 183, 184, 187, 193, 216, 287, 288

Granby, Kathleen (a daughter of Frank Tennant, q.v., and nicknamed 'Kakoo', she married in 1916 Lord Granby, q.v.), 67, 106, 125, 182, 187, 244, 287, 288, 289, 391, 412, 417, 464

Grant (chauffeur), 115, 398, 438

Granville-Barker, Harley, 391

Gray, Mrs, 376

Great Expectations (Dickens), 397

Green, Raymond, 301

Green, C. (Lady Cynthia's pseudonym as Barrie's secretary).

Green Mirror (Hugh Walpole), 429

Gregory, Lady, 307

Grenfell, Francis (d. 1915—awarded V.C. 1914), 31, 35

Grenfell, Hon. Imogen (second daughter of Lord Desborough,

q.v., she married in 1931 the 6th Visct. Gage), 260, 405

Grenfell, Hon. Ivo (1899–1926: youngest son of Lord Desborough, q.v. Escaping the war, he was killed in a motor accident), 189, 306, 313, 362, 365, 369, 374, 405, 424, 425, 432, 433

Grenfell, Hon. Julian (1888–1915: eldest son of Lord Desborough, q.v. He had joined the 1st (Royal) Dragoons in 1910, and served in South Africa, and after distinguishing himself in France died in a Boulogne hospital of a head wound, on 13th May 1915. His most famous poem was 'Into Battle'), 22, 23, 25, 29, 31, 32, 33, 59, 103, 152, 207

Grenfell, Hon. William (1890–1915: known as 'Billy', second son of Lord Desborough, q.v. He was killed in action. He and his elder brother Julian inherited their father's athletic ability, and were known as 'Castor and Pollux'), 41, 62, 74, 76, 91, 103, 203, 207, 258

Greville, Mrs, 458

Grey, Albert Grey, 4th Earl (1851–1917: he succeeded Jameson as administrator of Rhodesia after the notorious Jameson Raid, and was Governor-General of Canada 1904–11), 16, 128, 244

Grey, Sir Edward (1862–1933: created 1st Visct. Grey of Fallodon in 1916. He was Secretary of State for Foreign Affairs 1905–16), 30, 88, 228, 390, 442

Grey Smith, (Mrs) Lucy (sister of Margot Asquith), 99–100

Griffiths, D. W., 366, 468

Grimson (A.D.C. to Pershing), 468, 473

Grosvenor, Dorothy (Lady Dorothy Browne, a daughter of the 5th Earl of Kenmare, married in 1914 Lord Edward Grosvenor, q.v. In 1930 she married Sir Evan Charteris, q.v.), 38, 39, 160, 262, 273, 274, 289, 303, 308, 315, 316, 317, 318, 319, 320, 425

Index

Grosvenor, Lord Edward 'Ned' (1892–1929: at first a lieutenant in the Royal Horse Guards, he was later a squadron leader in the R.A.F.), 38, 39, 273

Grosvenor Gallery, 108, 196, 293, 309, 366

Guest, (Mrs) Flora, 133

Guinness, Clotilde 'Cloe' (daughter of Sir George Russell, 4th baronet, she married in 1903 the Hon. Ernest Guinness, second son of the 1st Earl of Iveagh. Their Irish home was Glenmaroon, Chapel Izod, Co. Dublin), 63, 64

Gunter's. *See* Bath Club.

Guy. *See* Charteris, Guy.

Gwendoline. *See* Osborne, Gwendoline.

Hackwood (country home of Lord Curzon near Basingstoke), 412

Haig, Sir Douglas (1861–1928: created 1st Earl Haig 1919. He succeeded French as C.-in-C. 1915), 85, 113, 235, 239, 294, 299

haircombing (talking session with one or more women-friends carried on in each other's rooms after bedtime, often till early in the morning: Lady Cynthia records Violet Asquith as being 'as good a listener as talker'), 14, 128, 129, 158, 334

Haldane, Richard Burdon, 1st Visct. (1856–1928: Lord Chancellor 1912–15), 16, 25, 26, 27, 36, 44, 53, 211, 408

Halliwell, Dr., xvii, 102, 108, 115, 123, 124, 378, 427, 428, 437

Hamilton, Cynthia, 420

Hamilton, General Sir Ian (1853–1947: Chief-of-Staff and deputy to Kitchener in the South African War, he was chosen March 1915 to command the Mediterranean Expeditionary Force, and when the attempt to force the Dardanelles by sea failed, undertook the Gallipoli operations), 16, 106, 124, 133, 135, 242, 323, 382

Hamilton, Lady (d. 1941: Jean Muir had married Sir Ian Hamilton, q.v., in 1887), 55, 133

Hamlet, 144, 301, 325

Handley and Jay (dressmakers), 221

Hankey, Maurice Pascal Alers (1877–1963: created 1st Baron 1939). The 'man of a million state secrets', he was appointed Secretary of the Cabinet by Lloyd George in 1916, the first 'outsider' regularly to attend its meetings: he was the only civilian to receive an award—£25,000—for assisting organisation of the Allied war effort), 26, 72, 112, 134–5, 142, 145, 147, 360

Hardinge, Henry Charles, 3rd Visct. (1857–1924: he had served in the Nile Expedition of 1885), 412

Hardy, Thomas, 89, 208, 426

harikro-wuh, 432

Harmsworth. *See* Northcliffe, Lord.

Harris (patient), 436, 437

Harris, Bogie, 146, 147, 154, 171

Harrisson, (Mrs) Hilda, 457, 458

Harrods, 5, 21, 89, 93, 196, 281, 287

Harrods Stores (game), 64

Hart-Davis, Richard Vaughan, 335

Hart-Davis, Sybil (elder sister of Duff Cooper, q.v., and wife of Richard Vaughan Hart-Davis), 86, 265, 278, 279

Hatchards (bookshop), 119

Hatchetts (restaurant), 473

Haunted Man (Dickens), 287

Hawtrey, Sir Charles (d. 1923: actor-manager and playwright, whose most famous role was in the comedy *The Private Secretary*), 138, 162, 268, 447

Hazelton, Richard (1880–1943: Hon. Secretary of the Irish Parliamentary Party 1907–18), 127

Headfort, Lady (d. 1958: in one of the fairy-tale stage romances of the time she had married in 1901 the 4th Marquess of Headfort, who died in 1943), 126, 303

Hearts of the World (D. W. Griffith), 468

Index

Index

Index

in 1919 Alfred Duff Cooper, q.v., later Lord Norwich, and after his death chose to be known as Lady Diana Cooper), 49, 52, 59, 82–3, 88, 89, 112, 119, 133, 134, 137, 138, 139, 153, 156, 157, 161, 165, 171, 173, 175, 177, 182, 187, 188, 196, 204, 210, 211, 223, 237, 238, 261, 264, 268, 278, 282, 283, 284, 288, 289, 290, 294, 301, 307, 309, 314, 340, 341, 342, 343, 344, 345, 346, 347, 366, 369, 375, 422, 456, 457, 476, 477

Manners, John Manners Sutton, 3rd Baron (1852–1927: nicknamed 'Hoppy'. Athletic, he once won the Grand National on his own horse, and favoured hockey as an after-lunch pastime. His children were John—killed in the war—Francis, and the 'Twins', who inherited his physique, Betty and Angie), 41, 191

Manners, Constance 'Con' (Constance Fane had married in 1885 the 3rd Baron Manners, q.v.), 14, 41, 187, 191, 207, 280, 408, 409, 431, 471

Manners, Lady Marjorie (a daughter of the 8th Duke of Rutland, she later became Marchioness of Anglesey), 183

Manners, Lady Robert (aunt of Lady Diana Manners), 342

Marigold. See Forbes, Marigold.

Marjorie. See Manners, Lady Marjorie.

Mark. See Tennant, Mark.

Markheim (R. L. Stevenson), 143

Marlborough, Charles Spencer-Churchill, 9th Duke of (1871–1934), 129, 335.

Marlborough, Duchess of, 269–70, 312, 353

Marne, Battle of, 442

Marsh, Sir Edward 'Eddie' (1872–1952: assistant private secretary to Asquith 1915–16, he then renewed an earlier link with Churchill and was his private secretary 1917–22. He was an art connoisseur, patron of literature, and an inspired translator of Horace), 12, 19, 31, 36, 50, 94, 117, 119, 124, 125, 150, 151, 154, 160, 222, 241, 245, 247, 258, 259, 260, 262, 263, 264, 266, 268, 284, 285, 291, 301, 309, 310, 311, 314, 323, 331, 335, 336, 337, 357, 400, 447, 471, 472

Martin. See Charteris, Sir Martin.

Martin Chuzzlewit (Dickens), 383, 464

Marx, General, 381–2

Mary. At the beginning of the diary Lady Cynthia's sister, soon to become Lady Mary Strickland; later often the Hon. Mrs Aubrey Herbert, Lady Cynthia's closest friend. Where confusion is likely, they are differentiated as Mary H. and Mary S., following Lady Cynthia's own occasional custom.

Mary, Princess (daughter of George V, the Princess Royal), 420, 455, 459

Mary, Queen (consort of George V), 327, 459

Masefield, John, 325, 399

Masterton Smith, Sir James (1878–1938: private secretary to McKenna, Churchill, Balfour, Carson and Geddes as First Lords of the Admiralty 1910–17 and Assistant Secretary, Ministry of Munitions, 1917–19), 43, 119, 455

Matheson, Dr, 81

Matthew, Sir. See Nathan, Sir Matthew.

Matthews (patient), 436

Maupassant, Guy de, 7, 472, 473

Maurice, General Sir Frederick (relieved of his post at the Foreign Office as Director of Military Operations, he wrote to the Press 7 May 1918 to challenge Lloyd George's statement on the strength of the British Expeditionary Force and the extension of the British front. Asquith pressed in the House for a Select Committee to inquire into the matter, but the debate ended against—293 to 106), 316, 441, 447

Maxwell, Sir John Grenfell (1859–1929: appointed C.-in-C., Ireland, he restored order in a few days,

Index

Index

Index

Osborne, Lady Moira (sister of Lady Gwendoline), 282, 289, 297, 301, 306, 307, 415, 474, 475

Othello (Shakespeare), 289

Ottoline. *See* Morrell, Lady Ottoline.

Our Mutual Friend (Dickens), 397

Oxford, 106, 230, 397

Pages from a Family Journal (Lady Desborough), 208

Paget, Lady, 171, 306, 460

Pamela. *See* Glenconner, Lady; Lytton, Lady; and McKenna, Pamela.

Pamela (Richardson), 5

Panshanger (country home of Lord Desborough in Hertfordshire), 208, 258

Papa. *See* Wemyss, 11th Earl of.

Papenheim, Countess, 138

Paradise Lost (Milton), 113

Parkinson, Sir Thomas (1863–1935: physician to the Marchioness of Milford Haven and Admiral Prince Louis of Battenberg), 7, 50, 67, 98, 99, 100–101

Parsons, Alan (d. 1933: dramatic critic), 156, 177, 211, 275, 282, 301, 302, 307, 309, 324, 341, 342, 343, 344, 345, 346, 476, 478

Parsons, Viola (daughter of actor-manager Sir Herbert Beerbohm Tree, and wife of Alan Parsons), 138, 156, 160, 162, 165, 177, 210, 211, 275, 282, 307, 343, 344, 345, 346, 347

Patmore, Coventry, 208

Patricia, H.R.H. Princess (1886–; daughter of Prince Arthur of Connaught, q.v., she married in 1919 Admiral the Hon. Sir Alexander Ramsey), 268

Patrick. *See* Shaw-Stewart, Patrick.

Pavlova, 414

Peacock, Miss, 208

Pease, Mack, 38

Pepinage (nickname for Lady Cynthia's London house in Sussex Place. Its origin is unknown, but

Herbert Asquith's pet name for his wife was Pepinetta), 21

Pepys, Samuel, 212, 354

Percy, Rt. Hon. Lord Eustace (son of the 7th Duke of Northumberland), 213, 291, 402

Pershing, General John (1860–1948: commander of the American Expeditionary Force in France), 468

Peter (cat), 134

Peter Ibbetson (George du Maurier), 11

Peter Pan (Barrie), 473

Peto, Ralph (1877–1945: he served with the Royal Hussars and later the R.A.F.), 49

Peto, Ruby (Ruby Lindsay had married Ralph Peto, q.v. in 1909: they were divorced 1923), 49, 154, 171, 175, 214, 302, 375, 380

Phipps, Norah, 313

Pickford, Mary, 410

Pickwick Papers (Dickens), 429

Pierpont Morgan, John (1837–1913: American financier), 276

Pioneer Society, 411

Pixton Park (country home of Aubrey and Mary Herbert, near Minehead), 96, 138, 206, 324, 325, 327, 329, 379, 429

Playboy of the Western World (Synge), 434

Playfair, Sir Nigel (d. 1934: actor-manager), 138

Please Help Emily (H. M. Harwood, Playhouse), 162

Pless, Princess (the former Daisy Cornwallis-West), 318

Plunket, Rt. Hon. Sir Horace (1854–1932: Commissioner of the Congested Districts Board for Ireland 1891–1918), 62

Plymouth, Irene, Countess of. *See* Charteris, Lady Irene.

Plymouth, Lady, 459

police strike (on 31st August the police struck over a wage rise and because the newly established National Union of Police and Prison Officers was not recognised), 470

Index

Index

Index

lapse of interest among holders of minor roles, or each taking a speech in turn, which led to regrettable cheating by those anxious to run off with the 'plum' speeches. In Lady Cynthia's earlier days confusion was often caused when lady members of the party happened to be using a bowdlerised edition), 16, 39, 182, 202, 216, 219, 326, 336, 381, 397, 417

Shaw, G. B., 177, 361

Shaw-Stewart, Patrick (d. 1917: a brilliant fellow of All Souls, he had been a managing director of Baring Bros. at twenty-four), 7, 258, 259, 260, 265, 266, 278, 283, 284, 290, 389, 392

Sheffield, Edward Stanley, 4th Baron (1839–1925: administrator and educational pioneer), 283, 393

Shelley, Percy Bysshe, 38, 391

Shuttleworth, Dr, 165, 174

Signature (D. H. Lawrence, it perished after the 3rd issue), 85, 88

Simon, Sir John (1873–1954: created 1st Visct. Simon 1940. Home Secretary 1915–16, he resigned in protest against conscription and served in the R.F.C. In later years he was Chancellor of the Exchequer 1937–40 and Lord Chancellor 1940–5), 88, 117, 120

Sitwell, (Dame) Edith (1887–1964), 279, 379

Sitwell, (Sir) Osbert (1892–), 264, 267, 275, 278, 379, 421

Sitwell, Sacheverell (1897–), 284, 318, 379

Sketch, 137

Slade School of Art, 364

Slave (film), 364. *See* Serra, Marquis Guido.

Smallbones, Richard, nicknamed 'Bones', 203, 248, 319, 466, 469, 471, 472, 473, 475, 480

Smith, Charles (a close friend and neighbour at Stanway), 115, 116, 230

Smith, F. E. (1872–1930: created 1st Earl of Birkenhead 1922. He became Attorney-General 1915 and was Lord Chancellor 1919–22), 227, 297, 300, 303

Smith, Margaret (artist-wife of Charles Smith, q.v.), 115, 141, 171, 230

Smith, Viva (sister of Charles Smith, q.v.), 115, 141, 230

Smuts, General Jan Christian, 325, 326

Sockiloff, Miss (Russian governess, nicknamed 'Sockie'), 95, 109, 140, 141, 143, 158, 166, 172, 175, 178, 188, 192, 197, 215, 225, 269, 272, 287, 378, 406, 410, 428

Somerset, Bobby (son of Henry and Kitty Somerset, qq.v.), 6, 48, 363

Somerset, Henry (1874–1945: nicknamed 'Summie', heir-presumptive to the 10th Duke of Beaufort, He married first in 1896 Katherine 'Kitty' de Vere Beauclerk, fourth daughter of the 10th Duke of St Albans—they were divorced in 1920—and in 1932 Brenda, the widowed Marchioness of Dufferin and Ava, q.v.), 224, 304, 412, 463, 469

Somerset, Kitty (wife of Summie Somerset, q.v.), 5, 6, 39, 48, 102, 213, 220, 238, 363

Somme, Battle of, 214

Sophocles, 259

Sorley, Charles (1895–1915: promising poet-son of the philosopher W. R. Sorley. He was killed in action), 379

Souls (the remarkable group of friends, among whom Lady Desborough, Lady Wemyss and Balfour had been leading members, their lighter activities including pencil-and-paper games which frightened their contemporaries. Lady Wemyss denied anything like a clique saying that they were 'merely a group of very intelligent, articulate people who happened to be friends and share a love of good talk; and that in so far as they were a "charmed circle", the line was drawn by those

Index

editor of *Spectator* till 1925), 86, 87, 123, 124, 125

Strachey, Lytton, 459

Strayte, Sylvia (pseudonym of Lady Cynthia for her intended film work).

Streatfield, Dr, 67

Strickland, A. H. P. (father of Tom Strickland), 70, 167

Strickland, Algernon Walter 'Tom' (1891–1938: he served in the Royal Gloucestershire Hussars Yeomanry in Gallipoli and Egypt, later becoming a partner in the banking firm of Hoare & Co.), xviii, 3, 68, 69, 70, 72, 75, 79, 86, 90, 108, 159, 160, 166, 180, 185, 186, 187, 188, 197,

Strickland, Barbara (sister of Tom Strickland), 167, 170, 351, 358, 424

Strickland, Mary (Lady Mary Charteris, second daughter of the 11th Earl of Wemyss, she married Tom Strickland in 1915. *See* family trees), xii, xvii, 3, 6, 17, 20, 21, 23, 39, 43, 49, 51, 54, 57, 58, 60, 61, 62, 63, 64, 66, 68, 69, 70, 71, 76, 79, 80, 81, 86, 87, 88, 90, 96, 102, 108, 110, 124, 160, 165, 166, 167, 169, 174, 178, 179, 180, 186, 188, 192, 193, 196, 197, 214, 229, 230, 235, 240, 241, 275, 299, 300, 324, 351, 358, 375, 377, 378, 383, 384, 385, 389, 404, 424, 427, 428, 429, 435, 437, 444, 448, 449, 450, 473

Stuart, Lord Colum Crichton (1886–1957: on the War Office staff from 1914, he became second Secretary in 1919), 363, 372, 401

Stuart-Wortley, Bettine, 261, 313

Stuart-Wortley, Major-General (son of), 282

Suggia, xii, 315

Sunday Pictorial (now *Sunday Mirror*), 113, 195

Sussex Place, No. 8 (London home of Herbert Asquith, *see* Pepinage), xii, 20–1, 202, 267, 268, 274, 276, 277, 311, 413

Sussex Square, No. 18 (Brighton home

of Lady Seymour), 195, 226, 227, 232

Suvla Bay, 110

Sweden, Crown Princess of, 337

Swettenham, Sir Frank, 239

Swift, Jonathan, 260

Swinburne, Algernon Charles, 283, 427

Swinton, Major-General Sir Ernest (1868–1951: official military correspondent in France, he initiated proposals for 'tanks' in 1914, and as secretary to the War Committee of the Cabinet worked on their preparation in 1915. Under the pseudonym of Ole-Luk-Oie, he wrote a popular book of short stories *The Green Curve*, 1909, and was professor of Military History at Oxford 1925–39), 215, 305–6

Sykes, Major-General Rt. Hon. Sir Frederick (d. 1945: commanded Royal Flying Corps in France 1914–15 and Royal Naval Air Service in E. Mediterranean 1915–16), 23, 35–6, 39

Sykes, Mark, 238

Sylvia. *See* Henley, Sylvia.

Sylvia Scarlett (Mackenzie), 476

Synge, John Millington, 39

tanks, 215, 218, 219, 220

Taplow Court (country home of Lord Desborough in Buckinghamshire, 'perched on a hill high above the Thames'), 59, 208, 260, 404, 407

Tate, Harry (1873–1940: music hall comedian, famous for 'motoring' sketch), 462

Taylor, Jeremy, 347

Tennant, Annie (Anne Redmayne married in 1886 Frank Tennant, q.v.), xv, 4, 13, 66, 67, 116, 117, 394, 426

Tennant, Bim or Bimbo (d. 1916, aged nineteen, in the Battle of the Somme), 220

Tennant, Sir Charles, 1st Bt. (1823–1906: Glasgow ironmaster, father

Index

Index